T0345181

SOME ASSEMBLY REQUIRED

Assembly Language Programming
with the AVR Microcontroller

SOME ASSEMBLY REQUIRED

Assembly Language Programming with the AVR Microcontroller

TIMOTHY S. MARGUSH

CRC Press
Taylor & Francis Group
Boca Raton   London   New York

CRC Press is an imprint of the
Taylor & Francis Group an **informa** business
A CHAPMAN & HALL BOOK

CRC Press
Taylor & Francis Group
6000 Broken Sound Parkway NW, Suite 300
Boca Raton, FL 33487-2742

© 2012 by Taylor & Francis Group, LLC
CRC Press is an imprint of Taylor & Francis Group, an Informa business

No claim to original U.S. Government works

Version Date: 20110818

International Standard Book Number: 978-1-4398-2064-3 (Hardback)

**Visit the Taylor & Francis Web site at
http://www.taylorandfrancis.com**

**and the CRC Press Web site at
http://www.crcpress.com**

My husband, Tim, died before completing the dedication page so I am writing this for him. To Michael Decker who put in hours of time proofreading text and code during a very busy time in his life. He is a credit to his profession and a blessing to our family. I would also like to dedicate this book to Tim's brother, Philip Margush, whom Tim loved very much.

—Gail Margush

Contents

Acknowledgments

I wish to extend my thanks to my students who have helped improve this book over the course of several semesters. Many have offered corrections and suggestions that have greatly improved the content and accuracy. I especially thank Michael Decker, who took this course as an undergraduate, and then later, taught the course as a graduate student. He dedicated hours to proofreading text and code during a very busy time in his life. His suggestions also have made this a better book that it could otherwise have been. He is a credit to his profession and a blessing to our family.

Thanks to Randi Cohen, Amber Donley, and others at Taylor & Francis for their suggestions and patience as this project moved toward completion.

My family has also been an encouragement to me, pushing me to go on when writing became difficult. Thanks to all of them.

Author

Timothy S. Margush, PhD (Bowling Green State University), was an associate professor of computer science at the University of Akron. He had more than 30 years of teaching experience in mathematics and computer science, including many courses in assembly language programming using a variety of hardware platforms. Dr. Margush passed away shortly after submitting *Some Asssembly Required: Assembly Language Programming with the AVR Microcontroller* with the satisfaction that he had served others interested in learning assembly language.

Introduction

WHAT IS ASSEMBLY LANGUAGE?

The functionality of every computer system is centered on a processor. The processor is responsible for controlling most aspects of the computer system. Its name indicates its function: processing data, performing arithmetic and logical operations, storing and retrieving information, and communicating with or controlling peripheral devices. Every processor has its own native language, called machine language. These are the processing instructions that are unique to each processor. Machine language instructions are simply binary codes that are interpreted by the processor's hardware and converted to a sequence of electrical signals that alter the state of the computer system. Machine language programming is accomplished by carefully devising sequences of bits, usually organized into bytes or words that need to be placed in appropriate memory locations before execution begins.

Programming at the machine language level requires knowledge of what is called the Instruction Set Architecture of the processor. This level of the processor's design is realized by an even lower level, called the microarchitecture. In some cases, the microarchitecture level is implemented using even more primitive instructions called microcode.

The Instruction Set Architecture of a processor includes its instruction set and the system components the instructions directly or indirectly affect. These components include registers, memory, addressing, interrupts, exceptions, and even the primitive data types that can be manipulated by the instructions.

For each particular machine language, an Assembly Language can be designed to aid a programmer in the process of writing a machine language program. Assembly Language is a plain text expression of a machine language program (Figure 0.1).

```
;Build key_code from stored data and make it a keyup event
lds     keyCode, lastdigit
sbr     temp, 1<<7              ;set bit 7 for event
or      keyCode, temp
ldi     temp, $0F              ;clear last digit
sts     lastdigit, temp
clr     temp
sts     keywasdown, temp       ;record no keys down
rjmp    exit
```

FIGURE 0.1 An excerpt from an assembly language program for the AVR processor.

It consists of instructions used by the assembler (the program that processes the assembly language source file) to generate the machine language representation of the program. Rather than directly writing machine instructions as binary codes, the assembly language programmer writes instructions using mnemonic codes that are easier to remember than the actual instruction numbers. The assembler is used to convert the assembly language instructions into machine instructions, ready to be executed by the processor.

Since each processor (or family of processors) has its own machine language, a particular assembly language closely parallels the machine language it targets. There may even be several distinct assembly languages targeting the same processor. These will likely share many similarities, but differ in capabilities and syntax details. Assembly language programs are not platform independent. Nevertheless, most assembly languages have many similarities that make learning a new assembly language easier after the first has been mastered.

WHY STUDY ASSEMBLY LANGUAGE?

The concept of an assembly language was invented in 1949. Maurice Wilkes, the coordinator of the Electronic Delay Storage Automatic Calculator (EDSAC) project at Cambridge University, is credited with this invention, which made programming less error-prone. The first successful high-level language was FORTRAN, released in 1957. This was designed under the direction of John Backus at IBM. For many years, computing professionals engaged in arguments as to whether programs generated by assembly language were more efficient than those generated by high-level languages. Modern optimizing compilers generate extremely efficient code, reducing the dependence on assembly language programming in many instances.

Assembly language was widely used through the 1980s to take full advantage of limited memory and to circumvent the limitations imposed by slow processing speeds of earlier computing systems. Even in the 1990s, assembly language was popular for game development. Currently, however, assembly language lags far behind more popular languages such as Java and C ++ for application programming, and even system programming. The source code for assembly language programs that accomplish relatively simple tasks is almost always much longer than their equivalent high-level language programs. There are, nevertheless, several advantages to studying an assembly language.

Because each assembly language closely parallels its processor's instruction set, a study of assembly language gives insight into the architectural details of that processor. When the focus is on the generic traits of assembly languages, assembly language programming can be used as a tool to study computer architecture. Every detail of the instruction set architecture of a particular processor is accessible through assembly language. Learning about the general design principles of processors helps to understand how high-level programs are translated and executed. This knowledge can help improve high-level language programming skills.

Since every high-level language program must be transformed into a sequence of machine language instructions, knowledge of the underlying machine capabilities is a prerequisite to understanding how compilers and interpreters work. Although these transformations may bypass the assembly language level and go directly to machine language, understanding assembly language provides the tools to examine the results of program translations. Whereas machine language programs can be translated relatively easily back to an assembly language form, it is generally very difficult, if not impossible, to recover the high-level language version of a program from the machine level representation. Without access to high-level source code, reading the assembly level representation of a program is the only way to discover how it is doing what it is doing.

On most general computing platforms, programs run under the control of a modern operating system that acts as a barrier between the program and the resources of the system. Operating systems must protect themselves and other programs from rogue programs, and must provide robust shared access to components such as ports and memory. This makes it difficult or impossible for programs to directly access all of the processor capabilities and system components. Even when the operating system is taken out of the picture, high-level languages, because they are designed to be somewhat portable, may not give direct access to all of the capabilities of each processor or system. Assembly language programs, give the programmer complete control over the instructions that are used and the resources they utilize. As long as the operating system allows it, assembly language programs can fully utilize their targeted processor's capabilities, and efficiently access the other components of the system. Assembly language programming also provides the ability to fine-tune segments of code in a way that is difficult or impossible using other techniques. Assembly language provides the tools to write the fastest and most efficient code for each situation. Some compilers provide the capability to include inline assembly language code.

A careful study of assembly language programming gives practical knowledge of memory use and allocation, stack functionality, procedure call and return mechanisms as well as parameter passing paradigms. Released from the specific methods imposed by a particular high-level language, assembly language programmers can create their own conventions for each of these program ingredients. Studying addressing modes available in a particular processor provides the basis for understanding how objects, arrays, and linked structures are implemented. This knowledge helps programmers understand when one data organization might be preferred over another.

The study of assembly language should not be undertaken with the goal of simply learning another programming language. Instead, this should be seen as laying a solid foundation to support the programming knowledge and skills already acquired. Studying assembly language will make you more aware of how computer systems work and how high-level language programming is used to control them. Knowledge about the details of a specific processor gained through the study of assembly language programming will ultimately make you a better computer practitioner.

TO THE READER ...

The best gifts come in a box with these words printed on the outside: "Some Assembly Required." Whether a bicycle, model airplane, bookcase, office chair, or baby toy, the challenge of assembly greatly increases the value ... at least, it does for me. Great enjoyment is derived from the process of taking things apart to see how they work, and then trying to put them back together again.

My first experience in programming introduced me to another type of assembly process—fitting a collection of basic FORTRAN statements into a meaningful sequence of operations. Understanding how high-level languages became another mystery to be explored. It was several years later that the secrets were revealed through the study of machine and assembly languages.

Computers (processors) are fundamentally very simple machines. Their capabilities are compactly represented through a mathematical construct called a Turing Machine. Layers of software bridge the chasm from simple hardware descriptions to extremely complex and capable high-level systems. Although we usually interface with computers at the higher levels, the real work gets done at the lowest levels which are understood only through machine or assembly language concepts.

Computer scientists need some understanding of the functionality of a basic processor, and how their capabilities support high-level languages and applications. Thus, the title of this book was born—*Some Assembly Required*. A study of any assembly language is the integration point for understanding the connection between hardware and software. This is the level that provides the foundation for understanding compilers, linkers, loaders, and operating systems, in addition to the processors themselves.

My first experience with programming was printing Fibonacci numbers using a programmable calculator in 1970. A wide variety of computing platforms provided a breadth of experience through college and graduate school. My first personal computer, the Commodore 64, opened up the world of assembly language programming for me in 1982. This was a pivotal point for my understanding of how hardware connected with software. Understanding this connection has been a crucial foundation for high-level programming concepts.

Studying assembly languages has made me a much better programmer. It is my hope that *Some Assembly Required* will provide a similar foundation for each of my readers.

CHAPTER 1

Computer Systems

BASIC PROCESSOR ARCHITECTURE

Every general purpose processor conceived since the Electronic Discrete Variable Automatic Calculator (EDVAC) and Electronic Delay Storage Automatic Calculator (EDSAC) of the 1950s operates on the principle of the basic fetch–execute cycle. A machine instruction is fetched from program memory, decoded, and then executed. This cycle is driven by a series of clock pulses and repeats ad infinitum, usually until the processor is powered down. Memory is usually organized as a series of bytes or words and is accessed by address. The processor keeps track of the address of the next instruction to be fetched in a register called the program counter (PC) or instruction pointer. As the instruction is fetched, the PC is updated to point to the next instruction; usually this is done by incrementing it by a fixed amount. Some processors have variable length instructions making the update of the PC a little more complicated. Figure 1.1 illustrates the fundamental components of a typical processor and program memory.

Decoding of the instruction occurs when it enters the environment of the processor. In simple processors, the instruction is stored in a special register, called the current instruction register. The bits of the instruction are used to select a sequence of logical control signals that are issued in a carefully timed pattern to affect the state of the machine, effectively executing the instruction.

This description is very general, and captures the basic functionality of all stored-program computers. Details vary depending on the specific processor architecture. For example, some processors actually interpret the instructions by executing lower-level instructions, called

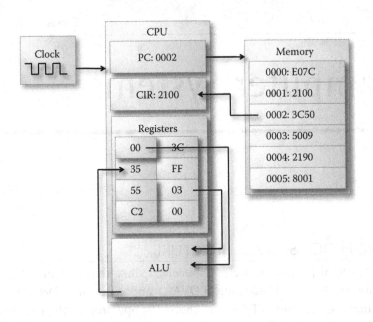

FIGURE 1.1   The basic components of a processor including memory.

microinstructions. These microinstructions achieve the necessary sequence of control signals required to emulate the machine language instruction in hardware. In other processors the logic signals are derived directly from the bits of the instruction's operation code and sequenced via hardware circuits. Processors also vary in terms of their internal structure, such as the number of registers and arithmetic capabilities.

COMPONENTS OF A COMPUTER SYSTEM

Processors are usually described as a collection of functional units, and generally as part of a larger system. The general computer system consists of five functional units, the control unit (CU), arithmetic logical unit (ALU), main memory, secondary storage, and input/output (I/O) devices. The CU and ALU together comprise what has historically been called the central processing unit (CPU).

Central Processing Unit

The CPU is the focus of the computational activity of a computing system. This is where machine instructions are executed and calculations take place. The CPU of older computers was composed of distinct components, but modern computers generally have their CPU on a single chip, often along with other subsystems. Large Scale Integration (LSI) is the technology that has made this possible.

The CU is responsible for fetching, decoding, and executing instructions. It is the control center for all activities in the system. The CU works in conjunction with a collection of registers that temporarily hold data values for immediate manipulation by the instructions.

The ALU is part of an internal data pathway that connects to the registers and provides access to other resources of the system such as main memory. The CU issues logic signals that enable registers to output to, or receive information from, this internal data pathway. Data can also be passed through the ALU and combined with other data or manipulated independently to implement arithmetic or logical operations.

Storage

Main memory is generally called RAM (Random Access Memory). Most RAM is volatile, meaning it requires the continual consumption of power to retain its data. RAM is used to hold the instructions of a program as well as the data that is being manipulated by the program. Most computer systems also include ROM (Read Only Memory). ROM is also RAM, but retains its contents even when no power is applied to the system. ROM memory makes it possible for computer systems to start up without operator intervention, since the initial instructions to be executed are available directly from ROM as soon as power is applied to the system.

Secondary storage is furnished by disk drives or other forms of non-volatile storage. In general, access to secondary storage is slower and is often not random. The term random access refers to the order in which information can be efficiently accessed. In particular, a device is called random access if the time to access information does not depend on the order in which the information is accessed. RAM devices can access the contents of any memory location in the same amount of time. Data in RAM can be accessed in any order without incurring a time penalty. Tape drives are clearly not random access. They are a classic example of a sequential access storage device, functioning efficiently only when reading/writing a stream of bytes from/to the tape as it moves past the read/write head. Disk drives are not technically random access either, but an index to the stored contents allows very fast access to any point in storage and creates an almost random access structure.

Secondary storage is typically used to hold programs and data needed by programs so it can be accessed without operator intervention when needed. Secondary storage capacity usually is much greater than main memory; the increased capacity at low cost justifies the penalty of slower access.

Input and Output

I/O devices vary widely depending on the type of computer system. Most personal computers support video and audio output, and keyboard and mouse input. Other systems may implement I/O in the form of digital control signals to operate external devices, or analog signals representing the state of an attached sensor.

At the processor level, I/O is generally very primitive. The most basic I/O capability is achieved through the execution of an instruction that causes a signal to be asserted outside the scope of the processor's major components (CPU and main memory), or to capture an external signal asserted by an external device or subsystem. The simplest output instruction would assert a binary value on one of the connections external to the processor; the simplest input operation would set a bit inside the processor to capture the current value of some external connection.

Each processor has its own specific I/O conventions and instructions. Some computer systems include more advanced I/O capabilities at the system level (unifying the processor and the I/O circuitry associated with standard devices immediately surrounding the processor). This provides richer I/O capabilities at the cost of specialized hardware.

When studying the characteristics of a single processor, I/O is a fairly primitive feature. It is common to discuss I/O in terms of ports on which the processor asserts or reads logical signals of external devices. Ports can connect to internal devices located on the same chip as the processor, or connect to pins, as shown in Figure 1.2, that can be connected to external devices.

I/O can be parallel (multiple binary signals asserted/read simultaneously on a collection of pins) or utilize a single pin for one bit of data or a stream of bits over time. Output, at this level of detail, is accomplished by asserting a logic signal on a port/pin and allowing an external device to respond to that signal; input is accomplished by copying a signal on an input port/pin into a register, or utilizing its value in some way to control processing.

Some computer systems implement variations on this basic I/O technique. For example, memory mapped I/O allows indirect control of I/O devices by simply reading from or writing to specific memory addresses.

FIGURE 1.2   A surface-mount microprocessor showing the pins that can form connections to external components.

The hardware translates these actions to device communication protocols. Some systems support Direct Memory Access (DMA) in which I/O devices are allowed to access memory independently of the processor. Memory locations are used for communications with the device.

CLASSIFICATION OF PROCESSORS

CISC versus RISC

Processors have historically been classified as either Complex Instruction Set Computer (CISC) or Reduced Instruction Set Computer (RISC) architectures. The CISC reflects the original development path of processors as capabilities were added over time. RISC is a design philosophy that aims to have a set of instructions that can all be executed very quickly. The term "reduced" refers to complexity; RISC instructions are generally very simple, and therefore easy to implement in hardware. CISC instructions range from very simple to very complex instructions; some execute quickly, others may take more time to complete their task. Most modern processors sport characteristics of both designs, so classifying a processor as CISC or RISC is seldom clear cut.

Functionality

Processors are also divided according to functionality. Microprocessors are the single-chip version of the earlier computer systems that were made up of many separate hardware components. Early computers had separate circuitry for the CU, ALU, memory, and I/O devices. Microprocessors, made possible by Very Large Scale Integration (VLSI) technology, combine the CU and ALU on a single chip. Microprocessors are the basic component of current personal computers. They are part of a larger circuit board that integrates their computing power with various I/O processing modules (video, audio, memory, etc.). Communication between the processor and these devices takes place over high-speed data pathways called busses.

Microcontrollers are designed for embedded applications. They include the processing power of a microprocessor but also integrate specific I/O devices and functionality on a single chip. Many include a limited amount of RAM, ROM, and serial or parallel I/O capabilities. Pins on the microcontroller chip are often used to directly control or accept input from external devices. Figure 1.3 shows a microcontroller plugged into a socket of a development board.

FIGURE 1.3 The Atmel ATmega16 microcontroller.

Architecture

There is one additional classification of processors that is related to how programs and data are organized in memory and accessed by the processor. When the EDVAC computer was developed at the University of Pennsylvania under the direction of John von Neumann, it incorporated the idea of storing program instructions in the same physical memory as the data to be processed. Both instructions and data were brought from memory into the processor using the same address and data buses. This organization is commonly called the von Neumann Architecture, Princeton Architecture, or more commonly, the Stored Program Computer. The CU alternates between fetching instructions and fetching or storing data.

In an alternative system architecture, instructions are stored apart from data, using different data pathways and storage for each. This is called the Harvard Architecture, deriving its name from the Mark I relay-based computer developed at Harvard. Mark I programs were encoded as a sequence of machine instructions represented by holes punched in a paper tape. The instructions operated on data located in main memory which consisted of electromechanical relays. This design allowed parallel access to instructions and data, implying the potential for increased throughput. Rather than alternating instruction fetching and data access, processors based on the Harvard architecture can fetch and decode the next instruction at the same time as the current instruction is reading or writing data in memory.

NUMERATION SYSTEMS

A numeration system is a language used to represent numbers. Most of us are comfortable using the decimal or base 10 numeration system. We have spent many years learning to express numbers using this system and developed skill at following paper and pencil algorithms to add, subtract, multiply, and divide numbers through the use of base 10 numerals. Although it is common to call things like 32 and −7 numbers, it is important to notice that these are simply symbols (or clusters of symbols) representing numbers. In computer science, we need to distinguish carefully between numeration systems and numbers. Numbers are an abstract concept that represents the size of a collection (we will temporarily limit ourselves to the natural number system). Numerals and numeration systems are a communication tool used to represent the abstract concept of a number. If we look at the letters of the word "four," we can see that they form a collection of a certain size, {"f," "o," "u," "r"}. The word "five" is made from letters chosen from an identically sized collection, {"f," "i," "v," "e"}. We can express this number (the size of the collection of letters in each of these words) in a variety of ways, including four, 4, quatro, 100, IV, and ||||.

The numeration system used in a particular situation is dictated by convention and simplicity. Roman numerals are elegant and traditionally used to record the copyright dates of old movies, but they are generally unsuitable for arithmetic calculations. The tally mark system is convenient when one counts a series of events, allowing the count to be easily updated without erasing and rewriting digits, and quickly summarized since the tally marks are visibly grouped in fives. Grammatical rules require the use of words when writing small numeric values such as seven, while larger numbers such as 12 may be written in the conventional decimal digit format. The rule is more complicated than this however, because five million is preferred over 5,000,000, and if 1024 starts a sentence, it must be written out as one thousand twenty-four, and commas are only used when there are more than 4 digits, as in 32,767. Amounts on checks are written in both decimal numeric form and as a lengthy text phrase, such as one hundred thirteen thousand, four hundred ninety-seven dollars.

Decimal (base 10) notation is commonly used by humans to represent numbers and to perform calculations, either by hand or with a calculating device. Because of our childhood training, it is the most readily accessible numeration system for expressing numbers. Alternative bases, such as binary, octal, and hexadecimal, are common in the realm of computing because of the nature of the logical signals used to represent data in the low-level processing tasks. In these cases, the binary, octal, or hexadecimal numerals allow immediate comprehension of the bit patterns represented by electrical signals in hardware. The computer scientist should be comfortable using a variety of numeration systems to represent data, choosing the one that best communicates the information in a particular context.

The Nature of Data

Data manipulated by a computer system is always most directly represented in binary form. At the logic level, every data value is a collection of 0's and 1's, called bits. The word bit is short for binary digit. This is a convenient way of thinking about the underlying hardware which is largely composed of bistable components that store and output two distinct electrical states, for example, a high or low voltage signal. The outputs of these components are used as inputs to other components in the circuit. The two distinct electrical states are represented by the binary numerals 1 and 0.

Usually, individual bits are only meaningful as part of a larger group. Common group sizes are 4 (nybble, also spelled nibble), 8 (byte), 16 (word), 32 (doubleword), and 64 (quadword). The meanings of these terms, especially word, doubleword, and quadword, have changed over time as the complexity (capability) of computing systems has increased, and often have different meanings in the context of different computer systems. In general, the size of a word is defined by the size of the fundamental computational unit used to process it. In a 64-bit processor world, you may use the term word when referring to a 64-bit data value. It is also common for a word to mean a 32-bit data value. The 16-bit word has its roots in the age of the 8- and 16-bit processors that were popular in the 1980s. It is also fairly consistent with the current usage in the world of many microcontrollers.

The origin of the term byte is not clearly known, however it seems that it was originally spelled bite and represented the number of bits in a character code ... a reasonable number to manage in one "bite." The spelling was changed at some point, presumably to avoid confusion if the trailing "e" were to be omitted. The term nybble is also a play on the word byte, indicating a small byte, specifically, half of a byte.

The contents of a byte may need to be viewed as a collection of independent bits, perhaps indicating whether individual sensors attached to the system are registering as on or off. Or, the meaning of the byte may require that all 8 bits be considered as a unit, perhaps representing one of 256 different characters. The bit pattern might represent an integer value, signed or unsigned. Or, a group of bits could represent a machine language instruction or contain address information.

Since the common ingredient in all of these representations is the underlying collection of bits, for communication purposes (human to human), we need a way to represent any particular bit pattern. It is convenient to allow the bits to represent a number. That is, to interpret the bits as a binary numeral. When the number of bits gets large, we have the option of switching to a different numeration base. Common bases used to represent bit patterns in their raw form are 2 (binary), 8 (octal), and 16 (hexadecimal). Binary representation is simplest way to express a bit pattern, directly representing each individual bit. However, it is somewhat inefficient for large numbers of bits. In such cases, octal and hexadecimal numerals provide an advantage, without making it too difficult to visualize the bits behind the digits of these numerals.

Binary, Octal, Hexadecimal, Decimal . . .

Before continuing with the representation of bytes and other sized groups of bits, it is important to review how the positional numeration system works. Base 10 numerals are composed of a sequence of digits (0–9). Each is a numeral representing one of the numbers zero through nine. The order of the digits is important as each digit's position in the sequence implies a certain place value (23 is not the same as 32). This so-called positional notation is directly connected with the expanded form, or polynomial representation, of numbers. The decimal numeral 3087 is simply a short-hand notation for the polynomial $p(x) = 3*x^3 + 0*x^2 + 8*x^1 + 7$ evaluated with $x = 10$. The digits correspond to the coefficients of the polynomial, and have the associated place value of x^k when in position k (positions are numbered from the right, starting with zero). The variable in the polynomial, x, is called the base or radix of the numeral. If this were a base 16 numeral, we would evaluate the polynomial at $x = 16$. The coefficients of a base b polynomial are restricted to the digits 0 through $b-1$. This guarantees a one-to-one correspondence between numerals in a given base and the numbers they represent.

The positions of the digits are numbered from the right (least significant digit) starting with 0. The place values for the digits in 3087 (base 10) are then one, ten, one hundred, and one thousand. The digit 7 is in position 0 having a place value of 10^0 or 1; the digit 3 is in position 3, having a place value of 10^3.

Returning to the representation of groups of bits, we will first focus on byte-sized groups. The 8 bits of a byte can be arranged in 256 distinct binary patterns. When we interpret the bits of a byte as a binary numeral, we form a natural correspondence between bytes and numbers. For example, the byte 10010010 is associated with the following base two positional polynomial:

$$P(2) = 1*2^7 + 0*2^6 + 0*2^5 + 1*2^4 + 0*2^3 + 0*2^2 + 1*2^1 + 0*2^0.$$

This polynomial is expressed and evaluated in our common base 10 notation, and in this case evaluates to 146 (one hundred forty-six). Thus we see a natural correspondence between a byte (a group of 8 bits) and a number.

There is no reason the place values have to be assigned as shown above, increasing in importance from right to left fashion. We treated the leftmost bit as the most significant, giving it a place value of 128. The choice to make the leftmost bit the most significant simply corresponds to our common left–right convention used in positional notation. Of course, the bits in a byte are not found in any particular spatial arrangement in memory or inside a processor, so any external representation of a byte's value is simply a notational convenience to describe how data is stored and manipulated by the computer system.

Even though the binary numerals 0 and 00000000 are numerically equivalent, it is sometimes important to represent data in a form that implies how many bits are involved as well as the bit values. It is also important to indicate the base used in the representation. The string of 8 0's could represent a byte (binary) or a 32-bit word (assuming the 0's were hexadecimal digits). It is sometimes necessary to use a prefix or suffix to clarify the representation used.

- Binary data is often represented with a 0b or % prefix, or b suffix.

- Hexadecimal data is usually specified with a 0x or $ prefix, or a suffix such as h. In the C programming language, hexadecimal numerals are written with a leading 0x.

- Octal data is often specified with a 0 (zero) or 0o (zero-oh) prefix or o suffix, however the similarity of o to 0 makes the latter conventions rather confusing. In C, any number written with a leading 0 is considered octal.

- Base 10 numerals are usually written with no special prefix or suffix.

Of course, a numeric subscript could also be used to specify the radix of the representation, as in 1001_2 or 372_8 or $4C_{16}$, but this is cumbersome when writing programs (plain text editors do not easily accommodate subscripts). There would also have to be an agreement that the subscripts be written in base 10 (or some other fixed base). Later, we will examine the notational conventions imposed by the assembler when representing numbers or bit patterns in assembly language programs.

It is sometimes important to be able to refer to specific positions within a group of bits. There are several competing conventions, but the most common follows the positional numeration convention, assigning the exponent in the polynomial as the position number of its coefficient. Thus, in the binary numeral, 0b00001000, the 1 is in position 3 since it corresponds to the term with 2^3 in the polynomial. In a word (16-bit), the positions would be numbered 15, 14, ..., 0, starting from the left. In a hexadecimal representation, each hex digit represents a nybble, and each nybble is a coefficient in the base 16 polynomial. So, in the hexadecimal numeral, 0xC325, C is in position 3 and 5 is in position 0. The C represents the nybble twelve (1010) and has place value 16^3; 5 represents the nybble five (0101) and has place value 1 (16^0). It is customary to number bytes in a word in the same way. This convention would correspond to the exponents of a base 256 polynomial; the least-significant byte, 0x25 (rightmost in the word 0xC325), is called byte 0.

Our discussion of data representation has focused on an external representation (written) of values stored in a bit, nybble, byte, word, and so on. When information is stored in memory, the order of bits, nibbles, and so on, can be rearranged according to the specific encoding scheme being used. When we store a word value, such as $1234, we will need to use two bytes of storage. These bytes are usually located in adjacent memory locations, but the order of the bytes may vary. The more significant byte ($12) may be stored first, or last. These two orders for multibyte numeric data are referred to as big-endian and little-endian, respectively. The terms refer to the fictional debate between the citizens of Lilliput and Blefuscu in *Gulliver's Travels* as to whether the soft-boiled egg was to be cracked on the little end or the small end.

We write our decimal numerals in big-endian format. The "big" end of the number comes first, followed by the less significant digits. When arranging the bytes of a 16-bit (or longer) representation of a number, you place the bytes in most significant to least significant order (left to right, or low address to high address) if you are a big-endian. If you subscribe to the little-endian philosophy, you list the bytes in the opposite direction.

Conversions

When discussing the low-level details of data representations, octal and hexadecimal representations are often preferred over binary as they are more compact and there is a simple conversion between these representations. Octal is compelling since it uses only the digits 0–7, requiring no additional symbols and can be typed on a conventional numeric keypad. But, it is awkward because a sequence of three octal digits can represent nine bits, and a nine-bit container is not very common in computing.

Hexadecimal numerals require 16 distinct symbols representing the numbers zero through 15. In this system, the usual 10 decimal digits represent the values zero through nine; a–f (or A–F) are used to represent the digit values 10 through 15. Two hex digits can represent 256 distinct numbers, and hence correspond naturally to the 256 variations possible in a single byte.

It is also very easy to convert either octal or hexadecimal to binary. The simplicity of conversion between binary and octal or hexadecimal is based on patterns in the grouping and the fact that 8 and 16 are powers of two. Consider the binary value 0b10010010 used earlier. The expanded form can be regrouped as a polynomial in powers of 8 or 16, without changing the bits of the original expression.

$$0b10010010 = 1*2^7 + 0*2^6 + 0*2^5 + 1*2^4 + 0*2^3 + 0*2^2 + 1*2^1 + 0*2^0$$

$$= (1*2^1 + 0*2^0) *2^6 + (0*2^2 + 1*2^1 + 0*2^0) *2^3 + (0*2^2 + 1*2^1 + 0*2^0) *2^0$$
$$= (1*2^1 + 0*2^0) *8^2 + (0*2^2 + 1*2^1 + 0*2^0) *8^1 + (0*2^2 + 1*2^1 + 0*2^0) *8^0$$
$$= (0b10) *8^2 + (0b010) *8^1 + (0b010) *8^0$$
$$= (2) *8^2 + (2) *8^1 + (2) *8^0$$
$$= 0222 \text{ or } 0o222 \text{ or } 222o$$

$$= (1*2^3 + 0*2^2 + 0*2^1 + 1*2^0) *2^4 + (0*2^3 + 0*2^2 + 1*2^1 + 0*2^0) *2^0$$
$$= (1*2^3 + 0*2^2 + 0*2^1 + 1*2^0) *16^1 + (0*2^3 + 0*2^2 + 1*2^1 + 0*2^0) *16^0$$
$$= (0b1001) *16^1 + (0b0010) *16^0$$
$$= (9) *16^1 + (2) *16^0$$
$$= \$92 \text{ or } 0x92 \text{ or } 92h$$

Binary to octal conversion is accomplished by grouping the bits in three's from right to left. Binary to hexadecimal uses groups of four. Each group is converted to the appropriate digit value.

```
0b11000111 => 11 000 111 => 0o307
0b11000111 => 1100 0111 => 0xC7
```

Three bits completely cover the range of the octal digits, 0–7. Four bits cover the range of the hexadecimal digits, 0 through F. Converting back to binary is as easy as expanding each digit to the correct number of bits, remembering to include leading zeros in each group if needed. The binary to octal conversion has the oddity that groups of three do not exactly fill out a byte or word, so the leftmost octal digit can only be a 0–3 for a byte, and a 0–1 for a 16-bit word. This might be seen as an argument to prefer hexadecimal notation, but octal has held an historic position. Base four numerals would also allow an easy conversion, but there is little benefit over binary in using this representation; hexadecimal and octal are more compact.

Conversions to other bases require a little more arithmetic. Although not required, conversions between bases (other than base 10) often use base 10 as an intermediate form. For paper and pencil conversions, there are two different algorithms that are commonly used, one for converting from base 10, and the other for converting to base 10. Only one of the algorithms is needed, but the calculations will be easier if you choose the algorithm based on the conversion task. Choosing the correct algorithm allows you to do all of the work in base 10 (our comfort zone).

Repeated Division Algorithm

From base (radix) 10 to base b, use the repeated division algorithm. This determines the digits of the equivalent base b numeral by performing repeated divisions by the value of b. Each division yields a quotient (used in the repeated step) and a remainder. Since we divide by b, the remainder is always a legal base b digit (0 through $b-1$), and is the next digit in the resulting base b representation. The digits are produced from right (least significant) to left (most significant). Leading zeros may be added if required for your particular application.

Example: Convert 232 (Base 10) to Base Three

```
232 / 3 = 77    r 1  (rightmost digit of the base 3 numeral is 1)
 77 / 3 = 25    r 2  (second digit, with place value 3¹)
 25 / 3 = 8     r 1
  8 / 3 = 2     r 2
  2 / 3 = 0     r 2  (stop − continuing would generate leading zeros)
232₁₀ = 22121₃
```

Polynomial Evaluation Algorithm

Converting from radix b to radix 10 uses the polynomial evaluation algorithm. This is as simple as evaluating a polynomial. The base b numeral represents a polynomial in powers of b, so if we write it out in base 10 notation, and carry out the indicated operations, we can determine the decimal value.

Example: Convert 0o37602 to Decimal

```
0o37602      = 3*8⁴ + 7*8³ + 6*8² + 0*8¹ + 2*8⁰
             = 16258
```

Horner's Algorithm

Evaluating polynomials is a common arithmetic task, and various algorithms have been devised to do this efficiently. One fundamentally important algorithm that has direct application here is known as Horner's Rule, named after William George Horner who formalized the method in 1819. Horner's Rule minimizes the number of additions and multiplications required to evaluate a polynomial, and are easily implemented using an iterative algorithm. If base 10 notation is used, and computations are performed in base 10, this algorithm can be used to convert from base b to base 10.

Horner's Rule is developed from a factored form of the positional polynomial. For example, consider the hexadecimal numeral 0x3CF which can be expressed as a polynomial with coefficients 3, C, and F, evaluated at $x = 16$ (the radix).

```
p(x) = 3*x² + C*x¹ + F
     = x*(3x¹ + C) + F
     = x*(x*(3) + C) + F
```

The last expression (resulting from Horner's factorization) is evaluated from the inside out. Notice that the innermost part of the expression consists of the most significant digit (leftmost) of the original numeral. We start with the most significant digit as the initial value of an accumulator (where the result will be accumulated). While there are more digits, we multiply by the value of x (the radix) and add the value of the next digit.

Example: Compute p(16) Using Base 10 Notation to Convert 0x3CF to Base 10

```
First digit is 3
Acc is set to 3
Next digit is C (12)
Acc is set to Acc*16 + digit = 3*16 + 12 = 60
Next digit is F (15)
Acc is set to Acc*16 + digit = 60*16 + 15 = 975
Result is 975
```

Since we carried out the computations in base 10, we see the result in base 10 notation. However, if you do all of the work in base b, you get the base b representation. Thus, this algorithm will suffice to convert any base to any other base (as long as you can work in the destination base numeration system). Note that processors usually do binary arithmetic in binary representations utilizing the processor's internal numeric processing standards, so implementing Horner's Rule in a looping structure will allow any stream of digits representing a number in any base to be converted to the processor's native internal representation of an integer. All that is needed is the ability to express the digits in binary, multiply by the base of the original numeral, and add two numbers.

Here is the same conversion, but carried out in base two notation. Since everything will be written in binary, the 0b prefix will be omitted.

Example: Compute p(16) in the Binary Numeration System to Convert 0x3CF to Base Two

```
First digit is 3 (11)
Acc is set to 11
Next digit is C (1100)
Acc is set to Acc*10000+digit = 11*10000+1100
= 110000+1100 = 111100
Next digit is F (1111)
Acc is set to Acc*10000+digit = 111100*10000+1111
= 1111000000+1111 = 1111001111
Result is 1111001111 (base two), which in hexadecimal is 0x3CF!
```

Thus, one simple algorithm can be used to convert a numeral expressed as a sequence of base b_1 digits to any other base b_2. Simply write the numeral in expanded form, as a polynomial, using only base b_2 numeration. Then evaluate the polynomial at $x = b_1$, preferably using Horner's Rule and doing all of the computations in base b_2. You can see why this works well on paper to convert to base 10 (all of the work is done in our comfort zone—base 10). If you are equally talented calculating in any base, you can use Horner's Rule to convert directly between any two bases.

Incidentally, the first algorithm, repeated division, can be used in other bases as well. To convert from base b_1 to b_2 you repeatedly divide by b_2. If you write everything in base b_1 it all works! Of course, when b_1 is base 10, the work is fairly easy. When you write a program to perform these calculations, all of the work is done inside the processor, using an internal representation of the numbers. This is natural for the processor, and allows conversion from its internal form to an external, easily read format, such as decimal, hexadecimal, octal, or binary. We will use both of these algorithms later to perform fundamentally important I/O translations.

BOOLEAN DATA

A byte can represent many things. Above, we treated the bits as the digits of a binary numeral. This is the common way to encode unsigned integers in a byte. Of course, the range of numbers that can be represented according to this scheme is limited allowing only numbers between 0 and 255 inclusive. Boolean data is another common data type. It is the foundation of the conditional and repetition control structures. In high-level languages, a byte or word is often used to encode Boolean data, even though it is wasteful in terms of space.

There are exactly two Boolean values, True, and False. Only a single bit is required to represent these two values. Usually, 1 represents True, and 0 represents False. Some programming languages provide support for the Boolean data type, but often utilize a word to represent Boolean information (all zeros for False, and some other value, possibly all 1's, for True). The space wasted (8, 16, or more bits to represent only two distinct values) is usually compensated for in speed and simplicity of access.

Microcontrollers commonly process single bit data, and may provide support for efficient processing of individual bits of a byte. In this case, Boolean data for one or more purposes can be grouped into bytes; the individual bits of the byte can be tested and modified by special bit-oriented instructions. This allows compact representation of Boolean information without a sacrifice of speed. Most general purpose processors do not include such specialized instructions.

The circuits that comprise ALUs and the CU, and all other parts of the digital computer system, ultimately perform Boolean operations. The fundamental Boolean operations are NOT, AND, and OR. A few additional operations, such as NAND, NOR, and XOR, are also realized in common logic circuits. Machine languages usually include instructions to perform some of these simple Boolean operations on the bits found in bytes or words.

Boolean Operations

The NOT operation is a unary (one operand) operation that simply reverses a Boolean value. In the context of data represented in a computer, this is called "flipping a bit." Symbolically, the NOT operation may be defined by a truth table as shown in Table 1.1.

In many cases, machine languages provide a NOT instruction that acts on a whole byte or word at one time. The NOT operation is applied to each

TABLE 1.1   The Boolean NOT Operation

a	NOT a
0	1
1	0

TABLE 1.2　The Boolean AND Operation

a	b	a AND b
0	0	0
0	1	0
1	0	0
1	1	1

bit in the container, performing 8 or 16 (or more) operations in parallel. This is sometimes called complementing the bits. High-level languages often provide operators that correspond to these bit-wise instructions. C, for example includes a bitwise NOT, called complement. The operator symbol is ~ (tilde) and this flips all of the bits in the value it is applied to. This should not be confused with C's logical operator, !, which negates a logical or Boolean value.

The AND operation shown in Table 1.2 is a binary operation (two operands). It combines its two operands to form a single Boolean value such that the result is 1 only when both operands are 1.

Table 1.3 defines the OR operation which is also a binary operation. Its result is 1 when either operand (or both) is 1.

The XOR (exclusive-or) operation provides a result of 1 only when either operand, but not both, is 1. Another way to describe XOR is *not equal*: a XOR *b* is 1 when a and *b* are not equal. Table 1.4 defines the exclusive-or operation.

Applications of Boolean Operations

Processors include logical instructions that perform Boolean operations on all of the bits in a byte (word) at the same time. By careful use of the operations, programs can access individual bits in a byte (word) to determine or change their value, without affecting the surrounding bits. These techniques are necessary when a processor lacks specialized bit-oriented instructions. They are also used to process groups of bits within a byte (word); these groups are sometimes called bit-fields.

TABLE 1.3　The Boolean OR Operation

a	b	a OR b
0	0	0
0	1	1
1	0	1
1	1	1

TABLE 1.4   The Boolean XOR (exclusive or) Operation

a	b	a XOR b
0	0	0
0	1	1
1	0	1
1	1	0

When a byte contains one or more bit-fields, the Boolean operations are the tools needed to isolate each part of the byte for independent processing. There are several basic Boolean principles that help to understand how this is accomplished. The letter "a" represents a bit or Boolean value.

```
a AND 0 is 0        ;used to force a bit to zero
a AND 1 is a        ;used to exclude bits from certain
                    ;operations

a OR 0 is a         ;used to exclude bits from certain
                    ;operations
a OR 1 is 1         ;used to force a bit to one

a XOR 0 is a        ;used to exclude bits from certain
                    ;operations
a XOR 1 is NOT a    ;used to toggle (flip, invert) a bit
```

The typical machine language instructions that perform these logical operations operate on all of the bits in a byte in parallel. That is, they perform eight independent AND, OR, NOT, or XOR operations in a single step. These fundamental instructions are often used with special pattern bytes, called bit masks, to isolate parts of the byte so only the desired bits are affected. To properly construct these masks, you must know the fundamental properties above.

To apply these Boolean properties, think of the 0 or 1 in each statement as a mask bit. Choosing the correct mask bit to get the desired result is the key to understanding how Boolean operations are used to manipulate selected bits in a container. Note that AND can be used to force a 0, or cause no change. OR is useful to force a 1, or cause no change. XOR is useful to toggle or flip a bit, or cause no change. The OR and XOR operations use a 1 mask bit to SET or TOGGLE a bit; AND uses the 0 mask bit to CLEAR a bit. The opposite mask bit causes no change.

Mask Out, Clear, Zero

The AND operation is often used to mask out (zero or clear) unimportant bits. A specific byte value is selected as a mask; 0's are placed in positions to be cleared and 1's in positions of importance. Note that the result of an AND with 0 is 0, and the result of an AND with 1 is just the other operand (identity). Thus the 0's mask out (zero) the unwanted bit positions, while the 1's cause no change to the important positions. To mask out bits 7-4, use $0F as a mask. To mask out all of the odd positioned bits, use $55 as the mask. To examine just bit 7, use $80 as the mask. Figure 1.4 illustrates the first two of these operations.

Another important use of AND is to clear specific bits, but leave the others unchanged. This is no different from masking out unimportant bits, except that this time the focus is on the bits being cleared, not the ones left unchanged. The term clear, as in "clear a bit," means to make it zero. Conversely, the term set, as in "set a bit," means to make it one. When using AND to clear specific bits, the focus is on the 0 bits of the mask. An AND with 0's will clear the bits, while the positions ANDed with 1 will be unchanged. To clear the upper nybble, use mask $0F. To clear bit 7, use mask $7F.

Set and Union

The OR operation is used to set specific bits. The 1 bits in a mask will force those positions to 1 when the OR operation is performed. To set bits 4 and 5, use the OR operation with a mask of $30.

Another application of the OR operation is to combine bit-fields from different bytes into a single byte. This is sometimes called union, as the result is a byte with 1's in positions where there was a 1 in one operand or the other. As an example, consider two 4-bit values that need to be combined to form a single byte, one value going into the upper nybble (bits

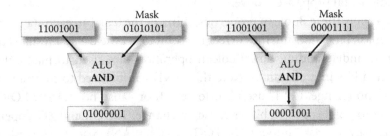

FIGURE 1.4   Using a mask with the AND operation to isolate portions of a byte.

7-4) and the other into the lower nybble (bits 3-0). For this to work properly, you need to have each value in its own container, already positioned in the correct bit positions. The other bits must be 0. Positioning the bits may require a shift operation that will be examined in the next section. Forcing the unimportant bits to 0 can be accomplished using AND as described above. After all of this preparation, simply OR-ing the bytes will combine them into a single container.

Example

The 4-bit value 0b1101 is to be combined with 0b1110, the first will be placed in the upper nybble (this is done using a shift operation which will be discussed soon). Each 4-bit value is in a byte with the opposite nybble cleared. Figure 1.5 illustrates the operation.

```
0b11010000 ;First value in upper nybble, lower nybble clear
0b00001110 ;Second value in lower nybble, upper nybble clear
0b11011110 ;The result of OR-ing the two bytes
```

Toggle

One important function of XOR is to toggle (flip, or invert) selected bits. The mask in this case uses 1's in positions to be toggled and 0's in positions to be unchanged. Figure 1.6 illustrates the exclusive-or operation with the mask value of $AA which will toggle all of the bits in odd positions.

Another interesting feature of the XOR operation is that if it is applied a second time with the same mask, it will undo the changes. This can be used as a simple encryption technique. The mask is the encryption key. It is used to encrypt (flip some bits to obscure the original byte value) and to decrypt (flip the bits back to restore the original byte) the data.

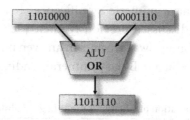

FIGURE 1.5   Using OR to combine opposite nybbles from two bytes into a single byte.

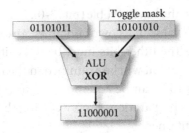

FIGURE 1.6   Using XOR to flip or toggle the bits selected by 1's in the mask byte.

Shifting and Rotating Bits

Shifting bits is technically not a Boolean or logical operation, but it is a bit-manipulation fundamental to the operation of digital computers. While the Boolean operations described previously are confined to independent column-wise manipulations, the shift operations allow movement of bits between columns or positions. A left shift moves bits to higher bit positions and a right shift moves them to lower bit positions.

The byte $5C, when shifted left is $B8, and when shifted right, is $2E. This is more obvious if the bytes are written in binary notation as shown in Table 1.5.

In these examples, a 0 was brought in to fill the vacated position on the left or right end. The bit that was shifted out of the other end was discarded. Processors provide several shift instructions that vary how the vacated position is filled. Usually, the bit that is shifted out is stored in a special flag register so it can be further processed by a program.

Another variation on shifting is rotation. In this case, the bit shifted out is circled around to the other end and shifted into the vacated position. A further variation on this is to rotate through an extra storage location for a single bit; this bit is used to fill the vacated position in the rotation, and then replaced by the bit rotated out of the byte.

Bit shifting can have numeric significance. If a byte represents an unsigned integer as discussed previously, then a left shift will double its value. Note that doubling always results in an even number, and a left shift always makes the last bit a 0. Binary numerals ending in 0 represent even

TABLE 1.5   Illustration of a Left and Right Logical Shift

Original Byte	Shifted Left	Shifted Right
$5C = 0b01011100	$B8 = 0b10111000	$2E = 0b00101110

numbers. Similarly, a right shift halves the numeric value, throwing away any remainder.

One historically important use of the bit shift operation was the implementation of a "multiply by ten" operation. Multiplication instructions in early processors often required special setups and took longer than many other instructions. When repeated multiplication by 10 was needed (remember Horner's Rule?), it was often implemented as a shift and add sequence to speed up the process. Although most modern processors provide highly efficient multiply hardware that has made this technique obsolete, you may still find this technique useful.

The trick is to break the multiplication by 10 into multiplications by powers of 2 (which are efficiently accomplished with a shift) and to use an add instruction. Here is one way to do this.

```
10a = 2a + 8a
```

Thus, to calculate 10a, we shift a once (to get 2a), and then shift 2 more times (to get 8a), and we add the results. For example, the byte representing 18 is $12 or 0b00010010. Call this a.

```
2a = 0b00100100 (obtained by shifting left once)
8a = 0b10010000 (obtained by shifting left twice more)
Adding we get
10a = 0b10110100 which is $B4 or 180.
```

EXERCISES

1. List the five functional units of a typical computer system.
2. Which functional unit of a computer system oversees the fetch–execute cycle?
3. Is main memory (primary storage) typically RAM or ROM? Why?
4. What is the fundamental distinction between the instructions in CISC and RISC architectures?
5. How does a microcontroller differ from a microprocessor.
6. What is the major distinction between the von Neumann and Harvard architectures?
7. Is a CDROM drive a random access or serial secondary storage device? Explain your answer. You may need to read about how these drives operate.
8. Is a mouse a serial or parallel input device? You may need to do some research to learn how a mouse communicates with a computer.

9. Is a printer attached to a PC, a serial or parallel output device? Are all printers the same with respect to this classification? Explain.

10. Is 10 a numeral or a number? Could this represent the number of eyes most animals have? Could this represent the number of eyes found in a jumping spider (family Salticidae)? Explain.

11. How many bits in a byte? In a word? How many nybbles in a doubleword? How many bits in a quadword?

12. Why is hexadecimal notation superior to octal when representing nybbles?

13. In what base is each expression equal to the number of bottles of root beer on the wall (one hundred)?
    a. $1*10000 + 2*100 + 1$
    b. $9*10 + 1$
    c. $2*100 + 4*10 + 4$
    d. $4*100$
    e. $1*100 + 4*10 + 4$

14. In the numeral 0x4C32CB, what digit is in position 4? What digit has a place value of 4096? If this numeral is translated to binary, how many 1's will be in the equivalent numeral?

15. Convert the following base 10 numerals to base two and base 16 using repeated division: 256, 32767, and 51983.

16. Convert the following base five numerals to base 10 using polynomial evaluation: 10, 44, and 243.

17. Convert these hexadecimal values to binary in the simplest way possible: 100, 2F, and AC.

18. Convert these octal values to binary and then hexadecimal without first converting to base 10: 377, 1037, and 4501.

19. Using Horner's Rule, show the step-by-step progress of converting the base seven numeral 62034 to base 10. Begin with zero; multiply by 7, add the next digit, and repeat.

20. Convert these base 15 numerals to base 10 using Horner's Rule. Process the digits from left to right. 9A2, 1000, and C07E.

21. Using Horner's Rule, show the steps to convert 734 (base 10) to base four. You will need to show all of your work in base four. Remember to convert the digits to base four before adding. You will need to know that 10, in base four, is written 22.

22. Determine the result of performing a bitwise AND operation on this pair of nybbles: 0b1011 and 0b0100.

23. Determine the result of performing a bitwise OR operation on this pair of nybbles: 0b1001 and 0b1100.

24. Determine the result of performing a bitwise XOR operation on this pair of nybbles: 0b1001 and 0b1101.
25. What mask and operation would be used to zero the upper nybble in a byte? To clear the lower nybble of a byte?
26. Give the mask and operation needed to round odd numbers (represented by the binary value in a byte) down to the next even number (and not alter even numbers). How could you round up to the nearest odd number?
27. Shift each byte to the left and tell the result in hexadecimal: $3C, $E9, $FF.
28. What happens if you shift a byte to the right, and then shift it back to the left?
29. Devise a way to multiply a byte by 6 using only shifts and one addition.

CHAPTER 2

The Atmel AVR Microcontroller Family

THIS CHAPTER FOCUSES ON assembly language principles in the context of a popular family of 8-bit microcontrollers produced by the Atmel® Corporation. The devices in the Atmel AVR® microcontroller family share a common machine level instruction set and core hardware design. Specific needs for memory size, processing speed, and I/O capabilities can be fulfilled by selecting the most appropriate device.

The AVR 8-bit RISC microcontrollers are designed around a common core architecture. This is a Harvard Architecture with program instructions stored in ROM. The family is roughly divided into the tinyAVR®, megaAVR®, and XMEGA™ series. Specialized members exist for automotive, lighting, networking, battery, and USB applications.

THE AVR CORE

The core of all these microcontrollers includes a CU that fetches instructions from flash (program) memory. Many of the microcontrollers include two additional memories, static RAM (SRAM) and Electrically Erasable Programmable Read Only Memory (EEPROM), which are used to store variable data being manipulated by the program. SRAM is a volatile memory that retains its information as long as it is supplied with power. This is where variable data will be stored during program execution. EEPROM might be considered a secondary storage device. The information stored in this memory will be retained when no power is present. Each byte of this storage area can be erased and rewritten with new information by the processor. The microcontroller's flash memory is also a form of EEPROM, but it usually must be erased and rewritten in larger sections, called blocks. Since erasing a block of flash might erase your program, flash memory is usually treated as read-only when applications are running. One downside to EEPROM storage is that it has a limited write/erase cycle lifetime. The AVR flash memory is good for at least 10,000 write/erase cycles, and the EEPROM for 100,000 cycles.

Instructions

The instructions that each AVR processor is able to execute are summarized in a datasheet provided by the manufacturer, Atmel. Roughly, the instructions can be divided into four categories: arithmetic/logical, memory access, branch, and I/O. Each instruction affects some part of the microcontroller's environment, so we need to become familiar with the basic components that are manipulated by machine instructions. This is the instruction set architecture level of the microcontroller.

Most instructions are 16-bits in length (some are 32-bits), and program memory is organized as a collection of 16-bit words. Program memory is word addressable. This means that the address 0 specifies the first word, address 1 the second, and so on. Each program memory address refers to a pair of bytes. The other AVR memories, SRAM and EEPROM, are byte addressable. Each byte has its own address. Since the AVR family uses different data pathways for program and data memory, the addressing and data transfer can be tailored differently to fit the needs of each.

Registers

The AVR processor has 32 general purpose 8-bit registers. These are named R0 through R31. Data that is currently being manipulated by the program must be located in these registers. Special purpose registers such as the program counter (PC), instruction register, and instruction decode register play an important role in the operation of the processor.

Figure 2.1 shows some of the core components of an AVR microcontroller. During each clock cycle, the address in the PC is used to fetch an instruction into the instruction register. At the same time, the previously fetched instruction moves into the instruction decode register where it is decoded and executed. The control signals generated from the decode register direct the flow of data from and to registers, the data bus, and ALU. They also control the operation performed by the ALU and which I/O device (if any) is being

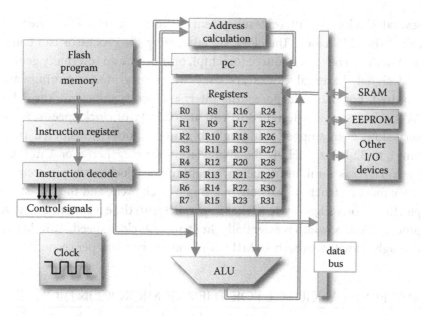

FIGURE 2.1 Some of the core components of a typical AVR microcontroller.

accessed. The data bus provides the data pathway to memory and other I/O devices that are part of the microprocessor's operating environment.

The PC always holds the address of the next instruction to be fetched. The PC register is usually a 16-bit register and holds a word address (as memory sizes vary, some models do not include all of the bits and some need more bits to accommodate large flash memories). A 16-bit PC register allows 65,536 distinct addresses; each address corresponds to a different word in program memory. Thus, the maximum addressable program space of most of the AVR processors is 64 kwords or 128 kbytes.

The instruction and instruction decode registers allow one instruction to be fetched while the previous is being decoded and executed. This creates a very simple, two-stage pipeline. With a single instruction register, one clock cycle would be required to fetch an instruction; it would be executed during the next clock cycle. The instruction pipeline makes it possible to fetch and execute in parallel. This, together with the fact that most instructions can be fetched and executed in a single clock cycle, allows the processor to achieve a throughput of close to one instruction per clock cycle.

Clock

The clock, mentioned above, is an oscillating (zero-one) signal that drives the processor's fetch–execute cycle. The AVR processor actually uses several clocks for different subsystems. The clock referred to here is called the CPU clock. The clock signal driving the processor can come from an external clock source (off chip), or it can be an internally generated signal. External clocks are used when very precise timings are required. For many purposes, the internal clock is sufficient. The 8-bit AVR processors are designed to run at a variety of clock speeds, from very slow, even stopped (although this might not be considered running), to 32 MHz. MHz is the abbreviation for megahertz, or 1 million hertz. Hertz is a unit of frequency, meaning one (clock) cycle per second. Since most instructions execute in a single clock cycle, and the two-stage pipeline allows single cycle fetches in parallel with the execution, the AVR processor's bandwidth is essentially the same as its clock speed. At 16 MHz, throughput will approach 16 MIPS (million instructions per second).

MACHINE LANGUAGE FOR THE AVR MICROCONTROLLER

Machine language programming is seldom done anymore because of the existence of many tools that avoid its tedious details. Assemblers allow programming at a level just above the machine level. Each assembly language instruction is translated by an assembler to a single machine instruction. Higher level languages, such as C, are translated by a compiler to assembly language, or directly to machine language. One high-level statement can take tens or hundreds of machine instructions to accomplish the intended result.

Programming directly in machine language requires a technical understanding of how instructions are represented and formed. The programmer has to pay careful attention to individual bits of the instructions and must perform many arithmetic tasks to determine the correct bit values for each instruction. Changes to one part of the program often affect the information in other instructions in the program, requiring many detail-oriented modifications every time a minor program edit is performed. Machine language programming is slow, tedious, and error prone. Nevertheless, it is a good starting point if you want to understand how a processor works and how an assembler functions.

One Plus One Equals?

Let us design a short machine language program for the AVR processor that will calculate 1 + 1. It will require just two instructions. When doing machine language programming, the programmer must decide where the instructions will be placed in memory so they can be correctly executed by the processor. Remember that the processor must fetch and execute instructions. We will place our program at consecutive memory locations starting at address 0. The reason for this choice will become apparent later.

The programmer also has to decide where the data used by the program will be stored, and where the results will appear. Since this is a very small program with little data, we will use a register for all of our processing needs. We have 32 to choose from. The sample program uses register r16. To fulfill the requirements of our addition program, we will place the constant 1 in register r16, add this register to itself, storing the sum back into register r16. That finishes the program; just two instructions are required.

```
;pseudocode of a program to compute 1 + 1
load register 16 with the number 1
add register 16 to register 16, storing the result in
register 16
```

The first instruction, when executed, places the number 1 in a register. The second adds the register to itself. Here are the machine language instructions represented in hexadecimal notation.

```
0000: E001
0001: 0F00
```

Most AVR instructions are 16-bits (a word) so four hex digits are used to represent each instruction. In the program above, each instruction is preceded by the address where it will be stored in flash memory; the first instruction will be located at address 0. Addresses are usually expressed as a word, so these are also written with four hex digits.

In order to execute this program, we need to actually place the values of the two words into program memory at the indicated addresses. The program itself is just 2 words (4 bytes) in length.

Before we attempt this, let us look into the encoding details of these instructions. We want to investigate how these particular bit patterns were determined and why they represent the actual instructions we want to put in our program.

Load Immediate

Most of the AVR machine instructions fit in a single word, and are conveniently expressed as a hexadecimal value (representing the bits of the actual instruction). The encoding details of the instructions are better understood if we break the bits of the instruction into fields. The locations and sizes and number of fields vary from instruction to instruction. The most important field of every instruction is the opcode (operation code). This determines what the instruction will do in general.

The first instruction of our simple program is named LDI, for load immediate. This is a simple instruction used to load a constant (byte) into a register. This instruction has three fields, the instruction opcode, the destination register, and the value of the constant byte (that is to be loaded into the register when this instruction is executed). The opcode is 4-bits in length and is located in the leftmost nybble, or bits 15–12. For the LDI instruction, these bits are 0xE, or 0b1110. Thus the instruction looks like this (so far).

```
1110 ???? ???? ????
```

(The nibbles are separated visually to make it easier to read.)

Once the opcode is determined (opcodes are listed in the microprocessor's manual), the operands must be coded. The destination register number in the LDI instruction is specified by 4 bits occupying the left nybble of the second byte, bits 7–4 of the word. You may recall that this processor has 32 registers, but 4 bits will only allow 16 combinations to be specified. Because the destination register field is only 4 bits in length, the LDI instruction can only specify 16 different registers; it is restricted to using registers r16 through r31. When the LDI instruction is decoded, a leading 1 is added to the four bits representing the destination register to make a 5-bit binary numeral. This corresponds to the register number. We want to use register 16, which in binary, is 10000. We strip off the leading 1 to determine the contents of the second field, the destination register. Now the instruction looks like this.

```
1110 ???? 0000 ????
```

The remaining eight bits represent the actual byte (0x01) that will be loaded into the designated register when this instruction is executed. The two nybbles of this byte are placed in nibbles 2 and 0 of the instruction. The byte is split into two parts, 0x0 and 0x1, and inserted into nybbles 2 and 0 respectively. This yields the actual code for the machine instruction.

```
1110 0000 0000 0001 or $E001
```

Figure 2.2 shows the effect of executing this instruction. The processor has gone through two clock cycles to move the LDI instruction into the instruction decode register. The second instruction in memory has been moved into the instruction register. The PC shows the address of the instruction just fetched into the instruction register but will be incremented before the next fetch occurs. Executing a LDI instruction consists of configuring a data pathway from the two nybbles of the instruction decode register (where the data byte is located) through the ALU (which is told by the control signals to simply pass this byte through unchanged), along the internal bus to the register file, to the register specified in nybble 1 of the instruction, in this case, r16.

The instruction to load the constant 0x3C into register R25 would be E39C (0x9 is the code for R25 since 25 = 0x19). The general form for this instruction in assembly language is

```
LDI Rd, K          1110 bbbb rrrr bbbb
16 <= d <= 31;  0x00 <= K <= 0xFF
Result: Rd = K
```

The LDI instruction is a simple form of an assignment statement. It is used to assign a byte value to a register (R16–R31). When you think of LDI as an assignment operation, you are thinking of the register as a variable.

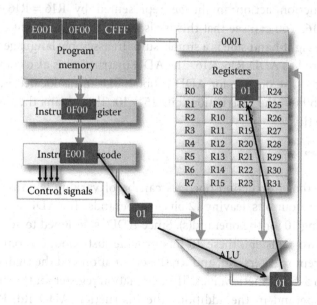

FIGURE 2.2   Executing the LDI R16, 1 instruction.

Many assembly language programs use registers in exactly this way. Using registers as variables is appropriate as long as you only need a few variables, and the data you are representing fits in a register. It would not be appropriate, for example, to store a string in a register; strings are sequences of bytes, but a register can hold only one byte at a time. When the number of variables exceeds the number of available registers, a different method must be used.

Analyze the following two sample LDI instructions, verifying that the instruction fields are correct.

```
LDI R16, 0x01      1110 0000 0000 0001
LDI R25, 0x3C      1110 0011 1001 1100
```

As you can see, encoding machine language instructions is a time consuming, tedious task. Fortunately, the assembler can do all of this encoding for us. The term, assembler, is quite descriptive of its major task: assembling the parts of an instruction into a single word.

Add

The second instruction in our program is called ADD. This adds the bytes in two registers and stores the sum back into one of them. In this case, the two registers are one and the same; register r16 is used twice. Symbolically, the instruction action might be represented by R16 = R16 + R16 or R16 += R16. You can see that this is also a type of assignment operation, where the right-hand side is a simple sum. In assembly language, it would be expressed as ADD R16, R16. The ADD instruction is also composed of three fields. The opcode for ADD is 0b000011 and is located in the leftmost six bits of the instruction, bits 15 − 10. This means the instruction looks like this.

```
0000 11?? ???? ????
```

Notice that instruction opcodes can be of varying lengths. The LDI opcode was four bits, leaving 12 bits for operands. The ADD opcode is six bits, leaving 10 for the operand(s). Since ADD is designed to add the contents of two registers, these 10 bits provide just enough room to name two different registers, Rd, and Rr, the destination and the right operand, using two 5-bit numeric values. The destination register for the sum is also the left operand in the addition. The instruction ADD Rd, Rr means Rd = Rd + Rr or Rd += Rr.

The register numbers are each expressed in 5 bits, but the leading bit for Rr is stored separately from the others. If the bits for Rd are **ddddd**, and the bits for Rr are **rrrrr**, then the bits of the ADD instruction will be arranged like this: 0000 11**rd dddd rrrr**. For our example, ADD R16, R16, we insert the bits for the destination register, the left R16, in the field marked with the d's.

```
0000 11?1 0000 ????
```

And then, since our destination register is the same as the register containing the other operand, insert the same register code (10000) into the field marked with the r's.

```
0000 1111 0000 0000, or 0x0F00.
```

Figure 2.3 illustrates the execution of the ADD instruction. Data pathways copy the value in R16 to the two inputs of the ALU. The ALU is set to perform an ADD operation. The result is stored back into R16, replacing the old value of 0x01 with the sum, 0x02.

If we wanted to ADD R4, R30, then the instruction would be 0000 1110 0100 1110, or 0x0E4E.

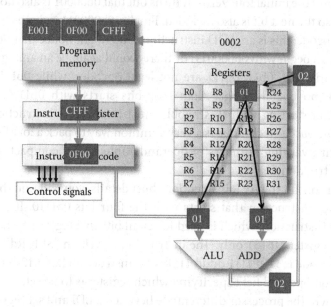

FIGURE 2.3   Executing the ADD R16, R16 instruction.

The general form for this instruction in assembly language is

```
ADD Rd, Rr    0000 11rd dddd rrrr
0 <= r <= 31;  0 <= d <= 31
Result  Rd = Rd + Rr
```

Verify that all of the fields are correct for these examples.

```
ADD R16, R16    0000 1111 0000 0000
ADD R4, R30     0000 1110 0100 1110
```

Expanding Opcodes

You should be asking how the processor "knows" whether the current instruction has a 4-bit or 6-bit (or other length) opcode. If opcodes are different lengths, how can the processor isolate the opcode to properly execute the instruction? The opcode in every AVR instruction begins in the leftmost bits of the word. Since the ADD instruction begins with 0b0000, the following cannot be valid opcodes: 0b0, 0b00, 0b000, and 0b0000. If any of these were valid opcodes, an ambiguity in the instruction design would exist. Thus, when the instruction starting 0b0000... is decoded (to determine what instruction it represents), the decoding must consider additional bits beyond the initial four zeros. It turns out that 0b00001 is also not a valid opcode, so the next bit is also included. Finally, 0b000011 is discovered to be a valid opcode; this is an ADD instruction. You might notice that no longer opcode can begin with 0b000011, or there would again be an ambiguity.

Similarly, 0b1, 0b11, 0b111 are not legal opcodes, while 0b1110 is. In addition, no opcode longer than four bits starts with 0b1110, so any instruction starting with this nybble must be the LDI instruction. This *expanding opcode* technique is a very common way to pack a lot of instructions (with varying numbers of operands) into a very compact and efficient instruction format.

If you consult the AVR instruction sheet details, you will find that there is another instruction that starts with the four bits 0b1110. It is the Set Register instruction, which is used to set all bits in a register to 1. It operates on registers 16–31 only. The instruction is written "SER Rd" and the machine code is 1110 1111 dddd 1111. This instruction has a 12-bit opcode and a 4-bit operand field specifying which register is to be set.

How will the processor differentiate between a LDI and set register? Let us decode the instruction both ways and see what happens. If we interpret the above machine instruction as if it is a LDI, we see that it corresponds to the assembly language statement, LDI Rd, $FF. This explains the mystery. This LDI does the same thing as a set register (sets all bits to 1). Thus, SER is just a special case of LDI. When programming in assembly language, you can use either form to get the desired instruction.

If you search the list of AVR machine instructions, you will find another instruction with the same opcode as ADD. It is the logical shift left instruction. You already know that a basic shift to the left will move the bits in a byte to the left one position and bring a zero into position 0. The left shift instruction is written "LSL Rd" and its machine code is 0000 11d**d dddd** dddd (the bold d's are replaced by the binary code for the register and the other d's are replaced by the same five bits). How can this be? Interpret this instruction as an ADD instruction and see what it really does. Compare this to the effect of a logical shift left. Is there a problem?

Execution Trace

Now that we understand how the instructions are assembled, and what they are supposed to do when executed, we can move on to actually testing it on a real processor. Our first step will be to place the two instructions in program memory. But now we have more questions to be answered. At what addresses should the instructions be placed? And in what order should they be arranged? Must they be in adjacent locations?

To answer these questions, we need to know a little more about how the AVR processor knows what program to run. Actually, this is a very simple answer. In normal operating mode, whenever the processor is powered on or receives a reset signal (this is a special pin on the processor that is asserted with a 0 or 1) it immediately performs a sequence of housekeeping operations before beginning or resuming its main duty, the fetch–execute cycle. One of those tasks is to load a zero into the PC. If you provide a reset signal to the processor, you can guarantee that it will fetch and execute the instruction at address zero. Thus, we should place our program's first instruction at address zero of program memory.

Upon fetching any instruction, the PC is incremented. Thus our second instruction should be located at address one.

If we can manage to get our program bytes into the proper memory locations, and then press reset, we should expect the following to happen. PC is set to zero. The instruction, 0xE001, is fetched into the current instruction register, and the PC is incremented to 0x0001. Since the PC was set to 0x0000 by the reset signal, no instruction is executed during this cycle. We will see that whenever the PC is changed by a mechanism other than its normal increment, the execute operation will be skipped on the next cycle. While the next instruction is being fetched (remember the two-stage pipeline), the first instruction is decoded and executed. Since the first four bits are 0b1110, the CU recognizes it as the LDI instruction. The control signals issued by the CU then cause bits 11-8, 3-0 of the instruction (the bits of the immediate byte) to be placed on the processor's internal data pathway, and received into register R16. At this point, the execution of the instruction is complete, and the fetch execute cycle repeats. Refer back to Figure 2.2 for a visualization of these details.

While the first instruction was executing, the second instruction of our program was fetched and the PC incremented. During the next clock cycle, it is decoded, and executed. Notice that each instruction requires two clock cycles to be executed: one to fetch it, the next to decode and execute. However, the two-stage pipeline overlaps the fetch and execute of adjacent instructions allowing an instruction to be executed during each clock cycle. Figure 2.4 illustrates the effect of the pipeline to essentially double the instruction throughput.

When the second instruction is decoded, the processor matches the first six bits of the instruction to the opcode for ADD. The appropriate remaining bits of the instruction are used to generate control signals that place the value of R16 on the two internal data pathways, leading to the ALU. R16 is placed on both pathways since it is being added to itself. The ALU is told to output the sum of its inputs, and the result is directed back into R16.

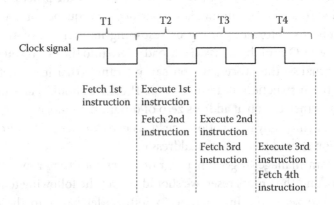

FIGURE 2.4   Parallel operation of the fetch and execute phases in a two-stage pipeline.

Our program is now complete, and if we could examine the contents of R16, we would see the value 0x02. However, the processor was simultaneously fetching the third instruction (from memory location two) while the ADD instruction was executing. It has no way to know that the program is finished; it has dutifully fetched the next "instruction." What will it find at address 0x0002? Since we did not place anything into this location, we will simply say "garbage." Whatever value is found there; it will be fetched into the current instruction register, decoded, and executed. The processor will probably proceed merrily through memory, fetching (and incrementing) and executing, oblivious to the fact that we are no longer interested in its computational efforts.

Jump

When a program is executed in a more sophisticated computing system, it is usually done so under the direction (oversight) of an operating system. In this case, programs are written to end with a special instruction that returns control to the operating system. You might signify this in high-level programs with a return (from the main program) or with an exit command.

In our example, our program is all that is running; there is no operating system to which we can return control. We could let the processor go on processing garbage, but a better ending would be to give it something specific to do. A simple solution is to create an infinite loop. The AVR instruction set includes a simple instruction to do this. The unconditional jump instruction, RJMP, can be used to change the normal behavior of the fetch–execute cycle. When an RJMP instruction is executed, it overwrites the just incremented PC value with a different address. This causes the next instruction to be fetched from a location other than the next sequential address of the program memory. If we place the RJMP instruction at address 0x0002 (right at the end of our program, and code this instruction so that the PC is overwritten by address 0x0002 (the address of the RJMP), then the processor will repeatedly (and contentedly) fetch and reexecute the RJMP. This is the tightest infinite loop possible in a program.

If you have been following the discussion carefully, you might notice a problem. While we were changing the PC (executing the RJMP), the fetch of the next instruction (at address three) has already been put into motion. Indeed, by the time the PC is changed back to two, the instruction at address three (more garbage) has already been brought into the pipeline and the instruction we actually want to execute will not be available until the end of the next clock cycle. This is a common "problem" with pipelined processors, but is easily solved by simply ignoring the extra instruction, waiting for the correct next instruction to be fetched (the RJMP at address two), and then executing it. As you can see, executing a jump instruction requires a second clock cycle to restock the pipeline. The processor automatically ignores the unnecessarily fetched instruction at address 0x0003 when the instruction at address 0x0002 changes the value in the PC.

To finish our program, we need to encode an RJMP that will jump to address two. The RJMP instruction causes the PC to be replaced by a computed value that depends on the address of the RJMP instruction itself. Our RJMP instruction will be located at the next address in our program, 0x0002, and to create our loop, we want to replace PC by this address. We need to encode an RJMP that will be fetched from address 0x0002, and that will jump to itself, address 0x0002.

The RJMP, Relative Jump, instruction looks like this:

```
RJMP K     1100 kkkk kkkk kkkk
-2048 <= K < 2048
```

According to the manufacturer specifications, this instruction causes this action:

```
PC = PC + 1 + K
```

In the AVR instruction set documentation, PC means the address of the current instruction, not the contents of the processor's PC. Here is the equation we need to solve and the solution is

```
0x0002 = 0x0002 + 1 + K
K = -1
```

We will see later that −1 is coded in binary as a string of all 1's. In this case, we need 12 bits for the value of K (see the instruction format above), so the required machine instruction will be 0xCFFF. Note that this same machine instruction can be used at any address to create a very tight infinite loop, an instruction that jumps to itself. Since the PC value of the RJMP instruction is used to compute the destination of the jump, this instruction always computes its own address, loads it in PC, and as a result, branches to itself.

Our complete program is now

```
0000: E001
0001: 0F00
0002: CFFF
```

When the third instruction is fetched, the PC is incremented from 0x0002 to 0x0003. The word at address 0x0003 will be fetched while the third instruction is decoded and executed. We will see soon that this "next instruction" is not needed and will eventually be discarded. Figure 2.5 illustrates the execution of the RJMP to put the processor in an infinite loop. Although the PC has already been incremented, the processor hardware adjusts it to 0x0002, the address of the RJMP instruction. The value 0xFFFF (−1) comes from the decode register, and the address computation hardware adds one to the sum, producing the new PC value of 0x0002. Because the PC is changed, the "instruction" in the instruction register is discarded as the RJMP instruction is fetched again from memory.

The processor decodes the instruction fetched from 0x0002 and since the first four bits match the RJMP opcode (0b1100), it sets up its internal data pathways to add together the number represented in its remaining 12-bits, the address of the instruction itself (0x0002) and the constant one. The result is directed back into PC. The computation is PC = PC + 1 + (−1) = 0x0002 + 1 + (−1) = 0x0002. Because of this change to the PC, the processor's instruction pipeline discards the instruction in the instruction

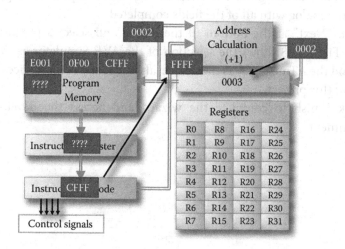

FIGURE 2.5   Executing a very tight infinite loop.

register (which was fetched from 0x0003) and does nothing for the next clock cycle as it waits for the instruction at address 0x0002 to be fetched and moved into the decode register. When that instruction is decoded, the processor, if it were capable of making remarks, would probably say, "Déjà vu!"

We will actually try out this program in the next section.

AVR STUDIO

Atmel provides a free development environment called AVR Studio® for the AVR family. This is an integrated editor, assembler/compiler, simulator/debugger, and downloader (to load the programs into the processor's flash memory). To introduce you to the AVR processor and programming techniques, we will start with a small program that uses only AVR studio. No actual AVR hardware will be required. By carrying out this exercise, you will learn how to write and execute (via a simulator) a machine language program.

New Project

Start up AVR studio; the New Project Wizard (see Figure 2.6) should appear. Click the New Project button.

We will be creating an AVR Assembly Language project. Name it Machine_Language_1, and have the studio create a folder and file for you. The folder and file will match the project name. You should select an appropriate Location folder to hold all of your AVR projects. Figure 2.7 shows the dialog with all of the fields completed.

Click "Next" at the bottom of the dialog and select a platform and device. Figure 2.8 shows the selection of the AVR Simulator as the platform and the ATmega16A as the device, although any of the devices would work for this project.

Click Finish to complete the wizard and access the development environment.

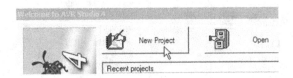

FIGURE 2.6 The New Project Wizard.

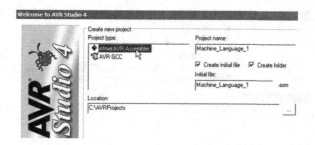

FIGURE 2.7   Select the project type, name, and location.

Editor

In the editor window, we will create a simple assembly language program that creates a sequence of word values. In the AVR assembly language, we tell the assembler to assemble a stream of bytes that will become our program. The assembler takes care of placing the bytes in a file in the appropriate format so we can download them to an actual processor, or simulate them in the Studio simulator. We will need only one Assembly Language command for this exercise, one that instructs the assembler to output a word value. Copy program 2.1 into the editor window as shown in Figure 2.9.

```
;Program 2.1
.dw 0xe001
.dw 0x0f00
.dw 0xcfff
```

Assembling

Save the file and assemble it (press F7 or choose Build under the Build menu). Compare the Build output on your screen to that shown in Figure 2.10. The Build output is a summary of the assembly process.

Select debug platform and device

Debug platform:	Device:
AVR Dragon	ATmega168
AVR ONE!	ATmega168P
AVR Simulator	ATmega168PA
AVR Simulator 2	ATmega169
ICE 200	ATmega169P
ICE 40	ATmega16A
ICE 50	ATmega16HVA

FIGURE 2.8   Choose the debug platform and the microcontroller type.

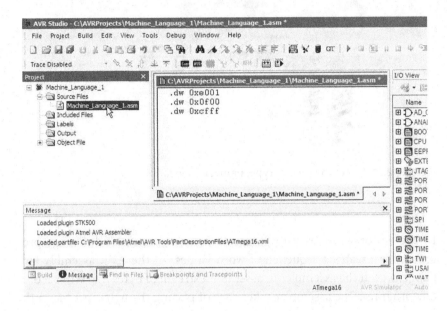

FIGURE 2.9   Using the editor to enter an assembly language program.

Debugger

Assuming no errors are detected, you can start the simulator (debugger). Figure 2.11 shows the Start Debugging command under the Debug menu. This will load your assembled program into the simulator's program memory; the simulator will pause at address 0x0000 awaiting your command to begin execution.

The editor should show a yellow arrow indicating the instruction about to be fetched. The left panel should show the Processor panel, where you can examine register and processor values. The PC should show 0x0000

```
Build

    AVRASM: AVR macro assembler 2.1.41 (build 1792 Jul 21 2009 12:30:27)
    Copyright (C) 1995-2009 ATMEL Corporation

    C:\AVRProjects\Machine_Language_1\Machine_Language_1.asm(4): No EEPROM data,

    Memory use summary [bytes]:
    Segment    Begin      End       Code   Data   Used    Size    Use%
    ------------------------------------------------------------------
    [.cseg] 0x000000 0x000006      0      6    6 unknown     -
    [.dseg] 0x000060 0x000060      0      0    0 unknown     -
    [.eseg] 0x000000 0x000000      0      0    0 unknown     -

 ⊛ Assembly complete, 0 errors. 0 warnings
```

FIGURE 2.10   Output from the assembly (build) process.

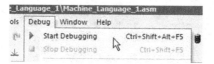

FIGURE 2.11 The Start Debugging command loads your program into the simulator.

as its current value. This is the address of the instruction about to be executed, not the value that would be in the PC of the actual hardware (which will be greater by one when the instruction is about to be executed because of the pipeline). Figure 2.12 shows the Processor window before execution begins.

Before executing any instructions, open the Memory window (Under the View Menu as shown in Figure 2.13) and verify that program memory contains the correct sequence of words that constitutes our program.

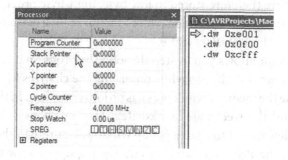

FIGURE 2.12 The simulator's view of the processor before execution begins.

FIGURE 2.13 Using the View menu to display Program Memory.

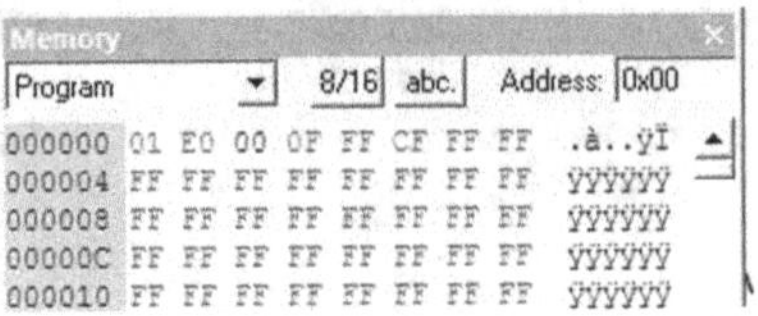

FIGURE 2.14 Program Memory showing the bytes of a machine language program to compute one plus one.

Be sure you are viewing Program Memory (use the selection dropdown to select which memory you want to view). You should see something like the display in Figure 2.14. The following sequence of bytes should appear beginning at address 0000: 01 E0 00 0F FF CF.

What seems wrong with this sequence? The instructions appear to have their bytes reversed. This is intentional. The AVR architecture prefers to store word data (including instructions) in reverse byte (little-endian) order. That is, the least significant byte is stored first. The usual 16-bit instructions are therefore stored in low-byte, high-byte order. If we translate these to normal presentation, we see the three instructions are exactly what we desired: E001 0F00 CFFF.

The simulator allows you to step through the program one instruction at a time. We want to do this while observing the changes to register R16. You can close the memory window as it is no longer needed. In the Processor panel, expand the tree node labeled Registers, or choose View/Register (from the View menu) to open a popup window. Figure 2.15 shows the register view in the Processor window and the popup window that appears when using the View/Register menu selection. Register 16 (R16) should be 0x00. The simulator initializes registers to 0x00 when you start a debugging session. You should never assume this occurs in the actual hardware!

Choose the Step Into option from the debug menu (or press F11—this is much simpler) to allow the program to fetch and execute the first instruction. You should observe the following changes. The yellow arrow in the editor jumps to the second instruction. As shown in Figure 2.16, register R16 now contains 0x01 (changed values appear in red). The PC is now 1.

Step Into again (F11) and observe the changes. Figure 2.17 illustrates the effect of executing the ADD instruction as the sum, 0x02, replaces the contents of register 16. The processor is ready to fetch our final instruction.

If you continue to single step (F11) you will observe no changes. Figure 2.18 shows the PC remaining at address 0x0002 even though 30 clock cycles have elapsed.

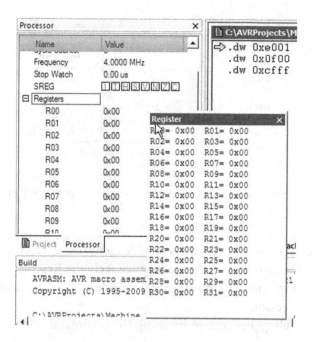

FIGURE 2.15   The General Purpose Registers before execution begins.

With each single-step command, the PC is incremented and then changed back to its original value as the relative jump instruction implements our tight loop. The only change seen in the Processor panel is the cycle count. This indicates the number of clock cycles that have elapsed during the simulated execution. The simulator also reports the elapsed time in simulated microseconds (based on the simulated clock speed). The relative jump instruction consumes two clock cycles for each execution. If you watch the Cycle Counter while executing the first two instructions,

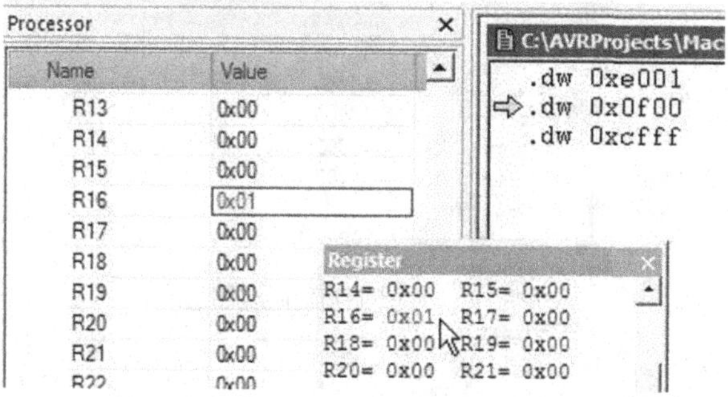

FIGURE 2.16   Executing the LDI instruction to place a 0x01 in register 16.

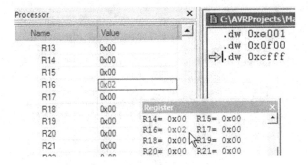

FIGURE 2.17   Executing the ADD instruction to compute 1 + 1 and store the result in register 16.

you will see that those instructions required only one clock cycle each (you can restart the program via the Debug menu; choose Reset). The ability to execute most instructions in a single clock cycle is a primary characteristic of a RISC processor.

Stop the debugging session by using the command under the Debug menu.

Mnemonics

Our assembly language program used a simple assembly language directive, .dw, to build our program. The assembler simply translated our numbers (the hexadecimal representations of the machine instructions) into a stream of bytes that were stored in files. In Figure 2.19 the assembler output is shown under the Output (Machine_Language_1.hex) and Object File (Machine_Language_1.obj) folders in the Project window. These files

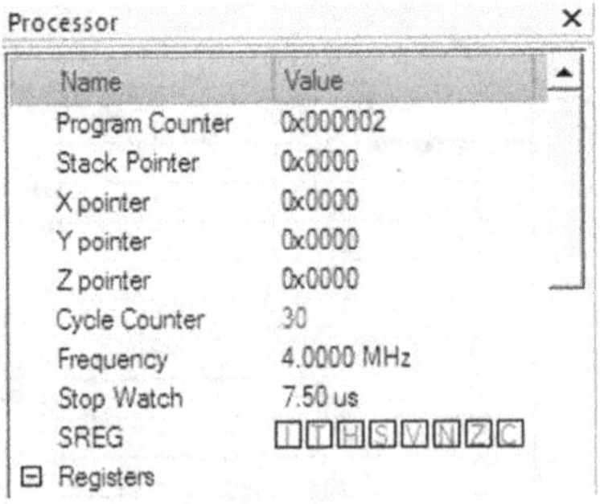

FIGURE 2.18   The Processor status as the RJMP is executed repeatedly at the end of our program.

FIGURE 2.19   Assembler output files are shown in the Project window under the Output and Object File folders.

contain details about the program bytes to allow the program to be simulated (.obj file) or downloaded (.hex file) to an actual processor.

We could better utilize the capabilities of the assembler by writing our program in machine instruction mnemonics and allow it to assemble the instruction words rather than doing the assembly by hand. But you will see that the results are the same. Replace your original program with the following, then save and build.

```
;Program 2.1 - Mnemonic Version
ldi R16, 0x01
add R16, R16
rjmp PC
```

This is a more typical assembly language version of the program we designed. Instructions are indicated by a mnemonic, a memory aid, representing the machine instruction to be assembled. The mnemonics used in the AVR assembler match the instruction names in the AVR instruction set. This is a common practice, but not all assemblers follow this convention completely. An AVR assembler designed by another company could require that you write LOADI for load immediate (instead of LDI).

The AVR assembler will recognize the machine instruction mnemonics and generate the appropriate machine instruction based on the operands. Notice the last instruction RJMPs to the address specified by PC. In AVR assembly language, PC represents the address of the instruction being assembled. The assembler will correctly compute the required displacement (−1) to cause this instruction to branch to itself when the program is executed. Be careful! You cannot write RJMP −1 as an assembly language instruction thinking you are telling the assembler to use the −1 for K (as the documentation of the RJMP instruction suggests). The Instruction Set Documentation is not an assembly language manual. Although the documentation contains statements that resemble assembly language, it is not assembly language. You need to refer to the assembly language manual (available through AVR Studio's Help menu) to see how to correctly write the operands for the instruction mnemonics.

After successfully assembling this program, start a debugging session and view memory as shown in Figure 2.20. You should see exactly the same memory contents as before.

The generated program does not include any hints as to how it was generated, as a sequence of numerals, or the equivalent mnemonics and operands. You can run the program and verify that the results are exactly the same.

AVR DEVELOPMENT PLATFORMS

Atmel manufactures several development and evaluation platforms for use with their microcontrollers. In this chapter we will assume you are using one of the following systems: the STK®-500 or the ATAVRXPLAIN (abbreviated XPLAIN).

STK-500 Development Kit

The STK-500 is a versatile and inexpensive kit designed for this purpose. It includes sockets for many of the AVR microcontrollers, and provides a standard set of I/O connections onboard, with extensive expansion capabilities. The AVR XPLAIN Demonstration Board is an even more inexpensive system, providing a different collection of I/O devices and providing USB support. The Atmel website provides links to vendors that can supply these and other Atmel hardware.

Both platforms include eight LEDs that provide visual feedback of the output state of some of the basic I/O ports of the AVR microcontroller.

FIGURE 2.20 Program Memory as loaded from the mnemonic version of the simple addition program.

There are also eight pushbutton switches that can be used for input to these ports. The STK-500 provides headers to interface to a variety of devices. The XPLAIN board includes several other I/O devices including a speaker and temperature sensor. In addition, it is a simple matter to setup serial I/O between the microcontroller and a remote RS-232 port (STK-500) or USB (XPLAIN).

After unpacking the STK-500, you will want to acquire a power supply (10–15 V) and connect some standard jumpers. Consult the manual for details of the usual configuration. Assuming you will be using a serial port for programming, you will need a 6-wire jumper from ISP6PIN header to appropriate SPROG header. The STK-500 is pictured in Figure 2.21 with a power supply and USB-Serial adaptor.

The microcontroller that ships with the STK-500 already has a program in flash. It will control the LEDs and accept input from the pushbuttons. You will need to connect the appropriate ports to these hardware items to make this work. Two 10 pin cables should be used to connect PORTB to the LEDs and PORTD to the switches. You should verify that everything works "out of the box" before attempting to download your own programs to the AVRmicrocontroller on the STK-500 board.

Although a microcontroller is supplied with the STK-500, you may want to purchase an ATmega16A. This chapter will use this microcontroller for

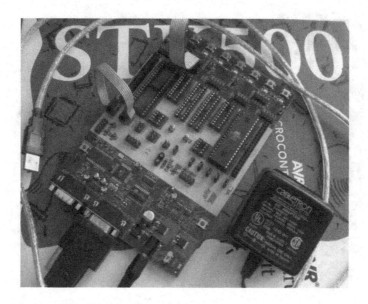

FIGURE 2.21   The STK-500 Development Kit.

examples and sample code. The ATmega16A is installed in a socket that requires the ISP connection to SPROG3. Be sure to consult the manual for proper installation. Figure 2.21 shows the correct location for the ATmega16A.

The ATAVRXPLAIN Demonstration Kit

The XPLAIN kit pictured in Figure 2.22 includes the more capable ATxmega128A1 microcontroller. Whereas the STK-500 supports the use of a wide variety of microcontrollers and allows jumpers to be used to connect devices to any of the microcontroller pins, the XPLAIN board comes prewired with the above processor and fixed connections to the onboard devices. Its main advantage is lower cost, USB support, and a wider variety of I/O devices. The XMEGA series of microcontrollers are the latest and most powerful of the 8-bit processors in the AVR family.

AVR Studio provides a simple programming interface allowing downloads to the AVR microcontroller used in either of the above platforms. Once programming is complete, the AVR processor can immediately execute the program. In the next sections you will write a simple assembly language program and execute it on an AVR microcontroller in the STK-500 environment or the XPLAIN Demonstration Board.

FIGURE 2.22 The Atmel ATAVRXPLAIN Demonstration Kit.

INTRODUCTION TO AVR ASSEMBLY LANGUAGE

You have already been introduced to a very simple AVR Assembler assembly language program for the AVR microcontroller. We used only the minimum of capabilities of the AVR Assembler to create a program consisting of three words (instructions). An assembler is needed to translate an assembly language program to the processor's machine language in a format it can be used.

Generally, an assembler outputs a file containing the machine language program along with information describing certain characteristics of the program. This file is usually called an object file; it contains the object code, the code that is the intended result of any translation process targeting a particular processor. The AVR Studio Simulator/Debugger uses the object file to support debugging tasks within the simulator. The AVR assembler also outputs a special file, called a hex file, which is actually used to download program information to the microcontroller's flash memory. These two files contain the same machine instruction information and data, but in different formats. If EEPROM data is specified in your assembly language program, a separate file will be created with this data.

Assembly languages for a specific processor can vary in their details, but there are usually many similarities. The manufacturer generally describes the processor instructions in an assembly-like language. Most assembly languages for that processor mimic features of the manufacturer's specifications. The mnemonics used to represent machine instructions are usually the same as those used by the manufacturer.

Other characteristics of the particular assembly language can vary substantially. Rules for creating identifiers, specifying operands for instructions, inserting comments, and issuing commands to the assembler about the assembly process, are all potentially unique to each assembly language. We will be using the AVR Assembler provided by Atmel as a developer tool for their AVR microcontrollers, so we will learn the details of this assembly language. The current version of the assembler is called AVR Assembler 2.1.

Assembly Language Source Files

Assembly language programs consist of a sequence of assembly statements, interspersed with comments (hopefully). Each program is stored in an ASCII text file; this file is called the source file. Any text editor can be used to create these files; AVR Studio includes an integrated text editor that is used for this purpose.

Statements are placed on separate lines of the file. In most cases, each statement must fit on a single line; however, there are some circumstances where this is not required.

Line Format

Each line of the source file is limited to 120 characters. In general, you want to keep your lines much shorter than this so the printed copies of your program are easily readable. Each line may begin with a label definition which is an identifier followed by a colon. A label is an identifier representing a memory location. They are used in other statements to refer to the specified memory location in place of an actual numeric address.

After the optional label there should be a directive or an instruction mnemonic. Instruction mnemonics represent machine instructions, and the assembler will translate these to the appropriate binary codes. Directives are used to tell the assembler to do something related to the assembly process, something other than translate an instruction. Most directives and instructions require operands which appear next on the line. A space or tab is used to separate the parts of each line.

Any line may end with a comment. Comments begin with the semicolon character and extend to the end of the line. A line may consist of only a comment; empty lines are also allowed and should be used appropriately to improve the visual presentation of your program. The AVR assembler also supports the comment format used in C ++ and Java: // for single line comments, and /* ... */ for multiline or block comments.

Here is a summary of the legal line formats. The items in [brackets] are optional. Operands are not required in all cases, but the format details for individual instructions or mnemonics indicate where they must be placed if required.

```
[label:] directive operands [;comment]
[label:] instruction operands [;comment]
[label:] [;comment]
```

Additional Features

There are a few additional features/details you may want to be aware of. There is a special preprocessor feature of the assembler that allows some text abbreviations for longer commands to be used. Preprocessor commands are preceded by the number-sign character (#). These lines are processed before the assembly process begins.

Statements that require very long lines may be carried onto subsequent lines by using the line continuation character. The backslash (\), when used at the end of a line, indicates the content of the current line continues on the next physical line of the file.

The AVR Assembler also supports macros. The preprocessor feature described in the previous paragraph is often called a macro facility, but its syntax is different from the assembly language macros. The general concept of a macro is that of text substitution. Once a macro is defined, the use of the macro (called a macro invocation) in the source code causes an expansion; the macro invocation is expanded into a series of new source code lines. The substituted text is assembled in place of the macro invocation. Macros support arguments that allow the substituted text to vary based on the invocation details. Macros are an historic part of assembly language programming. They are not essential to understanding the assembly process, but they do provide a useful tool for assembly language programmers. The use of macros is covered in Chapter 6.

SAMPLE AVR ASSEMBLY LANGUAGE PROGRAM

Programming in a new language requires learning a new syntax and the conventions practiced by most programmers that regularly use that language. There are lots of textbooks for the popular high-level languages and these generally introduce common stylistic conventions. If you look at a lot of AVR programs from different sources, you will see a wide variety of styles.

Assembly language programs and an assembler are simply tools to generate a sequence of bytes that need to appear in particular locations in memory. In the AVR world, we have two places where we want the assembler to place specific byte values: flash and EEPROM. Although many assemblers targeting other processors and computing systems allow bytes to be specified as initial contents of RAM, the AVR assembler does not allow this, and for good reason. AVR programs must reside completely in nonvolatile storage. They can utilize SRAM for storage during execution, but cannot assume SRAM contains anything in particular when execution begins. This is common in microcontroller systems. More general computing systems utilize a loader that will fill memory (volatile memory) with bytes (both data and instructions) needed to begin execution. AVR programs reside in ROM (flash), and are executed directly from there, so there is no load step required. There is a utility called the programmer that acts like a loader. It is used to copy (download) a program from the hex file produced by the assembler into flash and EEPROM memory.

When writing assembly language programs, the programmer must carefully choose flash or EEPROM as the destination of bytes that will be output by the assembler. In addition, AVR programs generally define labels that will refer to memory locations in each of the three memory areas, including SRAM. To switch between these three memory contexts as you write programs, AVR assembly language provides three special commands, called directives: .cseg (switch to the code segment or flash), .dseg (switch to the data segment or SRAM), and .eseg (switch to the EEPROM segment). These represent the three memories of the AVR microcontroller. The assembler begins each assembly task assuming output is to flash, as if an implicit .cseg directive was processed first. The programmer inserts a segment command as needed to switch contexts. It is good practice to explicitly specify which segment is intended as the initial segment in your program.

A Counting Program

Here is a sample program that will illustrate some of the basic assembly language features. The program will display numbers on one of the AVR microcontroller's output ports. Most AVR processors have a number of 8-bit ports that may be used for input or output with external devices. When configured for output, each bit of a byte independently controls the voltage level asserted on the associated pin of the microcontroller chip. This signal can be used to control many different types of devices. As a simple visual indicator of the output level asserted on the pins, each pin can be connected to control an LED. In the simulator environment, the state of each pin is visualized in the I/O view panel.

PROGRAM 2.2   A Program to Illustrate PORT Output and Counting

```
;Counter - A simple AVR program to illustrate output to a port
;Designed to be executed in a simulator under debug control

;This program counts from 0 to 255 (and repeats)
;The current counter value is output to PORTB of an ATMega16A.

;Programmer: TM
;Date: 5/2010
;Platform: STK-500
;Device: ATMega16A

.cseg           ;select current segment as code
.org    0       ;begin assembling at address 0
```

```
;Define symbolic names for resources used
.def    count   = r16        ;Reg 16 will hold counter value
.def    temp    = r17        ;Reg 17 is used as a temporary
                              register

.equ    PORTB   = 0x18       ;Port B's output register
.equ    DDRB    = 0x17       ;Port B's Data Direction Register

        ldi     temp,0xFF     ;configure PORTB as output
        out     DDRB,temp

        ldi     count,0x00    ;Initialize count at 0

lp:

        out     PORTB,count   ;Put counter value on PORT B
        inc     count         ;increment counter

        rjmp    lp            ;repeat (forever)
```

Explanation of the Statements

This entire program is to be contained in flash memory. The .cseg directive at the top of the program specifies this to the assembler. The bytes of the program begin at address zero; the .org directive specifies this fact. Program memory must contain a meaningful instruction at address zero. When the AVR processor is reset, it begins its fetch–execute cycle at address zero in flash memory. If there is not a meaningful instruction there, the results will not be predictable. Every program you write must locate its first instruction at address zero of flash (cseg).

The next group of directives is not required; it serves to give meaningful names (symbols) to hardware resources used by the program, making the meaning a little more clear. Registers R17 and R16 are renamed as temp and count to reflect their usage throughout this program. The I/O registers, 0x17 and 0x18, are specified by numeric literals in AVR Assembly language format; in this case they are written in hexadecimal. The two I/O registers used in this program are given names, PORTB and DDRB, by equating the identifiers (via the .equ directives) to the port numbers. The actual port numbers are specific to the ATMega16A. If you are using a different micro-controller, these numbers must be changed. Once equated, the I/O registers are referred to by name instead of number in the program.

The executable instructions begin after these initial directives. When the assembler reaches these statements, it still has not output any bytes to the hex file, so the location counter (which determines the address of the next piece of assembled data) is still zero. The assembly language mnemonics ldi, out, inc, and rjmp cause the assembler to output the actual words (assembled instructions) that will need to be placed in flash memory to execute the program. The assembled program is stored in two files, the object file and the hex file.

Assembling the Program

If you have not already done so, you should begin a new AVR Assembler project, naming it appropriately and locating it in a folder. Use the new project wizard to do this and to set the platform to AVR Simulator and device to ATmega16A. You can copy the program into the assembly language source file and then build it.

Assembling this file produces a build report similar to this one:

```
AVRASM: AVR macro assembler 2.1.41 (build 1792 Jul 21 2009 12:30:27)
Copyright (C) 1995-2009 ATMEL Corporation

C:\AVRProjects\Counter\Counter.asm(29): No EEPROM data, deleting
C:\AVRProjects\Counter\Counter.eep


Memory use summary [bytes]:
Segment    Begin        End       Code  Data  Used   Size     Use%
--------------------------------------------------------------------
[.cseg]   0x000000   0x00000c    12    0     12    unknown    -
[.dseg]   0x000060   0x000060     0    0      0    unknown    -
[.eseg]   0x000000   0x000000     0    0      0    unknown    -

Assembly complete, 0 errors. 0 warnings
```

From this report you can see that the entire program requires 12 bytes (six instructions at two bytes each). These are located at address 0x00000 up to (but not including) 0x00000c. These are byte addresses corresponding to program addresses zero through five. The assembler's full report, found in the listing file, contains the word addresses which are displayed as 000000 through 000005.

Obtaining a Listing File

The assembler does not automatically generate a listing file. You can turn on this feature under the Project menu. Choose Assembler Options and place a check in the box that indicates you want the assembler to Create a List file. When you build the project again, the listing file (it will have extension .lst) can be opened from the Output folder in the Project window.

```
000000 ef1f    ldi    temp,0xFF      ;configure PORTB as output
000001 bb17    out    DDRB,temp

000002 e000    ldi    count,0x00     ;Initialize count at 0

               lp:

000003 bb08    out    PORTB,count    ;Put counter value on PORT B
000004 9503    inc    count          ;increment counter

000005 cffd    rjmp   lp             ;repeat (forever)
```

Each generated word is shown in the listing, next to the address where that word will be located in memory. The listing file contains a number of other useful bits of information. Following the actual assembled program listing, where address information and generated bytes can be found (or error messages if applicable), is a summary of resources used by the program.

The Map File

If you want to know what symbols are used in the program, and their values, you should look at the map file. This file contains a report generated from the symbol table which is an internal table created by the assembler. As the assembler carries out its task, it builds a table of all the symbols defined in the program and the values assigned to them. Here are the symbols defined in the above program.

```
DEF count  r16
DEF temp   r17
EQU PORTB  00000018
EQU DDRB   00000017
CSEG lp    00000003
```

Simulating Execution

To execute the program, you can use the simulator, or download it to the actual processor and execute it there. This program is designed to be run at slow speed in a simulated environment, so you can observe how each instruction affects hardware resources.

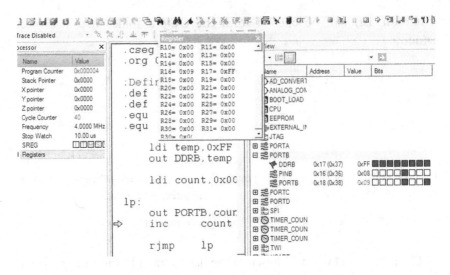

FIGURE 2.23   Simulating the Counter program (Program 2.2).

After a successful build, start the simulator by choosing Start Debugging from the Debug menu (Shortcut Ctrl + Shift + Alt + F5 or the start triangle). The yellow indicator arrow will appear on the first instruction, the one being fetched for execution. The I/O View window can be used to view the register contents, processor status, and Port B under the I/O node. Initially, these all contain zeros, but this will change as you step through the program.

Use the Debug Step Over command (F10) to view the result of executing each instruction. Observe the changes to R16, the PC (especially as the loop is executed), and the values of PORTB as each instruction is executed. Figure 2.23 is a screenshot of the simulator just after the counter value of nine (0b00001001) is output to PORTB.

Downloading to the AVR Processor

It is illuminating to see this program in action using the STK-500. If you are using the XPLAIN hardware, refer to the alternate project (Program 2.2a) and download instructions for that platform.

The output from PORTB of the microcontroller must be connected to the LEDs on the STK-500 board. This is accomplished by connecting a ribbon cable between the headers marked PORTB and LEDS as shown in Figure 2.24.

To download the machine code to the microcontroller, you will need to attach a serial cable between the computer's serial port and the STK-500 at the RS232 port labeled CTRL shown in Figure 2.25.

FIGURE 2.24   STK-500 with PORTB connected to the LEDs ready to run the counter program.

FIGURE 2.25   STK-500 serial programming and power connections.

FIGURE 2.26   STK-500 showing the proper ISP ribbon cable connection for the ATmega16A.

In addition, the ISP header must be connected to the target microcontroller. Figure 2.26 shows the correct ISP connection for the ATmega16A microcontroller.

Be sure the STK-500 is powered on and then activate the programmer using the Tools menu. Select Program AVR/Connect (Figure 2.27). Do not use the AVR Prog... choice at the top of the Tools menu.

The Program AVR application gives access to all of the STK-500 specific programming features. In the Connect dialog (Figure 2.28), be sure to select the STK-500 platform. If you know which COM port, select it otherwise let the program automatically connect.

Once connected, select the Main tab and be sure the correct device shows up in the Device dropdown and ISP is selected as the programming mode. Appropriate settings are shown in Figure 2.29. You may need to manually select the device. Click the Read Signature button to have the programmer ask the microcontroller for its unique signature bytes. This will confirm that communication is taking place between the PC, STK-500, and the target microcontroller.

FIGURE 2.27   Starting up the AVR programmer in preparation for downloading to the microcontroller in the STK-500 platform.

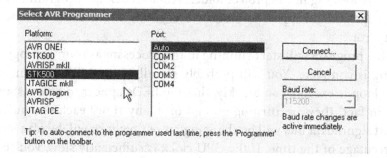

FIGURE 2.28   Selecting the Device and Programming Mode for downloading.

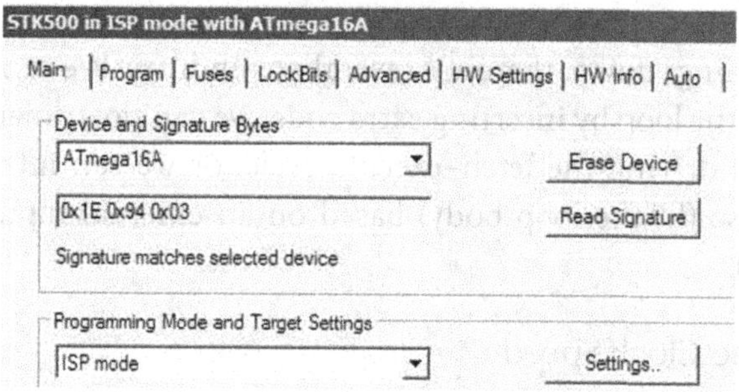

FIGURE 2.29   Selecting the Device and Programming Mode for downloading.

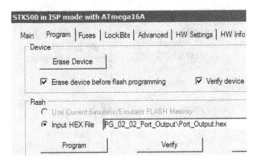

FIGURE 2.30   Selecting the correct machine language (.hex) file for download.

Next, select the correct hex file in the Flash section under the Program tab as shown in Figure 2.30. You can find the hex file in your project folder; it will have the same name as the project (which may be different from the name of the source file). The extension will be .hex. If the hex file is missing, be sure the program assembled with no errors, and that you are looking in the project folder. Finally, click the program button. Messages should appear to indicate everything was accomplished without error.

The program will start running in the processor as soon as programming is complete. You will probably see all of the LEDs illuminated. The loop is executed so quickly, that the LEDs appear to be constantly lit. In fact, they are turning on and off many times each second. The most significant bits will be changing more slowly, so will be off a larger percentage of the time. If the CPU clock is sufficiently slow, you could see the flickering of the LEDs as the counter advances, changing bits from 0 to 1 and back again. The most significant bits will toggle at the slowest rate. The least significant bit will toggle with every loop iteration. The loop repetitions must be relatively slow to observe these changes.

To slow things down, there are several possibilities. We can introduce a delay inside the loop by inserting extra code, we can slow down the system clock that is driving the fetch–execute cycle, or we can introduce some type of pause (in the loop body) based on an external input (such as a pushbutton).

Adjusting the Clock Speed

The CPU clock used by the microcontroller in the STK-500 is configurable. It can use an internal oscillator, or an external one on the STK-500 itself. Assuming the microcontroller is using its internal oscillator, and running at 4 MHz, and assuming one instruction per clock cycle, our loop of three instructions will be executing at $1*10^6$ repetitions per second (remember that the the RJMP instruction requires 2 clock cycles). The one-byte counter will overflow 3906 times per second; the most significant bit will toggle on and off once in each full 256-count cycle. If we change the clock speed to 1024 cycles per second, we should observe an overflow about once per second (1024 cycles/second * 1 loop repetition/4 cycles * 1 overflow/256 loop repetitions).

In the STK-500 programming window, under the Fuses tab, select the appropriate fuse setting to select Ext Clock (there are 3 such choices, any will be fine) as shown in Figure 2.31. You will use the dropdown labeled SUT_CKSEL. The external clock choices are at the top of the list.

Click the Program button at the bottom of the dialog to send these settings to the target processor in the STK-500 socket. Then on the Hardware Settings tab, enter 1024 Hz in the Clock Generator text box as shown in Figure 2.32. Click the Write button to send this setting to the STK-500.

You should immediately see the LEDs toggling at the expected rate. The most significant bit takes approximately 1 second to cycle on–off. Each successive bit toggles at twice the rate of the adjacent one.

Be sure to set the STK-500 Clock Generator value back to a larger number (such as 3.686 MHz) and Write this to the board. If the microcontroller is running at too slow a speed (relative to the serial communications), you will be unable to program the microcontroller.

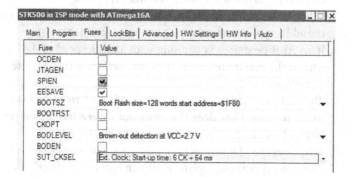

FIGURE 2.31 Setting the fuses on the ATMega16A to use the external clock signal provided by the STK-500.

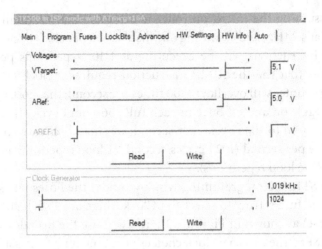

FIGURE 2.32   Slowing down the external clock signal provided by the STK-500.

EXERCISES

1. Name the three memories found in an AVR processor.
2. In which of the three memories are instructions (to be fetched and executed) stored?
3. What is meant by volatile memory? Which of the three AVR memories are volatile?
4. What is the usual length of an AVR machine instruction (in bits)?
5. The ATmega16A, a common member of the AVR family, has 16 KBytes of program memory (16,384 bytes). However, it has only 8 K distinct addresses (0-8191). Explain why this is OK.
6. How many general purpose registers are present in the AVR core? What is the size of each register (in bytes).
7. What is the name of the special register that always contains the address of the next instruction to be executed?
8. If an AVR processor is running with a clock speed of 4 MHz, what is the maximum number of instructions it can execute in a single second?
9. The LDI instruction causes a certain bit pattern to be loaded into a register. How does the processor determine the bit pattern to be loaded? That is, where are the bits found?
10. Why does the LDI instruction only work with half of the available general purpose registers? Which half can it affect?
11. The ADD instruction can utilize any general purpose register as the destination of the result (sum). What is different about

the encoding of the ADD and LDI instructions that makes this possible?

12. Is there any difference between ADD R0, R1 and ADD R1, R0? Explain.

13. How many bits is the opcode for the LDI instruction? For the ADD instruction?

14. How similar are these two instructions: LSL R2 and ADD R2, R2? Explain.

15. When the AVR processor is reset, what address is placed into the PC register? Do all processors work this way? Check on the Intel 8086 and the Motorola PowerPC.

16. The RJMP instruction used to create a very tight infinite loop uses a K value of −1. What would an RJMP with a K value of 0 do?

17. Hand assemble the following instructions. Express each machine language instruction in hexadecimal (4 hex digits)
    a. LDI R20, 45
    b. LDI R31, $C2
    c. ADD R18, R19
    d. ADD R0, R16
    e. RJMP 27 (Jumps to PC + 1 + 27)

18. Decode the following instructions (shown in hexadecimal notation) to a machine instruction and its operands. Write your answer in a format similar to that of the previous question.
    a. E43C
    b. 0E2E
    c. C002
    d. ECE0
    e. 0D00

19. What assembler directive can be used to assemble a machine language instruction if you know the instruction's binary representation?

20. What is an instruction mnemonic?

21. The AVR assembler stores the intended contents of flash memory in a file with what extension?

22. What is the file called that contains a report of the assembly process, including error messages?

23. How is a label defined in an AVR assembly language program?

24. When the assembler encounters a machine language mnemonic, it executes it. True or false?

25. Illustrate the three ways a comment can be placed in an assembly language program.

26. What directive indicates that the following statements are to be assembled into flash storage?
27. What directive is used to associate statements with SRAM?
28. Why is it important for address zero of flash to contain a valid (and meaningful) machine instruction?
29. What directive is used to bind a meaningful symbolic name to a general purpose register? Why is this done?
30. What information is found in the map file?
31. If the AVR processor uses a clock speed of 1 MHz, how many seconds will it take to execute a loop that counts from 0 to 255, assuming each loop iteration takes three clock cycles?
32. If the AVR processor uses a clock speed of 2 MHz, how many seconds will it take to execute a loop that counts from 0 to 65535, assuming each loop iteration takes four clock cycles?
33. If the AVR processor uses a clock speed of 1 MHz, how many loop iterations will be required to cause a 1 millisecond delay if each loop repetition requires five clock cycles? Can this be accomplished with a 1-byte loop counter variable? Explain.

PROGRAMMING EXERCISES

1. Setup the STK-500 to run the sample program in Figure 2.11. Use a clock speed slow enough so you can observe each value. When the program starts, a zero is asserted on the output port. Are the LEDs on or off when a zero bit is asserted on the port? What is the next byte value to be asserted? What LEDs are on?
2. Again, referring to the sample program in Figure 2.11, if you add a second inc count instruction immediately after the existing increment, how would that change the program's behavior? Try it out in the simulator.
3. Write an assembly language program to add three numbers together. The program must begin by loading the three numbers into three distinct registers. The sum is to be calculated in register zero using ADD instructions. You might need to investigate the CLR instruction. Assemble and test your program in the simulator. Try several different numbers, keeping in mind that the sum cannot exceed 255 (if it is to be correct).
4. Determine the machine language version of the following program. Use the assembler to help.

```
ldi r16, 15
add r16, r16
rjmp PC-1
```

Rewrite the program without using any instruction mnemonics (use only .dw). Assemble it. Verify that both programs do exactly the same thing when tested in the simulator. List the successive and distinct values of register 16 as the program executes. Which instruction is the target of the RJMP instruction? Rewrite the original version of the program to use a label (in place of PC-1). Verify that the assembled program has exactly the same machine language words.

ALTERNATE PROGRAMS FOR THE XPLAIN DEMONSTRATION KIT

Program 2.2a: Counter

The XPLAIN hardware has hard-wired connections between the ATxmega-128A1 and the IO devices on the demonstration board. The LEDs are connected to PORTE of the microcontroller. The ATxmega128A1 always starts up using an internal 2 MHz clock. Although the clock speed is adjustable via software, in this program we will simply accept the 2 MHz signal and use a delay loop to slow down the counting loop. The instructions to send data to the two port registers are also slightly different for the ATxmega-128A1. This change is needed because the port registers are located at a much higher address than those of the ATmega16A.

Create a new project in AVR Studio, naming it appropriately. Be sure to click the Next button to select the debug platform and device. When using the ATxmega128A1, you will need to choose the AVR Simulator 2 as the debug platform. The earlier version of the simulator does not support this device.

PROGRAM 2.2a   A Program to Illustrate PORT Output and Counting

```
;Counter - A simple AVR program to illustrate output to a port
;Designed to be executed in a simulator under debug control

;This program counts from 0 to 255 (and repeats)
;The current counter value is output to PORTE of an ATxmega128A.

;Programmer: TM
;Date: 5/2010
;Platform: XPLAIN
;Device: ATxmega128A
```

```
.cseg  ;select current segment as code
.org 0 ;begin assembling at address 0

;Define symbolic names for resources used
.def  count    =r16   ;Reg 16 will hold counter value
.def  temp     =r17   ;Reg 17 is used as a temporary register
.def  d_count_h=r25   ;counter for delay loop
.def  d_count_l=r24
.equ  PORTE_OUT=1668       ;Port E's output register
.equ  PORTE_DIR=1664       ;Port E's Data Direction Register
.equ  DELAY_C  =2048       ;Larger numbers mean slower counting
                           (1-65536)

        ldi    temp,0xFF      ;configure PORTE as output
        sts    PORTE_DIR,temp

        ldi    count,0x00     ;Initialize count at 0
lp:
        sts    PORTE_OUT,count       ;Put counter value on PORT E
        inc    count          ;increment counter

;delay loop to slow repetitions of the outer loop
        ldi    d_count_h, high(DELAY_C)
        ldi    d_count_l, low(DELAY_C)
delay:
        sbiw   d_count_h:d_count_l,1
        brne   delay

        rjmp   lp             ;repeat program (forever)
```

Once Program 2.2a has been entered and assembled, you can download it to the ATxmega128A1 using the AVRISP mkII programmer. Select the

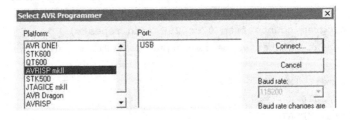

FIGURE 2.33   Selecting the AVRISP mkII Programmer.

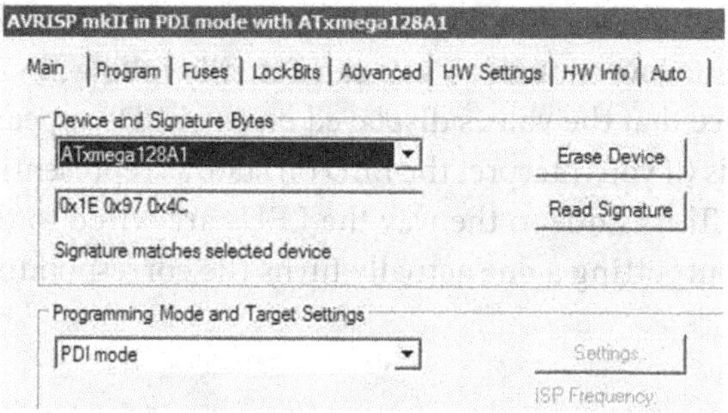

FIGURE 2.34   Reading the signature of the target microcontroller.

Program AVR/Connect choice from the Tools menu. When the Select Programmer dialog appears, select the AVRISP mkII programmer as shown in Figure 2.33. Be sure the XPLAIN board is connected via USB and is in programming mode.

The Main tab should show the proper device (ATxmega128A1). You can check that communications are working by reading the signature. The correct signature for this microcontroller is shown in Figure 2.34.

Under the Program tab, you must select the HEX file (in the Flash section) for the current project (Figure 2.35). This is located in the project folder. Once selected, click the Program button to download it and begin execution. The LEDs on the Xplain board should be flashing as the program counts from 0 to 255 and repeats. The most significant bit will cycle on/off approximately once per second.

You can change the speed of the counting by adjusting the value of the constant named DELAY_C in the program. Larger numbers will cause

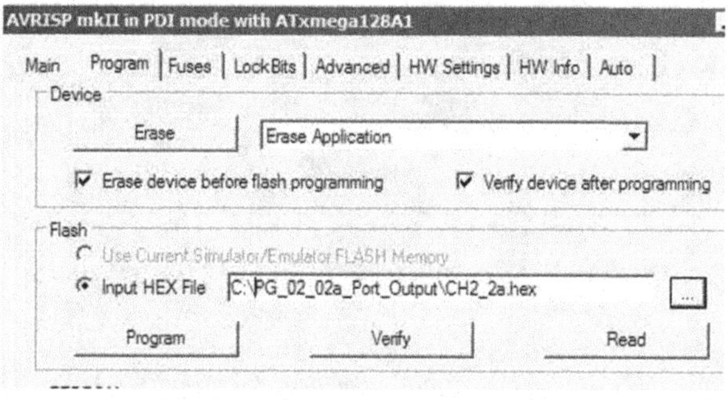

FIGURE 2.35   Selecting the correct HEX file for download.

the program to update the count (LEDs) more slowly. If you make the program count slow enough so you can actually follow along (in binary), you may notice that the values displayed on the LEDs appear to be counting backwards (if you interpret the LED on state as representing the binary digit of one). This is due to the way the LEDs are wired to the microcontroller pins; outputting a one actually turns the corresponding LED off.

CHAPTER 3

Assembly Language

A SSEMBLY LANGUAGE IS SIMPLY a programming tool to facilitate the generation of a sequence of bytes representing machine instructions and data. These bytes can be generated directly in memory or stored in a file that can be later loaded into memory in preparation for execution. The job of the assembly language programmer is to write instructions that will cause the assembler to generate the desired bytes. Frequently, there are several ways to accomplish this task. For example, the two-byte sequence 0x03, 0x95 can be generated using any of the following assembly language statements:

```
.db     0x03, 0x95
.dw     38147
inc     R16
```

Since the goal was to produce a sequence of two bytes, the first statement provides the most obvious and direct solution. It uses a single define byte directive specifying a sequence of bytes to be assembled in the order they are listed. This is the purpose of the define byte directive. The second statement defines a word (using the define word directive) representing the value 38,147. In hexadecimal, this is 0x9503. Because word data is assembled in reverse byte order (little-endian order), the first byte is placed last in the word; the end result is indistinguishable from that of the previous directive. The last statement uses an instruction mnemonic (INC) and a register operand. The assembler dutifully assembles the two-byte instruction which happens to correspond to the hexadecimal value 0x9503; this value is also byte reversed when placed in memory, resulting in the same pair of bytes.

The assembly language programmer should write statements that clearly communicate the intent. Although all of the statements in the above example result in the same word, one of them is usually preferred depending on the circumstances. If the problem was to generate an instruction to increment register 16, then clearly the third option would be best. If the problem was to assemble a 16-bit integer code representing the integer value 38,147, then the second would be preferred. You should note that the programmer can often express the value of an operand in several ways; the best choice will most clearly represent the meaning of the operand.

In addition to specifying what bytes are to be assembled, the programmer must also decide where the bytes will be placed in memory. Assembly language programs are typically divided into logical segments with related items grouped together. Instructions to be executed are placed in the code segment. Constant data values might be placed in the code segment as well, or stored in EEPROM. The AVR assembler generates two files containing the required contents of flash (cseg) and EEPROM (eseg). Space for variables is generally set aside in part of SRAM. Some of the memory available in SRAM will likely be used for the stack; in some cases, memory for variables can be allocated inside the stack dynamically as the program executes. No file is generated for SRAM contents as these are undefined when a program begins running; initialization of SRAM must be accomplished during execution. The assembler activity related to SRAM is purely to allocate addresses to identifiers. The results are recorded in the map file as well as the listing file.

As the assembler processes the instructions in an assembly language program, it keeps track of how many bytes in each segment have already been defined or allocated for some purpose (more accurately, it keeps track of where the next byte should be located). The AVR assembler allocates space in each of the three segments, code, data, and EEPROM, as needed. Directives are used to tell the assembler which segment it should be using at any time. These three segments correspond to the physically separate storage areas accessed by this processor.

Because of the Harvard architecture characterizing this processor, machine instructions must be stored in flash memory. Although instructions are assembled in what is called the code segment, the programmer is free to mix data in with instructions in this segment. The only difference between an instruction and a data value that is located in flash memory is that they are intended to be used differently. Instructions are meant to be fetched and executed; data values are intended to be loaded into registers.

Data values may be assembled to the flash or EEPROM segments. Data values cannot be assembled to SRAM. Although both EEPROM and SRAM are referred to as *data* storage or memory, SRAM is volatile and can only hold information while a program is running. Constants must be assembled to nonvolatile memory in the AVR system. Program instructions and data are programmed (downloaded) into flash and EEPROM by the AVR programmer utility. When power is supplied to the microcontroller, these bytes are immediately available to the processor for use.

Assembly language directives exist for many purposes. The next section lists the most common directives used in the AVR assembly language.

DIRECTIVES

In addition to generating machine language instructions, the assembler needs to generate constants needed by the program. It must also set aside memory locations for variable storage. In assembly language programming, the programmer is responsible for deciding where each instruction of the program and each byte of data will eventually be located. Directives are used for these and other purposes. Table 3.1 lists the most common AVR directives and briefly explains how they are used.

The use of these directives will be illustrated in the sample programs to come. Just keep in mind that the purpose of an assembly language program is to provide instructions to the assembler to generate a sequence of bytes that will need to be placed in particular memory locations in order for the program to be executed successfully. Directives are used to allow the programmer to completely control this process.

The Assembler's Location Counters

When assembling a program, the assembler maintains internal location counters to track the next available address in each memory segment. We will call these cloc, dloc, and eloc. An assembly language programmer must be aware of these counters since these are used to assign addresses to data values and instructions. Figure 3.1 illustrates how an assembly language program can switch between segments; the assembler sorts this all out and neatly arranges the bytes (words) sequentially in the appropriate memory.

The initial values for the segment registers in this example were $0000, $0060, and $0000. Remember that the cloc value is a word address while

TABLE 3.1   Common AVR Assembly Language Directives

Directive	Description	Example
.byte	Set aside addresses in SRAM or EEPROM where bytes can be stored during execution. No initial values can be specified.	buff: .byte 32 ;a 32 ;byte area count: .byte 2 ;a ;word-sized counter
.db .dw .dd .dq	Define a series of byte, word, doubleword, or quadword values that will be placed in flash or EEPROM when downloaded to the microcontroller	ages: .db 13, 18, 21, 30 sevens: .db 0x07, 0b00000111, 7 maxint: .dw 32767 bignum: .dq 0x123456789abcdef0
.def	Define a symbolic name for a register	.def sum = R16 .def counter = R24
.undef	Undefine a register name	.undef sum
.equ .set	Equate or set a symbol to a value or expression. Equated symbols are constant; set symbols can be reassigned	.equ tabsize = 14 .set flag = 1 .equ cr = 0x0D .set flag = flag + 1
.cseg .dseg .eseg	Switch to the specific memory segment: code (flash), data (SRAM), or EEPROM.	.cseg //program code comes next .dseg //.byte statements usually follow
.include	Include a file as part of the source code	.include "iodefs.asm"
.list .nolist	Turn listing output on (list) or off (nolist)	.nolist //This code does not appear in list file .list //This code will appear
.org	Set the location counter of the current memory segment to a specific value	.cseg .org 0x002A; set code segment loc ctr .dseg .org 64; set sram loc ctr

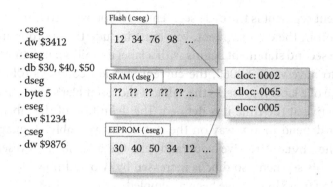

FIGURE 3.1   The use of segment directives during assembly.

the other counters represent byte addresses. Also remember that word data is assembled in little-endian order.

Consider the following assembly language program. The program does not do anything meaningful, but it will be useful to see how the assembler analyzes the program and what actions it takes with each statement.

```
        .dseg
total:
        .byte 2
        .cseg
        rjmp startup
        .org $2A
startup:
        rjmp PC
        .eseg
        .db $FF, $AA, $55, $00
        .dseg
sum:    .byte 1
```

When this program is assembled, the assembler initializes its three internal location counters representing addresses in the code (flash), data (SRAM), and EEPROM segments. The initial values for cloc and eloc are 0. The value of dloc is the first available RAM address. This varies between the AVR microcontrollers. For this example, we will assume the ATMEGA16A is in use; the lowest RAM address for this microcontroller is $0060.

The first statement in the program is a directive, causing the assembler to switch to data segment mode. The assembler always begins assuming the current segment is the code segment, so if you want to start your code generation in the data segment, you must include the appropriate directive. The second statement begins with a label definition; it defines a label, total, to have value $0060, the current location counter's (dloc) value. The value of a label represents the value of the assembler's location counter that is active at the time it is defined. The definition of the label, total, does not depend in any way on the rest of the assembly language statement. The .byte directive's operand tells the assembler to reserve two bytes in this segment, so dloc is increased by two and now has the value $0062. So far, no bytes have been assembled.

The next directive switches the assembler to code segment mode. The rjmp instruction is assembled and output to the hex file. This instruction is one word in length (16 bits); it will be placed at address 0 in program memory. The location counter, cloc, is increased to 1 because a word of program memory has been defined. Remember that cloc is a word address.

The .org directive changes the location counter (cloc) to $002A. The next statement simply defines the label named startup to have value $002A, the current location counter value. A label can be defined on a line by itself, or combined with another assembly operation (as illustrated by the definitions of total and sum). The next line of the program is an rjmp PC instruction which is assembled and output to the hex file. This word will be placed at address $002A, the current location counter value. The new value of cloc is now $002B. You have encountered this instruction before; it creates a very tight infinite loop when executed.

The next statement switches the assembler to EEPROM segment mode. The define byte directive causes the sequence of bytes listed to be placed in the EEPROM file for later downloading to the processor. The assembler produces a separate file for EEPROM and flash contents. The generated bytes will be stored at addresses $0000, $0001, $0002, and $0003 of EEPROM memory. Remember that eloc was initially set to $0000. The value of eloc after these four bytes are defined will be $0004.

Next, the assembler switches back to data segment mode, defines the symbol sum to have value $0062 (dloc's value which was remembered from its previous use), and increases dloc by 1 (the number of bytes reserved for the variable sum).

The end of the program has been reached, and the resulting machine language program is found in two files that were created by the assembler,

TABLE 3.2   Sample Contents of the Hex and Eep Files Produced by the Assembler

something.hex	something.eep
:020000020000FC	:04000000**FFAA5500**FE
:020000000**29C0**15	:00000001FF
:02005400**FFCF**DC	
:00000001FF	

something.hex and something.eep. These files contain the generated bytes and additional information to tell the AVR programmer utility where the bytes must be placed in flash and EEPROM. The actual file contents are shown in Table 3.2. The generated bytes are highlighted.

One point should be made about this process. When the rjmp startup command is assembled, the assembler will need to already know the address of the label startup (in order to calculate the displacement of the relative jump). As this label is defined later in the program, it is not obvious how the assembler can determine its address without looking ahead. All assemblers utilize some type of look-ahead methodology. The simplest such technique is employed by a two-pass assembler. On the first pass through the program, the assembler just defines symbols (and labels), using its location counters as described above. At the end of this pass, all symbols should be defined. On the second pass, the assembler can assemble all of the instructions and data since it now knows the values of all of the symbols.

EXPRESSIONS

Assemblers take over many of the tedious details of machine language programming. They are capable of performing numeric calculations that are needed to generate the correct bytes for program instructions and data. They can translate base 10 numerals to appropriate byte and word size codes and determine address details such as the number of words between two instructions. They can also determine the high and low bytes of larger numbers. The AVR assembler provides operators and functions to aid the programmer in these tasks. Here we will look at the basic expression syntax used in the operand fields of many instructions and directives.

Expressions are built from operands and operators. The AVR assembler expects expressions to be written in infix notation, much like C or Java. The assembler does all calculations using 64-bit data. The result is then interpreted as a byte or word (or other size data) as needed.

Here are a few examples of expressions that might be found in an AVR assembly language program.

```
(1 << RXEN) | (1 << TXEN)
(high(strloc) % 0x0F) << 8
(rpmi-rpms)/30
```

Most of the operators are the similar to those used in high-level languages. The simplest operands are symbols, literals, or the value of the code segment's location counter (PC).

Symbols and Literals

Symbols are either defined by their appearance at the beginning of a line with a colon termination or by a set or equ directive. When a symbol is defined using the colon, it is referred to as a label. Each label stands for a location in one of the memories.

Literals are bit patterns expressed in decimal, hexadecimal, octal, binary, string, or character format. Literals can (and usually do) represent numbers, however they can also simply represent bit patterns. Character literals represent the numeric values of the ASCII codes represented by the characters. String literals represent a sequence (or an array) of characters. Arrays in assembly language are just blocks of contiguous bytes.

In AVR Assembly language, hexadecimal literals must be prefixed with 0x or $. Binary literals are indicated by the 0b prefix; octal literals start with a leading zero. These literals are assumed to represent unsigned numbers. Numbers that begin with a nonzero digit are assumed to be in decimal format. The predefined symbol PC is used to represent the current value of the assembler's code segment (flash) location counter (regardless of what segment is currently active).

Character literals correspond to single bytes and are specified inside single quotes. There are a few escape sequences used to represent special ASCII codes. These can be used inside single quotes to represent special single byte values (Table 3.3).

The last two escape sequences, starting \x, and \(octal digit), may be used to represent a byte as a hexadecimal or octal value. If the value specified is too big for a byte, only the least-significant byte is used. Thus, '\651' (110101001B) will represent the byte 0xA9, and '\xFDEC' will simply be 0xEC. You should consider this "truncation" behavior as undefined and limit such expressions to legal byte values. There is very little reason

TABLE 3.3   Escape Sequences Recognized in Character Literals

Escape Sequence	Meaning
\n	0x0A (newline)
\r	0x0D (carriage return)
\a	0x07 (bell or alert)
\b	0x08 (backspace)
\f	0x0C (form feed)
\t	0x09 (tab or horizontal tab)
\v	0x0B (vertical tab)
\\	0x5C (backslash)
\0	0x00 (nul)
\'	0x27 (single quote)
\xhh	0xhh (hexadecimal value)
\ooo	0ooo (octal value)

to use these last two formats; you can always use the more conventional numeric literals to specify byte values that do not correspond to printable characters or do not have a standard escape sequence. On the other hand, you may want to emphasize that a byte value is intended to represent a character rather than a number. In this case, "\0" represents the null character, whereas 0 (which has the same value) represents the number zero.

A list of characters (actually an array of characters) can be represented as a string inside double quotes. No escape sequences are recognized in strings, and there is no end of string indicator included when the string is assembled. The string "abc" is just shorthand for the three byte sequence, "a", "b", "c". Although character literals may be used anywhere a numeric value is needed, the string format may only be used with the .db directive.

Two strings written next to each other (with no punctuation between) are simply concatenated. This convention, together with the line continuation character (backslash at end of line), allows long strings to be defined over several lines.

```
.eseg
.db "hello" "there"        ;same as "hello there"
.db "abcdefgh" \
    "ijklmno"      "pqrst" \
    "uvwxyz"               ;the alphabet in lower case
```

DATA DEFINITION DIRECTIVES

Data values can be assembled to flash or EEPROM storage using the .db, .dw, .dd, and .dq directives followed by a suitable expression. When we say the data is assembled to flash or EEPROM, we mean the assembler simply writes these bytes to files (the hex and EEPROM files). The AVR programmer utility actually places the bytes in the appropriate memory when the files are downloaded to the microcontroller.

The define byte directive needs an operand (or list of operands), each representing a byte. The value should be between –128 and 255. Larger values are simply truncated to the least-significant byte. Note that the values above 127 are considered unsigned as a byte. You may specify the values in any of the legal literal formats; you may also use more complex expressions. Word, doubleword, and quadword values must also be in an appropriate range, or the result will be truncated to fit the specified container (Table 3.4).

It is common to define a label in conjunction with the .db, .dw, .dd, .dq, and .byte directives. Labels defined in this way will have a value equal to the address of the associated byte (or first byte of a multibyte directive). Do not confuse the value of a label with the contents of the memory location the label represents. In assembly language, labels always represent addresses, never the values stored at the addresses. Thus,

```
myAge:       .dw 50
myName:      .db "Joe", '\0'
```

defines the label myAge to be the address of the word containing the number 50 (fifty), and the label myName to be the address of the byte with the ASCII code for the character "J" (0x4A), the first character of the string.

The assembler will allocate addresses sequentially when this pair of statements is processed. If the bytes are assembled in the flash (code) segment, then the addresses are word addresses, so the values of these two

TABLE 3.4 Minimum and Maximum Values for Common Data Types

Data Type	Minimum Value	Maximum Value
Byte	–128	255
Word	–32768	65535
Doubleword	–2147483648	4294967295
Quadword	–9223372036854775808	18446744073709551615

labels will differ by exactly 1. The label myName would be associated with the word containing the "J" (and the "o"). If these statements appear in the EEPROM segment, then the addresses will differ by 2; myAge will be the address of the first byte of the word containing the value 50 (and this will be stored in little-endian order), and myName will be the address of the byte containing "J".

When assembling data into the code segment, each new .db directive will define bytes starting at a word address. If necessary, a nul byte will be added to flash to get to a word address for the start of each new .db directive. This is called padding. The assembler issues a warning each time a padding byte is added. Because of the requirement for word alignment, the following are not equivalent (if located in the code segment) (Table 3.5).

The listing file contains a report of all of the bytes assembled by the assembler. You must enable the generation of the listing file in the project options or it will not be created when your project is assembled. All of the bytes generated in the code segment are displayed as words in the listing report. Since words are stored in little-endian order, the byte sequences will appear to be reversed. The assembler will report the assembly of above statements (possibly with different addresses) as:

```
warning: .cseg .db misalignment - padding zero byte
00005c 002f      .db 0x2F
warning: .cseg .db misalignment - padding zero byte
00005d 003c      .db 0x3C
00005e 3c2f      .db 0x2F, 0x3C
```

If we just listed the six bytes in order by byte address, we would see 2F 00 3C 00 2F 3C. As words, they appears as 002F 003C 3C2F. Little-endian format can be confusing; we just need to get used to it!

Operators Used in Expressions

Expressions are used in many places in assembly language programs. They relieve the programmer of the burden of carrying out many tedious

TABLE 3.5 Illustration of Padding of Data Values in the Code Segment

.db 0x2F	Generates 4 bytes: 2F, 00, 3C, 00
.db 0x3C	(or 2 words: 002F, 003C)
.db 0x2F, 0x3C	Generates 2 bytes: 2F, 3C
	(or 1 word: 3C2F)

hand computations. There are quite a few operators used to form expressions. The more common operators are listed in Table 3.6. Associated with each operator is a precedence or priority level. High precedence operators are evaluated first. Parenthesis may be used as required to enforce a particular order of evaluation. Operations are left associative (in the case of equal precedence).

A common misunderstanding regarding the use of operators in assembly language expressions is due to a fundamental difference in the

TABLE 3.6   AVR Assembly Language Expression Operator Reference

Operator	Name and Description	Example
!	Logical Not-0 if expression is non-zero, 1 if the expression is zero. Precedence: 12	!047 (equals 0) !0 (equals 1)
~	Bitwise Not-flip the bits Precedence: 12	~0x3F (equals 0xC0 as a byte, but actually it is 0xFFFFFFFFFFFFFFC0 since the assembler evaluates expressions in 64-bit mode)
-	Unary Minus-change the sign of the integer Precedence: 14	-2 (equals negative two)
+, -, *, /, %	The usual integer arithmetic operations. Division calculates the integer quotient only; % (modulo) calculates the remainder Precedence: 13 Precedence: 12 (+ and -)	PC + 2 (4 + 7)*size 35%2 (equals 1)
>>, <<	Shift Right/Left-Shift the bits right or left a specified amount Precedence: 11	0x44 << 1 (equals 0x88) 0b11110000 >> 2 (equals 0x3C)
<, <=, >, >=, ==, !=	The usual comparison/ equality operators that evaluate to 1 if true, 0 if false Precedence: 10 Precedence: 9 (== and !=)	.set OK = size < max (could be 0 or 1)

TABLE 3.6 (continued) AVR Assembly Language Expression Operator Reference

Operator	Name and Description	Example
&, |, ^	Bitwise logical operators and, or, and xor (exclusive or) Precedence: 8 (&) Precedence: 7 (^) Precedence: 6 (|)	0x0f & m (equals right nybble of m—upper nybble zeroed) 0xf0 | n (equals n with left nybble set to 1111)
&&, ||	Logical and/or operations that compute 0 or 1 for false and true. Precedence: 5 (&&) Precedence: 4 (||)	a && c (equals 1 if both a and b are non zero, otherwise equals 0)
?	Conditional Operator Precedence: 3	d ? 3 : 7 (equals 3 if d is true and 7 if d is false)

semantics of such expressions and expressions in high-level languages. When a compiler encounters an expression in a statement such as (3 * x + 1), it is not responsible for evaluating the expression, but instead generates machine instructions that cause the evaluation to occur at runtime. In high-level languages, most expressions imply execution sequences. Contrast this to the job of the assembler. Each expression found in an assembly language statement is completely evaluated by the assembler and the result used to determine the generated byte(s). Complex expressions never result in more than a single machine instruction. You will need to rethink the concept of expressions if you have not used an assembler before.

Calculations that involve labels (symbols representing locations in the program) or the PC are not always meaningful, but if used properly can be very useful. One common operation involving labels is the difference of two addresses. This is one way to represent the size of a block of memory. The addresses must be in the same segment (code, data, or eeprom) or the operation is meaningless. Subtracting two labels both located in the code segment represents the number of intervening words; subtracting two labels both located in one of the other memory areas gives the number of bytes between the addresses. Consider the following assembly language statements, assuming they appear in the code segment.

```
letters:    .db "abcdefg"
numLetters: .db PC-letters
```

The first statement creates an array of ASCII codes, beginning at the address represented by the label letters. You can see that 7 bytes are required for the letters; however, one extra byte is added to preserve word alignment. When the expression PC-letters is calculated by the assembler, the difference is 4. This is because the array occupies 7 (8 with padding) bytes which is exactly 4 words. Code segment addresses are always word addresses when assigned by the assembler. Thus, the byte labeled numLetters will hold the value 4. This value is computed by the assembler. You could fix the expression to represent the number of bytes in the string by writing (PC-letters)*2. In this case, the value 8 would be assembled to the memory location named numLetters. A program using this string would have to note that the last letter (in the group of eight) was null ($00) and not consider it to be part of the string.

Be careful of expressions involving PC. PC always represents the location counter in the code segment. It never refers to a position in SRAM (dseg) or EEPROM (eseg), so it is usually a mistake to use it in those segments. In the above example, numLetters would be totally meaningless if these statements appeared in the EEPROM segment. The following would, however, be correct:

```
.eseg
letters:     .db "abcdefg"
numLetters:  .db numLetters-letters     ;assembles a 7 in
                                        ;this byte
```

Functions Used in Expressions

In addition to the operators covered above, there are several functions that are useful in building expressions. The most common functions are the low and high functions which return the low and high order bytes respectively of an expression. The function byte2 is a synonym for the high function. There are also functions named byte3, byte4, lwrd, and hwrd. The abs function is another common function; it computes the absolute value of an expression.

```
high(0x1234) is $12
high(4660) is also $12  (4660 = 0x1234)
low(0x1234) is $34
hwrd(0x12345678) is $1234
abs(-1) is 1
```

The use of expressions will be illustrated in the programs that follow. You do not need to use all of these features to write assembly language programs, but effective use of them can make writing programs easier and more interesting. Expressions also document how a value is determined, eliminating mystery and ensuring accuracy. Most assembly language programmers make extensive use of the power of the assembler's expression evaluation facilities.

Keep in mind the fact that the use of expressions in the assembly language statements does not slow down the final program. All expressions are completely evaluated at assembly time. None are evaluated by the AVR processor. The actual instruction generated for these two statements will be exactly the same. Why?

```
ldi R16, 1
ldi R16, (45 + 92/7)%7−1
```

You must also resist the temptation to treat assembly language symbols as if they were variables. Symbols and expressions must be completely evaluated by the assembler used to assemble the statement at hand. They do not represent data being manipulated by the program; instead they represent addresses and numbers used in the assembly process.

INSTRUCTIONS

Assembly language programs are made up of two main parts: data, either defined or reserved, and machine instructions that are to be executed by the processor. Instructions to be executed are ultimately binary codes, but in assembly language are usually expressed with an instruction mnemonic. Each machine instruction is represented by at least one mnemonic. In some cases, two different mnemonics represent the same machine instruction; either may be used, but in different contexts one will better represent the intent of the programmer. Mnemonics may require operands to allow the assembler to fill in the required details of the instruction.

The purpose of each machine instruction, when executed, is to cause some change of state in one of the resources controlled by the processor. We have already discussed the fact that the AVR microcontroller has 32 8-bit registers and some amount of RAM where data can be stored during execution. The AVR processor has several instructions that can set or change the data in these registers or RAM.

We will look at the semantics of the following instructions in more detail in later chapters where they are grouped by functionality. Here we simply look at a few examples of common assembly language statements and their corresponding machine instructions. Using these statements in a program will cause the assembler to assemble the 16- or 32-bit machine code for each instruction and output it to the hex (and object) file. You can find a complete list of all of the AVR instructions in the manufacturer's documentation. This list is also available under the Help menu in AVR Studio (Figure 3.2).

When you read assembly language programs, you may notice that there are two conventions for defining labels. One is to place each label definition on a line by itself.

```
reset:
        ldi r16, high(RAMEND)
```

The other is to combine label definitions with another assembly language instruction (directive or instruction mnemonic).

```
reset:  ldi r16, high(RAMEND)
```

There is no difference in the result. A label on a line by itself refers to the next byte generated by a subsequent statement in the same segment. In

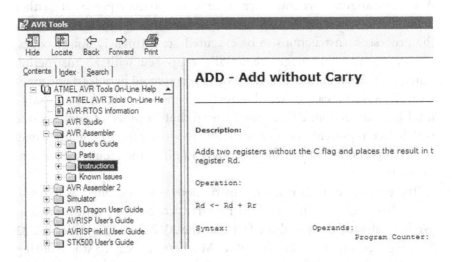

FIGURE 3.2 AVR Studio Help contains instruction documentation as well as information about the programming tools.

general, labels are used only at instructions (or data locations) that must be referred to by address from another place in the program. This will be used to conveniently implement loops, selection structures, and functions, as well as access data stored in the various memories.

Consider the following example of how a loop is implemented using a label. The loop is designed to count down from an initial value to zero. The last statement in the loop branches back to the label lp that designates the location in the code where the loop body begins. When the branch is not taken, the processor continues on to the next instruction in memory.

```
    ldi   r20,35  ;35 is the initial value for the counter
lp: dec   r20     ;the counter is decremented

;when the counter reaches zero, the Z flag is set
    brne lp       ;branch if Z is not set

;the next instruction is written here-no label is needed
```

The key to using the conditional branch instructions (such as BRNE) is to perform some operation first that sets or clears one or more flags. A common choice is an arithmetic instruction. In this loop, the z flag is set (to 1) when the result of the DEC operation is zero. It is cleared (to 0) when the result is not zero (most of the time this is the case). When the BRNE instruction is executed, it checks the z flag and, if clear (0), places the address of the label lp in the PC so the next instruction fetched is at the top of the loop. Each time execution reaches the BRNE instruction the same thing happens, that is, until the DEC instruction results in a zero. This time, the BRNE does nothing (because z is set). The next instruction in memory (the one following the BRNE in the program) is fetched and executed. This is how most loops are built.

Assembly language commands that correspond to machine instructions must be located in the code segment. Theoretically it should be possible to assemble machine instructions into EEPROM (after all, an instruction is just a couple of bytes), but the AVR assembler flags this as an error. The important thing to keep in mind is that assembling an instruction mnemonic is just another way the assembler outputs a sequence of bytes.

Zero-Operand Instructions

Some machine instructions are quite simple in their syntax requirements; they are represented by just a mnemonic alone. Such instructions are called

TABLE 3.7   AVR Instructions that Require No Operands

Syntax	Operands	Action	Description
CLC	None	C← 0	Clear (set to 0) the carry flag
NOP	None	None	No operation
SEZ	None	Z← 1	Set (to 1) the zero flag
RET	None	PC← Stack; POP value from stack	Return (from function)

zero-operand instructions. The resource they affect is implied by the instruction. Since there is no operand, assembling one of these instructions always results in the same pattern of bits. The operation code (opcode) for these instructions is a full 16-bits in length. Here are some examples of zero-operand mnemonics for AVR assembly language (Table 3.7).

One-Operand Instructions

Single-operand instructions require an operand that specifies a resource that will be affected by the instruction or a value used to affect a resource. This allows a single mnemonic to cause somewhat different actions, depending on the operand. Assembling one of these instructions combines bits representing the operation (opcode) with bits representing the operand. The opcode field and the operand field vary in length depending on the instruction. See Table 3.8 for some examples in the AVR assembly language.

Two-Operand Instructions

Two-operand instructions name two resources or a resource and a value. Assembling these instructions requires the combination of bits for the opcode with bits representing each operand. See Table 3.9 for some examples in the AVR assembly language.

The AVR assembler considers instruction mnemonics as keywords (or reserved words). They are recognized irrespective of letter case (unless the assembler is operated with the case-sensitive option turned on). You cannot use keywords for other purposes, such as symbols or labels.

THE TOGGLER PROGRAM: SAMPLE I/O

To finish this chapter on AVR assembly language, we will consider another sample program. This program will illustrate both input and output operations. We will revisit the use of the LEDs for output, and add the use of

TABLE 3.8   AVR Instructions that Require One Operand

Syntax	Operands	Action	Description
BCLR s	A bit number s 0 <= s <= 7	SREG(s)← 0	Bit s of status register is cleared (to 0)
BREQ label	A label representing an address in the code segment	if Z == 0 PC← PC + 1 else PC← label	Branch (to label) if zero flag is set (if previous operation indicated equality)
CALL label	A label representing an address in the code segment	Push PC on stack; PC← label value	Call a procedure
NEG Rd	A register	Rd← (-Rd)	Negate (change the sign of) the value in register Rd

the pushbutton switches as input devices. The program will display a binary value on the LEDs. Each pushbutton controls the LED adjacent to it. Pressing a button will toggle the state of the associated LED. The program begins with all LEDs on. Figure 3.3 shows a pushbutton and LED on the XPLAIN Demonstration board.

TABLE 3.9   AVR Instructions that Require Two Operands

Syntax	Operands	Action	Description
ADD Rd, Rr	Two registers, destination and source	Rd← Rd + Rr	Add registers
CPI Rd, k	Register (16-31) and byte value	SREG← result of comparing Rd to K	Compare register with immediate byte
LDS Rd, label	Register and memory (SRAM) address	Rd← (label)	Load register with byte from data space at specified address
OUT A, Rr	An I/O register (0 <= A <= 63) and a register	I/O(A)← Rr	Output byte (in Rr) to I/O register (A)

FIGURE 3.3   Pushbutton and LED on the XPLAIN Demonstration board.

Before going into the details of the program, a little background about LEDs and pushbuttons as I/O devices in this context seems appropriate. For those not interested in the electronics, you can skip ahead to the programming. All you need to know is that outputting a zero (bit) on a port connected to an LED on the STK-500 (or XPLAIN) will cause the LED to illuminate. The opposite, a one, will turn it off. Similarly, when a pushbutton is at rest (in the up position or not depressed), it will be read as a one (not zero).

AVR Digital I/O Ports and STK-500/XPLAIN LEDs

The eight bits (pins) of each of the general purpose I/O ports provided by the AVR microcontrollers can be configured for either input or output via software (your program). As an output pin, you can drive the signal high or low by outputting a 1 or 0 respectively to the bit controlling that pin. When the pin is driven high, a volt meter connected to the pin will register a high voltage (relatively to ground). When the pin is driven low, the meter will register a low voltage (like 0).

An LED (light-emitting diode) emits light when current passes through it. An LED has two leads, the anode and cathode. To induce a current through an LED, the anode is connected to the positive side of the power supply, and the cathode to the negative side. A resistor is usually added in series to limit the flow of electrons and prevent the LED from flashing very brightly one time, and then never working again. A typical LED requires about 20 mA and at least 2 V to function.

When the LEDs on the STK-500 or XPLAIN boards are connected to pins of an output port, one side of the LED (anode) is connected to a high-voltage source (in this case +5 V) through a resistor (to limit the current). The other side (cathode) is connected to a simple circuit that acts like an on/off switch controlled by the AVR's I/O pin. The details of this circuit are available in the STK-500/XPLAIN documentation. Placing a 0 on the I/O pin (output port) turns the switch on, effectively allowing current through the LED, causing it to emit light. Placing a 1 on the pin effectively turns off the switch and the LED (Figure 3.4).

The sample program will illustrate one way an output port can be configured, and how bits may be set (to 1) or cleared (to 0) to assert these values on the pins. The program uses a byte in a register to hold the desired values of the eight pins, and then outputs the byte to the port in one action. This allows any bit pattern to be changed to any other bit pattern in a single output operation. The AVR processor also has several specialized instructions that allow individual bits of a port to be set or cleared as required by your program.

Remember that on the STK-500 you must connect the 10-pin header for the microcontroller port to the 10-pin header for the LEDs if the port is to control the LEDs. For this example, PORTB is used to control the LEDs. On the XPLAIN, the LEDs are wired to PORTE.

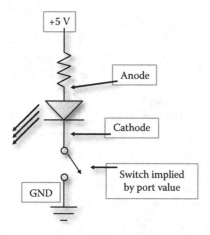

FIGURE 3.4 A typical LED activation switch with current limiting resistor.

AVR Digital I/O Ports and STK-500/XPLAIN Pushbuttons

For a port pin to function as an input, an external signal must be applied to the pin. This will be either low relative to ground, or high. The low signal will be read as a zero, and the high, as a one. The pushbutton switches on the STK-500 and XPLAIN can be used to provide this type of signal to the pins of a port configured for input. On the STK-500, you will need to connect the pushbuttons to the desired port using one of the ribbon cable connections. In this example, connect the pushbutton header to the PORTD header. The XPLAIN pushbuttons are hardwired to PORTF.

The pushbutton switches are of the normally open type (meaning you push them to make the connection between the switch contacts and release them to break the connection). One side of the switch is connected to ground (0 V) and the other to the input pin. A small resistor is added here to limit current. Pressing the switch pulls the input pin to a near-zero voltage level, causing a read of zero on the port's pin. Releasing the switch disconnects the pin from ground. In this state, the voltage read at the pin would be unreliable, except that another resistor in the circuit, the pull-up resistor, is used to connect the pin to the positive side of the voltage supply (called VTG). When the button is released, input pin is "pulled" to the high-voltage level by the so-called pull-up resistor.

The AVR microcontroller circuitry includes internal pull-up resistors that can be enabled via software. When using the STK-500 pushbuttons (Figure 3.5), the internal pull-up resistors are not needed because the board includes external pull-up resistors in the switch circuit. Enabling or

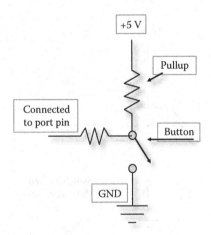

FIGURE 3.5 The STK-500 pushbutton input circuit.

disabling the internal pull-up resistors is just part of the I/O port configuration task.

The Toggler Program

Memory allocation in the Toggler program is very simple. There are essentially three variables that would be considered global to the program. Of course, the program does not have any functions, so talking about variable scope is rather meaningless in such a small program. No memory (RAM) is used by the program as the variables are bound to three general purpose registers (r16–r18). These registers are equated to symbols (leds, switches, and temp) so they can be referred to by a meaningful name, instead of a register number. There is no allocation associated with register bound variables; the programmer simply keeps track of the fact that certain registers currently represent certain variables.

Very small programs can get away with this simple realization of variables. As long as there are enough free registers, and the data is of the right size to fit in a register (or group of registers), registers can be dedicated to hold variable data for the entire life of a program. As complexity increases, it will be necessary to allocate space in RAM for variables and swap data in and out of registers as needed. Registers are the most limited storage resource and must be used carefully to avoid bottlenecks. We will explore more sophisticated memory allocation techniques in later chapters.

The Toggler program uses a register (equated to the symbol leds) to hold the current state of the LEDs. This is represented by the bits in a single byte; we will call this byte the LED status byte. This byte is output to port connected to the LEDs whenever it is changed by the program. By keeping the byte in asserted on the port synchronized with the status byte, the LEDs will always display the pattern the program expects them to display. The state of the switches is read and stored in another register labeled switches. This is updated frequently so it always represents the actual state of the pushbuttons.

The flow of control in the Toggler program is also fairly simple. The input section of the program is handled by two loops. The first loop repeatedly reads the input port (pushbuttons) until one of the buttons is pressed. At this point, the LED status byte is changed to reverse the state of the LED corresponding to the activated button. The new byte is output to the LED port so the LEDs display the new pattern. Note that only one bit of the status byte will be changed, but we reassert all eight bits when the byte is sent out to the port. The program then enters another loop and waits for the pushbutton to be released before repeating the whole process.

The LED Toggler program (Program 3.1) is written for the ATMEGA16A microcontroller. For the XMEGA version, see the alternate Program 3.1a.

PROGRAM 3.1 LED Toggler

```
;A simple AVR example to illustrate I/O using LED's and
;Pushbuttons

;Toggler - This program uses pushbuttons (PORTD) to
;toggle bits in a byte. The value of the byte is
;displayed on the LED's (PORTB)

;PORTB must be connected to the LEDS
;PORTD must be connected to the SWITCHES

;Programmer: TM
;Date: 5/2010
;Platform: STK-500
;Device: ATMega16A

.cseg          ;select current segment as code
.org  0        ;begin assembling at address 0

.def  leds     = r16    ;current LED state
.def  switches = r17    ;switch values just read
.def  temp     = r18    ;used as a temporary register

.equ  PORTB = 0x18  ;Port B's output register
.equ  DDRB  = 0x17  ;Port B's Data Direction Register
.equ  PIND  = 0x10  ;Port D's input register
.equ  DDRD  = 0x11  ;Port D's Data Direction Register

      ldi    temp,0xFF   ;configure PORTB as output
      out    DDRB,temp
      clr    temp   ;configure PORTD as input
      out    DDRD,temp

      ldi    leds,0x00   ;Initialize LED's all on
      out    PORTB,leds  ;Display initial LED's
```

```
;wait for switch to be pressed
;while (no button is depressed);
waitpress:
        in      switches, PIND
        cpi     switches, 0xFF      ;0xFF means none pressed
        breq    waitpress
;one or more switches are depressed (0's)
        com     switches ;flip all bits, now 1's indicate
                                ;pressed
        eor     leds,switches  ;toggle associated bits in
                                ;led status
        out     PORTB,leds  ;(Re)display LED's

;wait for all switches to be released
;while (at least one button is depressed);
waitrelease:
        in      switches, PIND
        cpi     switches, 0xFF  ;0xFF means none pressed
        brne    waitrelease

        rjmp    waitpress     ;repeat (forever)
```

There are several new ideas and techniques illustrated in this program. First is how the microcontroller knows if pins on a port are to be used for input or output. In the AVR MEGA series processor, each I/O port has three associated registers, the data direction register, output register, and input register. For the curious, these registers correspond to addresses in the data space accessible by the processor. Do you remember that SRAM begins at address $0060 on the ATMEGA16A? The 12 registers (three for each of four ports) occupy twelve addresses somewhere below address $0060. The OUT instruction (and the IN instruction) are special instructions to access these memory locations. The following information is specific to the MEGA series microcontroller. See the alternate project for details on the XMEGA series general purpose I/O ports.

Each bit (pin) of a port can be independently configured for input or output. In this program, all pins of port B are set to output. This allows them to drive the LEDs. A 1 in bit position n indicates pin n is used for output. Setting pins to output mode is done by storing 1's into all of the bits of DDRB (data direction port B). A load immediate followed by an OUT instruction accomplishes this task.

All of the pins of port D are configured for input. Thus, all of the bits of DDRD are set to 0. The CLR instruction is used to make temp (register 18) zero (instead of LDI temp, 0, which would have accomplished the same thing). The zero is then output to DDRD to configure its pins as inputs.

There are three loops in the program. One is an outer loop that repeats the three-step process:

```
do forever
        wait for a button press,
        update and output the new LED state,
        wait for the button release.
```

This loop executes forever. Note that microcontroller programs almost always have infinite loops. They are designed to continue doing their task until power is removed.

The inner wait loops simply read the input pins and wait for some change of level. When pins of port D are used for input, you read their values on the I/O register named PIND, not PORTD. The I/O registers corresponding to each port are located at three different addresses. You read the byte at the PIN register to determine the value on the external pins. You write a byte to the PORT register to assert values on the external pins. The PORT registers are for output; the PIN registers are for input (Figure 3.6).

Remember that the port pins will read as 1 if the buttons are at rest (not pressed). Thus the first loop iterates as long as the value read on port D is 0xFF (all 1's). This loop is waiting for a button to be depressed causing a change of state on PIND. The IN instruction copies the data from the PIND I/O register into a general purpose register. The loop control is

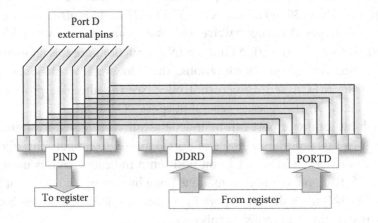

FIGURE 3.6 ATMEGA16A's general purpose I/O port control registers.

accomplished by comparing the read byte to 0xFF (using CPI—compare immediate), and branching back to the top of the loop while equal.

The other loop waits until the PIND value is again all 1's (all pushbuttons up). The structure is similar, except the repetition continues while the PIND value is not equal to 0xFF.

Between these two loops, the byte read from port D is complemented (using the COM instruction) so only the bit corresponding to the depressed button is a 1. This value is combined with the current LED state byte using the exclusive-or instruction (EOR). Exclusive or is convenient here as the effect of an exclusive-or with a 1 is to toggle the other bit. Thus, the bit (or bits) in the byte representing the LED state in the same positions as the 1 (or 1's) in switches, is toggled. The new LED value is then output to the LEDs via port B.

You can assemble, download, and run this program in the STK-500. Be sure the cables are connected correctly to attach the switches to port D and the LEDs to port B. When the program starts, all of the LEDs should be on. Pressing a button should immediately change the LED next to the button that was pressed. No further button presses are registered until all buttons are released.

There is one glitch that might be noticed when you test the program. Sometimes, it appears that pressing a button once results in no change of the LED state. This is due to a hardware problem commonly called switch bounce. Unfortunately, pressing or releasing a physical button can result in many state changes, all occurring within a few milliseconds. If the number of changes is even, you may not see any change on the LED. If the number of changes is odd, the LED will visibly change state.

As the physical contacts inside the switch change between the open and closed states, they make and break the electrical contact many times. Some switches exhibit little bounce, others are quite noisy. There are hardware and software solutions to switch bounce. Later, we will explore some software solutions that read the switch state multiple times to detect and eliminate bounce effects.

EXERCISES

1. All of the following directives assemble a byte representing negative one. Which most clearly represents this intent? Why?
   .db $FF
   .db –1
   db 255

2. Which memory area is always considered to be uninitialized when the AVR processor is powered on? Which memories can be affected by the AVR programmer utility?

3. Write an assembly language directive that will generate a sequence of four bytes representing Fred's name. Write another directive to generate the following sequence of four bytes: 70, 114, 101, 100. How do these two statements compare?

4. What directive would cause the assembly of the 16-bit code for the number represented by 076234 (octal notation)?

5. Use a directive to define the symbol minimum as an alias for register 27.

6. Use a directive to create a constant symbol named LPP that is used to specify there will be 66 lines per page.

7. Use a directive to define a symbol named isDefined as the number 0. This symbol may change value later in the program.

8. Which directive would be best to create a data value in memory representing a 5-digit U.S. zipcode? Why? Write an assembly language statement to assemble your zipcode.

9. If you create an assembly language source file with some common assembly language routines used in your AVR programs, what directive would be used to incorporate those routines in another assembly language program you are writing?

10. What is the value of the PC (representing the code segment's location counter) after the following statements are assembled?

```
.cseg
.org        $FF
.db         "abcd"
.dw         10
here: add   r2, r2
```

11. What is the value of the data segment location counter after the following statements are assembled?

```
.dseg
.org        $60
a: .byte    7
.byte       1
.org        $70
.byte       1
```

12. You are creating a table (two-dimensional array) in an assembly language program. The table needs half as many rows as columns. The number of columns should be set to 12.

a. Define two constant symbols (use directives) to represent the numRows and numCols in a table. Be sure that changing the 12 to another number will automatically adjust the number of rows.

b. What happens if the number of columns is odd?

c. Write a directive that sets the symbol numCells to the number of cells in a table with the above number of rows and columns.

d. Assuming you used the / operator in part a., redo it using the >> operator (otherwise redo it using /). What happens now if the columns value is odd?

13. Use the conditional operator to write an expression that represents the ASCII code for "A" or "a," depending on whether the symbol FLIP is even or odd, respectively.

14. What is the numeric value of each expression truncated to a single byte? You can answer in hex or unsigned decimal.

   a. !2
   b. ~0
   c. "\45"
   d. 2 + 7/3
   e. 0xFF << 0x04

15. When the following instruction is assembled, will other machine instructions need to be generated by the assembler to evaluate the expression? Explain, listing the required instructions if applicable.

   ldi   r16, a + 2/b

16. What constant will be assembled as a result of the following directives (give each answer in hexadecimal)?

   ```
            .eseg
   aa:   .db      256
         .dw      "A"
   bb:   .dd      1 << 31
         .db      bb-aa
   ```

17. Lookup the CLC instruction. How many bits are needed to represent this instruction? How long is the opcode?

18. Lookup the CALL instruction. How many bits are required to represent this instruction? What is the opcode for the CALL instruction?

19. Write an instruction to add register 3 to register 14 (the result is to be placed in R14). Write an instruction to subtract register 7 from register 9 and store the result in register 9. What complication would arise if the result needed to be stored in register 7 instead?

20. Design a loop using a conditional branch instruction that will repeat 255 times. What value will be used to initialize

the loop counter? What initial value would be used to repeat the loop 256 times? Include two nop instuctions in the body of the loop. If the microcontroller is running at 1 MHz, how long will the code take to execute 256 iterations (answer in milliseconds)?

21. The cpi and breq instructions are often used in sequence. That is, the processor performs a comparison and then the next instruction (breq) acts on the result of that comparison. Write a sequence of instructions that cause a branch to the label named *found* if register 20 contains the ASCII code for the letter "e."

22. The instructions that use labels for operands can also accept numbers (after all, labels represent numeric values). Write an instruction that copies the byte at address 0x00F0 of the data space into register 2.

23. Some might call the nop instruction an oxymoron. Why? Why would a processor have such an instruction (do a little research if necessary)?

24. Lookup the addresses of the I/O registers in the ATMEGA16A for the digital I/O port A. Write directives that correctly define the symbols PORTA, PINA, and DDRA.

25. What statements are needed to configure the ATMEGA16A's port B so all pins are outputs?

26. What statements are needed to configure the ATMEGA16A's port D so the even numbered pins are inputs and the odd numbered pins are outputs?

27. When using a port to control LEDs on the STK-500/XPLAIN, what bit value causes the LED to light up? Explain. When reading the state of a pushbutton, what bit value is read when the pushbutton is pressed? Explain.

PROGRAMMING EXERCISES

1. Using a loop to introduce a carefully timed delay is not uncommon in AVR program development. A loop controlled by an 8-bit counter can only delay for relatively short times. If it is embedded inside another loop, longer delays are possible. Use a nested loop to obtain a delay of 1/2 second, assuming the processor is running at 1 MHz. Run the program in the simulator. You can set the simulated clock speed to 1 MHz (Debug menu, Simulator Options, Frequency) and then examine the Stop Watch in the processor toolbar (View menu, Toolbars, Processor). By setting a breakpoint on an instruction following the loop, you can see exactly how long the loop will take.

2. Write a program to flash the LEDs of the STK-500/XPLAIN. The display should cycle through three patterns, OOOooooo, ooOOOOoo, and oooooOOO (where O is on, o is off) and repeat forever. Use a delay loop of 1/3 second between each pattern change. The processor should be set to run at 2 MHz using the internal oscillator (this is the default for the XPLAIN board).

3. Rewrite the counter program (Program 2.2) to pause in the loop when any switch (pushbutton) is depressed. When all switches are released, the program resumes. Ignore the problem of switch bounce.

4. Rewrite the counter program (Program 2.2) to pause in the loop at the end of each iteration. The counter will only advance when any switch (pushbutton) changes state (a state change means a button value changes from 0 to 1 or from 1 to 0). Ignore the problem of switch bounce. You can keep the previous button state in a register and use the cp instruction to compare the values in two registers.

5. Write a program to count the number of times button number 1 is pressed; the count should be displayed on the LEDs in base two notation (on = 1, off = 0). Design the program so the release of button 1 causes the advance of the count by one. Pressing button 0 should clear the count (back to 0). Do not worry about switch bounce. What happens if the count exceeds 255?

6. Write a program to "walk a bit" from position 0 to position 7 of a byte. Display the current position of the bit by illuminating the LED in the same position. Each time button 0 is pressed, the bit should move one position to the left. When the bit "falls out" of the left end of the register, the program should halt (enter an infinite loop). Try to eliminate switch bounce if it is observed during testing.

ALTERNATE PROGRAMS FOR THE XPLAIN DEMONSTRATION KIT

Program 3.1a: Toggler

The XPLAIN hardware has hard-wired connections between the ATxmega128A1 and the I/O devices on the demonstration board. This application accesses the LEDs and switches on the XPLAIN board. The LEDs are connected to PORTE of the microcontroller; the switches are connected to PORTF. Input port configuration for the XMEGA series microcontroller is much more flexible than that of the earlier processors. The XMEGA input ports allow pullup or pulldown resistor configurations for input. Each pin's configuration is set through its own configuration register. A multipin configuration option is also available and is used in this project.

Create a new project in AVR Studio, naming it appropriately. Be sure to click the Next button to select the debug platform and device. When using the ATxmega128A1, you will need to choose the AVR Simulator 2 as the debug platform. The earlier version of the simulator does not support this device.

PROGRAM 3.1a   A Program to Illustrate Use of the GPIO Ports with LEDs and Switches

```
;A simple AVR example to illustrate I/O using LED's and
;Pushbuttons
;Toggler - This program uses pushbuttons (PORTF) to
;toggle bits in a byte. The value of the byte is
;displayed on the LED's (PORTE)

;Programmer: TM
;Date: 5/2010
;Platform: XPLAIN
;Device: ATxmega128A1

.cseg          ;select current segment as code
.org  0        ;begin assembling at address 0

.def   leds       = r16    ;current LED state
.def   switches   = r17    ;switch values just read
.def   temp       = r18    ;used as a temporary register

.equ   PORTE_OUT  = 0x684  ;Port E's output register
.equ   PORTE_DIR  = 0x680  ;Port E's Data Direction
                           ;Register

.equ   PORTF_IN   = 0x6A8  ;Port F's input register
.equ   PORTF_DIR  = 0x6A0  ;Port F's Data Direction
                           ;Register
```

```
.equ    PORTF_PIN0CTRL = 0x6B0      ;Port F's Pin0 Control
                                    ;Register

.equ    PORTCFG_MPCMASK = 0xB0      ;Multi-pin Configuration
                                    ;Mask

;Configure all 8 input pins (PORTF) to use internal
;pullup resistors
        ldi     temp,0xFF
        sts     PORTCFG_MPCMASK, temp       ;configure all 8
                                            ;input pins
        ldi     temp, 0b00011000   ;code to enable pullups
                                            ;on input pins
        sts     PORTF_PIN0CTRL, temp        ;PORTF will read
                                            ;switches

;Configure port directions
        ldi     temp,0xFF
        sts     PORTE_DIR,temp      ;configure PORTE as
                                    ;output
        clr     temp
        sts     PORTF_DIR,temp      ;configure PORTF as input

        ldi     leds,0x00   ;Initialize LED's all on
        sts     PORTE_OUT,leds      ;Display initial LED's

;wait for switch to be pressed
;while (no button is depressed);
waitpress:
        lds     switches, PORTF_IN
        cpi     switches, 0xFF      ;0xFF means none pressed
        breq    waitpress

;one or more switches are depressed (0's)
        com     switches    ;flip all bits, now 1's
                                    ;indicate pressed
        eor     leds,switches       ;toggle associated bits
                                    ;in led status
        sts     PORTE_OUT,leds      ;(Re)display LED's

;wait for all switches to be released
;while (at least one button is depressed);
```

```
waitrelease:
      lds    switches, PORTF_IN
      cpi    switches, 0xFF      ;0xFF means none pressed
      brne   waitrelease

      rjmp   waitpress     ;repeat (forever)
```

Once Program 3.1a has been entered and assembled, you should download it to the ATxmega128A1 using the AVRISP mkII programmer. Be sure the XPLAIN board is connected via USB and is in programming mode. Under the Program tab, you must select the HEX file (in the Flash section) for the current project. This is located in the project folder. Once selected, click the Program button to download it and begin execution.

The LEDs on the Xplain board should all be on when the program begins. Pressing a button will toggle the corresponding LED off (or on if it was off).

Program Notes

There are several new ideas and techniques illustrated in this program. First is how the microcontroller knows if pins on a port are to be used for input or output. In the AVR XMEGA series processor, each I/O port has 32 associated configuration registers. We will focus on just 11, the data direction register, output register, input register, and the 8-pin configuration registers. These registers correspond to addresses in the data space accessible by the processor. Because the addresses of these registers are above $0060, the IN and OUT instructions cannot be used. Instead, programs accessing the GPIO ports in their assigned locations must use the more general load (LDS) and store (STS) instructions (or an equivalent).

Each bit (pin) of a port can be independently configured for input or output. In this program, all pins of port E are set to output. This allows them to drive the LEDs. A 1 in bit position n of the direction register (PORTE_DIR) indicates pin n is used for output. Setting pins to output mode is done by storing 1's into all of the bits of PORTE_DIR (data direction port E). A load immediate to place the constant $FF in a temporary register followed by an STS instruction accomplishes this task.

All of the pins of port F are configured for input. Thus, all of the bits of PORTF_DIR are set to 0. The CLR instruction is used to make temp (register 18) zero. The zero is then stored at PORTF_DIR to configure its pins as inputs. Incidentally, this is the default value for this port, so after a reset, explicitly selecting input mode is not necessary.

The switches on the XPLAIN board connect the pins of the XMEGA's port F to ground (when the switch is pressed). There is no pullup resistor in this circuit; when the pushbuttons are up, the pins on the micro-controller will float to an undefined level unless configured to use the internal pullup resistors. On the XMEGA, each pin has its own configu-ration register, PINnCTRL. The pin control registers are subdivided into four fields, Slew Rate Limit Enable (bit 7), Inverted I/O Enable (bit 6), Output and Pull Configuration (bits 5–3), and Input/Sense Configuration. The default value in these registers is 0, which is appro-priate for PORTE which is configured for output. However, this will not work for input of the switch values. Consulting the documentation, we learn that we need to place the code 0b011 into the third field, bits 5–3 to select pullup resistors.

Configuring all 8 pins would normally require 8 STS instructions how-ever the XMEGA hardware includes a facility to configure a group of pins with a single operation. By setting bits in the Multi-Pin Configuration Register (MPCMASK), we select which pins are included in the group (in our example, we use $FF to select all pins). After setting the mask, writing to one of the pin control registers causes a simultaneous write to all control registers in the group. In Program 3.1, all pins are configured to use pull-ups by writing 0b00011000 to PIN0CTRL.

When pins of port F are used for input, you read their values on the I/O register named PORTF_IN. Port E is configured for output, so you assert values by writing to PORTE_OUT. The LDS and STS instructions are used to transfer a byte between a general purpose register (r0–r31) and an I/O register. LDS transfers from an I/O register (at the specified address) to a general purpose register; STS stores a value from a general purpose regis-ter to an I/O register.

Program 3.1 complements the bits of the switch state as read from the ports IN register. This changes the raw data to a byte containing 1's for switches which are pressed (instead of 0's). The XMEGA's pin configuration register can do this automatically by setting the Inverted I/O Enable bit (bit 6). If the pins of port F are configured with the value 0b01011000, then the complement after the read can be eliminated. This change will also require that the wait loops compare the switch data to $00 instead of $FF.

One additional improvement can also be accomplished by taking advantage of the XMEGA's flexible port registers. Each port has an output toggle register. For port E, it is named PORTE_OUTTGL. Writing a bit-mask to this register with 1's in bit positions you want to toggle will toggle those bits in PORTE_OUT. This completely eliminates the need to keep the current LED state in a register and allows the two instructions to change the LEDs to be combined into one.

```
;one or more switches are depressed (0's)
      com    switches      ;flip all bits, now 1's
                           ;indicate pressed
      eor    leds,switches      ;toggle associated bits
                           ;in led status
      sts    PORTE_OUT,leds      ;(Re)display LED's
```

becomes

```
;one or more switches are depressed (1's)
      sts    PORTE_OUTTGL, switches    ;toggle associated
                                       ;bits in led port
```

Of course, the symbol PORTE_OUTTGL will need to be defined to represent the proper address. You should try to implement these changes to the program.

CHAPTER 4

Integer Data Representation

N OW THAT WE HAVE a way to describe a raw data item (bit, byte, word, etc.) we can discuss how different types of information are represented inside a computer system. The native data type is, of course, raw logical (binary) data, in which true and false are represented as 1 and 0. Ultimately, all computations are carried out at this level. Even addition is realized as a sequence of logical operations. We will cover logical data in more depth when we study logical operations and instructions.

Numbers are perhaps the most commonly used data type. Numeric types must be separated into integer and floating point types as the usual representations of these are quite different. Even plain integer data can be represented in a variety of ways. We begin with the simplest: unsigned integers.

UNSIGNED INTEGER DATA

Unsigned data is typically stored in a fixed-size container such as a byte or a word. Thus we must distinguish between 8-bit unsigned and 32-bit unsigned as distinct, but similar data types. Unsigned data is represented by expressing it in base two, appending leading zeros to get the right length to fit the container, and then storing the binary digits as bits. Thus if a byte contains 0b00000010 and is interpreted as an 8-bit unsigned integer, it would represent the decimal value 2 (10 in base two is 2).

This size container (8 bits) is capable of representing at most 256 ($256 = 2^8$) distinct values, the unsigned integers in the range 0 through

255. Larger containers have greater range; n-bit containers can represent 2^n distinct values. Conversion between different-sized unsigned integer formats is as simple as adding leading zeros, or removing leading bits. If nonzero bits are removed in an attempt to fit a value to a smaller container, the value represented will be changed. This is referred to as truncation. In this case, the truncated value will be mathematically equal to the original value modulo some power of two. For example, if 0b1011101111001011 which represents 48,075 is truncated to fit in a byte, the result is 0b11001011 or 203. Note that 203 is the remainder when 48,075 is divided by 256 (48075 % 256 = 203).

Fixed-size containers are the most convenient computationally, but always suffer from the danger of overflow and the limitation of a restricted range. Variable size numbers are more complex to represent, and less efficient computationally; however, they have their place in particular situations. Processors provide native support for fixed-size numbers, but usually not for variable ones.

The ALU in a computing system most likely includes the circuitry to perform unsigned addition and subtraction, and probably multiplication and division. You can examine the processor instruction set to see what numeric operations are supported and what sizes of data can be used. Addition and subtraction instructions usually produce a result of the same size as the operands. It is quite possible that such operations will result in overflow, and this is generally handled by producing the arithmetic result modulo a power of two (via truncation), and indicating that overflow occurred in case the programmer deems this important. In unsigned arithmetic, larger numbers cannot be subtracted from smaller numbers (e.g., 1 − 2); nevertheless, this operation is legal as far as the ALU is concerned. The result is obtained by simulating a borrow from the next higher bit position (outside the container). The result is correct (modulo a power of two), and the need for the simulated borrow is flagged (as unsigned overflow).

We will revisit the full arithmetic capabilities of the AVR processor in a later chapter; for now we will examine some of the more basic AVR arithmetic instructions, focusing on the arithmetic properties and representation of integers.

Before we can operate on numbers, we need to encode them in a supported numeric code (as a numeric data type) and place them into memory or registers. You can tell the assembler to generate unsigned integer codes for any number by using a literal or expression as the operand for a data definition directive. The value of the expression is evaluated (using 64-bits) and then encoded properly as an unsigned integer of the desired size. The following statements illustrate the generation of constant bytes and words in unsigned format. The data in this example is assembled to the code segment. Remember that the assembler cannot generate constant data to be placed in the data segment (dseg). Only flash and EEPROM can be used for this purpose.

```
.cseg
.dw $FFFF
.dw 65535
.db 0b10000001, 207, 0207, 0xFF, '9', high(45239)
```

You should determine the values the assembler will output for each of these statements. Remember that the easiest way to describe the content of a byte or word is to express it in hexadecimal. If you paste this code into an AVR Assembly language source file, assemble it, and examine the listing file, which will display each byte (word) in hexadecimal format, you can verify your analysis.

The assembler will translate the result of any expression that represents a nonnegative number into unsigned format to be incorporated in the assembly process. Remember that when you write programs, specify numbers in the most convenient and descriptive notation. The age of a newborn baby (in years) is usually written as 0, although 00, $00, and 0x00 all express the same value. The largest unsigned integer that fits in a word is correctly expressed as $FFFF, 65535, or 0177777. I find the hexadecimal representation easiest to remember.

The define data directives are used to assemble numeric values into flash memory locations (or EEPROM) for use when the program is executing. These numbers will need to be copied into one of the 32 registers before any arithmetic operations are performed on them. This is accomplished using a LPM (load from program memory) instruction. In many cases, it is simpler to use a LDI (load immediate) instruction to set a register to a specific value. When the LDI instruction is executed, it loads the specified register with bits taken right out of the instruction itself (which is in the current instruction register).

```
LDI register, expression
```

When the assembler assembles the LDI instruction, it combines the LDI opcode, the bits representing the destination register, and eight bits representing the value of the expression (the expression is truncated to fit an 8-bit container). Examine the following instructions:

```
ldi R16, $FF
ldi R17, 0b11111111
ldi R18, 255
ldi R19, 0377
ldi R20, $100-1
ldi R21, 0x12345678FF % 256
```

All of the above instructions load the unsigned integer representation for 255 into the specified register. You should assemble and run this program in the simulator, observing the values loaded into the registers. They should all be the same.

The AVR processor can perform addition, subtraction, and multiplication on unsigned data. The following instructions are commonly used for this purpose (multiplication will be covered later).

```
ADD Rd, Rr
SUB Rd, Rr
SUBI Rd, n
```

These all store the result of the operation into Rd. Rd is also one of the operands in the arithmetic operation. In C or Java syntax, these might be expressed as Rd += Rr, Rd -= Rr, and Rd -= n. The third instruction is subtract immediate. This instruction subtracts a byte value (0–255) from Rd and stores the result into Rd as shown in Figure 4.1. The byte is encoded as a field of the SUBI (Subtract Immediate) instruction itself. One

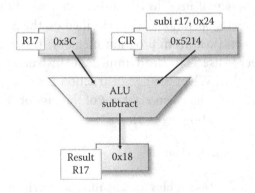

FIGURE 4.1   The AVR Subtract Immediate (SUBI) instruction.

could accomplish this in two steps (LDI followed by SUB), but SUBI does it in one step and without using a temporary register to hold the second operand.

There is also limited support for 16-bit unsigned arithmetic in the AVR instruction set.

```
ADIW Rd + 1:Rd, k
SBIW Rd + 1:Rd, k
```

These instructions allow a small constant (0–63) to be added to or subtracted from a 16-bit number stored in certain register pairs. Only registers R25:R24, R27:R26, R29:R28, and R31:R30 may be used in this way.

When 16-bit numbers are to be manipulated, they are often copied into a pair of registers (each 8 bits in length). The 16-bit immediate mode instructions (ADIW and SBIW) expect the high byte of the number to be in the odd numbered register. The register pair notation suggests this order. If the registers are thought to be arranged in numeric order, you can see that this storage convention is little-endian format. Note that these instructions are an exception to the general rule that the ALU adds or subtracts two operands of the same size. These instructions combine a 16-bit integer (in a register pair) and a 6-bit (immediate) unsigned integer. The result is always 16-bits (Figure 4.2).

If any of the arithmetic instructions overflow their result size (including the case of an illegal subtraction, that is, one in which the unsigned answer would need to be negative), the result modulo 256 (or 65536 in the 16-bit case) is stored, and the carry flag in the status register is set. If an

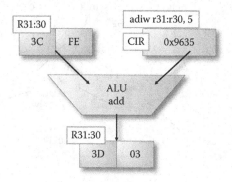

FIGURE 4.2 The Add Immediate Word (ADIW) instruction.

operation does not cause overflow, the carry flag is cleared. These instructions also set or clear other status flags, such as the zero flag which indicates when a result is zero. When an arithmetic operation is applied to unsigned data, the carry flag can be interpreted as the unsigned overflow indicator. Recall that the status flags form the basis for conditional branches, allowing different actions to be taken by placing an appropriate branch instruction after an arithmetic instruction in the program.

Because the AVR provides only very limited support for 16-bit arithmetic, if you need to add (or subtract) two 16-bit unsigned integers, you must do it one byte at a time. There are special instructions to take into account the carry between bytes. In the following example, registers R7:R6 and R5:R4 hold 16-bit unsigned integers.

```
;add the low bytes
ADD R6, R4
;add the high bytes (with carry)
ADC R7, R5
```

If the first add overflows, then the carry flag is set. The carry flag indicates unsigned overflow has occurred, but in this context, we use that fact to propagate the carry into the next add instruction; there is a carry from bit 7 to bit 8 in the 16-bit addition. In Figure 4.3 you can see the result being copied in R6 and the Carry flag waiting for use with the next instruction.

The ADC (add with carry) instruction adds the high-order bytes incorporating the carry flag (0 or 1) in the final sum as shown in Figure 4.3.

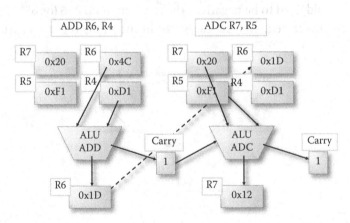

FIGURE 4.3 An ADD instruction followed by ADC to accomplish 16-bit unsigned addition.

When the two operations are complete, R6:R7 will hold the 16-bit sum. The carry flag will also indicate whether the sum was small enough to fit in a word. In the example shown here, there is a final carry of 1 indicated for with the result (0x1121D) which is too large to fit in 16-bits. The carry flag indicates overflow has occurred.

There is no reason that the two bytes of each word be in adjacent registers. The program must address each byte individually. In this example, we have maintained the convention of storing the high byte in an Rn + 1:Rn register pair where *n* is even.

Be careful if you need to test the result of a 16-bit addition carried out using these two steps against zero. The z flag will only reflect the second addition. That is, it will be set if the high byte of the result is zero. If the low byte is not zero, the z flag does not correctly indicate the status of the 16-bit result.

There is also a SBC (subtract with carry) instruction which is better described as subtract with borrow that allows 16-bit subtraction.

```
SUB R6, R4 ;subtract the low bytes
SBC R7, R5 ;subtract the high bytes (with borrow)
```

This sequence computes the subtraction, (R7:R6) -= (R5:R4). The zero flag in this sequence will always correctly represent the status of the 16-bit result. This is a very interesting feature of the SBC instruction. The zero flag is set if the high byte is zero and the z flag was previously set (presumably by an earlier subtract instruction). This behavior is different from the addition (ADC) instruction. There is also a subtract with carry immediate, SBCI, which also correctly sets the zero flag when used in a multibyte subtraction.

CHARACTER DATA

Before moving on to signed data, it should be noted that character information is stored as unsigned numbers. The ASCII table provides a popular numeric encoding for 128 different characters; this encoding has been the most common one used throughout computer history. ASCII codes are unsigned integers in the range 0–127. ASCII is a 7-bit code. Usually a leading zero is added to fill out a byte. Some computer systems use an extension of the ASCII character set, defining a mapping between the unused codes numbered 128–255 and special characters.

The Unicode Consortium has more recently taken on the job of cataloging all of the symbols that are used for writing text and developing representation schemes that are not limited in size to one or even two bytes. The AVR assembler provides support only for the basic ASCII character set, which is essentially equivalent to the first section of the UTF-8 Unicode translation format.

In UTF-8, certain 8-bit patterns (with values above 127) indicate that the character code is more than one byte in length. UTF-8 is another example of an expanding code, a technique used to encode opcodes in AVR instruction set. UTF-8 codes can be 1, 2, 3, or 4 bytes. If you need to use Unicode formats for characters in an AVR program, the assembler will not provide any direct support; you will need to specify the codes in hexadecimal or other numeric format.

SIGNED INTEGER DATA

Two's Complement

There are several conventions for representing signed integers. The most common is called two's complement notation. In this context, the word *complement* refers to *completing the whole*, as in complementary angles (two angles that add to 90 degrees; the one angle completes the other). Under the rules of complement encoding, the integers x and $-x$ (x's additive inverse) are represented by complementary numbers; together they complete the whole. Any "whole" can be used. For example, in our familiar base 10 notation, we could devise a hundred's complement notation in which 100 is the "whole." The codes for x and $-x$ would have to be chosen so they add to the whole, 100. In other words, once we choose the code for x, the code for $-x$ would be $100 - x$. If we decide that the code for twenty-three is 23, then its negative (negative twenty-three) would be represented by its complement, 77 ($77 = 100 - 23$). If we add these codes together (using normal addition of base 10 numerals) we get $23 + 77 = 100$. In the hundred's complement system, we would truncate this answer to 0, and get the correct result for signed addition ($23 + -23 = 0$). In *two-digit hundred's complement* representation, integers from -50 through 49 can be encoded. The complement technique splits the codes into two halves, representing an equal number of negative and nonnegative values.

Computers generally represent signed integers using n-bit two's complement notation. In this case, the "whole" is 2^n. In this system, positive numbers are represented by the unsigned code for their value. If x is a positive value, then its complement would be $2^n - x$, and this number (x's two's complement) would represent the integer $-x$. If you treat the codes for x and $-x$ as unsigned data, they will add to 2^n. Note that in an n-bit unsigned code, 2^n is beyond the range for this size container, so it would be truncated to zero when the sum is found. Thus adding the codes for x and $-x$ (treating the codes as if they were unsigned integers and truncating the result to the required number of bits) gives the result of zero.

Example: Determine the 8-Bit Two's Complement Codes for 37 and –37 and Demonstrate that They are Complements of Each Other

```
Since 8 is the container size, the whole is 2⁸ = 256
The complement of 37 is therefore 256 − 37 = 219.
The codes for 37 and −37 are the unsigned codes for these
numbers:
37  = 0b00100101 (37)
219 = 0b11011011 (−37)

If we add the codes together (in binary)
  0b00100101
+ 0b11011011
  ----------
0b100000000 = 256 or 2⁸
```

This illustrates that these are indeed complements of one another.

To encode a number in two's complement notation, simply write the magnitude (absolute value) of the number in binary form. This must, of course, fit in the fixed-size container. You must always add at least one leading zero to fill the container; if you cannot, the number is out of range (too big). If the original number was negative, then you must perform one additional step: find the two's complement of this code. In binary, this can be accomplished by changing all of the bits (1 becomes 0 and 0 becomes 1) and then adding 1 (truncate the result to fit the container).

Changing (or flipping) all of the bits results in what is called the one's complement of the original code. A few historically important computers used one's complement representation of integers, but two's complement is now the most prevalent system. If you add one's complements together, you will get a binary number that is all 1's. Essentially, corresponding bits are complements in the whole, 1 (one). This bit pattern of all 1's, interpreted as an unsigned integer, is one less than some power of two. Adding one to such a number gives a power of two.

All fixed-size representations have a limited range of numbers that can be represented. If you attempt to encode a number that is out of range, you will get a result that represents a different number than expected. To ensure the two's complement code you obtained by flipping the bits and adding one represents the correct number, there is one final check after encoding your integer. You must verify that the leftmost bit in your result is one if the number you are encoding is negative, and zero otherwise. If it is not, then the original number was out of the legal range for this size code. For an 8-bit code, the legal range of integers is –128 through 127. The number line below shows some of the 256 possible code values 00 through FF. Above the line are the integers corresponding to the 8-bit two's complement code immediately below.

```
  0   1    2  ...  126  127  –128  –127  –126  ... –3   –2  –1
 00  01   02  ...   7E   7F    80    81    82  ... FD   FE  FF
```

Notice that the negative numbers are represented by bytes with larger unsigned values. Also note that there is a –128, but no +128. The codes associated with the integers 0 and –128 are self-complements. That is, the complement of 0x80 is 0x80 (0x80 + 0x80 = 0x100 or 256) and the complement of 0 is 0. Technically, the complement of 0 is 256, but 256 cannot fit in a byte, so by ignoring the 9th bit, you get 0 as the complement. Thus 0 and –0 have the same code. This is fine arithmetically since 0 and –0 are equal. There would be a serious problem if we allowed 128 and –128 to have the same code, since numerically they are not equal. We eliminate this ambiguity by defining the range of integers that can be represented in 8 bits to include –128, but not 128.

The process of flipping the bits and adding one is sometimes called the *change sign rule*. You can simplify the change sign procedure if you simply flip the bits found to the left of the rightmost one (1). The end result is the same. This is the simplest way of manipulating the bits of a two's complement code to change the sign of the integer it represents.

Example: Apply the Change Sign Rule to the 16-Bit Two's Complement Code for 11,128. Verify that the Result is the Two's Complement of the First Code

```
In binary, 11,128 is 0b10101101111000.
Extending this to 16 bits, we get 0b0010101101111000.
This is the 16-bit two's complement code for 11,128.

To apply the change sign rule, we locate the rightmost bit
which is 1.
The rightmost '1' is in bit position 3, so we flip all of the
bits in positions 4 and above.
```

```
The result is 0b1101010010001000.
```

```
Compare the bits of these two codes:
    0010101101111000
    1101010010001000
```

```
The latter is the 16-bit two's complement code for -11,128.
This is verified by adding.
        0010101101111000
    + 1101010010001000
    ----------------
      10000000000000000 (which is 2¹⁶)
```

A second fact that is apparent when examining the correspondence between integers and their two's complement codes is that all of the negative integers have a binary code that begins with 1. Some people refer to the leftmost bit of a two's complement code as the sign bit. Indeed, if this bit is one, then the integer represented is negative; if it is zero, then the integer is nonnegative. It is also true that if you apply the change sign rule to any code, the sign bit will change, with two exceptions. Applied to the code for 0, there is no change; this is a reflection of the fact that 0 and –0 are the same. Applying the rule to the code for –128 also results in an unchanged code, still representing –128. Attempting to change the sign of this particular value results in signed overflow since the intended result (128) is out of range of the current code.

The change sign rule is the key to encoding and decoding integers in two's complement representation.

Example: Determine the Two's Complement Codes for 23 and –120

23 represented in 8-bit binary is 0b00010111 which is also the two's complement code for this integer. Note that the leading bit is 0.

120 represented in binary is 0b01111000. Applying the change sign rule (since the value we are encoding is negative) we get 0b10001000, which is the two's complement code for –120. Notice that the leading bit is 1 as required.

Example: Determine the Integers Represented by These Two's Complement Codes, 0b11110001 and 0b01000011

0b11110001 represents a negative number (as indicated by the sign bit). Applying the change sign rule we get 0b00001111 which is 15. Thus the original code represents –15.

```
The second code represents a positive value since the leading
bit is 0. Converting it to decimal gives the integer value it
represents, 67.
```

One of the reasons two's complement representation is so common in modern processors is that the circuitry for unsigned addition and subtraction is identical to that required for two's complement operations. That is, the machine instructions we discussed above for unsigned numbers are also used for signed (two's complement) integers. The only technical difference is that overflow must be detected differently. The status register contains an overflow flag (V) that is set when an addition or subtraction results in signed overflow, that is, an answer that would be out of range for the current container size. At the same time, the carry flag (C) is used to report unsigned overflow. In addition, there is a negative (N) flag and a sign (S) flag. The N flag is always the same as the most significant bit of the result (the sign bit). Normally N and S are the same, but when signed overflow occurs they are opposites. The S flag indicates the expected sign of the result (as if overflow did not occur).

```
Status Flags
      V = Signed overflow
      C = Carry
      N = Negative
      S = Sign
```

There is a special machine instruction to apply the change sign rule to a byte in a register.

```
NEG Rd
```

This flips all the bits to the left of the rightmost one (1). Actually it flips all the bits and then adds 1, but as we already discussed, the end result is the same. This instruction causes the V bit to be set if the register contains $80.

There are also special instructions to add or subtract the number one to a value in a register.

```
INC Rd
DEC Rd
```

When executing these arithmetic instructions, SUB, ADD, ADC, and so on how does the ALU know whether it is performing signed or unsigned arithmetic? It does not. Actually, it (almost) always does both. The result stored in the register is always the same regardless of whether the data is signed or unsigned. With every addition or subtraction, the processor sets the flags related to unsigned arithmetic (c and z) and the flags related to signed arithmetic (v, n, s, and z) allowing the programmer to use whichever are relevant. The representation of 0 is the same in both unsigned and signed formats, so the setting for z is the same whether the data is signed or unsigned.

There is one exception to the ALU simultaneously performing both signed and unsigned arithmetic. The INC and DEC are considered signed arithmetic instructions. These only affect the flag s, v, n, and z. You may use them on unsigned data, but they will not alter the carry flag if unsigned overflow (incrementing from $FF to $00) or borrow (decrementing from $00 to $FF) occurs.

One's Complement

One's complement code was a competing representation scheme for signed integers. The PDP-1 and CDC 6600 (1960s era) used this representation. In one's complement code, there are two representations of zero: 0b00000000 and 0b11111111 (8-bit version). This duplication avoids the oddity (of the two's complement encoding) of a negative value that has no additive inverse within the number set. The one's complement code has a symmetry not shared by the two's complement counterpart.

The range of values (for an 8-bit one's complement code) is –127 through 127. The change sign rule for one's complement codes is simply *flip all of the bits*, a logical NOT operation. The presence of two codes for zero, and a slightly more complicated addition algorithm, is probably why this code is now less common than the two's complement code. Neither the AVR assembler nor the AVR processor support one's complement representations. If you need to use this encoding scheme, you will have to write your own arithmetic operations using the existing AVR instruction set.

Sign and Magnitude

There are several other codes sometimes used for signed integers. The next corresponds to our normal base 10 signed notation, modified a bit to conform to the binary world. In this scheme, signed integers are encoded in two parts, their sign and magnitude, from which this code derives its name. One bit of the code is reserved as the sign indicator: zero indicates a nonnegative number and one indicates a nonpositive number (there are two representations for zero in this code). The remaining bits encode the magnitude (absolute value) of the integer being represented.

For example, the integers 100 and –100 would be represented in an 8-bit sign and magnitude code as

```
100:  01100100
-100:  11100100
```

The change sign rule in this encoding is simply "flip the sign bit."

Excess-N

Excess-N representation, sometimes written XS-n, and sometimes called biased encoding, adds a constant (the bias) to every integer to be encoded. The bias is chosen so the negative integers that need to be represented become positive after the bias is added. Once the integer is converted (biased) to a whole number, the result is encoded using the normal unsigned code. An 8-bit biased code would be called excess –128, using 128 as the bias, allowing an equal number of negative and nonnegative numbers to be represented.

```
-128 would be represented as 0x00  (-128 + 128 = 0)
 127 would be represented as 0xFF  (127 + 128 = 255)
```

The change sign rule in this system is "subtract from 2⊠bias."

Example: Determine the XS–128 Code for 47 and Apply the Change Sign Rule. Decode the Result to Verify it is –47

47 + 128 = 175. In binary, this is 10101111, the XS – 128 code for 47.

To apply the change sign rule, we subtract this from 2*128 = 256 (100000000). The result is 81 (256 – 175) or 01010001.

To decode, we start with the XS – 128 code 01010001 and interpret as an unsigned code. It represents the number 81 (base ten).

We subtract the bias (128) to determine the signed integer it represents. 81 – 128 = -47, as expected.

There is no reason this code has to be balanced (i.e., have approximately the same number of negative values as positive values) so a bias of 100 could be used, allowing the integers from −100 through 155 to be represented in an 8-bit biased code (XS–100). Normally, the bias for an n-bit code would be 2^{n-1}, producing a balanced set of representable numbers. XS-n code is often used to represent the exponent in floating point codes (which are based on scientific notation).

BINARY CODED DECIMAL

Another way to represent integers is as a sequence of decimal digits, in array fashion, each digit encoded in binary. This approach often employs variable-sized containers, allowing great flexibility in the range of numbers that can be represented. The elements of the array may be an array of bytes or nybbles. Since all of the possible digits (0–9) can be encoded by four bits (a nybble), it is very common to employ an array of nybbles to represent numbers in BCD (Binary Coded Decimal). Since nybbles cannot be directly addressed, this requires packing digit pairs into bytes. This scheme is called a Packed BCD representation. Signed numbers may be represented in packed BCD by adding a sign nybble; this is often placed at the end of the sequence of digits. Commonly, 0b1100 represents plus and 0b1101 represents minus. This special code also serves to mark the end of the string of digits when variable size containers are used.

Unpacked BCD, or simply BCD, representation means that each digit is stored in its own byte (as a 4-bit BCD code with leading zeros). This doubles the storage requirement for each number. A variation of this encoding standard is to simply store the number as a string of ASCII or EBCDIC characters representing the digits of the numeral. In these cases, the upper nybble of each byte is 0b0011 (ASCII) or 0b1111 (EBCDIC). The lower nybble is just the 4-bit BCD equivalent of the digit. Using the character form makes it very easy to perform I/O, but complicates arithmetic.

The BCD formats have the advantage of allowing highly efficient I/O. Translating between the internal BCD format and external decimal (base 10) formats is quite trivial and much faster than translating to a two's complement representation. On the other hand, most processors do not provide arithmetic instructions to perform computations on BCD data. BCD arithmetic routines often need to be implemented in software, usually as a collection of functions. BCD arithmetic will be less efficient than operations on two's complement and unsigned data.

The AVR add and subtract instructions affect one additional status register flag that plays an important role in the implementation of packed BCD arithmetic. The half-carry flag (H) is set when an addition requires a carry from bit 3 to bit 4. This is the boundary between the two digits packed in a BCD byte. By clever use of this flag, Packed BCD addition and subtraction can be implemented relatively easily. We will take this up again when we study the arithmetic operations of the AVR in more depth.

DATA VALUES IN PROGRAMS

To initialize or set variables in high-level programs, one often uses an assignment statement, such as $x = 0$; or $y = -1$. How does one do this in assembly language? A full treatment of this will take some time to develop as the answer depends on where the variables are located and what type of data is being used. Another, related, question is where does the processor get the numbers it needs to initialize the variables? Zero is pretty easy (there is a CLR instruction that zeros all the bits in a register), but other values cannot be so easily generated. When you write numeric values (literals) in programs that will be used at runtime, those values must be encoded and become part of the object file containing the program code. In the AVR setting, the numbers need to be encoded and downloaded to flash or EEPROM.

Define Byte, Word, and Others

The define byte directive along with its differently-sized counterparts (define word, doubleword, and quadword) is used to create data values that must be downloaded as part of the program. These values must be assembled to code memory (cseg) or EEPROM (eseg). The assembler does not allow these directives to be used in the data segment (dseg) since there is no way to start the processor with constants in SRAM (which is volatile storage). Remember that the assembler assembles bytes that will be downloaded to the AVR's flash and EEPROM memories. SRAM always starts with undefined contents when power is first applied to the microcontroller. Programs must always be designed with this assumption in mind. Reading from SRAM before the program stores meaningful data that will result in unpredictable behavior.

When using literals in your programs, keep in mind that any data value can be explicitly specified in binary, octal, or hexadecimal notation if you know the bit patterns required to encode it. Knowing that the 8-bit two's complement code for negative one (-1) is $FF, you might express this value as the literal 0xFF, 0b11111111, 0377, or even 255. Remember that the assembler can correctly translate from normal base 10 sign and magnitude representations, so writing the literal for negative one as − 1 is probably going to be much clearer.

Always write literals in an appropriate and self-documenting format. Numbers usually written in base 10 should be expressed using a decimal literal. Character data (ASCII) should be written using a character literal. String information should utilize the string literal representation. Bit patterns are best expressed in binary, octal, or hexadecimal forms.

For example, the numeric value representing the number of days in a long month (January, March, May, July, August, October, or December) can be stored as an unsigned integer code in a byte using any of the following directives:

```
.db 31
.db 0x1F
.db 0b00011111
.db 037
```

The negative quantity representing the temperature of absolute zero using the Celsius scale could be assembled as a 16-bit two's complement integer using any of the following:

```
.dw −273
.dw 0xfeef
.dw 0b1111111011101111
.dw 0177357
.dw 65263
```

Finally, the byte containing the ASCII code representing a newline character can be expressed as any of the following:

```
.db '\n'
.db 10
.db 0x0A
.db (1<<3) | (1<<1)
```

Which of the alternatives do you prefer? Which best communicates the programmer's intent? In each case, you should prefer the first choice listed.

Data Encoding

When you ask the assembler to assemble a byte (or word or larger), how does it know what encoding to use? Should it assemble an unsigned value, two's complement, sign and magnitude, or BCD? The AVR assembler uses the following rule. Evaluate the expression representing the value (using 64-bit arithmetic) and truncate it to the correct number of bits. The expression is evaluated internally using 64-bit two's complement/unsigned representation, so the bit patterns are correct for the AVR encoding. The assembler does not support any integer encoding other than unsigned and two's complement. Let us look at some examples.

Example: How are the following expressions encoded?

```
.dw 763 << 10, 60416, -5120
.db -1, 255
ldi r16, $3c-$5f
subi r25, -2
```

The 64-bit representation for 763 is $00000000000002FB. Shifting this left by 10 positions gives $00000000000BEC00. A word is desired, so we take just the last 16 bits, assembling $EC00 as the word data. The 64-bit representation for 60,416 is $000000000000EC00. This results in the exact same word. Finally, the 64-bit representation of 5120 is $0000000000001400. We apply the change sign rule (since it is negated in the expression) to get $FFFFFFFFFFFFEC00. This is truncated to the same value as before, $EC00.

The literal 1 is represented as $0000000000000001. We apply the change sign rule and get $FFFFFFFFFFFFFFFF. The last 8 bits are $FF, the encoded byte. The 64-bit code for 255 is $00000000000000FF. This is also truncated to get the same byte value, $FF. Note that there is no difference in how a –1 and a $FF are encoded when stored in a single byte.

The $3C – $5F is calculated as $000000000000003C – $000000000000005F which turns out to be $FFFFFFFFFFFFFFDD. The ldi instruction needs a singly byte value, so this is truncated to $DD. The instruction is encoded as $ED0D.

The internal representation for –2 is obtained by applying the change sign rule to the 64-bit code for two: $FFFFFFFFFFFFFFFE. The subi instruction's second operand is a byte, so we truncate this to $FE and encode it into the instruction code. When this instruction is executed, the processor will subtract 254 from the contents of register 25. The net effect is to add 2 (subtracting –2 is the same as adding 2). Try it! Pick any byte value, subtract $FE from it and truncate the result to one byte. The result will be two more than the original. As you can see from this, there is no need for an add immediate instruction in the AVR instruction set.

So, how does the assembler know whether you want the unsigned code or the signed (two's complement) code for a specific application? The answer is simply, "it doesn't know." It simply evaluates the expression, truncates the result to the proper size, and spits out the bits. Suppose you wanted to assemble the 16-bit two's complement code for the number twenty. You would probably write .dw 20. This would be correct. The assembler would dutifully assemble $0014. But wait! Is not this the unsigned code for twenty? Yes! Fortunately they are exactly the same. There is no need to distinguish between signed and unsigned representations of expressions in assembly language.

There is a potential problem however; the assembler will not always warn you if a signed value is out of range. For example, the directive .db −129 is clearly an attempt by the programmer to assemble an 8-bit two's complement code. The assembler correctly evaluates this as the 64-bit value, $FFFFFFFFFFFFFF7F (representing −129). This is truncated to the 8-bit value $7F. Unfortunately, this is not −129. It represents the integer 127 (regardless of whether you interpret the byte as signed or unsigned). In this case, the desired value was out of range of the storage container. The assembler does not generally issue warnings in such situations; it assumes you know what you are doing!

You can also use literals or expressions when writing instructions that require a constant as an operand. The LDI instruction, for example, needs a register and a constant byte value. If your intent is to load register 31 with the two's complement code for −1, then

```
    ldi R31, 0xFF
```

will work, but

```
    ldi R31, −1
```

will be much clearer. Similarly, you should use

```
    ldi R16, 'A'
```

instead of

```
    ldi R16, 65
```

(Assuming you are loading the ASCII code for the letter A, not a loop counter whose value starts at 65.)

Incidentally, the AVR assembler checks that the register you are specifying is legal for this instruction and that the value will fit in a byte. Remember that LDI can only load into registers 16 through 31. The expression must evaluate to a number between −128 and 255 inclusive.

You can write any expression as the second operand, but it must represent a value in this range.

The most important idea to keep in mind as an assembly language programmer is to try to write well-documented and straightforward code. Use literals and expressions that best convey the intent of each programming statement. Let the assembler do the work of determining the bits and bytes that make the program work.

ASSIGNMENT STATEMENTS

When designing assembly language programs, it is often helpful to think of how a problem would be solved in a high-level language or pseudocode. The resulting statements are then translated to assembly language instructions that implement the intended actions. Probably the most common statement found in high-level language programs is the assignment statement. The purpose of this statement is to store a value into a variable. The value is represented by an expression appearing on the right side of the assignment operator. We will see that accomplishing the seemingly simple effect of an assignment statement may require many assembly language statements.

To understand how an assignment statement is translated to the machine level, you must first understand several related topics: how variables are implemented at the machine level, how data is represented in binary codes, how data is changed in hardware, and how expressions are evaluated through a series of instructions.

In Figure 4.4, we need to understand where space for the variable x is allocated. Will it be stored in a register or memory? Which register or memory? Where in memory? We also need to know how the number 45 will be encoded when it is stored. Is it 8, 16, or 32 bits? Assembly language programmers need to make all of these decisions for every data value.

Simple Variables

Assemblers do not know anything of the concept of a variable as it exists in languages such as C and Java. Variables are really a high-level language

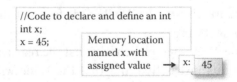

FIGURE 4.4   Visualizing an assignment statement.

concept. Assemblers deal with symbols that represent numbers, but the numbers are usually addresses, not data being manipulated by the program. In C or Java, when you use a variable in an expression, the normal interpretation is that it represents the current value of the variable. Thus the expression temp + 1 means calculate the sum of 1 and the number stored in temp; this operation would be done when the program runs, not at compile time. In an assembly language program, this expression would be evaluated by the assembler; temp would be a symbol representing perhaps an address or other numeric value. Depending on the context of the expression, the result would be used by the assembler to generate the details of an instruction or data value.

Symbols used in assembly language programs usually represent numbers. A label is a special type of symbol that represents an address. Recall that labels are defined by placing them at the beginning of a statement and appending a colon. Other types of symbols are defined using directives such as .set or .equ. Values of symbols are used only for the assembly process and are discarded after assembly is complete. Variables in high level languages, on the other hand, represent virtual storage locations; the compiler must create machine instructions that will allocate and deallocate storage for the variable at appropriate times while the program runs. Variables do not have any value until the program begins executing (and the variable is instantiated). The compiler does not evaluate expressions involving variables.

Translating the concept of a variable into an assembly language level program requires planning for some type of storage allocation. This in itself can be quite complex. There are many ways to allocate storage for variables. One common method of variable allocation is called static allocation. In this case, the assembler is told to reserve a specific memory location (or register) to hold the binary code representing the variable's run-time value. The variable is said to be bound to that location for the life of the program.

The AVR processor has three basic memories where static variables may be bound. The program memory (flash) is read-only while an application is running, so can only be used for constant variables. SRAM and EEPROM are both read/writable, and can be used for nonconstant variable storage. The AVR assembler does not allow an initial value for a variable in SRAM to be specified. Remember that when execution begins, SRAM contents are considered to be undefined. Variables in flash and EEPROM must be given an initial value; the assembler needs to store bytes into these memories when the microcontroller is programmed. Reading and writing to EEPROM requires some special techniques, so the use of this memory area will not be covered at this time.

SRAM is the easiest memory to use for variables; in addition, it is the fastest to access. To statically allocate storage for a variable in SRAM you should use the .byte directive. This will reserve a block of storage for a variable. A label is usually attached to this statement so you can refer to the memory location by name (instead of its numeric address).

Assignment

The storing action of an assignment statement, assuming the variable on the left of the assignment operator is bound to a specific SRAM location (is a static variable), is accomplished by executing a machine instruction to store a byte (or group of bytes) into SRAM. The basic store instruction copies one byte from a register into a memory location. The memory location is specified by its address. Although you can specify an actual address using a numeric literal, it is more convenient to refer to memory addresses using symbols (labels) or simple expressions.

The assignment action is accomplished using the store instruction, but the value to be stored must already be in a register (or group of registers). This value is determined by the expression on the right side of the assignment operator. In the simplest case, this expression is a simple literal, as in the statement x = 45. The AVR instruction set includes an instruction to place a literal value in a register, thus this assignment statement will require two assembly language instructions. For example, the assignment c = 'a', where c is a static variable (one byte in length) assigned to an appropriate address (represented by the label c_lab) in SRAM, would be accomplished by these two instructions:

```
ldi R16, 'a'
sts c_lab, R16
```

The first instruction places the ASCII code for the letter 'a' in register R16. This register now holds the result of the expression on the right side of the assignment. The sts instruction copies this byte to the memory location to which the label c_lab is bound. The assembly language statement to bind c_lab to an SRAM address is

```
.dseg
c_lab: .byte 1
```

This statement causes the assembler to set aside one byte and define the label c_lab to represent its address. The actual address assigned could be specified by the programmer (by adding a .org directive just before the label is defined), but usually it is left to be determined by the assembler as it takes into account other allocations of bytes in the data segment.

The use of the label c_lab in this example is about as close to the concept of a variable as you get in assembly language. Notice, however, that a statement such as

```
lds R16, c_lab + 1
```

will NOT add 1 to the byte in the memory location at address c_lab and load the result into R16. Instead, the assembler will evaluate the expression, c_lab + 1, which is the address of the next byte (at the next higher address) in memory. This address is used to assemble the lds (load direct from data space) instruction. When the instruction is executed, it will load the byte at address c_lab + 1 (the byte immediately after c_lab) into R16.

One immediate complication with this simple implementation of a variable in assembly language is that not all variables occupy a single byte. In many cases, data is stored in a group of bytes (word, doubleword, etc). This situation will require storing each byte separately since the AVR's store instruction is only capable of storing a single byte at a time. The following example carries out the assignment, a = 1, where a is a 16-bit integer bound to the word at label a_lab. The assignment is illustrated in Figure 4.5.

```
.dseg
a_lab: .byte 2
.cseg
ldi r16, 1
ldi r17, 0
sts a_lab, r16
sts a_lab+1, r17
```

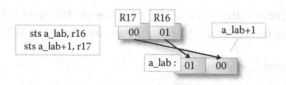

FIGURE 4.5   Assigning a 16-bit value to a static variable.

The label a_lab will be given a numeric value equal to the address of the next two available bytes in SRAM. The actual address is not specified in this program, but will be determined by the assembler based on other allocations of bytes in SRAM. The assembler expressions a_lab and a_lab + 1 are simply specifying the address at which the values in R16 and R17 are to be stored. The assembler evaluates these expressions and assembles the sts instructions with the correct addresses. The arithmetic expression representing the address of the second byte is not part of the runtime task of the program. It is completely evaluated by the assembler at assemble time. Although two bytes are involved, we do not attach labels to both bytes. In general, a label to the first byte in a group is sufficient. The other bytes are addressed by adding an offset (such as 1) to the value of the label.

The ldi (load immediate) instructions in the above code simulate the "evaluation" of the expression on the right side of the assignment (the literal 1). They create the binary code for this integer in a pair of registers. The two bytes are then stored to the required memory locations. Most assignments require additional instructions to determine the value to be stored. For example, the simple assignment a = a + 1 might be accomplished as follows. Notice that the word is stored in little-endian order per the AVR convention word data.

```
lds    R24, a_lab      ;get the low byte of the word
                       ;into R24
lds    R25, a_lab + 1  ;get the high byte of the word
                       ;into R25
adiw   R25:R24, 1      ;add one to the word (16-bit
                       ;add immediate)
sts    a_lab, r24      ;store both bytes back to the
                       ;proper locations
sts    a_lab + 1, r25
```

The adiw instruction adds 1 to the integer represented by the bytes in R25 and R24. The result is then stored back into memory. This sequence illustrates the common load, calculate, store sequence that is associated with assignment statements. If the assignment statement was a = a + 64, we would not be able to accomplish it quite as efficiently. Why?

Register-Based Variables

Not all variables are bound to a fixed memory location; some are not even bound to memory at all. Assembly language programs often use registers to hold the data representing a variable. In this case, the variable is not really bound to a memory location. Instead, it "lives" in a register, and is referred to using a register name. As long as there are enough registers, this approach to variable allocation will be fast and convenient. The AVR assembler provides a directive to allow the programmer to refer to a register by another name, making such register use for variables self-documenting.

```
.def age = R25
```

This represents naming register R25 by the symbol "age" for the purpose of assembling the statements following this directive. A later .undef age directive would indicate that the register is no longer going to be used to hold the data for this variable in the code that follows. These directives do not allocate or deallocate storage; they are merely a naming convenience so the assembly language statements you write will be somewhat self-documenting. It is also important to note that the defined name is only applied to the statements between the .def and .undef directives. If the enclosed code contains a function call, or a branch to statements outside the scope of the definition, the defined symbol will have no meaning in those other statements. It is incorrect to say that the .def directive binds the variable to a register. The actual binding occurs during execution, when the program reaches the point that the register begins to be used for the purpose of storing the variable. Unbinding occurs when the register begins to be used for a different purpose.

In larger programs, efficient register use is an important consideration. Each section of code has a limited number of variables that are referenced frequently. These should be allocated register space for the duration of that code, especially if a looping structure is used. When a few variables are referenced frequently in a loop, registers might be used to hold those variables values. At the start of the applicable section of code, the variable values are loaded into suitable registers. The assembly language program might define names for these registers using .def. When the registers are needed for another purpose, the current values of the variables must be stored from the registers back into memory. The assembly language program might .undef the register names after this action is taken. While the variables are held in registers, the data in SRAM is considered out-of-date; the program must take actions to synchronize the register value with the memory constants at appropriate times. Compilers generate code that manages such register use automatically. One of the special challenges of assembly language programming is the efficient allocation of registers to minimize memory access.

There are other ways to allocate space for variables in assembly language programs. We will examine two others when we discuss local variables in functions, and dynamic storage allocation.

Evaluating Expressions

Compilers need to parse high-level language expressions and generate code to cause the evaluation to occur at run-time. Assembly language programmers, translating pseudocode into assembly language, often are faced with a similar task. Consider, for example, the assignment statement

```
d = a - (3-b) + 4 - (c + 2) + d;
```

Let us assume the variables are all 8-bit signed numbers and they are represented by registers 16 through 19 (assume define directives are in effect that bind these symbols to these registers). The expression needs to be evaluated in separate registers, to avoid destroying the original values. Only register d will be altered by the assignment (and we need its original value for the last part of the computation).

We begin by usurping registers 20 through 22 for temporary results. If these registers are already in use we will need to choose different registers or save their contents temporarily until we have finished evaluating our expression. It is a good idea to use define directives to specify our usage of these registers. Not only does this document our intent, but it also makes it very easy to change the register assignments at a later time. The first subexpression is evaluated in register 20.

```
.def    tempexp1 = r20
ldi     tempexp1, 3          ;compute (3-b)
sub     tempexp1, b
```

Register 21 must be initialized to the value of c before adding two. The MOV instruction copies one register to another. Note how the add immediate operation is implemented using the SUBI instruction.

```
.def    tempexp2 = r21
mov     tempexp2, c          ;compute (c + 2)
subi    tempexp2, -2
```

Before going on, one might notice that c + 2 is the same as 2 + c, so the above sequence could have been written as

```
ldi    tempexp2, 2          ;compute (2+c)
add    tempexp2, c
```

This evaluation would be acceptable in this situation, but you must be careful that any application of the associative and commutative laws must not alter the result. For example, (a – b) + c might be mathematically the same as (a + c) – b, but one may cause overflow while the other does not (try a = 255, b = c = 1). This difference might be important in some situations.

Going on with our example, we can now calculate the final value of the expression in R22, applying the operations from left to right.

```
.def   tempresult = r22
mov    tempresult, a         ;begin with a
sub    tempresult, tempexp1  ;subtract (3-b)
subi   tempresult, -4        ;add 4
sub    tempresult, tempexp2  ;subtract (c+2)
add    tempresult, d         ;add d
mov    d, tempresult         ;copy to d
.undef      tempresult
.undef      tempexp1
.undef      tempexp2
```

The final MOV instruction copies the result into the destination register d. At this point the temporary registers are no longer needed, so they are undef'd.

Expression evaluation is not a trivial thing. It often requires the use of one or more temporary storage locations. When registers are at a premium, the technique we used in this example will not always be possible. A comprehensive treatment of expression evaluation will require the use of stacks.

BRANCH INSTRUCTIONS

Programs that use only the basic sequence structure are the simplest to write and understand. Sequencing is the default behavior for a processor; the PC is incremented after each fetch, ready to access the instruction at the next higher address in memory. Most programs, however, require more complex control structures. At the machine level, the ability to alter the sequential flow of execution is accomplished using a branch (or jump) instruction. High level languages use structured statements such as if and while to deviate from sequential flow of control. Ultimately, such control structures must be reduced to the machine-level branch instructions; the compiler is responsible for the proper translation. We will study control structures in more detail later, but the basic concept of decision making to affect the flow of control in assembly language is presented here. You will need these ideas to implement even the simplest assembly language programs.

We have already encountered the RJMP instruction. This is an unconditional jump. No decision, to jump, or not to jump, is made. The jump is unconditional. This marks a definite break in the sequential flow of the statements preceding the RJMP. We have also seen how a conditional BRNE instruction can be used to implement a loop. This instruction (and others) can also be used to implement selection structures.

The conditional branch instructions are used to conditionally alter the PC. Remember that the PC is always incremented as each instruction is fetched. The conditional branch instruction sometimes overwrites this value with a new value. If the PC is changed a branch occurs; if it is not changed, there is no branch and sequential execution continues. A conditional branch instruction, when executed, either causes a branch to an instruction at a specific address, or continues with the next instruction in memory. The processor "chooses" which action to take based on a bit in the status register. Many instructions cause bits in the status register to be set or cleared. For example, adding two numbers and getting a zero answer will set the zero (z) bit in the status register. This zero result flag can be used to alter the flow of control by following the add instruction (that sets or clears the z flag) by a branch if equal to zero instruction. A conditional branch that is executed later will depend on the result of the earlier calculation. Of course, you must be careful not to place any instructions that would change these flags between the addition and the conditional branch.

For example, the C if-statement,

```
if (a + b == 0) statement;
```

might be implemented in assembly language something like this. We will assume that a and b are single byte integer variables bound to memory locations in SRAM.

```
lds R24, a
lds R25, b
add a, b
brne not_equal
;assembly code to execute the body of the if statement
    . . .
not_equal:
;program continues here regardless of which branch was
taken
```

To determine if the sum is zero or nonzero, the values of the static variables must be brought into registers to be added. The AVR ADD instruction only adds numbers in registers. When the add instruction executes, the status register flags are set according to the result. If the sum is zero, the Z flag will be set; if the sum is nonzero, the Z flag will be cleared. The subsequent instruction (BRNE) tests the setting of the Z flag and either continues to the next instruction in memory, or branches to the instruction at label "not_equal." When the condition is not satisfied we say "the conditional branch was not taken," or "the conditional branch sequenced." When the condition is satisfied, we say "the branch was taken," or "the instruction branched."

Assembly language programmers are not constrained to the limited collection of control structures provided by high-level languages (if, if/ else, while, for, switch, etc.). They are free to create new control structures of arbitrary complexity through the use of labels and branch instructions. Unfortunately, this can make assembly language programs extremely difficult to understand and maintain. Unrestrained use of labels and branches can quickly result in what has been called "spaghetti code." We will look at standard patterns used to implement the common high-level control structures later. For now, try to keep related sections of code physically together as much as possible in your programs. Avoid branches to distant labels followed by a short section of code and a branch back. In general, fewer branches are better.

EXERCISES

1. What is the 8-bit unsigned code for 227? What is the 16-bit unsigned code for 3201? (answers in hexadecimal)
2. What is the largest 8-bit unsigned value? What is the largest 16-bit unsigned value? (answers in decimal)

3. What is the smallest value that can be added to 127 that will cause unsigned overflow assuming an 8-bit unsigned integer representation?

4. If x represents an unsigned value, why does the pseudocode, if (x >= 0) not make much sense?

5. What is stored in R20 after the instruction subi R20, 033 is executed if R20 is initialized by ldi R20, 33? Be careful to interpret the literals correctly.

6. What is stored in R16 after the instruction subi R16, $27 assuming R16 originally contained $E2? Is the carry (borrow) flag set (to 1) as a result of this operation?

7. Tell the value in R31:R30 after the indicated sequence of instructions.

```
ldi r30, $30
ldi r31, $21
adiw r31:r30, $1C
```

8. What is found in R18 after this sequence of instructions?

```
ldi r18, 0x80
add r18, r18
adc r18, r18
```

9. The AVR instruction set does not have an ADDI (add immediate) instruction. Write a sequence of two instructions that will add the number 7 to the value in register r16. You may use register 17 as a temporary register.

10. Design a loop that uses a 16-bit counter and the 16-bit subtract immediate instruction to repeat a nop instruction COUNT times. Use an equate directive to define the symbol COUNT to be 3987. Use the high and low functions to initialize your 16-bit counter (held in a suitable register pair). Analyze the number of clock cycles needed to completely execute the code you have written. You can find information about how many clock cycles each instruction takes in the AVR instruction set documentation (or in AVR Studio Assembler help). What is the maximum number of iterations you can achieve using this structure? What initial value (for COUNT) is used to achieve this maximum?

11. Design a loop that uses a 16-bit counter held in registers R17:R16. The loop does nothing except repeat COUNT times. Use an equate directive to define the symbol COUNT to be 3987. Use the high and low functions to initialize your 16-bit counter. Analyze the number of clock cycles needed to completely

execute the code you have written. What is the maximum number of clock cycles that this loop can consume (including the initialization statements)?

12. Write statements to place the ASCII code for a space character in register 20 and the asterisk (*) in register 21. Did you have to consult an ASCII table?

13. What are the 8-bit two's complement codes for the following integers? (answer in hexadecimal) 126, –105, and –2. Give the 16-bit codes for the same numbers.

14. What integers are represented by the following 8-bit two's complement codes? (answer in decimal) $7E, $80, and $E4.

15. Compare the 4-, 5-, 6-, and 7-bit two's complement codes for +3. Based on your observations, how would an 8-bit two's complement code for a positive number differ from the 16-bit code for that number?

16. Compare the 4-, 5-, 6-, and 7-bit two's complement codes for –3. Based on your observations, how would an 8-bit two's complement code for a negative number differ from the 16-bit code for that number?

17. If R16 contains $E2, a two's complement code for an integer, and the instruction INC R16 is executed, what is the new value in R16 and what integer does it represent?

18. If R16 contains $FF, a two's complement code for an integer, and the instruction INC R16 is executed, what is the new value in R16 and what integer does it represent? Did signed overflow occur? Explain by interpreting the signed values indicated by $FF and the result from the INC instruction.

19. The COM instruction flips all the bits in a register. What is the effect on a number stored in two's complement code in register 18 if the following two instructions are applied? Explain your reasoning.

```
com  r18
inc  r18
```

20. Shifting left (bringing a zero in) doubles the value of a number represented in unsigned code. What happens if you shift a two's complement code to the left? Illustrate with the code for –3, interpreting the result as an integer.

21. Shifting right (bringing a zero in) divides an unsigned value by two (truncating the result). What happens if you shift a two's complement code to the right? Illustrate by trying it on the code for –7 and interpreting the result.

22. Tell the 8-bit code for the integers +5 and –5 in one's complement, sign and magnitude, and excess –128 codes. Express each answer in hexadecimal.

23. A 10-digit number is encoded in packed BCD format. If a sign nybble is required, how many bytes are needed?

24. The directive `.db  117` creates a single byte value. If this byte is interpreted as an unsigned packed BCD value, what integer does it represent?

25. Write a define byte directive to assemble the packed BCD value for +297. Include a sign indicator in the last nybble. Note that this will require two bytes. Why would it be a bad idea to use a define word directive to assemble this value?

26. Write a define byte directive for the (unpacked) BCD code for `127` (no sign indicator). This will require three bytes.

27. How many numbers can be represented in a 3-byte container if unsigned integer representation is used? If packed BCD is used (including a sign nybble)? If unpacked BCD is used (no sign indicator)?

28. Write a statement to assemble the 16-bit two's complement code for `32,767`.

29. What happens if you write a statement to assemble the 16-bit two's complement code for `32,768`?

30. Write a statement to assemble an unsigned byte representing the minimum legal voting age in the United States (18). The byte should have a label, `minVA`.

31. Write a statement to assemble the two byte, carriage return, linefeed sequence commonly used to represent the end of a line of text in Microsoft text files. Attach the label `crlf` to the bytes.

32. Write a statement to assemble a constant representing the number of seconds in a day. Let the assembler do the calculations. Include a comment that explains the statement.

33. Write a statement to assemble the integer negative ten as an 8-bit two's complement code. Repeat for a 16-bit two's complement code.

34. Write a statement to assemble the number of cells in a matrix that has 23 rows and 47 columns.

35. What byte value is assembled by the statement `.db  128`? What about `.db –128`?

36. Is there any difference between `.db –1` and `.db $FF`? Explain.

37. Is there any difference between `.dw –1` and `.dw $FF`? Explain.

38. If a and b are labels of bytes in SRAM, write assembly language instructions to imitate the assignment statement:

    ```
    a = b;
    ```

39. If a and b are labels of unsigned bytes in SRAM, write assembly language instructions to imitate the assignment statement: a = a + b. Would your answer change if the bytes contained signed integers? Explain.

40. Can you subtract 1 from a word in R25:R24 by using adiw R25:R24, −1? Try it and then attempt to explain the error message. What number did the assembler think you were trying to add?

41. In writing an AVR program, a programmer tried to write an instruction to add 17 to the value in R20: ADDI R20, 17. Unfortunately the assembler issued an error on this statement. Why? The programmer decided to substitute the following instruction: SUBI R20, −17. Will this work? Try it in the simulator.

42. Write an assembly language equivalent to this for loop:

    ```
    for (a = 9; a! = 0; a--) b++;
    ```

    Assume a and b are defined as registers R16 and R17. You should not initialize b since the high-level code does not. Use a brne instruction at the end of the loop statements to branch back to a label marking the top of the loop.

43. Consult the machine instruction documentation to determine which flags are affected by the load immediate (LDI) instruction. What about the compare immediate instruction (CPI)? Does a BRNE affect any flags?

44. Suppose I need to branch to a label hot_spot if R17 is nonzero. Otherwise the program should continue to the next instruction in memory. Write a sequence of two assembly language statements to accomplish this.

45. Suppose I want to branch to hot_spot if R17 is nonzero, and branch to cold_spot if R17 is zero. Show how to do this in exactly three statements.

46. Write an assembly language equivalent for this if statement.

    ```
    if (b ! = 0) {
        a = a - b;
        b--;
    }
    a++;
    ```

Assume registers R16 and R17 are being used to hold the values of the variables a and b. You should not initialize either since the high-level code does not. Use a cpi instruction (or tst) and a breq instruction to construct your control structure.

PROGRAMMING EXERCISES

1. Write an assembly language program to add and subtract two 8-bit values. Use the simulator to determine how the status flags are affected by additions. Try the following operations:

```
255 + 1
127 + 1
−128 − 1
−127 + 127
```

2. Write an assembly language program to add two 16-bit numbers in registers R31:R30 and R29:R28. Run the program in the simulator. Pay attention to the carry flag as the two-step addition is simulated. Explain the status flags (H, S, V, N, Z, and C) at the completion of each example. Use these example values for testing.

```
1480 + 831
1480 + 64030
−32767 + 32767
128 + 128
```

3. Write a program to evaluate the following assignments in sequence. The symbols a0, b0, c0, and d0 should be equated to specific values (of your choice) at the top of the program; these represent the initial values of the variables a, b, c, and d. Use define statements to assign registers to represent the variables and temporary locations. Undefine temporary registers as appropriate. Your program must initialize the variables and then evaluate the expression. This program is designed to be executed in the simulator environment only.

```
a = a0;
b = b0;
c = c0;
d = d0;
c = a − (b + c) − d;
a = a − (b − (c − d));
d = (5 − a) + (7 − b) − (c + d);
```

4. Implement the following assembly language program and test it on a variety of numbers in the simulator. Represent the variables in registers, initializing them to test values before doing the assignments. The second assignment will require the temporary use of another register. What does this program do? Does it always work?

```
a = a + b;
b = a - b;
a = a - b;
```

5. Implement the following assembly language program and test it on a variety of byte values in the simulator. The ^ symbol stands for the EOR operation. Represent the variables in registers, initializing them to test values before doing the assignments. What does this program do? Does it always work?

```
a = a ^ b;
b = b ^ a;
a = a ^ b
```

CHAPTER 5

AVR Core

Startup, Reset, and Memories

O NE OF THE VERY interesting aspects of a computer system is what happens when power is first applied. What program will be run? How does it get into memory? Where in memory is it found? The term bootstrapping has been used to describe the process of using a very small program to load a larger one. From this comes the familiar phrase, "boot up your computer," which simply means execute a small program (the bootloader) to load a bigger program (the operating system) into memory. This does not answer the question of how the small program gets into memory.

Early computers required specific operator intervention to bootstrap the system. Remember that when power is removed from most RAMs, they lose their state. When power is reapplied, each binary component can potentially start with either a 0 or 1 value. Primitive computers required initial instructions to be entered manually into memory through a control panel giving access to the memory address register, memory data register, and the read/write control lines. This small program was called the bootstrap.

The control panel of the PDP8e is shown in Figure 5.1. The 12 switches in the middle are called the switch register bits. The operator would enter the twelve 0's and 1's of an address on these switches, and then press ADDR LOAD (just to the right of the group of 12 switches) copy the switch data (address) into the memory address register (CPMA). Then, the operator would reset the switches to represent an instruction or constant to be stored in memory. Lifting the DEP (DEPosit) switch (far right) would store the word represented by the switches into memory (at the address in

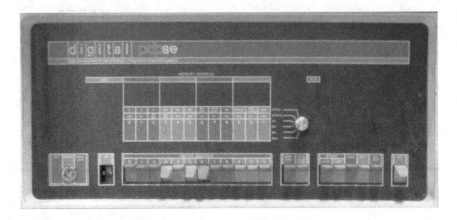

FIGURE 5.1   The control panel of a PDP8e.

CPMA) and increment the address. The next data word would then be toggled on the data switches and deposited into memory. In this way, a sequence of words could be easily stored in RAM. Note the color coding of the switches; they are grouped by three's to easily visualize the octets. Data, addresses, and instructions to be entered on the switches would usually be written in octal format. The CONT button (fifth from the right) starts the fetch–execute cycle at whatever address is currently in CPMA.

By positioning switches and pressing buttons in a specific sequence, an operator would quickly enter the first instructions of an initialization program called the bootstrap. Setting the CPMA to the address of the first of these instructions, and pressing the run button, would cause the fetch–execute cycle to begin at that address. This bootstrap program would typically initiate an input operation that would read data from a paper tape (Figure 5.2) or magnetic disk into the memory locations just above the bootstrap. This data would in turn be fetched and executed as the PC naturally incremented into the newly loaded section of memory, causing additional data to be loaded into storage. Through this process, a rudimentary utility program could be loaded into memory, and then used to perform additional and more complex tasks. This computer essentially picked itself up by its own bootstraps.

Modern computers store their bootstrap code in ROM. When power is first applied, the processor undergoes a reset cycle that forces a specific address into the PC. The system circuitry is designed so that this address is associated with the ROM, so the initial bootstrap code is already present and ready for execution. This code initializes the system and then usually

FIGURE 5.2 A paper tape that might contain instructions and data for a PDP computer.

loads an operating system from the secondary storage. When that task is complete, the computer is ready to respond to user commands.

AVR RESET SIGNAL

Since the AVR processor executes all of its instructions from ROM (actually this is flash memory which can be erased and rewritten, but during normal execution we will consider it to be read-only), it effectively bypasses the bootstrap phase. Processors are designed to respond to a reset signal that forces a specific value into the PC. This value is called the reset address. The reset address for the AVR processor is zero, but other processors may have a different reset address. When power is first applied to an AVR processor, the reset signal is asserted. After a short delay, the reset signal is negated and the fetch–execute cycle begins. At this instant, the PC contains the value 0, the address of the first instruction to be fetched.

This repeatable behavior of the AVR processor in response to a reset signal is the reason we need to always place our first instruction at address 0 of flash. Every time the reset signal is asserted, we can then be sure that the processor will fetch and execute this instruction. Everything that happens after the reset signal occurs can then be predicted by analyzing the instructions in flash, and accounting for other external signals that may affect execution decisions.

The AVR's reset signal can be received from several sources. Power on reset occurs when the supply voltage to the chip is below a specific level. This occurs, for example, when power is first applied to the chip (the voltage level rises from zero to the power supply level). An external reset is caused when the RESET pin is pulled low; this causes a reset to occur. The STK-500 board has a reset button that is connected to the RESET pin on the target processor. This button can be used to reset the processor. On the XPLAIN board, the JTAG XMEGA header exposes the reset pin of the XMEGA microcontroller; shorting it to ground (pin 2 to pin 6) will reset the microcontroller. The AVR microcontroller also includes a watchdog timer. If activated, this timer causes a reset signal if it is not updated by an application program at regular intervals. This allows the processor to restart in the event an application hangs for any reason. There is also a brown out reset that acts similarly to the power on reset if activated. Finally, the JTAG On-Chip Debug System can cause a reset via an internal reset register. JTAG is an initialism for Joint Test Action Group which specifies a debugging subsystem and interface that is very useful when working with microcontrollers and embedded systems. The AVR processors support this interface.

Interrupt Jump Table

The knowledge of interrupts is of great importance to a fundamental understanding of how computer systems operate. The interrupt system is a feature of the processor that allows for the interruption of the normal fetch–execute cycle. Normally, the point of interruption is unpredictable; the intent is to instantly respond to a high-priority request by interrupting the currently executing program to service the source of the interrupt, and then resume the previously executing program. Interrupt signals in the AVR can come from external (pins) or internal sources (counters and other subsystems). The code that handles an interrupt is called an interrupt service routine, or interrupt handler.

When the AVR processor is reset (responds to a reset signal), interrupts are disabled; interrupts must be enabled by your program only after specific housekeeping tasks have been completed. It is important to know, however, that the first instruction of each interrupt service routine must be located at a specific memory location. For example, the RESET service routine (the reset signal is considered an interrupt that cannot be disabled) always begins at address $0000. In the ATmega16A, the first instruction of the External Interrupt Request 0 service routine must be located at address $0002. In the ATxmega128A1, this address is for the Crystal Oscillator Failure Interrupt vector. Subsequent service routines begin at addresses $0004, $0006, and so on, up through $0028 in the ATMEGA16A and $00F8 in the ATxmega128A1. Although it looks like each service routine can only be two instructions long (two words), each service routine only *begins* at one of these addresses. Typically, the two words allocated for each interrupt routine are used for a JMP instruction that simply branches to the section of memory where the actual service routine is located.

The words at the beginning of program memory then contain what are commonly called interrupt vectors; they vector the processor to the actual interrupt service routine. Only the RESET vector is required for basic use of the processor. None of our programs thus far have used interrupts (other than the reset interrupt), so they began at the reset vector and occupied the interrupt vector table and beyond. If interrupts will be enabled in an application, then the RESET vector must actually transfer execution around the interrupt vector table to a safe area of memory. In the ATmega16A, the interrupt vector table occupies memory locations $0000 through $0029 (the ATxmega128A1 uses addresses $0000 through $00F9). It is customary to define a symbol such as INT_VECTORS_SIZE near the top of a program to document specific values and make it easy to change to a different device. We will see later in this chapter that there are files for each microcontroller supplied with the assembler that can be included in your program with a single include directive. These standard include files define hundreds of symbols specific to each microcontroller. To avoid the interrupt vector table area, a program will typically begin like this.

```
.include "one of the device include files.inc"
.cseg
jmp RESET; code the reset vector
        ;Define other interrupt vectors as needed.
        ;Each may be preceded by a .org to accurately
position it.
        ;Alternatively, all possible vectors can be inserted
by writing
        ;a sequence of jmp instructions.


;set cseg location counter at the first address past the
interrupt table
.org INT_VECTORS_SIZE
        ;Code or data can be safely placed here. At some
point you will
        ;need the RESET label to make the first jmp legal.
RESET:
        ;this is where execution will begin after each reset
signal.
```

BASIC SYSTEM ORGANIZATION

The AVR Processor is an example of the Harvard architecture. Separate busses for the program instructions and data access allow instructions to be fetched from flash at the same time as data is being manipulated in the RAM. Simple pipelining allows the next instruction to be fetched while the current instruction is executed. Most instructions are executed in a single clock cycle.

Program Memory

Program memory (flash) is divided into two areas, the Boot Loader Section (BLS), and the Application Program section. The BLS is needed to perform the in-system programming tasks that make this processor so versatile. Programs running in this section of memory can cause new bytes to be written into the Application Program section. This is how we are able to download an assembled program to the AVR processor. Our programs will run from the Application Program section. A study of the BLS is beyond the scope of this text.

General Purpose Registers

Many of the AVR instructions utilize some of the 32 × 8-bit general purpose registers located in what is called a fast-access register file. In the AVR assembly language, the registers are named R0 through R31. Each register is capable of providing input to the ALU, and the ALU can output its results into any register. This data cycle can be accomplished in a single clock cycle, allowing execution to keep pace with the speed instructions are fetched. Registers are also used as an intermediate location for transferring data between memory locations and I/O registers.

In the ATMEGA series microcontroller, the register file is also mapped into the first 32 bytes of the microcontroller's data memory, addresses $0000 through $001F. The load and store instructions can be used to access the general purpose registers using these addresses, however, at a price; the load and store instructions are slower than instructions that access registers by name. This mapping is not used in the XMEGA series.

I/O Registers and Data Space

The AVR processor also has a collection of registers that are used for I/O. Some I/O registers are paired to represent values requiring more than one byte. In the MEGA series microcontrollers, the register file and I/O registers, together with SRAM, form a contiguous address space, called the data space. The 32 general purpose registers are available as memory locations and may be accessed by their addresses 0x0000 through 0x001F. In the ATmega16A, there are 64 I/O registers. The I/O registers are numbered 0x00 through 0x3F and may be accessed at memory addresses 0x0020 through 0x005F. The data space address of each I/O register is obtained by adding $20 to its register number.

The data space in the XMEGA series consists of I/O registers, EEPROM, internal SRAM, and external memory. The ATxmega128A1 has 4096 I/O registers. They occupy addresses $0000 through $0FFF. The first 64 I/O registers (addresses $00 through $3F) can be accessed using the IN and OUT instructions. All others use the more general load and store instructions.

The first byte of SRAM in the ATmega16A begins at address 0x0060. This processor has 1024 bytes of SRAM (1K) so these are located at addresses 0x0060 through 0x045F. Access to memory locations in SRAM usually requires two clock cycles.

The first byte of SRAM in the XMEGA series always begins at $2000. The standard device include files define the symbol SRAM_START to be the first address in SRAM and SRAM_END to be the last address of internal SRAM. Using the standard include files and symbolic names for important addresses makes it easier to change devices without rewriting programs.

Stack

Function calls and interrupts utilize a stack storage structure located in SRAM. This is called the hardware stack. Unless an XMEGA series microcontroller is being used, the programmer must take care to initialize this structure before any instructions needing it are executed. The stack is initialized by setting the stack pointer to a specific address in SRAM. The XMEGA's stack pointer is automatically initialized to the highest address of internal SRAM (RAM_END) whenever a reset occurs.

The stack pointer is the address where the first byte will be written when something is pushed on the stack. The stack pointer is implemented as a pair of I/O registers; SPH (the high byte of the stack pointer) is I/O register $3E and SPL is I/O register $3D. The hardware stack is nothing more than an array in memory. The stack pointer indicates (indirectly) how much of the array is in use. Refer to Figure 5.3, which is a visualization of the stack in an ATmega16A. The stack bottom is located at $045F (the end of SRAM) and the stack pointer contains $0455. The stack therefore contains 10 bytes

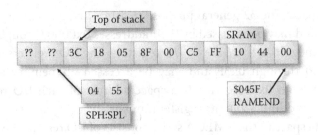

FIGURE 5.3   Visualization of a stack containing 10 bytes of data (ATMEGA16A).

of information ($045F-$0455 = $A). The stack contents are found at memory locations $0456 (top) through $045F.

If your program uses interrupts, functions, or any stack operations, then the stack pointer must be initialized before use. The following instructions are often found at the beginning of the code reached from the RESET vector. Here is the typical initialization code for the ATmega16A stack. It is common to use a symbol to represent the last address of SRAM so this code can be easily adapted to different processor memory sizes. It is also customary to use symbolic names for the stack pointer.

```
.equ RAMEND = $045F; for the ATmega16A
.equ SPL = $3D
.equ SPH = $3E
ldi R16, low(RAMEND)
out SPL, R16
ldi R16, high(RAMEND)
out SPH, R16
```

Register R16 is used to hold each byte of the initial value of the stack pointer so it can be sent to the appropriate I/O register using the out instruction. Once the stack pointer is initialized, stack operations may be used, interrupts can be enabled, and function calls can occur. Note that this code is not necessary when using the XMEGA series microcontroller. However, it may be included without harm. The stack pointer registers in the XMEGA are named CPU_SPL and CPU_SPH.

The AVR instruction set includes PUSH and POP instructions. Once the stack is initialized, a PUSH Rr instruction will copy the contents of Rr to the stack, increasing the size of the stack by one byte. This operation implicitly changes the stack pointer (decrements it by one). A subsequent POP Rd instruction will remove the last byte pushed (this is a stack data structure), copying it to the destination register, Rd. This instruction implicitly changes the stack pointer (increments it by one). There is no check for stack overflow or underflow.

Writing simple functions in assembly language is fairly straightforward. To define a function, create a label representing the function name. Write the function body, ending it with a RET instruction. To invoke the function from elsewhere in your code, use an RCALL instruction. This instruction requires the address of the function which is just the label you placed at the start of the function's code.

The function definition is usually placed after the main part of the application. There is no need to use any type of forward declaration. Here is a skeleton of a program using functions.

```
.cseg
;stack initialization code must be located here if needed

main:
;place your main application code here
. . .
rcall my_function
. . .
rjmp main ;assuming the main application repeats forever

my_function:
;function body goes here
    . . .
ret

;place more function definitions here
```

The program begins by initializing the stack and then enters the main loop. When execution reaches the RCALL instruction, the return address is pushed on the stack and the address of the function is placed in the PC. The next instruction will be fetched from the function body. Execution continues in the function until RET is reached. At this point, the return address is popped off the stack into the PC, causing execution to resume with the instruction immediately after the RCALL.

Be careful not to use a branch or jump to go from the main section into the function, or from the function back to the main section. We will explore functions in more detail in the next chapter.

EEPROM Storage

EEPROM is a nonvolatile, read/write memory. Nonvolatile means its contents are not erased when power is turned off. The ATmega16A's EEPROM is accessed as an I/O device through a collection of I/O registers. Individual bytes of this memory may be read or written, although it has a limited number of erase/write cycles (typically at least 100,000). Reading data from the EEPROM requires multiple clock cycles (around 10) and specific sequences of instructions. Writing data to EEPROM is much slower; it typically takes 8.5 ms to write a byte to EEPROM (compared to microseconds for SRAM or registers). It is still, however, an important resource because of its nonvolatile nature. One typical use of the EEPROM storage area is for configuration information needed by an application when power is applied; the information may be changed periodically by the application. You can specify bytes to be stored in EEPROM as part of an assembly language program. Simply define bytes in the eseg segment of the program. The assembler will create a file that includes these byte values (and their addresses) and they can be downloaded to the actual EEPROM on the AVR microcontroller by the AVR programmer utility.

The XMEGA series microcontroller includes the option of mapping EEPROM memory into the data space starting at address $1000. It also offers paged read and write operations.

Many of the other AVR features are important to specific uses of this microcontroller. Our focus is on the use of the AVR to study general assembly language programming concepts, so many of the special features are not covered in this text. However, we will examine some of the I/O capabilities, which include the use of timers and counters, the USART (Universal Synchronous and Asynchronous serial Receiver and Transmitter), external interrupts, and the general digital I/O ports introduced earlier.

PROGRAM MEMORY

During execution, the registers are the key players in all computations. But register space is limited. Programs must be able to move information between registers and storage. The AVR microcontroller has several different types of memory; each is accessed using a different technique.

Program Indirect Addressing

Data stored in program memory is of course constant. This is a convenient place to store string and numeric constants that are needed by the program. There is just one instruction that can be used to copy data from program memory to a register.

```
lpm Rd, Z
```

Load Program Memory (LPM) reads one byte from an address of program memory (flash) into the destination register. This instruction uses indirect addressing; the address is held in the Z register (R31:R30).

Indirect addressing is a powerful feature found in most processors. In its simplest form, a register holds the address to be accessed. The instruction to access the data at that address simply specifies the register holding the desired address. This is similar to the concept of a pointer in C, or a reference to an object in Java, the main difference being that in the high-level languages the address is stored in a variable instead of a register.

Although program memory uses word addresses (from the PC) when instructions are being fetched, the LPM instruction allows fetching of individual bytes, and actually requires a byte address to be held in Z (see Figure 5.4). The hardware converts this to a word address, copies the entire word from program memory, and then uses the least-significant bit of the address to select one of the bytes of the word to be copied into the register.

The following example illustrates how a numeric constant might be assembled into flash and then used by a program. The define word directive

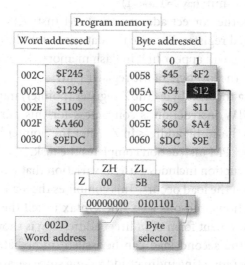

FIGURE 5.4　Word addressing versus byte addressing in program memory.

must not be assembled to a location in memory where it might be executed. The assembly language programmer must always be mindful of the flow of control created by the arrangement of instructions in the assembly language program.

```
myValue: .dw $1234
```

At some other part of the code segment we might find the following instructions that load the constant above into R25:R24:

```
ldi ZH, high(myValue*2)
ldi ZL, low(myValue*2)
lpm R24, Z
adiw Z, 1
lpm R25, Z
```

Since the data is 16-bits, it must be loaded in two steps, one byte at a time. To prepare for the load, the Z register (in AVR assembly language, Z refers the register pair, ZH:ZL, otherwise known as R31:R30) must be set to point at the desired location in program memory. The label of the word is used to specify the address; it is multiplied by two to convert it to the byte address. Remember that labels in the code segment are given word addresses by the assembler. LPM requires Z to hold the byte address of the flash memory location to be accessed. The multiplication by two is sometimes written as a shift: (myValue<<1).

Once Z holds the correct address, the LPM instruction can load the byte to the desired register. Because the data was stored as a little-endian word, the low byte will appear first in flash memory. Thus, the first byte is loaded into R24, the low byte of the register pair.

Before loading the next byte, The Z register (pointer) must be advanced by one. The ADIW instruction is convenient for this purpose, allowing 1 to be added to the 16-bit address in Z. After the pointer has been incremented, another LPM instruction completes the task.

The LPM instruction includes a useful variation that will automatically increment Z when the load occurs. This combines the load byte and increment address actions into one step. The syntax to tell the assembler you want the postincrement form of indirect addressing is shown next. Using this technique, the second load can be issued immediately; the second LPM uses nonincrementing indirect addressing since we are not interested in continuing on to the next byte.

```
lpm R24, Z+
lpm R25, Z
```

For completeness, you should be aware that the assembler allows an even shorter form of this instruction. The LPM mnemonic with no operands implies that R0 is the destination and Z holds the address. Thus, the following are equivalent in behavior:

```
lpm
lpm R0, Z
```

It is strange that the assembler would even require the specification of the pointer register Z in this instruction, as it is the only location the address may be placed; it would seem that LPM R4 should suffice. Remember that the design of an assembly language is somewhat arbitrary. The language should allow the programmer to express their ideas clearly and succinctly. The language should also be consistent and unambiguous, making it easy to do what the programmer needs. Requiring the Z to indicate the source of the load (a pointer in Z) is consistent with the syntax of other load register operations.

The LPM instruction, in any of its forms, requires three clock cycles to complete its task. Devices with more than 64K of flash also include an extended LPM (ELPM) instruction. To access addresses above $FFFF, an I/O register named RAMPZ is used. This register is concatenated with Z (RAMPZ:ZH:ZL) to form a larger address, up to 24 bits in size.

There is a complementary instruction, store program memory (SPM). However, this is not available to application programs. The SPM instruction can only be executed if it is fetched from the BLS of flash memory. This instruction can erase a section of flash and then copy bytes from SRAM into flash. To write into flash storage, an entire page (64 words) must be erased, and then new data written. This technique is used by the bootloader to write new programs into the application area. Each time you download your updated program to the processor, the bootloader is using this instruction to place the correct words in flash in preparation for running your application.

Program indirect addressing is also used when instructions are fetched by the control unit prior to being executed. In this case, the address is found in the PC. This is always a word address and the instruction fetch is for a whole word, not just a byte. Since the PC is always incremented after the fetch, you might call this program indirect with postincrement. The

PC can also be altered by a reset signal (causing PC to be set to zero), or by executing a branch, jump, call, or return instruction. An interrupt will also change the value in PC.

The difference between an instruction fetch and a data load (via LPM) is where the address is found, whether it is a byte or word address, where the data is sent, and the size of the data. An instruction fetch uses the PC as a word address and loads a word into the instruction queue. The LPM instruction converts the byte address in Z to a word address, copies the specified word from memory, and then selects one of the two bytes to be copied into the specified destination register.

DATA SPACE

The data space of the AVR processor is divided into three or four sections, accessible in a single, linear address space. The lowest 32 addresses of the ATMEGA16A ($0000–$001F) correspond to the general purpose registers. This section is not present in the XMEGA series. The next address section corresponds to the I/O registers. Each AVR device has different I/O needs so the size of this space varies. In the ATmega16A it consists of 64 bytes ($0020–$005F). The XMEGA microcontrollers all have the same size I/O space with addresses from $0000 through $0FFF.

The XMEGA series reserves addresses $1000 through $1FFF for memory mapped EEPROM and SRAM always begins at $2000. External memory addresses (if external memory is present) begin at the end of internal SRAM.

The next memory location after the I/O registers in the MEGA microcontrollers is the first byte of SRAM for these devices. SRAM in the ATMEGA16A begins at address $0060. The assembler automatically initializes its internal location counter for the data segment to the beginning of internal SRAM (based on the address in the standard include file for the target device), so labels declared in the data segment are assigned addresses in SRAM (unless the location counter is altered by an org directive).

Several addressing modes can be used to access bytes in the data space.

Data Direct Addressing

The AVR instruction set includes two types of instructions to access bytes in the data space (including all addresses starting at $0000). The first uses direct addressing. Direct addressing simply means that the address to be accessed is coded into the bits of the instruction as an unsigned integer.

When the instruction is decoded, some of the bits constitute address information and are placed on the memory address bus. The other bits in the instruction differentiate between read and write (load and store) and the register involved in the transfer.

```
lds Rd, K
```

This instruction is called load direct from SRAM (data space). The destination register is specified along with the actual address of the byte to be copied. The value of K is limited to a 16-bit unsigned integer, more than sufficient to access all of the ATmega16A data space (and more). Usually, the address is written as a label, or an expression involving a label, but the assembler will happily assemble an address that is represented by any arithmetic expression.

```
lds R0, aByte
lds R24, aWord
lds R25, aWord + 1
lds R31, 0
```

The symbols used above must either be labels of memory locations in SRAM or symbols representing numbers (that will be interpreted as addresses in the data space). The first load copies a byte from the location labeled aByte to general purpose register 0. The next two instructions load a word (low byte, high byte) at two consecutive memory locations into R25:R24. The last instruction copies whatever is found at address $0000 to R31. If executed by the ATMEGA16A, this will be the contents of general purpose register 0 (R0). If executed by an XMEGA, this will be an I/O register named GPIOR0.

The complementary instruction used to store the value in a register into a byte in the data space is STS.

```
sts K, Rr
```

Store direct copies the byte in Rr to the data space location with address K. Again, K is limited to a 16-bit unsigned integer. This is also a 32-bit instruction and requires two clock cycles to execute. The following examples illustrate the use of store direct:

```
sts aByte, R16
sts aWord, R30
```

```
sts aWord+1, R31
sts $38, R0
```

The first instruction copies the contents of R16 into the byte in the data space with label aByte. The next pair stores a word. The last instruction copies register R0 to the I/O register at address $38.

I/O Direct Addressing

The only instructions that use I/O Direct addressing are IN and OUT. These are used only to access the first 64 I/O registers in the I/O section of the data space. In the ATMEGA16A microcontroller, I/O registers begin at $0020; in the XMEGA series, they begin at $0000. The IN and OUT instructions specify the address of an I/O register as a 6-bit unsigned offset into the I/O space. In the ATMEGA16A, registers have numbers which are 32 ($20) less than their address in the data space. Thus, an address of $0038 corresponds to I/O register number $18. The ATmega16A documentation indicates that this is PORTB, the port we have been using to control the LEDs.

In the XMEGA series, I/O register numbers and addresses are the same (because I/O space starts at address $0000).

Although LDS and STS can be used for all of the I/O registers, normally, I/O registers with numbers/addresses below $40 are accessed using the IN or OUT instructions which require only 1 clock cycle and are more compact (one word instead of two). The following instructions are identical in function when executed on the ATMEGA16A, but each will access different I/O registers when executed on an XMEGA series microcontroller.

```
sts $38, R0
out $18, R0
```

Data Indirect Addressing

Direct addressing is good for accessing a few bytes at a labeled memory location defined in the assembly language program. In many cases, data is not labeled, or consists of a large collection of bytes for which a label provides only the address of the first byte. Arrays, stacks, queues, and linked lists are several data structures that require a more powerful form of addressing for efficient implementation. We have already encountered indirect addressing in the LPM instruction where Z holds a pointer to a byte in flash. The Atmel specifications actually call this "program memory constant addressing," but it truly is indirect addressing. Data indirect addressing allows instructions to access the data space through an address in a register.

The AVR processor has three register pairs that can be used for (data) indirect addressing. The address to be accessed must be preloaded into either X, Y, or Z. The AVR assembler uses these symbols to refer to the register pairs XH:XL, YH:YL, and ZH:ZL, otherwise known as R27:R26, R29:R28, and R31:R30. To load a byte from the specified address, the load (LD) instruction is used; the instruction requires that you specify the destination register and the register (pair) holding the address.

```
ld Rd, X
ld Rd, Y
ld Rd, Z
```

Load indirect from data space causes a byte from the data space to be copied into the destination register. This is a 16-bit instruction that takes two clock cycles to execute. The store instruction transfers data in the opposite direction, from register to memory.

```
st X, Rr
st Y, Rr
st Z, Rr
```

Store indirect to data space copies the contents of the specified register into the data space at the address in X (or Y or Z). Notice that in both cases, the destination of the transfer is written as the left operand.

Indirect addressing can also be used to access the I/O registers. Remember that the IN/OUT instructions are generally more efficient when the I/O register has an offset of less than 64.

Data Indirect Addressing with Postincrement or Predecrement

Because indirect addressing is commonly employed in a looping construct to access sequential storage locations, the load and store indirect instructions include variants that automatically increment or decrement the pointer. The only change in syntax is to append a plus (+) or prepend a minus (–) to the pointer register. Note that incrementing occurs after the address is used (postincrement) but decrementing occurs before the address is used (predecrement). The following loop pushes the 16 bytes located at addresses $0000 through $000F of data space onto the stack. The stack pointer will need to be initialized before this can work.

The LD instruction copies each byte in turn to r15 in preparation for pushing it on the stack.

```
;R15 is used as an intermediate location before each push
ldi ZH, high(16) ;we will start at the end of the array of 16 bytes
ldi ZL, low(16)
lp_1:
    ld r15, -Z    ;address next lower byte and copy to R15
    push r15      ;copy to stack
    cpi ZL, 0     ;when the address is 0, we stop
    brne lp_1
;16 locations saved
```

At some later time, the contents of these memory locations may need to be restored from the stack. The restore must go in the opposite direction ($0000 through $000F) due to the LIFO organization of the stack.

```
;during the restore, R15 is used as an intermediate loc for pop
ldi ZH, high(0)      ;Address of first byte is 0
ldi ZL, low(0)
lp_2:
    pop r15
    st Z+, r15    ;copy to register, then increment pointer
    cpi ZL, 16    ;stop when we have restored 16 locations
    brne lp_2
;16 locations restored
```

Data indirect addressing with the predecrement or postincrement option can utilize any of the three pointer registers, X, Y, or Z.

Data Indirect Addressing with Displacement

The Y and Z registers offer one additional addressing mode: (data) indirect with displacement. This mode allows a constant displacement to be added to the pointer in Y or Z to specify the data space address. In this form, the pointer register points to the beginning of a group of bytes, and the constant displacement selects one of the bytes inside the group. The load and store mnemonics require an extra "d" to indicate the displacement option for this addressing mode. Note that you may not use the X register as a pointer in this mode of the instruction.

```
ldd Rd, Y + q
ldd Rd, Z + q
std Y + q, Rr
std Z + q, Rr
```

Load/store indirect with displacement uses a pointer located in Y or Z and a fixed displacement, q, which must be between 0 and 63 (inclusive). The pointer is not changed by these instructions. The following examples indicate possible uses of this addressing mode:

```
ldi YH, high(aWord)    ;pointer to SRAM location labeled
                       ;aWord
ldi ;YL, low(aWord)
ldd R25, Y + 1         ;get high byte of word
ldd R24, Y             ;get low byte of word
in ZL, SPL             ;Z points to the byte above the
                       ;stack top
in ZH, SPH
std Z + 4, R0          ;overwrite 4th from the top byte in
                       ;the stack
```

The first part of the example loads a word into R25:R24 from memory using Y as a pointer to the word. The second example sets Z to point to the top of the stack (the address where the next byte would be pushed), and then stores a copy of R0 into the 4th byte from the top of the stack. These instructions assume SPH and SPL are suitably defined. With Z set to the stack pointer value, Z + 1 would reference the top byte of the stack, Z + 2 the next byte on the stack, and so on.

EEPROM

This program illustrates how data can be preloaded into EEPROM and then read by a program. In EEPROM, we will store a sequence of byte values that will be used as LED display patterns. The program will wait for a pushbutton to be depressed. Each button will correspond to a specific address in EEPROM where a byte defining the desired LED display pattern is located. The program will read that byte and then output it on the port connected to the LEDs. Pressing different buttons will display the associated bit pattern. If multiple buttons are pressed, the results will be undefined. There will only be eight preset data values.

This program is written for the ATMEGA16A microcontroller. For the XPLAIN/ATxmega128A version, see the alternate version, Program 5.1a.

PROGRAM 5.1 EEPROM Access

```
;LED Patterns: Illustrate reading of EEPROM data to
;control LED's

;This program uses pushbuttons (PORT D) to select an
;address
;in EEPROM. The byte at this address is displayed on the
;LED's
;(PORT B).

;PORTB must be connected to the LEDS
;PORTD must be connected to the SWITCHES


;Programmer: TM
;Date: 5/2010
;Platform: STK-500
;Device: ATMega16A

;This include file has all of the I/O addresses
;already defined via appropriate equ directives.
.include "m16def.inc"

.cseg          ;select current segment as code
.org   0       ;begin assembling at address 0


.def   leds        = r16 ;current LED state
.def   switches    = r17 ;switch values just read
.def   temp        = r18 ;used as a temporary register

       ldi    temp,0xFF    ;configure PORTB as output
       out    DDRB,temp
       clr    temp         ;configure PORTD as input
       out    DDRD,temp
       ldi    leds,0xFF     ;Initialize LED's all off
       out    PORTB,leds    ;Display initial LED's

;wait for switch to be pressed
```

```
;this will occur when one or more switches are depressed
waitpress:
        in      switches, PIND
        cpi     switches, 0xFF      ;0xFF means none pressed
        breq    waitpress

;one or more switches are pressed (0's)
;use this as an address into EEPROM (but flip bits
;first)
        com switches
        clr     temp
        out EEARH, temp         ;high bit of address is 0
        out EEARL, switches     ;low byte of address is in
                                ;switches
        sbi EECR, EERE          ;request a read of EEPROM
        in leds, EEDR           ;data is returned in EEDR

        out     PORTB,leds   ;(Re)display LED's

;wait for all switches to be released
waitrelease:
        in      switches, PIND
        cpi     switches, 0xFF      ;0xFF means none pressed
        brne    waitrelease

        rjmp    waitpress    ;repeat (forever)

;Define EEPROM data
.eseg
;set origin (address) then define byte
.org 1<<0    ;for switch 0
.db 0b00001111

;set origin (address) then define byte
.org 1<<1    ;switch 1
.db 0b11110000

.org 1<<2    ;switch 2
.db 0b10101010

.org 1<<3    ;switch 3
.db 0b01010101
```

```
.org 1<<4      ;switch 4
.db 0b10000001

.org 1<<5      ;switch 5
.db 0b00011000

.org 1<<6      ;switch 6
.db 0b11100111

.org 1<<7      ;switch 7
.db 0b01111111
```

This program includes a few new instructions, and incorporates the useful include file feature supported by the assembler. The flow of control matches that of the earlier Toggler program, repeating a main loop forever, one iteration per button press/release action.

The Standard Include File

The include file, m16def.inc, contains all of the equate directives needed to access the I/O registers of the ATmega16A processor. The ATxmega128 uses the include file ATxmega128A1def.inc. The include file contains statements that inform the assembler that the program is being assembled for a particular processor and defines several symbol values as are specific to this processor, such as the amount of SRAM, flash, and EEPROM. Here are a few statements found in the m16def.inc include file.

```
.equ   DDRB  = 0x17
.equ   PINB  = 0x16
. . .
.equ   EEARL = 0x1e
.equ   EEARH = 0x1f
.equ   EEDR  = 0x1d
.equ   EECR  = 0x1c
. . .
.equ   FLASHEND    = 0x1fff        ;Note: Word address
.equ   RAMEND      = 0x045f
.equ   EEPROMEND   = 0x01ff
```

Using the include file for the target processor simplifies the programmer's task and eliminates many errors. The symbols defined in the include file match the documentation for the processor and make programs readable by many programmers. It is good practice to always use the appropriate include file targeting the processor the application will run on.

EEPROM Read

The four statements that interact with EEPROM are found in the middle of the program.

```
out EEARH, temp        ;high bit of address is 0
out EEARL, switches    ;low byte of address is in
                       ;switches
sbi EECR, EERE         ;request a read of EEPROM
in leds, EEDR          ;data is returned in EEDR
```

Reading a byte from EEPROM requires placing its address in the EE Address Register. Since EEPROM addresses range from 0 to 512, 9 bits are required. We are only using a few addresses, namely 1, 2, 4, 8, 16, 32, 64, and 128 (all powers of 2 corresponding to a single button being pressed), so our addresses all start with a leading bit of 0. This is set in the first OUT instruction (temp contains 0). The rest of the address is set in the second OUT instruction. The register names are defined in the include file.

The third instruction, SBI, simply sets a bit (to 1) in the EEPROM control register. This is the Read Enable bit. This action causes the EEPROM to go into action and copy the requested byte into the EEDR (data register). This requires four clock cycles, but the processor knows this and actually halts execution for this period of time. The byte read from EEPROM is then immediately available to be copied into a general purpose register, in this case the one holding the LED display data. An IN instruction does the copying from I/O register to general purpose register. The IN and OUT instructions use I/O Direct Addressing mode. This means the I/O register number is coded as part of the instruction code. It directly specifies what I/O register is to be accessed.

Defining EEPROM Data

The last part of the program is pure data. Note the use of the .eseg directive to inform the assembler that the next part of the source code will contain instructions to generate bytes in the EEPROM segment.

```
.eseg
;set origin (address) then define byte
```

```
.org 1<<0    ;for switch 0
.db 0b00001111
```

There are just 8 bytes to be defined, but they must be at specific addresses; they are not simply stored sequentially in memory. The choice of addresses is made to make it very easy to translate switch (pushbutton) data to an address in EEPROM. Each define byte directive is therefore preceded by a .org directive to set the location counter for the assembly. The expression in the .org operand uses the left shift operator to create a value that represents the desired address. Each expression is simply a one (1) shifted left by the button number (0–7). These could just as easily been written out in many other ways. The following .org statements are all equivalent:

```
;set origin in several equivalent ways for button 5
.org 1<<5         ;using the left shift operator
.org 0b00100000   ;explicitly in binary
.org 0x20         ;explicitly in hex
.org 32           ;explicitly in decimal
```

Using EEPROM Data in the AVR Simulator

After assembling the program, you can run it in the simulator, or download it to the AVR processor. To use the simulator, you must Start Debugging (debug menu). The simulated EEPROM data must be manually loaded from the file created by the assembler. Start by viewing the EEPROM memory (View Menu). Select the EEPROM memory in the window that appears as shown in Figure 5.5.

To load the data you need for this program, choose the Up/Download Memory option from the Debug menu. Select EEPROM under Memory

FIGURE 5.5 Default EEPROM contents displayed in a memory window of the AVR Simulator.

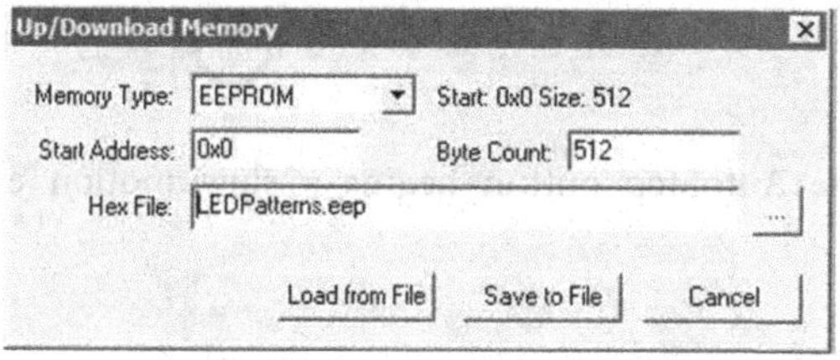

FIGURE 5.6   The Up/Download dialog for AVR Simulator memories.

Type. The Start address should be 0. The Byte Count can be ignored. Select the Hex file in the dialog as shown in Figure 5.6; this will be the EEPROM data file created by the assembler. It will have extension .eep and have the same base name as the hex file output by the assembler.

When you click the Load from File button, a warning indicating that the start address in the file is 0x01, and the available size is less than the Byte Count specified in the dialog. Simply ignore this message (click Yes) and then close the Up/Download dialog.

The EEPROM window should show the new contents (Figure 5.7). You will see the changes in red in the EEPROM memory window. Note that the EEPROM data loaded a lot of values not specified in your code. The EEPROM data file is loaded as a stream of bytes; many of the bytes will be garbage; the program specified only 8 specific byte values located at 8 different addresses. You can check that each address has the correct byte value.

Before starting the program, set port D's PIND value to $FF to simulate all 8 switches in the up position; remember that switch values are one when not pressed. You can start the simulation using the Auto AutoStep mode (ALT + F5 or click the icon on the toolbar as shown in Figure 5.8). This will repeatedly single step, showing the progress of the program at each step.

You can interact with the I/O ports while the program runs in this mode. In the I/O window, display the two relevant digital ports, B (LEDs)

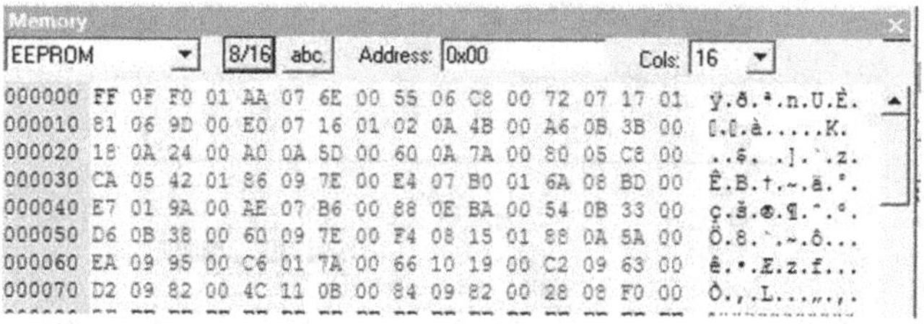

FIGURE 5.7   Updated EEPROM contents after the download process.

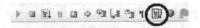

FIGURE 5.8 The AutoStep button begins a slow motion execution of the program.

and D (switches) as shown in Figure 5.9. Click on one of the PIND bits to change it (simulating a button press); observe how the program progresses through the EEPROM read section to the wait for button release loop.

By the time the program reaches the wait-release loop, the value in PORTB (Figure 5.10) should show the pattern selected by the specific button you pressed. You can allow the program to continue by toggling the bit in PIND back to a value of one.

You can also observe the EEPROM registers in the I/O view window as the program executes. You may want to pause the program, and then continue in single step mode so the changes do not occur too quickly.

The button data (read from PIND) is used as an address into EEPROM (after complementing it). If button four is pressed, PIND contains 0b11101111. This is complemented and then copied into EARL. The EEPROM returns the byte at that address to EEDR when the EEPROM

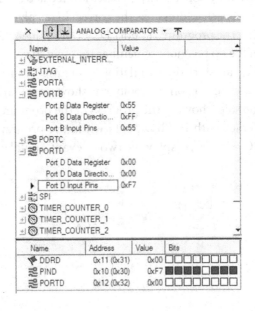

FIGURE 5.9 Simulating a button press by toggling a bit in the PIND register.

PORTA
PORTB
Port B Data Register 0x55
Port B Data Directio... 0xFF
Port B Input Pins 0x55
PORTC

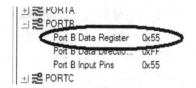

FIGURE 5.10 PORTB is updated to the value read from EEPROM.

read signal is asserted. You can see the byte returned is 0b10000001. This is exactly the byte assembled to EEPROM by these commands:

```
.org 1<<4     ;switch 4
.db 0b10000001
```

You can also set a breakpoint in the debugger to stop the AutoStep action at the beginning of the EEPROM read section so you can single step through the sequence.

Downloading EEPROM Data to the Microcontroller

To execute the program on the STK-500 platform, you must download the program and associated EEPROM data. The programmer software has two separate buttons for each memory as shown in Figure 5.11. Be sure to select the correct files (.hex for flash, .eep for EEPROM). Program Flash first, then program EEPROM. If you do this in the opposite order, it is likely that EEPROM will be erased when Flash is programmed!

To prevent the EEPROM erase during Flash programming, you need to change a fuse setting. Under the fuse tab (Figure 5.12), check the box named EESAVE. Then you only need to download the EEPROM contents if you change them in your program.

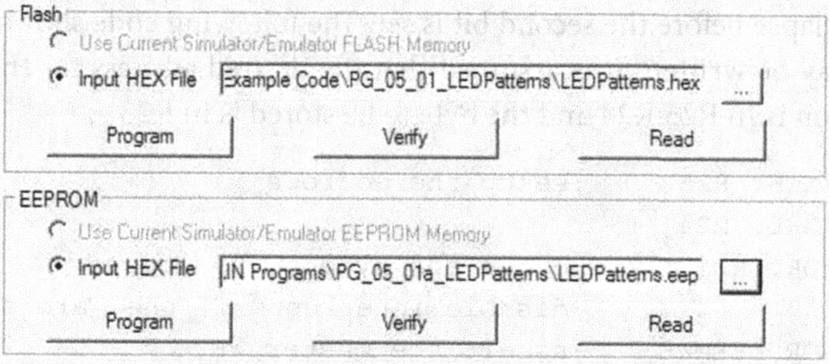

Flash
Use Current Simulator/Emulator FLASH Memory
Input HEX File
Example Code\PG_05_01_LEDPatterns\LEDPatterns.hex
Program
Verify
Read
EEPROM
Use Current Simulator/Emulator EEPROM Memory
Input HEX File
IN Programs\PG_05_01a_LEDPatterns\LEDPatterns.eep
Program
Verify
Read

FIGURE 5.11 Programming Flash and EEPROM using the AVR Programmer.

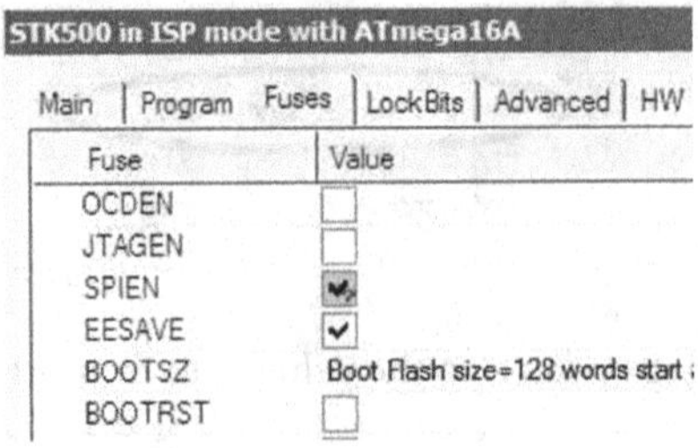

FIGURE 5.12   The EESAVE fuse will preserve EEPROM contents during the chip erase cycle that occurs during flash programming.

Note that by changing just the EEPROM contents, the program will be able to display different patterns in response to switch presses. No changes to the actual program code are needed. It would be possible for the program to alter EEPROM during execution. This might be used to allow you to configure an LED pattern via button presses and then save it in EEPROM, so it can be recalled at a later time by pressing the associated button. This is similar to programming station presets in a car radio.

Writing Data to EEPROM

Because EEPROM is limited in the number of writes that can occur (before the memory stops working), a special sequence of operations is required to cause a write into the EEPROM memory. The basic register setup is the same as for a read; the address must be loaded into EEARH and EEARL. In addition, the byte to be stored must be placed in EEDR. This is necessary because there is a byte we want to transmit to EEPROM. Two bits must be set in the control register to initiate the write, and they must be set in sequence. First, the EEMWE bit of the EECR must be set. Then, within four clock cycles, the EEWE bit must be set. If interrupts are enabled, they must be disabled during this sequence, or more than four clock cycles might elapse before the second bit is set. The following code shows how a byte may be written. It is assumed that the desired address for the store operation is in R25:R24 and the byte to be stored is in R23.

```
out EEARH, R25      ;setup the address
out EEARL, R24
out EEDR, R23       ;queue the byte to be stored
cli                 ;disable interrupts if they are active
sbi EECR, EEMWE     ;assert the master WE
sbi EECR, EEWE      ;assert the WE
sei    ;only do this if interrupts should be ;enabled
```

The EEWE (EEPROM Write Enable) bit will remain set until the byte is stored. This requires about 8.5 ms. If storing multiple bytes, you must wait until EEWE clears before placing the next byte into EEDR and starting the next write cycle. There is an interrupt signal that can be triggered when the write cycle is complete. This is covered in the chapter on interrupts. Without interrupts, you will have to poll the EEWE bit to see when it is clear.

EXERCISES

1. Give four sources of a reset signal for an AVR processor.
2. What is the common name for the section of code that is executed when an interrupt occurs?
3. In the AVR processor, at what address does the interrupt vector table usually begin?
4. Which interrupt cannot be disabled?
5. What does BLS stand for? What is usually stored there?
6. (ATMEGA16A) What is the data space address of general purpose register R31? What is the data space address of the I/O register called PORTB? (ATxmega128A1) What is the data space address of PORTB_OUT? What is the data space address of CPU_SPH and CPU_SPL?
7. In which of the three memories is the AVR hardware stack located?
8. (ATMEGA16A) What is the numeric value used to initialize the stack pointer in a program designed to run on the ATmega16A? Why is this particular value used (what does it represent)?
9. Write a short assembly language program to load three characters from flash into registers R0, R1, and R2, and then loop indefinitely. The characters are to be your initials defined in a statement like this:

```
myInitials: .db "JQS"
```

Test the program in the simulator.
10. Assume the following statements appear somewhere in the code segment of an assembly language program (they do not need to be sequential). Write a program to load the byte at secretaddr into R0 without using the symbols secretaddr or secretvalue. You may use the symbol publicaddr and you should use program indirect addressing (twice).

```
secretaddr: .db secretvalue
publicaddr: .dw secretaddr
```

11. What symbol in the standard include file represents the address of the last byte of flash? Write a loop to successively load every byte of flash into R0, starting at the uppermost address and working towards $0000. Exit the loop when the last byte has been loaded. Calculate the number of clock cycles required for the loop to execute. At 4MHz, how many seconds will this require?

12. The label lp is defined in a program and represents the address of the first instruction in some loop. Write a short assembly language sequence (part of the same program containing the loop) that will copy the most significant byte of this instruction into R0. Remember that instructions are words and are stored in little-endian order. When an instruction is 32-bits in length, it is considered as two separate words, not a doubleword, so each word is independently stored in little-endian order.

13. What symbol in the standard include file represents the first address of SRAM? Write a sequence of instructions that will store the word in R25:R24 into the first two bytes of SRAM. Store the word in little-endian order.

14. The label aNum represents the address of a 32-bit unsigned integer in SRAM (stored in little-endian order). Write a single instruction to load byte 2 (bytes are numbered starting with 0 as the least significant byte) of this integer into R0.

15. Your three initials are stored in R0, R1, and R2. Use the .byte directive to reserve storage in SRAM at address myInitials, and write a sequence of statements to store the initials into this area of memory. Use data direct addressing.

16. What instructions are needed to make Y point to the following SRAM location?

```
myInitials .byte 3
```

17. Assuming Y points to the first byte of the three-byte SRAM area labeled by myInitials, and your initials are already in R0, R1, and R2, show how to store your initials using only data indirect addressing (ST).

18. Write instructions to copy the stack pointer into Y and then use LDD, INC, and STD instructions to increment the 8-bit number on the top of the stack. Remember that SPH:SPL points to the byte just past the top of the stack (at the next lower address). This is why LDD is needed instead of LD. Do not use push or pop.

19. Register Y points to an array of words in SRAM (a sequence of words in consecutive memory locations). R1 contains an integer representing the number of words in the array. Write a loop to remove the first word from the array, shifting the

other words left one position (each position is a word in size). Decrement the array size when done.

20. Register Y points to an array of bytes in SRAM (a sequence of bytes in consecutive memory locations). R1 contains an integer representing the number of bytes currently in the array. Insert the byte value $AA at the front of the array, shifting the current bytes one position to their right. Be careful you do not destroy the entire array in the process!

21. Write a loop to fill the 32-byte string area in SRAM at the label dPtr with nul characters ($00).

22. Write a loop that will copy a string from one area of SRAM to another using indirect addressing with postincrement. The address of the source string is stored in SRAM at sPtr (as an unsigned word, little-endian). The address of the destination is stored in SRAM at dPtr. The length of the string is a constant:

```
.equ strLength = 32   ;the number of bytes in the
                      ;string
dPtr: .byte 2         ;points to the destination
sPtr: .byte 2         ;points to the source
```

23. Examine a listing of an assembly language program that includes the m16def.inc or ATxmega128A1def.inc file. Several symbols related to memory are defined. What is the value of each of the following symbols defined in this include file (state which include file you used)?

   FLASHEND
   SRAM_START
   SRAM_SIZE
   RAMEND
   EEPROMEND

The following four questions all refer to the LED Patterns program discussed in this chapter.

24. When is the selected pattern displayed on the LEDs: when the button is pressed, or when it is released? What causes this behavior? (answer by analyzing the source code)

25. Modify the program to display the selected pattern while a switch is pressed. The display should go blank when the switch is released. Hint: add a label and modify one jump.

26. Why is the switch data complemented (flipped) before it is used as an address?

27. If you remove the complement instruction (COM), how would you modify the .org statements so the program still works as before? Hint: use ~ and &.

PROGRAMMING EXERCISES

1. Rewrite the LED Patterns program to read the eight patterns from flash memory instead of EEPROM. This will be a little tricky as the addresses used for the data might conflict with the addresses where instructions are located. For example, you can hardly place pattern bytes at addresses 1 and 2 of flash if these locations already contain instructions of your program. Assuming that your program is not too large, you should be able to place the patterns in an unused area of memory, possibly starting at $0200. The switch data will still determine the lower byte of the address as before, but the upper byte would be $02 (instead of $00). Another possibility is to use an RJMP at address $0000 to jump past the pattern data to the actual start of your program. Do not forget that LPM uses byte addresses, but the assembler's location counter for the code segment is a word address.

2. Write a program to add the following 32-bit integers together. The result should appear in registers R3:R2:R1:R0. Use ADD and ADC instructions. The program should loop indefinitely when done. Test the program in the simulator.

```
.cseg
numbers:     .dd -234876543
             .dd 3487632465
```

3. Write a program that contains the following statements:

```
.cseg
f _ str: .db "This is a very interesting string."
                 "It has some characters.", 0
.equ STRLENGTH = (PC-f _ str)*2
.dseg
str .byte STRLENGTH
```

Your program should copy the string from flash to SRAM. Stop your loop when a nul byte is copied and stored. Test in the simulator (ignore any assembler warnings related to padding bytes), observing the progress.

4. Write a program to copy the EEPROM contents into SRAM (starting at the lowest SRAM address). Use symbols defined in the include file for your microcontroller. Run the program in the simulator, observing the contents of SRAM as the program executes. You should place something interesting in EEPROM so you will recognize the bytes in SRAM when you are successful (you can edit EEPROM in the memory window of the simulator).

5. Write a program that displays a pattern on the LEDs. The pattern is read from EEPROM. The program then waits for eight

button presses to define a new pattern. You press button 1 for ON and button 0 for OFF. The first button press sets LED7, the next sets LED6, and so on. The LEDs should be immediately updated as each bit is entered. When the last of the eight bits are entered, pressing 1 will store the new pattern in EEPROM and blank the display, entering an infinite loop; resetting the processor will show the new pattern. Pressing 0 will simply restart the program (without updating the EEPROM) causing the previously stored pattern to reappear.

ALTERNATE PROGRAMS FOR THE XPLAIN DEMONSTRATION KIT

Program 5.1a: LED Patterns

The XMEGA series microcontrollers provide two ways to access the on-board EEPROM. The Nonvolatile Memory (NVM) Controller module provides a command-based interface to access all of the nonvolatile memories: Flash Program Memory, User Signature, and Calibration rows, Fuses and Lock Bits, and EEPROM data memory. It is also possible to map EEPROM to the data space addresses beginning at address $1000; this allows EEPROM to read simply and efficiently using the usual load instructions.

Create a new project in AVR Studio, naming it appropriately. Be sure to click the Next button to select the debug platform and device. When using the ATxmega128A1, you will need to choose the AVR Simulator 2 as the debug platform.

PROGRAM 5.1a   A Program to Illustrate Reading EEPROM Data

```
;LED Patterns: Illustrate reading of EEPROM data to
;control LED's

;This program uses pushbuttons (PORT F) to select an
;address
;in EEPROM. The byte at this address is displayed on the
;LED's
;(PORT E).

;Programmer: TM
;Date: 5/2010
;Platform: XPLAIN
;Device: ATxmega128A1
```

```
;This include file has all of the I/O addresses
;already defined via appropriate equ directives.
.include "ATxmega128A1def.inc"

.cseg          ;select current segment as code
.org  0        ;begin assembling at address 0

.def  leds  = r16 ;current LED state
.def  switches = r17 ;switch values just read
.def  temp  = r18 ;used as a temporary register

;Configure all 8 input pins (PORTF) to use internal
;pullup resistors
    ldi temp,0xFF
    sts PORTCFG_MPCMASK, temp   ;configure all 8 input pins
    ldi temp, 0b00011000        ;code to enable pullups on
                                ;input pins
    sts PORTF_PIN0CTRL, temp    ;PORTF will read switches

;Configure port directions
    ldi    temp,0xFF
    sts    PORTE_DIR,temp    ;configure PORTE as output
    clr    temp
    sts    PORTF_DIR,temp    ;configure PORTF as input

;Initialize LED's
    ldi    leds,0xFF         ;Initialize LED's all off
    sts    PORTE_OUT,leds    ;Display initial LED's

;wait for switch to be pressed
;this will occur when one or more switches are depressed
waitpress:
    lds    switches, PORTF_IN
    cpi    switches, 0xFF    ;0xFF means none pressed
    breq   waitpress

;one or more switches are pressed (0's)
;use this as an address into EEPROM (but flip bits
;first)
    com switches

    ;load desired EEPROM address to NVM
    clr temp
```

```
    sts NVM_ADDR1, temp     ;high bit of address is 0
    sts NVM_ADDR0, switches         ;low byte of address is
                                    ;in switches


    ;select the NVM command (EEPROM read)
    ldi   temp, NVM_CMD_READ_EEPROM_gc ;NVM command to
                                       ;read EEPROM
    sts NVM_CMD, temp


    ;unprotect protected IO registers and execute command
    ldi temp, CCP_IOREG_gc ;code to unlock IO registers
    sts CPU_CCP,temp
    ldi temp, NVM_CMDEX_bm ;code to execute command
    sts NVM_CTRLA, temp     ;do it!


    ;Copy read data from NVM to leds register
    lds leds, NVM_DATA0     ;data is returned in the DATA
                            ;register


    sts   PORTE_OUT,leds    ;(Re)display LED's

;wait for all switches to be released
waitrelease:
    lds   switches, PORTF_IN
    cpi   switches, 0xFF    ;0xFF means none pressed
    brne  waitrelease

    rjmp  waitpress ;repeat (forever)

;Define EEPROM data
.eseg
;set origin (address) then define byte
.org 1<<0    ;for switch 0
.db 0b00001111

;set origin (address) then define byte
.org 1<<1    ;switch 1
.db 0b11110000

.org 1<<2    ;switch 2
.db 0b10101010
```

```
.org 1<<3      ;switch 3
.db 0b01010101

.org 1<<4      ;switch 4
.db 0b10000001

.org 1<<5      ;switch 5
.db 0b00011000

.org 1<<6      ;switch 6
.db 0b11100111

.org 1<<7      ;switch 7
.db 0b01111111
```

This program uses the standard include file feature supported by the assembler. The flow of control matches that of the earlier Toggler program (Program 3.1), repeating a main loop forever, one iteration per button press/release action.

The Standard Include File

The include file, ATxmega128A1def.inc, contains all of the equate directives needed to access the I/O registers of the ATxmega128A1 processor. The include file contains statements that inform the assembler that the program is being assembled for a particular processor and defines several symbol values as are specific to this processor, such as the amount of SRAM, flash, and EEPROM. Here are a few statements found in the ATxmega128A1def.inc include file.

```
.equ PORTE_DIR = 1664        // I/O Port Data Direction
.equ PORTE_OUT = 1668        // I/O Port Output

.equ PORTF_DIR = 1696        // I/O Port Data Direction
.equ PORTF_IN = 1704         // I/O port Input
.equ PORTF_PIN0CTRL = 1712       // Pin 0 Control
                                 Register

.equ PORTCFG_MPCMASK = 176       //Multi-pin
                                 Configuration Mask

.equ NVM_ADDR0 = 448         // Address Register 0
```

```
.equ NVM_ADDR1 = 449          // Address Register 1
.equ NVM_DATA0 = 452          // Data Register 0
.equ NVM_CMD = 458            // Command
.equ NVM_CMD_READ_EEPROM_gc = (0x06<<0) ;Read EEPROM

.equ NVM_CTRLA = 459          // Control Register A

.equ CCP_IOREG_gc = (0xD8<<0) ;IO Register Protection
.equ CPU_CCP = 52    // Configuration Change Protection
```

Using the include file for the target processor simplifies the programmer's task and eliminates many errors. The symbols defined in the include file match the documentation for the processor and make programs readable by many programmers. It is good practice to always use the appropriate include file targeting the processor the application will run on.

EEPROM Read

The statements that interact with EEPROM are found in the middle of the program.

```
;load desired EEPROM address to NVM
clr temp
sts NVM_ADDR1, temp      ;high bit of address is 0
sts NVM_ADDR0, switches  ;low byte of address is in
                         ;switches

;select the NVM command (EEPROM read)
ldi temp, NVM_CMD_READ_EEPROM_gc    ;NVM command to
                                    ;read EEPROM
sts NVM_CMD, temp

;unprotect protected IO registers and execute command
ldi temp, CCP_IOREG_gc ;code to unlock IO registers
sts CPU_CCP,temp
ldi temp, NVM_CMDEX_bm ;code to execute command
sts NVM_CTRLA, temp    ;do it!

;Copy read data from NVM to leds register
lds leds, NVM_DATA0    ;data is returned in the DATA
                       ;register
```

Reading a byte from EEPROM requires placing its address in the NVM Controller's address register, placing a command code in the CMD register to read from EEPROM, initiating the read sequence, and then copying the returned byte to a register.

We are only using a few addresses, namely 1, 2, 4, 8, 16, 32, 64, and 128 (all powers of 2 corresponding to a single button being pressed). The NVM Controller uses 24-bit addresses that must be loaded into the NVM registers ADDR2, ADDR1, and ADDR0. ADDR2 is not used when accessing EEPROM; ADDR1 will be 0 (since our addresses are no larger than 128). The standard include file prefaces each of these names with NVM_. The first two STS instructions above set the two byte EEPROM address to be read.

The next two instructions load the NVM's EEPROM Read code into the NVM's command register. To initiate the read action, bit 0 of the NVM's CTRLA register must be set. This is a protected register and a special procedure must be followed to unlock it. To unlock any protected I/O register, you must store the code $D8 (CCP_IOREG_gc) into the Configuration Change Protection (CCP) register. This unlocks the I/O registers for four clock cycles.

Reading from EEPROM causes the processor to skip four clock cycles (the time required for reading the byte). The data read is then immediately available in the DATA0 register of the NVM. The last statement in the code above copies it into the leds register.

Defining EEPROM Data

The last part of the program is pure data. Note the use of the .eseg directive to inform the assembler that the next part of the source code will contain instructions to generate bytes in the EEPROM segment.

```
.eseg
;set origin (address) then define byte
.org 1<<0    ;for switch 0
.db 0b00001111
```

There are just 8 bytes to be defined, but they must be at specific addresses; they are not simply stored sequentially in memory. The choice of addresses is made to make it very easy to translate switch (pushbutton) data to an address in EEPROM. Each define byte directive is therefore preceded by a .org directive to set the location counter for the assembly. The expression in the .org operand uses the left shift operator to create a value that represents the desired address. Each expression is simply a one (1) shifted left by the button number (0–7). These could just as easily been written out in many other ways. The following .org statements are all equivalent:

```
;set origin in several equivalent ways for button 5
.org 1<<5     ;using the left shift operator
.org 0b00100000    ;explicitly in binary
.org 0x20    ;explicitly in hex
.org 32      ;explicitly in decimal
```

Using EEPROM Data in the AVR Simulator 2

After assembling the program, you can run it in the simulator, or download it to the AVR processor. To use the simulator, you must Start Debugging (debug menu). The simulated EEPROM data must be manually loaded from the file created by the assembler. Choose the Up/Download Memory option from the Debug menu. Select EEPROM under Memory Type. The Start address should be 0. The Byte Count can be ignored. Select the Hex file; this will be the EEPROM data file created by the assembler. It will have extension .eep and have the same base name as the hex file output by the assembler.

When you click the Load from File button, a warning indicating that the start address in the file is 0x01, and the available size is less than the Byte Count specified in the dialog. Ignore the warning (click Yes) and the EEPROM data from the file will be loaded into the simulated EEPROM. You can view the EEPROM memory by selecting this option from the View Menu. Select the EEPROM memory in the window that appears. Note that the EEPROM may contain garbage at locations not specified in your program. Only 8 specific byte values located at 8 different addresses were actually defined in your code. You can check that each byte at addresses 1, 2, 4, 8, 16, 32, 64, and 128 is the correct value.

Set a breakpoint at the first statement in the waitpress loop; you can right-click on that statement and choose toggle breakpoint. A red circle on a line indicates a breakpoint.

Find PORTF in the I/O View window (Figure 5.13). Set its IN register to $FF to simulate all buttons up; remember that a button reads as a one when it is up and a zero when it is down.

Choose Run from the debug window. Execution will stop at your first breakpoint. Change one of the bits in PORTF as shown in Figure 5.14. This change would occur when you press a button.

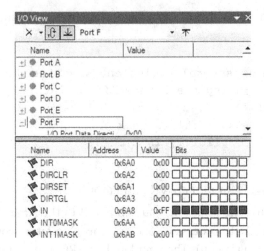

FIGURE 5.13 Setting PORTF pins (the IN register) to $FF to simulate all buttons up.

Single-step through the program until the EEPROM is read and the LED pattern is output to PORTE_OUT. You can view the NVM controller registers (Figure 5.15) as you step through the program.

When your program reaches the waitrelease loop, you will need to return the pin value to one to simulate the button release; your program waits for this event before looping back to the top to wait for another button press.

Downloading EEPROM Data

To execute the program on the XPLAIN platform, you must download the program and associated EEPROM data. The programmer software has two separate buttons for each memory. Be sure to select the correct files (hex for flash, .eep for EEPROM).

To prevent the EEPROM erase during Flash programming, you need to change a fuse setting. Under the fuse tab (Figure 5.16), check the box named EESAVE. Then you only need to download the EEPROM contents if you change them in your program.

Note that by changing just the EEPROM contents, the program will be able to display different patterns in response to switch presses. No changes to the actual program code are needed. It would be possible for the pro-

FIGURE 5.14 Changing a bit in PORTF's IN register to simulate a button press.

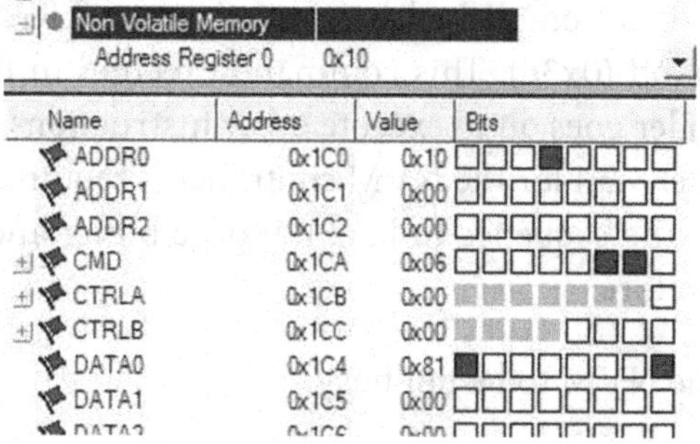

FIGURE 5.15   The NVM Controller registers just after reading a pattern.

gram to alter EEPROM during execution. This might be used to allow you to configure an LED pattern via button presses and then save it in EEPROM, so it can be recalled at a later time by pressing the associated button. This is similar to programming station presets in a car radio.

Writing Data to EEPROM

There are two steps to write to EEPROM: load the data to be written into the NVM's temporary page buffer and write the page buffer to EEPROM. The ATxmega128A1 has 64 32-byte pages. An EEPROM address is subdivided as a page number (bits 10:5) and a position within the page (bits 4-0). Up to 32 bytes can be loaded at one time for a single write to EEPROM operation. The bytes must be in the same page; their addresses must differ only in the last five bits.

There are two preliminary steps that are sometimes necessary before starting to load the page buffer. The NVM controller must not be busy performing another operation, and the page buffer must be empty. Erasing

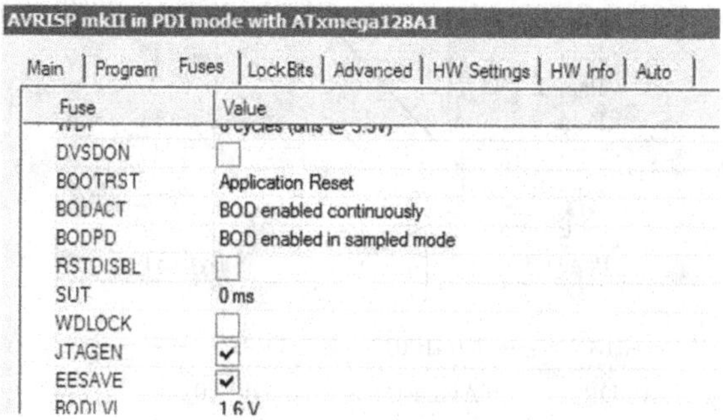

FIGURE 5.16   The EESAVE fuse will preserve EEPROM contents during the chip erase cycle that occurs during flash programming.

the page buffer is accomplished by executing the ERASE_EEPROM _ BUFFER command (0x36). This command executes in the background; the microcontroller goes on to execute other instructions while the NVM is busy, so another wait for the NVM controller is required before loading the page buffer. The sequence to load the page buffer and write it to the EEPROM is therefore:

1. Wait for the NVM to be not busy

2. Erase the page buffer

3. Wait for the NVM to be not busy

4. Load up to 32 bytes into the buffer

5. Write the page buffer to EEPROM

Each byte loaded into the temporary page buffer is tagged when loaded; only the tagged bytes are eventually written, so the EEPROM supports single byte writing if desired. When the buffer is cleared, all of the tags are cleared and the buffer contents are set to $FF. When loading bytes into the buffer, only the lowest 5 bits of the address are used; this specifies the byte position in the buffer. When writing the buffer to the EEPROM, only the upper bits are used to select the page. This address interpretation is illustrated in Figure 5.17.

The erase page buffer and write buffer to EEPROM steps both require access to a protected I/O register. The steps to access a protected register to execute a command should be abstracted to a function. The task of waiting

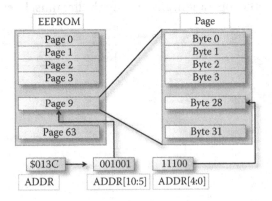

FIGURE 5.17   In the ATxmega128A1, EEPROM address $013C selects page 9 and the byte at offset 28 within that page.

for the NVM controller to become not busy is used in several places and also deserves to be implemented as a function.

```
;function: wait for NVM to become not busy
wait_nvm_busy:

   lds temp, NVM_STATUS
   andi temp, NVM_NVMBUSY_bm
   brne wait_nvm_busy
   ret

;function: execute protected NVM command
;(assumes pertinent NVM registers are already loaded)
execute_nvm_cmd:
   ldi temp, CCP_IOREG_gc ;code to unlock IO registers
   sts CPU_CCP,temp
   ldi temp, NVM_CMDEX_bm ;code to execute command
   sts NVM_CTRLA, temp    ;do it!
   ret
```

Loading a single byte into the page buffer is done in three steps:

1. Place the LOAD_EEPROM_BUFFER command (0x33) in the NVM command register

2. Select the byte address in ADDR0

3. Write the byte to DATA0

Writing the byte into DATA0 must be done last as it immediately triggers the action of copying the byte into the proper location of the buffer. More bytes can be loaded by simply changing the address and writing each byte to DATA0.

Once the data is loaded, the ERASE_WRITE_EEPROM_PAGE command (0x35) is executed to copy the tagged bytes in the buffer to the EEPROM. This action also erases the temporary page buffer. The sequence below shows all of the steps required to write the byte value $AA to EEPROM address $013C.

```
;write a single byte ($AA) to EEPROM at address $013C
rcall wait_nvm_busy

ldi   temp, NVM_CMD_ERASE_EEPROM_BUFFER_gc
sts NVM_CMD, temp
```

```
rcall execute_nvm_cmd
rcall wait_nvm_busy

;select the NVM command to load data into the page buffer
   ldi temp, NVM_CMD_LOAD_EEPROM_BUFFER_gc
   sts NVM_CMD, temp
;set address
   ldi temp, high($013C)
   sts   NVM_ADDR1, temp
   ldi   temp, low($013C)
   sts   NVM_ADDR0, temp
;load the data to be written into NVM's data register
   ldi   temp, $AA
   sts   NVM_DATA0, temp  ;triggers the load buffer action
;write the page buffer (containing just one byte) to EEPROM
   ldi   temp, NVM_CMD_ERASE_WRITE_EEPROM_PAGE_gc
   sts NVM_CMD, temp
   rcall execute_nvm_cmd
```

The program will continue executing while the NVM is busy writing
the page to EEPROM. You must avoid performing other NVM operations
until its BUSY flag is cleared (as shown in the wait_nvm_busy function).
This process will take about 12 ms to complete.

CHAPTER 6

The Stack and Function Calls

O NE OF THE FUNDAMENTAL data structures studied in computer science is the stack. This last in first out (LIFO) storage structure is also of fundamental importance in the procedure call mechanism, interrupt system, and the design of processors. Most processor designs include hardware support for at least one stack. The AVR processor includes a stack pointer (SP) register (in the I/O register area) and a few explicit stack instructions. The use of the stack by AVR programs is required for interrupts and procedure calls.

The stack is useful for several purposes. The most basic is temporary storage of a register value to free the register for another use. Instructions that call procedures implicitly affect the stack, using it to store a return address. When designing functions, the stack may also be used for local variable storage and as a storage area for parameters. The stack is also used when an interrupt handler is invoked.

STACK

The AVR's stack resides in SRAM memory. The SP keeps track of the top of the stack, holding the address where the next byte would be placed by a push operation. The stack instructions decrement the SP when data is pushed onto the stack, so the stack grows downward from a fixed point. Often, the bottom of the stack is set to the end of SRAM.

Stack and Pointer

The SP requires initialization before the stack can be used. The XMEGA series microcontrollers automatically initialize the SP to the highest address of internal SRAM whenever a reset signal occurs. The MEGA series (and earlier) require a manual initialization. The following statements can be included in the RESET routine (at the start of every program that uses the stack). They set the bottom of the stack to the last byte of SRAM. Initially, the SP will hold the address where the top byte (when it is pushed) will reside; since the stack is empty, there is no meaningful data at this address when the stack is initialized. After information is pushed on the stack, the SP is decremented, so it never points to data actually on the stack.

```
;MEGA Version
;RAMEND is defined in the appropriate include file
ldi R16, high(RAMEND)
ldi R17, low(RAMEND)
out SPL, R17
out SPH, R16

;XMEGA Version (optional)
ldi R16, high(RAMEND)
ldi R17, low(RAMEND)
sts CPU_SPL, R17    ;always write low byte first
sts CPU_SPH, R16
```

Just keep in mind that the SP always points to the address where the next byte will be stored when pushed onto the stack. The actual top of stack location (if the stack is not empty) is (SP) + 1.

Push and Pop

The two basic stack operations are push and pop. These are also AVR machine instructions that allow a byte from any register to be pushed onto the stack, or the top item to be popped off the stack and copied into any register.

```
push Rr
```

This instruction stores the byte in Rr to the address found in SP, then decrements SP. There is no check for stack overflow. The application must verify that SP has not decreased so much that it encroaches on storage used for other purposes, or is decremented past the start of SRAM.

```
pop Rd
```

This instruction first increments SP, then loads the byte from the address found in SP into Rd. No check is made for an empty stack. The application may choose to verify that SP is not equal to its initial value (stack is not empty) before performing a pop operation. It is possible to increment the SP right past the last SRAM address.

One important use of the stack is to temporarily hold register values when the registers are needed for another use. The values stored on the stack can be restored when the registers are again free.

Example

Suppose registers 16–31 are holding important data during some computation, but there is a need to output the value $FF to PORTB. Since the LDI command can only use these registers, we need to free a register to accomplish the task.

```
push R16       ;save register value
ldi R16, $FF   ;use register freely
out PORTB, R16    ;XMEGA version: sts PORTB_OUT, R16
pop R16        ;restore register value before continuing
```

One could also use the stack as temporary storage when swapping the contents of two registers:

```
;swap R5 and R6
push R5        ;R5 moved to temporary location on stack
mov R5, R6
pop R6         ;temp location removed from stack to R6
```

FUNCTIONS

In assembly language, you can use the term procedure, function, or sub-routine interchangeably, although a common distinction is sometimes made; a function returns a value, whereas a procedure or subroutine usu-ally does not. Regardless of which name you prefer, a function call implies a transfer (branch, jump) to an address representing the entry point of the function, causing execution of the body of the function. When the function is finished, another transfer occurs to resume execution at the statement following the call. The first transfer is the function call (or invocation); the second transfer is the return. Together, this constitutes the processor's call-return mechanism.

Historically, the call-return mechanism has been implemented in two fundamentally different ways. The simplest is to have the return address loaded into a register when the call is executed. This same register is used to carry out the return action. The programmer must then decide what to do with the return address. It may be left untouched or it may be altered (to return to some location other than the instruction immediately following the call). If another function call is to be made before the return is effected, the return address must be safely stored away while the other function carries out its task. A stack structure is often utilized to facilitate nested function calls.

The second implementation of the call-return mechanism implicitly utilizes a stack that is part of the architectural description of the processor. Note that nested function calls require the use of a stack, but the first case was a stack implemented out of necessity as part of the application. In the second model, the stack is supported through the hardware and automatically used for return address storage. The AVR processor uses a hardware stack in this way.

The AVR processor provides three or four call instructions to invoke a function, and one return (RET) instruction to return to the caller. The call instructions vary only in how the address of the function is specified.

Defining a Function

When writing assembly language programs, a function need not be declared in any way, although it is a good idea to document it as a function. We might conceptually define a function as a group of interrelated statements with one entry point (indicated by a label) and one exit point, implemented by a RET instruction. The entry point is the target of the call instruction. Once entered, the flow of control continues normally through the function's code until a RET instruction is encountered. This is the exit point.

You are not actually restricted to this *narrow* interpretation of a function. Functions can have multiple entry points, multiple exit points, and it is even possible to enter a function without a call and to leave a function without executing a return statement. This flexibility must be used with caution, however, or you risk corruption of the stack.

To create a function in AVR assembly language, simply start writing the function body. You will want to affix a label at the entry point (usually at the top of the function body), as it is convenient to refer to the function by a meaningful name. Be sure that the function cannot be entered inadvertently by executing a statement that is written immediately before the function's code in the source file, and "falling into" the function.

Functions may include decision structures resulting in multiple control paths. When a control path in the function reaches the logical end of the function's task, you may immediately insert a RET instruction. This may result in multiple return points within the function. An alternate design is to ensure that all control paths lead to a single, common return point. This is a good way to ensure consistency. Be sure that every path through the function will eventually reach a RET instruction.

To invoke a function from any point in your program, use one of the call instructions with the address specified by the function's entry point label. When the call instruction is executed, the processor will push the return address onto the stack and then jump to the function by loading the function's address into the PC. When a RET instruction is reached, the PC is loaded from the address popped off the stack, causing execution to resume at the instruction following the call.

Never allow execution to enter the code of a function via a sequence (*falling into* the function) or via a branch or jump, either to the entry point or some other label inside the function. Doing so will very likely cause stack corruption or underflow (from executing returns with no corresponding calls). Do not exit a function except through a RET instruction or you risk eventual stack overflow (from return addresses being pushed but never removed).

Function Call Instructions

There are four instructions that are used to call or invoke a function. These all perform the same operation; they differ only in how the address of the function is specified.

```
call function_address     ;long call
rcall function_address    ;relative call
icall                     ;indirect call
eicall                    ;extended indirect call
```

The CALL instruction uses direct addressing to specify the entry point of the function. RCALL uses another addressing mode, PC-relative. In the AVR, this addressing mode is specific to addressing of instructions; it involves adding a signed integer (displacement) to the processor's PC to calculate the destination address. The ICALL instruction uses indirect addressing. The address of the function must be preloaded into Z. EICALL is available only for microcontrollers with more than 128KB of flash; it uses an extra I/O register to form a 24-bit address (EIND:ZH:ZL).

The (long) CALL instruction is a 32-bit instruction. This is because the address portion may require up to 22 bits, already overflowing the space in a 16-bit instruction. The only disadvantage of the CALL instruction is its size and slightly slower speed; it requires one extra clock cycle to execute (compared to RCALL).

```
call k: 1001 010k kkkk 111k kkkk kkkk kkkk kkkk
(-4194304 <= k <= 4194303)
```

The relative call is the most common function call instruction. As long as the destination (function's entry point) is not too far away from the point of the call, this instruction should be preferred over CALL. The RCALL instruction encodes a 12-bit signed displacement into the 16-bit instruction.

```
rcall k: 1101 kkkk kkkk kkkk
(-2048 <= k <= 2047)
```

In assembly language, you will never specify k directly. Instead you use an address for the argument of RCALL. The assembler calculates the proper value for the displacement k and informs you if it is out of range. The equation, $k = destAddr-(PC + 1)$, is used to determine k. In this equation, PC is the address of the RCALL instruction being assembled. The entry point of the function, destination of the call, is indicated by destAddr. This is the only operand for the RCALL instruction. At execution time, the PC will hold the value (PC + 1) when the RCALL is executed. The value of k (from the instruction code) is sign-extended and added to the processor's PC; the result is placed back into the PC, effectively causing a branch to the function's entry point. The next fetch will bring the first instruction of the function into the instruction pipeline.

Since the displacement is 12 bits, the range of the value k in the RCALL instruction is −2048 to 2047 (words). The ATmega16A's program memory is only two times this range, so only very large programs or programs with code scattered around in memory will need to resort to the long call format. Of course, the ATxmega128A1 has a much larger flash memory; the rcall instruction's range can easily be exceeded when working with this microcontroller.

The indirect call instruction (ICALL) is useful when the address of the function is determined through some calculation, or if you have a table of functions. The target of the call is implied to be in Z.

```
icall: 1001 0101 0000 1001
```

Since the address must be loaded into Z before executing ICALL, this instruction requires no operands. Because Z contains an address, this instruction utilizes (program) indirect addressing. For processors having more than 128KB flash, this instruction can only call functions with entry points in this lower portion of memory since Z is limited to a 16-bit value.

The extended indirect call instruction (EICALL) uses a 24-bit address found in EIND:ZH:ZL. EIND is an I/O register located with other CPU registers.

```
eicall: 1001 0101 0001 1001
```

Return Address and RET Instructions

When any of the above call instructions are executed, a jump to the function's entry point occurs. However, a call instruction differs from a simple jump in that the return address (the address of the instruction following the call) must be saved so the function return can be executed. In the AVR processor, the return address is saved by pushing it onto the stack (Figure 6.1). This of course requires that the application has appropriately initialized the SP before any calls occur. When the call instruction is fetched, the PC is automatically incremented (so it points to the next instruction in memory). Pushing the return address on the stack is as

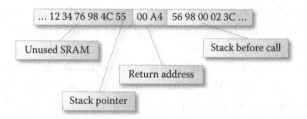

FIGURE 6.1 Return address on the top of the stack just after executing a call instruction.

simple as pushing the value of the updated PC. The low byte is pushed first. If the processor has a PC of more than 16-bits (as does the ATxmega128A1), then 3 bytes are pushed, otherwise only two bytes are placed onto the stack. Once the PC is safely placed on the stack, the address of the function (specified by the call instruction) is loaded into the PC.

The RET instruction is used to remove the return address from the stack and place it back into the PC. This restores the stack to its state just before the call, and causes execution to resume with the instruction immediately after the call. When a RET instruction is executed, the top bytes of the stack are popped into the PC, setting up the fetch of the instruction following the function call statement. The RET instruction requires four clock cycles in the ATmega16A and five in the ATxmega128A1.

ARGUMENTS, PARAMETERS, AND RETURN VALUES

Assembly languages generally provide little support for standard function call mechanisms such as arguments or parameters, or provision for local variables or a return value. All of these options are left to the programmer to decide how they are to be accomplished. In this section we examine how arguments, parameters, local storage, and return values can be implemented in assembly language programs.

Return Values

Return values are probably the easiest to dispense with. A common way to return a value as the result of a function is to have the function place the return value in a register. If the return value is a word, a register pair can be used. For more complicated return types, the return value could be placed somewhere in memory; the function would simply return its address in a register pair. The stack is another possible place to leave a return value, however this is a bit more complicated. Just before executing the RET instruction, the top of stack value must be the return address. If a function pushes a return value onto the stack before reaching the RET instruction, it will cause the return to fail; the return value would be used as (part of) the return address.

If the function is to leave its return value on the stack, it cannot simply be pushed on the stack. The return value will either have to be placed on the stack below the return address, or an alternate method of returning from the function needs to be devised.

Let us explore the possibility of placing the return value (a single byte) inside the stack, just below the return address (which is on the top of the stack). We will need to make space inside the stack to do this. Consider the following solution. Assume R24 holds the return value that has just been calculated by the function. Registers R31 and R30 will be used as scratch registers.

```
;assuming a 2-byte return address
pop R31; get high byte of return address
pop R30; get low byte of return address
push R24; put return value on the stack
push R30; replace the return address
push R31
ret; return to caller
```

After the three push instructions, the stack will look like the diagram of Figure 6.2. Notice how the return value has been inserted into the stack, underneath the return address. If the return address is three bytes, you will need an extra register and another pop/push instruction pair.

When the RET instruction is executed, the return address will be removed from the stack and the return value will be found on the top of the stack. The code immediately following the call would simply pop the return value from the stack into an available register as needed.

A good question to ask at this point is what benefit there is in placing the return value on the stack if it is just going to be popped into some register before it can be used. Why not just use a specific register? The key to the answer is in the question. If the function leaves the return value in a *specific* register, that register is tied to that usage. The calling program may need to move important data out of the designated register before the function is called. Otherwise, the function will overwrite important data. If the return value is on the stack, the caller can pop it into any register it desires, and a specific register is not tied up as a return value storage

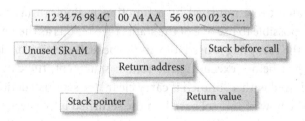

FIGURE 6.2 The stack with a return value (byte value $AA) inserted below the return address.

location. The advantage is increased flexibility, and not tying up any particular register for this purpose. The disadvantage is extra instructions required to shuffle things on and off the stack.

Actually, the last three instructions of the above sequence can be shortened to a single instruction. When the return address was popped, it was placed in Z. Thus, Z holds the address to which we must return, and the IJMP (Indirect Jump) instruction Z as the target of a jump. Executing an IJMP instruction simply copies Z into the PC. Once the return address has been removed from the stack and is in Z, we can effect the return from the function by an IJMP to the address in Z. Here is the alternative method of returning from a function with the return value left on the stack.

```
;assuming a 2-byte return address
pop R31; get high byte of return address
pop R30; get low byte of return address
push R24; put return value on the stack
;return address is in Z and has been removed from the stack
ijmp; return to caller
```

A similar sequence will accomplish the same thing for a three byte return address. The first byte popped will need to be placed in EIND and the EIJMP (extended indirect jump) instruction used to perform the IJMP at the end of the sequence.

Despite the noted advantage of leaving the return value on the stack, the influence of C on AVR programming has resulted in the designation of certain registers as a conventional return value location. It is not uncommon to establish conventions for register usage. In AVR programming, the register pair R25:R24, or simply R24, is often used as the designated return value register. For return values requiring more than 2 bytes, additional registers may be used.

If the value to be returned by a function is Boolean (a true or false result), it is possible to use one of the status register bits as the return value; frequently the carry flag is used for this purpose. By setting or clearing the carry flag just before executing the return statement, the call statement may be followed with a "branch if carry clear" (or set) instruction, thereby changing the flow of control based on the returned bit value.

A variation of this technique allows a function to return a Boolean and a data value. The Boolean is indicated by a status flag, and the returned value might be found in R25:R24. In this case, the carry flag usually provides additional information, such as "the search was successful," or "some type of error condition was encountered inside the function." The caller can interpret the returned value in the register in light of the additional piece of Boolean information.

Arguments and Parameters: Call by Value/Call by Reference

The most powerful aspect of the function call mechanism is the ability to pass information to a function. The information passed to the function is referred to as the function's arguments. These are generally expressions that represent values or addresses. The arguments can vary from call to call making the function much more flexible.

Arguments are passed to functions and received in corresponding parameters. There are a variety of ways to establish this correspondence. This process often requires memory allocation. A clarification of terminology is important. Arguments belong to the calling function; parameters belong to the called function. The distinction is based on ownership. Actual parameters require storage locations separate from that of the arguments. Because parameters belong to the called function, they are often classified as part of the function's local storage. Local storage is expected to be allocated when the function is called and released when the function is finished. This is how local variables and parameters in C functions and Java methods are implemented.

The two main methods of passing arguments to a function are called call by value and call by reference. Call by value means the argument is copied into the parameter, allowing the function to use the value represented by the argument without ever knowing where the argument was located. Call by reference means the caller makes the address of the argument available to the function, copying the address into the parameter. In this case we could say that the address of the data is passed by value. Using the address provided in this way, the function is able to alter the actual argument, without knowing in advance where it would be located. Implementing this technique will use indirect addressing. In assembly language, the programmer can choose to pass information by either method, call by value or call by reference, and can even devise other schemes if they are convenient. Figure 6.3 illustrates the difference between these two calling methods. In call by value, the argument, $AA, which is stored at memory location $203C, is copied to another location allocated for the parameter. In call by reference, the parameter holds the address of the argument. It is a pointer to the argument.

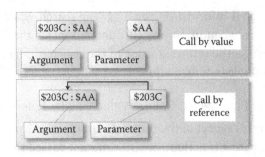

FIGURE 6.3 Call by value copies the argument; call by reference copies the address of the argument.

In C, functions always receive copies of the argument values (call by value). To accomplish call by reference, the caller must pass the address of the argument explicitly. C provides the address of operator (&) to make this possible. If s is a simple variable, &s represents the address of s. Thus, the function call f1(s) passes a copy of the value stored at s (call by value), whereas the function call f2(&s) passes the address of the variable s, resulting in call by reference.

Java uses the same convention; all arguments are passed by value; however, Objects are always referred to be a reference (address) so Objects are passed by reference (by copying their reference to a parameter). C ++ is an example of a language that allows the programmer to choose between call by value or call by reference. A small change in syntax where the function parameters are declared is all that is needed to switch between call by value and call by reference modes.

There are other mechanisms used for passing arguments to parameters. These include call by value return, call by name, and call by result. We will leave those topics for a course in programming languages.

Memory Allocation for Parameters

Besides the option to use call by value or call by reference, the assembly language programmer must also decide where the arguments will be placed (how storage for the parameters will be allocated). It is generally the responsibility of the caller to copy arguments (either values or addresses) into the storage that will be used for the function's parameters.

If there are only a few arguments required by a function, then registers are convenient containers for the parameters. The caller simply loads arguments into specific registers and then calls the function. The function "takes ownership" of the registers (they are now considered parameters) until it is finished with its task.

Passing arrays or large objects by value via one or more registers is not practical as such data will generally not fit in the registers; large objects are therefore often passed by reference for this reason; the address of the array or object might be passed in a register pair.

The second possible location for parameter storage is memory, but where in memory? Once again we are faced with several alternatives. The stack is perhaps the most common choice; arguments are pushed onto the stack just before the call. This is simple way to allocate storage for the arguments, whether they are values or addresses. The function can then access this information inside the stack.

Arguments could also be placed into some other area of memory that the function can access, usually in a contiguous block. This can be at an agreed upon (fixed or static) location, or it might be allocated dynamically and the address of the argument block made available via one of the already mentioned techniques. It is even possible to place the arguments into program memory; in this case they are usually stored immediately after the call statement (sometimes called inline parameters). Special care is required to avoid returning into the middle of this data! In the case of the AVR architecture, program memory is considered read-only, so only constant arguments can be handled in this manner.

Since there is no formal assembly language support for functions, the assembler does not enforce any particular argument passing methodology. It does not provide any means to check that the programmer actually passes the correct number of arguments to a function; it does not check that the arguments are the correct type; it does not even know about arguments! All of the responsibility for ensuring a proper call and return sequence and correct implementation of argument passing falls on the programmer. This also affords a great deal of flexibility, allowing different numbers of arguments for each call and a variety of parameter passing techniques tailored to specific needs. It also creates the opportunity for many subtle errors. The following sections will explore the many possibilities in more detail.

Register Parameters

The following function computes the sum of two signed words and an unsigned byte. The arguments will be passed by value in registers r25:r24, r23:r22, and r20.

PROGRAM 6.1   A Function to Add Three Values, Returning the Sum, Arguments Passed in Registers

```
;Function definition
;word addThree(word a, word b, unsigned byte c)
;define parameter registers and temp register
.def word_aH = r25        ;parameter a
.def word_aL = r24
.def word_bH = r23        ;parameter b
.def word_bL = r22
.def byte_c = r20         ;parameter c
.def temp_zero = r21      ;needed for internal use

addThree:
     push temp_zero            ;save this register to be
                               ;restored later
     ldi temp_zero, 0          ;high byte of 16-bit version of c
     add word_aL, byte_c       ;add c to r25:r24
     adc word_aH, temp_zero
     add word_aL, word_bL      ;add b
     adc word_aH, word_bH      ;return value is now in place
     pop temp_zero             ;restore register
     ret

.undef temp_zero
.undef word_aH
.undef word_aL
.undef word_bH
.undef word_bL
.undef byte_c
```

This function returns the result in r25:r24, overwriting the argument that was passed to the function in that register pair. It also leaves all of the other registers unchanged. Register r21 is used temporarily to hold a zero to facilitate the addition of the unsigned byte (to allow propagation of the carry). The original value in r21 is preserved on the stack, and restored before returning.

In general, registers should be left unchanged by functions. The exception to this rule would be any registers agreed upon for return values, and any registers agreed upon to be scratch registers which can be freely used for temporary results of calculations. The function above also provides symbolic names for registers to aid the programmer in proper use of the parameters. The names are needed only for the function, so the corresponding undef directives appear after the last instruction in the function.

To call this function, arguments must be loaded into the proper registers (parameters) according to the call by value rules. As an illustration, we will use immediate mode addressing to load sample arguments into the registers. The arguments are constants representing the values of the integers to be added. They would likely be defined using the .equ directive. In a real application, it is more likely that the data would be copied into the parameter registers from SRAM, flash, EEPROM, other registers, or from one of the registers in the I/O area.

PROGRAM 6.1 (continued)   Calling a Function to Add Three Values

```
;call function
;word d = addThree(-3, 458, 'a');
;place copies of arguments in registers used as parameters
     ldi r25, high(-3)     ;arg 1 (word)
     ldi r24, low(-3)
     ldi r23, high(458)    ;arg 2 (word)
     ldi r22, low(458)
     ldi r20, 'a'          ;arg 3 (byte)
     rcall addThree

     sts d + 1, r25        ;complete the assignment, r25:r24
                            holds the result
     sts d, r24
```

Versions of this program for both the ATMEGA16A and ATxmega-128A1 have been provided for you. You should run this program in the simulator and observe the register values, SP, and data memory as it executes. Don't forget to add the stack initialization and the space to store d before you run the program. Use the step into command to single step through the program. You should see the bytes $28 and $02 at memory locations $0060 and $0061 ($2000 and $2001 in the XMEGA version). The sum of the three arguments is $0228. Change the argument values and then run the program a second time using the step over command to execute the function call in one simulator step. Perform the calculations by hand and verify the answer.

When arguments are going to be passed to a function in registers, storage for the parameters has already been allocated (registers are always available).

However, the registers designated as parameter locations may already be in use by the calling function. This is, of course, one of the disadvantages to using registers for this purpose. A convenient place to temporarily save register contents is the stack. Adding push instructions to store the necessary registers before the parameters are loaded, and adding the complementary pops to restore registers after the return value is used may be necessary.

The parameters (designated registers) are considered part of the local storage for the function, and it is possible for the function to utilize these registers as needed to perform its task. Although in general, functions should save and restore registers needed for internal computations (except for return values of course), it is reasonable to establish other conventions for any given function. Indeed, if the registers containing copies of the arguments are considered local storage for the function, then the function should be free to change them. If the registers are to be left unchanged, then the function will need to take appropriate steps to comply with this convention. If the function will be changing registers to carry out its task, it will probably push those registers onto the stack and then restore them using pops just before returning.

Stack Parameters

Another common method of passing arguments to a function is to use the stack. This does not require the use of a block of registers and is therefore more flexible. It does however take more time. To pass arguments on the stack, the caller pushes the arguments before calling the function. Parameters are allocated in SRAM; each push allocates (and initializes) a byte of a parameter. Here is the call to the addThree function presented above, modified to use stack-based parameters. Register R16 is used as a conduit to place the arguments on the stack.

PROGRAM 6.2   Calling a Function to Add Three Values, Arguments Passed on Stack

```
;word d = addThree(-3, 458, 'a');
;place copies of arguments on stack as parameters
.def temp = r16
     ldi temp, high(-3)      ;arg 1 to stack
     push temp
     ldi temp, low(-3)
     push temp
     ldi temp, high(458)     ;arg 2 to stack
```

```
    push temp
    ldi temp, low(458)
    push temp
    ldi temp, 'a'      ;arg 3 to stack
    push temp
    rcall addThree_S
    sts d+1, r25      ;complete assignment, r25:r24 holds the
                       result
    sts d, r24
;the stack has 5 extra bytes (the arguments) that need to be
 removed
    pop temp
    pop temp
    pop temp
    pop temp
    pop temp
```

The calling sequence is quite a bit longer because of all of the push instructions. In addition, the final pop instructions are required to restore the stack to its previous condition. The only advantage is that the call requires only the use of one register (to facilitate the push).

Using the stack for parameters requires copying the arguments (values or addresses) into the stack area. This part of the stack then becomes part of the local storage used by the function. The caller allocates and initializes the parameter storage for the function, and after the return is executed, the caller deallocates the parameter storage area. There is a common variation of this that shares the allocation/deallocation responsibilities between the caller and the called function. We will look at this technique in a later section.

One final note regarding pushing a word onto the stack. It is customary (but not required) to push the high byte first. Because of the orientation of the stack, this results in the word being placed on the stack in little-endian order. If you consistently use this convention, you will be less likely to make mistakes when accessing multibyte data. However, the return address is an exception to this convention. The call instruction places the return address on the stack in big-endian order! We will need to know this in the following section. Unless noted otherwise, we will always follow the little-endian convention for data on the stack.

Of course, our original addThree function will not work if the arguments are passed on the stack; the original was written to expect the arguments to be in specific registers. The following version expects arguments to be passed on the stack.

PROGRAM 6.2 (continued)   Function to Add Three Values, Parameters on Stack (ATMEGA16A Version)

```
;word addThree_S(word a, word b, unsigned byte c)
;using stack based parameters
.def word_rvH = r25     ;return value
.def word_rvL = r24
.def word_tempH = r17  ;temp word
.def word_tempL = r16

addThree_S:
     push word_tempH  ;save these registers to be restored later
     push word_tempL
     push YH
     push YL
     in YL, SPL         ;Make Y point to stack top
     in YH, SPH

;parameters are offset into stack by 7 bytes
.set p_offset = 7
     ldd word_rvH, Y+p_offset+3+1  ;copy param a (offset 3)to rv
     ldd word_rvL, Y+p_offset+3
     ldi word_tempH, 0         ;copy param c (offset 0)to word_
                                    temp (0 extend)
     ldd word_tempL, Y+p_offset+0

     add word_rvL, word_tempL          ;add c to retval
     adc word_rvH, word_tempH
     ldd word_tempH, Y+p_offset+1+1   ;copy param b (offset 1)
                                         to rv
     ldd word_tempL, Y+p_offset+1

     add word_rvL, word_tempL          ;add b to r25:r24
     adc word_rvH, word_tempH

     pop YL       ;restore registers
     pop YH
     pop word_tempL
     pop word_tempH
     ret
```

This function saves and restores all of the registers it uses (except the return value registers). Since it has to access parameters that are buried in the stack, it first establishes a pointer (in Y) to the byte just below the top of the stack. This is accomplished by copying the SP into Y. Then Y + 1 is the top of stack. Since the function pushed four bytes, and the return address is two bytes, the offset to the last argument pushed is seven. Thus, parameter c is accessed using indirect addressing with displacement at Y + 7. A symbol is set to this value for use inside the function. Figure 6.4 shows the stack contents after the function establishes the pointer Y; the return address in the stack reflects the ATMEGA16A version of the program.

You should take the time to run one of the two versions of this program provided for you. Observe the stack and register contents as the program executes. You can see the stack by opening the memory window, selecting Data (as the memory to view) and scrolling to the bottom of the window (end of SRAM). The ATxmega128A1 version defines the offset to the parameters to be eight instead of seven. Why is this change needed?

Although this method of parameter allocation seems like a lot of work, it is quite common. It affords the greatest flexibility as it is not limited by the number and size of available registers.

Inline Parameters

Inline parameters are allocated in the middle of the executable code. The call instruction in the program is immediately followed by data allocation, leaving space in program memory for the function parameters. In a typical application, the statements leading up to the call will copy arguments into the parameter area.

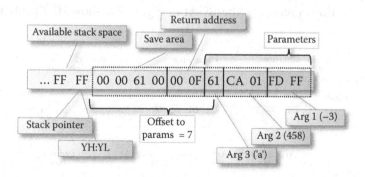

FIGURE 6.4 Stack contents when addThree_S is ready to compute the sum of its three parameters.

Once the call occurs, the function can access the return address (which is on the stack) and use it as a pointer to the parameters. Because the parameters reside in program memory, this technique, when applied to an AVR microcontroller system, can only utilize constant arguments which must be determined at assembly time. The arguments are evaluated by the assembler and placed into the parameter locations inline with the program instructions. Consider the following example of a call to the addThree_I function that uses inline parameters.

PROGRAM 6.3   Calling a Function to Add Three Values Using Inline Parameters

```
;word d = addThree_I(-3, 458, 'a');
;all arguments must be assembly time constants
     rcall addThree_I
;inline parameters go here
     .dw -3
     .dw 458
     .db 'a'
;program continues
     sts d+1, r25      ;complete assignment, r25:r24 holds
                        the result
     sts d, r24
```

Notice that the calling sequence is very simple; in this example, the arguments are already placed in the parameter area by the assembler. If program instructions could be executed from SRAM, arguments would be copied into the memory area immediately after the RCALL instruction by instructions preceding the RCALL. Figure 6.5 shows the contents of

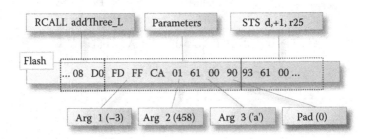

FIGURE 6.5   Program memory showing a function call, inline parameters, and the instruction to be executed upon return.

flash memory from the RCALL to the STS instruction (which is the statement to be executed when the function addThree_I is finished).

When the RCALL is executed, the processor jumps to the function named addThree_I. This action also pushes the "return address" on the stack. This is not actually the correct return address in this instance. It is, however, the address of the parameter block! The following implementation of the addThree_I function gets this address off the stack, and uses it to access the arguments and complete the function task. This is the ATMEGA16A version. The ATxmega128A1 version will need to pop a three byte return address.

PROGRAM 6.3 (continued)   ATMEGA16A Version of addThree_I Illustrating Inline Parameter Access

```
;inline parameter version of the addThree_I function
;assumes 2-byte return address
;word addThree_I(word a, word b, unsigned byte c);
;this function changes Z
addThree_I:
;Load Z with pointer to parameters (in flash)
      pop ZH          ;place return address in Z
      pop ZL          ;remember the return address is big-endian
      add ZL, ZL      ;double the word address to make byte address
      adc ZH, ZH

;define registers for this function
.def return_H = r25
.def return_L = r24

.def temp = r16
      push temp               ;save register for later restore

;copy parameters into registers for calculations
      lpm return_L, Z+        ;return_value = arg1
      lpm return_H, Z+

      lpm temp, Z+            ;return_value += arg2
      add return_L, temp
      lpm temp, Z+
      adc return_H, temp
      lpm temp, Z+           ;return_value += arg3
      add return_L, temp
```

```
    ldi temp, 0              ;use 0 for high byte of agr3
    adc return_H, temp       ;return value ready

;Adjust Z so it is the correct return address
    adiw ZH:ZL, 1    ;move Z past padding byte
    lsr ZH               ;shift Z right to divide by 2 (convert to
                          word address)
    ror ZL


    pop temp            ;restore saved value
    ijmp                ;simulate the ret from the function
.undef temp
.undef return_L
.undef return_H
```

The first four statements of addThree_I copy the return address into Z and double it. The return address is a word address; doubling it converts it to a byte address. After doubling, Z points to the byte address of the first parameter in flash. This byte immediately follows the two bytes of the RCALL instruction.

You should also take note of the fact that the return address is no longer on the stack (we moved it to Z and then doubled it!). We will deal with this problem after we perform the required calculations. Note that the function documentation informs the reader that this function will destroy Z (R31 and R30). Functions should always document registers that will be clobbered.

The next part of the function names registers we will be using and then begins to systematically access and use the five bytes of the parameters. The temp register is preserved on the stack so it can be restored before exiting the function.

The parameters are accessed, using indirect addressing (via Z) with the postincrement option. The first parameter is loaded into the return register pair. As each byte of the subsequent parameters is loaded into the temp register, it is accumulated into the proper byte of the sum. Note the use of ADD and ADC to effect the 16-bit additions. The last parameter (a byte) is zero-extended to a word for its addition.

After all of the parameters have been accessed, the Z register is left pointing to the byte just before the return address; this was a padding byte added to preserve word alignment. One is added to Z to bypass this byte. Now Z contains the return address (in byte pointer form). It is halved to convert it to a word address. Dividing a word by two is easy to do with a right shift and rotate. The high byte (ZH) is shifted right; the least significant bit falls into the carry flag. The subsequent rotate right brings that bit into the most significant bit of ZL.

The final steps are to restore the temp register and use the pointer in Z with an IJMP to return to the instruction following the inline parameter area.

Inline parameters are not commonly used. However they do provide good practice in the use of addressing modes. There are many methods of passing arguments to functions. Assembly language allows the programmer to take complete control of this task.

Innovative stack manipulation (such as removing a return address and using it in a nonstandard way) is not uncommon in assembly language programs. It does require great care and planning. Performing stack operations incorrectly can result in serious errors related to control flow. Messing up the stack often causes RET to return to unexpected locations, often where there is no real code to be executed. You will also experience this undefined behavior if the SP is not properly initialized before calling a function or processing an interrupt.

LOCAL STORAGE

If a function needs local storage in addition to the storage for its parameters, it may be allocated in registers (saving and restoring the original values if necessary) or from SRAM. Local storage is intended to be used only while the function is executing, so it should be allocated as the function is called and deallocated as the function completes its task.

Usually the function manages its local storage internally. That is, local storage is allocated and initialized at the beginning of the function body. The function also includes code to deallocate local storage that must be executed prior to the RET instruction. If a function uses registers that must not be changed, their contents are generally saved on the stack. This is one type of local storage that is needed by nearly every function. When local storage needs exceed what is easily available in registers, additional storage must be allocated from SRAM.

The most common place to allocate local storage from SRAM is in the stack. The portion of the stack used by a function during its lifetime is called a stack frame. The stack frame generally contains the parameters (when the arguments are passed on the stack), return address, and additional local storage required by the function. Allocation and initialization of the stack frame usually begins when the caller pushes arguments onto the stack, allocating parameter storage. The CALL instruction adds the return address to the stack frame. At this point, the function takes over to allocate an additional block for local storage. This is usually accomplished by subtracting a constant from the SP to reserve a block of additional local storage. Local storage is then initialized as needed.

Although the function may also utilize more of the stack for temporary storage (using push and pop instructions during execution), this is usually called temporary storage and is generally not considered part of the stack frame. The stack frame size is unique to each function (varying with different parameter and local storage needs). The stack frame does not (usually) change in size during the function's lifetime.

The following instructions demonstrate the allocation of local storage in the stack. These instructions are commonly found at the beginning of any function that needs more storage than can be easily provided by the registers. Figure 6.6 is a visualization of the stack after local storage has been allocated; the bytes of local storage are not yet initialized and simply contain what was in those locations of the stack.

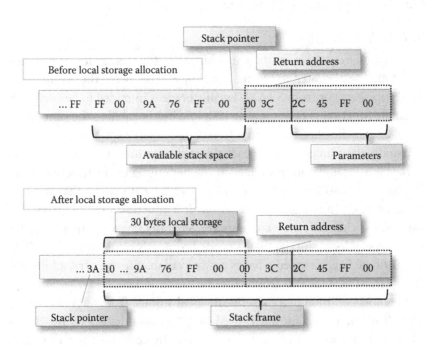

FIGURE 6.6 A stack frame for a function requiring 30 bytes of local storage; before and after local storage is allocated.

```
;-------
;allocate local storage (ATMEGA16A version)
        in r24, SPL        ;get stack pointer
        in r25, SPH
        addiw r25:r24, 30  ;prepare to reserve 30 bytes local storage
        in r16, SREG       ;store interrupt flag state
        cli
        out SPL, r24       ;establish new top of stack
        out SPH, r25
        out SREG, r16      ;restore previous interrupt state


;-------
;allocate local storage (ATxmega128A1 version)
        in r24, CPU_SPL    ;get stack pointer
        in r25, CPU_SPH
        addiw r25:r24, 30  ;prepare to reserve 30 bytes local storage
        out SPL, r25       ;establish new top of stack (write to SPL
                           ;first)
        out SPH, r25
```

The CLI instruction disables interrupts during the modification of the SP. If you are not using interrupts, this is not required. This step is not needed in the XMEGA series; writing to CPU_SPL automatically disables interrupts for four clock cycles or until the next write to I/O memory.

Disabling interrupts prevents possible memory corruption while the SP is being modified. This is a common problem when modification of a shared resource requires a sequence of operations that place the resource in an undefined state while the modification is effected. The SP is a shared resource. It is shared by the currently executing code, and the interrupt system. The SP is being modified, but each byte of the pointer is handled separately. When the first byte is changed, the SP may be invalid until the second byte is also changed. If this sequence is interrupted, the interrupt system will use a corrupt SP, placing the address used to return from the interrupt at an unpredictable location in SRAM, possibly overwriting important data.

This is an important concept, so it is worth restatement. If an interrupt should occur after the high or low bytes of the SP is modified, but before the other byte is changed, half of SP is wrong. In this state, the interrupt will push the return address at an unpredictable memory location, possibly corrupting data. Thus, interrupts must be disabled during the critical section of the SP modification. To ensure that this code works whether interrupts are enabled or not, the current interrupt enable state is saved in R16 and then restored after the critical section. The CLI instruction disables interrupts (if active); the final OUT restores the original interrupt enable state. The global interrupt flag is found in bit 7 of the status register, so saving and restoring the status register in this way will restore the original global interrupt flag setting. Remember that interrupts are disabled in the XMEGA series by a write to CPU_SPL, so the extra instructions to guard the SP access are not needed with this microcontroller.

This snippet of code uses registers 16, 24, and 25. If r16 is used as a scratch register (program wide) and r25:r24 will hold a return value (and not an argument), then these registers can be freely used without saving their original contents. Otherwise, some means of saving and restoring these registers will need to be devised. One option is to push these registers onto the stack before allocating the local storage, and restoring them at the end of the function, after local storage is released, just before the return is executed. This places the register data in the middle of the stack frame, and complicates the overall design of the stack frame allocation and utilization. Nevertheless, this is sometimes necessary.

Part of the stack frame may be used for register storage as just described (incorporating the register data to be saved in the stack frame) or saving registers may be considered a temporary storage need in which case the register values are pushed onto the stack on top of the stack frame after it is allocated. You are free to choose the method that works best in each function. Writing functions that adhere to a single convention, however, will reduce the incidence of programming errors.

Before a function returns to the caller, it must clean up the stack frame. This requires removing any temporary data from the stack, adding the appropriate constant to the SP to release local storage, and executing the return (which removes the return address from the stack). Unfortunately, this still leaves all of the parameters on the stack. Some processors have a special return statement that increment the SP an additional amount during a return to release the parameter area. Unfortunately the AVR processor lacks such an instruction. The intended effect, however, can be simulated by copying the return address into Z, then releasing the entire stack frame (by adding the stack frame size to the SP), and executing an (E)IJMP (to complete the return). The alternative is to pass the responsibility for removing the parameters on to the caller. The caller did allocate the parameter storage when it placed the arguments on the stack before the call, so it seems reasonable to require that it reverse this allocation when it resumes execution following the call. The drawback to this is the parameter removal code must be duplicated at the point of each function call. This sometimes results in larger programs.

Parameter and Local Storage Access in Stack Frames

So far we have ignored the subdivision and initialization of local storage to imitate local variable usage. Local storage is accessed just like the parameters were in Program 6.2: data indirect addressing with displacement. Once local storage is allocated, the beginning of the stack frame is known. It is placed in an appropriate pointer register (Y) to access all parts of the stack frame. Remember that this addressing mode is limited to a 63 byte offset, so it can only be used if the entire stack frame does not exceed 64 bytes. The need for indirect addressing with displacement limits us to the use of Y or Z. Since Z is the only register that can be used for accessing flash, it is common to use Y as a stack frame pointer.

It is also good practice to provide names for the memory locations (containing parameters and local variables) inside the stack frame. The names will simply be symbols whose value is the offset of the variable into the frame. Using symbols provides good documentation and allows changes to the locations of parameters and local variables without having to edit every instruction accessing the data.

Fibonacci Numbers Example

Consider the following example of a function to calculate a Fibonacci number. We will explore an inefficient recursive implementation. The Fibonacci numbers are defined by the following recurrence relation.

```
fib(0) = fib(1) = 1
fib(n) = fib(n - 1) + fib(n - 2)  if  n > 1
```

The function Fibonacci has one argument and will use two local variables. Because the function is recursive, we cannot use registers for local storage (unless we save them on the stack when making recursive calls). Each recursive call requires its own local storage area; you cannot use static memory locations for this purpose. Recursive functions are great examples to illustrate the use of the stack for local storage. Each recursive call gets its own stack frame with local storage separate from that of other invocations. We will assume the parameter, n, is an unsigned byte, and is passed by value on the stack. The argument is therefore pushed on the stack by the caller. The function will return the *n*th Fibonacci number as a 16-bit unsigned word in r25:r24.

Here is how the argument is prepared and the function called. We will assume that r16 is a scratch register throughout this example. The code illustrates a call requesting the fifth Fibonacci number, Fibonacci (5).

PROGRAM 6.4   Fibonacci Numbers Computed by a Recursive Function

```
;word k = fibonacci(5);
    ldi temp, 5
    push temp        ;put argument on stack
    rcall fibonacci
    pop temp         ;discard parameter
;store the result in k
    sts k, r24
    sts k + 1, r25
```

The function code might look like this.

PROGRAM 6.4 (continued)   The Function Prolog, Standard Code to Set Up the Stack Frame (ATMEGA16A Version)

```
;word fibonacci(byte n) return the n-th Fibonacci number
fibonacci:
;allocate local storage
    push YH; save Y for later
    push YL
    in YL, SPL       ;point Y to stack
    in YH, SPH
    sbiw YH:YL, 4    ;reserve 4 bytes local storage
;set new top of stack
    in temp, SREG
    cli        ;ensure atomic operation
    out SPL, YL
    out SPH, YH
    out SREG, temp
```

Note that allocation of local storage could be more efficiently accomplished (in this case) by a sequence of 4 push instructions (using any register value since the allocated space is not actually initialized). Remember the importance of protecting the SP from corruption; writing to SPH:SPL must be an atomic operation. The instructions shown are for the ATMEGA16A. The XMEGA version automatically disables interrupts when CPU_SPL is written. Remember to write to it first when changing the SP.

Also of importance is the fact that Y now points to the beginning of the stack frame (actually the byte just below the stack frame). If we maintain this fixed reference point while the function is active, all of the stack frame can be accessed using indirect addressing with displacement. Because we must (to be polite) preserve the contents of the Y register for the caller, the two bytes, YH and YL, are pushed on the stack before Y is used to manipulate the SP to reserve local storage. The word pointer is pushed high-byte first so the value is stored in little-endian order in the stack. Figure 6.7 shows the stack frame after local storage has been allocated. Both Y and SP point to the same place. While the function executes, SP may change (as the stack is used for temporary storage) but Y will remain fixed.

To calculate the nth Fibonacci number, we will apply the recursive definition. If n is 0 or 1 return 1; otherwise, return the sum of the two previous Fibonacci numbers. The local storage is used to hold the two previous Fibonacci values when a calculation is needed. Local storage starts at offset 1 from Y's reference point. We will return to this diagram after looking at the pseudocode for the function.

```
int fibonacci(int n){
    if (n<2) return 1;
    int a=fibonacci(--n);
    int b=fibonacci(--n);
    return a+b;
}
```

Each step of the algorithm will be completed by a block of assembly language statements. This will result in a lot of memory access that could

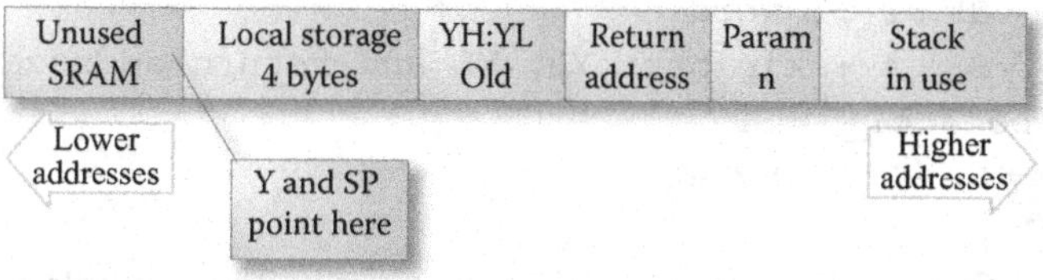

Unused SRAM	Local storage 4 bytes	YH:YL Old	Return address	Param n	Stack in use

Lower addresses ← → Higher addresses

Y and SP point here

FIGURE 6.7 The stack frame for the Fibonacci function.

be avoided if registers were utilized efficiently; the focus of the example is not efficiency, but how local storage is managed by a function.

Stack Frame Naming Conventions

The function has one parameter and two local variables. These are located at specific offsets into the stack frame. Rather than referring to these locations by their numeric offsets (which would be prone to error and difficult to maintain if the layout of the stack frame is changed), it is a good idea to provide names for the offsets. The equate directive is the best way to do this. The stack frame begins at offset one (with respect to Y).

PROGRAM 6.4 (continued) Equate Directives to Define Offsets to Variables in the Stack Frame

```
.equ fibonacci_a = 1 ;local storage (2 words)
.equ fibonacci_b = 3
.equ fibonacci_y_save = 5   ;save area for callers Y
                            ;register
.equ fibonacci_retaddr = 7
.equ fibonacci_n = 9 ;the parameter n (1 byte)
```

Each offset must be manually determined by careful examination of the intended layout of the stack frame. If you insert another local variable, the offsets will need to be recalculated by hand.

You can use the set directive to perform the calculations automatically. An identifier is defined to simulate a location counter; its value is incremented by the size of each variable in the stack frame:

```
;establish stack frame location counter
.set SF = 1
.equ fibonacci_a = SF
.set SF = SF + 2 ;1 word
.equ fibonacci_b = SF
.set SF = SF + 2 ;1 word
.set SF = SF + 4 ;skip over YH, YL and return address
.equ fibonacci_n = SF
.set SF = SF + 1 ;1 byte
```

Each of these techniques gives the same result. The symbols representing local variables and the parameter are defined as the offsets 1, 3, and 9.

The symbol definitions allow local storage to be accessed by name (as an offset to the stack frame base address which must be in Y or Z). For example, the instruction

```
ldd R16, Y + fibonacci_b
```

loads the local variable Fibonacci_b into R16 (assuming Y contains the address of the byte just below the stack frame as described earlier).

Note that the symbols used in the Fibonacci function are prefaced by the function name. This allows the same symbols (a, b, n) to be used in other functions (the function prefix will always be different). Remember that the assembler uses global scope for all symbols. Naming conflicts between functions are avoided by prefixing the function name to the symbols intended to be local to the function.

Function Fibonacci Continued

Establishing Y as a pointer to the function's stack frame provides a reliable way to access the local variables and parameter. Now we can get to the actual function computation. First, the value of the argument n is checked. If it is less than two, we immediately know the answer. The BRLO instruction (branch if lower) tests the result of an unsigned comparison; it branches if R16 contains a lower (smaller) value than the immediate value 2. This is the comparison made in the instruction just before the conditional branch.

PROGRAM 6.4 (continued)   Function Fibonacci Control Structure

```
;if (n < 2) ... else ...
ldd temp, Y + fibonacci_n
cpi temp, 2
brlo fibonacci_return_1  ;base cases for recursion

;The parameter n is 2 or more - use recursion to
 calculate the result
    ;(see details below)
    rjmp fibonacci_return

;For small n (less than 2), the return value is 1
fibonacci_return_1:
    ldi return_L,low(1)
    ldi return_H,high(1)
```

```
;common exit code - clean up stack frame
fibonacci_return:
    ;(see details below)
```

The middle section uses recursive calls to calculate the two previous Fibonacci numbers.

```
;The parameter n is 2 or more - use recursion to calculate the
 result
    ;a = fibonacci (--n)
    ldd temp, Y+fibonacci_n  ;copy n into temp register
    dec temp  ;calculate n-1 and then store back into parameter
    std Y+fibonacci_n, temp  ;param n is now (n-1)

    push temp        ;place argument (n-1) on stack for call
    call fibonacci
    pop temp         ;discard parameter

    std Y+fibonacci_a, return_L      ;store low byte of result
    std Y+fibonacci_a+1, return_H    ;store high byte of result

    ;b = fibonacci (--n)
    ldd temp, Y+fibonacci_n
    dec temp
    std Y+fibonacci_n, temp          ;param n is now (n-2)

    push temp        ;setup the parameter for the call
    call fibonacci
    pop temp         ;discard parameter

    std Y+fibonacci_b, return_L      ;b = return value
    std Y+fibonacci_b+1, return_H

    ;return a+b
    ldd return_L, Y+fibonacci_b      ;setup return value
    ldd return_H, Y+fibonacci_b+1
    ldd temp, Y+fibonacci_a          ;start with low byte
    add return_L, temp
    ldd temp, Y+fibonacci_a+1        ;follow up with high byte
    adc return_H, temp
    rjump fibonacci_return
```

This is the else part of the if $(n < 2)$ statement. It calculates the two previous Fibonacci numbers (storing them in local variables a and b) and then loads the return value register pair with their sum. This section of code is ended with an unconditional jump to the common return code.

The if and else parts both load the return value into R25:24 and then the flow of control joins at the common return code. All that remains is to remove the local variables from the stack, restore registers, and return to the caller.

PROGRAM 6.4 (continued)   The Common Return Code for Function Fibonacci

```
;clean up stack frame, restore registers and return
fibonacci_return:
    in temp, SREG
    cli
    adiw YH:YL, 4 ;calculate end of local storage
    out SPL, YL ;restore stack pointer
    out SPH, YH
    out SREG, temp
    pop YL ;restore Y
    pop YH
    ret ;return to caller (caller must remove argument)
```

Putting this all together you can see the general structure of a robust function call. The caller pushes arguments onto the stack. This action begins the allocation of the function's stack frame, allocating storage for the parameters. The call statement adds the return address to the stack frame. The function immediately saves Y on the stack, and then allocates local storage by decrementing the SP, which has been copied into Y, by the correct amount. This leaves Y pointing at the start of the stack frame (actually it points to the byte just in front of the frame). Cleanup reverses the process, deallocating local storage by adding a constant to SP, restoring Y, and returning to the caller. This leaves the responsibility to remove the arguments from the stack with the caller. You can see this in the program each place function Fibonacci is called (three locations).

Stack Cleanup: Automatic Parameter Removal

When the responsibility for removing parameters from the stack remains with the caller, every place the function is called you must insert duplicate code to effect the parameter removal. With a little trick, the function can remove the parameters from the stack before returning, making the calling sequence a little simpler. This technique will eliminate the need to follow each function call with parameter removal details.

The following modified exit routine performs the return and finishes the stack cleanup by also removing the parameters. It does need to use

R16, Z, and X, so this would need to be understood by all callers; it would be the caller's responsibility to save these registers (if necessary) before making a call to a function that utilizes this technique. It is not unusual to require the function and the caller to share the responsibility to save some registers. The expectations just need to be clearly understood.

PROGRAM 6.4 (continued) **Alternate Version of the Common Exit Code, Taking Over the Responsibility of Parameter Deallocation from the Caller**

```
;clean up entire stack frame - modified - destroys R16, X, and Z
fibonacci_return:
     ;remember return address is big-endian
     ldd ZH, Y + fibonacci_return_address (must be defined)
     ldd ZL, Y + fibonacci_return_address + 1
     ldd XL, Y + fibonacci_Y_save (must be defined)
     ldd XH, Y + fibonacci_Y_save + 1
     in r16, SREG
     cli
     adiw YH:YL, 4 + 2 + 2 + 1 ;local + Y + ret_addr + arguments
     out SPL, YL ;output new stack pointer
     out SPH, YH
     movw YH:YL, XH:XL ;restores Y to original value
     out SREG, r16
     ijmp        ;return to caller using an indirect jump
```

The X register is used to set the SP to the end of the stack frame after copying the return address into Z and the saved Y register into X (X is used temporarily until Y is done being used as the stack frame pointer). The stack frame is removed completely by adding the size of the stack frame to the value that is in Y. This address is placed into SP effecting the deallocation. The return address has also been removed from the stack, so the IJMP instruction completes the return to the caller. Note that this code will not work correctly if the return address is three bytes instead of two. This is only a problem in processors with a 22-bit PC (such as the ATxmega128A1).

Preprocessor Macros

The use of offsets to access the stack frame is a necessity, but the notation is still a little cumbersome. Having to write Y + local_a obscures the fact that you are simply accessing a variable named local_a; the Y+ is superfluous (but necessary for proper operation). Preprocessor macros can be used to further simplify this notation and allow local storage to be accessed as simply as a variable stored in static storage. The macro command needed is #define.

```
#define sym_name sym_value
```

This preprocessor macro defines the symbol *sym_name* to represent *sym_value*. Values in this context are simply strings (and may include spaces); a simple string substitution takes place throughout the program before it is assembled, names defined by these #define macros are replaced by their values.

Using this preprocessor macro, local variables and parameters can all be defined as simple variable names representing the string consisting of the pointer register and offset.

```
;layout 2 words in local storage and
;set the location of the parameter
#define fibonacci_a Y + 1 //1 word local
#define fibonacci_b Y + 3 //1 word local
#define fibonacci_n Y + 9 //the parameter
```

This allows the load and store indirect with displacement to be written very succinctly. The pointer register and displacement are completely represented by the defined symbol.

```
ldd temp, fibonacci_n
std fibonacci_b, temp
```

You must still use the instruction mnemonic for indirect with displacement addressing mode, but the address information is easily expressed by a single symbol. You can even use a displacement to access an adjacent byte.

```
ldd temp, fibonacci_b + 1
```

This is changed to the following before it is assembled:

```
ldd temp, Y + 3 + 1
```

The assembler correctly evaluates the $3 + 1$ expression and inserts the offset of 4 into the assembled instruction.

Symbols defined in this way can be undefined by the undef macro:

```
#undef fibonacci_n
```

The use of #define to represent the pointer register and displacement might be discouraged since the syntax obscures the fact that indirect addressing with displacement is being used. Of course, the operation mnemonic specifies this is the case, but the argument does not clearly indicate which pointer the displacement is added to. Nevertheless, the utter simplicity makes it a compelling technique, especially in functions where the use of Y as a pointer to the stack frame might be a well-established convention.

AUXILIARY DATA STACK (SOFTWARE STACK)

The fact that the return address is in the middle of the stack frame and the lack of a specialized RET instruction that can automatically add a constant to the SP as part of the return action makes it awkward for functions to remove parameters before returning. The sample code presented above is complicated, and destroys five registers (temp, X, and Z) in the process. On the other hand, forcing the caller to remove the parameters often requires a lot of duplicate code, and forces the caller to manage cleanup details when it should be processing the results of the function call. This awkwardness and additional complexity can be avoided through the use of an auxiliary stack.

The stack maintained by the SP (and used by the stack related instructions) is referred to as the hardware stack. We will continue to use it to for return addresses and temporary storage for registers. To facilitate parameter allocation and deallocation, we will create a second stack. The second stack is referred to as the data stack. It will be used for stack frames (without the return address since this is already on the hardware stack). Stack frames will hold parameters and local storage. One of the registers Y or Z must be used for the data SP because we want to take advantage of indirect addressing with displacement (and X does not support the displacement option). Since Z is the only register that can access program memory, it is customary to set Y aside as the pointer to the data stack. This leaves X and Z free to be used for indirect addressing as the application needs them.

The data stack will have to share SRAM with the hardware stack. Deciding how much space to allocate to each is nontrivial, however, the hardware stack will only need to be large enough to handle return addresses for the most deeply nested function calls, plus incidental over-head for temporary storage and memory needed by interrupt handlers. Of course, if recursive functions are used, the stack will need to be much larger to allow for the deepest expected levels of recursion.

With two stacks, SRAM is usually divided into four areas. Static stor-age, the heap, the data stack, and the hardware stack. Figure 6.8 illustrates this arrangement. The expected size of the hardware stack is used to deter-mine the beginning (bottom) of the data stack. The following statements initialize both stacks:

```
.equ HSTACK_MAXSIZE = 64
;initialize hardware stack pointer
ldi r16, low(RAMEND)
out SPL, R16
ldi r16, high(RAMEND)
out SPH, r16
;initialize data stack pointer
ldi YH, high(RAMEND-HSTACK_MAXSIZE + 1)
ldi YL, low(RAMEND-HSTACK_MAXSIZE + 1)
```

Figure 6.8 shows freshly initialized stacks. SP points to the last byte of SRAM, where the first push will store its data. The SP is decremented after it is used to determine the location of the pushed data. Y points to the byte just past the end of the data stack. It will be decremented before it is used to determine the address of the pushed byte. We will use the ST instruc-tion with predecrement to effect a push onto the data stack.

Keep in mind that SP points to the next available byte on the hardware stack. Y, the data SP, points to the top byte on this stack.

There is another advantage to having Y point to the actual top of stack. Since Y will point directly at the byte on the top of the stack data, and this

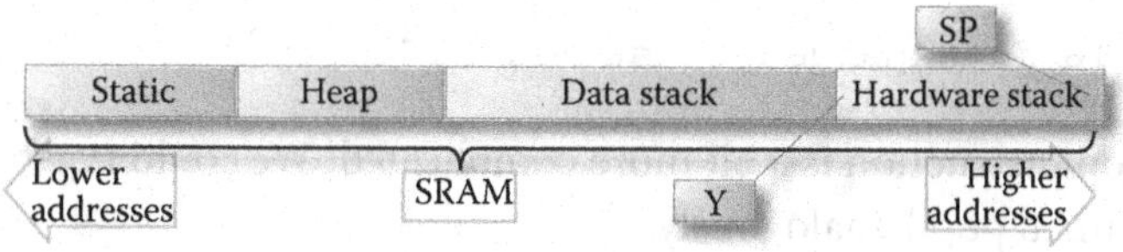

FIGURE 6.8 The data stack and hardware stack areas in SRAM.

will be the first byte of a stack frame, all of the 64 offsets allowed in indirect-offset addressing are used, including an offset of 0.

Now that the stacks are initialized, we need to see how we can store and retrieve data in the stacks. Of course, we will continue to use push and pop for the hardware stack. We already saw how to use indirect addressing with displacement to address bytes within the hardware stack. To implement the push and pop operations in our data stack, we will use the indirect mode instructions LD and ST.

To push a byte in a register onto the data stack, use `st -Y, Rr`

To pop a byte from the data stack into a register, use `ld Rd, Y+`

To access a byte at displacement d within the stack, use `ldd Rd, Y + d` or `std Y + d, Rr`

Macros for the Data Stack

The instructions used to implement push and pop operations in the data stack do not look like push and pop instructions. We can correct this through the use of a macro. Consider the following preprocessor macro:

```
#define pushd st -Y,
```

Once this is macro is defined you can forget about writing

```
st -Y, R16
```

when you intend to push R16 onto the data stack. Instead you will use the macro, indicating the push in a very natural way.

```
pushd R16
```

The preprocessor replaces *pushd* with *st -Y*, and the assembler assembles this (with the R16 following it) as the actual intended instruction. Note that the register that is written after the macro name is still there on the line; it becomes the rest of the actual instruction.

```
pushd r16 is expanded to st -Y, r16
```

The pop instruction is a bit more complicated. We could try to define a macro named popd analogously.

```
#define popd ld Y+,
```

Unfortunately, this would not give the desired result. A popd instruction

```
popd R16
```

would be expanded to

```
ld Y+, R16
```

Unfortunately, the operands are in the wrong order. We need the macro to insert the register into the middle of the expansion. Fortunately, the define macro supports the use of arguments, but parentheses will need to be used when invoking the macro. For consistency, both macros should be written using the same format. Here are the new macros and sample uses.

```
#define pushd(Rr) st -Y, Rr
#define popd(Rd) ld Rd, Y+
...
pushd(R21)
popd(R0)
```

The assembler also has its own macro facility that is independent of the preprocessor macros just described. Assembly language macros are defined using an assembler directive in a block structure. Here are the pushd and popd definitions using this type of macro. These definitions should be placed at the top of the source file. Assembler macros must be defined before they are used (must appear above the invocations in the source file). This is also required for preprocessor macros.

```
.macro pushd
st -Y, @0
.endmacro

.macro popd
ld @0, Y+
.endmacro
```

The @0 represents the first (and in this case, only) argument to the macro. Macros defined in this way are expanded when used later in the source code. The expansion is done by the assembler, not a preprocessor. The arguments are written after the name of the macro, separated by commas. This follows the same syntax used with instruction mnemonics, making this type of macro easy to use in assembly language programs. A macro essentially expands the assembly language instructions. Simple text substitution is used when the macro is expanded. Here are examples of macro invocations.

```
pushd R21
popd temp
```

The arguments R21 and temp replace the @0 as each macro is expanded. The actual code that is assembled is the ST and LD instruction with the appropriate substitution for @0.

```
st -Y, R21
ld temp, Y+
```

Assembler macros allow a single command to be expanded to a sequence of instructions. As you can see, this type of macro preserves the usual assembly language notation, and should be preferred in most cases where an argument must be passed to the macro. We will look into the macro facility of the assembler again.

Fibonacci with Data Stack

Here is the entire Fibonacci function, rewritten to use the two stack model. No macros are used so the code explicitly illustrates the use of indirect addressing with displacement, and indirect addressing with predecrement and postincrement as the data stack is accessed and manipulated. We start with the calling sequence. The argument must be pushed onto the data stack, not the hardware stack. Remember that Y and SP must both be initialized prior to the execution of these instructions.

PROGRAM 6.5 **The Fibonacci Program Rewritten to Use an Auxiliary Data Stack for Stack Frames**

```
;Fibonacci - ATMEGA16A version

;k = fibonacci(5);
    ldi temp, 5
    st -Y, temp ;put argument on stack
    rcall fibonacci
```

```
;function removes the argument... so just store the result in k
    sts k, return_L
    sts k+1, return_H
    rjmp PC

;The stack frame will contain 2 words of local storage and one
; parameter, a byte. The offsets are ...
.equ fibonacci_a=0 ;1 word
.equ fibonacci_b=2 ;1 word
.equ fibonacci_n=4 ;the parameter (byte)
.set local_size=4
.set param_size=1
.set frame_size=local_size+param_size

fibonacci:
;allocate local storage
sbiw YH:YL,local_size  ;Y is now the stack frame pointer

;if (n<2) return 1
ldd temp, Y+fibonacci_n
cpi temp, 2
brlo fibonacci_return_1

;this section computes the previous two fibonacci
;numbers and then adds them

    ;a=fibonacci(--n)
    ldd temp, Y+fibonacci_n
    dec temp
    std Y+fibonacci_n, R16 ;complete the side effect of --n
    st -Y, temp ;put argument on stack
    call fibonacci
    std Y+fibonacci_a, return_L ;store low byte of result
    std Y+fibonacci_a+1, return_H ;store high byte of result

    ;b=fibonacci(--n)
    ldd temp, Y+fibonacci_n
    dec temp
    std Y+fibonacci_n, R16 ;complete the side effect of --n
    st -Y, temp ;put argument on stack
    call fibonacci
    std Y+fibonacci_b, return_L ;store low byte of result
    std Y+fibonacci_b+1, return_H ;store high byte of result
```

```
    ;return a+b
    ldd return_L, Y+fibonacci_b ;get a into return registers
    and add b
    ldd return_H, Y+fibonacci_b+1
    ldd temp, Y+fibonacci_a ;start with low byte
    add return_L, temp
    ldd temp, Y+fibonacci_a+1  ;follow up with high byte
    adc return_H, temp
    rjmp fibonacci_return
;for small n, the return value is 1
fibonacci_return_1:
    ldi return_H,high(1)
    ldi return_L,low(1)

;clean up stack frame
fibonacci_return:
    adiw YH:YL,frame_size ;Removes local storage and parameter
    ret
```

Notice how much cleaner this approach is with respect to the stack frame allocation and deallocation. There is no need to worry about interrupts and manual manipulation of SP. The hardware stack is readily available for temporary register storage if needed, and the local data is arranged in sequential locations, without the intervening return address.

CALL BY REFERENCE EXAMPLE

So far, the examples have only illustrated call by value. The next example uses call by reference. The function etyb must reverse the bits in the byte argument. The byte to be reversed is passed by reference on the data stack. This means that the address of the byte is pushed onto the stack. The address is a word; word data is generally stored in little-endian order, so the high byte will be pushed first. The following code shows how to call the function passing (by reference) a byte in the data space. It is presumed these data locations have been initialized elsewhere in the program. Macros to access the data stack are also illustrated in this example.

PROGRAM 6.6   Calling Sequence for a Function to Reverse a Byte which is Passed by Reference

```
.dseg
theByte:        .byte 1         ;the byte to be reversed
```

```
.cseg
;theByte = readByte();
rcall readByte
sts theByte, return_L

reverse:

;etyb(&theByte) - pass the address of the variable to the function
ldi temp, high(theByte)
pushd temp
ldi temp, low(theByte)
pushd temp
rcall etyb
;the function stores directly into the argument's storage space
```

The main program reads a byte into a variable in SRAM. The calling sequence for the reverse byte function requires the address of the argument to be pushed on the data stack. The function will use this address to access the original argument value. It will also use this address to store the reversed byte into the same memory location.

PROGRAM 6.6 (continued)   The Reverse Byte Function Illustrating Call by Reference

```
;void etyb(byte * a){a = (a with bits reversed)}
.equ etyb_a_ptr = 0 ;Offset to pointer parameter in the stack frame
.set framesize = 2        ;stack frame is just the pointer

.def b = r19      ;byte being reversed
.def bitcount = r20       ;counter for bits to be reversed
.def newb = r21 ;the reversed byte

etyb:
push XL           ;save registers used in this function
push XH
push b
push bitcount
push newb

;access argument by reference
ldlocalptr X, etyb_a_ptr       ;set X to point to the argument
ld b, X           ;access the actual byte via its address
```

```
;perform the reversal
ldi bitcount, 8          ;number of bits to reverse
;newb is used to receive the bits in reverse order
etyb_nextBit:
     lsr b ;first bit out is the one on the right
     rol newb ;it becomes first in (on right)
     dec bitcount
     brne etyb_nextBit  ;repeat 8 times


;store result to actual argument location
st X, newb


;exit code
adiw YH:YL,framesize ;Removes argument (address; 1 word)
pop newb ;restore registers
pop bitcount
pop b
pop XH
pop XL
ret
.undef newb
.undef bitcount
.undef b
```

The function's stack frame consists of a single word containing the address of the actual argument. The ldlocalptr macro is used to load the pointer parameter into the XH:XL pair. This macro is defined as follows:

```
;ldlocalptr - load pointer from local storage in data stack to
  @0L:@0H
;usage: ldlocalptr R, offset (R is X or Z)
.macro ldlocalptr
ldd @0L, Y + @1
ldd @0H, Y + @1 + 1
.endm
```

Once the pointer is loaded into X, indirect addressing is used again to load the byte (the argument) into a register to be reversed. When the reversal is complete, the new byte is stored back to the same location using the address still in X. Call by reference allows the function to modify the argument in its original location.

Take time to run this program in the simulator and on the actual hardware. A version is provided for the STK-500 platform and the ATMEGA16A and the XPLAIN board.

EXERCISES

1. (ATMEGA16A) Show how to initialize the SP so the first item pushed onto the stack will be located at address $00FF. What will be in SPL after the first push occurs? (ATxmega128A1) Show how to initialize the SP so the first item pushed onto the stack will be located at address $20FF. What will be in CPU_SPL after the first push occurs?

2. Write a sequence of instructions to push the word stored in ZH:ZL onto the stack. Design your solution so the word is stored in little-endian order in SRAM.

3. Rewrite the swap sequence

```
push  r5
mov   r5, r6
pop   r6
```

to accomplish the task using only push and pop instructions. How many clock cycles does each solution require?

4. Write a sequence of instructions to interchange the top two bytes on the stack. You may assume there are at least two bytes on the stack.

5. Write a sequence of instructions to add one to the value on the top of the stack. The new top of stack value should be one more than the old top of stack value when finished. You should assume there is a byte on the stack.

6. Write a sequence of instructions to add the top two bytes of the stack (removing them) and then push the result byte.

7. Write an instruction that could be used to call a function located at address $003C. This instruction should work no matter where it is located in flash.

8. Write a sequence of instructions to call a function located at address $003C using indirect addressing. This sequence should work no matter where it is located in program memory.

9. The address of a function has been stored as a word in SRAM. The label faddr represents the address of this word. Write a sequence of instructions to call the function. The word is stored in little-endian order, as expected.

10. When the return address is pushed onto the stack by a call instruction, its two/three bytes are at adjacent memory

locations. Is the address stored in memory in big-endian or little-endian order?

11. (ATMEGA16A) In an ATmega16A, if an RCALL instruction is fetched from address $014C and executed, what byte is on the top of the stack just after the call? What byte is next on the stack? (ATxmega128A1) In an ATxmega128A1, if an RCALL instruction is fetched from address $00014C and executed, what byte is on the top of the stack just after the call? What byte is next on the stack?

12. What difficulty would be encountered if you wrote a function to add two bytes passed on the stack using the strategy of simply popping the top two bytes off the stack and then pushing their sum?

13. Write a function named average that will accept two unsigned bytes (passed by value) and return the average of the bytes. Remember that you can divide by two without actually dividing. You should return the average in R24. The function expects the arguments to be passed in R25 and R24.

14. In the previous problem, if the bytes being averaged overflow when the sum is found, using LSR to divide by two will give the wrong answer. Would ROR be a better choice? Trace the calculation using LSR and again using ROR following the ADD of the two bytes $F7 and $E5 to illustrate the incorrect and correct answers.

15. Write the instructions necessary to accomplish the following assignment statement (using the average function defined above):

```
byte avg3 = average (average (5, 27), 29);
```

This will require two function calls; the first call is to calculate the average of 5 and 27. The next call should calculate the average of the result of the previous call and the number 29. Assume the following allocation in SRAM:

```
avg3: .byte 1
```

16. If the function average is designed to use inline parameters (instead of register parameters), then it is straightforward to implement a call such as

```
average (5, 27);
```

but implementation of a call that looks like this

```
average(average(5, 27), 29);
```

would not be possible. Explain why not.

In the following exercises, the stack referred to is the AVR stack represented by the SP I/O register.

17. If a caller pushes an argument on the stack, then makes the call to a function, can the function simply pop the argument into a register to access it? Explain why this is not possible, or why it would be difficult.

18. To pass an argument by reference, the argument must be located somewhere in memory. Suppose the byte at label sss (in SRAM) is to be passed by reference to the function comp. Let us assume comp expects the address of its only argument to be in ZH:ZL (a register parameter). Write the statements leading up to (and including) the call: comp(&sss).

19. The function comp (described in the previous problem) is supposed to complement its argument. Write this function. It should copy the actual argument into a free register (you may need to use push to save the original register contents), complement it, and then store it back into its original location. Be sure to restore the register before returning to the caller.

20. If comp (see above) is written using stack parameters, write the statements leading up to (and including) the call: comp(&sss). You should ensure that the argument is stored in little-endian order on the stack.

21. If comp (see above) is written using an inline parameter, write the statements necessary to implement the call and parameter definition: comp(&sss);

22. A certain function takes one argument (a word, located on the stack) and needs four local variables. Their names are a, b, c, and d. The types are byte, word, doubleword, and byte respectively. Draw a diagram showing the intended stack frame layout (label the return address, Y's save area, each local variable, and the parameter which should be named e) and indicate where Y will be pointing after the stack frame is allocated. Write .equ directives representing the total size of local storage and the offsets to each local variable and parameter (assume the return address is 2 bytes).

23. Continue the previous problem by writing the code to save Y and then allocate space on the stack for the local variables. At the conclusion of the sequence, Y should be pointing to the same location as SP.

24. Continue the previous problem by adding code to initialize a to 0, c to –1, and d to the ASCII code for the percent (%) sign. Use appropriate literals and byte functions.

25. Continue the previous problem by adding code to copy the parameter e into the local variable b. The argument is passed by value.

26. Consider the use of .set to define symbols representing offsets in the stack frame for the fibonacci function (Program 6.4):

```
.set  S = 1
.equ  fibonacci_a = SF
.set  SF = SF + 2  ;1 word
(and so on)
```

Write a single .equ directive that would come at the end of these statements to define the symbol fibonacci _ framesize representing the size of the stack frame (in bytes). Design your answer so the addition of a parameter or local variable will be automatically accounted for in the calculations.

27. Write statements to define the two symbols used in the Fibonacci function's (Program 6.4, alternate cleanup) stack cleanup code assuming a 2-byte return address:

```
fibonacci_return_address and
fibonacci_Y_save.
```

28. Rewrite the stack cleanup section of fibonacci (Program 6.4, alternate cleanup) so R16 is not needed and X's original value is preserved. Assume a 2-byte return address. Follow this outline:

a. Copy Y into Z and use Z as the stack frame pointer for the cleanup operation. This frees Y for temporary usage.

b. Copy the return address from its location within the stack frame to the last two bytes of the stack frame (overwriting parameters).

c. Save the status register in the stack frame to the byte just below the return address.

d. Restore Y from the stack frame.

e. Make SP point to the saved status register. Z is now free for temporary usage.

f. Restore the status flags (from the byte now on the top of the stack).

g. Execute the return.

The following questions refer to a properly initialized data stack with Y pointing to the top value (if any).

29. Assume the preprocessor macro:

```
#define fibonacci_a Y + 1
```

What will `fibonacci_a + 1` represent (tell its expanded value)? If Y is appropriately positioned to access the stack frame in the data stack, write instructions to load the word value `fibonacci_a` into `R25:R24`. Be sure to order the bytes correctly.

30. When pushing a word onto the data stack, it is customary to place it in memory in little-endian order. Illustrate the proper way to do this by writing instructions to "push" `XH:XL` on the data stack. Do not use any macros in your answer.

31. a. Write a preprocessor macro that requires an integer argument. The result is an expression representing 2 raised to that power. For example, `pow(3)` would expand to the parenthesized expression `(1<<3)`.

    b. What values do `pow(pow(0))` and `pow(pow(1))` represent?

    c. What value would be loaded into R16 by the statement

```
ldi  R16,  pow(2)|pow(6)|pow(7)
```
(Give your answer in binary)?

32. Write a preprocessor macro that will expand to an instruction to load a number representing a power of 2 into a register. For example,

```
ldipow2(R16, 3)
```

should expand to

```
ldi R16, (1<<3)
```

You may use the previous macro in your solution.

33. Write an assembly language macro that will expand to an instruction to load a number representing a power of 2 into a register. For example,

```
ldip2      R16,   3
```

should expand to

```
ldi  R16,    (1<<3)
```

You need to use @0 and @1 for the two parameters in the macro definition.

34. Write an assembly language macro definition named pushxy that will expand to the instructions required to push the four registers (xh, xl, yh, and yl) onto the hardware stack. Write another macro named popxy that will restore these registers if previously pushxy'd

35. Write a function to initialize a block of bytes in SRAM to a particular value. The function is passed the starting address, the number of bytes, and the byte value used for initialization. The starting address is passed in X, R16 holds the number of bytes (up to 255), and R17 holds the byte to be written into the block.

36. Write a function to copy a string from flash to SRAM. The function is passed two 16-bit addresses on the data stack. One is the word address of a null-terminated string in flash; this is pushed first, high byte then low byte. The other address is the byte address of a block of bytes in SRAM large enough to receive the characters of the string. This address is also pushed high byte first. The fact that the string is null-terminated means that you should copy characters up to and including the first byte holding the value $00.

37. Functions can be passed a variable number of arguments. Write a function that can calculate the maximum of any group of bytes. This function is passed an arbitrary number of unsigned byte values on the data stack. The last value pushed on the stack is the number of bytes to be processed (up to 255). Return the largest (assuming unsigned) byte from the set in R24. The data stack should be emptied before returning. You can determine the larger of two bytes after a comparison (cp) by using the brlo (branch if the first is lower than the second) or brsh (branch if the first is the same or higher than the second).

PROGRAMMING EXERCISES

1. Write a program to calculate a postfix expression using the stack. The expression will include only addition and subtraction operations and single digit BCD values. Addition is indicated by " + ," subtraction by " − ," and the end of the expression by "$." You will do all computations using 8-bit 2's complement format. Process each expression left to right, pushing values on the stack and replacing operands by the result of the operation

when an operation is encountered. Pop the final result into R0, display it on the LEDs (in binary of course) and halt. The following example should clarify the process:

```
expression .db 3,9,4,6,'+','-',2,'-','+','$'
```

push 3, 9, 4, 6 (stack: 6 4 9 3)
pop 6 and 4, add, push 10   (stack: 10 9 3)
pop 10 and 9, subtract, push −1   (stack: −1 3)
push 2   (stack: 2 −1 3)
pop 2 and −1, subtract, push −3   (stack: −3 3)
pop −3 and 3, add, push 0   (stack: 0)
pop the result (0) into register 0, display, and stop

2. Write a macro addwords that will allow you to add two words stored in SRAM and store the result back to SRAM. The macro should take the names of the three memory locations: addwords c, a, b would perform the assignment: c = a + b; Include a test program that stores some values into variables in SRAM and then adds different ones together. Use the simulator to test.

3. Write a function that uses call-by-reference to interchange the contents of two memory locations. The memory locations are doublewords. The arguments are passed on the data stack. The function must swap the data at the two SRAM locations. Include a test application to swap several doublewords and observe the progress using the simulator.

4. Write a function that uses call-by-reference to interchange the contents of two memory locations. The memory locations are doublewords. The arguments are passed using inline parameters. The function must swap the data at the two SRAM locations. Include a test application to swap several doublewords and observe the progress using the simulator.

5. Write a function to multiply a word and a byte (unsigned data). The arguments are passed on the data stack. The return value, a word, is left in R25:R24. The multiplication algorithm is repeated addition:

```
word multiply(byte n, word a){
 word answer = 0;
 while (n-- > 0) answer += a;
 return answer;
}
```

Define and use a macro that takes four arguments, the registers holding the two words: addw ah, al, bh, bl.

6. Write a program to calculate *n*-factorial. It must use a factorial function that is recursive. Pass all arguments on the data stack. Your factorial function should use the multiply function designed in the previous exercise. Your program should accept a value for *n* from the switches, *n* is restricted to the range 1 through 8. Button 0 should calculate 1 factorial; button 1 should calculate 2 factorial, and so on. Display the answer on the LEDs, high byte, then low byte. A press of any button should toggle between the bytes.

CHAPTER 7

Serial Communications Using the Universal Synchronous and Asynchronous Serial Receiver and Transmitter

THE USART INCLUDED IN the ATmega16A and ATxmega128A1 provides a convenient way to communicate serially with other devices. This I/O unit is controlled through a collection of I/O registers. Before delving into the details of this device, we must cover the principles of serial communication commonly used with an RS-232 interface.

RS-232

RS-232 is a standard developed by the Electronics Industry Alliance. It specifies the physical properties of an interface designed to support serial communications between two devices. The devices are classified as either DTE (data terminal equipment) or DCE (data communications equipment). In its early uses, the DCE device was typically a modem and the

FIGURE 7.1   A typical DE-9 male connector on a serial cable.

DTE was a terminal. The RS-232 specifications include the electronic signaling levels, sizes and shapes of the connectors as well as pin assignments, and the functions of the circuits included in the interface.

The simplest subsystem of the RS-232 standard provides the basic receive–transmit function through a subset of the many possible connections. It is commonly referred to as the PC Signal Set, because it was used in many of the early IBM PC/AT and compatible computers. The proper name for this standard is EIA/TIA-574. In this standard, the personal computer acts as the DTE and provides a DB-9 (actually a DE-9, but commonly called DB-9) male connector to which a cable is attached (Figure 7.1).

Connections between a DTE and DCE device is accomplished with a straight through cable connecting pin x to pin x. Table 7.1 names the important pins for this type of communication. When connecting two DTE devices directly, a null-modem cable is used. This cable crosses the

TABLE 7.1   Pin Assignments for PC Signal Set and DE-9 Connectors

Equipment Type	Pin 2	Pin 3	Pin 5
DTE	Transmit Data (TD)	Receive Data (RD)	Ground (G)
DCE	Receive Data (RD)	Transmit Data (TD)	Ground (G)

transmit and receive lines (and related signals) so the transmit pin on one end corresponds to the receive pin on the opposite end. The simplest receive–transmit connection requires only three wires joining TD and RD, RD and TD, and the grounds.

The RS-232 standard does not specify how communications are to take place. These details are left up to the user of the RS-232 connection. Many AVR microcontrollers include a standard communication component called a USART. This I/O device will handle the low-level details of sending and receiving signals across the serial line. Many serial devices share the protocol used by this system. Our programs can control this I/O device by exchanging messages in its control registers.

SERIAL COMMUNICATION BASICS

Before looking at the control details of the USART, it is important to understand how the transmission of serial data is commonly accomplished by this type of device. This is necessary in order to understand the commands the USART responds to. We will describe the more common asynchronous mode of transmission. This means that the two devices do not share a clock signal, and need to take special measures to stay in sync with each other.

Using the RS-232 interface, transmission and reception of data can occur simultaneously; separate wires are used for each direction. Consider the communication between a DTE and DCE device with a typical straight through cable shown in Figure 7.2. The DTE device's transmitter asserts a signal on its TD connection (pin 2 of a DE-9). The serial cable connects

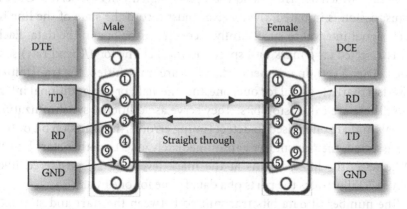

FIGURE 7.2   Straight through cable joining DTE and DCE devices via DE-9 connectors.

this to pin 2 of the DE-9 at the DCE end. This is the receiver's RD connection; the receiver senses the state of the line. The DCE's transmitter can simultaneously assert data to be transmitted in the opposite direction on its TD output (pin 3). This signal, carried across the serial cable to pin 3 of the DE-9 at the DTE device, is sensed by the receiver in the DTE via its RD input.

Mark and Space

The RS-232 specifications provide for two possible signals on the transmit lines: +12 V and −12 V. The +12 V signal is named space; the −12 V signal is named mark. The space signal corresponds to a zero (0); a mark corresponds to a one (1).

When no transmission is taking place, the TD pin is asserted with the mark signal (1 or −12 V). This is considered the idle state of the line. As long as this line is in an idle state the receiver does nothing but wait for the beginning of a transmission.

Serial Data Frame

When data is ready to be sent, the transmitter asserts a space (0) on the TD line. This is called a start bit. This is a synchronization signal telling the receiver that a series of data bits will follow. The 0/1 data values (individual bits of the binary data) will be asserted sequentially by the transmitter, each in turn and each for a specific time interval. The time interval each bit value is asserted varies according to the baud rate; the baud rate is the number of signal intervals in a second. The receiver will need to know the baud rate, which determines how long each signal will be asserted. Once a transmission is initiated, the receiver must record the state of the line in each signal interval to successfully reconstruct the bits in the data. Each bit is asserted (as a mark or a space) on the TD line for 1/(baud rate) seconds. After a certain number of data bits are transmitted, the transmitter asserts a mark (1) signal for one, one and one-half, or two additional intervals. These are called stop bits. They serve as additional synchronization signals and are often used to detect timing errors. After the stop bit or bits are asserted, the transmitter can immediately assert another start bit (0). Otherwise, the line remains at the mark level and is considered idle. Figure 7.3 illustrates the parts of a data frame for one byte.

The number of data bits transmitted between the start and stop bits can vary. The USART built into the AVR can set this to a number from 5 through 9. Keeping the number of data bits small allows the two devices

FIGURE 7.3   A serial data frame with eight data bits and one stop bit.

to stay in synchronization. If there are too many data bits, the two device's clocks may drift apart, resulting in corrupted data. Remember that the transmitter and receiver synchronize on each start bit, and then their clocks run asynchronously, hence the term asynchronous communication mode.

Serial communication can also take place in what is called synchronous mode. In synchronous mode, the transmitter supplies a copy of its clock signal to the receiver in the opposite device. Sharing a clock signal allows the receiver to stay in complete synchronization with the transmitter so there is no need for limiting the number of data bits or for using stop bits.

The AVR USART module uses a variation of this synchronous communication scheme, utilizing a single shared clock line. The clock signal is controlled by one USART operating in master mode. The other USART operates in slave mode, using the same clock signal as the master.

Other than the shared clock signal, and a few other configuration issues, the rest of the AVR USART functionality remains the same. The clock connection is not part of the PC Signal Set, and is therefore not available via a standard DE-9 connector. We will not cover the synchronous serial communication mode any further.

In addition to the 5–9 data bits, the USART can transmit one additional bit called the parity bit. This is a value sometimes used to verify the integrity of the received byte. There are two parity types supported by the AVR USART, even and odd. In even parity, the parity bit is set to 0 or 1 to force an even number of 1's to be transmitted between the start and stop bit. Thus, an 8-bit data value 0b00110011 would require a zero parity bit as the number of 1's is already even. Odd parity means the parity bit is set to force an odd number of 1's. So using odd parity, the byte 0b00110011 would require a 1 for the parity signal. The USART in the AVR can be configured to use even, odd, or no parity (meaning the optional parity bit is not transmitted).

The start bit, data bits, optional parity bit, and stop bit(s) constitute a serial data frame. Information is transmitted and received in these frames.

At the start of each frame, the receiver synchronizes to the transmitter, allowing the receiver to correctly decode the sequence of signals into the appropriate data bits. If the receiver does not see stop bits at the expected time, it reports this as a framing error. The receiver can also report a parity error (PE), and a data overrun error (DOR). A DOR means that an incoming data frame could not be properly processed because the receiver's queue had no more room for the new data.

AVR USART CONFIGURATION

Now that we have covered one of the basic serial communication protocols, we can turn to the matter of controlling the USART to perform serial communications tasks. Before transmission or reception can occur, the USART must be configured so it can properly interpret the stream of signal changes observed on its RD line, and assert appropriate signals (at the right times) on the TD line. The first configuration option is the baud rate.

Baud Rate

The USART in the AVR uses the clock signal of the AVR to time the transmission and reception of bits. To do this, it must count off a specific number of "ticks" to determine how long each signal is asserted (or will be valid in the case of reception) to transmit at a specific baud rate. The USART has a baud rate register that must be loaded with the proper number, the baud rate parameter. This value will depend on the desired baud rate and the clock speed of the microcontroller. There is a formula to calculate the baud rate parameter.

```
UBRR = clockSpeed/(16*baudRate) - 1 (round to the nearest
integer)
```

Baud rates are usually one of the following: 300, 1200, 2400, 4800, 9600, and so on.

The baud rate parameter to communicate at 1200 baud when the processor is running on a 4 MHz clock is:

```
UBRR = 4000000/(16*1200) - 1 = 207.33 (rounded to 207)
```

Notice that the rounding implies that the USART (operating under a 4 MHz clock signal) will not be able to generate an exact 1200 baud signal.

Therefore, its internal clock may not exactly match that of the other device. Keep in mind that the processor's clock may not be very accurate either (unless an external crystal is used for the clock signal). This can aggravate the timing issues. This is why the frames need to be resynchronized on each data frame, and why the data portion cannot be too long. The greater the roundoff amount in the UBRR value, the more likely that framing errors might occur.

Here are the formulas for the actual baud rate and percentage error given the baud rate parameter.

```
ActualBaudRate = clockSpeed/(16*(UBRR+1))
PercentError = ((ActualBaudRate/NominalBaudRate) - 1) * 100%
```

For example, the percentage error for the 4 MHz clock and UBRR = 207 (1200 baud) is

```
ActualBaudRate = 4000000/(16*(207+1)) = 1201.92
PercentError = ((1201.92/1200) - 1) * 100 = 0.16%
```

You should only use a baud rate parameter that results in less than 0.5% error. Higher values may work, but there will be an increased chance of corruption. The ATMEGA16A Data Sheet includes a table listing the UBRR values for various baud rates and clock speeds that indicates an accuracy figure. You should consult this table for specific applications.

The baud rate selection register is a 16-bit register. In the ATMEGA16A it is named UBRRH and UBRRL, and referred to collectively as UBRR. The ATxmega128A1 microcontroller has eight independent USARTS. We will focus on just the first, which is named USARTC0. Its baud rate selection registers are named USARTC0_BAUDCTRLB and USARTC0_BAUDCTRLA and collectively is called the BSEL (baud select) value.

The baud rate parameter (baud selection value) is restricted to 12 bits. The low byte is placed in UBRRL or USARTC0_BAUDCTRLA. The high byte's least-significant nybble is placed in bits 3:0 of UBRRH or USARTC0_BAUDCTRLB. The upper nybble of these registers are used for a special purpose. The usage of the upper nybble differs between the XMEGA series and the earlier microcontrollers. For our purposes, the upper nybble should be a 0 when storing the high byte of the baud rate parameter (baud selection value).

You must load the baud rate parameter in two steps. Here is the code required to document the meaning of the baud rate parameter, and to load it into the UBRR (ATMEGA16A).

```
.equ BRP = 207  ;1200 baud for a 4MHz clock speed
ldi R16, high(BRP)&0x0F
out UBRRH, R16
ldi R16, low(BRP)
out UBRRL, R16
```

If using the ATxmega128A1, then the following sequence should be used:

```
.equ BSEL = 12  ;9600 baud for a 2MHz clock speed
ldi R16, high(BSEL)&0x0F
sts USARTC0_BAUDCTRLB, R16
ldi R16, low(BSEL)
sts USARTC0_BAUDCTRLA, R16
```

Be sure that any application using serial communications includes appropriate documentation stating the intended clock speed and baud rate. It is customary to use symbols to define these parameters and then perform the necessary calculations at assembly time to make everything work.

Data, Parity, and Stop Bits

The next configuration option is the number of data bits, parity, and the number of stop bits. These are defined using the USART Control and Status Register C (UCSRC) in the ATMEGA16A. This register is subdivided into several fields containing information about the USART (Table 7.2).

Bit 7 is a special bit in this register. In the ATmega16A, two USART registers share the same I/O location (address). UCSRC and UBRRH are both numbered as I/O register $20. When writing data to UCSRC, bit 7 of the data must be set (1), otherwise the byte will be written to the high byte of the baud rate parameter register (UBRRH). Because the values to be written into UBRRH are never very large (the baud rate parameter is 12 bits, and therefore the high byte is limited to values between $00 and $0F), sending the high byte of the baud rate parameter to I/O register $20 will always update the UBRR in the USART. Just be careful that bit 7 is set when a byte sent to I/O register $20 is to be copied into the USART's Control and Status Register C instead.

TABLE 7.2 Bit Definitions for the UCSRC

Bits	Name	Function	Settings
7	URSEL	Register select	1 for UCSRC
6	UMSEL	Mode select	0 = asynchronous 1 = synchronous
5:4	UPM1:0	Parity mode	00 = disabled 01 (reserved) 10 = even parity 11 = odd parity
3	USBS	Stop bits	0 = 1 stop bit 1 = 2 stop bits
2:1	UCSZ1:0	Data size (if UCSZ2 is 0. This bit is in UCSRB and is set (1) to get 9 data bits)	00 = 5 data bits 01 = 6 data bits 10 = 7 data bits 11 = 8 data bits
0	UCPOL	Clock polarity	Used in synchronous mode only

In the ATxmega128A1, the corresponding control register is named XMEGA Control Register C (CTRLC). The fields are different for the XMEGA series (Table 7.3).

The following instructions will configure the USART to communicate in asynchronous mode, parity disabled, 1 stop bit, and 8 data bits.

```
;ATMEGA16A Version
ldi r16, 0b10000110
out UCSRC, r16

;Atxmega128A1 Version
ldi r16, 0b00000011
sts USARTC0_CTRLC, r16
```

To document the settings of each field, this is often written as follows. Note the line continuation character allowing the long expression to be broken across several lines for readability.

```
;ATMEGA16A Version
ldi r16, (1<<URSEL) \
      |(0<<UMSEL) \
      |(0<<UPM1)|(0<<UPM0) \
      |(1<<USBS) \
      |(1<<UCSZ1)|(1<<UCSZ0)
out UCSRC, r16
```

TABLE 7.3   Bit Definitions for the CTRLC

Bits	Name	Function	Settings
7:6	CMODE[1:0]	Communication Mode	00 = Asynchronous 01 = Synchronous 10 = InfraRED Communication 11 = Master SPI
5:4	PMODE[1:0]	Parity mode	00 = disabled 01 (reserved) 10 = even parity 11 = odd parity
3	SBMODE	Stop bits	0 = 1 stop bit 1 = 2 stop bits
2:0	CHMODE[2:0]	Character size	000 = 5 data bits 001 = 6 data bits 010 = 7 data bits 011 = 8 data bits 100 = reserved 101 = reserved 110 = reserved 111 = 9 data bits

The 0's shifted do not affect the result, but provide a place to modify the settings easily. The last bit, UCPOL, will be zero in this expression; it is omitted since we will have no reason to ever change it.

When bit fields in a byte are in groups, the values are sometimes specified with a single shift. Compare the above sample with the following. This sample also documents the bit settings which makes it easy to modify.

```
ldi r16, (1<<URSEL) \
  |(0<<UMSEL) /*mode 0(asynchronous) 1(synchronous)*/ \
  |(0b00<<UPM0) /*parity 00(disabled) 10(even) 11(odd)*/ \
  |(1<<USBS) /*stop bits (0=one, 1=two)*/ \
  |(0b11<<UCSZ0) /*data bits 00(5), 01(6), 10=(7),
     11(8)*/
out UCSRC, r16
```

The parity bits and mode select are adjacent, so shifting a 0, 1, 2, or 3 to position UPM0 and UCSZ0 will place both bits of each pair in the correct location. Beware of using this technique if the bits of a field are not adjacent!

The include file for the ATxmega128A1 contains additional symbols that makes it even easier to define the USART settings. This is the equivalent XMEGA version.

```
;Atxmega128A1 Version
ldi r16, USART_CMODE_ASYNCHRONOUS_gc \
     |USART_PMODE_DISABLED_gc \
     |(0<<USART_SBMODE_bp) \
     |USART_CHSIZE_8BIT_gc
sts USARTC0_CTRLC, r16
```

The symbols (along with others) are defined using equate directives. Here are some samples.

```
.equ USART_CHSIZE_8BIT_gc = (0x03<<0)    ;Character size:
                                         ;8 bit
.equ USART_CHSIZE_9BIT_gc = (0x07<<0)    ;Character size:
                                         ;9 bit
.equ USART_CMODE_ASYNCHRONOUS_gc = (0x00<<6)   ;Asynchronous
                                               ;Mode
.equ USART_CMODE_SYNCHRONOUS_gc = (0x01<<6)   ;Synchronous
                                              ;Mode
```

Physical Connections

The USART embedded in the AVR microcontroller can be controlled via the I/O registers, but requires some external connection to be useful. The USART is connected to three pins on the exterior of the AVR. The ground of the AVR is also used as a reference point for these signals. The three logical connections are TD, RD, and XCK (XCK is only used for synchronous mode). These external connections share physical pins with some of the general purpose digital port bits. The names RxD and TxD are used instead of RD and TD to distinguish between the microcontroller pins and the actual RS-232 signal lines. On the XMEGA series, a USART identifier is appended: RXDnx and TXDnx.

```
RxD is the same as PD0
TxD is the same as PD1
XCK is the same as PB0
RXDC0 is the same as PC2
TXDC0 is the same as PC3
```

When the transmitter, receiver, or synchronous mode is enabled, the corresponding pin cannot be used for digital I/O; it is taken over by the USART. The XCK pin is not affected by the USART unless synchronous mode is selected. In the XMEGA series, the pins must also be specifically configured for input or output; this is automatic in the ATMEGA16A.

There is one additional problem that has to do with signal levels. The voltages on the AVR pins are not compatible with the RS-232 standards. The AVR produces 0 and +5 (typically) V. RS-232 specifies a symmetric signal of −12 V and +12 V. A simple level-converter device is needed between the AVR pins and the RS-232 connector to make this switch. The STK-500 board contains a MAX202CSE chip to perform the level conversion.

The XPLAIN hardware connects the TXDC0 and RXDC0 pins to pins on another microcontroller, the AT90USB1287. The signal levels for these connections are already compatible. The LUFA Bridge software, running on the USB chip translates the RS232 serial communication to USB format. As far as the PC connected to the XPLAIN board is concerned, the USB cable is emulating an RS-232 communications device. It appears as a standard serial COM port to the PC.

To accomplish serial communications using the STK-500, you will need to jumper pins PD0 and PD1 to the level converter, which is already connected to the RS-232 DE-9 connector labeled RS232 Spare. Use jumpers to connect PD0 and PD1 to the pins labeled RXD and TXD of the two-pin header labeled RS232 Spare, right next to the PORTD header as shown in Figure 7.4. Be sure PD0 is connected to RXD. Using these connections, the STK-500 RS232 Spare connector acts like a DTE device; the USART transmits on pin 2 and receives on pin 3 of the DE-9.

Once a null-modem cable is connected from the RS-232 spare connector to another DTE device (such as a serial port on a PC), and the remote serial communication application is configured to match the settings of the USART in the AVR, communications can begin. Any terminal program such as HyperTerminal may be used on the PC side. Simply configure it to the same settings as the AVR's USART and connect. If you are using the same COM port to program the ATMEGA16A and to communicate with the application, be sure to close the programmer utility before connecting to the terminal program. You will also need to disconnect the terminal program before activating the programmer. Do not forget to switch the serial cable to RS232 SPARE (Figure 7.5) when running the application and to RS232CTRL to program the ATMEGA16A. Also remember to jumper PD0/1 to RxD/TxD.

FIGURE 7.4   Connecting the USART TxD and RxD pins to the RS232 Spare header.

When designing an application that uses serial communication on the STK-500, PORTD is no longer available to use for pushbutton input (our examples so far have used PORTD to access the switches). You can choose the ATMEGA16A's PORTA, PORTB, or PORTC to connect to the switches. If you choose PORTC, be aware that this port has a special function on the ATMEGA16A; it serves as the JTAG interface. There is a fuse that enables/disables the JTAG interface. When the JTAG interface is enabled, you cannot use all of the pins on PORTC for your own purposes. To disable the JTAG interface, simply find the correct fuse via the programmer and disable it.

Terminal Programs

As an alternative to HyperTerminal, you may wish to download PuTTY, a free terminal program. It is available at http://www.putty.org/. When you run PuTTY, you will need to select Serial for the connection type

FIGURE 7.5 Serial cable connected to STK-500 RS232 SPARE in preparation for communication with an application.

(see Figure 7.6). You can then enter the COM port (Serial Line) and baud rate (Speed). Additional configuration is available under the Category named Serial.

XPLAIN Programming Notes

When using the XPLAIN hardware, you must remove the jumper from pins 9 and 10 of the JTAG USB header, and then disconnect and reconnect the USB cable (or reset the AT90USB1287). This will cause the XPLAIN board to enumerate as the LUFA Bridge, creating a virtual COM Port. You can determine which port it is using by opening the device manager and examining the list of COM ports.

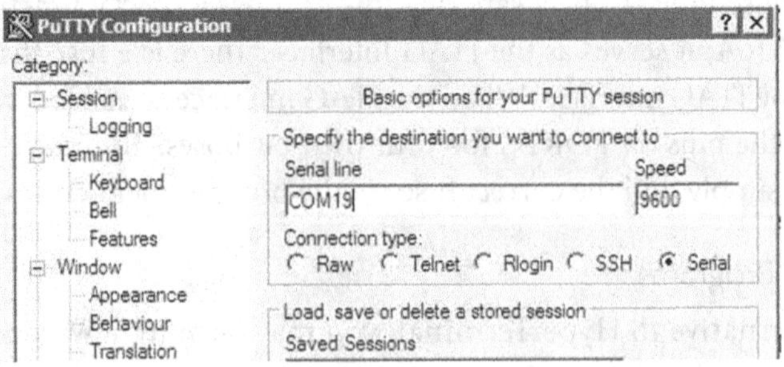

FIGURE 7.6 PuTTY terminal configuration for serial communication.

To download programs to the XMEGA, you must replace the jumper and reset the USB processor (or disconnect and reconnect the USB cable). Just remember which mode the LUFA software is operating in: jumper on, programming mode (AVRISP-MKii clone), jumper off, bridge mode (Serial to USB). The LUFA USB-Serial Bridge communicates with USARTC0 at 9600 baud (N-8-1).

AVR USART TRANSMIT AND RECEIVE

After the AVR USART is configured and connected to a remote serial device, it is ready to begin transmitting and receiving. The USART has separate transmit and receive subsystems. You must explicitly enable one or both to participate in serial communications.

Enabling the Transmitter and Receiver

Once the USART serial communication parameters are set, you may enable the transmitter, receiver, or both. To enable the transmit or receive functions of the ATMEGA16A's USART, the USART Control and Status Register B is used. The XMEGA series calls this register CTRLB. Each function has a single enable bit in this register. The following instructions enable both transmit and receive functions. The XMEGA series also requires configuring the transmit pin for output. The receive pin defaults to input unless your application has changed this setting.

```
;ATXMEGA16A Version
ldi r16, (1<<RXEN)|(1<<TXEN)
out UCSRB, r16

;ATxmega128A1 Version
;Set the transmit pin to one (idle) and as output
ldi r16, 1<<3          ;PC3
sts    PORTC_OUT, r16      ;configure TXDC0 as 1
sts    PORTC_DIR, r16      ;configure TXDC0 as output
;enable transmit and receive
ldi r16, USART_TXEN_bm | USART_RXEN_bm
out USARTC0_CTRLB, r16
```

Notice that in the above approach, all eight bits of the byte are written even though we are interested in setting/clearing only the bits in specific fields of the I/O registers. Is it appropriate to simply write zeros to the other bits? Sometimes this will not be a problem, but in other cases you may be changing settings that should not be changed. To set or clear some bits, leaving others unchanged, you should either use the special bit set/clear instructions for I/O registers, or read the byte, use bit operations to alter the required bits, and then write the new byte back to the register. Here is how the USART transmitter and receiver would be enabled using these two methods.

```
;using the set bit in I/O register instructions in the
;ATMEGA16A
sbi UCSRB, RXEN
sbi UCSRB, TXEN

;using bit manipulation instructions in the ATxmega128A1
;Set the transmit pin to one (idle) and as output
lds    r16, PORTC_OUT  ;load byte for bit modifications
ori r16, 1<<3          ;PC3 - configure TXDC0 as 1
sts    PORTC_OUT, r16
lds    r16, PORTC_DIR  ;load byte for bit modifications
ori r16, 1<<3          ;PC3 - configured for output
andi r16, ~(1<<2)   ;PC2 - configured for input
sts    PORTC_DIR, r16
;enable transmit and receive
lds r16, USARTC0_CTRLB
ori r16, USART_TXEN_bm | USART_RXEN_bm
sts USARTC0_CTRLB, r16
```

Once the receiver is enabled, bytes received are buffered in the USART awaiting pickup by an application. They can be read from an I/O register named the USART Data Register: UDR (or in the XMEGA, USARTxn_DATA). When the transmitter is enabled, a byte written to the USART Data Register will be queued for output in the transmit buffer. The USART has a one byte transmit buffer (queue) and a two byte receive buffer. This is in addition to two internal shift registers, one for transmit and one for receive, used during the actual transmission or reception of a byte. The USART Data Register is the single I/O register (address) used to access both transmit and receive buffers.

Transmitting Data

When the transmitter is enabled, the transmit line is held in an idle state (mark) until a byte is placed in the transmit buffer. To transmit a byte (or part of the byte depending on the number of data bits selected in the setup), all that needs to be done is to send the byte to the USART's data register (an I/O register). The data register is named UDR in the ATMEGA16A and USARTnx_DATA in the XMEGA series. Data can only be written to this I/O register when the USART's transmit buffer is empty. There is a flag (bit field) in one of the USART's status registers to indicate this condition.

The data register empty flag is located in the ATMEGA16A USART's Control and Status Register A (UCSRA) or the XMEGA's Status register (USARTnx_STATUS). The bit is named USART Data Register Empty (UDRE) (in the ATMEGA16A) and USART Data Register Empty Interrupt Flag (USART_DREIF) (in the XMEGA). Writing to the USART's data register should only be done when this bit is set, indicating the USART can accept the next byte into the transmit buffer. Writing a byte to this data register will clear the empty flag. The flag will be set again as soon as the USART copies the byte into the transmit shift register and begins sending its bits serially.

The transmitter's internal shift register is used to shift the bits of the byte onto the TxD pin, effecting the serial transmission. Figure 7.7 shows the registers of the transmitter section of the USART. When a byte has been completely transmitted, the transmit buffer is empty. If no byte is waiting in the transmit buffer (the Data Register Empty flag is set), then the USART enters idle mode and reports this by setting another bit, the

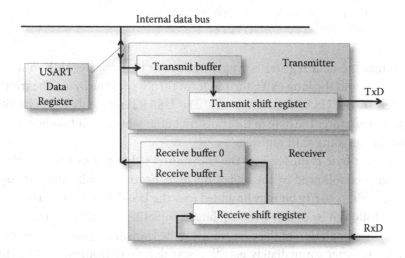

FIGURE 7.7   USART transmitter and receiver registers.

Transfer Complete Flag (TXC in the ATMEGA16 and USART_TXCIF in the XMEGA). This flag is located in the same status register as the Data Register Empty flag. On the other hand, if another byte is waiting in the transmit buffer, it is immediately copied into the transmit shift register and transmission begins. This action also sets the Data Register Empty bit to allow the application to queue up another byte.

As mentioned above, before writing to the USART's data register, the application must check to see if it is empty. The following loop waits for the empty signal, and then places the byte in r16 in the USART's transmit buffer.

```
;wait for data register empty, then enqueue the byte to
;be transmitted
;(ATMEGA16A version)
transmit:
        sbis UCSRA, UDRE
        rjmp transmit       ;not empty
        out UDR, r16
```

```
;wait for data register empty, then enqueue the byte to
;be transmitted
;(ATxmega128A1 version uses r17 as a temp register)
transmit:
        lds r17, USARTC0_STATUS
        sbrs r17, USART_DREIF_bp
        rjmp transmit       ;not empty
        sts USARTC0_DATA, r16
```

When the data register is empty, the ready bit indicates this with the value one and the loop exits; the program then writes the byte to be transmitted to the USART data register. The USART responds to this write action, and stores the byte in the transmit buffer where it waits to be moved into the outgoing shift register.

When a byte is moved into the transmitter's shift register, a start bit is transmitted followed by the bits of the byte, beginning with the least significant bit. A parity bit may be added (per the USART configuration) and this is followed by one or two stop bits, completing one data frame.

At the completion of the data frame, if the transmit buffer is not empty, the transmitter immediately gets the next data byte from the buffer and begins transmitting it. Otherwise, it transmits the idle signal and sets the Transmit Complete flag.

Receiving Data

Receiving is quite similar, but has more options because of the possibility of errors. An application can monitor the state of the receive queue by checking the Receive Complete (RXC) bit in USART Status and Control Register A (or the USART_RXCIF bit in the USARTxn_STATUS Register). This bit is set to one (1) whenever a byte has been received (receive complete) and has been placed by the USART into the receive queue. The byte can be read by an application through the I/O register named UDR (USARTxn_DATA). This is the same I/O location used to specify bytes to be transmitted. Figure 7.7 shows the registers of the receiver section of the USART. When the processor writes to this I/O register, the USART copies the data into the transmitter's transmit buffer. When the AVR reads from this I/O register, the USART dequeues a byte from the receive queue (possibly clearing the Receive Complete flag) and makes the byte available on the AVR's internal data bus where it becomes available to the CPU. The following loop illustrates how to wait for a byte to appear in the receive queue, and then read it into a register.

```
;ATMEGA16 version
receive:
        sbis UCSRA, RXC
        rjmp receive   ;nothing in the receive queue yet
        in r16, UDR    ;received byte dequeued into r16
;ATxmega128A1 version (uses r17 as a temporary register)
receive:
        lds r17,USARTC0_STATUS
        sbrs r17, USART_RXCIF_bp
        rjmp receive
        lds r16, USARTC0_DATA      ;dequeue one byte into r16
```

When the byte is dequeued, the receive complete flag will be cleared unless there is a second byte already in the queue. In this case, the receive complete flag remains set so the application can retrieve that byte when it checks the USART again. The receive queue can hold up to two bytes.

Disabling the Transmitter or Receiver

When the transmitter is disabled by clearing the Transmit Enable bit, any pending bytes are transmitted before the transmitter actually enters the idle state and shuts down. The Transmit Complete Flag is used to determine when this occurs. When the transmitter is disabled and has finished transmission of queued bytes, the port pin used for the transmit function reverts to the usual port control settings.

When the receiver is disabled by clearing the Receive Enable bit, the receiver immediately stops and data still in the receive buffer is discarded. At this time, the port pin used for received data also reverts back to normal port control.

SERIAL TRANSMISSION ERRORS

Only the receiver subsystem of the USART reports errors. An error is reported by setting a bit in the USART Control and Status Register A (USARTxn_STATUS in the XMEGA). There are three error bits corresponding to three errors that can be reported.

The first is a frame error (FE). This occurs when the receiver thinks it is time for a stop bit (mark) but a space is read instead. A FE is reported by setting the FE bit (FE or USART_FERR). The USART only looks for one stop bit regardless of the USART configuration. The number of stop bits specified in the USART configuration affects the transmitter only. Regardless of whether a stop bit is detected or not, the receiver interprets the next space signal as a start bit and begins the reception of another byte.

The second type of error is called a data overrun error (DOR or USART_ BUFOVF). This is a buffer overflow error. It occurs when the receive buffer is full (contains two bytes), a third byte has been completely received and is in the internal shift register, and a start bit is detected. In order to receive the bits streaming in, the data in the shift register must be moved into the queue, but it is full. When a data overrun occurs, the Data OverRun (Buffer Overflow) bit is set and the byte in the receive shift register is discarded.

The third error is a parity error (PE or USART_PERR). If odd or even parity is expected (according to the USART configuration), a PE is reported when the number of ones in the data (including the parity bit) is incorrect. If the USART is configured for no parity, the PE flag will always be clear.

Detecting Errors

Accessing the error flags is another very interesting process in the AVR. These are available by reading from I/O register USCRA (USARTxn_ STATUS). However, remember that there are up to three bytes in the USART pending dequeueing, and each has its own error information. When the receiver buffers a received data byte, it also buffers the associated error flags. The error flags must be read first (if the application is interested in examining them), because when the data is dequeued (reading from the USART Data Register), the associated error flags are discarded. The following code illustrates the proper way to receive a byte with error information:

```
;ATMEGA16A version
receive:
      sbis UCSRA, RXC
      rjmp receive     ;empty queue
      in r17, USCRA   ;read error flags first
      in r16, UDR     ;read data (and dequeue both)
;mask out unrelated bits
      andi r17, (1<<FE)|(1<<DOR)|(1<<PE)
;if not zero, an error occurred
      brne receiveErrorOccurred


;ATxmega128A1 version
receive:
      lds r17,USARTC0_STATUS
      sbrs r17, USART_RXCIF_bp
      rjmp receive   ;empty queue
      ;R17 also contains the error flags for the
      ;following byte
      lds r16, USARTC0_DATA  ;dequeue data and error flags
;mask out unrelated bits
      andi r17, USART_FERR_bm|USART_BUFOVF_bm|USART_
      PERR_bm
;if not zero, an error occurred
      brne receiveErrorOccurred
```

When a PE or FE is reported for a byte, you must assume that one or more bits of the data (which is about to be accessed via the data register) are corrupt. When a DOR is reported, it means there were one or more bytes lost between the previous byte read from the data register and the one about to be read. Remember that you must access the error flags from the status register before you read the data from the data register.

One note about the XMEGA example above. The XMEGA include file defines many constants that specify locations of bits in I/O registers. The field names are often suffixed with _bm or _bp. These stand for bit mask and bit position. For example, the Buffer Overflow field in the STATUS register is USART_BUFOVF, and is bit position three. USART_BUFOVF_bp is therefore defined to be 3 and the bit mask is a byte with a one at this position.

```
.equ USART_BUFOVF_bp = 3
.equ USART_BUFOVF_bm = (1<<3)
```

POLLED I/O

The transmit and receive loops illustrated so far utilize a polled I/O method. To be efficient, an application should constantly monitor the status of the transmitter so no time is wasted between transmission of consecutive bytes. It should also monitor the status of the receiver so no data is lost due to a DOR. However, waiting for the data register to become empty, or waiting for byte to be received, can be wasteful, burning CPU cycles that might be used for better purposes. A possibly more efficient method of interaction between the application and the USART involves the use of interrupts. Once the necessary interrupt handler is in place, the USART can interrupt the current application when a byte is available in the receive queue. The interrupt handler can check error info and remove the byte from the USART queue. The byte might be placed in a larger input queue used by the application. This interrupt controlled input method avoids the need to waste clock cycles polling the RXC flag.

The USART can also cause an interrupt when the transmit buffer is empty. This allows an application to keep bytes in the transmit queue without polling the Data Register Empty flag. The transmit complete event can also trigger an interrupt. This interrupt handler could respond to this condition by disabling the transmitter to restore the normal functionality of the port pins.

Interrupt-driven USART control will be examined when we cover interrupts and interrupt handlers in general.

SERIAL COMMUNICATIONS EXAMPLE

The following example uses polled I/O to receive characters through the USART. Each character is converted to upper case and transmitted back to the other device. There is an alternate version for the ATxmega128A1.

PROGRAM 7.1   Serial Echo: Echo Received Characters Back to the Sender, Converting Lowercase to Uppercase

```
;Program 7.1 - Serial Echo
;Illustrate serial communications
```

```
;Programmer: TM
;Date: 5/2010
;Platform: STK-500
;Device: ATMega16A
.include 'm16def.inc'

;Serial communications between the STK and PC
;Echo received characters (converting to uppercase)
;Receive error displayed on LED's

;2 mhz clock speed, 9600 baud UBRR = 12
.equ UBRRvalue = 12

.def temp = r16

.cseg
      ;Stack initialization
      ldi temp, low(RAMEND)
      out SPL, temp
      ldi temp, high(RAMEND)
      out SPH, temp

      ;leds display RXD counter or receive error flags
      ldi temp, $FF
      out DDRB, temp
      out PORTB, temp     ;initially clear

      ;initialize USART
      ldi temp, high (UBRRvalue)      ;baud rate
      out UBRRH, temp
      ldi temp, low (UBRRvalue)
      out UBRRL, temp

      ;URSEL 0 = UBRRH, 1 = UCSRC (shared port address)
      ;UMSEL 0 = Asynchronous, 1 = Synchronous
      ;USBS 0 = One stop bit, 1 = Two stop bits
      ;UCSZ0:1 Character Size: 0 = 5, 1 = 6, 2 = 7, 3 = 8
      ;(UCSZ2 is in UCSRB, but is only needed for 9 data
      ;bits)
      ;UPM0:1 0 = none, 1 = reserved, 2 = Even, 3 = Odd

      ;8data, 1 stop, no parity
```

```
        ldi temp, (1<<URSEL)|(0<<UMSEL)|(0<<USBS)|(3<<UCSZ
        0)|(0<<UPM0)
        out UCSRC, temp

        ldi temp, (1<<RXEN)|(1<<TXEN)
        out UCSRB, temp; enable receive and transmit

        ;USART initialization complete

.def    rxCount=r0   ;holds the complemented receive count
        ;this is stored in 1's complement for easy display
        ;on LED's
        clr rxCount
        com rxCount  ;initial value is ~0

;loop until a byte is received
lp:
        rcall receive  ;poll receiver for byte
        brcc lp        ;carry set indicates byte received

;count received byte and display receive count
        dec rxCount  ;subtract 1 since this is the
                     ;complemented count
        out PORTB, rxCount

;r25 holds error flags - Check if an error occurred
;Mask out non-error flags
        andi r25,(1<<FE) | (1<<DOR) | (1<<PE)
        brne receiveError  ;halt program on error

        rcall toUpperCase  ;convert letters to uppercase
        rcall transmit     ;echo converted character
        rjmp lp

;Receive error - display error message on LEDs
;r25 has error codes
;      bit    2 = PE
;             3 = DOR
;             4 = FE
receiveError:
        com   r25; display error code
```

```
        out PORTB, r25
        rjmp pc         ;halt execution

;Function definitions—

;Translate lowercase characters to uppercase
;Character is in r24, return value is r24
.def theByte = r24
toUpperCase:
        cpi theByte, 'a'    ;screen out non-lowercase
        brlo   toUpperCase_ret
        cpi theByte, 'z'+1
        brsh   toUpperCase_ret
        andi theByte, ~('A'^'a')  ;only alter lowercase
                                  ;letters
toUpperCase_ret:
        ret
.undef theByte

;Receive byte - non-blocking implementation
;return the byte received (if any) in r24
;return error flags in r25
;return with carry clear if no byte was ready
.def rec_byte = r24
.def rec_err = r25
receive:
        clc
        sbis UCSRA, RXC; is byte in Rx buffer?
        ret; not yet
        in rec_err, UCSRA   ;error flags
        in rec_byte, UDR    ;received byte
        sec     ;to indicate a byte was received
        ret
.undef rec_byte
.undef rec_err

;Transmit byte - blocks until transmit buffer can accept
;a byte
;The param, byte to transmit, is in r24
.def byte_tx = r24
transmit:
        sbis UCSRA, UDRE; wait for Tx buffer to be empty
```

```
        rjmp transmit  ;not ready yet
        out UDR, byte_tx  ;transmit character
        ret
.undef byte_tx
```

This program illustrates a nonblocking version of polled input. The receive function returns with the carry flag clear if there was no data ready in the USART's receive buffer. This allows the application to go on to do other tasks before checking for a received byte again. In this application, there is no other task, so the program simply calls the receive function again.

The transmit function is designed differently. It blocks until it can place the byte into the transmit queue. If for some reason, the transmit queue never becomes empty, this function will never return and the application will not be able to perform any other tasks. This could lead to a DOR in this application.

Transmit Time

It may be important to know how long the application may need to wait for the transmit buffer to became available again or how long it will take to transfer a certain number of bytes at a specific baud rate. The maximum wait for the transmit shift register to become empty will be the time required to transmit one frame at the current baud rate. If eight data bits, a parity bit, and two stop bits are included in the frame (along with the required start bit), each frame will occupy 12 timeslots. At 9600 baud, each RS-232 signal is asserted for 1/9600, or approximately 0.0001 seconds. The transmission of the 12-bit frame requires 1.25 ms. A lot of instructions can be executed during this time! Polled I/O using a blocking approach should only be used if the application can afford to be delayed significantly by this operation.

EXERCISES

1. At 1200 baud, how long is each signal asserted on the TD pin?
2. Assuming 7 data bits and even parity, tell the parity bit that will be sent with each of the following data values: 0b0000000, 0b1111111, and 0b0101100.
3. Assuming 6 data bits and odd parity, which of the following 7-bit values received by a USART would cause a PE? 0b1101101, 0b0000001, and 0b1010101.

4. Determine the baud rate parameters needed for 9600 baud communication at three different clock speeds: 1, 2, and 4 MHz. Calculate the percent error for each case.

5. (ATMEGA16A) Consult the tables in the AVR ATmega16A specification sheets to determine the baud rate parameter for a 3.6864 MHz clock speed to achieve a baud rate of 14.4k. Compare this to the calculated value.

6. What is the maximum standard baud rate that can be achieved with a 1 MHz clock speed? This figure can be determined from the equations. Baud rate parameters can be any value between 0 and $2^{12} - 1$. What is the percentage error for this configuration?

7. Use an equate directive to define BR300, the baud rate parameter needed for 300 baud for an application running with a clock speed CLK. Assume CLK, representing the actual clock speed in MHz (not Hz), is already defined in another .equ.

8. Write a sequence of assembly language statements to set the baud rate register to the value BR300 just determined in the previous question.

9. (ATMEGA16A) If $A2 is written to UCSRC, what asynchronous communication parameters are being specified? (parity, stop bits, and data bits) (ATxmega128A1) if $21? Is written to USARTC0_CTRLC, what asynchronous communication parameters are being specified? (parity, stop bits, and data bits).

10. Write an assembly language statement to load register 16 with the proper byte value to configure the USART to communicate with 7 data bits and even parity. One stop bit will be sufficient. Use an expression that will determine the correct byte value using bit-wise or, the bit shift operator, and appropriate names for the fields.

11. Write a function named txEnabled that returns with the carry flag clear if the USART transmitter is disabled, or the carry flag set if the transmitter is enabled. This is just about the transmitter, not the receiver.

12. Write a queueByte function that attempts to store the byte in R24 into the USART transmit queue. If the queue is full, the function returns with carry set (as an error indicator). If the byte is successfully queued, the function returns with carry clear.

13. Write a function named skipErrors that clears the receive queue of any data with a frame or PE associated with it. Upon return from this function, either the receive buffer is empty, or it holds a byte received without a parity or FE. Note that this does not clear DORs.

14. Write a function called flushRX to completely empty the receive buffer of all data. Return a count of the number of bytes discarded in r24 (an 8-bit unsigned int).

15. Write a function isDOR that checks if a DOR occurred since the previous data byte was removed from the USART. It should return with the carry flag set if this error is detected, and with carry clear if the error has not occurred. If no byte is in the receive queue, there is no error information to read.

16. (ATMEGA16A) A programmer wants to transmit the byte in R16 via the USART and also copy the byte into register zero. What is wrong with the solution?

```
out UDR,    r16
in R0, UDR
```

(ATxmega128A1) A programmer wants to transmit the byte in R16 via the USART and also copy the byte into register zero. What is wrong with the solution?

```
sts USARTC0_DATA, r16
lds R0, USARTC0_DATA
```

17. What is the minimum time to transmit 1000 characters at 300 baud? What USART configuration would be used in this case?

PROGRAMMING EXERCISES

In the following exercises, use a 2 MHz clock speed and perform serial communications at 9600 baud, 8 data bits, 1 stop bit, and no parity. Use a suitable terminal program such as HyperTerminal or PuTTY to test the applications. If your program's first task is to output on the serial line, you may miss that output while switching between programming and running, especially if you are using the XPLAIN board. Consider having such programs wait for a character to be received over the serial communications line before it actually starts.

1. Write a program to transmit a character each time a pushbutton is pressed. Button 0 should transmit the digit "0," button 1 the digit "1," and so on. If you are using the ATMEGA16A and the STK-500, use PORTA or PORTC to connect to the pushbuttons. Remember to be sure the JTAG interface is disabled in the ATMEGA16A's fuses.

2. Write a program to accept input via the serial port. Input will be a sequence composed of only the characters "0" and "1." You

are to put these together to form a nybble, and then output the character representing the hexadecimal value of the nybble on the serial port. For example, entering 1, 0, 1, 0, should cause the letter "A" to be output and entering 0, 0, 1, 0, would output the letter "2." Output your hexadecimal characters to two per line. That is, after each pair, automatically output a carriage return and linefeed character, and then process more nybbles, repeating this process forever.

3. Write a function called readLine that accepts characters on the serial port, echoing each as it is received, storing them at successive locations in SRAM. The function receives the address for storage in X. When a carriage return is received, store a null character instead and echo a carriage return line feed sequence. The function should return the string length in R25:R24 (the number of characters stored, not counting the null character). Include a brief test program that stores two lines in different locations. You may assume that no input string will exceed 79 characters in length.

4. Write a function named `printFlash` that will transmit a string (null-terminated) on the serial port. The string will be located in flash. Assume the address (byte address) of the string will be in Z when the function is called. The function outputs characters from sequential bytes until a `nul` character is encountered. Write a test program to call `printFlash` on several strings of your choosing. Include a string consisting of a carriage return and line feed as one of the strings, and call `printFlash` to output this string after each other string is printed.

5. Use the Serial Echo program (Program 7.1) to experiment with errors. Make a slight change to the program to display the character received instead of a count on the LEDs. You may also want to loop back to the receive loop from the error reporting section instead of halting the program. Change the baud rate parameter to 13. What baud rate will this select? Type the letter a. What is received? What is echoed? Type the letter !. What is received? What is echoed? Can you explain? What error occurs on reception if the baud rate parameter is set to 11? What happens if it is set to 9? Set the baud rate parameter back to 12 and change the serial configuration to expect even parity. What characters are correctly received? Which ones cause an error? Why? Introduce a delay loop in your program to cause a data overrun (buffer overflow) error. You should be able to enter characters slowly without error, but if you type three in a row, you should get a DOR.

ALTERNATE PROGRAMS FOR THE XPLAIN DEMONSTRATION KIT

Program 7.1a: Serial Echo

The only differences between the two versions of this program are the I/O register access conventions. The LEDs are on PORTE and USARTC0 is used for serial communication.

PROGRAM 7.1a   Atxmega128A1 Version of Serial Echo

```
;Program 7.1a - Serial Echo
;Illustrate serial communications

;Programmer: TM
;Date: 5/2010
;Platform: XPLAIN
;Device: ATxmega128A1
.include "ATxmega128A1def.inc"

;Serial communications between the XPLAIN and PC
;using LUFA Bridge
;Echo received characters (converting to uppercase)
;Receive error displayed on LED's

;2 mhz clock speed, 9600 baud BSEL = 12
.equ BSEL = 12

.def temp = r16

.cseg
;Set the LEDS as OFF and PORT as output
;leds display RXD counter or receive error flags
ldi temp, $FF       ;led's off
sts PORTE_OUT, temp
sts    PORTE_DIR,temp

;set baud rate
ldi temp, high(BSEL) & 0x0F
sts USARTC0_BAUDCTRLB, temp
ldi temp, low(BSEL)
sts USARTC0_BAUDCTRLA, temp
```

```
;data packet format
;select, asynchronous, no parity, 1 stop, 8 data bits
ldi temp, USART_CMODE_ASYNCHRONOUS_gc|USART_PMODE_
DISABLED_gc|(0<<USART_SBMODE_bp)|USART_CHSIZE_8BIT_gc
sts USARTC0_CTRLC, temp

;Set the transmit pin as output and set high, receive
;pin as input (default)
ldi temp, 1<<3      ;PC3
sts    PORTC_OUT,temp    ;configure TXD as 1
sts    PORTC_DIR,temp    ;configure TXD as output

;enable bi-directional communication
lds temp, USARTC0_CTRLB
ori temp, USART_TXEN_bm | USART_RXEN_bm
sts USARTC0_CTRLB, temp

;USART initialization complete

.def   rxCount = r0   ;holds the complemented receive count
       ;this is stored in 1's complement for easy display
       ;on LED's
       clr rxCount
       com rxCount   ;initial value is ~0

;loop until a byte is received
lp:
       rcall receive  ;poll receiver for byte
       brcc lp        ;carry set indicates byte received

;count received byte and display receive count
       dec rxCount   ;subtract 1 since this is the
                     ;complemented count
       sts PORTE_OUT, rxCount

;r25 holds error flags - Check if an error occurred
;Mask out non-error flags
       andi r25,USART_FERR_bm|USART_BUFOVF_bm|USART_PERR_
       bm
       brne receiveError; halt program on error
```

```
        rcall toUpperCase   ;convert letters to uppercase
        rcall transmit      ;echo converted character
        rjmp lp
.undef temp

;Receive error - display error message on LEDs
;r25 has error codes
;       bit    2 = PE
;              3 = DOR
;              4 = FE
receiveError:
        com    r25; display error code
        sts PORTE_OUT, r25
        rjmp pc        ;halt execution

;Function definitions—

;Translate lowercase characters to uppercase
;Character is in r24, return value is r24
.def theByte = r24
toUpperCase:
        cpi theByte, 'a'    ;screen out non-lowercase
        brlo   toUpperCase_ret
        cpi theByte, 'z'+1
        brsh   toUpperCase_ret
        andi theByte, ~('A'^'a')  ;only alter lowercase
                                  ;letters
toUpperCase_ret:
        ret
.undef theByte

;Receive byte - non-blocking implementation
;return the byte received (if any) in r24
;return error flags in r25
;return with carry clear if no byte was ready
.def rec_byte = r24
.def rec_err = r25
receive:
        clc
        lds rec_err, USARTC0_STATUS
        sbrs rec_err, USART_RXCIF_bp  ;is byte in Rx
                                      ;buffer?
```

```
        rjmp receive_no
        lds rec_byte, USARTC0_DATA        ;received byte
        sec    ;to indicate a byte was received
receive_no:
        ret
.undef rec_byte
.undef rec_err

;Transmit byte - blocks until transmit buffer can accept
;a byte
;The param, byte to transmit, is in r24
.def byte_tx = r24
.def temp = r16
transmit:
        push temp
transmit_wait:
        lds temp, USARTC0_STATUS
        sbrs temp, USART_DREIF_bp  ;wait for Tx buffer to
                                   ;be empty
        rjmp transmit_wait  ;not ready yet
        sts USARTC0_DATA, byte_tx  ;transmit character
        pop temp
        ret
.undef byte_tx
.undef temp
```

CHAPTER 8

Logical Operations

L OGICAL AND ARITHMETIC INSTRUCTIONS are fundamental to the operation of every processor. The ALU plays the central role in executing these instructions, accepting one or more values as input, and outputting an arithmetic or logical result. Although the operands for the basic logic instructions are from registers or immediate data, the AVR processor also provides several special instructions for checking and manipulating bits in the I/O registers. This design conserves registers for other purposes and allows efficient implementation of I/O operations.

BITWISE LOGICAL OPERATIONS

The bitwise logical operations are implemented in hardware by fundamental digital devices called gates, the same devices that are used as building blocks for more complex circuits. There are four basic logical or Boolean operations supported by most processors, including the AVR: complement, AND, OR, and EOR. The following AVR instructions are used to perform these operations on the bits of a byte (Table 8.1).

In addition to these standard logical operations, the AVR includes some specialized bit-oriented instructions that are convenient for many operations required of embedded processors. The ability to check, set, clear, and move individual bits is necessary when performing many I/O operations. These instructions allow quick manipulation of individual bits of a byte. None are required, as the results could be obtained by using one or more of the above instructions (Table 8.2).

TABLE 8.1   Bitwise Logical (Boolean) Instructions

Syntax	Operands	Action	Description
com Rd	A register	Rd ← NOT Rd	One's complement; all of the bits are "flipped"
and Rd, Rr and i Rd, K	Two registers or a register (16-31) and a constant ($00-$FF)	Rd ← Rd AND Rr Rd ← Rd AND K	The bitwise (logical) AND is computed and stored in Rd
or Rd, Rr ori Rd, K	Two registers or a register (16-31) and a constant ($00-$FF)	Rd ← Rd OR Rr Rd ← Rd OR K	The bitwise (logical) OR is computed and stored in Rd
eor Rd, Rr	Two registers	Rd ← Rd XOR Rr	The bitwise (logical) Exclusive-OR is computed and stored in Rd

Status Flags

When using any instruction, it is important to note how that instruction affects the status flags in the status register (SREG). Remember that the status flags are the basis for all of the conditional instructions in machine language. The conditional branches depend on how other instructions affect the status flags. The AVR SREG contains six flags that are commonly affected by logical and arithmetic operations. These are located in bits 5-0 of the SREG. All of the bits of the SREG are shown in Figure 8.1. Each flag is represented by a letter: H, S, V, N, Z, and C.

- H is the Half Carry flag. It is not affected by any of these logical instructions. It is affected only by some of the addition and subtraction operations. This flag is helpful in implementing BCD arithmetic.

- S is the Sign flag. It is always the EOR of two other flags (S = N xor V). It is generally only relevant after a signed arithmetic operation, but it is also set by many logical operations.

- V is the twos complement overflow flag. It indicates when an arithmetic operation with signed numbers overflows. Most of the logical operations set this flag to zero (thus S will always match N after a logical instruction that affects N).

TABLE 8.2   Specialized Bit Manipulation Instructions Available in the AVR Processor

Syntax	Operands	Action	Description
sbr Rd,K	A register (16-31) and constant ($00-$FF)	Rd ← Rd OR K	Set bits in register; this is identical to ORI
sbi P,b	One of the lower I/O registers (0-31) and bit position (0-7)	I/O(P,b) ← 1	Set bit in I/O register
cbr Rd, K	A register (16-31) and a constant ($00-$FF)	Rd ← Rd AND (COM K)	Clear bits in register; this clears bits in Rd that correspond to 1's in the mask, K. This is identical to ANDI
cbi P,b	One of the lower I/O registers (0-31) and bit position (0-7)	I/O(P,b) ← 0	Clear bit in I/O register
tst Rd	A register	Rd ← Rd AND Rd	The register is unchanged; only status bits are affected
clr Rd	A register	Rd ← Rd XOR Rd	The register is cleared (all bits are 0); identical to eor Rd, Rd
ser Rd	A register (16-31)	Rd ← 0xFF	All bits in register are set (all bits are 1)
swap Rd	A register	Rd(7:0) ← Rd (0-3):Rd(7:4)	Swap nybbles in register

Status Register (SREG)							
I	T	H	S	V	N	Z	C

FIGURE 8.1   The AVR SREG showing the arithmetic and logical flags as well as the Global Interrupt Enable flag (I) and Bit Copy Storage flag (T).

- N is the Negative flag. It simply is a copy of the most-significant bit of a result. For signed integer data (twos complement), bit 7 indicates if the number is negative. For unsigned integer data, this bit indicates the number is 128 or greater. For logical data, it simply indicates the state of the most significant bit. Logical operations generally affect this bit even though the data may not represent a number.

- Z is the Zero flag. It is set if a result is zero and cleared if a result is not zero.

- C is the Carry flag. It is named after an arithmetic phenomenon, but is also meaningful after a shift and rotate instruction is executed. It is generally not altered by the logical operations.

The effects on the flags of the bitwise logical and special bit manipulation instructions are detailed in Table 8.3. A dash (–) indicates that that flag is not affected by the instruction.

USES OF LOGICAL INSTRUCTIONS

The logical instructions have common uses that may not be immediately apparent. Many embedded applications require the setting/clearing/ testing of individual bits in a byte to control or respond to an I/O device. For example, choosing the direction of some of the pins of a general purpose I/O port requires setting or clearing just one of the bits in the direction register, leaving the other bits unchanged. The set bit in I/O register instruction (SBI) or clear bit in I/O register instruction (CBI) provide an easy way to accomplish this.

```
sbi DDRB, 3   ;set Pin3 as output
```

TABLE 8.3   Affect of Logical and Special Bit Instructions on the Status Flags

Instruction	H	S	V	N	Z	C
and, andi, or, ori, eor, cbr, sbr, tst	–	N xor V	0	Copy of bit 7 of result	1 if all bits are zero	–
com	–	N xor V	0	Copy of bit 7 of result	1 if all bits are zero	1
clr	–	0	0	0	1	–
ser, sbi, cbi, swap	–	–	–	–	–	–

Unfortunately, this will not work on the ATxmega128A1. The SBI (and CBI) instruction is limited to addressing only the first 32 I/O registers; PORTE_DIR is at I/O address 0x680. The XMEGA microcontrollers provide a mapping of real ports to virtual ports (up to four at one time) that essentially move the general purpose I/O port addresses to a lower position. At the virtual port locations, four registers are available for each mapped port: IN, OUT, DIR, and INTFLAGS.

To map PORTC to Virtual Port 0, you do the following:

```
lds temp, PORTCFG_VPCTRLA    ;current mappings for virtual
                             ;ports 0 and 1
cbr temp, $0F                ;clear low nybble which is
                             ;port 0's mapping
sbr temp, $02                ;PORTC is number 2
sts PORTCFG_VPCTRLA, temp    ;mapping in effect
```

The above sequence leaves the current mapping for virtual port 1 (in the high nybble) unchanged. From this point on, access PORTC's main registers as follows:

```
sbi, VPORT0_DIR, 3    ;Pin 3 of PORTC set as output
in temp, VPORT0_IN    ;read PORTC
sbi VPORT0_OUT, 3     ;output a 1 on pin 3 of PORTC
sbic VPORT0_IN, 3     ;skip next instruction if pin3 of
                      ;PORTC is clear
```

PORTC's control and pin configuration registers are not accessible through the virtual port; only the most frequently used registers are made available at the lower address. This allows use of IN, OUT, SBI, CBI, SBIS, and SBIC instructions. These instructions are more efficient than the alternative load and store instructions coupled with bit manipulate/test instructions.

The SBI instruction is a convenient instruction affecting only one bit in an I/O register. When using this instruction, it is a good idea to use the standard names for the I/O registers and bit positions. In the ATmega16A, setting pin 3 of port B as output could be written:

```
sbi 0x17, 3 ;set pin 3 of DDRB (0x17) for output
```

Although the comment does explain the meaning of the "magic number," 0x17, using DDRB in its place makes the instruction self explanatory.

Using literal values in instructions like this is prone to error and makes it difficult to port the program to a different device in the AVR family. The I/O register locations and bit assignments are not the same for every member of the AVR family. When a program uses the standard include file for a specific microcontroller, the I/O register names and bit positions are correctly defined for that microcontroller. This will allow for easy conversions between different MEGA series microcontroller, or between different XMEGA series. As we have seen, the register names are quite different between these two series, so converting a program from the ATMEGA16A to the ATxmega128A1 requires quite a bit of work.

Clearing, Setting, and Toggling

The AVR includes special instructions to manipulate and test bits in the I/O registers. These affect only single bits at a time. The logical instructions can affect some or all of the bits in a byte in a single operation. Next we will explore how the AND, OR, and EOR instructions can be used to clear, set, or toggle one or more bits in a byte.

One common application of "bit-twiddling" involves manipulation of the ASCII codes for character data. The ASCII codes for uppercase and lowercase letters differ in exactly one position, bit five. For example, the ASCII codes for "J" and "j" are 0b1001010 and 0b1101010. If an application needs to convert all letters to uppercase (or lowercase), a simple logical operation to clear (or set) bit five will suffice; toggling case is as easy as toggling bit five. Of course, you should verify that the code represents a letter and not some other character before changing bit five, or surprising things might happen.

The process of setting, clearing, and toggling a bit (or several bits) is commonly accomplished through the use of a logical instruction and a constant value called a bit mask. The bit mask is a string of bits of the same size as the data being manipulated. In the AVR processor, all of these operations apply to bytes, so the bit masks are also a byte.

- To set a bit (or multiple bits), create a mask with 1's in the positions to be set (0's elsewhere). Perform a logical OR operation.

- To clear a bit (or multiple bits), create a mask with 0's in the positions to be cleared (1's elsewhere). Perform a logical AND operation.

- To toggle (flip) a bit (or multiple bits), create a mask with 1's in the positions to be flipped (0's elsewhere). Perform a logical EOR operation.

Masks

Masks are often created via expressions in assembly language programs. For example, the mask needed to convert letters to lowercase (set bit five) is the result of the expression 1 ≪ 5. To clear bit five, you need the complement of this, ~(1 ≪ 5). The mask to toggle bit five is the same as the one used to set bit five.

To create a mask with several bits set, use the bitwise or operator. Thus, the mask 0b01001000 would be written (1 ≪ 6)|(1 ≪ 3). The complement could be expressed as ~((1 ≪ 6)|(1 ≪ 3)). Note that these expressions are evaluated by the assembler; they are not logical instructions executed by the processor.

Another task that can be accomplished using logical instructions is the extraction of a digit value from a digit character. The ASCII codes for the characters "0" through "9" are 0x30 through 0x39. Masking out (clearing) the upper four bits will convert the ASCII code to unsigned 8-bit data. This mask is usually written as 0x0F rather than constructing it using an expression. To convert in the opposite direction (unsigned byte to ASCII), you would simply set bits five and four, as in ori Rd, 0x30. This might also be written as ori Rd, '0', since the ASCII code for "0" is 0x30; the latter operand format provides a clue to the reader regarding the intent of the operation. This conversion is only valid if the original byte represents one of the numbers 0 through 9.

Similarly, the right and left nybbles of a byte can be isolated using masks 0x0F and 0xF0 with ANDI instructions.

The ANDI instruction can be used to test if particular bits in a register are 0 or 1. In this application, the mask includes 1's in positions to be tested. The ANDI instruction will set the zero flag if all of the corresponding (unmasked) bits in the register are 0. If any are 1, then the result will be nonzero.

The OR instruction is often used to combine bits in two bytes. When used in this way, the bits being combined must be in different parts of the bytes, and the unused bits of each byte must be zero. For example, the two bytes 0xC0 and 0x04 might contain two independent 4-bit values, one in the upper nybble, the other in the lower. An OR instruction will combine these into a single byte, 0xC4. The swap instruction is useful to reposition the low nybble of a byte as the high nybble in preparation for combining two nybbles in a single byte.

For completeness, the instructions SBR, CBR, SBRS, and SBRC should be mentioned here. The set bits in register (SBR) instruction is simply another name for *or immediate* (ORI). The assembler generates the same machine instruction for SBR as for ORI.

The clear bits in register (CBR) instruction is functionally equivalent to an *and immediate* with the complementary mask. That is, the following instructions are assembled to the same machine instruction:

```
cbr temp, $3C
andi temp, ~$3C
```

The skip instructions, SBRS and SBRC, test a single bit in a register and skip the next instruction if it is set or clear. These are efficient conditional branch instructions, combining the test and branch in a single statement, however, the branch is limited to skipping around a single instruction which immediately follows the SBRS or SBRC instruction.

SHIFT AND ROTATE

Some operations require the shifting of bits to different positions with a byte or word. The SWAP instruction is a special case of this, shifting the upper nybble to the lower and vice versa. The more common shift instructions allow all of the bits of a data unit to be moved to the left or right by one or more positions. This type of shifting also has important arithmetic applications. Processors generally include several types of shift instructions in their basic instruction set.

Basic shifting can be to the left (bits move to more significant positions in the byte) or right (bits move to less-significant positions). Bits can be shifted one position, or multiple positions in either direction. The AVR processor only supports single position shifts, so you must repeat the shift operation to shift multiple positions. When a shift occurs, there are several options regarding the bit positions on the ends of the data. When shifting one position to the left or right, one bit is shifted out of the data; what happens to it? A one-position shift also vacates one-bit position; what value is used to fill the vacancy?

Processors generally include several variations of shifts to allow the programmer to select between these options. The bit shifted out of the data is commonly copied into the Carry flag. This allows the programmer to use that bit to affect the flow of control in an application. The bit shifted out may also be carried around the end of the data, so to speak, and used to fill in the vacated position. This is often called a rotate instead of a shift. A variation of this includes the Carry flag in the rotation. The term rotate through carry is sometimes used to describe this variation.

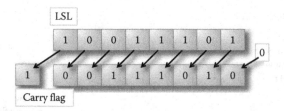

FIGURE 8.2 The LSL instruction brings a zero into the least-significant bit.

The AVR processor includes only the rotate through carry version of a rotate.

The other variations are differentiated by the behavior of the vacated bit position. There are three possibilities: the vacated bit can be 0, 1, or unchanged. The AVR processor includes three different shift instructions to account for the most useful of these options. The LSL (logical shift left) instruction (Figure 8.2) clears the vacated position (to 0). There are two right shift instructions. The LSR (logical shift right) clears the vacated bit (the most significant bit). The ASR (arithmetic shift right) leaves the vacated bit (most significant bit) unchanged. The differences are shown in Figure 8.3. The rotate instructions shown in Figure 8.4 (ROL and ROR) always include the Carry flag in the rotation, filling the vacated bit with what was in the Carry flag; the Carry flag is replaced by the bit shifted out of the register (Table 8.4).

Each of these instructions also affect the flags differently (Table 8.5).

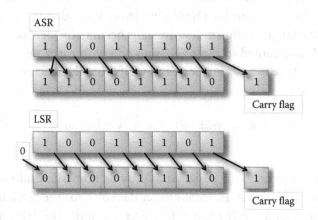

FIGURE 8.3 The logical and ASR differ in how the most significant bit is determined.

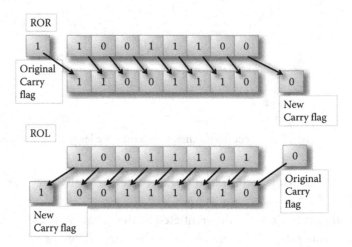

FIGURE 8.4 The rotate instructions rotate the eight bits of the byte along with the bit in the Carry flag.

Arithmetic Shifting

Although the AVR's right shift has logical and arithmetic variations, there is no separate arithmetic version of the left shift. LSL serves as a logical and arithmetic left shift. In fact, in the AVR, the LSL instruction is actually implemented as an ADD instruction. That is, `lsl  Rd` is actually assembled as `add  Rd,  Rd`. When you think of the left shift in this way, it is obvious that it simply doubles the result whether the data is in unsigned or two's complement format. The numeric result may overflow; this is detected using the usual flags (C for unsigned and V for signed). Note that V is 1 if the new sign bit (N) differs from the old sign bit (doubling should not change the sign unless overflow occurs). Incidentally, rotate left (ROL) is implemented in the AVR as an add with carry instruction. Try assembling these two instructions and verify that the machine code is the same for each.

```
rol r7 ;these are assembled exactly the same
adc r7,r7
```

The ASR instruction is designed to provide numeric results consistent with dividing two's-complement integer data by two. The remainder (0 or 1) is actually found in the Carry flag after the shift. The arithmetic shift instruction always preserves the sign of the data (assuming it is signed data). Note that dividing an odd negative number by two, rounds to the left

TABLE 8.4   AVR Shift and Rotate Instructions

Syntax	Operands	Action	Description
lsr Rd lsl Rd	A register	$0 \to Rd \to C$ $C \leftarrow Rd \leftarrow 0$	Logical shift right/ left. Carry gets the bit shifted out, and a zero is shifted in.
asr Rd	A register	$Rd(7) \to Rd \to C$	Same as lsr except most significant bit is unchanged
ror Rd rol Rd	A register	$C \to Rd \to C$ $C \leftarrow Rd \leftarrow C$	Old Carry flag is the bit shifted in, carry is replaced by the bit shifted out

on the number line, just as it does for positive numbers. Thus an ASR of –7 will result in –4 (not –3), and –1 shifted right will remain –1. Contrast this to the result of a right shift applied to the positive numbers, 7 and 1. A right shift applied to the code for 7 will yield 3, and 1 will be changed to 0.

To divide unsigned data by two, use the LSR instruction.

Other Applications of Shift and Rotate

In addition to doubling and halving numbers, shift and rotate operations have numerous additional applications. One is to cycle through the bits of a value. In a looping structure, this allows you to easily process each bit in turn. One simple application is to count the number of ones in the byte. A shift in the loop body places each bit in turn in the Carry flag, allowing it to be easily analyzed. Rotating (instead of shifting) the byte nine times (eight bits plus carry) will actually restore the data to its original state, so the operation is nondestructive. The following code segment uses the branch if carry clear (C == 0) instruction to count the ones in a byte.

TABLE 8.5   Affect of the Shift and Rotate Instructions on the Status Flags

Instruction	H	S	V	N	Z	C
lsl Rd rol Rd	Bit 3 of original Rd	N xor V	N xor C	Copy of bit 7 of result	1 if all bits are zero	Bit 7 of original Rd
lsr Rd	–	N xor V	N xor C	0	1 if all bits are zero	Bit 0 of original Rd
asr Rd ror Rd	–	N xor V	N xor C	Copy of bit 7 of result	1 if all bits are zero	Bit 0 of original Rd

Register R16 will be the loop counter, R17 will contain the byte whose bits are being counted, and R18 will hold the count of the number of ones found in the byte.

```
;non-destructive bit counter
.def loopcounter = R16
.def databyte    = R17
.def bitscounted = R18
clr bitscounted            ;set bit counter to 0
ldi loopcounter, 8         ;8 loop repetitions needed
nextbit:
    ror databyte           ;next bit shifted to carry
    brcc iszero            ;carry clear means the bit was 0
    inc bitscounted        ;count the 1
iszero:
    dec loopcounter        ;decrement loop counter
    brne nextbit           ;while loopcounter > 0

ror databyte               ;final shift restores data and
                           ;carry flag
;bitscounted contains the number of 1's in databyte
```

Rotating and shifting can be used to reverse the bits in a byte. The strategy is to shift each bit in turn to the Carry flag, and then use the rotate command to bring the bit in the Carry flag back into a different register.

```
;bit reversal
.def loopcounter   = R16
.def databyte      = R17
.def reversedbyte  = R18
ldi loopcounter, 8     ;8 loop repetitions needed
nextbit:
    lsr databyte        ;next bit shifted to carry
    rol reversedbyte    ;bit brought into position 0 of
                        ;reversed byte
    dec loopcounter     ;decrement loop counter
    brne nextbit        ;while loopcounter > 0
```

This strategy destroys the original data byte. If we had used the ROR instruction instead of LSR, in hope of preserving the value in the data-byte register (as in the previous example), we would be disappointed at the end. The value in databyte would end up being a reversed copy of the original contents of the reversedbyte register! Trace through the sequence of operations to see why. You will need to add a final ror databyte after the loop terminates to finish off the last bit of the double reversal.

Shifting multibyte data requires the use of the Carry flag. It temporarily stores a bit shifted out of one of the bytes so it can be rotated into the adjacent byte. The following sequence shifts a 16-bit number in R25:R24 to the left one position. This doubles the numeric value represented by the 16-bit code.

```
lsl R24     ;shift low byte first
rol R25     ;shift high byte, bringing in bit 7 from R24
```

A similar strategy can be used to shift such data to the right. You must be careful to begin with the most significant byte, using ASR or LSR, depending on whether the data is signed or unsigned. The rest of the bytes use ROR.

SPECIAL BITWISE OPERATIONS

The AVR microcontroller contains a few special instructions that facilitate the manipulation of the SREG flags. The SREG is affected by many machine instructions, but this is more like a side-effect. In some cases, an application simply needs to set or clear a status flag directly. The BSET and BCLR instructions allow direct control of each bit in the SREG, allowing any bit to be set or cleared (Table 8.6).

To avoid having to look up what flag is in what position in the SREG, all eight possibilities of each of these instructions can be coded using a mnemonic alias (Table 8.7).

In addition, there are special instructions to copy any bit from any general register to the T bit of the SREG or from the T bit to any bit of any general register. These are called the bit store and load instructions (Table 8.8).

TABLE 8.6   Special Instructions Affecting SREG Bits

Syntax	Operands	Action	Description
bclr s	A bit position	SREG(s) ← 0	Clear/Set bit in
bset s		SREG(s) ← 1	Status Register

TABLE 8.7   Aliases for Status Flag Set and Clear Instructions

Syntax	Action	Description
sec	$C \leftarrow 1$	Set/Clear C (carry) flag in status register
clc	$C \leftarrow 0$	
sez	$Z \leftarrow 1$	Set/Clear Z (zero) flag in status register
clz	$Z \leftarrow 0$	
sen	$N \leftarrow 1$	Set/Clear N (negative) flag in status register
cln	$N \leftarrow 0$	
sei	$I \leftarrow 1$	Set/Clear I (Global Interrupt) flag in status register
cli	$I \leftarrow 0$	
ses	$S \leftarrow 1$	Set/Clear S (signed test) flag in status register
cls	$S \leftarrow 0$	
sev	$V \leftarrow 1$	Set/Clear V (signed overflow) flag in status register
clv	$V \leftarrow 0$	
set	$T \leftarrow 1$	Set/Clear T flag in status register
clt	$T \leftarrow 0$	
seh	$H \leftarrow 1$	Set/Clear H (half carry) flag in status register
clh	$H \leftarrow 0$	

The above instructions are used to directly set or clear individual bits in the SREG. The conditional branch instructions are used to alter the flow of control based on the value of specific status bits.

AVR TIMER/COUNTER

The AVR ATMEGA16A microcontroller includes three distinct timers (also called counters), all capable of running from the system clock signal or from an external clock source. The ATxmega128A1 has eight timers. The basic purpose of a timer is to count up or down independent of the execution of a program. The timer will have some way of notifying the processor when a certain counter related event (such as reaching zero or a predetermined value) has occurred. For now, we will explore the basic capability of one of the AVR counters, the one known as Timer/Counter 1. This timer has a 16-bit resolution meaning it can count through 65,536 states. The counter is incremented by a user selectable clock source. The clock signal can be from an external source (supplied via one of the pins on the microcontroller), or it can utilize the same clock signal that is

TABLE 8.8   The Bit Store and Load Instructions

Syntax	Operands	Action	Description
bst Rd, b	Any register and bit position	$T \leftarrow Rd(b)$	Store bit b of Register Rd into T flag
bld Rd, b	Any register and bit position	$Rd(b) \leftarrow T$	Load bit b of Register Rd from T flag

TABLE 8.9   TCCR1 (Timer/Counter 1 Control Registers A and B; ATMEGA16A)

TCCR1A	7:6 - COM1A [1:0]	5:4 - COM1B [1:0]	3 - FOC1A	2 - FOC1B	1:0 - WGM1 [1:0]
Meaning	Output Compare Mode Channel A	Output Compare Mode Channel B	Force Output Compare Channel A	Force Output Compare Channel B	Waveform Generation Mode
TCCR1B	7 - ICNC1	6 - ICES1	5 - Reserved	4:3 - WGM1[3:2]	2:0 - CS1[2:0]
Meaning	Input Capture Noise Canceler	Input Capture Edge Select	Reserved	Waveform Generation Mode	Clock Select

supplied to the CPU. The CPU clock signal can also be prescaled (divided) by selected powers of two; the prescale unit allows the timers to run longer before overflowing, even at fast clock speeds.

The AVR timers are considered I/O devices, and as such are controlled via the I/O registers. In the simplest configuration, the timer is configured with a particular value called TOP. It begins counting at zero (BOTTOM); incrementing with each count pulse. When the timer reaches the TOP it resets on the next pulse to BOTTOM and signals this event by setting a flag bit in a register.

Timer/Counter 1 Configuration: ATMEGA16A

Configuration of the timers is accomplished by setting various bits in the associated Timer/Counter Control Registers. Timer/Counter 1 in the ATMEGA16A is configured via TCCR1A and TCCR1B. The ATxmega128A is treated in its own section as shown in Table 8.9.

As you can see, there are a lot of configuration options. We will only explore a single operating mode for now, which means most of these bits will all be zero. We want to select Clear Timer on Compare (CTC) Match mode. This is selected using the WGM1 field which is split across both registers. The correct value for this mode is 0b0100. Two of these bits are placed in the field WGM1[1:0] in TCCR1A and two in WGM1[3:2] in TCCR1B. All of the other bits (except for the clock select bits) should be zero. For our purposes, we will simply set WGM1[3:2] and CS1[2:0].

The last three bits control the clock source.

```
;Clock source selection codes for Timer / Counter 1
000 = Clock disabled  ;timer is stopped
```

```
001 = I/O clock (same frequency as CPU clock)
010 = /8 prescale
011 = /64 prescale
100 = /256 prescale
101 = /1024 prescale
110 = External clock on pin T1, falling edge trigger
111 = External clock on pin T1, rising edge trigger
```

Once the clock source is established (as something other than 0b000) the counter will immediately begin counting upwards towards TOP. Each pulse of the counter's clock will advance the counter by one. When the counter matches TOP, it is reset on its next pulse to 0 and the cycle repeats. The value of TOP is specified in Output Compare Register 1A (OCR1A). This is a 16-bit register; the parts are named OCR1AH and OCR1AL. When writing to this register, you must write the high byte first (MEGA series convention).

The counter's current count value is located in another 16-bit register: TCNT1H:TCNT1L. When writing to this register, it is also important to write the high byte first. The timer hardware includes an 8-bit TEMP register that is used to buffer the high byte when writing or reading any of the timer's 16-bit registers. Writing to TCNT1H or OCR1AH simply stores the byte in TEMP. Writing to the low byte of either of these registers causes the entire 16-bit value to be placed into the timer's 16-bit register. When reading TCNT1 or OCR1A, read the low byte first; this will return the low byte of the current count, and buffer the high byte in TEMP. Reading the high byte retrieves the value in TEMP.

If the processor clock is running at 1 MHz, and the clock select bits are 0b001 (divide by one prescaler), then the counter will count at the same speed (one million pulses per second). If the select bits are 0b011, then a divide by 64 prescale is selected, so the counter pulses (counts once) for every 64 CPU cycles. The counter would be running at 1,000,000/64 pulses per second, or 15,625 Hz. Using the full range of the counter (0 through $FFFF) it would take 4.194304 s (65,536/15,625) for the counter to reset.

Timer/Counter 1 Compare Match (ATMEGA16A)

The Timer Interrupt Flag Register (TIFR) is used by all of the timers to report events (Table 8.10).

Only bits 5:2 in TIFR are related to Timer/Counter 1. We are interested in the one called Output Compare Flag 1A (OCF1A). This is the flag that reports that a match occurred between the timer's count register and

TABLE 8.10   Timer Interrupt Flag Register

Bit	7	6	5	4	3	2	1	0
Meaning	OCF2	TOV2	ICF1	**OCF1A**	OCF1B	TOV1	OCF0	**TOV0**

OCR1A. When running in CTC mode, the timer sets this flag when a match occurs on its next count pulse; rather than incrementing the counter past the matched value (called TOP), it resets the counter value to zero as it sets the output compare flag. The output compare flag will remain set until your program clears it.

Do not think of the TIFR I/O register as a byte in memory. Instead, think of it as a collection of eight control lines and eight status lines. When you read from TIFR, you are getting status information from all of the timers. When you write to the I/O register, TIFR, you are sending a signal to the associated timers. Do not expect to read back what you write! In particular, the protocol for clearing any of the TIFR flags is to send a signal to the timer on the specific flags' control line. The signal to clear the flag is a one (1). After writing a one to a bit in this register, it will normally read back as a zero! If the following instructions are executed, it is very likely that R16 will contain $00 after the IN instruction.

```
ldi r16, $FF        ;command to clear all flags
out TIFR, r16       ;send the command
in r16, TIFR        ;request flag info from all timers
```

This may seem a little odd, but the confusion can be cleared up if you remember that the timer is an I/O device. You can send information to it, and you can request information from it. Sending information does not imply that the information is stored, only that the device responds to the message it receives. When you request information, you get a report from the device. What makes this confusing is that you perform this device communication through something that looks like an address (accessed via IN and OUT instructions), and we tend to think of this address as corresponding to a storage location.

The following code illustrates how to poll the status of Timer/Counter 1, waiting for an output compare match. The loop repeats until the flag is a one. When the loop terminates, the flag is cleared by sending a clear signal to the timer. This is done by writing a one to the OCF1A bit in TIFR.

```
ocwait:
    in r16, TIFR          ;request status from timers
    andi r16, 1<<OCF1A    ;isolate the output compare flag
    breq ocwait           ;repeat while it is 0
```

```
ldi r16, 1<<OCF1A        ;write a 1 to clear the flag
out TIFR, r16
```

The last OUT sends signals to all of the timers; only one of the signals is nonzero. The timers ignore a zero signal. Only Timer/Counter 1 gets a one (1) as its command to clear its OCF1A flag. If you read the same flag after this signal is sent, it will be read as a zero (unless the timer happens to match again on the next count before you read TIFR).

You might wonder why the simpler bit manipulation instructions were not used in the sample code. It seems clumsy to load a whole byte just to check one bit. Certainly it would be easier to write instructions such as

```
sbis TIFR, OCF1A
sbi TIFR, OCF1A
```

to accomplish what is required by several instructions. Unfortunately, TIFR is at I/O address $38, and the special bit test and set instructions can only be used with the lower numbered I/O registers (up to $1F). In this case, the only option was to copy the entire byte into a register in order to check the specific flag. To assert the clear signal for the overflow flag, an entire byte must be written. The 0-bits are ignored by the timer hardware.

Timer/Counter Configuration: ATxmega128A1

The ATxmega128A1 has eight 16-bit counters named TCC0, TCC1, TCD0, TCD1, TCE0, TCE1, TCF0, and TCF1. They are all pretty similar and offer a lot of configuration options. We will start with the clock selection which is managed by each timer's Control Register A (Table 8.11).

The clock select bits select the prescaler value. Load this register with one of the following:

```
0000 = Clock disabled; timer is stopped
0001 = Peripheral clock (same frequency as CPU clock)
0010 = /2 prescale
0011 = /4 prescale
0100 = /8 prescale
```

TABLE 8.11 CTRLA: Timer/Counter Control Register A (ATxmega128A1)

CTRLA	7	6	5	4	3:0
	– Reserved	– Reserved	– Reserved	– Reserved	– CLKSEL[3:0]
Meaning	Reserved	Reserved	Reserved	Reserved	Clock Select

```
0101 = /64 prescale
0110 = /256 prescale
0111 = /1024 prescale
1xxx = Event Channel xxx (0-7)
```

We will be using this counter to count to a TOP value and then reset (to zero). Assuming a 2 MHz clock and clock select value of 0b0101, the counter will increment each 2,000,000/64 = 31,250 times per second. The counts will be 1/31,250 = 0.000032 s apart. Using 65,535 as TOP, it will take 65,536*0.000032 = 2.097152 s to reach TOP and reset. Notice that counting to TOP means TOP + 1 counts will occur before the reset; the reset occurs on the next clock pulse after reaching TOP.

Control Register B contains fields to select the waveform generation mode (Table 8.12).

We will configure this timer to operate in Normal mode, which is coded as a zero in WGMODE. The other bits should be written to zero. As this is the default, it will probably be unnecessary to do anything with this register.

Timer/Counter Period: ATxmega128A1

In Normal mode, the XMEGA timer counts to a value called TOP and then resets. The value for TOP is specified in the Period Register (PER). This is a 16-bit register (PERH:PERL) and requires special care in accessing it. To complicate matters, access conventions are different from those of the ATMEGA16A. In the XMEGA series, when accessing 16-bit registers, always access the low byte first. When the low byte is written, it is buffered until the high byte is written. When the low byte is read, the high byte is buffered and the buffered value is returned when the high byte is read. We encountered this convention earlier when modifying the stack pointer in the XMEGA.

TABLE 8.12   CTRLB: Timer/Counter Control Register B (ATxmega128A1)

CTRLB	7 – CCDEN	6 – CCCEN	5 – CCBEN	4 – CCAEN	3 – Reserved	2:0 – WGMODE[2:0]
Meaning	Compare or Capture Enable CH D	Compare or Capture Enable CH C	Compare or Capture Enable CH B	Compare or Capture Enable CH A	Reserved	Waveform Generation Mode

The counter value is accessed through the 16-bit register CNT (CNTH:CNTL). Again, observe the access low byte first when reading or writing this register.

To use the XMEGA Timer/Counter C1 to time a 1 s interval, you must determine an appropriate clock prescale value and TOP value. In general, you want to use the smallest feasible prescale divisor. At 2 MHz, with a prescale divisor of 1, the maximum interval we can time will be $(1/2,000,000)^*$ 65,536 = 0.032768 s. Using a divisor of 2, $(1/(2,000,000/2))^*65,536 = 0.065$ 536 s is the maximum interval. Using Algebra we can eliminate the trial and error approach:

```
Let DIV be the prescale divisor.
(1/(2000000/DIV))*65536 >= 1 (second)
DIV >= 2000000/65536
DIV >= 30.5
So we choose DIV = 64, the smallest prescale divisor
available over 30
```

With the prescale divisor 64, each count is 0.000032 s (64/20,00,000). To get 1 s, we need 31,250 counts (1/0.000032). This will be the value for TOP.

```
;Using timer TCC1
;set TOP
.equ TOP = 31250
ldi temp, low(TOP)
sts TCC1_PER, temp
ldi temp, high(TOP)
sts TCC1_PER + 1, temp
;select clock
ldi temp, 5  ;divide by 64
sts TCC1_CTRLA, temp
```

When the timer reaches TOP (as specified by the value in PER), the next clock pulse resets the timer and sets a flag in the INTFLAGS register (Table 8.13).

In Normal mode, the timer counts up to TOP. The Overflow flag (OVFIF) is set on the next clock pulse and the count is reset to zero. The overflow flag will remain set until cleared by your program. The bit is cleared by writing a one.

TABLE 8.13   Timer Interrupt Flag Register (INTFLAGS)

Bit	7 – CCDIF	6 – CCCIF	5 – CCBIF	4 – CCAIF	3:2	1 – ERRIF	0 – OVFIF
Meaning	Compare or Capture Channel D Flag	Compare or Capture Channel C	Compare or Capture Channel B	Compare or Capture Channel A	Reserved	Error	**Overflow/ Underflow**

TIMER/COUNTER EXAMPLE: LED BLINKER

The following application illustrates the use of a 16-bit Timer/Counter to perform an action approximately two times per second. The application loops continuously, only entering the action block when the timer's compare match overflow event has occurred. The timer is configured so it takes 0.5 s to reach TOP. Any additional processing can be inserted in the main loop as long as it does not take too long; the counter's flag register needs to be checked frequently. This is the ATMEGA16A version. An alternate version for the ATxmega128A1 can be found at the end of the chapter.

PROGRAM 8.1   LED Blinker Flashes the LEDs Using a Timer

```
;Program 8.1 - LED Blinker
;Illustrate the use of a Timer/Counter to blink an LED

;Programmer: TM
;Date: 5/2010
;Platform: STK-500
;Device: ATMega16A
.include "m16def.inc"

;LED's on PORTB
;Clock speed 2 MHz

;Timer Counter 1 is used to count off a 0.5 second
;interval.
;At the end of each interval, the LED's are toggled.

.def temp = r16
.def leds = r17                 ;current LED value

.cseg
;Stack initialization
ldi temp, low(RAMEND)
out SPL, temp
```

```
ldi temp, high(RAMEND)
out SPH, temp

;leds display alternating pattern
ldi temp, $FF
out DDRB, temp
ldi leds, $AA
out PORTB, leds            ;alternating pattern

#define CLOCK 2.0e6        ;clock speed
.equ PRESCALE = 0b011      ;/64 prescale
.equ PRESCALE_DIV = 64
#define DELAY 0.50  ;seconds
.equ WGM = 0b0100     ;Waveform generation mode: CTC
;you must ensure this value is between 0 and 65535
.equ TOP = int(0.5 + (CLOCK/PRESCALE_DIV*DELAY))
.if TOP > 65535
.error "TOP is out of range"
.endif

;On MEGA series, write high byte of 16-bit timer
;registers first
ldi temp, high(TOP)        ;initialize compare value (TOP)
out OCR1AH, temp
ldi temp, low(TOP)
out OCR1AL, temp
ldi temp, ((WGM&0b11) << WGM10) ;lower 2 bits of WGM
out TCCR1A, temp
;upper 2 bits of WGM and clock select
ldi temp, ((WGM>>2) << WGM12)|(PRESCALE << CS10)
out TCCR1B, temp           ;start counter

main_lp:
    in temp, TIFR          ;request status from timers
    andi temp, 1<<OCF1A    ;isolate only timer 1's match
    breq skipoverflow      ;skip overflow handler

;match handler - done once every DELAY seconds
ldi temp, 1<<OCF1A ;write a 1 to clear the flag
out TIFR, temp
    ;overflow event code goes here
    ldi temp, $FF
```

```
        eor leds, temp
        out PORTB, leds
skipoverflow:
        ;main application processing goes here

rjmp main_lp
```

The #define statements are preprocessor commands that define a symbol to stand for a string. In this case, CLOCK stands for "2.0e6" (2 MHz) and DELAY stands for "0.5." These symbols cannot be equated to these values as the assembler only allows symbols to be equated to integer values.

The assembler's expression evaluator does perform floating point calculations (if a floating point value is used) and then truncates the result to an integer when necessary. The division, CLOCK/PRESCAL _ DIV, converts Hz (the CPU clock speed) to counter ticks (per second). Multiplying by DELAY calculates the number of ticks equivalent to DELAY seconds of time. To round (instead of truncate) the expression adds 0.5 before truncating the value to an integer. Because this value is loaded into the 16-bit counter, care must be taken to ensure it is between 0 and 65,535. The program uses a conditional assembly directive to issue an error message when this condition is not satisfied.

```
.if TOP > 65535
.error "TOP is out of range"
.endif
```

The condition after .if is evaluated; if it is true then the statements up to the .endif directive are assembled, otherwise they are skipped. In this case, a value for TOP that is out of range will cause an assembler error.

EXERCISES

1. The SBR and SBI instructions are similar in that they are used to SBRs. One affects a general purpose register, the other an I/O register. Although they look very similar, the second operands are very different. Explain the difference in meaning (or effect) of the three (3) in these two instructions:

```
sbr R20,3
sbi $18,3.
```

2. Tell the status flag values (HSVNZC) after `tst r0` is executed for each of the following R0 contents: $CF, $7F, and $00.

3. Lookup the instruction code for CLR and EOR. What do you notice about these instructions?

4. SER could be accomplished by ORI with a mask of $FF. Compare the operation codes for these two instructions. Are they the same instructions? If not, what is the difference in their actions?

5. SER could be accomplished using a LDI instruction. Compare the instruction codes for these alternatives. What do you find?

6. If R6 contains the ASCII code for an uppercase letter, show how to convert it to lowercase in three different ways: using ORI, SBR, and SUBI.

7. Toggling a bit can be accomplished using EOR, but this requires another register to hold the mask. Write a sequence of instructions to toggle bit 2 of R3 without using any other registers. You will probably need to use a conditional branch.

8. Write an instruction to clear bits 0 through 3 of the byte in register R16.

9. Write instructions to clear bits 0 through 3 of the byte in register R15.

10. Write instructions to divide a 16-bit unsigned integer (in R31:R30) by two.

11. Write instructions to divide a 16-bit signed integer (in R31:R30) by two.

12. Write instructions to shift R16 to the left, but fill the vacated position with a one instead of zero.

13. Write instructions to shift R16 to the left, but leave the least-significant bit unchanged.

14. Write a loop that shifts bits in R19 to the left while bit 7 is non-zero. Be sure to test the byte before performing the first shift. When the loop exits (moves on to the next instruction after the end of the loop) R19 will have a zero in bit 7.

15. Write instructions to divide a 32-bit twos complement coded number stored in R31:R30:R29:R28 by two.

16. Assemble the BSET instruction with operands 0, 1, 2, and 3. Also assemble the SEC, SEZ, SEN, and SEV instructions. Compare the instruction codes. What do you notice?

17. Show how to use BST and BLD to copy bit 7 to bit 0 in R20 in two steps. Does the following sequence do the same thing?

```
asr r20
bst r20, 7
rol r20
```

18. If R5 contains two BCD digits (packed BCD), write a sequence of instructions to separate the digits into registers R4 and R5. In particular, if R5 contains $39, then after the instructions are executed, R4 will contain $03 and R5 will contain $09.

19. Write a sequence of statements to pack the BCD digits in R4 and R5 to a single byte in R5. In particular, if R4 contains $01 and R5 contains $03, then after the instructions are executed, R5 will contain $13.

20. Assuming the processor is running at 4 MHz, and the clock select value for Timer/Counter 1 is 4, how much time is there between counter ticks (increments)?

21. Assuming the processor is running at 4 MHz, determine the time it will take until Timer/Counter 1 resets (starting at zero) given the following values for TOP and clock select. Assume the counter is running in CTC mode (ATMEGA16A) or Normal mode (ATxmega128A1). Specify which processor you are using.

```
TOP = 250      Clock Select = 1
TOP = 0        Clock Select = 2
TOP = 53200    Clock Select = 3
TOP = 1        Clock Select = 5
```

22. Write instructions to configure Timer/Counter 1 (ATMEGA 16A) or Timer/Counter C1 (ATxmega128A1) and start it running so it will overflow in 357 µs. Assume the processor clock speed is 8 MHz. Show your calculations and discuss your choice of prescaler value.

PROGRAMMING EXERCISES

1. Modify Program 8.1 to output the sequence of numbers 0, 1, 2, etc. in binary on the LEDs. Use the overflow event to output each successive value on the LEDs. The count should change every 0.1 s. Experiment with different delays. How long of a delay is possible? Change the PRESCALE _ DIV to 256 (you need to modify two constants). How long of a delay is possible using this setting? Hint: Look in the map file to determine the value the assembler assigns to TOP. You are looking for a DELAY that makes this number as large as possible.

2. Write a program to play a Simon like game. Your program will flash LEDs 0 through 3 in a progressively longer sequence. Each LED will remain on for one second. At the end of the sequence, the LEDs will blank and wait for button input. The

player must press the buttons corresponding to the LEDs in the same sequence. The LED corresponding to the button pressed is displayed ON until the next button is pressed. If the correct sequence is entered, the program flashes the LEDs ON and OFF once (one second each) and then restarts the sequence, lengthening it by one. If the player does not enter the correct sequence, the LEDs flash an alternating pattern ($AA - $55) and then the game starts over. If the player echos the longest sequence, they win—the game flashes $0F - $F0 forever). The sequence is fixed and is defined by a series of LED positions found in flash. The definition should look something like this.

```
LED: .db 0, 3, 2, 1, 2, 0, 3, $FF ;$FF ends the
sequence.
```

Place this definition somewhere in the code segment where it will NOT be executed! Use a 2 MHz clock.

3. Use a timer/counter to build a reaction timer. The LEDs should flash a countdown, 7, 6, 5, 4, 3, 2, 1, 0, by illuminating the corresponding LED for one second. When LED 0 is illuminated, the program should wait for a button press. If the button is pressed before the countdown reaches zero, flash the LEDs in some type of error pattern and wait for a button press to restart the program. Otherwise, flash the LEDs all ON for one second and then display the high byte of the reaction time (in ms) in binary. When a button is pressed, the low byte should be displayed. The next button press restarts the program. You should use a timer/counter that increments each millisecond to determine the reaction time. Read and display the count value when the button is pressed.

The following exercises use serial communications between the AVR microcontroller and a PC running a program such as HyperTerminal or PuTTY. Use a 2 MHz clock speed and 9600 baud 8-N-1 for the serial settings.

4. Write a program to encrypt characters in a line of input data. As each character is received, it is encrypted by toggling certain bits. The first character is modified by toggling bits 3 and 1; the second character has bits 2 and 0 toggled. The encrypted pair is transmitted back to the PC. The next pair is modified in the same way. Continue until a CR is received. You should simply echo the CR and then add a LF to the output. Restart the process

as more data is received. Check that an encoded message can be decoded by sending it through the program a second time.

5. Write a program to accept any character as input. As each character is received, it's ASCII code is transmitted back to the PC. For each character received, output eight "0" or "1" characters representing the ASCII code in binary. Output should be eight characters per line.

6. Write a program to accept a series of characters representing hexadecimal digits. Each digit received causes output of four "0" or "1" characters representing the binary version of the digit, followed by a space. Be sure your program handles upper or lower case digits such as "a" or "A." The input 0F2c would cause output 0000 1111 0010 1100. Have your program respond to a CR by outputting a CR and LF.

ALTERNATE PROGRAMS FOR THE XPLAIN DEMONSTRATION KIT

Program 8.1a: LED Blinker

The ATxmega128A1 has eight 16-bit counters. This application uses Timer Counter C1 (TCC1), There are only minor changes related to the port and timer configuration and access. There are minor differences between the XMEGA timer counters labeled 0 and 1, so bit positions and masks are prefaced by TC0_ or TC1_ to distinguish. This program uses this notation to specify the mask for the overflow interrupt flag, TC1_OVFIF_bm. The ATxmega128A1 include file does not define H and L versions of the 16-bit timer registers, so TCC1_PERH must be written as TCC1_PER + 1. Remember that the XMEGA hardware requires that the low bytes of 16-bit registers always be accessed first. This program also illustrates the use of a virtual port to control the LEDs.

PROGRAM 8.1a: LED Blinker Flashes the LEDs Using a Timer

```
;Program 8.1a - LED Blinker
;Illustrate the use of a Timer/Counter to blink an LED

;Programmer: TM
;Date: 5/2010
;Platform: XPLAIN
;Device: ATxmega128A1
.include "ATxmega128A1def.inc"
```

```
;LED's on PORTE
;Clock speed 2 MHz

;Timer Counter C1 is used to count off a 0.5 second
;interval.
;At the end of each interval, the LED's are toggled.

.def temp = r16
.def leds = r17      ;current LED value


.cseg

;Setup PORTE as Virtual Port 0
lds temp, PORTCFG_VPCTRLA  ;current mappings for virtual
                              ;ports 0 and 1
cbr temp, $0F ;clear low nybble which is port 0's mapping
sbr temp, $04 ;PORTE is number 4
sts PORTCFG_VPCTRLA,temp ;mapping in effect

;Configure port direction
ldi    temp,0xFF
out    VPORT0_DIR,temp     ;configure PORTE as output
;leds display alternating pattern
ldi leds, $AA
out VPORT0_OUT, leds            ;alternating pattern

#define CLOCK 2.0e6             ;clock speed
.equ PRESCALE = 0b0101          ;/64 prescale
.equ PRESCALE_DIV = 64
#define DELAY 0.50 ;seconds
.equ WGMMODE = 0b000  ;Waveform generation mode: Normal

;you must ensure this value is between 0 and 65535
.equ TOP = int(0.5 + (CLOCK/PRESCALE_DIV*DELAY))

.if TOP > 65535
.error "TOP is out of range"
.endif

;On XMEGA series, write low byte of 16-bit timer
;registers first
ldi temp, low(TOP)              ;Set the period
```

```
sts TCC1_PER, temp
ldi temp, high(TOP)
sts TCC1_PER+1, temp
ldi temp, WGMMODE              ;other bits are zero
sts TCC1_CTRLB, temp
ldi temp, PRESCALE << TC1_CLKSEL0_bp  ;clock select
sts TCC1_CTRLA, temp           ;start counter

main_lp:
     lds temp, TCC1_INTFLAGS      ;request status from
                                  ;timer
     andi temp, TC1_OVFIF_bm      ;isolate overflow flag
     breq skipoverflow            ;skip overflow handler

;match handler - done once every DELAY seconds
ldi temp, TC1_OVFIF_bm                 ;write a 1 to clear the
                                       ;flag
sts TCC1_INTFLAGS, temp
     ;overflow event code goes here
     ldi temp, $FF
     eor leds, temp
     out VPORT0_OUT, leds

skipoverflow:
     ;main application processing goes here

rjmp main_lp
```

See the comments following Program 8.1 for a description of the features of this program.

CHAPTER 9

Control Structures

A LARGE PERCENTAGE OF STATEMENTS in a high-level program are part of the fundamental control structure called sequence. That is, they are executed in the same sequence they appear in the program. The sequence structure is used inside methods, functions, and subroutines. It is used inside blocks and loop bodies. Sequence structures are entered at the top and exited at the bottom. There is no branching into or out of a sequence structure.

Most high-level languages provide four basic control structures: sequence, selection, repetition, and call–return. These are indicated by keywords such as if, else, for, while, and by symbols representing a function name. The call–return control structure is usually treated separately under the topic of functions or methods. It is nevertheless, a control structure that serves an important role in programming. In conjunction with recursive techniques, it also provides a powerful iteration structure.

Assembly language provides the necessary tools to implement all of these higher-level language constructs. It also allows any number of arbitrarily complex control structures to be developed. Programmers have learned from experience that restricting programming practices to a few well-understood and carefully implemented structures makes programming, debugging, and maintenance much easier and more efficient.

Since you are already familiar with the basic control structures used in popular high-level languages, this chapter will demonstrate how to translate those structures into assembly language. Remember that the basic fetch–execute cycle includes a step that automatically increments the PC. This is how sequential execution is accomplished. Instructions intended to be executed in sequence are located in successive memory locations so the fetch–execute cycle naturally fetches and executes them in sequence. The fundamental instruction needed to break out of a sequential flow of control at the machine level is one that can alter the state of the PC, allowing the next instruction to be fetched from a totally different location. The process of changing the PC is called branching. The term sequencing is applied when the PC is simply incremented in the normal manner to fetch the next instruction. Branching instructions provide the means to implement nonsequential control structures.

ALTERING THE FLOW OF CONTROL

Because the normal function of the fetch–execute cycle includes incrementing the PC, the default control structure for machine language programs is sequence. To alter the flow of control, something must interrupt the default sequential execution by changing the value in the PC before the next instruction is fetched. Jump, branch, and call instructions, and interrupts can all cause a change to the PC and interrupt the sequential execution path.

Jump

The AVR processor has several instructions that can affect the PC. The simplest is the unconditional jump instruction. This simply places a new address in the PC (after it has been dutifully and unnecessarily incremented). This address becomes the target of the next fetch. The following instruction creates a very short, but infinite loop:

```
rjmp PC
```

The assembler evaluates the target address and codes the instruction so the target of the jump is the RJMP instruction itself (PC is assembly language syntax that means the address of this instruction—try not to confuse the symbol PC used by the assembler with PC when it is used as an abbreviation for a processor's program counter register). When the instruction is fetched, the processor's PC is incremented, and the next instruction is prefetched. When the RJMP is executed, the updated PC is replaced with the target address of the RJMP; the prefetched instruction (next in sequence) is discarded, and the RJMP instruction is executed again. Once this loop begins, nothing else can happen unless the program is interrupted.

Call and Return

The call–return mechanism is a special case of the unconditional jump. Before branching to a new location when a CALL instruction is executed, the processor saves the current PC value (this will be the address of the next instruction in sequence). This address is called the return address. After the called function completes its task, a special instruction (RET, which is short for return) can replace the PC value with the saved return address, effecting the return portion of the call–return mechanism. Both instructions (CALL and RET) modify the PC, causing a deviation from the normal sequential flow of control.

Conditional Branch

In addition to the unconditional jumps, there are conditional jumps or branches. These instructions have the same effect as a jump, except that in some circumstances the PC value is not altered. Thus, the branch is conditional. When the PC is changed to a new target address, we say that the branch is taken. If it is unaffected, we say the branch instruction sequenced. Remember that the PC is always incremented in anticipation of sequencing. If a conditional branch's condition is not satisfied, then the value of the PC is already correct; no further action is needed.

Conditional branches usually depend on one or more bits in the processor SREG. These bits generally reflect the result of some past instruction. It is important to know that some instructions do not modify the SREG while others do. To determine what previous instruction will determine the outcome of a conditional branch, it is sometimes necessary to trace backwards in a program. Good documentation will be appreciated by anyone that has to read your program and determine what prior instruction affects a particular branch.

Tracing backwards in an assembly language program is not always easily done. Simply considering the instructions in reverse sequence ignores the possibility that a branch to any of the prior instructions may be possible. This necessitates careful scrutiny of the entire program to locate the targets of every branch instruction. Unlike high-level language control structures with single entry and exit points, assembly language code can be entered at any point from many different places. Due to the potential complexities of this type of programming, it is important to resist the urge to create overly complex structures. Well documented entry and exit points make assembly language programming and debugging much easier.

JUMP AND CONDITIONAL BRANCH INSTRUCTIONS

The AVR processor provides several different jump instructions. The basic difference between them is how the destination address is encoded. The most common jump is the relative jump.

```
rjmp address
```

The only limitation to this instruction is that the address must be within 2048 words of the instruction itself. This limitation is due to the fact that twelve bits are used to encode the displacement ($2^{12} = 4096$) inside the instruction. The assembler determines the displacement to the target of the jump (from the current address) and codes that signed number into the instruction. When an RJMP is executed, the processor adds the displacement (found in the instruction code) to the current value of the PC to determine the new PC value, the target of the jump. This addressing mode is known as PC relative addressing.

The other jump instructions are:

```
ijmp    ;Indirect addressing: target address must be in Z
eijmp   ;Extended Indirect addressing: target in EIND:Z
jmp address  ;Direct addressing into 4Mwords of program
             ;memory
```

The JMP instruction is two words in length. The entire second word and six bits of the first word of the instruction comprises the target address. This allows up to 2^{22} addresses (4 million word addresses). The penalty for the extended address space is the increased instruction size and an extra clock cycle of execution time.

The conditional branch instructions either sequence, or branch, based on the current value of a single status flag. These are always preceded by some instruction that affects the flags to setup the reason for the conditional jump. Executing a conditional branch does not change any flags in the SREG, so you can have a sequence of branch instructions that rely on a single SREG setting.

The addressing mode used to specify the destination of the conditional branches (if successful) is PC-relative. The range is −64 to +63 words from the instruction following the conditional branch. The displacement is calculated by the assembler and is stored in the instruction as a 7-bit, two's complement integer.

The AVR microcontroller has only two conditional branch instructions that are based on flags in the SREG. One branches if a bit in the SREG is clear (BRBC), the other if it is set (BRBS). To use these properly, you must know the positions of the bits in the SREG (carry flag is bit zero, signed overflow is bit three, etc.) and what each means in a variety of situations. To simplify the selection of the correct bit, and avoid confusion and potential errors, there are aliases for the conditional branches connected with each bit of the SREG. These instructions (aliases) should always be used in place of the general conditional branch instructions (Table 9.1).

TABLE 9.1 AVR Conditional Branch Instructions Based on the SREG Flags

Syntax	Operands	Action	Description
brbc s, k	A bit number and address	PC ← SREG(s)? PC + 1 : PC + 1 + k	Branch if bit in status register is clear
brbs s, k	A bit number and address	PC ← SREG(s)? PC + 1 + k : PC + 1	Branch if bit in status register is set
brcc k brcs k	An address	Same as brbc/s 0, k	Branch if carry clear/set
brsh k brlo k	An address	Same as brbc/s 0, k	Branch if same_ or_higher/lower (as unsigned integer)
brne k breq k	An address	Same as brbc/s 1, k	Branch if not_ equal/equal
brpl k brmi k	An address	Same as brbc/s 2, k	Branch if plus/ minus
brvc k brvs k	An address	Same as brbc/s 3, k	Branch if oVerflow clear/ set
brge k brlt k	An address	Same as brbc/s 4, k	Branch if greater_or_ equal/less (as signed integer)
brhc k brhs k	An address	Same as brbc/s 5, k	Branch if half carry clear/set
brtc k brts k	An address	Same as brbc/s 6, k	Branch if T flag is clear/set
brid k brie k	An address	Same as brbc/s 7, k	Branch if global interrupt disabled/ enabled

Notice that the carry flag is the condition in two pairs of branches. These instructions are completely interchangeable (BRCC and BRSH, BRCS and BRLO). It is customary to use the branch if same or higher (or branch if lower) after a comparison of two unsigned values. The branch if carry clear (or set) is used when the programmer wants to explicitly check the value in the carry flag.

Comparisons

The compare instructions are commonly used to set the SREGs in preparation for a conditional branch. The test (TST) instruction is also used for this purpose. None of these change any general purpose registers; they only affect the status flags. However, remember that the arithmetic and logical instructions also affect status flags, so a conditional branch may immediately follow one of these instructions; a compare (or TST) is not always necessary (Table 9.2).

Following a compare, any of the conditional branches based on the six status flags (HSVNZC) are valid. After a TST, only the branches that depend on N or Z should be used (BREQ, BRNE, BRMI, BRPL).

Conditional branches after an INC or DEC cannot rely on the carry flag (BRCC, BRCS, BRLO, BRSH) as it is not affected by these instructions.

When comparing numbers, be sure to follow the comparison with the correct conditional branch for the data types. Use BRLO and BRSH only after a comparison of unsigned numbers; use BRLT and BRGE only after a comparison of signed numbers.

TABLE 9.2   Compare and TST Instructions that Often Precede a Conditional Branch

Syntax	Operands	Action	Description
cp Rd, Rr	Two registers	Affects status flags the same as sub Rd, Rr (Rd − Rr)	Compare Rd to Rr
cpc Rd, Rr	Two registers	Affects status flags the same as sbc Rd, Rr (Rd−Rr−C)	Compare Rd to Rr with carry
cpi Rd, k	Register (16–31) and byte value	Affects status flags the same as subi Rd, k (Rd−k)	Compare Rd with immediate constant
tst Rd			Test for zero or minus

TABLE 9.3   Conditional Skip Instructions

Syntax	Operands	Action	Description
cpse Rd, Rr	Two registers	PC ← (Rd = Rr)? PC + 2(3):PC + 1	Compare Rd with Rr and skip if equal
sbic A, b	I/O register (0-31 only) and bit number (0-7)	PC ← (SREG(b) = 0)? PC + 2(3):PC + 1	Skip if bit in I/O register is clear
sbis A, b	I/O register (0-31 only) and bit number (0-7)	PC ← (SREG(b) = 1)? PC + 2(3):PC + 1	Skip if bit in I/O register is set
sbrc Rr, b	Register and bit number (0-7)	PC ← (Rr(b) = 0)? PC + 2(3):PC + 1	Skip if bit in register is clear
sbrs Rr, b	Register and bit number (0-7)	PC ← (Rr(b) = 1)? PC + 2(3):PC + 1	Skip if bit in register is set

Logical instructions may be followed by branches that depend on the zero flag (BREQ or BRNE). The shift and rotate instructions are sometimes also followed by decisions based on the carry flag (BRCC, BRCS). When shifts are used to multiply/divide by two, the S, V, and N flags may also contain meaningful information.

Conditional Skip Instructions

There are a few special conditional branches that can skip one instruction (or not) according to some condition. Since the next instruction may be 1 or 2 words in length, these so-called skip instructions perform one of the following actions:

```
If condition false: PC = PC + 1          (sequence, no skip)
If condition true: PC = PC + 2 (or 3)    (skip)
```

None of these instructions affect the status flags or general purpose registers (Table 9.3).

SELECTION

Selection structures provide the ability to choose one of several alternative paths of execution. The common selection structures provided by many programming languages are if, if/else, and a switch or select case statement.

C and Java also provide a conditional expression that allows one of two expressions to be evaluated based on a logical condition. This is simply a restricted version of an if/else structure, condensed to a single expression evaluation semantic.

If The fundamental selection structure is the if statement. When the condition is true, the then-part is executed, otherwise it is skipped. The if statement has one entry point (where the condition is evaluated) and one exit (after the then-part). To translate an if statement into assembly language, you need to reverse (negate) the condition, as the action is to branch around (skip) the then-part when the original condition is false. The following examples illustrate how simple if statements might be translated to assembly. In each case, note how the condition of the if statement is negated to branch around the conditional action. In some cases the condition must be rewritten in an equivalent form due to the limited number of conditional branch variations.

The examples assume the variables names have been equated to appropriate registers. The variables a and b are unsigned bytes, m and n are signed bytes (all based in registers) (Table 9.4).

If Else

If/else structures are implemented in a similar way. Since there is an if-part and an else-part, the programmer has the choice of placing either one first in the code. If the else-part is listed first, the if's condition need not be negated (as required by the translation of the simpler if statement) in the assembly language version. The disadvantage of this approach is that it is inconsistent with the normal presentation order encountered in the high-level language if/else structure.

Regardless of which part of the structure is placed first, there must always be an unconditional branch to skip over the second part of the statement. The examples here place the if-part first, negating the condition as illustrated in the if statement translations (Table 9.5).

Notice that in each case, the flow of control out of the else-part naturally sequences to the next statement of the program; there is no additional jump instruction needed to complete the control structure.

Compound Conditions

Compound conditions (those involving && and || operators) require a little more work. Compound conditions are usually evaluated using what

TABLE 9.4   Translating IF Structures to Assembly Language

High Level	Assembly Equivalent
if (a >= b) b ++;	cp a, b ;skip if a < b brlo skip inc b skip:
if (a > b) a--;	cp b, a ;skip if a <= b, i.e. b >= a brsh skip dec a skip:
if (m >= n) m -= n;	cp m, n ;skip if m < n brlt skip sub m, n skip:
if (m == 0) n = 0;	tst m ;skip if m != 0 brne skip clr n skip:

if (a > 9) {
  b ++;
  a = 0;
  }
	cpi a, 10 ;skip if a <= 9, i.e. a < 10
	brlo skip
	inc b
	clr a
	skip:

if (m != n + 1) a = 255;	push n inc n ;temp expression value (n + 1) cpse m, n ;skip if m == n + 1 ldi a, 255 pop n ;restore n

TABLE 9.5   Translating IF/ELSE Structures to Assembly Language

High Level	Assembly Equivalent

if (a >= b)
  b ++;
else
  a ++;
	cp a, b ;skip to else if a < b
	brlo else
	inc b
	rjmp end_if
	else:
	  inc a
	end_if:

if (a == 0)
  a = b;
else
  b ++
	tst a ;skip to else if a! = 0
	brne else
	mov a, b
	rjmp end_if
	else:
	  inc b
	end_if:

is called short-circuit evaluation common to C and Java. Short-circuit evaluation means:

> When evaluating compound conditions involving &&, the parts are evaluated left to right. As soon as one part is detected to be false, the entire condition is false, and the appropriate branch occurs without evaluating the rest of the parts.

> When evaluating compound conditions involving ||, the parts are evaluated left to right. As soon as one part is detected to be true, the entire condition is true, and the appropriate branch occurs without evaluating the rest of the parts.

In some cases, you will need to negate compound conditions to make the assembly language cleaner. Negating compound conditions requires the application of DeMorgan's Law.

```
~(a && b) == ~a || ~b
~(a || b) == ~a && ~b
```

Remember that after applying DeMorgan's Law, you will be evaluating the negation of the original if condition. This means that you want to skip over the if-part when the new (negated) condition is true.

Writing a sequence of TSTs that implement short-circuit evaluation of a compound condition involving OR operations is fairly straightforward. For example, to branch to a specific location when A || B || C is true is easily accomplished with a sequence of TSTs. The first TST to give a true result short-circuits immediately to the destination:

```
;skip to end_if when A||B||C (is true)
    Setup test A
    Branch if true to end_if
    Setup test B
    Branch if true to end_if
    Setup test C
    Branch if true to end_if
;This is the if-part, reached only when ~(A||B||C)
;so 'do something' here
end_if:
```

The above structure would be a plausible implementation of an if statement with a compound condition involving AND operators.

```
if (~A && ~B && ~C) do something
```

The condition would be negated using DeMorgan's Law so we can skip over the if-part when the original condition is false, or when A || B || C is true.

It is easy to become confused and build extremely complicated structures to correctly evaluate complex conditions and direct the execution path to the correct location. In general, choose the solution that requires the least amount of branching around; such structures will be more likely to be correct (and understood).

When the original compound condition of an IF includes OR operations, it is generally translated without negation. The first true condition encountered in the sequence causes a branch to the if-part. Each false condition simply falls into the next TST (as in the sequence described above). The last TST is reversed, causing a branch around the if-part (to the end-if) if it is also false. Look carefully at the examples involving OR operations in the translations below to see the technique used in practice.

In general, compound expressions involving AND conditions are more easily implemented by negating the entire condition, while those involving OR conditions are left alone, reversing only the final TST (Table 9.6).

To improve readability and maintenance, it is a good idea to imitate the layout of high-level language control structures. Include comments showing control structures in pseudo-code. Clearly label the then and else parts. The use of indentation is generally of little use in assembly language,

TABLE 9.6   Translating Selection Structures with Compound Conditions to Assembly Language

High-Level	Comment	Assembly Equivalent

if (a >= b)
|| m < n)
  a++;
	No negation of the compound condition is necessary	cp a, b ;if a >= b do if-part
		brsh if_part
		cp m, n ;if ⊠ (m < n) skip to end_if
		brge end_if
		if_part:
		  inc a
		end_if:

if (a >= b
&& m < n)
b++;
	Negated condition:
	(a < b || m >= n)
		cp a, b ;if a<b skip to end_if
		brlo end_if
		cp m, n ;if m >= n skip to end_if
		brge end_if
		;then part
		  inc b
		end_if:

(continued)

TABLE 9.6 (continued) Translating Selection Structures with Compound Conditions to Assembly Language

High-Level	Comment	Assembly Equivalent

if (a == 0
&& b!=0)
  m = n;
else
  n = m;
	Negated
	condition:
	(a! = 0 ||
	b == 0)
	
	else-part
	listed
	second in
	code
		tst a ;if a! = 0 skip to else
		brne else
		tst b ;if b == 0 skip to else
		breq else
		;then part
		  mov m, n
		  rjmp end_if ;skip around else-part
		else:
		  mov n, m
		end_if:

if (m > 0
|| n > 0)
  a++;
	Not negated	cpi m, 1 ;if m > 0 (i.e. m >= 1)
		  skip to then
		  brge then
		  cpi n, 1 ;if☒ (n > 0) (i.e. n < 1) ...
		  brlt end_if
		  then: inc a
		end_if:

if (m > n
|| m >= 0)
  a = b = 0;
else
  m--;
	Not Negated
	
	Else-part
	will be
	listed first
	in code to
	simplify the
	structure
	(this avoids
	reversing the
	last test)
		cp n, m ;if (m > n) (i.e. n < m)
		  brlt then ;...skip to then-part
		  tst m ;if (m >= 0) skip to
		  then-part
		  brpl then
		;else part
		  dec m
		  rjmp end_if
		then:
		  clr a
		  clr b
		end_if:

if (a > b
&& b > 9)
  m++;
else
  n++
	Negated
	condition:
	(a <= b ||
	b <= 9)
	Note reversal
	of a and b
	to use brsh
	(there is no
	branch if
	lower or
	equal)
	Note that cpi
	b, 10 with
	just brlo
	could be
	used in
	place of the
	2 branches
		cp b, a ;if b >= a skip to else
		  brsh else
		  cpi b, 9 ;if b <= 9 skip to else
		  brlo else ;this is the < case
		  breq else ;this is the == case
		;then part
		  inc m
		  rjmp end_if
		else:
		  inc n
		end_if:

so vertical separation and comments provide the best documentation of your flow of control. Try to avoid complex control structures; use functions when possible to keep code segments short and easily traced.

Before going on, another approach to the evaluation of a conditional expression should be considered. Rather than creating a sequence of TSTs, the entire condition could be evaluated to a final Boolean value. Consider the following example evaluation of the expression (a > b && b > 10). In this example, all parts of the condition are evaluated; short-circuit evaluation is not performed.

```
;if (a>b && b>10) ... else ...
;r16 will be the Boolean result of the expression
ser r16  ;assume true when processing &&'s
;evaluate first part: a>b (unsigned)
    cp b, a  ;carry set when b<a
    in r17, SREG
    sbrs r17, SREG_C  ;skip if condition is true
    clr r16  ;condition is false
;evaluate next part: b>10 (unsigned)
    cpi b, 11
    in r17, SREG
    sbrc r17, SREG_C  ;skip if condition is true
    clr r16
;act on condition
    tst r16  ;$00 means false, $FF will be true
    breq elsePart
;then part
    . . .
    rjmp end_if
else:
    . . .
end_if:
```

In the case of a Boolean expression including the OR operation, begin with a false result and set the result to true when either condition is true.

```
;if (a>b || b>10) ... else ...
;r16 will be the boolean result of the expression
    ldi r16, 0  ;assume false when processing ||'s
;evaluate first part: a>b (unsigned)
    cp b, a  ;carry clear when b>=a
    in r17, SREG
```

```
    sbrc r17, SREG_C  ;skip if condition is false
    ser r16  ;condition is false
;evaluate next part: b > 10 (unsigned)
    cpi b, 11
    in r17, SREG
    sbrs r17, SREG_C  ;skip if condition is false
    ser r16
;act on condition
    tst r16
    breq elsePart
. . .
```

This approach performs a full evaluation of the Boolean expression; no short-circuit evaluation is performed. In some cases, this may be desired. For example, a condition that causes a side effect, such as (a > 0 && ++b < limit) may require b to be incremented even if a is not greater than 0. Using short-circuit evaluation, this would not happen.

You can see that there are two approaches to implementing condition evaluation for the purposes of control-flow decisions. The first uses SREG flags to branch appropriately. The value of the Boolean expression is never explicitly generated; the branches are taken based on the implicit Boolean result. This approach is best suited for situations where short-circuit evaluation is needed, or the conditions are very simple. The flow of control through the condition evaluation section is sometimes rather complex, especially for complex conditions.

The second approach actually generates a Boolean value (in a register) representing the result of the expression. Once the final Boolean value is determined, the program uses this value to determine the appropriate branch. This approach is better suited to full evaluation of a compound expression. The control logic of the expression evaluation is a simple sequence, followed by a final branch to the appropriate section of the program. The simplicity of this structure may be an advantage when a condition is very complex.

Multiway Selection Structure

A multiway selection structure, similar to the switch statement in C or Java, is easily implemented in assembly language by creating a series of comparisons followed by branches to the appropriate case. For example, compare the following case structure in C ++ and assembly (Table 9.7).

The above structure could also be implemented by negating the conditions and branching around each case to the next test/case pair. This

TABLE 9.7   Implementation of a Multiway Selection Structure

High Level	Assembly Equivalent
```switch (m) {```	```;start switch(m)```
```case 1: case 3:```	```cpi m, 1```
``` m++;```	```breq case1```
``` break;```	```cpi m, 3```
```case 2:```	```breq case3```
``` n++;```	```cpi m, 2```
``` break;```	```breq case2```
```case 4:```	```cpi m, 4```
``` m+=n; //no break```	```breq case4```
```default:```	```rjmp casedefault```
``` n=0;```	
```}```	```;cases```
	```case1:```
	```case3:```
	``` inc m```
	``` rjmp end_switch```
	```case2:```
	``` inc n```
	``` rjmp end_switch```
	```case4:```
	``` add m, n```
	``` ;intentionally fall into```
	``` ;next case```
	```casedefault:```
	``` clr n```
	```end_switch:```

approach would be more like a nested if/else structure, and would make it awkward to simulate the fall-through effect (between cases) that may be desired in some situations.

Computed Goto

Assembly language provides some interesting selection structures that are not commonly used in modern high-level languages. One is the computed goto. This structure uses an address calculation to determine the destination of a jump. Some case statements are easily implemented using this type of structure. Consider the following implementation of the switch statement using this technique. The code begins by eliminating m values that are too high. Then Z is set to point to the start of a jump table, a collection of relative jumps to the actual case code. The value of m is added to the table address to index into the table by the correct amount (the value

TABLE 9.8   Implementation of a Multiway Selection Using a Jump Table

High Level	Assembly Equivalent
```switch (m){```	```;start switch```
```case 1: case 3:```	``` cpi m, 5```
``` m++;```	``` brsh casedefault```
``` break;```	``` ldi ZH, high(jtab)```
```case 2:```	``` ldi ZL, low(jtab)```
``` n++;```	``` add ZL, m```
``` break;```	``` brcc no_carry```
```case 4:```	``` inc ZH```
``` m+=n; //no break```	```no_carry:```
```default:```	``` ijmp```
``` n=0;```	```;jump table```
```}```	```jtab:```
	``` rjmp casedefault```
	``` rjmp case1```
	``` rjmp case2```
	``` rjmp case3```
	``` rjmp case4```
	```;cases```
	```case1:```
	```case3:```
	``` inc m```
	``` rjmp end_switch```
	```case2:```
	``` inc n```
	``` rjmp end_switch```
	```case4:```
	``` add m, n```
	```casedefault:```
	``` clr n```
	```end_switch:```

of *m*). The indirect jump transfers to the appropriate RJMP which then transfers to the correct case code (Table 9.8).

This approach takes a little more code for the small example shown above, however, it is easily extended to a large number of cases. This is the same technique used to dispatch interrupts by the AVR interrupt system. The interrupt vector table is a table much like this; the interrupt number serves as the index into the table to transfer control to the correct interrupt handler.

LOOPING

In assembly language, loops are created using the jump and branch instructions; when these are used to jump to an instruction previously executed they create a repetition structure.

```
;statements before loop
;start of loop structure
top_of_loop:
    ;loop body
    ...
    rjmp top_of_loop
```

The loop illustrated above may look like an infinite loop; there is no obvious way to exit the structure. In assembly language, the exit can occur from any point of the loop body. Discipline must be exercised to prevent complicated looping control structures.

Implementation of conditional looping structures is accomplished by applying the same principles used to implement selection. The evaluation of the loop condition can be at the top of the loop, bottom of the loop, or even in the middle of the loop. The loop can be entered at the top, or a jump may precede the loop body to enter it at some other point. The choices will be made by the programmer. Just remember to keep everything as simple as possible.

While, For, and Do Until

The most common high-level language pretest loops (in which the condition is tested before each potential iteration) are the while loop and the more specialized for loop. You can think of the for loop as an enhanced while; it includes (as part of the syntax) an initialization expression (an expression that is evaluated before the loop TST is made for the first time), and an update expression (evaluated before each successive TST of the loop condition). Both the for loop and the while loop terminate if the loop condition is false when it is tested (at the top of the loop).

The do until (or do while) structure provides for one iteration of the loop body before the loop condition is evaluated. This is called a posttest loop. The do while and do until structures are identical except for the semantics of the condition. The do until loop executes until the condition becomes true (iterates while the condition is false). The do while structure implies the opposite; the loop iterates while the condition is true (terminates when the condition becomes false). The only real difference between the pretest while loop and the post-test do while is the initial evaluation of the condition. In both cases, the loop condition is evaluated between iterations; the while loop adds one extra evaluation which occurs before the first iteration (which might be skipped).

When possible, loops should be coded to closely mirror the high-level language structure that best describes the loop function. However, in assembly language, loops are most efficiently coded with the TST at the end of the loop body, branching back to the top only if the loop will be repeated. Such loops will closely resemble the do-while or do-until high-level language counterparts.

This structure below illustrates a posttest loop. This is the typical way a do-until or a do-while loop is written in assembly language. This structure also would be used for any loop that might be commonly written as a while loop in which at least one iteration is intended.

```
;statements before loop

;start of loop structure
top_of_loop:
    ;loop body
    . . .
    ;evaluate condition
    brne top_of_loop  ;or appropriate test

;continue with statements after loop
```

If a loop must account for the possibility of zero repetitions, then some type of pretest loop must be constructed. There are two common alternatives to implementing this structure. The first follows the layout of a typical while loop; the condition is placed at the top of the loop with a branch to the statement after the end of the loop body when the loop is to terminate. This also requires an unconditional jump at the end of the loop body back to the top of the loop.

```
;statements before loop

;start of loop structure
top_of_loop:
    ;evaluate condition
    brne exit  ;or appropriate test

    ;loop body
    . . .
    rjmp top_of_loop

exit:
;continue with statements
;after loop
```

The other implementation is to leave the condition at the end of the loop body. To ensure the loop condition is evaluated before the loop body, the entrance to the loop is at the bottom. This is effected by adding an unconditional jump just before the start of the physical loop.

```
;statements before loop
;start of loop structure
rjmp loop_test

top_of_loop:
    ;loop body
    . . .
loop_test:
    ;evaluate condition
    brne top_of_loop   ;or appropriate test

;continue with statements after loop
```

The implementation of a for loop requires the extra steps of writing the code that corresponds to the initialization and the update steps. Common loop translations are illustrated in the following examples. Once again, *a* and *b* are unsigned bytes, *m* and *n* are signed bytes; all are located in registers (Table 9.9).

The last example illustrates the flexibility of assembly language to allow the loop TST to occur in the middle of an iteration. This structure is sometimes referred to as a do-while-do statement. It might be expressed in high-level pseudocode as follows:

```
do{
    first half of loop
}while (condition) {
    second half of loop
}
```

Since this structure is not provided in most high-level languages, several approaches are used to code it. One duplicates the code for the first half of the loop.

```
first half of loop
while (condition) {
    second half of loop
    first half of loop
}
```

TABLE 9.9   Common Translations of Looping Structures to Assembly Language

High Level	Assembly Equivalent

<pre>while (m > 0){
  n +=m--;
}</pre>
	<pre>;while (m > 0)
	while_test:
	  cpi m, 1 ;exit when m < 1 (m <= 0)
	  brlt end_while
	;loop body
	  add n, m
	  dec m
	  rjmp while_test
	end_while:</pre>

<pre>while (m > 0){
  n +=m--;
}</pre>
	<pre>;alternate implementation
	  rjmp while_test
	;while (m > 0)
	lp:
	  add n, m
	  dec m
	while_test:
	  cpi m, 1 ;repeat while m >= 1 (m > 0)
	  brge lp
	;end while</pre>

<pre>do{
  a--;
  b++;
} while (a!=0)</pre>
	<pre>do:
	  inc b
	  dec a ;note reordering for test
	         ;below
	;until a ==0
	  brne do ;repeat while a!=0</pre>

<pre>for (m=0; m < 10; m++)
  a++</pre>
	<pre>;for(...)
	  ldi m, 0 ;initialization step
	for:
	  cpi m, 10 ;while m < 10
	brge end_for ;exit when m >= 10
	inc a
	inc m ;update part of for structure
	  rjmp for
	end_for:</pre>

<pre>while (m < n && a < b){
  a++;
  m++;
}</pre>
	<pre>;while(...)
	while_test:
	  cp m, n ;test at top
	  brge end_while ;short circuit to
	exit if m >= n
	  cp a, b ;next part of test
	  brsh end_while ;exit if a >= b
	  ;loop body
	  inc a
	  inc m
	  rjmp while_test
	end_while:</pre>

TABLE 9.9   (continued) Common Translations of Looping Structures to Assembly Language

`n--;`	`;loop and a half`
`while (m < n) {`	`lp:`
`  m++;`	`  dec n`
`  n-;`	`;while test in middle of loop`
`}`	`  cp m,n`
`or equivalently...`	`  brge end_while`
`while(1) {`	`;continue loop`
`  n--;`	`  inc m`
`  if (m >= n) break;`	`  rjmp lp`
`  m++;`	`end_while:`
`}`	

The other solution is to use a break statement.

```
while (true) {
    first half of loop
    if (!condition) break;
    second half of loop
}
```

With assembly language, the evaluation of the condition in the middle of the loop is easily written, matching the do while do structure almost exactly. It is even possible to move the condition to the end of the loop body, and simply enter the loop in the middle. This approach is illustrated in Table 9.10.

Implementing looping structures is a little more complicated than selection structures, however, with a disciplined approach, and the use of

TABLE 9.10   Alternate Implementation of the Loop and a Half

High Level	Assembly Equivalent
`do {`	`;loop and a half`
`  n--;`	`rjmp lp_entry`
`} while (m < n) {`	`lp:`
`  m++;`	`  ;second half of loop`
`}`	`  inc m`
	`lp_entry:`
	`  ;first half of loop`
	`  dec n`
	`;loop test`
	`  cp m,n`
	`  brlt lp ;repeat while m < n`
	`;loop exit`

functions if needed to keep the loop body short and easy to understand, loops can be reliably designed. Be sure to document the control structures, and verify that something in the loop will cause the loop to eventually terminate.

Also remember that in a microcontroller, an infinite loop is not necessarily a bad thing. Most embedded applications run as long as power is applied. This implies some sort of infinite loop is intentionally placed in the code. It is the unintentional infinite loops that cause real problems.

PSEUDOCODE DEVELOPMENT: A CHECKSUM PROGRAM

To illustrate development of an assembly language program using pseudocode, we will write a program to generate and verify checksum digits. The checksum digit will be the last digit of any sequence of characters. It is calculated according to the following algorithm:

```
cs = 0
for each char x {
    action = x mod 3
    switch action
        case 0: cs += x; break
        case 1: cs = cs <<1 + x; break;
        case 2: cs -= x ;break;
        case 3: cs = cs >>1 + x; break;
    }
}
cs = cs & 0x1f | 0x40
```

The checksum value is a single byte, initialized to zero. As each character of the incoming sequence is received, the checksum is modified according to the last two bits of the character. This is implemented as a switch statement. The final checksum value is turned into a character by retaining the least-significant five bits, and forcing the upper three to be 0b010. This generates one of the following checksum characters: @ ($40), A ($41), ..., Z ($5A), [($5B), ..., _ ($5F).

In pseudocode, the algorithm is fairly straightforward. Since it represents a task of the application, it should abstracted to one or more functions. We will abstract the inner part of the loop to a function called process _ char, which will process the next character of the sequence. Before the character is processed, the function check _ cs will determine if the character is the correct check character for the sequence already received. The action of converting the checksum to a character will be implemented as a function, finalize _ cs, since it is needed in two places. The outer control structure (the loop) will be abstracted to a function called process _ case, which will also handle the I/O and differentiate between generating and verifying the checksum.

Using the techniques of this chapter, each of these functions can be turned into an assembly language function and integrated into the final application.

The application will accept input via serial communication and output to the LEDs and also over the serial line. The LEDs will display the progress of the checksum calculations by showing the current checksum value (cs) as each character is processed. Each input sequence is terminated with enter ("\r") or a question mark ("?"). The question mark indicates that the input was a sequence with a checksum character to be verified. The application will respond by printing OK or BAD. Otherwise, the correct checksum character is printed at the end of the input sequence. The following pseudocode captures the application details:

```
void process_case(){
    byte cs = 0; //current cs (checksum) value
    ledOut(cs);
    boolean chk_ok = false;
    char cx = receive(); //current character
    while(cx != '\r' && cx != '?'){
        transmit(cx);
        chk_ok = check_cs(cs, cx);
        cs = process_char(cs, cx);
        ledOut(cs);
        cx = receive();
    }
    if (cx == '\r')
        cs = finalize_cs(cs);
        transmit(cs);
        print_crlf();
    } else {
        if (chk_ok)
            print_OK();
        else
            print_BAD();
    }
}
```

Thinking through the details of the application at this level allows potential problems to be identified more easily than if this had simply been written in assembly language. High-level code that is modular is much easier to trace and debug (by hand) than the equivalent assembly language version. Careful translation of the pseudocode to assembly language can result in a working program with minimal effort.

The pseudocode version is included in the assembly language program to provide a high-level view of the underlying algorithm. Comparing it to the actual assembly language code can help identify logical errors.

Program 9.1 shows the entire application for the ATMEGA16A. An alternate version for the XPLAIN platform can be found at the end of the chapter. The only differences between the two programs are related to I/O.

PROGRAM 9.1: A Checksum Calculation

```
;Program 9.1 - Checksum calculator
;Illustrate pseudocode development of an assembly
;language program

;Programmer: TM
;Date: 5/2010
;Platform: STK-500
;Device: ATMEGA16A
.include "m16def.inc"

;Characters are received over the serial port for which
;a check digit must be calculated. The calculations are
;preformed according to this algorithm.
;cs = 0
;for each char x {
    ;action = x mod 3
    ;switch action
        ;case 0: cs += x; break
        ;case 1: cs = cs << 1 + x; break;
        ;case 2: cs -= x; break;
        ;case 3: cs = cs >> 1 + x; break;
    ;}
;}
;cs = cs & 0x1f | 0x40
```

```
;For each input case, characters are echoed until a CR
;or '?' is received.
;If a CR is received, then the calculated checkdigit is
;transmitted followed by a CR LF.
;If a '?' is received, the preceeding character should
;be the checkdigit and the program sends either "-OK" or
;"-BAD" followed by CR LF.
;The LED's should constantly display the partially
;calculated cs value (from the algorithm) each time it
;is updated.

;LEDS on PORTB

;Set the LEDS as OFF and PORT as output
;leds display RXD counter or receive error flags
.def temp = r16
ldi temp, $FF  ;led's off
out PORTB, temp
out DDRB,temp

;Stack initialization
ldi temp, low(RAMEND)
out SPL, temp
ldi temp, high(RAMEND)
out SPH, temp
.undef temp

;Initialize the USART
rcall initUSART
;Wait for a received char to ensure terminal connection:
;receive();
;while (1) {
;issue instructions
;process one checksum case
;}
rcall receive
cs_mainloop:
    rcall instructions
    rcall process_case
    rjmp cs_mainloop
;Function definitions--
```

```
;void process_case(){
;byte cs = 0; //current cs (checksum) value
;ledOut(cs);
;boolean chk_ok = false;
;char cx = receive(); //current character
;while(cx != '\r' && cx != '?'){
    ;transmit(cx);
    ;chk_ok = check_cs(cs, cx);
    ;cs = process_char(cs, cx);
    ;ledOut(cs);
    ;cx = receive();
;}
;if (cx == '\r')
    ;cs = finalize_cs(cs);
    ;transmit(cs);
    ;print_crlf();
    ;} else {
    ;if (chk_ok)
        ;print_OK();
    ;else
        ;print_BAD();
    ;}
;}
process_case:
;byte cs = 0; //current cs (checksum) value
;ledOut(cs)
;boolean chk_ok = false;
;char cx = receive(); //current char
.def cs = r17
.def cx = r20
.def chk_ok = r19
push cs   ;preserve registers
push cx
push chk_ok
push r24
push r25
ldi cs,0
mov r24, cs  ;parameter to ledOut
rcall ledOut
ldi chk_ok, 0  ;false
rcall receive
mov cx, r24   ;return value from receive
```

```
;while(cx != '\r' && cx != '?'){
process_case_while:
    cpi cx,'\r'
    breq process_case_endwhile
    cpi cx,'?'
    breq process_case_endwhile
    ;transmit(cx);
        mov r24,cx  ;parameter for transmit
        rcall transmit
    ;chk_ok = check_cs(cs, cx);
        mov r25,cs  ;parameters for check_cs
        mov r24,cx
        rcall check_cs
        mov chk_ok, r24  ;return value
    ;cs = process_char(cs, cx);
        mov r25,cs  ;parameters for process_char
        mov r24,cx
        rcall process_char
        mov cs, r24  ;return value
process_case_skip:
    ;ledOut(cs);
        rcall ledOut  ;r24 is already the argument
    ;cx = receive();
        rcall receive
        mov cx, r24
        rjmp process_case_while
;}
process_case_endwhile:
;if (cx == '\r')
    cpi cx, '\r'
    brne process_case_else
    ;cs = finalize(cs);
        mov r24, cs
        rcall finalize_cs
    ;transmit(cs);
        rcall transmit  ;argument already in r24
    ;print_crlf();
        rcall print_crlf
        rjmp process_case_endif
;} else {
process_case_else:
    ;if (chk_ok))
```

```
        tst chk_ok
        breq process_case_else_inner
    ;print_OK();
        rcall print_OK
        rjmp process_case_endif_inner
    ;else
process_case_else_inner:
    ;print_BAD();
        rcall print_BAD
process_case_endif_inner:
;}
process_case_endif:
;}
pop r25  ;restore registers
pop r24
pop chk_ok
pop cx
pop cs
ret
.undef cs
.undef chk_ok
.undef cx

;Convert checksum to check character
;char finalize_cs(byte cs){
;return cs & 0x1f | 0x40
;}
;param and return value are in r24
finalize_cs:
    andi r24, 0x1f
    ori r24, 0x40
    ret

;Check if current check character matches cx
;boolean check_cs(byte cs, char cx){
;ret finalize(cs) == cx;
check_cs:
.def cs = r25
.def cx = r24
.def temp_cx = r18
    push cs
    push temp_cx
```

```
    mov temp_cx, cx
    mov r24, cs
    rcall finalize_cs
    mov r25, r24   ;r25 is expected check character:
                   ;finalize_cs(cs)
    clr r24        ;return value initialized to false
    cp r25, temp_cx  ;compare expected to actual char
    brne check_cs_wrong
    com r24   ;make return value true
check_cs_wrong:
    pop temp_cx
    pop cs
    ret
.undef cs
.undef cx
.undef temp_cx

;Update and return checksum with next character
;byte process_char(byte cs, char cx){
    ;byte action = cx mod 3
    ;switch action
        ;case 0: cs += cx; break
        ;case 1: cs = cs << 1 + cx; break;
        ;case 2: cs -= cx; break;
        ;case 3: cs = cs >> 1 + cx; break;
    ;}
    ;return cs;
;}
.def cs = r25
.def cx = r24
.def action = r17
process_char:
        push action
    ;byte action = cx mod 3
        mov action, cx
        andi action, 3
    ;switch action
    ;case 0: cs += cx; break
        cpi action, 0
        brne process_char_case1
        add cs, cx
        rjmp process_char_endswitch
```

```
    ;case 1: cs = cs << 1 + cx; break;
process_char_case1:
        cpi action, 1
        brne process_char_case2
        lsl cs
        add cs, cx
        rjmp process_char_endswitch
    ;case 2: cs -= cx; break;
process_char_case2:
        cpi action, 2
        brne process_char_case3
        sub cs, cx
        rjmp process_char_endswitch
    ;case 3: cs = cs >> 1 + cx; break;
process_char_case3:
        lsr cs
        add cs, cx
;}
process_char_endswitch:
;return cs;
    mov r24, cs                 ;return value
    pop action
    ret
.undef cx
.undef cs
.undef action

;void ledOut(byte r24){
;PORTE_OUT = ~r24
;}
ledOut:
    com r24
    out PORTB, r24
    com r24
    ret

;Receive byte - blocking implementation
;return the byte received in r24
;byte receive(){
.def rec_byte = r24
receive:
```

```
;while(RXC flag is clear){}
    sbis UCSRA, RXC          ;is byte in Rx buffer?
    rjmp receive             ;not yet
    ; return USARTC0_DATA
    in rec_byte, UDR         ;received byte
    ret
.undef rec_byte


;Transmit byte - blocks until transmit buffer can accept
;a byte
;The param, byte to transmit, is in r24
;void transmit(byte byte_tx){
.def byte_tx = r24
.def temp = r16
transmit:
    push temp
transmit_wait:              ;while(!data register empty){}
    sbis UCSRA, UDRE         ;wait for Tx buffer to be
                            ;empty
    rjmp transmit_wait       ;not ready yet
    ;USARTC0_DATA = byte_tx;
    out UDR, byte_tx         ;transmit character
    pop temp
    ret
.undef byte_tx
.undef temp


;void print_crlf(){
print_crlf:
    push r24
;transmit('\r');
    ldi r24, '\r'
    rcall transmit
;transmit('\n');
    ldi r24, '\n'
    rcall transmit
;}
    pop r24
    ret
```

```
msg_instructions: .db "Checkdigit generator/
  calculator",'\r','\n', \"terminate input with Enter
  (to calculate checkdigit) or ? to check", \'\r','\n',
  ">",0
msg_bad:  .db "-BAD",'\r','\n', 0
msg_OK:  .db "-OK",'\r','\n', 0

;void print_BAD(){
;sendsting(&msg_bad)
;}
print_BAD:
push ZH
push ZL
;Z = address of message
ldi ZH, high(msg_BAD << 1)
ldi ZL, low(msg_BAD << 1)
rcall sendstring
pop ZL
pop ZH
ret

;void print_OK(){
;sendsting(&msg_OK)
;}
print_OK:
push ZH
push ZL
;Z = address of message
ldi ZH, high(msg_OK << 1)
ldi ZL, low(msg_OK << 1)
rcall sendstring
pop ZL
pop ZH
ret

;void instructions(){
;sendsting(&msg_instructions)
;}
instructions:
push ZH
push ZL
```

```
;Z = address of message
ldi ZH, high(msg_instructions < <1)
ldi ZL, low(msg_instructions < <1)
rcall sendstring
pop ZL
pop ZH
ret

sendstring:
.def theChar = r24          ;use r24 so it matches the
                            ;transmit function
parameter
;while(*Z != 0) print *(Z++);
push theChar
sendstring_nextchar:
    lpm theChar, Z +        ;(Pointer is incremented
                            ;here)
    tst theChar             ;check next character for nul
    breq sendstring_done
    rcall transmit          ;print
    rjmp sendstring_nextchar

sendstring_done:
pop thechar
.undef theChar
ret

;void initUSART()
;2 mhz clock speed, 9600 baud UBRRvalue = 12
.equ UBRRvalue = 12

initUSART:
.def temp = r16

;initialize USART
ldi temp, high (UBRRvalue)  ;baud rate
out UBRRH, temp
ldi temp, low (UBRRvalue)
out UBRRL, temp

;URSEL 0 = UBRRH, 1 = UCSRC (shared port address)
```

```
;UMSEL 0 = Asynchronous, 1 = Synchronous
;USBS 0 = One stop bit, 1 = Two stop bits
;UCSZ0:1 Character Size: 0 = 5, 1 = 6, 2 = 7, 3 = 8
;(UCSZ2 is in UCSRB, but is only needed for 9 data bits)
;UPM0:1 0 = none, 1 = reserved, 2 = Even, 3 = Odd

;8data, 1 stop, no parity
ldi temp,
   (1 << URSEL) | (0 << UMSEL) | (0 << USBS) | (3 << UCSZ0) | (0 << UPM0)
out UCSRC, temp

ldi temp, (1 < <RXEN) | (1 < <TXEN)
out UCSRB, temp; enable receive and transmit

.undef temp
ret
```

EXERCISES

1. What register is modified by a processor's jump instruction?
2. Write a sequence of instructions to pop a return address off the stack and use an indirect jump to transfer to that address. The return address is two or three bytes; the byte on the top of the stack is the high byte of the address. State whether the code is for the ATMEGA16A or ATxmega128A1.
3. If a `breq` instruction is immediately followed by a `brne` instruction, is it possible that neither branch will be taken? Explain.
4. Write the more common alias for each of the following instructions:
   a. `brbc 4, loc`
   b. `brbs 2, loc`
   c. `brbc 0, loc`
   d. `brbs 7, loc`
5. Registers 16 and 17 contain unsigned data; r16 is $3C and r17 is $5F. What will the carry flag contain after `sub r16, r17` is executed? Which instruction would branch (not sequence) after this subtraction: `brcc` or `brcs`?
6. Immediately after an `inc r16` instruction, a programmer has placed a `brcs someLabel` instruction. The intent is to branch when the counter in r16 increments from $FF to $00. Why will this technique fail? What branch should be used?

7. Write a sequence of instructions to branch to one of two locations. Branch to `loczero` if R7 contains a zero; branch to `locnotzero` otherwise. Use exactly three instructions.

8. Write a sequence of instructions to branch to one of two locations. Branch to `locnegative` if r25:r24 (a 16-bit two's complement value) contains a negative value; branch to `locnonnegative` otherwise. Use exactly three instructions.

9. Use a conditional skip instruction followed by an INC instruction to increment r16 only when r17 is odd.

10. (MEGA) Write a sequence of two instructions that will set bit 3 in PORTB only when bit 4 of PIND is clear. (Use a conditional skip and the set bit in I/O register instruction). (XMEGA) Write a sequence of two instructions that will set bit 3 in VPORT0_OUT only when bit 4 of VPORT0_IN is clear. (Use a conditional skip and the set bit in I/O register instruction.)

11. Write a sequence of two instructions that will clear bits 6 and 7 in r16 only when bit 4 of r17 is clear. (Use the clear bits in register instruction.)

12. (MEGA) In the ATmega16A, why cannot you use `sbic SREG, 0` to skip the next instruction when the carry flag is clear? (assume the proper include file has defined `SREG` as the status register). (XMEGA) In the ATxmega128A1, why cannot you use `sbic CPU_SREG, 0` to skip the next instruction when the carry flag is clear? (assume the proper include file has defined `CPU_SREG` as the SREG).

13. Use a conditional skip followed by a CALL that will call the function `isNegative` only if r16 (as a signed integer) is less than zero. The CALL instruction is a two-word instruction; will the conditional skip work correctly in this case? Explain.

14. Write short assembly language segments to implement the following high-level control structures. Assume the following data segment declarations are in effect. You will need to move data between memory and registers to accomplish the tasks.

```
.dseg
counter:    .byte 1        ;unsigned byte
limit:      .byte 1        ;unsigned byte;
a:          .byte 2        ;signed 16-bit int
b:          .byte 2        ;signed 16-bit int
```

a. if (limit > 130) counter ++;

b. if (a < b) limit = counter;

c. if (counter < limit) a++; else b++;

d. if (limit > 0 && counter == 3) b += a;

15. Simplify the following groups of statements (parts a–e) by eliminating unnecessary steps. Identify the parts of your solution that are equivalent to each of the parts shown here.

```
;part a:
        dec r16
        brne aaa
        breq bbb
aaa:

;part b:
bbb:
        add r16, r24
        push r16
        andi r16, $80
        pop r16
        breq bbb

;part c:
        cp r0, r1
        brlt ddd
        cp r0, r1
        breq ddd
        cp r0, r1
        brge eee

;part d:
ddd:
        cp r16, r16
        breq eee
        rjmp aaa

;part e:
eee:
        dec r16
        cpi r16, -1
        breq ddd
        brlt ddd
```

16. Write pseudocode (C- or Java-like) for the following assembly language program segment. Assume that the variables used are stored in registers defined as follows:

```
.def r16 = count      ;unsigned 8-bit integer
.def r17 = sum        ;signed 8-bit integer
.def r18 = limit      ;signed 8-bit integer


one: cpi count, $A
     brsh two
     inc sum
two: cp sum, limit
     brlt three
     dec limit
     rjmp four
three:  add sum, limit
     sub sum, count
four:  inc count
```

17. Write short assembly language segments to implement the following high-level control structures. Assume the following register definitions:

```
.def counter = r16; unsigned byte
.def limit = r17; unsigned byte  ;a = r25:r24
                                 ;signed 16-bit int
.def aH = r25
.def aL = r24 ;b = r23:r22 signed 16-bit int
.def bH = r23 .def bL = r22
```

a. do {counter++; limit−; } while (counter < limit);
b. while (a < b){a += limit;} // beware of data sizes
c. while (true){a++; if (a < b) break; b−}

18. Write pseudocode (C- or Java-like) for the following assembly language program segment. Assume that the variables used are stored in registers defined as follows:

```
.def r16 = count      ;unsigned 8-bit integer
.def r17 = sum        ;signed 8-bit integer
.def r18 = limit      ;signed 8-bit integer
```

```
one:      cpi count, $A
          brsh two
          inc sum
          rjmp one
two:      dec count
          cp sum, limit
          brlt one
three:    dec limit
          cpi limit, 0
          brne four
          add sum, count
          rjmp three
four:  inc count
```

19. Write a function to return the sum of the ASCII codes of characters found in consecutive SRAM locations. The function is named `checksum1`. It expects the address of the first character to be passed in YH:YL and the number of characters to be passed in r24. The 16-bit sum (of the character codes) is to be returned in r25:r24. You may assume there is at least one character to be summed.

20. Repeat the previous problem with the following changes. The name of the function is `checksum2`. The number of characters is not passed. Instead, the end of the data is marked by a "$" character (a sentinel, not to be counted). Before the next character is added to the checksum (so far) the checksum is doubled. Ignore any overflow that may occur.

PROGRAMMING EXERCISES

Use pseudocode to design each program, then expand the pseudocode into assembly language using the techniques found in this chapter. Retain the pseudocode as comments in your program.

1. Write a program to compute a checksum of a line of characters received over the serial port. For this program, the checksum is the EOR of all of the ASCII codes of the characters. Immediately echo each received character. Display the checksum on the LEDs as it is being computed. When the end of line character is detected, zero the checksum before processing the next line. Add a linefeed when appropriate. Use a 2 MHz clock and 9600 N-8-1 communications parameters.

2. Design a credit card number validity checker for 16-digit card numbers that utilize the Luhn formula for integrity checking. The last digit is a check digit and must be compared to a checksum computed from the other 15 digits. Starting from the left, number the digits 0, 1, 2, and so on. The digits in even positions are doubled and replaced by the sum of the digits making up the doubled value. Thus 4 is replaced by 8 ($2 \boxtimes 4 = 08$, $0 + 8 = 8$) and 5 is replaced by 1 ($2 \boxtimes 5 = 10$, $1 + 0 = 1$). The odd positioned digits are unchanged. The sum of the 15 resulting digits is calculated modulo 10. The last digit (check digit) should be (10-checksum)%10 if the card is valid. Your program must input credit card numbers (via serial communication) and display the progress of the Luhn algorithm calculations. After each digit is received, display on the LEDs, \$xF, where x is the checksum calculated so far (modulo 10). When the check digit is received, if the credit card number passes the Luhn integrity check, display \$xy where x is the calculated checksum and y is the actual check digit. If fraudulent, display \$Fy, where y is the required checkdigit. Your program should echo all of the received characters back to the terminal and restart processing each time a newline character is received. Use a 2 MHz clock and 9600 N-8-1 communications parameters.

Example 6011 2345 7329 8755
Becomes 3021 4385 5349 7715 (after digit replacement)
Successive checksums (x): 3, 3, 5, 6, 0, 3, 1, 6, 1, 4, 8, 7, 4, 1, 2
Final output \$F8 (illegal, check digit 5 should be 8)
(If the last digit was 8, then \$28 would be displayed)

3. Write a function to add numbers in sequential memory locations in flash. These are to be signed bytes. Return the sum in R24. Stop summing when a 0 is encountered, or just before signed overflow occurs (i.e., stop summing if adding the next number would cause overflow). Assume the byte address of the array (in flash) is passed to the function in Z. Include a small TST program that calls the function for two different sequences (one that will add all the numbers up to the zero, the other that will halt because of pending overflow). The program can display the sum on the LEDs and then wait for a button press to go to the next array.

4. Write a function called sumAll. It is passed a set of numbers (all signed bytes) on the stack. The number of values to

be summed (the number of bytes pushed onto the stack) is passed in R24. The function should remove the numbers from the stack before returning and return the 16-bit (two's complement) sum in R25:R24.

5. Write a program to play Character HILO. Use a terminal program for I/O via serial communication (9600 N-8-1). The HILO program thinks of a secret character and then the player tries to guess it. After each guess, the program responds with "Too high," "Too low," or "Just right." When the secret character is guessed, the program displays the number of guesses and begins again. Restrict the secret characters to the lower case alphabet. To generate a secret character, the program asks the player to press a key to begin. While waiting, an 8-bit counter increments freely until the character is received. Use the counter value to pick a "random" character between "a" and "z."

ALTERNATE PROGRAMS FOR THE XPLAIN DEMONSTRATION KIT

PROGRAM 9.1a: A Checksum Calculator

The XPLAIN/ATxmega128A1 version of the checksum calculator differs only in the I/O details. The pseudocode is identical.

```
;Program 9.1a - Checksum calculator
;Illustrate pseudocode development of an assembly
;language program

;Programmer: TM
;Date: 5/2010
;Platform: XPLAIN
;Device: ATxmega128A1
.include "ATxmega128A1def.inc"

;Characters are received over the serial port for which
;a check digit must be calculated. The calculations are
;preformed according to this algorithm.
;cs = 0
;for each char x {
;action = x mod 3
;switch action
;case 0: cs += x; break
;case 1: cs = cs << 1 + x; break;
```

```
;case 2: cs -= x; break;
;case 3: cs = cs >>1 + x; break;
; }
; }
;cs = cs & 0x1f | 0x40

;For each input case, characters are echoed until a CR
;or '?' is received.
;If a CR is received, then the calculated checkdigit is
;transmitted followed by a CR LF.
;If a '?' is received, the preceeding character should
;be the checkdigit and the program sends either "-OK" or
;"-BAD" followed by CR LF.
;The LED's should constantly display the partially
;calculated cs value (from the algorithm) each time it
;is updated.

;Set the LEDS as OFF and PORT as output
;leds display RXD counter or receive error flags
.def temp = r16
ldi temp, $FF  ;led's off
sts PORTE_OUT, temp
sts PORTE_DIR, temp
.undef temp
;Initialize the USART
rcall initUSART
;Wait for a received char to ensure termional
;connection:
;receive();
;while (1) {
;issue instructions
;process one checksum case
;}
rcall receive
cs_mainloop:
    rcall instructions
    rcall process_case
    rjmp cs_mainloop

;Function definitions--
;void process_case(){
```

```
;byte cs = 0; //current cs (checksum) value
;ledOut(cs);
;boolean chk_ok = false;
;char cx = receive(); //current character
;while(cx != '\r' && cx != '?'){
;transmit(cx);
;chk_ok = check_cs(cs, cx);
;cs = process_char(cs, cx);
;ledOut(cs);
;cx = receive();
;}
;if (cx == '\r')
;cs = finalize_cs(cs);
;transmit(cs);
;print_crlf();
;} else {
;if (chk_ok)
;print_OK();
;else
;print_BAD();
;}
;}
process_case:
;byte cs = 0; //current cs (checksum) value
;ledOut(cs)
;boolean chk_ok = false;
;char cx = receive(); //current char
.def cs = r17
.def cx = r20
.def chk_ok = r19
push cs                 ;preserve registers
push cx
push chk_ok
push r24
push r25

ldi cs,0
mov r24, cs             ;parameter to ledOut
rcall ledOut
ldi chk_ok, 0           ;false
rcall receive
mov cx, r24             ;return value from receive
```

```
;while(cx != '\r' && cx != '?'){
process_case_while:
    cpi cx,'\r'
    breq process_case_endwhile
    cpi cx,'?'
    breq process_case_endwhile
;transmit(cx);
        mov r24,cx   ;parameter for transmit
        rcall transmit
;chk_ok=check_cs(cs, cx);
        mov r25,cs   ;parameters for check_cs
        mov r24,cx
        rcall check_cs
        mov chk_ok, r24    ;return value
;cs=process_char(cs, cx);
        mov r25,cs   ;parameters for process_char
        mov r24,cx
        rcall process_char
        mov cs, r24  ;return value
process_case_skip:
;ledOut(cs);
        rcall ledOut        ;r24 is already the argument
;cx=receive();
        rcall receive
        mov cx, r24
        rjmp process_case_while
;}
process_case_endwhile:
;if (cx == '\r')
    cpi cx, '\r'
    brne process_case_else
;cs=finalize(cs);
        mov r24, cs
        rcall finalize_cs
;transmit(cs);
        rcall transmit      ;argument already in r24
;print_crlf();
        rcall print_crlf
        rjmp process_case_endif
;} else {
process_case_else:
```

```
  ;if (chk_ok))
      tst chk_ok
      breq process_case_else_inner
  ;print_OK();
                   rcall print_OK
                   rjmp process_case_endif_inner
  ;else
process_case_else_inner:
  ;print_BAD();
                   rcall print_BAD
process_case_endif_inner:
;}
process_case_endif:
;}
pop r25                 ;restore registers
pop r24
pop chk_ok
pop cx
pop cs
ret
.undef cs
.undef chk_ok
.undef cx

;Convert checksum to check character
;char finalize_cs(byte cs){
;return cs & 0x1f | 0x40
;}
;param and return value are in r24
finalize_cs:
    andi r24, 0x1f
    ori r24, 0x40
    ret
;Check if current check character matches cx
;boolean check_cs(byte cs, char cx){
;ret finalize(cs) == cx;
check_cs:
.def cs = r25
.def cx = r24
.def temp_cx = r18
    push cs
```

```
    push temp_cx
    mov temp_cx, cx
    mov r24, cs
    rcall finalize_cs
    mov r25, r24      ;r25 is expected check character:
                        finalize_cs(cs)
    clr r24            ;return value initialized to false
    cp r25, temp_cx ;compare expected to actual char
    brne check_cs_wrong
    com r24            ;make return value true
check_cs_wrong:
    pop temp_cx
    pop cs
    ret
.undef cs
.undef cx
.undef temp_cx


;Update and return checksum with next character
;byte process_char(byte cs, char cx){
;byte action = cx mod 3
;switch action
;case 0: cs += cx; break
;case 1: cs = cs << 1 + cx; break;
;case 2: cs -= cx; break;
;case 3: cs = cs >> 1 + cx; break;
;}
; return cs;
;}
.def cs = r25
.def cx = r24
.def action = r17
process_char:
    push action
;byte action = cx mod 3
    mov action, cx
    andi action, 3
;switch action
;case 0: cs += cx; break
        cpi action, 0
        brne process_char_case1
        add cs, cx
```

```
        rjmp process_char_endswitch
;case 1: cs = cs << 1 + cx; break;
process_char_case1:
        cpi action, 1
        brne process_char_case2
        lsl cs
        add cs, cx
        rjmp process_char_endswitch
;case 2: cs -= cx; break;
process_char_case2:
        cpi action, 2
        brne process_char_case3
        sub cs, cx
        rjmp process_char_endswitch
;case 3: cs = cs >> 1 + cx; break;
process_char_case3:
        lsr cs
        add cs, cx
;}
process_char_endswitch:
;return cs;
    mov r24, cs      ;return value
    pop action
    ret
.undef cx
.undef cs
.undef action
;void ledOut(byte r24){
; PORTE_OUT = ~r24
;}
ledOut:
    com r24
    sts PORTE_OUT, r24
    com r24
    ret

;Receive byte - blocking implementation
;return the byte received in r24
;byte receive(){
.def rec_byte = r24
receive:
;while(RXC flag is clear){}
```

```
    lds rec_byte, USARTC0_STATUS
    sbrs rec_byte, USART_RXCIF_bp      ;is byte in Rx
                                       ;buffer?
    rjmp receive
;return USARTC0_DATA
    lds rec_byte, USARTC0_DATA  ;received byte
    ret
.undef rec_byte


;Transmit byte - blocks until transmit buffer can accept
;a byte
;The param, byte to transmit, is in r24
;void transmit(byte byte_tx){
.def byte_tx = r24
.def temp = r16
transmit:
    push temp
transmit_wait:       ;while(!data register empty){}
    lds temp, USARTC0_STATUS
    sbrs temp, USART_DREIF_bp   ;wait for Tx buffer to
                                ;be empty
    rjmp transmit_wait          ;not ready yet
    ;USARTC0_DATA = byte_tx;
    sts USARTC0_DATA, byte_tx   ;transmit character
    pop temp
    ret
.undef byte_tx
.undef temp


;void print_crlf(){
print_crlf:
    push r24
;transmit('\r');
    ldi r24, '\r'
    rcall transmit
;transmit('\n');
    ldi r24, '\n'
    rcall transmit
;}
    pop r24
    ret
```

```
msg_instructions: .db "Checkdigit generator/
calculator",'\r','\n', \ "terminate input with Enter
(to calculate checkdigit) or ? to check", \ '\r','\n',
"> ",0
msg_bad:                .db "-BAD",'\r','\n', 0
msg_OK:.db "-OK",'\r','\n', 0

;void print_BAD(){
;sendsting(&msg_bad)
;}
print_BAD:
push ZH
push ZL
;Z = address of message
ldi ZH, high(msg_BAD<<1)
ldi ZL, low(msg_BAD<<1)
rcall sendstring
pop ZL
pop ZH
ret

;void print_OK(){
; sendsting(&msg_OK)
;}
print_OK:
push ZH
push ZL
;Z = address of message
ldi ZH, high(msg_OK<<1)
ldi ZL, low(msg_OK<<1)
rcall sendstring
pop ZL
pop ZH
ret

;void instructions(){
;sendsting(&msg_instructions)
;}
instructions:
push ZH
push ZL
;Z = address of message
```

```
ldi ZH, high(msg_instructions<<1)
ldi ZL, low(msg_instructions<<1)
rcall sendstring
pop ZL
pop ZH
ret


sendstring:
.def theChar = r24    ;use r24 so it matches the transmit
                      ;function
parameter
;while(*Z != 0) print *(Z++);
push theChar
sendstring_nextchar:
    lpm theChar, Z+        ;(Pointer is incremented here)
    tst theChar           ;check next character for nul
    breq sendstring_done
    rcall transmit        ;print
    rjmp sendstring_nextchar


sendstring_done:
pop thechar
.undef theChar
ret


;void initUSART()
;2 mhz clock speed, 9600 baud BSEL = 12
.equ BSEL = 12


initUSART:
.def temp = r16


;set baud rate
ldi temp, high(BSEL) & 0x0F
sts USARTC0_BAUDCTRLB, temp
ldi temp, low(BSEL)
sts USARTC0_BAUDCTRLA, temp


;data packet format
;select, asynchronous, no parity, 1 stop, 8 data bits
ldi temp,
```

```
USART_CMODE_ASYNCHRONOUS_gc|USART_PMODE_DISABLED_
gc|(0<<USART_SBMODE_bp)|US
ART_CHSIZE_8BIT_gc
sts USARTC0_CTRLC, temp

;Set the transmit pin as output and set high, receive
  ;pin as input

(default)
ldi temp, 1<<3      ;PC3
sts PORTC_OUT,temp  ;configure TXD as 1
sts PORTC_DIR,temp  ;configure TXD as output

;enable bi-directional communication
lds temp, USARTC0_CTRLB
ori temp, USART_TXEN_bm | USART_RXEN_bm
sts USARTC0_CTRLB, temp

.undef temp
ret
```

CHAPTER 10

Interrupts

THE INTERRUPT SYSTEM OF a microprocessor is the key to allowing programs to respond immediately to external events. An *interrupt* is an event (technically, a signal) that can interrupt the flow of the currently running program. Interrupts can be triggered by external or internal signals; they can be caused by software or hardware. The interrupt system provides a mechanism whereby a normally executing program can be suspended temporarily (between instructions) to allow a high-priority task to run. When the task is completed, the original program resumes. This is a bit like a function call and return, however, in the case of interrupts, there is no explicit call statement, and the interrupt invocation can occur at virtually any location in a program. When a program is interrupted, the routine that is executed in response to the interrupt is called an *interrupt service routine*, or *interrupt handler*. The process of interrupting the current program, executing the interrupt handler, and returning, is called *servicing the interrupt*.

The AVR processor can respond to interrupts from a variety of sources. For example, when using the USART for serial communication, an interrupt can be used to signal the fact that a byte has been received and is available in the buffer to be picked up. This technique can avoid buffer overflows which might occur using a polled approach if a program is busy performing other tasks and does not get around to checking the receive buffer quickly enough.

INTERRUPT PROCESSING

The ATmega16A processor can respond to 21 different interrupt signals. The interrupts have different priorities based on their interrupt number;

high-priority interrupts have lower numbers. Each interrupt can be individually enabled or disabled. The specific interrupt enable bits are located in various registers scattered throughout the I/O register file. Writing a one (1) to an interrupt enable bit will enable that specific interrupt service. A zero (0) will disable that interrupt.

The ATxmega128A1 has a much richer programmable, multilevel interrupt control system (PMIC). In addition to individual interrupt priorities, interrupts can be classified as having high-, medium-, or low-level importance, allowing higher level interrupts to interrupt lower level interrupts. There are 150 different interrupt sources. In addition to enabling individual interrupts, each level of interrupt can be independently enabled.

The global interrupt enable bit in the SREG, when cleared, will disable the entire interrupt system. Interrupt signals are still active, but the interrupts are not serviced while interrupts are disabled globally. When global interrupts are enabled again, the processor will immediately interrupt the program to service the highest priority pending interrupt.

When the interrupt system is enabled, the processor checks for the presence of an interrupt signal each time an instruction finishes. If more than one interrupt is asserted at that time, one is chosen based on priority. The processor then interrupts its current task to service the interrupt.

Interrupt routines are activated when the address of an associated interrupt vector is loaded into the program counter. The original program counter value is pushed on the stack for safe keeping. It is the interrupt's return address. This action is the same as a call to a function, except that there is no call instruction.

While an interrupt is being serviced, other interrupts at the same and lower levels are prevented from interrupting the current interrupt service routine. In the ATMEGA16A, when an interrupt occurs, the processor first clears the global interrupt flag (disabling all interrupts so the interruption is not interrupted). This does not occur in the XMEGA processor due to the multilevel interrupt system. Since higher level interrupts are allowed to interrupt lower interrupts, the global interrupt flag is not affected when an interrupt is serviced. In the XMEGA series, it is the job of the PMIC to prevent interruption of an interrupt routine by other interrupts at the same or lower levels.

Each interrupt has an associated vector in a special location in memory called the Interrupt Vector Table (IVT).

Interrupt Vector Table

Interrupt vectors are simply jump instructions that transfer to an actual interrupt routine. Interrupt vectors normally reside in program memory, beginning at address $0000 (fuse settings allow other configurations). Each vector is two words in length and typically holds a long jump (JMP) to the interrupt handler instructions. The JMP instruction is used (instead of RJMP) so interrupt handlers can be reached wherever they are located in memory. The following code segment illustrates a typical IVT definition in an ATMEGA16A assembly language program:

```
.cseg
jmp RESET
jmp ext_int_0
.org OVF0addr
jmp timer0_overflow
. . .
RESET:
```

Each JMP instruction in the table is called *an interrupt vector*. It is used to transfer control to code located elsewhere in program memory. The vectors are numbered 1 through *n*, where *n* is the number of interrupts available for the specific processor. For the ATMEGA16A, *n* is 21. In all of the AVR processors, vector 1 is called the reset vector. The collection of vectors is called the IVT. Figure 10.1 shows the interrupt vectors located at the beginning addresses in flash memory for the ATxmega128A1 and ATMEGA16A.

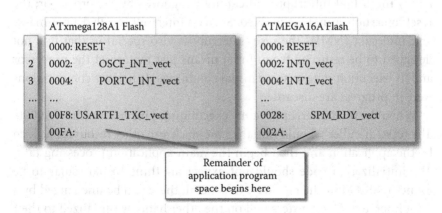

FIGURE 10.1 Interrupt vectors and their numbers located at the beginning of flash memory.

It is not necessary to specify every interrupt vector. Only the ones being used need to be entered in the table. The .org directive is used to skip unused entries and position vectors at the correct address. The first two vectors in the example above happen to be consecutive entries in the table. The third entry is positioned using the .org directive.

When interrupt number k occurs, the processor calculates the address of the corresponding vector:

```
vector_address = (k - 1) * 2
```

This calculated address is loaded into the program counter (which is first pushed onto the stack) causing a branch to the interrupt vector. This in turn branches to the actual interrupt service routine. When the service routine is finished, it typically executes a RETI (return from interrupt) instruction. This is identical to a return instruction, except that it also reenables global interrupts in the ATMEGA16A (which were disabled automatically when the interrupt occurred), or restores the state of the PMIC in the XMEGA series processors.

Upon return from an interrupt service routine, at least one program instruction will be executed before another interrupt can occur.

Interrupt Signals

The reset signal is a special type of interrupt. This signal can be triggered by a level change at the reset pin on the microcontroller package. It can also be triggered by several other conditions related to power levels. This is a very important interrupt, and cannot be ignored by the processor; the reset interrupt cannot be disabled. Such an interrupt is called a nonmaskable interrupt (NMI). The reset interrupt is also special in that it is not designed to be returned from. Reset means just that; reset the processor and its execution state to some initial conditions. Whatever computations were in progress are discarded.

When the reset interrupt occurs, execution begins from address $0000. The reset "handler" should initialize the stack and other resources needed by the application and then begin the main application processing task. The initialization code should not expect anything in particular to be found in SRAM or the registers. In general, these will be unchanged by a reset interrupt. I/O registers will on the other hand be initialized to their default states.

The AVR processor responds to two distinct types of interrupt signals. The first type of interrupt is something like a fire alarm. The alarm is activated by the outbreak of a fire. The alarm will sound and continue to sound until it is reset. When the alarm sounds, you expect the firemen to immediately drop what they are doing and rush to service your interrupt. However, the firemen might be busy at another fire, or they might be on strike. One would hope that the firemen eventually come to put out your fire and reset the alarm (as part of their service). Possibly, the fire will burn itself out in which case there is no real need for servicing the interrupt. However, the alarm will continue to sound until the alarm is reset. If the firemen never come, you might need to reset the alarm yourself.

In the context of the AVR microcontroller, the fire alarm type of interrupt functions as follows. Some condition triggers an interrupt flag to be set. This flag is simply a bit in an I/O register. The bit is set to one when the microcontroller notices the presence of the interrupt condition. The bit will remain set (even if the interrupt condition disappears) until one of two things occurs. The flag will be automatically cleared if the interrupt is serviced. The flag can also be cleared manually. This is done by writing a one (1) to the interrupt flag bit. Yes, writing a one (1) will clear the interrupt flag. Remember that I/O registers are not all like storage locations. When you write a one to an interrupt flag, you are signaling the interrupt hardware to clear that flag. If you subsequently read the interrupt flag, you are requesting information about the state of the interrupt. Since the flag was just cleared, it should read as a zero (unless the interrupt condition is still present or has immediately reasserted itself causing the flag to be set again). We have already encountered this version flag in the Timer/Counter units. In the ATMEGA16A, it was the OCF1A; in the ATxmega128A1, it was the OVFIF. These flags were cleared manually by writing a one to their position. If we had implemented an interrupt handler, servicing the interrupt would have automatically cleared the flag.

The second type of interrupt is more like a screaming child. The screams continue as long as the child needs service. We notice the child needs service because we hear the screams. When the child no longer needs service, the screams stop. No actual servicing may take place, and no manual resetting of the scream detector is required. If the parent is out of the room while the screams occur, and the screaming stops before they return, they may be completely oblivious to the fact that the child had been screaming. In some cases, servicing the child will not completely remove the reason for the screaming, and screams may continue after servicing; in other words, the interrupt remains asserted after servicing.

In the AVR, the screaming child interrupt will be triggered repeatedly while the interrupt condition is present. To clear the screaming child interrupt, you need to remove the reason for the screaming (or wait for it to stop on its own).

As long as the condition asserting the interrupt is present and the interrupt is enabled, it will continually request service. If a condition triggering this type of interrupt is present while interrupts are disabled, but disappears before interrupts are enabled, then it will not be serviced. No manual resetting of a flag is needed for this type of interrupt.

Global Interrupt Flag

The global interrupt flag is located in bit 7 of the SREG. This flag is cleared immediately when a reset occurs, and remains clear (rendering interrupts disabled) until set (enabled) by the program. Interrupts are enabled (globally) by setting the global interrupt enable flag. The SEI instruction is the easiest way to do this. The CLI instruction clears this flag, disabling all interrupts except for NMIs.

In the ATMEGA16A, the global interrupt flag is automatically cleared when any interrupt occurs. Once an interrupt service routine is underway, the routine can choose to reenable global interrupts, allowing the interrupt routine to be interrupted. Care must be taken to avoid unexpected recursive interrupts which would possibly overflow the stack. Usually interrupt routines execute very quickly and terminate, reenabling interrupts only when they are completely finished with their task. Interrupt routines that allow interruptions are only used when the interrupt routine needs to perform a time consuming task, or some very important time-sensitive interrupt must be allowed to occur during processing. The XMEGA PMIC facilitates this type of interrupt system through its multi-level interrupt categories.

When a program executes the CLI instruction, interrupts are immediately disabled. This means a pending interrupt, even if its condition is asserted while the CLI is being executed, will not interrupt the program until global interrupts are reenabled. When the SEI instruction is executed, globally enabling interrupts, the instruction following SEI will always be executed before an interrupt can occur. The same is true when exiting an interrupt handler via the RETI instruction; at least one instruction will be executed before another interrupt can occur.

The XMEGA microcontrollers require an extra step to enable interrupts. Since there are three independently enabled interrupt levels, you must also enable the levels you are using. This is done by setting the appropriate bits in the PMIC Control Register (PMIC_CTRL). The following code enables all three levels of interrupts and then activates the interrupt system:

```
ldi temp, PMIC_LOLVLEN_bm | PMIC_MEDLVLEN_bm | PMIC_
    HILVLEN_bm
sts PMIC_CTRL, temp
sei  ;enabled interrupts can occur now
```

Interrupts and the SREG

Since an interrupt can occur between any two instructions, it is essential that each interrupt service routine preserves essential details related to the state of the running program. Consider for example, the following instruction sequence:

```
cpi r16, 0
breq somewhere
```

If an interrupt occurs between these instructions, and an instruction in the interrupt handler changes the Z flag in the SREG, then this decision structure will sometimes fail (Figure 10.2). When writing interrupt handlers, we must be certain this will not happen. At the very minimum,

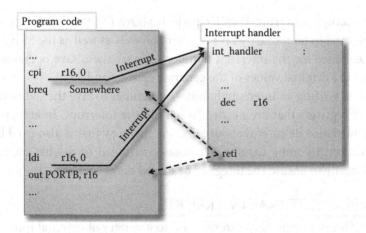

FIGURE 10.2 An interrupt handler that might alter flags and registers will cause programs to fail.

interrupt handlers must preserve the SREG contents. This is typically done using the following pattern:

```
interruptHandler:  ;ATMEGA16A version
     push r16  ;save r16
     in r16, SREG  ;Use CPU_SREG for XMEGA versions
     push r16  ;save status register's value
     . . .
     pop r16  ;restore status register
     out SREG, r16  ;Use CPU_SREG for XMEGA versions
     pop r16  ;restore r16
     reti
```

As you can see, the SREG is immediately saved on the stack and restored just before the RETI instruction is executed. Do not execute any instructions that change the SREG before it is saved, or after it is restored.

Each interrupt handler should also save registers that it needs for its task. It would be equally disconcerting to load a zero into r16, and then find that r16 contains something else when the next instruction is executed. If an interrupt handler is not careful to preserve register contents, anything can happen. Imagine your surprise if the following sequence sometimes produced random patterns on the LEDs connected to port B (Figure 10.2):

```
ldi r16, 0
out PORTB, r16  ;might not output a zero!
```

The sample interrupt handler pattern above illustrates how the stack can be used to temporarily save register contents as well as the SREG. The exit sequence for the interrupt handler reverses these save operations to restore the original values of the general registers and SREG.

When writing an interrupt handler, remember to save the status values and all registers that are needed to handle the interrupt. Interrupt handlers must also be careful about affecting memory that is also used by an application. In some cases, applications will need to disable interrupts temporarily to ensure the integrity of shared data.

GENERAL EXTERNAL INTERRUPTS

The AVR microcontroller can respond to a variety of external interrupts. These signals are made available to the microcontroller on specific pins. We have already covered the reset signal which is both an external and

TABLE 10.1   ATMEGA16A External Interrupts and Pin Assignments

External Interrupt	Shared Pin
INT0	PD2
INT1	PD3
INT2	PB2

internal interrupt. That is, this interrupt can be triggered by a logic signal applied to a pin, the RESET pin, or the reset interrupt can also be triggered by internal sources.

The AVR processor has several additional pins that can be connected to external devices to allow them to trigger a general interrupt. On the ATMEGA16A, the pins INT0, INT1, and INT2 are used for this purpose. These pins actually serve a dual rule, sharing functionality with the I/O ports (Table 10.1). Each of the I/O ports of the XMEGA series has two general interrupts; any collection of port pins can be configured to trigger these interrupts.

Usually, when a port pin is used to monitor an interrupt request for an external device, the pin is set as an input in the associated digital I/O port. This allows the external device to assert its interrupt signal on the pin. It is, however, possible to configure the pin as an output, in which case the program itself will output the value that is being monitored. This can be used to allow a program to trigger an interrupt by asserting a value on the associated digital port pin. This is called a software interrupt: an interrupt triggered by an explicit instruction. Some processor instruction sets include a specific software interrupt instruction. For example, the X86 microprocessor family includes the INT instruction. This instruction will trigger a software interrupt when it is executed. The AVR processor does not have any explicit software interrupt instruction, but writing to specific hardware locations can sometimes trigger an interrupt.

External Interrupt Behavior

Each external interrupt pin can be configured to trigger its associated interrupt according to specific conditions. The interrupt can be triggered while the pin is low (0), when a change of state occurs, or when one of the transitions, low to high or high to low, occurs.

When the external interrupt pin is configured to request an interrupt when the pin is low (0), the signal must be low at the instant the current instruction finishes executing, or the interrupt will not occur. This is like the screaming child interrupt; it must be asserted when the interrupt

TABLE 10.2   MCUCR—ATMEGA16A MCU Control Register

7	6	5	4	3:2	1:0
SM2	SE	SM1	SM0	**ISC1[1:0]**	**ISC0[1:0]**

conditions are checked, or it will be missed. This particular interrupt will continue to be asserted as long as the voltage level on the pin remains low.

When an external interrupt pin is configured as a level change or edge-triggered interrupt, the specific transition will set an interrupt flag that will remain set until cleared. The interrupt flag may be cleared manually (by writing a 1 to that bit), or automatically by the act of servicing the interrupt. This is the fire alarm type of interrupt.

When configured for level change or edge-triggered mode, the external interrupt's flag will be set, and remain set, as soon as its triggering condition occurs. The interrupt flag will be set even while the interrupt is disabled. The interrupt will not be serviced until interrupts are enabled. In some cases, it is important to clear this type of flag before enabling interrupts (to ignore past triggers).

Port pins are read synchronously according to the I/O or Peripheral clock signal. This clock is by default the same as the CPU clock, but may be configured to run at a faster rate for some devices. The XMEGA microcontrollers also support asynchronous latching of edge changes on specific pins. This provides greater flexibility so quickly changing external signals are not missed.

External Interrupt Control Registers (ATMEGA16A)

Here are the details for configuring and using the AVR external interrupts on the ATMEGA16A. The relevant control and status bits are in registers MCUCR, MCUCSR, GICR, and GIFR.

The MCU Control Register (Table 10.2) is used to select the type of trigger for INT1 and INT0. This is determined by the setting of the Interrupt Sense Control bits. These allow four configurations for the external interrupts on pins PD2 and PD3 (INT0 and INT1) as shown in Table 10.3.

TABLE 10.3   Interrupt Sense Control Bits for INT0 and INT1 (ATMEGA16A)

ISCn[1:0]	Triggered by
00	Low level
01	Change
10	Negative (falling) edge
11	Positive (rising) edge

The other external interrupt, INT2, has its configuration bit in a different I/O register, MCUCSR. It is also only capable of edge-triggered mode. Bit ISC2 is set to 1 to trigger the interrupt when the pin transitions from zero to one (positive edge-trigger) and is cleared to select negative edge-triggered mode (Tables 10.4 and 10.5).

The external interrupts are all independently enabled. The enable bits are located together in the General Interrupt Control Register (GICR, Table 10.6). Set an interrupt's enable bit (to one) to enable the specific interrupt; clear the bit to disable it. The default value for these bits is of course, zero.

When one of the external interrupts is configured to detect change, rising edge, or falling edge, the General Interrupt Flag Register (Table 10.7) is used to determine if one of the interrupts has been triggered. Remember that in these modes, the interrupt flag is set when the interrupt condition is met. The flag remains set until cleared manually or automatically via an interrupt occurrence. These flags are cleared by setting the corresponding bit in the I/O register.

Because the interrupt pins are sampled only once per clock cycle, it is possible that very short pulses will be missed. This is a circuit design issue

TABLE 10.4   MCUCSR—ATMEGA16A MCU Control and SREG

7	6	5	4	3	2	1	0
JTD	ISC2	—	JTRF	WDRF	BORF	EXTRF	PORF

TABLE 10.5   Configuration Bit for INT2 to Select Positive or Negative Edge Triggering (ATMEGA16A)

ISC2	Triggered by
0	Negative (falling) edge
1	Positive (rising) edge

TABLE 10.6   GICR—ATMEGA16A General Interrupt Control Register

7	6	5	4	3	2	1	0
INT1	INT0	INT2	—	—	—	IVSEL	IVCE

TABLE 10.7   GIFR—ATMEGA16A General Interrupt Flag Register

7	6	5	4	3	2	1	0
INTF1	INTF0	INTF2	—	—	—	—	—

TABLE 10.8   INTCTRL—XMEGA Digital I/O Port Interrupt Control Register

7	6	5	4	3:2	1:0
—	—	—	—	INT1LVL[1:0]	INT0LVL[1:0]

that cannot be accounted for in software. The interrupt signal must be present long enough to be detected by the microcontroller hardware.

The interrupt flag bit is always clear if the interrupt is configured with a level trigger. In this case, an application can test the associated bit (2 or 3) from I/O register PIND to determine if the interrupt condition is asserted or not.

Enabling the external interrupts does not affect the normal use of the associated pins (either for input or output) in PORTB or PORTD. It simply adds the feature that writing to these ports can cause a software interrupt. If the port is configured as an output, an application can write a 0 or 1 to the appropriate bits in PORTB or PORTD which will cause the PINB or PIND bits to change, thereby potentially triggering an interrupt. When an instruction triggers an interrupt, it is called a software interrupt. The AVR processor can issue software interrupts only indirectly (as just described).

External Interrupt Control Registers (XMEGA Series)

The XMEGA microcontroller has two general interrupts for each port: INT0 and INT1. Each port has an Interrupt Control Register (INTCTRL, Table 10.4) which is used to set the interrupt level for each of these interrupts. In the XMEGA, interrupts are assigned one of the levels OFF, LOW, MEDIUM, or HIGH (Tables 10.8 and 10.9).

Two additional registers, INT0MASK and INT1MASK select which pins are used to trigger each of these interrupts. The following code would select pins 0 and 1 of PORTF to trigger INT0 and pin 3 to trigger INT1:

```
ldi r16, (1 <<0) | (1 <<1)  ;mask for pins 0 and 1
sts PORTF_INT0MASK, r16
ldi r16, (1 <<3)  ;mask for pin 3
sts PORTF_INT1MASK, r16
```

TABLE 10.9   Interrupt Level Field Values (XMEGA)

INTnLVL[1:0]	Interrupt Level
00	Off
01	Low
10	Medium
11	High

TABLE 10.10   Interrupt Sense Control Bits for PINnCTRL (XMEGA)

ISC[2:0]	Configuration
000	Both Edges (Change)
001	Positive (Rising) Edge
010	Negative (Falling) Edge
011	Low Level
101–110	Reserved
111	Input Disabled (PORTA-F only)

Pins used to generate interrupts are usually configured as input. The input sense configuration is selected by each pin's individual PINnCTRL register via its Input Sense Configuration field: ISC[2:0]. The configuration settings are shown in Table 10.10.

Each port has an associated Interrupt Flags Register (INTFLAGS, Table 10.11).

The specific interrupt flag INTnIF is set if a change (according to the input sense configuration) on an associated pin (as selected in INTnMASK) is detected. You can clear the flag by writing a one to its position. The interrupt flag is cleared automatically if the associated interrupt is serviced.

Other External Interrupts

In addition to the external interrupts discussed above, some pins have special uses that trigger other types of interrupts. These utilize the alternate functions of specific pins of the digital I/O ports. One example is associated with the Timer/Counter units. A Digital I/O Port pin can be used to signal an input capture action. When a change to the associated pin (according to its input sense configuration) is detected, the timer's count is copied into a capture register. This action can optionally trigger an input capture interrupt. On the ATMEGA16A, there is only one such capture mechanism; it is triggered from PD6 (IPC1) and associated with Timer/Counter 1. The XMEGA series provides much greater flexibility at the cost of more complex configuration requirements.

TABLE 10.11   INTFLAGS—XMEGA Digital I/O Port Interrupt Flags Register

7	6	5	4	3	2	1	0
—	—	—	—	—	—	INT1IF	INT0IF

INTERRUPT-CONTROLLED UP/DOWN COUNTER

Program 10.1 illustrates the use of two general external interrupts to create an up/down counter. Switches are connected to two pins of a digital I/O port (on the ATMEGA16A, the only option is to use the pins labeled INT1 and INT0). Recall that the switches are normally open, and the processor pins are pulled up to a one (1) level by pull-up resistors (must be software configured in the ATxmega128A1 on the XPLAIN board). Pressing a switch will therefore assert a zero at the processor pin.

In this application, the interrupts are configured as positive edge-triggered, so releasing the switch button (causing a transition from zero to one) will trigger the interrupt. Only switches 2 and 3 are active—these are the pins used for external interrupts INT1 and INT0. Incidentally, this program will likely exhibit bad behavior due to switch bounce. You may explore ways to eliminate this. Refer to the XPLAIN version of Program 10.1 if you are using that platform.

PROGRAM 10.1   Up/Down Counter Implemented Using External Interrupts: ATMEGA16A STK-500 Version

```
;Program 10.1 - External Interrupt driven counter
;Illustrate use of external interrupts to implement an
;up/down counter

;Programmer: TM
;Date: 5/2010
;Platform: STK-500
;Device: ATMega16A
.include "m16def.inc"

;Counter value is displayed on LEDS
;External interrupts are used to change the counter
;value

;LED's on Port B
;Switches on Port D (only switches 2 and 3 are used)

;Up/down counter, interrupt controlled
.def count = r16   ;count is changed via interrupt handlers

;Interrupt Vector Table (IVT)
jmp reset
jmp countup   ;int0
jmp countdown   ;int1
```

```
;Program code overlaps the rest of the IVT as it is not
;used
countup:  ;int0 handler
      inc count  ;increase count
      reti


countdown:  ;int1 handler
      dec count  ;decrease count
      reti


.def temp = r17
reset:
ldi temp, high(RAMEND)  ;stack initialization required
                        ;for interrupts
out SPH, temp
ldi temp, low(RAMEND)
out SPL, temp


;configure INT0 and INT1 sense
ldi temp, (0b11 <<ISC10) | (0b11 <<ISC00)  ;positive edge
                                           ;triggers
out MCUCR, temp
;enable int0, int1
ldi temp, (1 <<INT0) | (1 <<INT1)
out GICR, temp


ldi temp, $FF  ;set PORTB for output
out DDRB, temp


clr count  ;initialize count
sei  ;enabled interrupts can occur now

lp:
      cli  ;disable interrupts for this critical section
      com count
      out PORTB, count
      sei  ;enable interrupts after next instruction
      com count
      rjmp lp
```

The reset interrupt takes care of the stack initialization, interrupt configuration and enabling, and the initialization of the application's only variable, count. The application simply loops forever, displaying the current value of count on the LEDs. It looks as though nothing ever changes count; the application complements it for output, but immediately restores it to its previous value.

Changes to count do occur, however. Every time an interrupt occurs (one of INT0 or INT1), the associated interrupt handler changes the value of count, either adding or subtracting one. The next time the main loop outputs count on PORTB, the LEDs will show the new value.

When the specified edge transition is detected on the INT0 or INT1 pin, the associated interrupt flag is set. At the first opportunity, the program will be interrupted to service the interrupt. Note that the external interrupts are enabled above the loop, so as long as the global interrupt flag is set, the interrupt can occur. The SEI instruction just above the main loop sets this flag, allowing the interrupt system to function.

In the main program loop, the variable count (R16) contains an unsigned integer. This must be complemented before it is sent to PORTB. The complement changes the numeric code to an LED display code so the bits of the number that are 1 will appear as on (asserting a 0 on the port) and the 0's will appear as off (asserting a 1 on the port). The second complement simply restores the count to a numeric value.

The interrupt handlers expect count to be in unsigned form; if they were to process an LED display code, they would not perform the correct operation. For example, if count is $03, the INT0 handler would change it to $04 (correctly). However, if the interrupt occurred while count contained a display code ($FC is the display code for $03), it would increment this code to $FD; This will display as the binary number 2. When $FD is complemented back to numeric format, it will be $02. In other words, the INT0 handler would have incorrectly decremented count (by incrementing its complement).

The application therefore needs to ensure that no interrupt can occur while count contains a display code rather than a number. This is accomplished by disabling interrupts during this critical section of code. Before R16 is complemented, interrupts are disabled (CLI). When R16 has been restored to a numeric code, the SEI instruction reenables interrupts. In this way, the application avoids the possibility of an interrupt corrupting data. Note that the SEI is placed before the last instruction of the critical section. Interrupts cannot occur on the instruction following the SEI instruction; at least one additional instruction will always be executed.

The potential corruption problem occurs in this case because the count variable is used by the application and the interrupt system; it is a shared resource. Shared resources must be carefully managed to avoid corruption. An alternate approach would be to use a different register for the LED pattern, never changing the data in count to a display code. The application would simply copy count to another register, complement it, and send it to PORTB. Interrupts could be left on throughout this process.

The interrupt handlers in the previous example do something very dangerous. Can you spot the potential problem?

Suppose we wanted the main application to only update the LEDs approximately five times per second. We might add a delay loop to implement this new behavior.

```
lp:
;assume a 1MHz clock speed, .2 second requires 200,000
 clock cycles
.def delayH = r25
.def delayL = r24
.equ dlp_init = 50000  ;inner loop = 50000 * 4 = .2 sec
       ldi delayH, high(dlp_init)
       ldi delayL, low(dlp_init)
dlp:  ;loop requires dlp_init * 4 clock cycles
       sbiw delayH:delayL, 1
       brne dlp

cli  ;disable interrupts for this critical section
com count
. . .
```

An interrupt can occur while the loop is running, but the interrupt handler does not use any of the registers used in the delay loop. At first glance there does not appear to be any conflict. However, the INC and DEC instructions in the interrupt handler can affect the Z (zero) flag in the SREG. The delay loop in the main application relies on the Z flag to correctly control the delay loop.

Consider what will happen if the delay loop has just started and reached the SBIW instruction, decrementing delay from 50,000 to 49,999. This subtraction will clear the Z flag (the result is not zero) and should cause the subsequent BRNE instruction to branch back to the top of the loop.

Now, what if INT0 occurs just after the SBIW instruction in the delay loop and the INT0 interrupt handler just happens to increment count from $FF to $00, causing the Z flag to be set (the result of the increment is zero). After returning from the interrupt, the BRNE instruction will sequence rather than branch sinze Z is set (the last result was zero). The delay loop will terminate early because of the interference of the interrupt.

Remember that interrupt routines should never alter the status flags. In general, interrupt handlers should not alter registers either, but our example is an exception to this rule. The interrupt handlers must alter the value of count; this is an intended effect. Here is a rewrite of the INT0 handler illustrating how the status flags can be preserved.

```
.def temp = r17
countup:
        push temp
        in temp, SREG   ;use CPU_SREG for XMEGA
        inc count
        out SREG, temp  ;use CPU_SREG for XMEGA
        pop temp
        reti
.undef temp
```

The interrupt handler uses a temporary register to save and restore the status values. The original value in temp is saved on the stack and also restored just before the return. With this correction applied to both interrupt handlers, the delay loop will always function correctly.

This sample program also suffers from switch bounce. When the switch is pressed or released, many 0–1 transitions can occur as the contacts stabilize. This can result in the counter increasing or decreasing by more than one for each switch release. To eliminate this behavior, we will examine the use of timers and another interrupt to mask out the unwanted signals.

TIMER COUNTER INTERRUPTS

The Timer/Counter units in the AVR microcontrollers can be configured to generate interrupts when certain events occur. One simple application of this capability is to use a timer interrupt to perform a specific action at predetermined intervals. In this section we will utilize a 16-bit Timer/Counter unit to generate a regularly recurring interrupt and an application to eliminate switch bounce.

AVR Timer/Counters Interrupts

The Timer/Counter units can generate interrupts in response to several different events. The most common is an overflow event. Other events include input capture and compare match. We will focus on the compare match interrupt on the ATMEGA16A and the overflow interrupt on the XMEGA microcontroller.

Suppose we want to trigger an interrupt every 0.1 s. We will need to configure a Timer/Counter to repeatedly match/overflow at this rate and generate an interrupt when the event occurs. The interrupt handler will then contain the code to perform a specific task every 0.1 s. This task might update the LEDs, attempt to transmit a character on the serial port, check for a received character, or read the switches.

The timer's clock selection and its TOP value must be determined in order to adjust its interrupt frequency. The prescaler unit provides clock division factors; in general you want to select the smallest divisor which will supply a faster clock impulse to the timer. This will require a larger TOP value to attain the correct interrupt frequency. Using a larger TOP value increases the resolution of the counter.

The interrupt frequency is the reciprocal of its period. That is, an interrupt with frequency 10 times per second will have a period of 0.1 s. To determine the appropriate TOP and prescaler divisor (DIV) values, consider the formulas that relate the interrupt PER in seconds, clock speed (CLK) in Hertz, prescaler DIV, and TOP. We will use the equation to choose the smallest available DIV value that satisfies the right-hand side of the last inequality.

```
PER = (TOP + 1) * DIV / CLK
DIV = PER * CLK / (TOP + 1)
TOP = PER * CLK / DIV - 1
0 <= TOP <= 65535 (16-bit counter limitation)
PER * CLK >= DIV >= PER * CLK / 65536
```

If our desired period is 0.1 s and the input to the prescaler unit (the clock speed) is 2 MHz, then

```
0.1 * 2000000 >= DIV >= (0.1 * 2000000)/65536
200000 >= DIV >= 3.1
```

The prescaler DIV selected would therefore be 8 for the ATMEGA16A or 4 for the XMEGA microcontroller. The value of TOP is calculated using the formula above.

```
TOP = PER * CLK/DIV - 1
ATMEGA16A: TOP = 0.1 * 2000000 / 8 - 1 = 24999
XMEGA: TOP = 0.1 * 2000000 / 4 - 1 = 49999
```

The TOP value is loaded into the ATMEGA16A Timer/Counter 1's OCR1A or the PER register of any counter in the XMEGA microcontroller. The appropriate Waveform Generation Mode is selected, and the timer is started by placing the correct value in the clock select field.

To utilize an interrupt when the counter resets to zero, the appropriate interrupt must be enabled. We will also have to write an interrupt handler and link the handler into the IVT. We will also need to enable Global Interrupts.

The ATMEGA16A has one Timer/Counter Interrupt Mask (TIMSK) that controls which timer interrupts are enabled. Recall that the ATMEGA16A has three timer units numbered 0, 1, and 2. Set the bits of TIMSK defined in Table 10.12 corresponding to the interrupts you want to enable. Each interrupt must have its own interrupt handler.

In our example, the desired interrupt is the Output Compare for Channel A on Timer/Counter 1 (OCIE1A). The following instructions will enable the desired interrupt without affecting the other interrupt settings:

```
;ATMEGA16A Output Compare A Timer 1 Interrupt Enable
in r16, TIMSK
sbr r16, 1 <<OCIE1A
out TIMSK, r16
```

In the XMEGA microcontroller, each Timer/Counter has its own pair of Interrupt Control Registers (INTCTRLA and INTCTRLB). Each possible interrupt has a two bit field used to select the interrupt level (Off, Low, Medium, or High). We want to select the Overflow Interrupt (located in Control Register A), and we will choose High for its

TABLE 10.12   TIMSK—ATMEGA16A TIMSK Register

7	6	5	4	3	2	1	0
OCIE2	TOIE2	TICIE1	OCIE1A	OCIE1B	TOIE1	OCIE0	TOIE0

level. The following instructions enable this interrupt for Timer/ Counter C0:

```
;XMEGA Timer/Counter C0 Overflow Interrupt Enable
lds r16, TCC0_INTCTRLA
andi r16, ~TC0_OVFINTLVL_gm  ;clear bits in field
ori r16, TC_OVFINTLVL_HI_gc  ;select level
sts TCC0_INTCTRLA, r16
```

The interrupt handler must be written and linked into the IVT. Here is a skeleton for each version of the interrupt handler.

```
OCI1A_Interrupt:  ;ATMEGA16A Output Compare T/C 1A
                  ;Interrupt handler
      push r16
      in r16, SREG
      push r16
;place the interrupt task here
      pop r16
      out SREG, r16
      pop r16
      reti
TCC0_Overflow_Interrupt:  ;XMEGA T/C C0 Overflow
                          ;Interrupt handler
      push r16
      in r16, CPU_SREG
      push r16
;place the interrupt task here
      pop r16
      out CPU_SREG, r16
      pop r16
      reti
```

To link the handler into the IVT, the following code can be inserted at the top of the program:

```
;IVT ATMEGA16A Version
jmp reset  ;reset vector
.org OC1Aaddr
jmp OC1A_Interrupt
reset:
```

```
;IVT XMEGA Version
jmp reset  ;reset vector
.org TCC0_OVF_vect
jmp TCC0_Overflow_Interrupt
reset:
```

The only missing step is to enable Global Interrupts (and in the XMEGA microcontroller, set the bit to enable the High-Level Interrupt group).

```
sei
;enable HI Interrupt Level group (XMEGA Only)
ldi r16, PMIC_HILVLEN_bm
sts PMIC_CTRL, r16
```

Prescaler Units

In the ATMEGA16A, there are two distinct timer prescaler units. Timers 0 and 1 share one prescaler; Timer 2 has its own. The prescalers are usually driven by the I/O Clock (which is usually the same as the CPU Clock). The prescaler for Timer 2 can also be driven from a signal asserted on an external pin (TOSC1).

The prescaler is essentially a clock signal divider and selector. The input is used to increment a counter. Each cycle of the input signal increments the counter. The ones place of the counter will cycle at one-half the frequency as the input; the twos place at one-fourth the frequency, and so on.

Picture a clock signal used as a pulse to increment a simple 10-bit counter. This counter can count from zero to 1023 before it overflows. At 1 MHz, the counter will increment 1,000,000 times per second. This means the one's digit oscillates at a frequency of 0.5 MHz; it requires two clock pulses to complete its 0–1 cycle. The next binary digit (in the 2's place) cycles at one-half of this rate, or 0.25 MHz. By connecting an output line to these digits in the counter, we can divide the original clock speed by any power of two. The Timer/Counter clock selection field is used to select one of these lines to be used as the input to the timer (Figure 10.3).

The XMEGA microcontrollers have one prescaler unit driven by the Peripheral Clock signal (which matches the CPU clock). The prescaler is shared by all of the Timer/Counter units.

The prescaler units are free running counters. When the clock select bits are written, the prescaler counter could be in any state. The first clock pulse to the Timer/Counter may be shortened (depending on how close the associated bit is to changing). In general, this anomaly may be ignored.

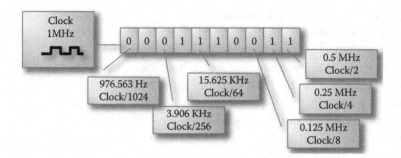

FIGURE 10.3   Timer/Counter Prescaler Unit counter and sample divider taps.

INTERRUPT-BASED SWITCH BOUNCE ELIMINATION

One very simple method of eliminating switch bounce is to sample the switch data less frequently. If a specific switch generally exhibits less than 10 ms of bounce, then if we sample the switch at 10 ms intervals, we will never obtain multiple changes due to the bounce effect. In this example, we will use a Timer/Counter to generate an interrupt every 10 ms. The interrupt handler will read the switch information and store it in a location accessed by the application.

For this example, we will assume that the processor is running at 2 MHz and apply the formula for clock signal selection.

```
PER * CLK >= DIV >= PER * CLK / 65536
* 2000000 >= DIV >= 0.01 * 2000000 / 65536
20000 >= DIV >= 0.30517578125
```

This means we should select DIV = 1. With this choice, we calculate TOP.

```
TOP = PER * CLK/DIV - 1
TOP = 0.01 * 2000000 / 1 - 1 = 19999
```

The following code will configure the ATMEGA16A Timer/Counter1 to generate an Output Compare interrupt every 10 ms (assuming the processor is running at 2 MHz):

```
#define CLOCK 2.0e6  ;clock speed
.equ PRESCALE = 0b001  ;/1 prescale
.equ PRESCALE_DIV = 1
```

```
#define PER 0.01   ;seconds
.equ WGM = 0b0100   ;Waveform generation mode: CTC

;you must ensure this value is between 0 and 65535
.equ TOP = int(0.5 + (PER * CLOCK/PRESCALE_DIV-1))
.if  TOP > 65535
.error "TOP is out of range"
.endif

;On MEGA series, write high byte of 16-bit timer
;registers first
ldi temp, high(TOP)   ;initialize compare value (TOP)
out OCR1AH, temp
ldi temp, low(TOP)
out OCR1AL, temp
ldi temp, ((WGM&0b11) << WGM10)   ;lower 2 bits of WGM
out TCCR1A, temp

;select interrupt
ldi temp, 1<<OCIE1A  ;TC 1 Compare Match Channel A
                     ;interrupt
out TIFR, temp  ;clear the overflow flag (if it was
                ;previously set)
out TIMSK, temp  ;enable the overflow interrupt

;upper 2 bits of WGM and clock select
ldi temp, ((WGM >> 2) << WGM12) | (PRESCALE << CS10)
out TCCR1B, temp  ;start counter
```

The interrupt handler itself is fairly simple. It will check the switches and store information related to switch activity. This could be as simple as copying the data from the switches to a global storage location, or the interrupt handler could interpret switch signals and place switch events in a queue for the application to use as needed.

Our example will implement a switch read system of intermediate complexity. The interrupt handler will call a function called sw_update that will maintain flags for each switch that indicate if a switch has been pressed. The application can call a function (switchread) to determine which button (if any) was pressed. If multiple switches have been pressed, the function will return the one that is highest numbered, and clear its flag.

The switchread function will return the number of the switch that was pressed (0–7) in R24. It will also clear the associated flag so the application does not get the same information on subsequent calls. The function will return a negative one ($FF) if no new switch presses have occurred.

The sw_update function will need to store enough information to fulfill these requests. It will need to be able to determine which switches have just been pressed and which were previously pressed. A new press will of course set the associated flag. The flag will be set only once for each press-release cycle.

By storing the previous state of the switches (obtained 10 ms earlier), sw_update can correctly differentiate between a new press and one that was flagged earlier. The switch flags and previous interrupt's switch status will be the only data needed by the function. Since the handler runs at 10 ms intervals, switch bounce should be eliminated.

We will incorporate this approach to switch debouncing in a simple application that will add a pressed switch's number to an accumulator. Pressing switch 0 will clear the counter. The application will never have to worry about switch bounce. Program 10.2 is the ATMEGA16A/STK-500 version. The ATxmega128A1/XPLAIN version is found at the end of this chapter.

PROGRAM 10.2   Switch Number Accumulator Illustrating Switch Debouncing via Timer Interrupt

```
;Program 10.2 - Interrupt Based Debounce

;Programmer: TM
;Date: 5/2010
;Platform: STK-500
;Device: ATMEGA16A
.include "m16def.inc"

;The timer counter unit is used to read switches at
;regular
;intervals, thereby eliminating switch bounce problems.

;Each switch press adds the switch number to the
;accumulator
;which is displayed on the LED's
;SW0 clears the accumulator.
```

```
;2 MHz clock
;PORTB to LEDS
;PORTD to Switches

;IVT ATMEGA16A Version
jmp reset  ;reset vector
.org OC1Aaddr
jmp TC1_CompareMatch_Interrupt

.def temp = r16
reset:
;Initialize stack
ldi temp, low(RAMEND)
out SPL, temp
ldi temp, high(RAMEND)
out SPH, temp

;Set the LEDS as OFF and PORTB as output
ldi temp, $FF  ;led's off and all outputs
out PORTB, temp
out    DDRB,temp

ldi temp, $00  ;all inputs
sts    DDRD,temp

;Configure timer for 0.01 second interrupt frequency
;(Clock speed is 2 MHz)
#define CLOCK 2.0e6  ;clock speed
.equ PRESCALE = 0b001  ;/1 prescale
.equ PRESCALE_DIV = 1
#define PER 0.01  ;seconds
.equ WGM = 0b0100  ;Waveform generation mode: CTC

;you must ensure this value is between 0 and 65535
.equ TOP = int(0.5 + (CLOCK/PRESCALE_DIV * PER))

.if TOP > 65535
.error "TOP is out of range"
.endif

;On MEGA series, write high byte of 16-bit timer
;registers first
```

```
ldi temp, high(TOP)  ;initialize compare value (TOP)
out OCR1AH, temp
ldi temp, low(TOP)
out OCR1AL, temp
ldi temp, ((WGM&0b11) << WGM10)  ;lower 2 bits of WGM
out TCCR1A, temp
;upper 2 bits of WGM and clock select
ldi temp, ((WGM >> 2) << WGM12)|(PRESCALE << CS10)
out TCCR1B, temp  ;start counter

;Enable Compare Match interrupt
;select interrupt
ldi temp, 1 <<OCIE1A  ;TC 1 Compare Match Channel A
                     ;interrupt
out TIFR, temp  ;clear the overflow flag (if it was
                ;previously set)
out TIMSK, temp  ;enable the overflow interrupt

;Enable global interrupts
sei

.def count = r17
ldi count, 0

repeat:
;Check for button press
rcall switchread  ;r24 = switch number or −1
cpi r24,−1  ;return value −1 means no button press
breq repeat
cpi r24, 0  ;0 means clear
brne noclear
clr count
noclear:
add count, r24
mov r24, count
rcall ledOut  ;display char on LED's
rjmp repeat
.undef count

TC1_CompareMatch_Interrupt:
;ATMEGA16A Compare Match Interrupt on T/C 1 A
     push r16
```

```
        in r16, SREG
;place the interrupt task here
        rcall sw_update
        out SREG, r16
        pop r16
        reti
.undef temp

;void ledOut(byte r24){
;   PORTE_OUT = ~r24
;}
ledOut:
        com r24
        out PORTB, r24
        com r24
        ret


.dseg  ;switch data
sw_lastread: .byte 1
sw_flags: .byte 1


.cseg
.def sw_current = r17
.def sw_lastread_reg = r18


sw_update:
        push sw_current  ;save registers
        in sw_current, SREG
        push sw_current
        push sw_lastread_reg
;set flags for new switch press events
        in sw_current, PIND  ;current switch info
        lds sw_lastread_reg, sw_lastread  ;previous switch
                                            info
        sts sw_lastread, sw_current  ;prev = current
        eor sw_lastread_reg, sw_current  ;compare!
;sw_lastread_reg becomes an indicator of changed switches
;we want to know which just changed to 0 (press)
;sw_current has 0's in positions corresponding to
;pressed buttons
        com sw_current  ;sw_current becomes a mask for
                        ;buttons currently pressed
```

```
;sw_current is now only pressed switches
      and sw_current, sw_lastread_reg  ;mask out the
                                       ;changes that
                                       ;were releases
;sw_current is now the pressed and changed switches
;combine the new and old flags to add newly pressed
 switches
      lds sw_lastread_reg, sw_flags
      or sw_lastread_reg, sw_current
      sts sw_flags, sw_lastread_reg
;restore registers and exit
      pop sw_lastread_reg
      pop sw_current
      out SREG, sw_current
      pop sw_current
      ret
.undef sw_current
.undef sw_lastread_reg

;byte switchread()
;return (in r24) highest number of switch with a switch-
;down event
;return −1 if none
;clear the switch-down event that is returned (if any)
.def sw_mask = r23
.def sw_num = r24  ;return value
.def sw_flags_reg = r25
switchread:
      push sw_mask
      push sw_flags_reg
      ldi sw_mask, (1 <<7)
      ldi sw_num, 7  ;process switch 7 first
      lds sw_flags_reg, sw_flags
switchread_lp:
      lsl sw_flags_reg  ;looking for a 1 (press event)
      brcs switchread_foundflag
      dec sw_num
      lsr sw_mask  ;becomes 0 when all flags have been
                   ;checked
      brne switchread_lp

      rjmp switchread_exit  ;none found
```

```
switchread_foundflag:
      com sw_mask
      cli  ;protect critical section
      lds sw_flags_reg, sw_flags  ;get the current flags
      and sw_flags_reg, sw_mask   ;clear the one about to
                                  ;be returned
      sei
      sts sw_flags, sw_flags_reg
switchread_exit:
      pop sw_flags_reg
      pop sw_mask
      ret

.undef sw_mask
.undef sw_num
.undef sw_flags_reg
```

The interrupt vector for Timer/Counter 1 Output Compare cannot be located immediately after the RESET vector. Therefore, a .org directive was used to place it at the correct address. The device include file contains names for all of the interrupt routines to help with the correct positioning of these vectors.

The sw_update function, called every 0.01 s, identifies those switches that are currently down, and were not down the last time they were checked. A flag is set in the global variable sw_flags for such switches. The flag is cleared only when the application receives a pressed switch's number when calling switchread.

The switchread function locates the leftmost 1 in the sw_flags byte by shifting it left and examining the bit that falls into the carry flag. Register sw_num is used to track which bit is being examined. Register sw_mask holds a mask that is later used to clear that bit in the original sw_flags byte. It is shifted to the right to position the 1 at the bit position being examined.

Note that interrupts are disabled while the sw_flag data is modified. We do not want an interrupt to set a bit in sw_flags after it is copied into sw_flags_reg for modification. If this were allowed, the event would be lost when switchread stores the new value into sw_flags.

We do not have to disable interrupts throughout the entire function even though we read sw_flags at the beginning. If an interrupt sets additional switch flags after we read sw_flags, we will base our return value on the flags read at the start. An interrupt will never clear a bit, but it may set additional bits. That is why it is important to disable interrupts and read the latest version of sw_flags before clearing the flag associated with the returned switch event. Events added after the switchread function begins will be reported in the next call of this function.

USART INTERRUPTS

Another useful set of interrupts are those related to USART functions. Polled serial I/O requires constant checking of the USART SREGs to determine when the next byte can be placed in the transmit queue, or when a received byte is available. If polling is too frequent, time is wasted that could be devoted to other processing tasks. If polling is too infrequent, time is wasted between transmittal of a sequence of bytes, or a data overrun error may occur in reception.

Rather than polling the USART to determine if a byte has been received, or if a byte can be transmitted, interrupts can be used to signal these conditions. To utilize interrupts for the output of a sequence of characters, a buffer or transmit queue must be used. These queues will buffer bytes between the USART and the application. Bytes to be transmitted are placed in the transmit queue. Bytes received by the USART (already placed in the receive queue) can be retrieved at any time by the application.

Each time the USART data register becomes empty, an interrupt handler can take the next character from the transmit queue and write it to the USART Data Register; this will keep the transmission going at full speed. A similar setup is used for reception. The USART has a two byte receive buffer, but this may be insufficient for many applications. Instead, a larger receive queue is established in SRAM. When there is a byte in the USART's little receive buffer, an interrupt handler can copy it into the larger software managed receive queue. The program can then access these characters at its convenience. A larger queue has less risk of overflow, and the interrupt-based receive keeps the USART's limited receive buffer empty to avoid data overrun errors.

The main advantage of the interrupt-based USART control is that it frees the program to perform its other tasks without having to deal directly with the USART in a polling style. This also simplifies the control flow for an application. Without interrupts, careful planning is required to ensure the polling functions are called frequently enough to be both efficient and to avoid loss of data.

The USART can generate interrupts for the following conditions:

- USART Data Register Empty
- Transmit complete
- RXC

Two of these interrupts are triggered while the associated status flag is set. In the XMEGA datasheets, these flags are referred to as interrupt flags even though they can be used in polling mode. The Data Register Empty interrupt will occur while the DREIF is set. The RXC interrupt will occur as long as the RXC flag is set. These flags cannot be cleared by writing a one to their position and they cannot be automatically cleared when their associated interrupt occurs. The interrupt handler must take a specific action to clear these flags. When the Data Register Empty interrupt occurs, the handler must either place another byte in the data register (for transmit) or disable the associated interrupt. When a RXC interrupt occurs, the interrupt handler should read the data register to remove the byte from the USART receive buffer, thereby clearing the RXC flag, or it should disable the interrupt (at the risk of a data overrun error).

The third USART interrupt is the Transmit Complete interrupt. A transmit complete event means the transmitter has entered an idle state: the transmit buffer is empty and the last bit of the current frame has been shifted out the transmit pin. This event is signaled by a one in the TXC flag. The Transmit Complete flag is automatically cleared when this interrupt is serviced. Alternatively, it can be cleared by writing a one to the TXC bit.

If transmit or receive queues are utilized in conjunction with interrupt-driven USART actions, special care must be taken when the application adds or removes bytes from these queues. The queues are shared memory, shared between the application and the interrupt system. There will be critical sections of code that must be completed without interruption or the queues will become corrupted.

The following instructions will configure the USART to trigger interrupts for the USART. The XMEGA version uses USARTC0:

```
;ATMEGA16A USART Interrupts
;Establish vectors to interrupt handlers
.org URXCaddr
jmp enqueue_received_byte
.org UDREaddr
jmp deque_and_transmit
...
;Enable the Data Register Empty and Receive Complete
;interrupts
sbi UCSRB, UDRIE
sbi UCSRB, RXCIE
```

```
;XMEGA USART Interrupts
;Establish vectors to interrupt handlers
.org USARTC0_DRE_vect
jmp deque_and_transmit
.org USARTC0_RXC_vect
jmp enqueue_received_byte
. . .
;Enable the Data Register Empty and Receive Complete
 interrupts
;Disable the TXC Interrupt
ldi r16, USART_RXCINTLVL_MED_gc \
      | USART_DREINTLVL_MED_gc \
      | USART_TXCINTLVL_OFF_gc
sts USARTC0_CTRLA, r16
```

The following functions could be used to configure an interrupt controlled send/receive system:

bool sendByte(byte b)

> Place a byte in the transmit queue and enable the USART Data Register Empty interrupt. Return with carry set if the queue is full (and the byte could not be placed into it).

byte getByte()

> Return a byte from the receive queue. If there is no byte, this might return a null character. The carry flag will be returned set if there is no byte in the queue.

void udrEmpty()

> This interrupt handler must dequeue a byte from the transmit queue and place it into the USART's data register. If the transmit queue is empty, it must disable the Data Register Empty interrupt.

void receiveInterrupt()

> This interrupt handler must copy a byte from the USART's receive buffer and place it in the receive queue. If the queue is full, it should discard the byte and possibly set a flag that can be checked by the application.

Program 10.3 illustrates interrupt controlled reception and transmission of characters. The application simply updates a counter displayed on the LEDs to keep itself busy. It employs a simple delay loop for this purpose. Meanwhile, the interrupt system echoes received characters back to the PC over the serial line. Every time the counter reaches a multiple of 16, a message is output to the PC using interrupt controlled transmission. The XMEGA version is at the end of the chapter.

PROGRAM 10.3   Interrupt   Controlled   USART–ATMEGA16A Version

```
;Program 10.3 - Interrupt Controlled USART
;This program displays a counter on the LED's. It also
;communicates serially, echoing received characters.
;Each time the counter reaches a multiple of 16, a
;message is sent over the serial line. The USART
;operations are all interrupt driven.


;Programmer: TM
;Date: 5/2010
;Platform: STK-500
;Device: ATMEGA16A
.include "m16def.inc"


;Serial communications between the STK-500 and PC
;PORTB connected to LEDS
;PD0 and PD1 to RXD and TXD


;Interrupt vector table
jmp reset
.org URXCaddr
jmp rxc_interrupt
.org UDREaddr
jmp dre_interrupt


;Data register empty interrupt
;Transmit next byte of a string or disable interrupt
;when done
;byte_ptr is the byte address of next character in flash
;to be sent
;nul terminates string
```

```
.dseg
byte_ptr: .byte 2   ;points to next byte in flash to be
                    ;transmitted
.cseg


.def temp = r16
dre_interrupt:
        push zh  ;save status and registers used
        in zh, SREG
        push zh
        push zl
        push temp

        lds zh, byte_ptr+1   ;get byte pointer into Z
        lds zl, byte_ptr
        lpm temp, Z+   ;load next byte
        tst temp  ;is it zero?
        breq send_done  ;br if zero to end task
        out UDR, temp  ;transmit
        sts byte_ptr+1, zh  ;save new pointer
        sts byte_ptr, zl
        rjmp dre_exit
send_done:
;turn off interrupt
        cbi UCSRB, UDRIE

dre_exit:
        pop temp  ;restore registers
        pop zl
        pop zh
        out SREG, zh
        pop zh
        reti

;Receive complete interrupt
;Echo received character, poll data register until empty
;and echo
rxc_interrupt:
        push temp  ;save registers and status
        in temp, SREG
        push temp
```

```
transmit_wait:
        sbis UCSRA, UDRE  ;is byte in Tx buffer?
        rjmp transmit_wait  ;not ready yet
        in temp, UDR  ;receive and echo
        out UDR, temp

        pop temp  ;restore registers
        out SREG, temp
        pop temp
        reti

reset:
;Stack initialization
ldi temp, low(RAMEND)
out SPL, temp
ldi temp, high(RAMEND)
out SPH, temp

;2 mhz clock speed, 9600 baud UBRR = 12
.equ UBRRvalue = 12
;Set the LEDS as OFF and PORT as output
ldi temp, $FF  ;led's off
out    PORTB, temp
out    DDRB, temp

;set baud rate
ldi temp, high (UBRRvalue)  ;baud rate
out UBRRH, temp
ldi temp, low (UBRRvalue)
out UBRRL, temp

;serial parameters
;URSEL 0 = UBRRH, 1 = UCSRC (shared port address)
;UMSEL 0 = Asynchronous, 1 = Synchronous
;USBS 0 = One stop bit, 1 = Two stop bits
;UCSZ0:1 Character Size: 0 = 5, 1 = 6, 2 = 7, 3 = 8
;(UCSZ2 is in UCSRB, but is only needed for 9 data bits)
;UPM0:1 0 = none, 1 = reserved, 2 = Even, 3 = Odd

;8data, 1 stop, no parity
ldi temp, (1 <<URSEL) | (0 <<UMSEL) | (0 <<USBS) | (3 <<UCSZ0) |
 (0 <<UPM0)
out UCSRC, temp
```

```
;enable bi-directional communication
ldi temp, (1 <<RXEN)|(1 <<TXEN)
out UCSRB, temp  ;enable receive and transmit
;USART initialization complete

;wait for PC to transmit a character
receive:
        sbis UCSRA, RXC  ;is byte in Rx buffer?
        rjmp receive

;enable receive interrupt
sbi UCSRB, RXCIE
;Enable global interrupts
sei

.equ DELAY = 60000
.def one = r17
ldi one, 1  ;constant to add one to counter
main_lp:
        in temp, PORTB  ;get current LED pattern
        com temp
        add temp, one  ;increment counter
;inc does not set half carry flag, so add is used
        brhc no_message  ;half carry sends message
        rcall startmessage
no_message:
        com temp  ;output current count in binary
        out PORTB, temp
        ;delay
        ldi r25, high(DELAY)
        ldi r24, low(DELAY)
delay_lp:
        sbiw r25:r24, 1
        brne delay_lp
        rjmp main_lp

msg: .db '\r','\n',"Message",'\r','\n',0
;initialize byte_ptr and enable DRE Interrupt to
;transmit string
startmessage:
        push temp
        ldi temp, high(msg * 2)  ;byte address of message
        sts byte_ptr + 1, temp
```

```
ldi temp, low(msg * 2)
sts byte_ptr, temp
sbi UCSRB, UDRIE  ;enable DRE Interrupt
pop temp
ret
```

The program waits for one character to appear in the USART receive buffer before entering the main loop. This action triggers the enable of the RXC interrupt. One instruction after the SEI, this interrupt will be handled causing the echo (reception and transmission) of the character.

In the main loop, the counter is incremented until a half carry occurs. This signals the fact that the counter has reached a multiple of 16. The startmessage function is called at this time to initiate the transmission of a message.

The message is not transmitted using a polling technique, or the counter updates would be delayed until the transmission finished. Instead, a pointer to the string is initialized and the Data Register Ready interrupt is enabled. Whenever the data register is empty, this interrupt will take the next character from the string and place it in the transmit buffer. When a null is encountered, the interrupt is disabled until it is time for another message to be sent.

EXERCISES

The following questions refer to the ATmega16A or ATxmega128A1. Some questions require consultation of the microcontroller's datasheet.

1. (ATmega16A) At what address must the vector for external INT1 be located? If the handler for this interrupt is extInt1, show how to define the appropriate vector in flash using the .org directive. (ATxmega128A1) At what address must the vector for PORTC's INT0 interrupt be located? If the handler for this interrupt is named portCInt0, show how to define the appropriate vector in flash using the .org directive.

2. (ATmega16A) At what address must the interrupt vector for interrupt number seven be located? This is Timer/Counter 1's Compare Match A Interrupt. (ATxmega128A1) At what address must the interrupt vector for interrupt number 15 be located? This is Timer/Counter C0's Overflow Interrupt.

3. (ATmega16A) Write two statements to enable External INT1. (ATxmega128A1) Write two statements to enable PORTC's INT1 as a medium-level interrupt.

4. (ATmega16A) Write an instruction to manually clear the interrupt flag for Timer/Counter 1's channel B output compare interrupt. Look for a description of TIFR. (ATxmega128A1) Write an instruction to manually clear the interrupt flag for Timer/Counter C0's compare or capture channel A interrupt.

5. In the previous problem, can the SBI or CBI instruction be used to clear the flag? Explain.

6. (ATmega16A) What is interrupt 13? What causes this interrupt to occur? What register and bit indicates that this interrupt needs servicing? (ATxmega128A1) What is interrupt 13? What causes this interrupt to occur? What register and bit indicates that this interrupt needs servicing?

7. How does RETI differ from RET?

8. Show how the SREG is generally preserved during execution of an interrupt handler. Write instructions to place it on the stack and then show how the registers are restored just before the RETI instruction.

9. (ATmega16A) Write a sequence of instructions to configure INT0 for low-level sensing and INT1 so it is edge-triggered, on the rising edge. Enable both interrupts. (ATxmega128A1) Write a sequence of instructions to configure pin 3 on PORTC for low-level sensing and to utilize its internal pullup resistor. Also write instructions to configure pin 7 of the same port to be edge-triggered, on the rising edge.

10. (ATmega16A) When INT0 is configured with ISC01:0 as 00, what value will be read from the INTF0 bit in GIFR if PIND(2) is zero? What if PIND(2) is one? Explain. (ATxmega128A1) When pin 2 of PORTC is configured with ISC[2:0] as 011, and this pin is associated with INT1 for PORTC, what value will be read from the INT1IF bit in PORTC_INTFLAGS if pin 2 is zero? What if pin 2 is one? Explain.

11. (ATmega16A) Show how to change the current enable state for INT1. Your statements should enable this interrupt if it is currently disabled, and disable it if it is currently enabled. Try to accomplish this without any branch instructions and do not change any other settings. (ATxmega128A1) Show how to change the current enable state for PORTC's INT1. This interrupt should be configured as a high-level interrupt. Your statements should disable this interrupt if it is currently enabled and enable it to level high if it is disabled.

12. (ATmega16A) If the CPU clock is running at 8 MHz, what frequency will be obtained from the prescaler associated with

Timer/Counter 1 if the clock select bits are 100? How much time elapses between Timer/Counter ticks? (ATxmega128A1) If the CPU clock is running at 8 MHz, what frequency will be obtained from the Timer/Counters' prescaler if its clock select bits are 0110? How much time elapses between Timer/Counter ticks?

13. (ATmega16A) What is the maximum interval that can be timed using Timer0 (consult the data sheet for information on this timer) with a 1 MHz processor clock speed and no prescaling? With Timer 1? (ATxmega128A1) What is the maximum interval that can be timed using just one Timer/Counter unit in normal mode with a 1 MHz clock speed and no prescaling?

14. (ATmega16A) What is the maximum interval that can be timed using Timer0 with a 1 MHz processor clock speed and maximum prescaling? With Timer 1? (ATxmega128A1) What is the maximum interval that can be timed using just one Timer/Counter unit in normal mode with a 1 MHz clock speed and maximum prescaling?

15. (ATmega16A) Determine an appropriate prescaler DIV and TOP value for Timer/Counter1 to time a 0.75 s delay with a 1 MHz clock signal using CTC mode. In a situation such as this, always choose the smallest prescaler DIV for greatest accuracy. (ATxmega128A1) Determine an appropriate prescaler DIV and TOP value for a Timer/Counter to time a 0.75 s delay with a 1 MHz clock signal using normal mode and the overflow interrupt. In a situation such as this, always choose the smallest prescaler DIV for greatest accuracy.

16. (ATmega16A) Write a sequence of instructions to load 27,345 into TCNT1. (ATxmega128A1) Write a sequence of instructions to load 27,345 into Timer/Counter C1's CNT register.

17. (ATmega16A) Timer/Counter 1 is running freely. Write a function called halfway that will return with 0 in R24 if the counter value is less than $8000 and return 1 otherwise. (ATxmega128A1) Timer/Counter C1 is running freely. Write a function called halfway that will return with 0 in R24 if the counter value is less than $8000 and return 1 otherwise.

18. Why would it be better to use a smaller prescaler DIV rather than a larger one if the same delay could be attained (using different initial counter values)?

19. Using a smaller prescaler DIV means the timer updates more frequently. Would this impact the execution speed of the application

program (slow it down) because of the frequent counter increments? Explain.

20. The USART is associated with three interrupts. Only one is cleared automatically when the interrupt occurs. Which one?

PROGRAMMING EXERCISES

1. Modify the main program in the original up/down counter application, Program 10.1, to copy count to a temporary register and complement the copy instead of the original before outputting it to the port driving the LEDs. Remove the unneeded cli and sei instructions from the loop. Verify that the program still works as before.

2. In the original up/down counter application, Program 10.1, modify the main loop so it looks like this:

```
lp: rjmp lp
```

Modify the interrupt handlers so they display the correct pattern on the LEDs whenever count is changed. To avoid writing duplicate code, each interrupt handler will exit at a common RETI instruction.

3. In Program 10.1, switch bounce might be eliminated by disabling the external interrupts for about 20 ms each time the interrupt is triggered. Add a timer to cause an interrupt in 20 ms. The timer interrupt handler should reenable the external interrupts and disable the timer interrupt. Be sure to clear the external interrupt flags before manually reenabling the interrupts. The external interrupt handlers should enable the timer interrupt so it occurs in 20 ms. Verify that forgetting to manually clear the external interrupt flags will sometimes cause a double increment or decrement.

4. Modify Program 10.1 to use (low) level-triggered external interrupts to process switch presses. Each time one of these interrupts occurs, the application's counter should be incremented or decremented by one and the interrupt disabled. The external interrupt should also start a timer to interrupt after 0.5 s. When the interrupt occurs, the timer should be disabled and the external interrupt reenabled. There is no need to worry about switch bounce in this application. Write the program to run correctly at 2 MHz. What happens if one switch is held down for a long time? What happens if both

switches are held down? Explain why only one of the switches appears to be processed in this case (Hint: which interrupt is occurring?).

5. In Program 10.1, make a modification so the program responds to level changes instead of edge-triggers. How does this change the behavior of the switches? What happens if you choose level-triggering?

6. In Program 10.1, eliminate switch bounce by skipping over the actual increment/decrement steps if a timer is running. Start the timer when a switch press occurs. Stop the timer 20 ms after it was started (use an interrupt).

7. Write a program to create a binary timer. The timer value should be displayed on the LEDs. It should count down from 10 to zero (in binary), and then stop. Use a Timer/Counter to generate an interrupt once every second. The interrupt should be used to update the LEDs. Use a pushbutton to start the timer. When the button is released, the program should start the timer at 10 (even if it is currently running).

8. Add a pause feature to the timer in the previous problem. Releasing the pause button will pause the timer. Releasing it a second time will restart it. You will need to debounce this button!

9. Write a program that starts a 16-bit Timer/Counter at zero and allows it to run freely. Your main program should simply display the value in the high byte of the timer's count on the LEDs while the timer is running. No interrupts are used. Choose the maximum prescale value for the counter and a 2 MHz clock. Approximately how often does the display change?

10. Design a USART Data Register Empty interrupt handler to transmit a null-terminated string located in flash via the USART. The handler assumes the USART transmitter is enabled and all of the communications parameters are already set. The interrupt handler uses one word located in SRAM.

```
sPtr: .byte 2
```

When the Data Register Empty interrupt occurs, use sPtr as a byte pointer into flash. If the character at this address is null, simply disable the UDRE interrupt and store a 0 in sPtr. Otherwise, transmit the character at that location and increment sPtr. Remember to preserve registers and status.

11. Enhance the interrupt handler in the previous problem. It should be able to handle strings in flash or SRAM. If sPtr's most significant bit is set, the address is assumed to be in flash, otherwise it is in SRAM.

12. Write an application to communicate via RS-232 serial at 9600 baud. Your application will simply send several strings using the interrupt handler described in the previous problem. You must define several strings in flash, and copy some of them into RAM when the program starts. To transmit a string, wait until the Data Register Empty Interrupt is disabled (so the interrupt handler is not busy transmitting a string), then store the address of the next string into sPtr and enable the interrupt. Repeat for each string, using some from flash and some from SRAM. When finished, start again with the first string. You could create an array of string addresses and implement the main program as a simple loop.

13. Declare storage in SRAM for a queue (circular queue in an array). It should be MAXQL bytes long (define a constant). You will need to keep track of the offset to the first byte (q_front) and the size (q_size) of the queue. You can calculate the location for the rear of the queue from this information. Write an initialization function named q_reset that makes the queue empty. Provide functions named q_add and q_remove that either add or remove a byte. These functions should return with carry set whenever the operation is illegal (remove from empty or add to full) and carry clear otherwise. Adding to the queue increases q_size and copies the parameter into the end of the queue. Removing from the queue increases q_front and decreases q_size, returning the front byte. Use R24 for the parameter.

14. Write an application to use your queue to perform interrupt-driven RS-232 data reception. The RXC interrupt should place the received byte into the queue. Your application will simply monitor the queue size (q_size) and whenever it is over 70% full, it will remove all of the bytes to a buffer area and then transmit them out the serial port. Use the interrupt-based string transmitter developed in an earlier exercise to accomplish this part of the task. Note that you should disable interrupts before calling q_remove (and reenable them after the call) since q_add is called from an interrupt. Use 9600 baud communication.

ALTERNATE PROGRAMS FOR THE XPLAIN DEMONSTRATION KIT

PROGRAM 10.1a: External Interrupt-Driven Counter

The XMEGA series microcontrollers allow any digital I/O port pins to be used to trigger general external interrupts. Each port supports two different external interrupts. The sample program uses PORTF since it is hardwired on the XPLAIN board to the switches. Pins 2 and 3 are used for INT0 and INT1 to keep the program as similar to the STK-500 version as possible.

```
;Program 10.1a - External Interrupt driven counter
;Illustrate use of external interrupts to implement an
;up/down counter

;Programmer: TM
;Date: 5/2010
;Platform: XPLAIN
;Device: ATxmega128A1
.include "ATxmega128A1def.inc"

;Counter value is displayed on LEDS
;External interrupts are used to change the counter
;value

;LED's on Port E
;Switches on Port F (2 and 3)

;Up/down counter, interrupt controlled
.def count = r16  ;count is changed via interrupt handlers

;Interrupt Vector Table (IVT)
jmp reset
.org PORTF_INT0_vect
jmp countup  ;int0
.org PORTF_INT1_vect
jmp countdown  ;int1

;Program code overlaps the rest of the IVT as it is not
;used
countup:  ;PORTF, INT0 handler
```

```
        inc count  ;increase count
        reti

countdown:  ;PORTF, INT1 handler
        dec count  ;decrease count
        reti

.def temp = r17
reset:
;stack initialization is automatic

;Assign pin 2 to PORTF INT0
ldi temp, (1 <<2)  ;pin 2
sts PORTF_INT0MASK, temp
;Assign pin 3 to PORTF INT1
ldi temp, (1 <<3)  ;pin 3
sts PORTF_INT1MASK, temp

;Configure pins 2 and 3 (PORTF) to use internal pullup
;resistors and Interrupt Sense Control for positive
;edge trigger
ldi temp, (1 <<2) | (1 <<3)
sts PORTCFG_MPCMASK, temp  ;configure pins 2 and 3 only
ldi temp, PORT_OPC_PULLUP_gc | PORT_ISC_RISING_gc
sts PORTF_PIN2CTRL, temp  ;PORTF pins 2 and 3 will read
                          ;switches

;Configure port directions
ldi    temp,0xFF
sts    PORTE_DIR,temp  ;configure PORTE as output
clr    temp
sts    PORTF_DIR,temp  ;configure PORTF as input

;enable PORTF's INT0 and INT1 interrupts as low priority
ldi temp, PORT_INT0LVL_LO_gc | PORT_INT1LVL_LO_gc
sts PORTF_INTCTRL, temp

clr count  ;initialize count

;Enable low level interrupts
ldi temp, PMIC_LOLVLEN_bm
sts PMIC_CTRL, temp
sei  ;enabled interrupts can occur now
```

```
lp:
      cli  ;disable interrupts for this critical section
      com count
      sts PORTE_OUT, count
      sei  ;enable interrupts after next instruction
      com count
      rjmp lp
```

The IVT contains vectors to PORTF's INT0 and INT1 interrupt handlers. Remember that each port has two such vectors.

The interrupt mask registers assign pins to interrupts. In this example, pins (switches) 2 and 3 were assigned to INT0 and INT1. You might experiment assigning several switches to each interrupt.

The pins used are directly connected to the switches, so internal pullup resistors must be used. The same registers (PINnCTRL) are used to select the interrupt sense control mode. The Multipin Configuration mask allows several pins to be configured identically by selecting the pin mask and writing to one of the pins in the group; in this case we write to pin 2.

Each interrupt is assigned a priority level; in this case, low was chosen. We want both interrupts to be at the same level so that one is not interrupted by the other. Any level could be used in this application. Whichever level is used, it must be enabled in order for the interrupt requests to be active. The global interrupt flag is enabled at the end of the initialization sequence.

PROGRAM 10.2a: Interrupt-Based Switch Debounce

The XMEGA version uses Timer/Counter C0 and ports E and F. Otherwise, there are few differences from the ATMEGA16A version.

```
;Program 10.2a - Interrupt Based Debounce

;Programmer: TM
;Date: 5/2010
;Platform: XPLAIN
;Device: ATxmega128A1
.include "ATxmega128A1def.inc"

;The timer counter unit is used to read switches at
;regular intervals, thereby eliminating switch bounce
;problems.
```

```
;Each switch press adds the switch number to the
;accumulator
;which is displayed on the LED's
;SW0 clears the accumulator.

;IVT XMEGA Version
jmp reset  ;reset vector
.org TCC0_OVF_vect
jmp TCC0_Overflow_Interrupt

reset:

;Set the LEDS as OFF and PORTE as output
.def temp = r16
ldi temp, $FF  ;led's off
sts PORTE_OUT, temp
sts    PORTE_DIR,temp

;Configure PORTF (switches) as input with pullups
;All 8 input pins (PORTF) to use internal pullup resistors
ldi temp,0xFF
sts PORTCFG_MPCMASK, temp  ;configure all 8 input pins
ldi temp, 0b00011000       ;code to enable pullups on
                           ;input pins
sts PORTF_PIN0CTRL, temp  ;PORTF will read switches

ldi temp, $00  ;all inputs
sts PORTF_DIR,temp

;Configure timer for 0.01 second interrupt frequency
;(Clock speed is 2 MHz)
#define CLOCK 2.0e6  ;clock speed
.equ PRESCALE = 0b001  ;/1 prescale
.equ PRESCALE_DIV = 1
#define PER 0.01  ;seconds
.equ WGMMODE = 0b000  ;Waveform generation mode: Normal

;you must ensure this value is between 0 and 65535
.equ TOP = int(0.5 + (PER * CLOCK/PRESCALE_DIV-1))
.if TOP > 65535
.error "TOP is out of range"
.endif
```

```
;On XMEGA series, write low byte of 16-bit timer
;registers first
ldi temp, low(TOP)  ;Set the period
sts TCC0_PER, temp
ldi temp, high(TOP)
sts TCC0_PER+1, temp
ldi temp, WGMMODE   ;other bits are zero
sts TCC0_CTRLB, temp
ldi temp, PRESCALE<<TC0_CLKSEL0_bp  ;clock select
sts TCC0_CTRLA, temp  ;start counter

;Enable Overflow interrupt
lds temp, TCC0_INTCTRLA
andi temp, ~TC0_OVFINTLVL_gm  ;clear bits in field
ori temp, TC_OVFINTLVL_HI_gc  ;select level
sts TCC0_INTCTRLA, temp

;Enable high level interrupts and global interrupts
ldi temp, PMIC_HILVLEN_bm
sts PMIC_CTRL, temp
sei

.def count=r17
ldi count, 0

repeat:
;Check for button press
rcall switchread  ;r24=switch number or -1
cpi r24,-1  ;return value -1 means no button press
breq repeat
cpi r24, 0  ;0 means clear
brne noclear
clr count
noclear:
add count, r24
mov r24, count
rcall ledOut  ;display char on LED's
rjmp repeat
.undef count

TCC0_Overflow_Interrupt:  ;XMEGA Overflow Interrupt
                          ;on T/C C0
```

```
        push r16
        in r16, CPU_SREG
;place the interrupt task here
        rcall sw_update
        out CPU_SREG, r16
        pop r16
        reti
.undef temp

;void ledOut(byte r24){
; PORTE_OUT = ~r24
;}
ledOut:
        com r24
        sts PORTE_OUT, r24
        com r24
        ret

.dseg  ;switch data
sw_lastread: .byte 1
sw_flags: .byte 1


.cseg
.def sw_current = r17
.def sw_lastread_reg = r18

sw_update:
        push sw_current  ;save registers
        in sw_current, CPU_SREG
        push sw_current
        push sw_lastread_reg
;set flags for new switch press events
        lds sw_current, PORTF_IN  ;current switch info
        lds sw_lastread_reg, sw_lastread  ;previous switch
                                         ;info
        sts sw_lastread, sw_current  ;prev = current
        eor sw_lastread_reg, sw_current  ;compare!
;sw_lastread_reg becomes an indicator of changed
;switches
;we want to know which just changed to 0 (press)
;sw_current has 0's in positions corresponding to
;pressed buttons
```

```
        com sw_current   ;sw_current becomes a mask for
                           ;buttons currently pressed
;sw_current is now only pressed switches
        and sw_current, sw_lastread_reg  ;mask out the
                                          ;changes that
                                          ;were releases
;sw_current is now the pressed and changed switches
;combine the new and old flags to add newly pressed
 switches
        lds sw_lastread_reg, sw_flags
        or sw_lastread_reg, sw_current
        sts sw_flags, sw_lastread_reg
;restore registers and exit
        pop sw_lastread_reg
        pop sw_current
        out CPU_SREG, sw_current
        pop sw_current
        ret
.undef sw_current
.undef sw_lastread_reg

;byte switchread()
;return (in r24) highest number of switch with a switch-
;down event
;return -1 if none
;clear the switch-down event that is returned (if any)
.def sw_mask = r23
.def sw_num = r24   ;return value
.def sw_flags_reg = r25
switchread:
        push sw_mask
        push sw_flags_reg
        ldi sw_mask, (1<<7)
        ldi sw_num, 7  ;process switch 7 first
        lds sw_flags_reg, sw_flags
switchread_lp:
        lsl sw_flags_reg  ;looking for a 1 (press event)
        brcs switchread_foundflag
        dec sw_num
        lsr sw_mask  ;becomes 0 when all flags have been
                      ;checked
        brne switchread_lp
```

```
        rjmp switchread_exit  ;none found

switchread_foundflag:
        com sw_mask
        cli  ;protect critical section
        lds sw_flags_reg, sw_flags  ;get the current flags
        and sw_flags_reg, sw_mask  ;clear the one about to
                                   ;be returned
        sei
        sts sw_flags, sw_flags_reg
switchread_exit:
        pop sw_flags_reg
        pop sw_mask
        ret

.undef sw_mask
.undef sw_num
.undef sw_flags_reg
```

PROGRAM 10.3a: Interrupt-Controlled USART–XMEGA Version

```
;Program 10.3a - Interrupt Controlled USART

;This program displays a counter on the LED's. It also
;communicates serially, echoing received characters.
;Each time the counter reaches a multiple of 16, a
;message is sent over the serial line. The USART
;operations are all interrupt driven.

;Programmer: TM
;Date: 5/2010
;Platform: XPLAIN
;Device: ATxmega128A1
.include "ATxmega128A1def.inc"

;Serial communications between the XPLAIN and PC
;using LUFA Bridge

;Interrupt vector table
jmp reset
.org USARTC0_RXC_vect
```

```
jmp rxc_interrupt
.org USARTC0_DRE_vect
jmp dre_interrupt


;Data register empty interrupt
;Transmit next byte of a string or disable interrupt
;when done byte_ptr is the byte address of next
;character in flash to be sent nul terminates string


.dseg
byte_ptr: .byte 2  ;points to next byte in flash to be
                   ;transmitted
.cseg


.def temp = r16
dre_interrupt:
        push zh  ;save status and registers used
        in zh, CPU_SREG
        push zh
        push zl
        push temp

        lds zh, byte_ptr + 1  ;get byte pointer into Z
        lds zl, byte_ptr
        lpm temp, Z +  ;load next byte
        tst temp  ;is it zero?
        breq send_done  ;br if zero to end task
        sts USARTC0_DATA, temp  ;save new pointer
        sts byte_ptr + 1, zh
        sts byte_ptr, zl
        rjmp dre_exit

send_done:
;turn off interrupt
        lds temp, USARTC0_CTRLA
        cbr temp, USART_DREINTLVL_gm
        sbr temp, USART_DREINTLVL_OFF_gc
        sts USARTC0_CTRLA, temp

dre_exit:
        pop temp  ;restore registers
```

```
        pop zl
        pop zh
        out CPU_SREG, zh
        pop zh
        reti

;Receive complete interrupt
;Echo received character, poll data register until empty
;and echo
rxc_interrupt:
        push temp  ;save registers and status
        in temp, CPU_SREG
        push temp
transmit_wait:
        lds temp, USARTC0_STATUS
        sbrs temp, USART_DREIF_bp  ;wait for Tx buffer to
                                   ;be empty
        rjmp transmit_wait  ;not ready yet

        lds temp, USARTC0_DATA  ;receive and echo
        sts USARTC0_DATA, temp

        pop temp  ;restore registers
        out CPU_SREG, temp
        pop temp
        reti

reset:
;2 mhz clock speed, 9600 baud BSEL=12
.equ BSEL=12

;Set the LEDS as OFF and PORT as output
ldi temp, $FF  ;led's off
sts PORTE_OUT, temp
sts PORTE_DIR, temp

;set baud rate
ldi temp, high(BSEL) & 0x0F
sts USARTC0_BAUDCTRLB, temp
ldi temp, low(BSEL)
sts USARTC0_BAUDCTRLA, temp
```

```
;data packet format
;select, asynchronous, no parity, 1 stop, 8 data bits
ldi temp, USART_CMODE_ASYNCHRONOUS_gc|USART_PMODE_
    DISABLED_gc|(0 <<USART_SBMODE_bp)|USART_CHSIZE_8BIT_gc
sts USARTC0_CTRLC, temp

;Set the transmit pin as output and set high, receive
;pin as input (default)
ldi temp, 1 <<3  ;PC3
sts PORTC_OUT,temp  ;configure TXD as 1
sts PORTC_DIR,temp  ;configure TXD as output

;enable bi-directional communication
lds temp, USARTC0_CTRLB
ori temp, USART_TXEN_bm | USART_RXEN_bm
sts USARTC0_CTRLB, temp
;USART initialization complete

;wait for PC to transmit a character
receive:
        lds temp, USARTC0_STATUS
        sbrs temp, USART_RXCIF_bp  ;is byte in Rx buffer?
        rjmp receive

;enable receive interrupt
lds temp, USARTC0_CTRLA
cbr temp, USART_RXCINTLVL_gm
sbr temp, USART_RXCINTLVL_HI_gc
sts USARTC0_CTRLA, temp

;Enable high level interrupts and global interrupts
ldi temp, PMIC_HILVLEN_bm
sts PMIC_CTRL, temp
sei

.equ DELAY = 60000
.def one = r17
ldi one, 1  ;constant to add one to counter
main_lp:
        lds temp, PORTE_OUT  ;get current LED pattern
        com temp
        add temp, one  ;increment counter
```

```
      ;inc does not set half carry flag, so add is used
        brhc no_message  ;half carry sends message
        rcall startmessage
no_message:
        com temp  ;output current count in binary
        sts PORTE_OUT, temp
        ;delay
        ldi r25, high(DELAY)
        ldi r24, low(DELAY)
delay_lp:
        sbiw r25:r24, 1
        brne delay_lp
        rjmp main_lp

msg: .db '\r','\n',"Message",'\r','\n',0
;initialize byte_ptr and enable DRE Interrupt to
;transmit string
startmessage:
        push temp
        ldi temp, high(msg * 2)  ;byte address of message
        sts byte_ptr + 1, temp
        ldi temp, low(msg * 2)
        sts byte_ptr, temp
        lds temp, USARTC0_CTRLA  ;enable DRE Interrupt
        cbr temp, USART_DREINTLVL_gm
        sbr temp, USART_DREINTLVL_HI_gc
        sts USARTC0_CTRLA, temp
        pop temp
        ret
```

CHAPTER 11

Arithmetic Operations

ADDITION AND SUBTRACTION

The fundamental numeric encodings for integers supported by most microprocessors are unsigned and two's complement. The circuits for performing addition and subtraction on numbers encoded in these formats are the same. All that is needed is an adder component. We will explore the structure of a simple adder that might be incorporated in the ALU unit of the AVR processor. Ultimately, the ALU can only perform Boolean operations, so addition and subtraction must be accomplished using logical formulas.

Half-Adder

Table 11.1 describes a Boolean function with two inputs that generates the sum (as a single binary digit) and the carry (as a second binary digit). The Boolean equations that generate the results are

```
Sum = A XOR B
Carry = A AND B
```

The combinational circuit that implements this pair of functions (Boolean functions can always be realized as simple logic circuits) is called a half-adder (Figure 11.1). This circuit is sufficient for summing the bits in each place-value column of a multibit binary addition problem. To incorporate the carry in the sum of the subsequent column, we need an additional input.

TABLE 11.1 Boolean Functions for a Half-Adder Circuit

A	B	Sum	Carry
0	0	0	0
0	1	1	0
1	0	1	0
1	1	0	1

Full-Adder

A full-adder circuit adds another input, called *carry in*, to the functions described above. This circuit will produce a two-bit value representing the sum of three bits. The least-significant bit of the result is called the sum; the most-significant bit is called the carry. Table 11.2 defines the sum and carry outputs for the addition of three bit values.

It is possible to construct a full-adder from a pair of half-adders. The first pair of inputs are added using the first half-adder, then the third input is added to the sum with a second half-adder. This provides the output for the sum of the full-adder. The two carry signals from the half-adders are logically or'd together to provide the carry output of the full-adder. These formulas reflect this implementation. Figure 11.2 illustrates this circuit.

```
Sum = (A XOR B) XOR C
Carry = (A AND B) OR ((A XOR B) AND C)
```

Ripple Carry Adder

Eight full-adders can be used to generate the sum of two bytes. The resulting circuit is called a ripple carry adder. This eight-stage ripple carry adder has 17 inputs (eight bits of one byte, eight bits of a second byte, and a carry in). Figure 11.3 shows a 4-bit ripple carry adder; double this to get a ripple carry adder that can add two bytes.

When the AVR processor executes an ADD instruction, it asserts the values of the bits in two registers (Rd and Rr) on the 16 adder inputs, and

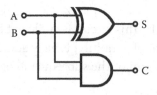

FIGURE 11.1 A half-adder circuit using an AND gate to compute the carry and an XOR gate to compute the sum.

TABLE 11.2 Boolean Functions for a Full-Adder Circuit

A	B	C	Sum	Carry
0	0	0	0	0
0	0	1	1	0
0	1	0	1	0
0	1	1	0	1
1	0	0	1	0
1	0	1	0	1
1	1	0	0	1
1	1	1	1	1

asserts a zero on the carry in input of the first stage. The adder produces a 9-bit result. Eight bits (representing the least-significant byte of the answer) are directed back to Rd. The other output, the carry out, is stored in the carry flag of the SREG.

If the ALU incorporates a ripple carry adder (there are other circuits that compute the same result more quickly), the result is computed as follows. All 17 inputs receive their values simultaneously and the circuit begins its logical computation. Each full-adder asserts its *carry out* signal on the *carry in* line of the next full-adder. The last full-adder outputs its *carry out* into the SREG's C (carry) flag. See Figure 11.4 for the complete diagram.

As each full-adder subsystem generates a carry and sum, the carry is propagated to the next stage of the ripple carry adder. This causes that stage to recalculate its result (if the carry in changed). The effect of these changing carries *ripples* through the circuit until the result stabilizes. The final carry is stored in the carry flag bit of the SREG and the sum bits are channeled back into the destination register. The circuit would also have logic to generate the other SREG flag values (N, V, S, H, and Z).

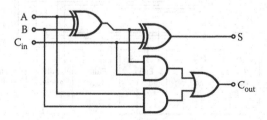

FIGURE 11.2 A full-adder circuit constructed from two half-adders.

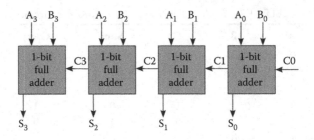

FIGURE 11.3   A 4-bit ripple carry adder constructed from four full-adders.

The adder design described above is called a ripple-carry adder because the output of each stage must ripple into the next stage. This ripple effect continues until all of the bits are determined and can be received by the destination register and status flags.

Example: An 8-Bit Ripple Carry Addition

To add the binary values 0b01001110 and 0b01001011 by hand, we start on the right (least-significant end) and add the bits in each column. As we complete each column, we propagate the carry into the next column. If we added all of the columns first (assuming no carry), then went back and adjusted the columns with carries, we would in fact be doing what a ripple carry adder does; it performs all of the column additions in parallel, but the carry input is likely to change a few times before the full 8-bit result is completed. As each carry is recalculated, it is applied to the adjacent column, causing an adjustment of the result. This in turn may create another carry, causing a ripple effect. At some point, the carry ripple subsides and the sum is correct. Follow through the changes that might occur in a ripple carry adder.

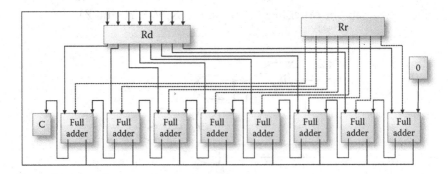

FIGURE 11.4   Ripple carry adder to support the ADD RD, RR instruction.

```
Initially all carries are 0:
000000000
01001110
01001011
--------
00000101 the carry flags in each column would be
01001010
```

Shift these over to the next column and then recalculate all of the columns that had a change in the carry flag (the initial carry will remain 0 throughout):

```
010010100
01001110
01001011
--------
10010001 and the new carry flags will be 01001110 (just
one change).
```

Again, these are applied to the column to the left and the adder recalculates where changes occur:

```
010011100
01001110
01001011
--------
10011001 with new carry flags 01001110
```

These carry flags are the same as before, so the circuit stabilizes. In the worst case, the carry may propagate through all stages (11111111 + 00000001).

The leftmost carry value (The leftmost 0 in 01001110) would be copied into the C flag of the SREG.

If these binary values represent unsigned data, the calculation would be interpreted as $78 + 75 = 153$. If they represent signed data, it would still be $78 + 75$, but the result would also be considered a signed integer, in this case, -103. This is an example of signed overflow. When signed overflow occurs, the oVerflow flag in the SREG is set (to 1). Notice that $-103 + 256$ is 153, which is the expected sum; the S flag will be 0 in this example, indicating that the sign of the expected sum is positive. The N flag will report the sign of the actual result which is −103, so the N flag will be 1 (indicating negative).

Status Flags

The AVR microcontroller's ALU can perform 8-bit addition and subtraction of numbers stored in registers. The results of the arithmetic operations are always stored back into a register, but information about the operation is also stored in the SREG. The SREG is a collection of bits named for the condition each represents.

An ALU must give indication regarding the result of each arithmetic operation. These additional status signals are stored in the SREG of the processor so subsequent instructions can take appropriate action in the event of certain results. Status flags set by addition (and subtraction) in the AVR processor are:

- C carry (unsigned overflow).

- Z zero (result is zero).

- N negative (result is negative).

- V overflow (signed overflow).

- S sign (expected sign).

- H half-carry (carry for lower nybble).

The V flag is set when the carry out of column seven is different from the carry into column seven. The Z flag is set when all bits of the answer are zero. The N flag is just a copy of bit seven of the result and C is the carry out of column seven. The H flag is the carry out of column three, indicating the sum of the lower nybbles was more than 15 (0xF). The S flag is always the EOR of N and V. This means N and S are the same unless signed overflow has occurred, in which case they are opposites.

Addition

Table 11.3 shows several examples of 8-bit addition, indicating the sum and the most important status flags (the H and S flags are omitted). Both the signed and unsigned interpretation of each calculation is shown to the right. Note that the ALU does exactly the same thing in each case regardless

TABLE 11.3 Sample 8-Bit Additions Showing Signed and Unsigned Interpretations

Calculations	Flags	Unsigned	Signed
00011110	Overflow: 0	78 + 27 = 105	Same
01001110	Carry: 0		
00011011	Zero: 0		
--------	Negative: 0		
01101001			
11111111	Overflow: 0	219 + 237 = 200	–37 + –19 = –56
11011011	Carry: 1	Unsigned overflow	
11101101	Zero: 0		
--------	Negative: 1		
11001000			
11111111	Overflow: 0	255 + 1 = 0	–1 + 1 = 0
11111111	Carry: 1	Unsigned overflow	
00000001	Zero: 1		
--------	Negative: 0		
00000000			
00000111	Overflow: 0	129 + 119 = 248	–127 + 119 = –8
10000001	Carry: 0		
01110111	Zero: 0		
--------	Negative: 1		
11111000			
01111111	Overflow: 1	127 + 127 = 254	127 + 127 = –126
01111111	Carry: 0		Signed overflow
01111111	Zero: 0		
--------	Negative: 1		
11111110			

of whether the data is signed or unsigned. In fact, the ALU is not aware of the programmer's intended interpretation of the data.

Subtraction

Binary subtraction often requires borrowing. The carry flags act as borrow indicators. If the carry flag is set after a subtraction, then the subtrahend (top number) was smaller than the minuend (bottom number) (interpreted as unsigned data). For example,

```
$93 − $10 = $83 carry flag 0
$93 − $A1 = $F2 carry flag 1
```

The second example results in a carry flag of one. This might be interpreted as a borrow from bit position eight (which does not exist).

The half-carry flag indicates a similar borrow condition, except the borrow occurs across the nybble boundary.

```
$93 - $13 = $80 H flag 0, C flag 0
$93 - $A4 = $EF H flag 1, C flag 1
```

Subtraction Using Addition

Subtraction can utilize the addition circuitry discussed earlier, resulting in a simpler circuit in the ALU. The key to reusing the addition circuit is to restate the subtraction, a − b, as an addition, a + (−b). Using two's complement codes, the negation of the second operand (b) is accomplished by flipping the bits and adding one. If the inputs from the minuend (b) are inverted, and the initial carry is set to 1, then the ripple carry adder will output the difference of the two inputs. Study the equivalent operations in Table 11.4. The first column obtains the result using subtraction. The third column shows how the same result is obtained using addition; the initial carry is set to 1, and the minuend is complemented before adding. Complementing the minuend and adding one (by setting the carry flag before adding) effectively negates the minuend. The unsigned and signed interpretations are shown in the final column. Note that if you perform the subtraction by adding, the carry flag (and half-carry) will be opposite of the result obtained when subtraction is performed.

In the subtraction column, a one in the borrow position indicates a borrow is required to carry out the subtraction in the next bit position to the left. If you compare the borrows (in the subtraction column) to the carries (in the add negative column), you will notice that they are opposites (complements). When subtracting using addition, the ripple carry adder's carry flags are complemented to produce the correct half-carry and carry flag values for the SREG.

AVR ADDITION AND SUBTRACTION

The AVR processor supports 8-bit unsigned and signed (two's complement) addition, subtraction, and multiplication, It also offers limited support for 16-bit addition and subtraction. The basic addition and subtraction instructions are ADD and SUB.

```
add Rd, Rr          Rd = Rd + Rr
sub Rd, Rr          Rd = Rd - Rr
```

TABLE 11.4 A Comparison between Subtracting and Adding the Negative; Invalid Answers (Overflow) are Shown in Italics in the Right Column

Subtraction	Flags	Add Negative	Unsigned/Signed
00110011	Overflow: 0	110011001	78 − 27 = 51
01001110	Carry: 0	01001110	78 − 27 = 51
−00011011	Zero: 0	+ 11100100	
-------	Negative: 0	-------	
00110011		00110011	
11101100	Overflow: 0	000100111	219 − 237 = *238*
11011011	Carry: 1	11011011	−37 − −19 = −18
−11101101	Zero: 0	+ 00010010	
-------	Negative: 1	-------	
11101110		11101110	
00000000	Overflow: 0	111111111	255 − 1 = 254
11111111	Carry: 0	11111111	−1 − 1 = −2
−00000001	Zero: 1	+ 11111110	
-------	Negative: 1	-------	
11111110		11111110	
01111110	Overflow: 1	100000011	129 − 119 = 10
10000001	Carry: 0	10000001	−127 − 119 = *10*
−01110111	Zero: 0	+ 10001000	
-------	Negative: 0	-------	
00001010		00001010	
10000000	Overflow: 1	011111111	127 − 255 = *128*
01111111	Carry: 1	01111111	127 − −1 = *−128*
−11111111	Zero: 0	+ 00000001	
-------	Negative: 1	-------	
10000000		10000000	

These instructions affect the six status flags (HSVNZC) as described above.

16-Bit Addition and Subtraction

Integers beyond the range of a single data byte are commonly represented in two or more bytes. The same numeric code is used (unsigned or two's complement), but the bits are spread across several bytes. Because the AVR registers and data pathways are only 8-bits, handling integers stored in multiple bytes requires sequences of instructions. The main difficulty in performing multistep arithmetic operations is propagating the carry (or borrow) between bytes.

To perform extended precision addition and subtraction (on two or more bytes), we begin by adding (subtracting) the low-order bytes. Follow the initial ADD or SUB instruction with the ADD/SUB *with carry* instruction applied to the pair of next higher-order bytes. This propagates the carry (borrow) flag into the next byte.

```
adc Rd, Rr          Rd = Rd + Rr + C
sbc Rd, Rr          Rd = Rd - Rr - C
```

A macro is a useful tool if a program regularly needs to perform sixteen (or more) bit arithmetic. The following macro will perform the proper steps to add 16-bit data in registers named aH:aL and bH:bL (where the *a* and *b* parts can be filled in by macro arguments which are restricted to X, Y, or Z).

```
;add word macro
;usage addw a, b (a and b must be chosen from X, Y, or Z)
.macro addw
add @0L, @1L
adc @0H, @1H
.endm
```

It is important to understand how the status flags are affected by a typical multibyte addition or subtraction. The status flags reflect the last operation (ADC/SBC) only. Since the overflow, sign, negative, and carry flags are all determined by just the leftmost bits, this works quite well. The two troublesome flags are the zero and half-carry. In general, the half-carry flag is of little importance when performing multibyte arithmetic, but the zero flag is a different matter. Consider, for example, a decision based on whether the sum of two numbers is zero or not.

```
add locL, amountL
adc locH, amountH
breq is_zero
```

The branch will be incorrectly taken any time the high bytes add to zero; the branch will not take into account the low byte of the result. This is clearly a trap you must be careful not to fall into!

One of the interesting features of the SBC instruction is that it correctly handles the setting of the zero flag in situations just like this. The SBC instruction sets the zero flag only if the subtraction yields zero and the zero flag was also set before the SBC executed. In other words, a SUB, followed by a series of SBC's, will set the zero flag only if all the partial results are zero (i.e., the multibyte result is zero).

Without this feature, subtracting $0001 from $0002 would clear the zero flag when the low bytes are subtracted (the result is not zero), but then set the zero flag when the high bytes are subtracted ($00 − $00).

```
ldi  r25, $00 ;R25:R24 = $0002
ldi  r24, $02
ldi  r27, $00 ;R27:R26 = $0001
ldi  r26, $01
sub  r24, r26 ;answer is 1,  Z = 0
sbc  r25, r27 ;answer is 0,  Z = 1 (without special feature)
breq zeroResult    ;R25:R24 = $0001
```

Without this special feature of the SBC instruction, the above code sequence would incorrectly branch to the zeroResult label because the high bytes subtract to 0. Fortunately, this does not happen in the AVR when using the SBC instruction; the zero flag correctly indicates a multibyte zero result. But, beware: The ADC instruction does not have this feature.

Immediate Data

The SUBI instruction allows any byte value to be subtracted from a register, without first placing the byte in another register. This uses immediate addressing mode (the data byte is part of the instruction code).

```
subi Rd, K  ;Rd = Rd - K (K is any byte, signed or unsigned)
```

This instruction is only available for registers R16–R31. Interestingly there is no corresponding add immediate instruction. However, adding K is the same as subtracting negative K (−K), so this is not really a limitation at all. Thus, to add one (using immediate mode) to a register (R16 or higher), just subtract negative one.

```
;add 1 to register
subi R16, -1
```

Do not confuse SUBI with SBI. These are very different instructions.

Using a negative number to add by subtracting does not limit you to signed data. You can add an unsigned immediate value to a register by subtracting its (signed) opposite. For example, suppose R16 holds the unsigned value 129 ($81) and we want to add the unsigned value 1. We accomplish this by writing `subi r16, -1`. Subtracting −1 ($FF) places the result of $81 − $FF in R16.

```
11 (borrow indicators for each nybble)
81
- FF
----
82
```

The unsigned interpretation of $82 is 130; the effect of subtracting −1 from the unsigned value correctly increased the unsigned value by one.

You can even add large unsigned numbers, such as 130, by writing `subi R16, -130`. Even though −130 is out of range of a signed byte, the assembler will correctly translate this to $7E, truncating the actual value to 8 bits. Subtracting this will be equivalent to adding 130. For example, $00 − $7E is $82 (130).

There is also a *subtract with carry immediate* instruction. In conjunction with SUBI, this allows a multibyte constant to be subtracted from a multibyte number in registers. The SBCI instruction also incorporates the prior value of the zero flag in determining the new zero flag value, so BREQ and BRNE work correctly following the subtraction of a multibyte constant. Only registers R16 and higher can be used with this instruction.

```
sbci Rd, K  ;Rd = Rd - K - 1 (K is any byte, signed or
                ;unsigned)
```

The following example shows how SUBI and SBCI instructions can be used to subtract (or add) any 16-bit immediate data from (to) a 16-bit value currently stored in two registers. To add 783 to the 16-bit integer (signed or unsigned) in R25:R24, the following instructions will suffice.

```
subi r24, low(-783)
sbci r25, high(-783)
```

If you need to use the carry flag to control a conditional branch after this sequence, you will need to know that it will be the opposite of what it would be if you actually had added.

To subtract and branch when zero, the following sequence may be used since the zero flag will correctly represent the resulting multibyte value.

```
subi r16, low(100)
sbci r17, high(100)
breq is_zero
```

You might also see the usefulness of this to subtract a small number from a large number. Consider a 32-bit integer that needs to be decremented by one until it reaches zero.

```
lp_top:
subi r22, 1
sbci r23, 0
sbci r24, 0
sbci r25, 0
brne lp_top
```

The SBCI instructions simply handle the borrow between bytes. If you want to add one (or any other value) to a multibyte value (signed or unsigned), you can still subtract the negative. This loop will increment by one until the 32-bit counter overflows (to zero).

```
lp_top:
subi r22, byte1(-1)
sbci r23, byte2(-1)
sbci r24, byte3(-1)
sbci r25, byte4(-1)
brne lp_top
```

Be careful not to confuse SBCI with SBIC (skip if bit in I/O register is clear).

Comparisons

The AVR compare instructions allow the comparison of two values. The comparison is accomplished by subtracting. The result of the subtraction is not actually stored, but the status flags are affected as if the subtraction had taken place. Comparisons set status flags; they are usually intended to be followed by conditional branch instructions.

There are three compare instructions, paralleling the subtract instructions: SUB, SBC, and SUBI.

```
cp Rd, Rr      ;Rd - Rr
cpc Rd, Rr     ;Rd - Rr - C
cpi Rd, K      ;Rd - K (Rd is R16 or higher, K is any byte)
```

The CP instruction, together with CPC, provides the ability to perform 16-bit comparisons. The comparison sequence can be followed by any of the conditional branches based on signed or unsigned comparisons. Zero propagation (as discussed for the SUB and SBC instructions) makes this possible.

Comparison of a 16-bit value in a register (pair) with an immediate value requires an extra register because there is no compare *with carry* immediate (the analog of SBCI). The following example illustrates how to perform a 16-bit compare immediate; it branches if R25:R24 is greater than or equal to 1000. R16 is used as a temporary register.

```
;we want to do this
cpi R24, low(1000)     ;this will not work
cpci R25, high(1000)   ;no such instruction!
;do this instead
ldi R16, high(1000)
cpi R24, low(1000)
cpc R25, R16
brge somewhere
```

Of course, the entire constant could be loaded into registers for the comparison, but if registers are in heavy use, this shows how to accomplish the task with just one extra register.

16-Bit Support

There are special instructions to add or subtract small constants to 16-bit integers, but only if the integers are in the upper four register pairs (R25:R24, XH:XL, YH:YL, or ZH:ZL). The constant must be unsigned, and less than 64.

```
adiw Rd + 1:Rd, K     ;Rd = Rd + K (0 <= K <= 63)
sbiw Rd + 1:Rd, K     ;Rd = Rd - K (0 <= K <= 63)
```

The half-carry flag is not affected by these instructions, but the other flags are all set to reflect the details of the 16-bit result.

Increment and Decrement

The increment and decrement instructions do exactly what their name implies. They are considered signed integer instructions (although they also work on unsigned bytes). The only idiosyncrasy is that these do not affect the carry flag (which is used to indicate unsigned overflow). They also have no effect on the half-carry flag.

```
inc  Rd ; Rd = Rd + 1
dec  Rd ; Rd = Rd − 1
```

These instructions are often used to implement count-controlled loops in which the carry flag must be preserved across the loop termination test. You can follow an increment/decrement by any conditional branch except those associated with unsigned data (BRCC, BRCS, BRSH, BRLO). The following increment and test at the bottom of a loop will branch back to the top of the loop while the counter (R16) is still negative. Thus, to iterate n times, the counter would be initialized to $-n$. The initial value must be no less than -129 or R16 will not be negative after the first increment.

```
looptop:
. . .
inc R16
brlt loopTop
```

The importance of DEC (INC) not affecting the carry flag is illustrated by the following situation. Suppose X and Y contain addresses of two 32-bit integers in SRAM and we want to compute X += Y. The numbers are assumed to be in little-endian order. The following loop will accomplish the task:

```
clc    ;initial carry must be 0
ldi r16, 4   ;four bytes to be added, r16 is the loop
             ;counter
lp:
     ld r17, X    ;get the next pair of bytes
     ld r18, Y +
     adc r17, r18
     st X+ R17    ;store the sum
     dec R16      ;does not affect the carry flag
     brne lp      ;loop control
```

If DEC changed the carry flag, the carry between bytes of the 32-bit addition would be corrupted.

Incrementing or decrementing 16-bit data is most conveniently done using the ADIW and SBIW instructions. Just remember that these affect the carry flag. If the carry flag must be preserved during the counter increment, then the following sequence of instructions might be used. This sequence increments a 16-bit integer in R17:R16 without affecting the carry flag.

```
        inc R16
        brne noCarry
        inc R17
noCarry:
```

Decrementing is a little more complicated. If we simply translate the above pattern to perform a decrement, we will get the following incorrect code:

```
;warning - incorrect code
        dec R16
        brne noBorrow
        dec R17
noBorrow:
```

Unfortunately, this approach borrows when the low byte becomes zero, not when the borrow is required (on the next decrement when the low byte becomes $FF). Inserting a `cpi r16, $FF` after the decrement will affect the carry flag which we are trying to avoid.

One way to solve the problem is to pretest the low byte (before decrementing) for zero with the TST instruction (which does not affect the carry flag). If the low byte is zero, then the decrement will require a borrow, so the high byte is decremented when this condition is detected.

```
;Correct 16-bit decrement that does not affect C
        tst R16
        brne noBorrow
        dec R17; borrow from high byte
noBorrow:
        dec R16
```

Consider the following 16-bit increment sequence that also branches to the label is_zero when the result is zero.

```
        inc R16
        brne noCarry
        inc R17
        breq is_zero
noCarry:
```

The BREQ instruction will correctly branch to is_zero exactly when the 16-bit counter becomes zero. If R16 is not zero, the BREQ is skipped. Only when R16 is incremented to zero and R17 is incremented to zero, will the BREQ statement branch to is_zero.

If one of the signed branches (BRGE or BRLT) is used in place of the BREQ, the branch will also execute correctly. Branches based on sign depend only on the high byte of the word; the INC instruction sets the flags required to detect if the new word value is negative or nonnegative.

Where would the breq is_zero instruction be placed in the 16-bit decrement above to accomplish similar processing?

Sometimes a word must be explicitly tested independent of an arithmetic operation to implement a selection or repetition structure. The compare instructions may be used if the carry flag value need not be preserved. However, if the carry flag should not be altered, then the TST instruction is used instead.

```
;test R17:R16 for zero without affecting the carry flag
        tst R16
        brne nonzero
        tst R17
        brne nonzero
;zero case here

;test R17:R16 for less than zero without affecting the
;carry flag
        tst R17
        brlt negative
;greater than or equal to zero case here
```

Both bytes must be tested to determine if the result is zero. The branch to nonzero occurs if either byte is nonzero; the code falls through to the zero case only if both bytes are zero. When checking if a value is positive or negative, only the most-significant byte needs to be considered. The second sequence uses the high byte to split processing into the negative and nonnegative cases.

Negation

The negate instruction negates the number stored in a register. Obviously, the register should hold a signed integer code for this instruction to make sense.

```
neg Rd        ;Rd = -Rd
```

Negating a 16-bit integer cannot be accomplished by simply negating the two bytes separately. Instead, the following sequence demonstrates how to perform the negation of the integer in R25:R24 using the basic two's complement change sign rule, *flip the bits and add one.*

```
com R25
com R24              ;one's complement
subi R24, low(-1)    ;add 1
sbci R25, high(-1)
```

If the 16-bit value being negated is in one of the upper four register pairs, ADIW can be used instead of the two immediate subtractions. The last two instructions above can be combined as follows:

```
adiw R25:R24, 1
```

Widening and Narrowing Conversions

When performing arithmetic operations on integer data of different sizes (e.g., 8- and 16-bit), it is important to *widen* or *narrow* the data correctly. Unsigned data is *widened* (converted to a representation with more bits) by adding leading zeros. If R24 contains an unsigned (8-bit) value, then it is widened to R25:R24 by this instruction.

```
clr R25
```

This is sometimes called *zero extension.* Unsigned data is *narrowed* to fewer bits by throwing away the extra leading bits (truncation). As long as all of the discarded bits are zero, this will not affect the numeric value.

Signed data is *widened* using sign-extension. That is, the sign bit is copied into the extra bits. If R24 contains an 8-bit signed integer, then it is *widened* to R25:R24 by the following sequence of instructions. The sign bit of R24 is used to change $00 to $FF if the original value is negative.

```
clr  R25
sbrc R24, 7
com  R25
```

Signed data is *narrowed* by discarding the extra bits. As long as these bits are all equal to the narrowed data's sign bit, there is no loss of information.

BCD ADDITION AND SUBTRACTION

Adding BCD numerals is not directly supported by the AVR instruction set. However, through clever use of the carry and half-carry flags, it can be implemented relatively painlessly. We will assume unsigned packed BDC notation and focus on two-digit numerals. When adding two BCD digits, the result must be another BCD digit. For example, adding seven and eight, we must get a two digit BCD numeral, 15 ($15 not $0F). In base 10, 7 + 8 produces 5 with a carry, however, the ADD instruction yields 15 ($0F) when $07 + $08 is computed.

The underlying problem to be solved in order to implement BCD arithmetic is the proper detection and application of carries. The addition of two nybbles only produces a carry to the next nybble if the sum is greater than 15; we need to carry when the sum is greater than 9.

To facilitate automatic carries, we add 6 to each nybble of one of the addends before the actual addition occurs. When the actual add is performed, there is a carry from each nybble with a sum of 10 or more (because the adjusted sum is really sixteen or more). As a desired side effect, when a carry is generated, the nybble value will be between 0 and 9 and is the correct BCD digit for the sum. If no carry occurs, the sum is six more than it should be; we can easily subtract six to recover the correct BCD digit in these cases.

Here is one way to implement the addition in the AVR instruction set. The BCD bytes to be added are passed in R25 and R24. R18 is used as a temporary location. The sum is returned in R24 and the SREG C, H, and Z flags will reflect the result of the addition. The S, N, and V flags are not relevant in this application.

```
;BCD_add:
        push r18
        ldi  r18,$66
        add  r24,r18            ;prepare for addition
```

```
        add r24,r25          ;add bytes
;this correctly implements carries across the digit
;boundaries
;but some digits may now be illegal (A-F)
;C, H, and Z flags are correct and must be saved
;Note - The XMEGA version should substitute these
;symbols:
;CPU_SREG for SREG, CPU_H_bp for SREG_H, and CPU_C_bp
;for SREG_C
        in r18,SREG          ;XMEGA use CPU_SREG
        sbrs r25,SREG_H      ;test H and C flags for
                             ;adjustments
        subi r24,$06         ;adjust low nybble
        sbrs r25,SREG_C
        subi r24,$60         ;adjust high nybble
        out SREG, r18        ;restore C,H, and Z flag
        pop r18
        ret
```

To facilitate multibyte addition, the first ADD may be changed to ADC. The initial call to the function must then be made with the carry flag clear, as it now becomes an implicit argument to the function. Subsequent calls use the carry flag produced by the previous call.

BCD subtraction is actually a little easier. When you subtract two BCD digits, the answer is always correct if no borrow is required. If a borrow occurs, the digit will be six greater than it should be. Thus the carry and half-carry flags can be used to decide if an adjustment to each digit is needed. Once again, the initial subtract could be SBC to facilitate multibyte subtraction. In this case, the initial call must be made with the carry flag clear.

```
BCD_sub:
    push r18
    sub r24,r25     ;could be sbc if c = 0 on initial call
;this correctly borrows across the digit boundaries
;but digits where borrow was needed are now be incorrect
;C, H, and Z flags are correct and must be saved
;Note - The XMEGA version should substitute these symbols:
;CPU_SREG for SREG, CPU_H_bp for SREG_H, and CPU_C_bp
for SREG_C
    in r18,SREG
```

```
sbrc r18,SREG_H   ;test H and C flags for adjustments
subi r24,$06      ;adjust low nybble
sbrc r18,SREG_C
subi r24,$60      ;adjust high nybble
out SREG, r18     ;restore C,H, and Z flag
pop r18
ret
```

As you can see, the ALU indirectly provides support for BCD arithmetic by reporting the half-carry flag produced by addition or subtraction. Software is used to adjust the nybbles to simulate true BCD arithmetic. Software simulation of arithmetic operations is not uncommon. We will see this again when we learn how to divide integers. The AVR processor does not include a divide instruction.

BINARY/BCD CONVERSION

Converting from an unsigned byte to packed BCD requires determining the 10s digit and ones digit of the base 10 representation of the unsigned value. Typically this would require dividing by 10 to get the quotient and remainder.

```
N = any value 0 through 99
Tens digit of BCD = N/10
Ones digit of BCD = N%10
```

Unfortunately, division is not directly supported by the AVR processor and must be simulated. For our conversion process a relatively inefficient division algorithm may be used (since the quotient is not too big); we can divide by repeatedly subtracting 10 until only the remainder is left (the remainder is 0–9). The quotient is the number of times we subtract 10 from the original number to find the remainder. This relationship comes directly from the division algorithm:

```
N = 10Q + R
N - 10Q = R
```

The algorithm to perform the conversion of a byte to BCD can only succeed if the original value is in the range 0 through 99. Larger numbers could be handled if a third digit (0, 1, or 2) is also returned. Here is the conversion routine assuming the argument, passed in R25, is in the legal range, 0 through 99. The result is computed and returned in R24. While R25 is at least 10, the algorithm adds $10 to R24 (initially zero) and subtracts 10 from R25. This reduces R25 to the remainder, R25 mod 10 and calculates the quotient in R24.

```
;Convert byte in r25 to BCD notation assuming
;0 <= r25 <= 99
;Return value is in r24
  bin2BCD:
      push r25
      ldi r24,0     ;answer appears here
;Division loop
dec2BCD_tens:
      cpi r25,10    ;stop loop when remainder is < ten
      brlo dec2BCD_done
      subi r24,-$10      ;add one to tens place of
                         ;answer
      subi r25,10        ;remove 10 from number
      rjmp dec2BCD_tens
dec2BCD_done:
      add r24,r25   ;add remainder (ones place)
      pop r25
      ret
```

Conversion from BCD to decimal requires multiplication. For the small numbers encountered here, we can simulate the multiplication by repeated addition. The 10's digit of the BCD value is used to add the correct multiple of 10 and then the units digit is added to the result.

```
;Convert BCD in r25 to unsigned byte, returned in r24
BCD2bin:
      push r25
      ldi r24,0     ;answer computed here
;Multiplication loop
BCD2bin_tens:
      cpi r25, $10   ;while r25 >= $10
      brlo BCD2bin_done
      subi r24,-10   ;add ten to result
      subi r25,$10   ;subtract ten (BCD) from r25
      rjmp BCD2bin_tens
```

```
BCD2bin_done:
        ;r25 is 0-9, the units digit
        add r24,r25
        pop r25
        ret
```

This algorithm should be revisited and implemented more efficiently once the AVR multiply instruction is covered.

MULTIPLICATION AND DIVISION

Although the AVR instruction set includes multiply instructions, it does not provide any division instruction. Early microprocessors did not include multiply or divide instructions, so these were often implemented in software using an appropriate algorithm. The simplest algorithms are based directly on the traditional techniques used to do multidigit multiplication and division on paper. Knowing the algorithm and basic multiplication tables, a little work is all that is required to multiply or divide large numbers.

8-Bit Multiplication

There are three integer multiply instructions provided in the AVR instruction set. The different instructions are needed to differentiate between signed and unsigned data. The instructions are described in Table 11.5.

In each case, the result of a multiplication is a 16-bit number and is stored in R1:R0. Note that MULS and MULSU can only use some of the registers for their operands. The only flags affected by the multiplication instructions are Z and C. Z is set only if the 16-bit result is $0000. The carry flag is always a copy of bit 15 of the result (a sign indicator for signed multiplication).

TABLE 11.5   AVR Multiplication Instructions

Syntax	Operands	Action	Description
mul Rd, Rr	Two registers	R1:R0 ← Rd ⊠ Rr	Multiply unsigned bytes
muls Rd, Rr	Two registers (16-31)	R1:R0 ← Rd ⊠ Rr	Multiply signed bytes
mulsu Rd, Rr	Two registers (16-23)	R1:R0 ← Rd ⊠ Rr	Multiply signed with unsigned bytes

Consider the product of two bytes, $98 ⊠ $37 (assume R16 is $98 and R17 is $37). Depending on whether these represent signed or unsigned data, there are several possibilities.

- If these are unsigned bytes, they represent the product 152 ⊠ 55 and the result of MUL R16, R17 is $20A8 or 8360 (R1 is $20, R0 is $A8).

- If these are signed bytes, they represent −104 ⊠ 55 and the result of MULS R16, R17 is $E9A8 or −5720 (R1 is $E9, R0 is $A8). The same result would be obtained by MULSU R16, R17 since $37 is 55 whether the code is signed or unsigned.

- The result of MULSU R17, R16 (now R17 is considered signed 55 and R16 is considered unsigned 152) is the same as the first case, $20A8 or 8360.

The following examples illustrate the range limits of multiplication in the AVR:

- Unsigned: $FF ⊠ $FF = $FE01 (255 ⊠ 255 = 65025).

- Signed: $80 ⊠ $80 = $4000 (−128 ⊠ −128 = 16384).

- Signed: $7F ⊠ $7F = $3F01 (127 ⊠ 127 = 16129).

- Signed: $80 ⊠ $7F = $C080 (−128 ⊠ 127 = −16256).

- Signed with unsigned: $80 ⊠ $FF = $8080 (−128 ⊠ 255 = −32640).

- Signed with unsigned: $7F ⊠ $FF = $7E81 (127 ⊠ 255 = 32385).

As you can see, overflow is impossible when multiplying.

Extended Precision Multiplication

Multiplication of larger values requires partial products and additions, similar to the multiplication algorithm written out on paper. Because the ALU can multiply bytes, we will treat each byte as a digit in our algorithm. The ALU knows its multiplication tables up to 255 times 255!

Figure 11.5 is an outline of the multiplication of an unsigned word by an unsigned byte. The word is located in R6:R5, the byte in R7, and the 24-bit result is stored in R4:R3:R2.

unsigned word ⊠ unsigned byte: AH:AL ⊠ B = (AH ⊠ B) << 8 + (AL ⊠ B)

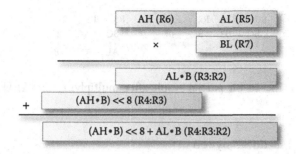

FIGURE 11.5   Multiplication of an unsigned word and an unsigned byte.

The steps of the multiplication will be illustrated with a specific example. Assume R6:R5 is the 16-bit number $A43C, and R7 is the byte $21. The result may require 3 bytes, so we will place the result in R4:R3:R2 (avoiding R1:R0 which is used each time for the result of MUL). The result of the multiplication will be $A43C ☒ $21 = $152BBC. We start by multiplying the least-significant bytes.

```
mul  R5,R7
movw R3:R2, R1:R0
clr  r4
```

The MOVW (move word) instruction can be used to copy the contents of one pair of registers (odd:even) to another pair of registers (odd:even). We also need to clear R4 before going to the next step. Figure 11.6 shows the 24-bit partial result for AL ☒ B in R4:R3:R2 where the final product will be accumulated. When examining these figures you need to keep in mind the little-endian format used in this processor. The high bytes are always on the right in the diagrams. The 24-bit contents of R4:R3:R2 are $0007BC in Figure 11.6.

The next step is to multiply AH ☒ B. The result, $1524, is in R1:R0 after the multiplication as shown in Figure 11.7.

```
mul R6,R7 ;second partial product
```

Because AH is the significant byte of the multiplicand, its place value is AH ☒ 256. So the product is really (AH ☒ 256) ☒ B. In other words, the partial product is really $152,400. When adding R1:R0 to R4:R3:R2, we add R1:R0 to R4:R3. The value in R2 is unchanged. The result of adding the partial products is shown in Figure 11.8.

R0	R1	R2	R3	R4	R5	R6	R7
BC	07	BC	07	00	3C	A4	21
					AL	AH	B

FIGURE 11.6   The 24-bit partial result after multiplying the AL ⊠ B and zero extending.

```
add R3,R0 ;middle bytes
adc R4,R1 ;high bytes (remember to include carry from
          ;previous add)
```

In this example, the result is $152BBC as expected.

Multiplication of larger values simply requires more steps. For signed data, the multiplication is a little more difficult to accommodate the sign information. A simple approach to the problem is to make the negative numbers positive, multiply, then adjust the sign of the result (negative times negative is positive, etc.). Changing the sign of a multibyte number can be accomplished by complementing all of the bytes, and then adding 1 to the result (propagating the carry through each byte if necessary).

Multiplication Algorithm

The inclusion of multiply instructions in the AVR instruction set is a real convenience to the programmer. But what if you need to perform multiplication with a processor that has no multiplication instruction? In this case, multiplication must be simulated in software. Of course, multiplication can be implemented as repeated addition: a ⊠ b = a + a + a + ⋯ + a (b times). This is not very efficient when b is a large number. A more efficient technique imitates the algorithm we use to multiply multidigit numbers on paper.

To understand how this will work, we will implement the AVR unsigned multiply instruction as a function. We will require that the numbers to be

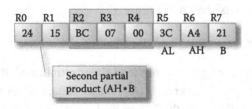

FIGURE 11.7   The result of AH ⊠ B is placed in R1:R0 by the unsigned multiply instruction.

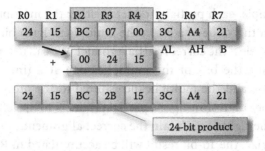

FIGURE 11.8   Adding the two partial products yields the final 24-bit result.

multiplied together are already in registers R16 and R17 (parameters). The product will be placed in R1:R0 (return value). No multiplication instructions will be used to calculate the product.

The algorithm is actually the same as the one we used to multiply a word by a byte. The solution required shifting and adding (and multiplying, but the multiplication was only needed because we treated a byte like a digit). To avoid multiplication, we need to treat each bit as a digit. Actually, we will still multiply, but only by zero or one, and these are really easy problems!

The algorithm is based on the long multiplication technique where partial products are lined up in the proper columns and added together. This will require shifting and adding. The required multiplication facts are quite trivial:

```
0 ⊠ n = 0, and 1 ⊠ n = n
```

Let us review the long multiplication algorithm using a 4-bit example. The twist is that it is all in binary.

```
    1001 (multiplicand)
   ⊠1010 (multiplier)
   ------
    0000 (partial products)
   1001
  0000
 1001
 ---------
 01011010 (product)
```

The implementation of this algorithm uses a loop to add each partial product into the 8-bit result (initialized to 0 at the start). As you can see from the example, each partial product is either the multiplicand or zero (depending on the value of a bit in the multiplier). Each bit of the multiplier is used to select the correct partial product. We can use a shift instruction to examine the bits of the multiplier one at a time. This bit will determine if we add the multiplicand (shifted to the proper column) or add zero. Rather than shifting the partial products to the left, we will shift the result to the right to maintain the correct alignment.

To summarize, the 16-bit result will be accumulated in R1:R0. As each partial product is determined, we will add it to R1 (the high byte of the result) and then shift R1:R0 to the right. This aligns the result for the next partial product. We will have to be careful about the addition, because if a carry out of the leftmost position occurs, it must be brought into the result when we shift it to the right (by using a rotate).

```
;8-bit unsigned multiplication
;R1:R0 = R16 ☒ R17
.def multiplicand = R16
.def multiplier = R17
.def counter = R18
clr R1
ldi counter, 8   ;loop counter
next_bit:
lsr multiplier        ;examine and discard next bit
brcc zero_partial     ;no carry means 0 times: no addition
add R1, multiplicand ;1 times case
zero_partial:
ror R1  ;shift result right, bringing in carry flag
ror R0
dec counter
brne next_bit
;multiplication complete
```

Most of the algorithm is fairly straightforward. In the next_bit loop, the next bit of the multiplier is shifted to the carry flag; the BRCC skips adding the multiplicand since the partial product would be zero. If the branch is not taken, the ADD instruction is executed. This addition may have a carry; examine the rotate instructions to see how this is handled.

What will the carry value be if the ADD is skipped? It should be zero if the rotates are going to do the right thing, but can you be sure it is zero if the ADD is skipped? Yes! Be sure you can see from the code why this is true.

Multiplication of signed data can utilize the same basic algorithm, multiplying the absolute values of the signed numbers, and then negating the result if required (if the original numbers had opposite signs). The algorithm is also easily extended to larger numbers. You just need to loop more times and use more registers.

Division Algorithm

Now that we have tackled the shift and add algorithm for multiplication, we are ready to move on to integer division. The AVR processor does not include a division instruction. This means that division must be implemented algorithmically. The process imitates the long division algorithm. Fortunately the trial division process is much simpler in binary. Rather than guessing a number from 0 to 9 for how many times the divisor goes into the current part of the dividend, in binary the guess is either 0 or 1. A simple comparison makes this decision easy. If you recall the steps of long division, you may guess that shifting of bits will be an important part of the algorithm. You might also guess this since division is the undoing of multiplication, and we just saw how multiplication could be accomplished using shifts and adds.

Signed division is accomplished by converting to unsigned data, carrying out the division, then adjusting the sign of the result. So, we can concentrate on the division of unsigned data. When performing integer division, there are actually two results: the quotient and remainder. The standard algorithms generate both at the same time.

The details of the division algorithm will vary depending on the sizes of the operands. We will look only at the division of two bytes.

Because division is the inverse of multiplication, and a byte times a byte can give a word, it might be expected that we would attempt to divide a word by a byte and get a byte. But, what if you divide by one? Then the result is still likely to require a whole word. When processors include divide instructions, they will likely have variants for different sizes of data.

When performing division, the bits of the result will be determined beginning with the most significant. As each bit is determined, it is rotated left into the quotient register. The algorithm shown here uses an extra register to extend the dividend working area to a 16-bit value. This is used to isolate the part of the dividend that is involved in the current division step (allowing the trailing bits to be ignored). We will call this extra register the dividend window. The dividend (as a word) is shifted left repeatedly as the quotient is determined.

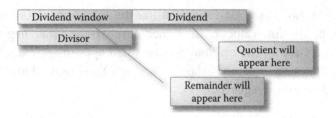

FIGURE 11.9 The dividend, dividend window, and divisor used in the division algorithm.

Think of the divisor being oriented directly below the dividend window, ready to subtract. This arrangement is pictured in Figure 11.9. At each step, if the divisor is less than or equal to the high byte of the dividend, then the next bit of the quotient is 1 and we subtract the divisor away from the dividend. The carry bit is set to the next bit of the quotient, and is rotated back into the dividend (on the right). Thus, the quotient gradually replaces the original dividend (which is shifting into the dividend window).

The process is illustrated in this example where 218 is divided by 41. The initial register contents are shown in Figure 11.10.

Begin by shifting the dividend left until we can legally subtract the divisor. This requires six shifts. At this point, the registers contain the values shown in Figure 11.11. The boxed 0's in the divisor area are the bits shifted in as the dividend was shifted left. These are the leading bits of the developing quotient. Each shift followed the decision to append a 0 to the quotient as the divisor was smaller than the current dividend window.

Since the divisor is now smaller than the dividend window, subtraction occurs and the next bit of the quotient is determined to be one. When the dividend is shifted, a 1 is therefore shifted in to take its place in the developing quotient. Figure 11.12 shows the register contents after the subtraction (dividend window minus divisor) and then after the shift, bringing in the 1 into the quotient.

Examining the dividend window and the divisor, you can see that the next bit of the quotient is zero. The next shift again makes the dividend window larger than the divisor so a subtraction occurs and a 1 is shifted into the quotient. Figure 11.13 illustrates this progress.

Note that at this last step, the remainder is found in the dividend window and the shift is only performed on the quotient register. The dividend window, which is now the remainder, is unchanged. The quotient has replaced the dividend byte. The iterative process requires one initial shift

FIGURE 11.10   Initial register contents for 218 divided by 41.

to setup the first potential subtraction, a loop of eight steps, plus a final step to rotate the last bit of the quotient into place.

```
218/41 = 5 r 13
```

Note that the shift operation requires a 16-bit shift. This is accomplished by a pair of rotates. The first rotate brings in the next bit of the quotient which will be in the carry flag. It also puts the high bit of the remaining part of the dividend into the carry flag. The subsequent rotate into the dividend window brings in this bit from the carry flag, completing the 16-bit shift.

Here is the algorithm sketched out in high-level pseudocode. Note that the comparison is replaced by a subtraction that is undone (by addition) if the result turns out to be negative.

```
R16 = 0                         //dividend window
R19 = 9                         //loop counter
R17 <<= 1; C = msb              //start the 16-bit shift
while (-R19 != 0) {
R16 = (R16 << 1) + C            //complete the shift
R16 -= R18                      //trial div
if (R16 is negative) {
R16 += R18                      //undo subtraction
C = 0                           //next quotient bit is 0
}
else {
C = 1                           //next quotient bit is 1
```

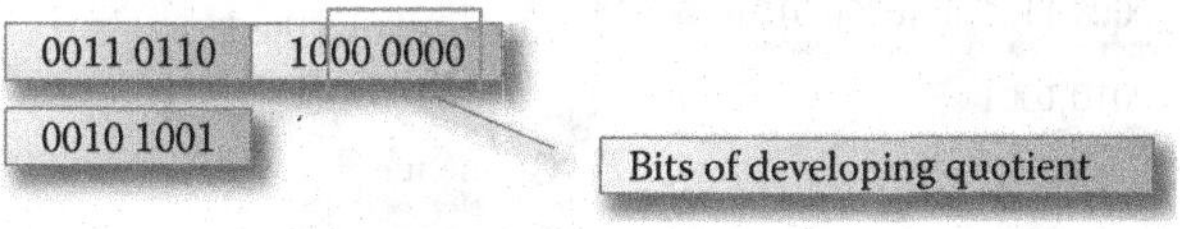

FIGURE 11.11   Register contents after six left shifts for which the dividend window was less than the divisor.

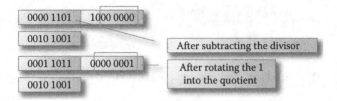

FIGURE 11.12   Register contents after the subtraction and then after the shift.

```
}
R17 = (R17 << 1) + C;  C = msb      //shift in quotient bit
                                   //and start 16-bit shift
}
```

Note the duplicated rotate instruction at the bottom of the loop. The duplication can be removed if the loop test is placed in the middle of the loop. The assembly language version does this.

```
;Compute the quotient and remainder r17/r18
;r16 = remainder
;r17 = quotient
clr r16          ;for remainder
ldi r19, 9       ;loop counter
lp:
rol r17          ;store quot bit and start 16-bit shift
dec r19          ;loop test here
breq exit        ;exit on 9th iteration
rol r16          ;complete shift into dividend window
sub r16, r18     ;trial division
```

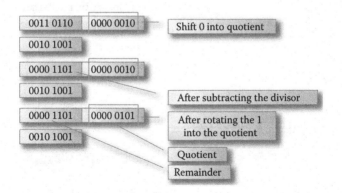

FIGURE 11.13   Register contents after a shift, subtraction, and shift.

```
brcc goesinto   ;cc means quot bit is 1
add r16, r18    ;undo subtraction
clc             ;next quot bit is 0
rjmp lp
goesinto:
sec             ;next quot bit is 1
rjmp lp
exit:
```

As long as the divisor is a byte, the above technique will work quite well, requiring just one extra byte to act as the dividend window and the final remainder. If the divisor is a word, the dividend window should be a word; the algorithm remains the same, but each step requires multibyte arithmetic (SUB, SBC) for the subtraction.

NUMERIC I/O AND TYPE CONVERSIONS

One of the fundamental tasks of most programs is the translation of information between external formats, possibly human readable, to the internal format required for processing. Integers are most efficiently handled internally when they are stored in the processor's native, signed or unsigned, formats. Externally, numbers are more commonly represented as a sequence of ASCII characters. In this section, we will examine typical conversion routines. These will convert numbers in ASCII format to one of the more usable internal formats, and vice versa. Our algorithm to convert from ASCII format will assume a numeral is already located in SRAM as a string and will process the digits sequentially, beginning with the most significant. Although base 10 is assumed as the external data format standard, adjustments to handle hexadecimal, octal, or binary (or any other base) are fairly simple to make.

Unsigned to ASCII

The task is to convert an unsigned byte (0–255) to 1, 2, or 3 ASCII characters representing the value as a base 10 numeral. The algorithm requires repeated division by 10 to determine the digits of the base 10 numeral and generates the digits beginning with the one's place. The conversion function pseudocode is as follows:

```
// x is the byte to be converted
do{
nextdigit = x % 10
```

```
x = x/10
while(x != 0)
```

The digits will need to be converted to the proper ASCII character and stored somewhere. We will write a function to store them into a three byte area in SRAM, padding with leading spaces if needed. Another choice might be to create a string with just the digits (no padding), or simply push them on a stack to be output in reverse order to some I/O device.

We will use indirect addressing, with predecrement; at the beginning of the function, X will be assumed to point to the beginning of the storage area where the ASCII characters will be stored. We will assume we have a division function (div8by8) that divides r17 by r18 placing the quotient in r17 and the remainder in r16.

```
;R17 holds the unsigned byte to be converted
;X points to a 3 byte storage area where the ASCII
;numeral is to be stored
u2a:
        adiw XH:XL,3 ;point past end of array
        ldi r18, 10  ;divisor for base 10
        ldi r20, 3           ;number of digits
u2a_next:
        rcall div8by8       ;get digit and remainder
        ori r16,'0'         ;BCD to ASCII
        st -X, r16          ;store next digit
        dec r20
        breq u2a_done
        tst r17             ;quotient 0 means done
        brne u2a_next

        ldi r16, ' '        ;add leading spaces
        u2a_leading:
        st -X, r16
        dec r20
        brne u2a_leading
u2a_done:
```

The division produces a remainder (0–9) in BCD form in R16. The ORI instruction inserts the bits needed to produce the ASCII equivalent. The counter in R20 is used to add leading spaces if required. The division loop ends when either three digits are stored, or the quotient is zero. In the latter case, one or two leading space characters will need to be stored.

By changing the divisor and the number of loop iterations, conversion to any base can be accomplished. Notice that conversions to base 2, 8, or 16 can be accomplished using shifts. This will be much more efficient than calling a division function.

Because division is so costly, conversion to ASCII is sometimes implemented using repeated subtraction. For a 16-bit unsigned value, we begin by subtracting 10,000 until the result would fall below zero. We will be able to do this 0, 1, 2, 3, 4, 5, or 6 times (max 16-bit value is 65,535). Then we subtract 1000. This will result in the next digit. The process continues until the last digit is determined. The powers of 10 are generally placed in a table and accessed as needed by the looping process.

Fewer loop iterations will be required by this approach compared to the cost of repeated division by 10. If a fast hardware divide instruction was available, then the previous algorithm would be preferred.

ASCII to Unsigned

Translation from the ASCII form to an unsigned representation requires repeated multiplication by 10. Horner's Rule is appropriate here to efficiently effect the translation. Processing begins with the most-significant digit, the first to be available in the case where the digits are streaming into view from a file or keypad. If the digits are part of a string in memory, they could be processed in either order; Horner's Rule requires that we start with the most significant.

In this function, we will assume X points to the first digit of the ASCII representation of a base 10 numeral. The algorithm will process digits until a nondigit is encountered. The unsigned equivalent (modulo 256) will be found in R0 when finished.

```
;X points to a string of ASCII digits terminated with a
;non-digit
;R0 will accumulate the result
a2u:
    clr r0
    ldi r18, 10
a2u_next:
    ld r16, X+      ;next character
```

```
        cpi r16,'9'+1    ;detect non-digits above '9'
        brsh a2u_done
        subi r16, '0'    ;convert ASCII to BCD
        brcs a2u_done    ;detect non-digits below '0'
        mul r0, r18      ;multiply accumulator by radix (10)
        add R0, r16      ;add in next digit value
        rjmp a2u_next
a2u_done:
```

Of course, if the number is greater than 255, the value in R0 will be truncated by this algorithm (reduced modulo 256). With a little work, this algorithm can be used to convert ASCII into a 16-bit integer or larger. The multiplication and addition will need to be upgraded to handle the wider data.

Conversion from other bases is accomplished using the base as the multiplier. Digits above nine must be converted into a numeric value in a separate case. If R16 holds a digit or a character, then the following sequence will extract the digit value:

```
        cpi r16,'A'
        brsh letter
        andi r16,$0F
        rjmp converted
letter:
        andi r16, $1F
        subi r16, -9
        converted:
```

The processing separates digits from letters. Digits are converted by masking the upper nybble. Letters are converted by masking the upper three bits (merging the upper and lower case letters to a single value, 1 through 26 (if we allow letters through z). Adding nine completes the conversion.

SIEVE OF ERATOSTHENES

Generating a list of prime numbers can be efficiently accomplished using The Sieve of Eratosthenes. The sieve is a large Boolean array, each entry indicating whether its index is prime or composite. The sieve is initialized to false (zero) indicating all numbers are prime. The algorithm eventually changes the values corresponding to composite numbers to true.

To conserve space, the sieve will be implemented as an array of bits. Each byte of memory will store eight Boolean values. Byte 0 of sieve array will hold the bits for the integers 0 through 7. When the algorithm finishes, this byte will contain 0b01010000, since 7, 5, 3, and 2 are prime (two bits are wasted as one and zero are not processed by this algorithm. To locate the Boolean value for an integer n, we first locate the index of the byte containing this value by computing $b = n/8$. Then, we isolate the bit in position $n\%8$.

The algorithm itself begins with the integer 2, and marks all multiples of 2 as composite (stores a 1 in the sieve at positions 4, 6, 8, ..., 2i, ...). Then it moves on to the next integer that the sieve indicates is prime (which would be 3). All multiples of 3 are marked (6, 9, 12, ..., 3i, ...). The next integer, 4 is marked as composite; the next prime is 5. Multiples of 5 are marked, and so on.

The sieve of course is finite in size. If S is the number of integers whose primeness is stored in the sieve, then the marking process can stop when the integer $m = \text{floor}(\text{sqrt}(S))$ has been processed. At this time the sieve will be completed. All multiples of $m + 1$ ($2(m + 1)$, $3(m + 1)$, ..., $m(m + 1)$, ...) have already been marked (as multiples of the other factor). The next multiple, $(m + 1)(m + 1)$ is too large for the sieve.

The program below includes a lot of pseudocodes to illustrate the use of high-level design in order to implement an assembly language program. The program outputs (via serial) each prime number as it is determined. There is a version for the XPLAIN hardware at the end of the chapter.

```
;Program 11.1
;Sieve of Eratosthenes - determining some prime numbers

;Use the sieve to determine all of the prime numbers up
;to a preset limit. The limit is determined by available
;memory and the limit imposed by 16-bit data.

;The sieve is implemented as a bit-array

;Output the list of primes to a terminal program using
;serial communication

;Programmer: TM
;Date: 5/2010
;Platform: STK-500
```

```
;Device: ATMEGA16A

;Serial communications between the STK-500 and PC

.include "m16def.inc"

;const int maxPrime = min(avail memory, 65535);
;const int maxCandidate = sqrt(maxPrime);
.equ STACK_SIZE = 64 ;leave room for stack

;there will be maxPrime + 1 bits in the sieve
;(0..maxPrime)
.set sievesize = SRAM_SIZE-STACK_SIZE
.set maxPrime = sievesize * 8 - 1
.if maxPrime > $FFFF
        .set maxPrime = $FFFF
        .set sievesize = (maxPrime + 1)/8
.endif

;find approximate square root of maxPrime
;square root will be < 256 since maxPrime < 65536
.def maxPrimeH = r23
.def maxPrimeL = r22
.def sqrt_candidate = r16

ldi maxPrimeL, low(maxPrime)
ldi maxPrimeH, high(maxPrime)
ldi sqrt_candidate, 1  ;start with 2 as the square root
maxCand_lp:
        inc sqrt_candidate
        cpi sqrt_candidate, 255
        breq maxCand_found
        mul sqrt_candidate, sqrt_candidate  ;square
                                            ;candidate
        cp r0, maxPrimeL  ;see if it equals or exceeds
                          ;maxPrime
        cpc r1, maxPrimeH
        brlo maxCand_lp
maxCand_found:
.undef maxPrimeH
.undef maxPrimeL
```

```
.def maxCandidateH = r23
.def maxCandidateL = r22
mov maxCandidateL, sqrt_candidate        ;low byte of sqrt
ldi maxCandidateH, 0                      ;high byte is 0
.undef sqrt_candidate

;Sieve organization:
;Composite numbers will be marked with 1's. Initially
;the sieve is all zeros.
;There are 8 numbers encoded per byte
;sieve[k] bit j is for n = k⊠8 + j  (0 <= j <= 7)

;unsigned byte sieve[(sievesize];
.dseg
sieve: .byte sievesize

.def temp = r16
.cseg
ldi temp, high(RAMEND)
out SPH, temp
ldi temp, low(RAMEND)
out SPL, temp

rcall initUsart
;wait for receipt of character from terminal
lp:
        sbis UCSRA, RXC     ;is byte in Rx buffer?
        rjmp lp
in temp, UDR                ;received byte

;mark all as prime to start (0 = prime)
;for (unsigned word i = 0; i < sievesize; i++) sieve[i] = 0;
.cseg
ldi temp, 0
ldi XH, high(sieve)
ldi XL, low(sieve)

.def countH = r25
.def countL = r24
ldi countH, high(sievesize)
ldi countL, low(sievesize)
init_lp:
```

```
        st X+ , temp
        sbiw countH:countL, 1
        brne init_lp
.undef countL
.undef countH

.def next_prime_H = r25
.def next_prime_L = r24
;unsigned word next_prime = 1;
;find_next(&next_prime);
;while (next_prime != 0){
; println next_prime;
; if (maxCandidate >= next_prime)
; markmultiples(next_prime);
; find_next(&next_prime);
;}

ldi next_prime_L, low(1)
ldi next_prime_H, high(1)

ldi temp, 0
main_lp:
        rcall find_next   ;advance to next prime number
        cp next_prime_L, temp
        cpc next_prime_H, temp
        breq main_done
        rcall printnum  ;display it
        cp maxCandidateL, next_prime_L
        cpc maxCandidateH, next_prime_H
        brlo main_lp
        rcall markmultiples  ;mark multiples if prime <=
                             ;square root
        rjmp main_lp
main_done:
        rjmp PC
.undef temp
.undef maxCandidateL
.undef maxCandidateH
.undef next_prime_L
.undef next_prime_H

;Functions -------
```

```
;void transmit(char c){
; while(!(usart data register ready));
; usart data register=c;
;}
;Transmit byte - blocks until transmit buffer can accept
;a byte
;The param, byte to transmit, is in r24
.def byte_tx=r24
.def temp=r16
transmit:
      push temp
transmit_wait:
      sbis UCSRA, UDRE    ;wait for Tx buffer to be empty
      rjmp transmit_wait ;not ready yet
      out UDR, byte_tx    ;transmit character
      pop temp
      ret
.undef byte_tx
.undef temp

;void printnum(word n){
;n is passed in r25:r24
;digits are pushed on the stack, then popped and
;transmitted followed by cr lf

;push lf
;push cr
;do{
; push n%10+'0'
; n=n/10
;}while(n>0)
;while(c=pop != '\n')
; transmit c
;}
.def param_nL=r24
.def param_nH=r25
.def remainder=r23
.def divisor=r18
printnum:
push param_nL
push param_nH
push remainder
```

```
push divisor

ldi divisor, 10            ;base 10 numerals
ldi remainder, '\n'        ;place lf on stack
push remainder
ldi remainder, '\r'        ;place cr on stack
push remainder
printnum_div_lp:
        rcall divWordbyByte    ;get digit and remainder
        ori remainder,'0'      ;BCD to ASCII
        push remainder
        tst param_nL           ;quotient 0 means done
        brne printnum_div_lp
        tst param_nH
        brne printnum_div_lp
;pop digits off stack and transmit
printnum_prt_lp:
        pop param_nL           ;argument for transmit
        rcall transmit
        cpi param_nL, '\n'     ;newline is last character
        brne printnum_prt_lp
pop divisor
pop remainder
pop param_nH
pop param_nL
ret
.undef param_nL
.undef param_nH
.undef remainder
.undef divisor

;Divide word by byte
;Compute the quotient and remainder r25:r24/r18
;Return values:
; r23 = remainder
; r25:r24 = quotient
.def quotient_H = r25   ;also parameter
.def quotient_L = r24
.def remainder = r23
.def divisor = r18
.def counter = r16
```

```
divWordByByte:
push counter
clr remainder        ;for remainder
ldi counter, 17      ;loop counter
div_lp:
        rol quotient_L              ;store quot bit and start
                                    ;24-bit shift
        rol quotient_H
        dec counter                 ;loop test here
        breq exit                   ;exit on 9th iteration
        rol remainder               ;complete shift into
                                    ;dividend window
        sub remainder, divisor      ;trial division
        brcc goesinto               ;cc means quot bit is 1
        add remainder, divisor      ;undo subtraction
        clc                         ;next quot bit is 0
        rjmp div_lp
goesinto:
sec   ;next quot bit is 1
rjmp div_lp
exit:
pop counter
ret
.undef divisor
.undef counter
.undef quotient_H
.undef quotient_L
.undef remainder


;void find_next(word ⊠ p){
;locate next prime number in table, set p to 0 if none
; do{
; if (⊠p == maxPrime)
; ⊠p = 0;
; else
; (⊠p) ++;
; while(⊠p != 0 && isComposite(⊠p)){
;}
.def param_pH = r25  ;argument and parameter are both in
                     ;this register
.def param_pL = r24
```

```
.def temp = r16


find_next:
        push temp
find_next_do:
        ldi temp, low(maxPrime)
        cp param_pL, temp
        ldi temp, high(maxPrime)
        cpc param_pH, temp
        brne find_next_else
        clr param_pH
        clr param_pL
        rjmp find_next_exit
find_next_else:
        adiw param_pH:param_pL, 1
;find_next_endif:
        rcall isComposite
        brcs find_next_do


find_next_exit:
        pop temp
        ret
.undef param_pL
.undef param_pH
.undef temp

;void markmultiples(word n){
; word c = n;
; while (c <= maxPrime-n){
;       c += n;
;       setcomposite(c);
; }
;}
.def param_nL = r24
.def param_nH = r25
.def cL = r22
.def cH = r23
.def maxpH = r21
.def maxpL = r20
markmultiples:
push cL
```

```
push cH
push maxpL
push maxpH
push param_nL
push param_nH
movw cH:cL,param_nH:param_nL
ldi maxpH, high(maxPrime)
ldi maxpL, low(maxPrime)
sub maxpl, param_nL
sbc maxpH, param_nH

markmultiples_while:
        cp maxpL, param_nL
        cpc maxpH, param_nH
        brlo markmultiples_endwhile
        add param_nL, cL
        adc param_nH, cH
        rcall setComposite
        rjmp markmultiples_while


markmultiples_endwhile:
pop param_nH
pop param_nL
pop maxpH
pop maxpL
pop cH
pop cL
ret
.undef param_nL
.undef param_nH
.undef cL
.undef cH
.undef maxpL
.undef maxpH


;boolean isComposite(word n){
;return true (CC set) if is composite
; return sieve[n/8] & (1 << (n & 0x0007)) != 0
;}
.def param_nL = r24
.def param_nH = r25
```

```
.def sieveByte = r16
isComposite:
push XH
push XL
push sieveByte
push param_nL
movw XH:XL, param_nH:param_nL    ;determine address of
                                 ;byte for n's flag
lsr XH                           ;X = n/8
ror XL
lsr XH
ror XL
lsr XH
ror XL
;add start address of sieve
subi XL, low(-sieve)
sbci XH, high(-sieve)


ld sieveByte, X     ;copy sieve byte into register
andi param_nL, 7    ;isolate bit position from n


isComposite_lp:     ;shift selected bit into carry flag
      lsr sieveByte
      dec param_nL
      brge isComposite_lp
      ;carry flag has required bit from sieve

pop param_nL
pop sieveByte
pop XL
pop XH
ret
.undef param_nL
.undef param_nH
.undef sieveByte

;void setComposite(word n){
;set the bit for value n to indicate it is composite
; sieve[n/8] |= (1 << (n & 0x0007));
;}
```

```
.def param_nL = r24
.def param_nH = r25
.def bitPos = r18
.def bitMask = r19
.def temp = r16
setComposite:
;bit position is least significant 3 bits
push bitPos
push bitMask
push XH
push XL
push temp

;bitPos = n && 0x07
mov bitPos, param_nL
andi bitPos, 0x07
;bitMask = 1 << bitPos; will require a loop
;implemented as:
;bitMask = 1
;while (bitPos > 0){
; bitMask << 1
; bitPos -;
;}
ldi bitMask, 1
tst    bitPos
breq setComposite_lp1_exit

setComposite_lp1:
      lsl bitMask
      dec bitPos
      brne setComposite_lp1

setComposite_lp1_exit:
;Move address to X in prep for indirect addressing
;divide X by 8 to get address
;X = X >> 3
movw XH:XL, param_nH:param_nL
lsr XH
ror XL
lsr XH
ror XL
lsr XH
```

```
ror XL
;add start address of sieve
subi XL, low(-sieve)
sbci XH, high(-sieve)

;sieve[n/8] |= bitMask
;set bit to indicate composite
ld temp, X
or temp, bitMask
st X, temp

pop temp
pop XL
pop XH
pop bitMask
pop bitPos
ret
.undef temp
.undef param_nL
.undef param_nH
.undef bitMask
.undef bitPos

;Initialize USART for bi-directional communication
initUSART:
;2 mhz clock speed, 9600 baud UBRR = 12
.equ UBRRvalue = 12
.def temp = r16

ldi temp, high (UBRRvalue)  ;baud rate
out UBRRH, temp
ldi temp, low (UBRRvalue)
out UBRRL, temp

;URSEL 0 = UBRRH, 1 = UCSRC (shared port address)
;UMSEL 0 = Asynchronous, 1 = Synchronous
;USBS 0 = One stop bit, 1 = Two stop bits
;UCSZ0:1 Character Size: 0 = 5, 1 = 6, 2 = 7, 3 = 8
; (UCSZ2 is in UCSRB, but is only needed for 9 data bits)
;UPM0:1 0 = none, 1 = reserved, 2 = Even, 3 = Odd

;8data, 1 stop, no parity
ldi temp,
(1 << URSEL) | (0 << UMSEL) | (0 << USBS) | (3 << UCSZ0) | (0 << UPM0)
out UCSRC, temp
```

```
ldi temp, (1 << RXEN) | (1 << TXEN)
out UCSRB, temp; enable receive and transmit
;USART initialization complete
ret
```

EXERCISES

1. Carry out the addition of the two bytes below using the ripple carry model. That is, begin with all of the columns having a carry in of zero. Add all columns and note which ones have a change in their carry (as a result of the column to their right). Increase the sum in all of these columns accordingly, and note the changes in carry again. Continue until no changes occur. Tell the new carry values at the end of each cycle.
   0b10110110 + 0b01110011

2. Add the following bytes telling the result and the flag values (V, N, Z, and C only). Interpret the results (in base 10) assuming unsigned data. What flag indicates overflow?
   a. $E2 + $3C
   b. $7F + $01
   c. $80 + $80
   d. $B5 + $4B

3. Interpret the results for the previous problem assuming the data is signed. In the case of signed overflow, tell the sign of the expected (not the actual) answer.

4. Subtract the following bytes (by negating and adding) telling the result and the flag values (V, N, Z, and C only) associated with the subtraction (not the addition). Interpret the results assuming unsigned data.
   a. $80 − $01
   b. $10 − $20
   c. $AF − $32
   d. $62 − $82

5. Interpret the results for the previous problem assuming the data is signed. What flag indicates overflow? In the case of signed overflow, tell the sign of the expected (not the actual) answer.

6. The contents of registers R25:R24 and R23:R22 are $A3C4 and $C15F respectively. Tell the new contents of R25:R24 after the following instructions are executed.
   ```
   add r24, r22
   adc r25, r23
   ```

7. The addw macro discussed in this chapter only worked for registers X, Y, and Z. Rewrite it so it works for any four registers. All four registers will need to be listed as separate arguments.

For example, `addw r17, r16, r3, r2` will add r3:r2 to r17:r16. Include usage documentation.

8. Why will the following code (which uses the `addw` macro in the previous exercise) sometimes fail to take the branch when the result is zero? Rewrite the `addw` macro so this problem will not occur.

```
addw XH, XL, YH, YL
breq zero_result
```

9. Write a subtract word macro modeled after the add word macro in the previous exercise. This macro should allow a subsequent branch if equal (or not equal) to function correctly.

10. An unsigned integer named `count` is in R25:R24 and R23 contains an unsigned byte. Write instructions to add R23 to `count`. You will find it useful to use one additional register. Follow the addition with a branch to label `done` if (unsigned) overflow occurs.

11. What value will be in R25:R24 and what will the zero flag contain after the following instructions are executed if R25:R24 initially contains $8001?
```
add r24, r24
adc r25, r25
```

12. What value will the zero flag contain after the following instructions are executed if R16 initially contains $40?
```
add r16, r16
adc r16, r16
```

13. What value will the zero flag contain after the following instructions are executed if R16 initially contains $01?
```
add r16, r16  ;yes, this is an add instruction
sbc r16, r16
```

14. An unsigned integer named `count` is in R25:R24 and R23 contains an unsigned byte. Write instructions to add R23 to `count`. Follow the addition with code to cause a branch to label `zero` if the answer is $0000.

15. Write a single instruction to decrease the value in R16 by 25 (R16 currently contains an unsigned integer greater than 25).

16. Write a single instruction to increase the value in R16 by 25 (R16 currently contains an unsigned integer smaller than 225).

17. Write a pair of instructions to increase the value in R25:R24 (containing a 16-bit two's complement number) by 1000. Ignore the possibility of overflow.

18. Write a pair of instructions to decrease the value in R25:R24 (containing a 16-bit two's complement number) by 1000. Ignore the possibility of overflow.

19. Is this instruction legal? If so, what does it do?

```
sbic r16, -1
```

20. Write a series of two instructions to branch to label not_bigger if the signed integer in R25 is less than or equal to the signed integer in R24. Use only two instructions!

21. Write a series of two instructions to branch to label smaller if the signed integer in R25 is less than 10.

22. Write a series of three instructions to branch to label smaller if the unsigned integer in R25:R24 is smaller than the unsigned integer in R23:R22.

23. Write a series of three instructions to branch to label bigger if the signed integer in R25:R24 is strictly larger than (strictly larger means larger, but not equal) the signed integer in R23:R22. Use only three instructions!

24. Explain why version one of the following loop functions correctly, but version two does not.

```
;version 1 loops ten times
ldi r16, 9
lp:
      subi r16, 1
      brsh lp
;version 2 loops ten times (not!)
ldi r16, 9
lp:
      dec r16
      brsh lp
```

25. The NEG instruction will change the sign of an 8-bit number in a register. Another way to change the sign of a number is to subtract it from 0. Write a sequence of instructions to negate the signed integer in R25:R24 using this idea. You may use only one additional register.

26. Another way to negate a number is to multiply it by negative one. Use this idea to negate the signed integer in R25:R24.

27. Negating a 16-bit integer using a sequence of two NEG instructions seems so simple, yet does not always give the correct result. Give an example of a nonzero value (in R25:R24) for which the following sequence correctly negates the value, and a second example where it does not. In each case, tell the actual and expected values (in hex and decimal).

```
neg r25
neg r24
```

28. Write a sequence of instructions to widen (sign extend) the signed integer in R25:R24 to a 32-bit integer in R27:R26:R25:R24.

29. Another way to widen a byte to a word is to multiply by one. Use this idea to widen R24 to R25:R24 assuming R24 is a signed byte. What would need to be changed if R24 is unsigned?

30. If R23:R22 contains $3CC2, tell the contents of R1:R0 after each instruction.

   a. `mul R23, R22`

   b. `muls R23, R22`

   c. `mulsu R23, R22`

   d. `mulsu R22, R23`

31. Assuming R23 and R22 contain nonzero signed integers, use a multiplication instruction followed by a conditional branch to jump to label `same` if the two numbers have the same sign or to label `different` if they have different signs.

32. Trace the byte by byte unsigned multiplication of $27C5 ⊠ $D3 by completing the following diagram:

		$27	$C5
		⊠	$D3
		Partial product	
Partial product			
	Final product		

33. Write a function to multiply the unsigned word in R25:R24 by the unsigned byte in R22. Return the result in R25:R24:R23.

34. Write a function to multiply signed data, R25:R24 * R22. Call the function from the previous problem to accomplish the task.

35. Write a function to compute the product of two unsigned words. The arguments are passed in R25:R24 and R23:R22. The result will be 32 bits, and should be returned in these same registers. Begin by drawing a diagram showing the partial products that must be computed.

36. What happens in the division algorithm if the divisor is zero?

PROGRAMMING EXERCISES

1. Write a program that will add two bytes using only logical instructions. Write a function that implements a single-bit full-adder. The three arguments are passed in bit 0 of R25, R24, and R23. The sum and carry are returned in bit 0 of R1 (sum) and R0 (carry). Implement a ripple carry adder function that adds the bytes passed in R22 and R21, returning the result in R20. This function should begin with the least-significant bits. By calling the full-adder function eight times, it determines the

result one bit at a time. Write a test application that calls the ripple carry function for a sample pair of bytes. This program should be tested in the AVR simulator for a variety of bytes.

2. Implement the multiplication algorithm covered in the reading as a real function. Verify the results are correct by testing it with several values, comparing the result to that obtained using the `mul` instruction. Run the program in the AVR simulator.

3. Implement the division algorithm (for two unsigned bytes) as a function named `div8by8`. Use the simulator to test the algorithm on a variety of numbers.

4. Implement the division algorithm for unsigned word divided by unsigned byte. The quotient should be a word and the remainder a byte. Test your algorithm using the simulator.

5. Implement the u2a and a2u algorithms and design a test application to perform several conversions. First, convert a byte into ASCII. Next, determine the address of the first digit (skip over the leading blanks) and pass this to the other function to convert it back. Be sure there is a nondigit after the last digit of the ASCII string.

6. Write 16-bit versions of the two conversion algorithms (see previous exercise) and test. Name them `a2uw` and `uw2a`.

7. Write a function named `sw2a` that creates a string representing the value of a signed word. Place the result in a 6-byte array with leading spaces if required. Negative values need a minus sign before the leading digit. Use the `uw2a` function to do most of the work.

8. Write a function named `a2sw` that converts a signed ASCII numeral into a signed word. The function should skip leading spaces. If a minus sign is encountered before the first digit, the result must be negative. Stop when a nondigit is encountered. Design your function to call the `a2uw` function.

9. Write a simple calculator that uses a terminal program and serial communication as an I/O device. The user will type problems like 345 + 6027 − 302 and then press enter. The program will echo the characters typed, but when enter key is pressed it will output an equal sign and the result, followed by a carriage return and line feed. The program should repeat this forever. Support only + and −. Everything is 16-bit unsigned. Assume input is valid and ignore overflow.

10. Write a simple calculator that uses a terminal program and serial communication as an I/O device. The user will type problems in postfix format. For example,

    345 −627 29 + −107 − +

and then press enter. The program will echo the characters typed, but when enter is pressed, it will output an equal sign and the result, followed by a carriage return and line feed. Exactly one space is used as a delimiter between tokens. The program should repeat this forever. Support only + and −. Everything is 16-bit signed. Assume input is valid.

ALTERNATE PROGRAMS FOR THE XPLAIN DEMONSTRATION KIT

PROGRAM 11.1a: Sieve of Eratosthenes

The XMEGA/XPLAIN version of this program will produce a much longer list of prime numbers due to the larger SRAM. Other than that, the only differences are references to the I/O ports.

```
;Program 11.1a
;Sieve of Eratosthenes - determining some prime numbers

;Use the sieve to determine all of the prime numbers up
;to a preset limit. The limit is determined by available
;memory and the limit imposed by 16-bit data.

;The sieve is implemented as a bit-array

;Output the list of primes to a terminal program using
;serial communication

;Programmer: TM
;Date: 5/2010
;Platform: XPLAIN
;Device: ATxmega128A1

;Serial communications between the XPLAIN and PC
; using LUFA Bridge

.include "ATxmega128A1def.inc"
;const int maxPrime = min(avail memory, 65535);
;const int maxCandidate = sqrt(maxPrime);
.equ STACK_SIZE = 64 ;leave room for stack
```

```
;there will be maxPrime + 1 bits in the sieve
;(0..maxPrime)
.set sievesize = SRAM_SIZE-STACK_SIZE
.set maxPrime = sievesize ⊠ 8 - 1
.if maxPrime > $FFFF
        .set maxPrime = $FFFF
        .set sievesize = (maxPrime + 1)/8
.endif


;find approximate square root of maxPrime
;square root will be < 256 since maxPrime < 65536
.def maxPrimeH = r23
.def maxPrimeL = r22
.def sqrt_candidate = r16


ldi maxPrimeL, low(maxPrime)
ldi maxPrimeH, high(maxPrime)
ldi sqrt_candidate, 1  ;start with 2 as the square root
maxCand_lp:
        inc sqrt_candidate
        cpi sqrt_candidate, 255
        breq maxCand_found
        mul sqrt_candidate, sqrt_candidate  ;square
                                            ;candidate
        cp r0, maxPrimeL  ;see if it equals or exceeds
                          ;maxPrime
        cpc r1, maxPrimeH
        brlo maxCand_lp
maxCand_found:
.undef maxPrimeH
.undef maxPrimeL


.def maxCandidateH = r23
.def maxCandidateL = r22
mov maxCandidateL, sqrt_candidate       ;low byte of sqrt
ldi maxCandidateH, 0                     ;high byte is 0
.undef sqrt_candidate


;Sieve organization:
;Composite numbers will be marked with 1's. Initially
;the sieve is all zeros.
;There are 8 numbers encoded per byte
```

```
;sieve[k] bit j is for n=k⊠8+j  (0<=j<=7)

;unsigned byte sieve[(sievesize];
.dseg
sieve: .byte sievesize

.def temp=r16
.cseg

rcall initUsart
;wait for receipt of character from terminal
lp:
        lds temp, USARTC0_STATUS
        sbrs temp, USART_RXCIF_bp ;is byte in Rx buffer?
        rjmp lp
lds temp, USARTC0_DATA              ;received byte

;mark all as prime to start (0=prime)
;for (unsigned word i=0; i<sievesize; i++) sieve[i]=0;
.cseg
ldi temp, 0
ldi XH, high(sieve)
ldi XL, low(sieve)

.def countH=r25
.def countL=r24
ldi countH, high(sievesize)
ldi countL, low(sievesize)
init_lp:
        st X+, temp
        sbiw countH:countL, 1
        brne init_lp
.undef countL
.undef countH

.def next_prime_H=r25
.def next_prime_L=r24
;unsigned word next_prime=1;
;find_next(&next_prime);
;while (next_prime != 0){
; println next_prime;
; if (maxCandidate >= next_prime)
```

```
; markmultiples(next_prime);
; find_next(&next_prime);
;}

ldi next_prime_L, low(1)
ldi next_prime_H, high(1)

ldi temp, 0
main_lp:
        rcall find_next  ;advance to next prime number
        cp next_prime_L, temp
        cpc next_prime_H, temp
        breq main_done
        rcall printnum   ;display it
        cp maxCandidateL, next_prime_L
        cpc maxCandidateH, next_prime_H
        brlo main_lp
        rcall markmultiples  ;mark multiples if prime <=
                             ;square root
        rjmp main_lp
main_done:
        rjmp PC
.undef temp
.undef maxCandidateL
.undef maxCandidateH
.undef next_prime_L
.undef next_prime_H

;Functions --------

;void transmit(char c){
; while(!(usart data register ready));
; usart data register=c;
;}
;Transmit byte - blocks until transmit buffer can accept
;a byte
;The param, byte to transmit, is in r24
.def byte_tx=r24
.def temp=r16
transmit:
        push temp
transmit_wait:
```

```
        lds temp, USARTC0_STATUS
        sbrs temp, USART_DREIF_bp  ;wait for Tx buffer to
                                   ;be empty
        rjmp transmit_wait         ;not ready yet
        sts USARTC0_DATA, byte_tx  ;transmit character
        pop temp
        ret
.undef byte_tx
.undef temp

;void printnum(word n){
;n is passed in r25:r24
;digits are pushed on the stack, then popped and
;transmitted followed by cr lf

;push lf
;push cr
;do{
;  push n%10 + '0'
;  n = n/10
;}while(n > 0)
;while(c = pop != '\n')
;  transmit c
;}
.def param_nL = r24
.def param_nH = r25
.def remainder = r23
.def divisor = r18
printnum:
push param_nL
push param_nH
push remainder
push divisor

ldi divisor, 10       ;base 10 numerals
ldi remainder, '\n'   ;place lf on stack
push remainder
ldi remainder, '\r'   ;place cr on stack
push remainder
printnum_div_lp:
        rcall divWordbyByte  ;get digit and remainder
        ori remainder,'0'    ;BCD to ASCII
```

```
        push remainder
        tst param_nL          ;quotient 0 means done
        brne printnum_div_lp
        tst param_nH
        brne printnum_div_lp
;pop digits off stack and transmit
printnum_prt_lp:
        pop param_nL          ;argument for transmit
        rcall transmit
        cpi param_nL, '\n'  ;newline is last character
        brne printnum_prt_lp
pop divisor
pop remainder
pop param_nH
pop param_nL
ret
.undef param_nL
.undef param_nH
.undef remainder
.undef divisor

;Divide word by byte
;Compute the quotient and remainder r25:r24/r18
;Return values:
; r23 = remainder
; r25:r24 = quotient
.def quotient_H = r25      ;also parameter
.def quotient_L = r24
.def remainder = r23
.def divisor = r18
.def counter = r16


divWordByByte:
push counter
clr remainder             ;for remainder
ldi counter, 17           ;loop counter
div_lp:
        rol quotient_L  ;store quot bit and start 24-bit
                        ;shift
        rol quotient_H
        dec counter  ;loop test here
        breq exit  ;exit on 9th iteration
```

```
        rol remainder  ;complete shift into dividend window
        sub remainder, divisor    ;trial division
        brcc goesinto        ;cc means quot bit is 1
        add remainder, divisor    ;undo subtraction
        clc                       ;next quot bit is 0
        rjmp div_lp
goesinto:
 sec          ;next quot bit is 1
 rjmp div_lp
exit:
pop counter
ret
.undef divisor
.undef counter
.undef quotient_H
.undef quotient_L
.undef remainder


;void find_next(word ☒ p){
;locate next prime number in table, set p to 0 if none
; do{
; if (☒p == maxPrime)
; ☒p = 0;
; else
; (☒p) ++;
; while(☒p != 0 && isComposite(☒p)){
;}
.def param_pH = r25 ;argument and parameter are both in
                    ;this register
.def param_pL = r24
.def temp = r16


find_next:
        push temp
find_next_do:
        ldi temp, low(maxPrime)
        cp param_pL, temp
        ldi temp, high(maxPrime)
        cpc param_pH, temp
        brne find_next_else
        clr param_pH
```

```
        clr param_pL
        rjmp find_next_exit
find_next_else:
        adiw param_pH:param_pL, 1
;find_next_endif:
        rcall isComposite
        brcs find_next_do

find_next_exit:
        pop temp
        ret
.undef param_pL
.undef param_pH
.undef temp
;void markmultiples(word n){
; word c=n;
; while (c <= maxPrime-n){
;       c += n;
;       setcomposite(c);
; }
;}
.def param_nL = r24
.def param_nH = r25
.def cL = r22
.def cH = r23
.def maxpH = r21
.def maxpL = r20
markmultiples:
push cL
push cH
push maxpL
push maxpH
push param_nL
push param_nH
movw cH:cL,param_nH:param_nL
ldi maxpH, high(maxPrime)
ldi maxpL, low(maxPrime)
sub maxpl, param_nL
sbc maxpH, param_nH

markmultiples_while:
        cp maxpL, param_nL
```

```
        cpc maxpH, param_nH
        brlo markmultiples_endwhile
        add param_nL, cL
        adc param_nH, cH
        rcall setComposite
        rjmp markmultiples_while

markmultiples_endwhile:
pop param_nH
pop param_nL
pop maxpH
pop maxpL
pop cH
pop cL
ret
.undef param_nL
.undef param_nH
.undef cL
.undef cH
.undef maxpL
.undef maxpH

;boolean isComposite(word n){
;return true (CC set) if is composite
; return sieve[n/8] & (1 << (n & 0x0007)) != 0
;}
.def param_nL = r24
.def param_nH = r25
.def sieveByte = r16
isComposite:
push XH
push XL
push sieveByte
push param_nL
movw XH:XL, param_nH:param_nL   ;determine address of
                                ;byte for n's flag
lsr XH                          ;X = n/8
ror XL
lsr XH
ror XL
lsr XH
ror XL
```

```
;add start address of sieve
subi XL, low(-sieve)
sbci XH, high(-sieve)

ld sieveByte, X      ;copy sieve byte into register
andi param_nL, 7     ;isolate bit position from n

isComposite_lp:      ;shift selected bit into carry flag
      lsr sieveByte
      dec param_nL
      brge isComposite_lp
  ;carry flag has required bit from sieve

pop param_nL
pop sieveByte
pop XL
pop XH
ret
.undef param_nL
.undef param_nH
.undef sieveByte

;void setComposite(word n){
;set the bit for value n to indicate it is composite
; sieve[n/8] |= (1 << (n & 0x0007));
;}
.def param_nL = r24
.def param_nH = r25
.def bitPos = r18
.def bitMask = r19
.def temp = r16
setComposite:
;bit position is least significant 3 bits
push bitPos
push bitMask
push XH
push XL
push temp

;bitPos = n && 0x07
mov bitPos, param_nL
andi bitPos, 0x07
```

```
;bitMask = 1 << bitPos; will require a loop
;implemented as:
;bitMask = 1
;while (bitPos > 0){
; bitMask >> 1
; bitPos -;
;}
ldi bitMask, 1
tst   bitPos
breq setComposite_lp1_exit

setComposite_lp1:
      lsl bitMask
      dec bitPos
      brne setComposite_lp1

setComposite_lp1_exit:
;Move address to X in prep for indirect addressing
;divide X by 8 to get address
;X = X >> 3
movw XH:XL, param_nH:param_nL
lsr XH
ror XL
lsr XH
ror XL
lsr XH
ror XL
;add start address of sieve
subi XL, low(-sieve)
sbci XH, high(-sieve)

;sieve[n/8] |= bitMask
;set bit to indicate composite
ld temp, X
or temp, bitMask
st X, temp

pop temp
pop XL
pop XH
pop bitMask
pop bitPos
```

```
ret
.undef temp
.undef param_nL
.undef param_nH
.undef bitMask
.undef bitPos

;Initialize USART for bi-directional communication
;initUSART:
;2 mhz clock speed, 9600 baud BSEL = 12
.equ BSEL = 12
.def temp = r16

;set baud rate
ldi temp, high(BSEL) & 0x0F
sts USARTC0_BAUDCTRLB, temp
ldi temp, low(BSEL)
sts USARTC0_BAUDCTRLA, temp

;data packet format
;select, asynchronous, no parity, 1 stop, 8 data bits
ldi temp, USART_CMODE_ASYNCHRONOUS_gc|USART_PMODE_
DISABLED_gc \
        |(0<<USART_SBMODE_bp)|USART_CHSIZE_8BIT_gc
sts USARTC0_CTRLC, temp

;Set the transmit pin as output and set high, receive
pin as input (default)
ldi temp, 1<<3  ;PC3
sts    PORTC_OUT,temp  ;configure TXD as 1
sts    PORTC_DIR,temp  ;configure TXD as output

;enable bi-directional communication
;lds temp, USARTC0_CTRLB
ori temp, USART_TXEN_bm | USART_RXEN_bm
sts USARTC0_CTRLB, temp
;USART initialization complete
ret
```

CHAPTER 12

Arrays

A RRAYS ARE COLLECTIONS OF homogeneous data stored in memory at consecutive addresses. Elements of the collection are indexed by an integer; indexing is commonly zero-based, but this is a high-level language decision. At the machine level, all arrays are arrays of bytes (or smallest addressable units). How the bytes are grouped and used is up to the application. Access to individual array elements requires address computations supplied by the programmer.

DECLARING AND USING ARRAYS

Creating an array in assembly language is quite easy. Usually a label is attached to the beginning of the array. This represents the base address of the array. Elements in the array will be located by calculating an offset from this reference point. Indirect and indexed addressing modes are the tools used for array access.

An array in SRAM is allocated using the .byte directive. The operand is the size of the array (in bytes). Arrays contents, like other variables based in SRAM, cannot be initialized before execution begins; the .byte directive simply reserves space. It is also possible to allocate array space dynamically on the hardware stack or the data stack (see local storage for functions) or the heap. Arrays declared in EEPROM can be initialized or not. The .byte directive reserves space; the .db directive reserves and initializes space.

Initialized arrays can also be created in program memory. This is how string literals are typically stored. This type of array might also hold a lookup table to support the needs of an algorithm.

Element Access

High-level languages provide access operators for arrays. These hide most of the details of address computation from the programmer. C allows pointers to arrays to be directly manipulated to access individual elements. Assembly language programs rely on the programmer to utilize the processor capabilities in a variety of ways to process arrays.

The primary tool for array access is indirect addressing. In this case, a register is loaded with the base address of an array and an offset to the specified element is added to it. Array address computations must consider the base address of the array, the index of the element to be located, and the size of the individual data items stored in the array. Array address computations rely on the fact that all elements occupy the same number of bytes. Assuming the zero-based indexing scheme, a typical address computation looks like this.

```
some_array[j] is at address:
base_address_of_some_array + (j * size_of_array_data)
```

Consider an array of words with the label numbers attached to the start of the array. To access numbers[j], we would use an offset of 2j (each word is two bytes). If this array is in SRAM, the following code will access numbers[j], loading the selected array component into register r25:r24. The index of the element to be accessed is assumed to be in R16.

```
clr r25
ldi xH, high(numbers)
ldi xL, low(numbers)
lsl r16 ;*2 since each element is 2 bytes
add xL, r16
adc xH, r25 ;r25 holds a zero
ld r24, x+
ld r25, x
```

Register R25 is cleared to use as a zero for the possible carry in the 16-bit addition. X is set to point to the base address of the array. The array index (R16) is doubled since each element takes two bytes. Once X points to the desired element, it is loaded into R25:R24 using two consecutive indirect loads. Remember that integers are generally stored in little-endian order.

Array Traversals

Indirect addressing with postincrement provides an efficient way to traverse an array from index 0 to the end. Once the pointer is initialized to the base address of the array, postincrementing can be used to sequentially access the bytes of the array. Of course, if the data requires multiple bytes, this will access the bytes of each element one at a time in the order they are found in memory.

Alternatively, when dealing with arrays of multibyte data, programmers often choose to use indirect addressing with displacement. The indirect addressing register always points to the first byte of an array element; a displacement is added to select specific bytes of the data. This allows the bytes of each component to be accessed in any order. In the following example, the second byte of an array element is accessed first. Since X does not support indirect with displacement addressing, a different pointer register (Y or Z) must be used.

```
clr  r25
ldi  zH, high(numbers)
ldi  zL, low(numbers)
lsl  r16
add  zL, r16
adc  zH, r25
ldd  r25, z + 1  ;access high byte first
ldd  r24, z + 0  ;or simply ld r24, z
```

To move to the next element of the array, the program would need to add two to Z; in this example, each array element is two bytes. The adwi instruction is often used for this purpose.

Arrays in program memory (flash) are accessed using Z and the load program memory instruction. Remember that the labels in program memory are word addresses, but LPM requires a byte address. Assuming R16 again contains the index of the element to be accessed, and that astring is an array of characters (bytes) in program memory, the following would load the specified byte into R17:

```
clr  r17
ldi  zH, high(astring <<1)
ldi  zL, low(astring <<1)
add  zL, r16
adc  zH, r17
lpm  r17, z
```

Many processors support an addressing mode not found in the AVR family. This mode, called base-index addressing, is especially suited for array access. One register, called the base register, is set to point to the base address of an array. Another register, called the index register, is set to the desired offset (in bytes) into the array. The base-indexed mode load or store instruction automatically performs the addition of the base and index values to determine the effective address. Only the index register is changed to select different array elements. Some processors even include a variation of this addressing mode that includes an offset in addition to the index and base registers. The hardware adds all three values to determine the effective address of the array element.

In the AVR processor, the base-index calculation is done manually, and the calculated location is placed in one of the registers supporting indirect addressing (X, Y, or Z). When a displacement is used in addition to the element address, the programmer must choose between registers Y and Z, as X does not support a displacement component.

MULTIDIMENSIONAL ARRAYS

High-level languages generally support multiple dimensioned arrays. However, there are two fundamentally different ways to organize such arrays in memory. The simpler organization "flattens" the array to a linear arrangement of data in memory. That is, a multidimensional array is actually stored in a one-dimensional array. For a two-dimensional array organized in this fashion, the elements of the first row might be stored sequentially, followed by the elements of the second row, and so on. The elements could be stored in other orders. For example, the array could start with the elements in the first column, followed by the second column, and so on. The first organization is called row major order (C implements arrays in this way); the second organization is called column major order (FORTRAN uses this organization). Figure 12.1 shows an array with three rows and four bytes in each row stored in row major order. From left to right, the elements would be arr[0][0], arr[0][1], arr[0][2], arr[0][3], arr[1][0], and so on.

Since each element of the array is a fixed size, and all rows or columns have the same number of elements, the address of any element can be efficiently computed.

Assuming row major order, the address of the item at row j and column k is:

```
base_address + (j * number_of_columns + k) * size_of_data
```

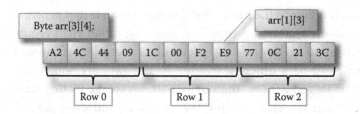

FIGURE 12.1   A two-dimensional array stored in row major order.

This formula can be easily extended to more than two dimensions. Arrays stored in the manner just described occupy one contiguous block of memory.

Assuming names is a two-dimensional array of characters flattened to row major order, the following code would load the character at names[j][k] into R16. Assume R17 is the row, j, and R18 is the column, k. Each row is 10 characters long.

```
;r16 = names[j][k]
ldi xH, high(names)
ldi xL, low(names)
;multiply row index by 10
ldi r16, 10
mul r16, r17
;add to X to point to row
add xL, r0
adc xH, r1
;next add k, the offset into the row
clr r16  ;high byte of widened r18
add xL, r18
adc xH, r16
ld r16, x
```

Many languages provide another form of multidimensional array organization that does not require the rows (or columns) of the array to be stored near each other (in contiguous memory locations). This hierarchical organization represents a multidimensional array as an array of (pointers to) arrays. At the outermost level, there is an array of pointers or references to other arrays; each address/reference is that of another array which is either another array of arrays, or an array of actual data items (or references to data items). Figure 12.2 shows how this type of array might be stored in memory.

One advantage to the hierarchical organization is that arrays can have their contents scattered throughout memory, rather than requiring the entire array to be in one contiguous block. Another advantage is that each row can be a different length. Such arrays are sometimes called ragged or jagged arrays. The obvious disadvantage to this structure is the extra storage required for the arrays of addresses and the time required to follow references through several levels of indirection to get to the actual data.

Address computations in hierarchical arrays are iterative. The first subscript, usually called the row, is used to access the address of the array containing the elements of that row. The second subscript, often called the column, is used to index into this array to find either data or the address of another array. This process repeats until the last subscript is used and the address of the actual data is found.

Assuming `names` is a hierarchical array of characters in SRAM, the following code would load the character at `names[j][k]` into R16. Assume R17 is the row, j, and R18 is the column, k.

```
;r16 = names[j][k]
clr  r16
ldi  xH, high(names)
ldi  xL, low(names)
lsl  r17  ;the outer array is an array of words
add  xL, r17
adc  xH, r16
```

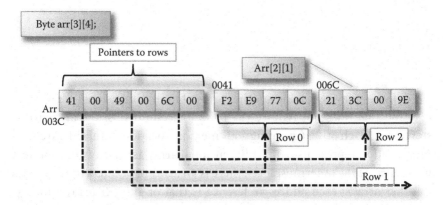

FIGURE 12.2   A two-dimensional array represented as an array of arrays.

```
ld yL, x+
ld yH, x  ;Y now points to the row array of char
add yL, r18  ;index to column
adc yH, r16
ld r16, y
```

The original array is an array of addresses, each requiring two bytes, so j is doubled before indexing into the array. The address of the specified row (an array of characters) is then copied into Y. The index into this array (the second subscript) is added, and then the character is accessed. The names (rows) do not have to be the same length, however, if they are not, there must be some way to determine the length of the array of characters in each row.

Array Sizes

None of the address computations illustrated so far considered whether the calculated address was inside the physical storage allocated to the array. Checking the legality of actual subscripts is called *bounds checking*. If array bounds are to be respected, additional care must be taken at each array access to ensure legal addresses are used.

When reserving space for an array, it is customary to define a constant that indicates the maximum number of elements of the array. For example,

```
.equ MAX_ELTS = 12
.equ ELT_SZ = 2
numbers:  .byte MAX_ELTS*ELT_SZ
```

This constant can be used in the program to verify that a subscript is within range before calculating an address. If R16 holds the desired array subscript, then testing legality is quite easy. In this example, MAX_ELTS must be no greater than 255.

```
cpi R16, MAX_ELTS
brsh bad_subscript
```

The test uses an unsigned compare since subscripts should be nonnegative integers. Another way to ensure legal access in a one dimensional array is to compare the computed address of the data item against the address at the end of the array. To facilitate this, a symbol is used to record the ending address of the array.

```
numbers: .byte MAX_ELTS*ELT_SZ
numbers_end:
```

The symbol `numbers_end` represents the address just past the end of the array. If X holds the computed address of an array element, then it should be smaller than `numbers_end` (and greater than or equal to the base address of the array). This type of comparison is sometimes used in array traversals to avoid the overhead of a loop counter; X is initialized to the base of the array, and incremented to access successive elements. When it reaches the ending address, the loop terminates. To facilitate the repeated comparison, the array's ending address is generally loaded into a register (pair) before starting the loop.

```
;sequentially process all elements of an array of words
ldi yH, high(numbers)
ldi yL, low(numbers)
ldi r25, high(numbers_end)
ldi r24, low(numbers_end)

next_item:
. . .
;Array processing
. . .
adwi yH:yL, ELT_SZ  ;increment pointer to next element
cp yL, r24
cpc yH, r25
brlo next_item
```

If registers are at a premium, the compare of the low part of the address could be replaced with a compare immediate:

```
cpi xL, low(numbers_end)
```

However, there is no compare immediate *with carry* instruction to finish the comparison, so two compares are needed, each with their own conditional branch:

```
cpi xL, low(numbers_end)
brne next_item
```

```
cpi xH, high(numbers_end)
brne next_item
```

Of course, a counter could also be used to terminate the loop when the end of the array is reached. There are generally no markers in memory that will allow a program to determine where an array begins or ends, or how many rows it has or the size of a row. It is up to the programmer to keep careful track of the dimensions and bounds of each array.

STRINGS

One very common data type manipulated by programs is a *string*. Fundamentally, strings are stored as arrays of characters. The array can be sized to exactly fit the string, or it may be larger than necessary to allow the string to expand (e.g., if characters are to be appended). Determining where a string ends can be accomplished in several ways. These variations lead to different string representations.

Fixed-Length Strings

If all strings in a program are of the same length, then the amount of storage for each string will exactly match the string's length. For example, if all strings are 10 characters, then the following would allocate space for one string, and an array of five such strings:

```
.equ strlen = 10
name: .byte str_len
.equ namelist_SZ = 5
namelist: .byte str_len*namelist_SZ
```

In this case, all strings will need to be exactly 10 characters. If shorter strings are needed, they could be padded with a special character, such as the space (0x20) character. This type of string representation is sometimes referred to as *fixed length*.

Variable Length Strings

It is far more common for string sizes to vary widely in a program, requiring the so-called *variable length* strings. In this case, two sizes must be known for each string: the size of the container (array) and the length of the string currently stored in the container. In some representations, the container size can be calculated from the string size.

Strings in C are stored in an array of char. The end of the string is marked by the nul character (ASCII value 0: '\0'). Usually, the container size is one more than the length of the string it contains (to account for the null), however, in some cases the container is larger than the space needed for the contained string. The C language supports this representation through a string function library and string literals. In C, the literal "abc" represents the address of an array of four characters; the last byte will contain nul. Using a literal in C causes storage allocation for the array and produces code to initialize it (if necessary).

Sometimes null-delimited strings are called ASCIIZ strings. Note that such strings can be stored in an array exactly matching the length of the string (plus one), or the array can be larger. Bytes following the nul character are simply not part of the string. Again, it is up to the programmer to keep track of the physical bounds of the array containing a string.

If strings can only contain ASCII characters, then the fact that ASCII codes (which range from $00 through $7F) all have a zero in bit 7 can be exploited to eliminate the trailing nul byte. The last character of a string could be marked as such by setting bit 7 in its binary code. The original character is easily recovered by clearing bit 7.

Determining the length of strings in the above representations requires counting the characters until the sentinel is located. This is inefficient if the string length must be calculated frequently. Another string representation encodes the length of each string along with the array of characters. The first byte (or two bytes) of the array can hold an unsigned integer.

Alternatively, a string could be a pair of items: a length (int) and a pointer to the array of characters (char *). This makes every string value the same size, which is nice for an array of strings. Note that a string in this case does not include storage for the characters themselves; this must be allocated separately and linked to the string through the pointer field. The arrays holding the characters of the strings can be any length, but they are stored apart from the actual string information. Java String objects are implemented in this way; the String object contains a reference to an array of characters.

Some extensions of the standard Pascal language represented strings as an array of bytes. The length of the string was stored in the first byte (or first two bytes) of the array. Such strings are sometimes called Pascal strings (or P-strings). P-string arrays can be sized exactly to the string, or have a fixed size array (partially used) to simplify storage allocation and facilitate changes to the strings that alter their lengths.

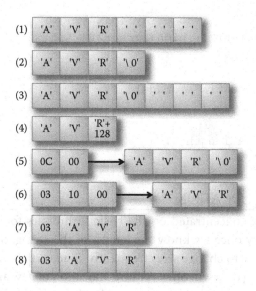

FIGURE 12.3   Memory allocation for various string representations: (1) fixed size with padding, (2) ASCIIZ, (3) ASCIIZ with extra space, (4) high-bit delimiter, (5) pointer to ASCIIZ, (6) length and pointer to char array, (7) p-string, and (8) p-string with extra storage.

Examples of the definition of each of these types of string literals in program memory is shown here. The memory allocation is shown in Figure 12.3.

```
;Define string literal "AVR" in program memory

;Fixed size (6 bytes, space padded)
.db "AVR"

;ASCIIZ version (max length 3)
.db "AVR", 0

;ASCIIZ version with extra space (max length 6)
.db "AVR", 0, " "

;High-bit delimiter version (max length 3)
.db "AV", 'R' + 128

;Pointer to ASCIIZ string (max length 3)
.dw avrstr1
avrstr1: .db "AVR", 0
```

```
;Length and Pointer to array (max length 3)
.db 3, low(avrstr2), high(avrstr2)
avrstr2: .db "AVR"

;P-string (no extra storage)
.db 3, "AVR"

;P-string (max length 5)
.db 3, "AVR"
```

STORAGE ALLOCATION

So far, we have concentrated on the basic techniques for storing string data in memory once we know the length of the string. Strings in programs often have to change sizes frequently. Since arrays are a fixed size, changes to string data will often require allocation of new arrays. In high-level languages, programmers use variables to gain access to strings. The variable can either represent the location of the string itself, or it can represent the address of information used to indirectly access the string data. Remember that variables do not exist in assembly language. If you wish to refer to a string that will be at a fixed memory location, then a label can be used. However, the memory dedicated to that string will be fixed at assembly time and cannot be expanded during execution to accommodate longer strings.

Dynamic Memory Allocation

To allow a string to grow or shrink, we need to have the ability to allocate new storage containers during execution. This chore is generally handled automatically by high-level languages (or the language provides explicit tools to accomplish the task). In assembly language, we will have to invent a scheme to manage our own memory. If the location of a string must change during execution, we will need to use a pointer to access it. If a string's length is changed, then we often will need to allocate new space for the new string, copying some or all of the characters from the old to the new, and adjusting a pointer to point to the new string instead of the old. The old string will perhaps not be needed any more and its storage can be reclaimed for other use.

Strings, and more generally arrays, are the second situation we have encountered that requires sophisticated memory allocation at runtime. The first encounter was parameters and local variables in a function. This was solved using a stack structure. Strings and arrays can be allocated in the stack, but this is not always desirable. Stack space should be considered a premium; arrays and strings often require a lot of space. In addition, the need to resize arrays at almost any time does not fit well with the allocation model used for stack-based parameters and local storage.

The term *dynamic memory allocation* refers to management of memory in which blocks can be randomly allocated and deallocated (to potentially be reused) while a program is running. According to the traditional C program model, RAM is divided into three sections, static storage, the stack, and the heap. Static storage is used for variables that can stay at the same address for the entire life of the program. Allocation of static storage is determined before execution begins. Fixed-length strings can easily be allocated in this manner. The stack is generally used for parameters and local storage. If these include arrays or strings which are large, or whose size will change during the function call, only space for a pointer to the structure will be allocated in the stack. The heap is then used for the data areas that must grow or shrink (in a manner more complex than that of a stack) during execution.

String Constants and String Initialization

In AVR programs, string literals are initially defined in program memory, effectively creating string constants. If string data must be changed by the program, space in SRAM must be allocated for the strings. The SRAM strings must then be suitably initialized by the program. Storage in SRAM for the string variable can be allocated statically (at assemble time) using the .byte directive, or dynamically (during execution) on the stack or elsewhere in free memory. If the string is to be initialized from a string literal in program memory, then the characters of the string must be copied into the allocated storage from program memory where they were placed by the assembler.

The following code illustrates the declaration and initialization of a string variable in SRAM. In this example, p-string representation is used:

```
rcall copyPStr
rjmp pc

.dseg
;var pstring[10] input_string = "AVR"
input_string: .byte 10
```

```
.cseg
input_string_LITERAL: .db 3, "AVR"  ;p-string format

copyPStr:
;initialize SRAM array from literal in cseg
ldi zH, high(input_string_LITERAL*2)
ldi zL, low(input_string_LITERAL*2)
ldi xH, high(input_string)
ldi xL, low(input_string)
lpm r16, Z+  ;get the length of the string
st X+, r16
tst r16
lp:
   breq done
   lpm r17, Z+
   st X+, r17
   dec r16
   rjmp lp
done:
   ret
```

The call to the copyPStr function would likely be located whenever the microcontroller is reset. In this example, the working storage for the string is 10 bytes of static storage. This memory is set aside by the assembler and cannot be expanded at runtime (other variables may occupy the bytes immediately before or after this area). Note that the allocation statement reserves enough space for any string of, at most, nine characters, the first byte holding the current length of the string. The initialization loop uses the first byte of the literal as a counter to copy only the actual characters of the string. The remaining bytes of the allocated array are uninitialized and should not be expected to contain any particular values.

Storage for a string variable local to function might be allocated in the function's stack frame (allocation record). The allocation may be a block of bytes to hold the characters of the string, or simply a pointer to an array. If a pointer is used, then the actual array must be allocated elsewhere, probably from the heap. The copyPStr function could be modified to accept arguments for the source and destination arrays to facilitate initialization of the array where appropriate within the function.

Dynamic allocation of storage for strings (or arrays) is a fairly complex task. A basic discussion of this technique will be covered in a later section.

String Operations

Typical string operations include determining the string length, concatenating strings, searching for substrings, extracting substrings, and comparing strings. The implementation of these operations depends on the string representation in use. Determining the length of a P-string, for example, is trivial. If ASCIIZ representation is used, then a counting loop must be employed. Concatenation operations must take into account the size of the container used to hold the string and avoid overwriting memory belonging to other variables. If strings can grow and shrink during their lifetime, enough storage for each must be allocated initially to meet these needs, or some type of dynamic allocation will be required.

The following function illustrates how an ASCIIZ string's length can be determined. The address of the string (located in SRAM) will be passed in R25:R24, which will also serve as the return value.

```
stringlen:
        movw zH:zL, r25:r24        ;make Z point to string
        ldi r25, high(-1)          ;count = -1
        ldi r24, low(-1)
strlen_nextchar:
        adiw r25:r24, 1            ;count ++
        ld r23, Z+                 ;get next char
        tst r23                    ;look for nul
        brne strlen_nextchar
ret
```

The function begins with –1 as the count since the loop body is always executed at least once and does not count the nul byte which is not part of the string. The return value is a 16-bit integer even though most strings in the AVR environment will be much smaller.

The following function concatenates two ASCIIZ strings. It is assumed the first string is stored in an array that is large enough to accommodate the extra characters from the other string. The function receives two pointers: R25:R24 is string one, R23:R22 is string two. It freely uses registers X, Z, and R23.

```
concat:
        movw zH:zL, r25:r24  ;make Z point to first string
        movw xH:xL, r23:r22  ;make X point to second string
concat_nextchar:
        ld r23, Z+   ;locate the end of first string
```

```
        tst r23
        brne concat_nextchar
        sbiw Z, 1     ;back up to the nul byte
concat_copychar:
        ld r23, X+    ;copy characters (incl. nul) from
                      ;second string
        st Z+, r23    ;to the end of the first string
        tst r23
        brne concat_copychar
ret
```

Here is the same routine, but designed to work for p-strings. It also uses R22 for temporary storage.

```
concatP:
        movw zH:zL, r25:r24   ;make Z point to first string
        movw xH:xL, r23:r22   ;make X point to second string
        ld r23, X    ;get length of second string
        ld r22, Z    ;get length of first string
        add r23, r22   ;calculate new string length
        st Z+, r23    ;and store at front of first string
        clr r23
        add zL, r22    ;advance Z to end of first string
        adc zH, r23
        ld r23, X+    ;get second string's length again
concatP_nextChar:
        tst r23    ;check if all characters copied
        breq concatP_exit
        ld r24, X+    ;copy next character of second string
        st Z+, r24    ;to the end of the first string
        dec r23
        rjmp concatP_nextChar
concatP_exit:
ret
```

You should take time to write a program to test these functions on a variety of strings in the simulator environment.

DYNAMIC MEMORY ALLOCATION

When an assembly language program is designed, care must be taken that variables will be assigned to appropriate memory locations during each variable's lifetime. High-level languages classify variables accord-ing to scope and lifetime. Variables that are local to a function generally have a lifetime that corresponds to the time the function is active. This type of storage allocation is easily achieved by reserving space in the function's stack frame, or binding the variable to a register for the dura-tion of the function. Such variables are sometimes called *automatic*, and may live in different memory locations at different times during the life of the program.

Some variables local to functions must retain their values between function invocations. Such variables are termed *static local* variables. Storage for these variables must be allocated and initialized before the function code is executed for the first time. Allocation is usually per-formed by the assembler (with .byte); however, dynamic allocation could occur when the function is called for the first time. Once such a variable is bound to a memory location (or register), it remains at that location for the rest of the program's lifetime.

Global variables are those that can be accessed from any place in a pro-gram. They are generally static by nature and occupy storage reserved by the assembler, and possibly initialized during the startup code of the appli-cation. The difference between static local and global is really a scope issue; access to the memory associated with a variable name is limited by scope. In assembly languages, there are generally no scoping rules, so a static memory location can be accessed from anywhere.

Another type of memory use is called *dynamic allocation*. Storage that is dynamically allocated is typically not named (labeled), but is managed by keeping track of the allocated and unallocated areas. Functions to allocate and deallocate different sized memory areas can be provided by an operating system, or managed directly by the program. This type of allocation is very flexible, but more difficult to manage than the ones described earlier.

A Heap for Strings

To illustrate dynamic allocation, a very simple memory management model will be presented. SRAM will be divided into three areas: the static area in the lower addresses, the stack in the upper area, and the dynamic area in the middle. We will refer to the dynamic area as the *heap*. A label, heap_start will represent the address of the first byte of the heap, and heap_end will represent the address just past the last byte of the heap. The heap will contain heap_end - heap_start bytes.

One of the difficult aspects of memory management in the heap is distinguishing between addresses that are currently in use, and those that are available. The complication occurs because the parts in use are usually scattered throughout the heap. Our heap will be used only for strings. To facilitate our very simple heap management technique, the only restriction we will place on the string contents is that the character 0xFF may not be used in a string currently allocated by an application.

We will use this byte value, 0xFF, to distinguish between used and unused space in the heap. To initialize the heap allocation system, we will write 0xFF to all of the bytes in the heap area. We will write functions to allocate space for a string and to deallocate that space when the string is no longer needed.

A function named salloc will allocate space for a string when called. It expects the size of the memory block required (*n*) to be passed in R24. This function will simply find (*n* + 1) consecutive bytes in the heap that are not currently in use (these bytes will all have $FF in them). All but the last byte will be replaced with nul values. A single 0xFF will be left at the very end of the allocated area to allow us to later identify the extent of this specific block. The function returns the address of the allocated string (or 0 if it was unable to fill the request) in R25:R24.

The sfree function will expect an address of a previously allocated string in R25:R24. Its job is to return the previously allocated block to the available heap. It will write 0xFF into the string area until it encounters an existing 0xFF which marks the end of the returned memory block.

PROGRAM 12.1   Heap Management for Strings

```
;Program 12.1
;Heap for string allocation

;Heap management for strings is illustrated by a simple
;application that
;creates an array of strings, removes some strings from
;the array freeing
;memory in the heap, and then adds more strings.

;The array of pointers to strings is located in lower SRAM
;The stack is at the end of SRAM
;The heap is in between

;Programmer: TM
```

```
;Date: 5/2010
;Platform: STK-500
;Device: ATMEGA16A

;Simulator execution only - no I/O

.include "m16def.inc"

rjmp main

;A list of P-strings for testing
names: .db \
        3,"Tim", \
        6,"Jeremy", \
        4,"Roni", \
        7,"Charles", \
        5,"Jamie", \
        6,"Esther", \
        0
;These strings will be added to the list after some are
removed morenames: .db \
        7,"Abigail", \
        2,"Um", \
        8,"Francine", \
        2,"Jo", \
        6,"Justin", \
        0

;MAX_NAMES is the sum of the number of names in the
;above lists
.equ MAX_NAMES = 6 + 5

.dseg
;P-string * name_list[MAX_NAMES]
name_list: .byte MAX_NAMES*2

.equ STACK_SIZE = 64
.equ STATIC_SIZE = MAX_NAMES*2

.cseg

.def temp = r16
```

```
main:
ldi temp, high(RAMEND)
out SPH, temp
ldi temp, low(RAMEND)
out SPL, temp

;initialize the heap of strings
rcall sinit

.def numNames = r18
ldi numNames, 0      ;the name list starts empty

;Load names from CSEG into SRAM, allocating space in
;heap
ldi zH, high(names*2)      ;pass source of string list
ldi zL, low(names*2)
ldi yH, high(name_list)   ;pass address of name array
ldi yL, low(name_list)
rcall addNames
add numNames, r24

;Remove all names with initial letter < 'M'
mov r24, numNames
ldi yH, high(name_list)   ;pass address of name array
ldi yL, low(name_list)
rcall removeSmaller
mov numNames, r24

;Add morenames to list
ldi zH, high(morenames*2) ;pass source of string list
ldi zL, low(morenames*2)
ldi yH, high(name_list)   ;address of name array
ldi yL, low(name_list)
ldi temp, 2  ;calculate end of array to append more names
mul numNames, temp
add yL, r0
adc yH, r1
rcall addNames
add numNames, r24

rjmp PC
.undef numNames
```

```
.undef temp

;int addNames(P-string * src, string * dest)
;src (Z) points to list of P-strings in flash terminated
;with null
;dest (Y) points to empty array of pointers to strings
;returns number of strings added to the array
addNames:
.def str_len = r16
.def count = r17
.def tempchar = r18
      push zH
      push zL
      push xH
      push xL
      push tempchar
      push count
      push str_len
      ldi count, 0 ;count number of names added
addNames_next:
      lpm str_len, Z+    ;get string size
      tst str_len
      breq addNames_exit ;zero length ends function

      ;allocate space for string
      mov r24, str_len
      inc r24        ;need str length + 1 bytes
      rcall salloc
      st Y+, r24  ;store address of string into array
      st Y+, r25

      ;copy string to array
      movw X, r25:r24
      st X+, str_len     ;string length into first byte
addNames_copy:
      lpm tempchar, Z+   ;copy string characters
      st X+, tempchar
      dec str_len
      brne addNames_copy

      inc count     ;one more name is in the list
      rjmp addNames_next
```

```
addNames_exit:
      mov r24, count        ;return value
      pop str_len
      pop count
      pop tempchar
      pop xL
      pop xH
      pop zL
      pop zH
      ret
.undef tempchar
.undef count
.undef str_len

;int removeSmaller(string * list, int size)
;remove names in list with first letter < 'M'
;return new list size in r24
;list is in Y
;size is passed in r24
removeSmaller:
.def size = r24
.def index = r16
.def temp = r17
.def endlistH = r9
.def endlistL = r8
      push index
      push temp
      push endlistH
      push endlistL
      push zH
      push zL
      push yH
      push yL
      push r0
      push r1
      movw endlistH:endlistL, Y
      ;calculate address past end of array
      ldi temp, 2  ;array elements are 2 bytes
      mul size, temp
      add endlistL, r0
      adc endlistH, r1

      ldi index, 0 ;current array index
```

```
removeSmaller_nxt:
        ;if (index < size) check current name
        cp index, size
        brsh removeSmaller_exit
        ;check first letter of name
        ld zL, Y        ;point Z to name
        ldd zH, Y + 1
        ldd temp, Z + 1      ;get first character of name
        cpi temp, 'M'        ;find and remove names < 'M'
        brsh removeSmaller_not

        ;remove current name
        push r24
        push r25
        movw r25:r24, Z     ;free storage associated with
                            ;name
        rcall sfree
        pop r25
        pop r24
        ;copy last pointer in array to current location
        movw Z, endlistH:endlistL
        sbiw Z, 2     ;Z is new end of list address
        ld temp, Z    ;namelist[index] = namelist[size-1]
        st Y, temp
        ldd temp, Z + 1
        std Y + 1, temp
        movw endlistH:endlistL, Z   ;update end of list
                                    ;address
        dec size        ;one less name in list
        rjmp removeSmaller_nxt   ;Y and index are
                                 ;unchanged

removeSmaller_not:
        ;Do not remove this name, advance Y and index
        inc index
        adiw Y, 2
        rjmp removeSmaller_nxt
removeSmaller_exit:
        pop r1
        pop r0
        pop yL
        pop yH
```

```
        pop  zL
        pop  zH
        pop  endlistL
        pop  endlistH
        pop  temp
        pop  index
        ret
.undef size
.undef index
.undef temp
.undef endlistL
.undef endlistH


;----------------------------------
;Heap management routines

;Our heap should not be so large it bogs down the
;simulator
.equ MAX_HEAP = 300
.set HEAP_SIZE = SRAM_SIZE - (STACK_SIZE + STATIC_SIZE)
.if HEAP_SIZE > MAX_HEAP
.set HEAP_SIZE = MAX_HEAP
.endif

.equ EMPTY = $FF  ;used to mark unused locations in heap

.dseg
heap_start: .byte HEAP_SIZE
heap_end:
.cseg

;Initialize the heap
sinit:
.def temp = r16
        push XH
        push XL
        push temp
        ldi  XH, high(heap_start)
        ldi  XL, low(heap_start)
        ldi  temp, EMPTY
sinit_lp:
        st   X+, temp
```

```
        cpi XH, high(heap_end)
        brne sinit_lp
        cpi XL, low(heap_end)
        brne sinit_lp

        pop temp
        pop XL
        pop XH
        ret
.undef temp

;char * salloc(byte sz)
;r24 is size of block to allocate, allocate r24+1 bytes
;last byte will have EMPTY terminator
;return address of block in R25:R24 (0 if none found)
salloc:
.def count = r24
.def temp = r23
        push XH
        push XL
        push temp
        ldi XH, high(heap_start)
        ldi XL, low(heap_start)
        subi count, -2      ;need n+2 consecutive EMPTY's
        push count   ;save n+2 on stack
        dec count    ;first allocation area needs only n+1
                     ;EMPTY's
salloc_nextfree:
        ;fail if past the end of the heap
        cpi XH, high(heap_end)
        brne salloc_nextfree1
        cpi XL, low(heap_end)
        brne salloc_nextfree1

;heap did not contain a large enough block
        pop count
        pop temp
        pop XL
        pop XH
        clr r24      ;failed
        clr r25
        ret
```

```
salloc_nextfree1:   ;count off EMPTY's til count==0
     ld temp, X+
     cpi temp, EMPTY
     brne salloc_restart
     dec count
     brne salloc_nextfree
     rjmp salloc_found


salloc_restart:
     pop count
     push count
     rjmp salloc_nextfree


;found a large enough block
salloc_found:
     sbiw X, 1  ;back up to last EMPTY
     pop count
     subi count, 2  ;fill n bytes with $00
     clr r25
salloc_allocate:
     st -X, r25
     dec count
     brne salloc_allocate


;copy address to return registers
     movw r25:r24, X
     pop temp
     pop XL
     pop XH
     ret
.undef temp
.undef count


;void sfree(char * blk)
;Free the block of memory passed as an argument by
;filling it with EMPTY
;Arg is in r25:r24
sfree:
.def temp = r24
.def empty_code = r25
     push XH
```

```
        push XL
        push temp
        push empty_code

        movw X, r25:r24  ;X points to start of block
        ldi empty_code, EMPTY
sfree_deallocate:
        ld temp, X
        cp temp, empty_code  ;stop when byte in array is
                             ;EMPTY
        st X+, empty_code  ;mark heap memory as free
        brne sfree_deallocate

        pop empty_code
        pop temp
        pop XL
        pop XH
        ret
.undef temp
.undef empty_code
```

Program 12.1 is designed for execution in the simulator only. Watch the heap area as the program adds strings to the name list and the removes some of them. When the second set of names is added to the list, some of the freed memory will be reused.

This simple heap management scheme will support dynamic allocation of any type of storage. It is subject to corruption by the application if a 0xFF byte is stored anywhere in the allocated memory block by the application, the 0xFF marker at the end of the allocation area is overwritten by some other value, or an invalid address is passed to sfree.

The heap is likely to become fragmented over time; there may be a lot of free space, but it may only be available in small chunks. In this case, requests for memory to hold a long string will fail. On the other hand, if a newly freed block is adjacent to a free area, the two areas are automatically joined into a single larger area that may be reused. The allocation scheme is also somewhat inefficient, requiring a sequential search of all of the bytes of the heap to fulfill allocation requests.

STRUCTURES

Arrays are a fundamental nonscalar data type. They allow a homogeneous collection of data to be stored in a large block of storage, referred to by a single name or address. Structs (structures) are a second fundamental nonscalar data type. The term struct is a keyword in C and C++ used to declare this type of data collection. A struct allows the combination of heterogeneous data under a single address or variable name. Structs are the foundation for objects. They are also similar to a simple database record. The members of a struct are sometimes called fields. Although fields may be named, the essential organizational detail is that a particular field will be located at a specific offset from the address of the struct. Indirect addressing with displacement can be used to access a struct: one register holds the address of the struct and a displacement is used to access items within the struct.

A simple struct to represent a date would combine three fields: the day, the month, and the year. Suppose the day is represented as a 2-digit BCD value, the month as three characters, and the year as a 4-digit BCD value. One Date would occupy 6 bytes. The following declaration sets up storage for two Date structs. It also defines symbols that represent the offsets into the struct for each field. Figure 12.4 depicts two Date structs in memory.

```
.dseg
.equ DATE_LEN = 6
a_Date: .byte DATE_LEN
.equ date_day = 0    ;1 byte (2 digits)
.equ date_mon = 1    ;3 bytes
.equ date_year = 4   ;2 bytes (4 digits)
b_Date: .byte DATE_LEN
```

The offsets, defined just once, are for any Date struct allocated in a program. The following code segment sets the two Date variables to 3 JAN 2006 and 31 DEC 2009, respectively.

```
ldi r16, $03
sts a_Date + date_day, r16
ldi r16, 'J'
```

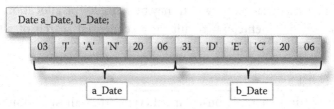

FIGURE 12.4   Two Date structs initialized to 3 JAN 2006 and 31 DEC 2009.

```
sts a_Date + date_mon, r16
ldi r16, 'A'
sts a_Date + date_mon + 1, r16
ldi r16, 'N'
sts a_Date + date_mon + 2, r16
ldi r16, $20
sts a_Date + date_year, r16
ldi r16, $06
sts a_Date + date_year + 1, r16

ldi r16, $31
sts b_Date + date_day, r16
ldi r16, 'D'
sts b_Date + date_mon, r16
ldi r16, 'E'
sts b_Date + date_mon + 1, r16
ldi r16, 'C'
sts b_Date + date_mon + 2, r16
ldi r16, $20
sts b_Date + date_year, r16
ldi r16, $09
sts b_Date + date_year + 1, r16
```

In this case, the offsets are added directly to the address of each Date variable by the assembler. Direct addressing is used. This is not possible if the address of the struct is not known by an assembly label. The next example illustrates a function that can initialize a Date struct. The function receives the address of a Date struct in R25:R24. The day, month, and year are passed in other registers. Indirect addressing with displacement is used to access the date fields.

```
;void dateset(Date * date, byte day, byte[3] mon,
;byte[2] yr);
date_set:
      movw Z, R25:R24
      std Z + date_day, R23   ;params in R23,22,...
      std Z + date_mon, R22
      std Z + date_mon + 1, R21
      std Z + date_mon + 2, R20
      std Z + date_year, R19
      std Z + date_year + 1, R18
      ret
```

Accessing fields in this way can also be applied to an array of Dates. If Z points to any element of such an array, the offsets can be used to get or set the fields. Array indexing would take into account that each element is DATE_LEN bytes.

Linked Lists

A struct (or at least the struct concept) is needed to implement linked lists. Each element of a linked list must contain some data and an address (pointing to the next element in the list). Here is a simple struct for a linked list of bytes:

```
.equ Listnode_LEN = 3   ;size of node
.equ Listnode_data = 0  ;a single byte
.equ Listnode_nextL = 1  ;an address (word)
.equ Listnode_nextH = 2
```

If Z points to a Listnode, the following statements will copy the current Listnode's data into R16 and then make Z point to the next node of the list. This is the foundation of a linked list traversal.

```
ldd R16, Z + Listnode_data
ldd R25, Z + Listnode_nextH
ldd R24, Z + Listnode_nextL
movw zH:zL, R25:R24
```

Note that the pointer cannot be copied directly into Z or the reference would be incorrect after the first half of the address is changed. Registers 25 and 24 are used as a temporary location to accomplish the change to Z. This code might appear be in a loop to iterate through the nodes of the list. When Z is zero, the end of the list has been reached (assuming a standard single linked list implementation and zero representing a null pointer).

Allocating storage for Listnodes can be done using a dynamic approach as discussed in the section on dynamic storage, or an array of Listnodes can be created, and used to manage the Listnode storage. In this case, the Listnodes in the array would be initially linked together to form the free list. Nodes are removed from this list when allocated, and returned to this list when freed by the application. Maintaining a free list eliminates the need to search for a memory location of the correct size for a Listnode. The following code allocates an array of 10 Listnodes:

```
.equ MAXNODES = 10
ln_space: .byte MAXNODES * Listnode_LEN
ln_free: .byte 2; pointer to first free node
```

This function initializes the free space list. The first free node will be at the end of the array. The variable ln_free will point to this node. The first node in the array will be the last node in the linked list. Its next field is set to null. Figure 12.5 shows the initialized free list.

```
Listnode_init:
      ldi zH, high(ln_space)    ;Z points to first node
      ;in array
      ldi zL, low(ln_space)
      clr xH  ;this holds address of next free
             ;(initially null)
      clr xL
      ldi r25, MAXNODES   ;count the number of nodes to
                         ;be initialized
Listnode_init_loop:
      std Z + Listnode_nextL, xL ;store address of next
                                ;free
      std Z + Listnode_nextH, xH
      movw X, Z ;X points to 'previous' node
      adiw Z, Listnode_LEN ;Z points to next node in array
      dec r25
      brne Listnode_init_loop
      sts ln_free,xL     ;pointer to the first node in
                        ;the free list
      sts ln_free + 1,xH
ret
```

Methods to allocate nodes and to free nodes need to be written. Allocating a node is accomplished by removing the first node from the

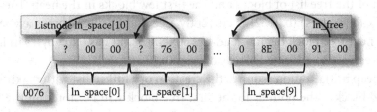

FIGURE 12.5   A linked list of 10 free Listnodes, just initialized.

free list, and returning its address. Freeing a node (this function is passed the address of the node to be returned to the free list) is accomplished by inserting the node into the free list at the beginning. The free list acts like a stack of available nodes.

If the number of available nodes is less than 256, then some memory conservation can be realized by using an array index instead of an address for each node's next field. If the next field is k, then it references the node at ln_space[k]. This adds a small array index calculation to linked list traversals to convert the index to an address.

A BETTER HEAP

The simple heap management routine presented earlier in this chapter is especially inefficient as every byte of a block of memory must be scanned to determine the size of the block. Additionally, as more blocks are allocated, the used blocks must also be scanned in the search for free memory locations. Using linked lists, we can create a much more efficient heap memory management routine. We will maintain a list of free memory blocks as a linked list. This will allow us to locate an appropriately sized memory block to fill allocation requests. The blocks can be used for any purpose, not just string data, and there will be no restrictions on what values can be stored in the bytes of the allocated blocks. The blocks will be maintained in order by address to facilitate merging of adjacent free blocks to minimize the impact of fragmentation.

We will limit the size of blocks to 256 total bytes. Each free block will begin with an unsigned byte representing the size of the data in the block (maximum 255 bytes), followed by a 2-byte pointer to the next available block. The smallest block will be 3 bytes total (2 data bytes). When a block is allocated, the pointer will be overwritten with data, so there is only a single byte of overhead for blocks in use. The size of the block must be retained in the allocated block to correctly free the block when it is no longer needed by the application. Figure 12.6 depicts the pointer to the start of the free list of blocks and the first few blocks in the heap. The first block (at address 0x0062) is currently free and has 0x34 bytes available. The next free block begins at address 0x00C5 and has 0x05 bytes in it. In between are to allocated blocks of sizes 0x10 and 0x1C.

Heap initialization requires the creation of a linked list with maximally sized blocks. The pointer to the first free block will be stored in the first two bytes of the heap area in storage. In this example, there will be 252 bytes allocated to the heap (2 bytes for the pointer to the head of the free

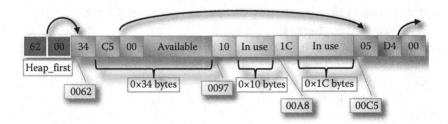

FIGURE 12.6   A heap with a linked list of free blocks is shown after some allocation and deallocation activity has occurred.

list). This will be subdivided into blocks of 31 bytes each (allowing allocation of a maximum of 30 bytes for data in each block). The last block would be 2-bytes long (250%31), but this is smaller than the minimum block size, so these bytes are wasted.

```
.dseg
;define number of bytes allocated to heap management
.equ HEAP_SIZE = 250
;reserve heap storage
heap_first: .byte 2
heap_start: .byte HEAP_SIZE
;define constants related to heap block structs
.equ    heap_struct_MAX_SIZE = 31  ;max is 256
.equ    heap_struct_MAX_DATA_SIZE = heap_struct_MAX_SIZE - 1
.equ    heap_struct_MIN_SIZE = 3    ;size field + next field
.equ    heap_struct_MIN_DATA_SIZE = heap_struct_MIN_SIZE - 1

.equ    heap_struct_sz_offset = 0
.equ    heap_struct_next_offset = 1
.equ    heap_struct_data_offset = 1
```

Initially, the heap will be a list of maximally sized blocks. The following routine will initialize the heap, assuming R25:R24 contains the desired heap size in bytes:

```
.cseg
;void lhinit(int heapsize) (passed in 25:r24)
;initialize the heap area to a linked list of maximally
;sized blocks
;filling the available heap
lhinit:
```

```
.def blocksize_H = r17      ;size of current block
.def blocksize_L = r16
.def heapMemLeft_H = r25    ;parameter - initially this is
                            ;the total
.def heapMemLeft_L = r24    ;memory avail to heap
      push XH
      push XL
      push ZH
      push ZL
      push blocksize_H
      push blocksize_L
      push r25
      push r24
;point to first free block in the heap
      ldi XH, high(heap_start)
      ldi XL, low(heap_start)
      sts heap_first, XL ;initialize head of heap
                         ;freelist
      sts heap_first + 1, XH

lhinit_next:
;do    {;create next block
      ldi blocksize_H, high(heap_struct_MAX_SIZE)  ;try
      ;max size block
      ldi blocksize_L, low(heap_struct_MAX_SIZE)
      sub heapMemLeft_L, blocksize_L
      sbc heapMemLeft_H, blocksize_H
      brcc lhinit_block  ;no borrow means block will fit

      ;recover partial block size
      add blocksize_L, heapMemLeft_L
      adc blocksize_H, heapMemLeft_H

      clr heapMemLeft_L  ;no more blocks after this
      clr heapMemLeft_H
lhinit_block:
      subi blocksize_L,1 ;data size is one less than
                         ;physical size
      sbci blocksize_H,0
      st X+, blocksize_L  ;store the block size (<= 255)
      movw Z, X    ;Z points to next field of this block
      add XL, blocksize_L      ;X points past end of
                               ;this block (to next)
```

```
        adc XH, blocksize_H
        st Z, XL      ;store addr of next into this block's
                      ;next field
        std Z + 1, XH
;do above while heapMemLeft >= heap_struct_MIN_SIZE
        cpi heapMemLeft_H, 0
        brne lhinit_next     ;still >256 bytes remaining
        cpi heapMemLeft_L, heap_struct_MIN_SIZE
        brsh lhinit_next     ;still >= heap_struct_MIN_SIZE
                             ;bytes remaining

        ;no more blocks, change next field to null
        st Z, heapMemLeft_H       ;which is 0
        std Z + 1, heapMemLeft_H

        pop r24
        pop r25
        pop blocksize_L
        pop blocksize_H
        pop ZL
        pop ZH
        pop XL
        pop XH
        ret
.undef blocksize_L
.undef blocksize_H
.undef heapMemLeft_L
.undef heapMemLeft_H
```

The complete program with some test memory allocations is available as Program 12.1. Keep in mind that the ATMega16A has a very limited SRAM so it is impossible to create a very large heap on this device.

EXERCISES

1. Arrays are collections of ___ data. Elements of an array are arranged in _____ storage locations.
2. Arrays declared in ___ cannot be initialized before execution begins.
3. Arrays declared in ___ are always initialized before execution begins.
4. If the base address of an array named arr is $2100 and the array contains word data, what is the address of arr[0]? arr[1]? arr[23]?

5. If the base address of an array of doublewords named dword is $0030, what is the address of dword[0]? dword[1]? dword[23]?

6. Write a directive for the data segment that will allocate an array of 20 words. Name the array data. Use an equ directive to represent the number of elements the array can hold.

7. Write a directive for the code segment that will allocate and initialize an array containing the powers of 2 (from 2^0 through 2^7. Name the array pow2.

8. Write statements to copy the contents of the pow2 array (previous question) into SRAM (using a loop). Allocate space for the array and name it pow2_s.

9. Write a function to return a word from an array that is stored in flash. The function is passed the byte address of the array (in z) and the index to be accessed (in r24). Return the word in r25:r24.

10. Write a function to determine the address of an array element given the base address of the array (in SRAM and passed in Z), the index (passed in r25:r24) and the size of each element (passed in r22). Return from the function with Y pointing to the desired element.

11. Write a function to store a word into an array in SRAM. The address of the array is passed in Z. The index is passed in R24. The word to be stored is in R23:R22.

12. Write a function summer to calculate the sum of the bytes (considered as signed integers) in an array found in SRAM. The function is passed the address of the array in Y and the address of the byte just past the end of the array in Z. The sum is returned in R25:R24 (signed word).

13. Write statements to use the function summer to calculate the sum of the bytes in the following arrays. Store them in the variables s1 and s2.
```
s1: byte 2
s2: byte 2
byte1data: .byte 35
byte1end:
byte2data: .byte 17
byte2end:
```

14. Write a function to calculate a checksum of the words in an array found in flash. The function is passed the byte address of the array in Z. The length of the array (number of words) is passed in R25:R24. The checksum is the EOR of all of the words in the array. Return the checksum in R25:R24.

15. A two-dimensional array named a2d with eight rows and 10 columns is organized in row major order has base address $100. If the array contains bytes, what is the address of a2d[3] [7]? If the array is organized in column major order, what is the address of a2d[3][7]?

16. A two-dimensional array named b2d with six rows and four columns is organized in row major order has base address $200. If the array contains words, what is the address of b2d[2] [1]? If the array is organized in column major order, what is the address of b2d[2][1]?

17. A two dimensional array stored in row-major order is, declared in flash as:
```
equ fdata_COLSIZE = 3
fdata: .dw 3245, 6784, 2345, 7321, 1254, 2387,\
2345, 876, 9874, 2145, 3412, 2904
```
What is stored at fdata[2][1]? At fdata[3][0]?
What is stored at fdata[2][1]? At fdata[3][0]?
Write a function to return (in r25:r24) the value fdata[i][j] if i is passed in r24 and j is passed in r25. Assume the arguments are legal.

18. Define a jagged array in flash with five rows. The rows contain the binomial coefficients.
```
1
1 1
1 2 1
1 3 3 1
1 4 6 4 1
```
Name the array binom. The array will contain pointers (byte addresses) to each row of bytes. The entire array should occupy 25 bytes (five pointers and 15 data bytes).

19. A list of ASCIIZ strings is found in flash beginning at the label strdata. The number of strings in the list is represented by the symbol STR_LEN. Declare space for the destination array in SRAM and write a segment of code to create an array of pointers to these strings in SRAM named strptr. Each element of this array should contain the byte address of one of the strings in flash. Here is a sample definition for a typical list of strings.
```
.equ STR_LEN = 4
strdata: .db "a string",0,"another",0,0,"last
one",0
```

20. Write a directive to store your name in flash at the label name in ASCIIZ format.

21. Write a directive to store your name in flash at the label name in P-string format.

22. Write a directive to store your name in flash at the label `name` in fixed-length format (padded with space characters to 20 characters).

23. Write a directive to store your name in flash at the label `name` with the high bit of the last character set.

24. Write a function to determine the length of a string in flash. The string's byte address is passed in Z. Return the length in r25:r24.

    a. int strlen_a(byte * addr); //the string is in ASCIIZ format

    b. int strlen_b(byte * addr); //the string is in P-string format with a single byte length field

    c. int strlen_c(byte * addr); //the string is terminated with a byte whose high bit is set.

25. An ASCIIZ string is stored in SRAM. Write a function to return the index of the first occurrence of a character in the string. Return the index if found, or −1 if not found. The return value is a signed word in r25:r24. The address of the string is passed in X.

26. Write a function `remove` that will remove a substring from an ASCIIZ string in SRAM. The function is passed the address of the string (in X), the starting position (in r24) and the ending position (in r25). If the string at `str` is "language", then `remove(str,0,3)` should change the string to "guage" (removing positions 0, 1, and 2). Assume all arguments are legal.

27. Structs contain a __ collection of data while arrays contain a __ collection.

28. The members of a struct are called __.

29. Write statements to store your birth date in the struct at a_Date (Figure 12.4).

30. Define a struct for a `Time` that contains a packed BCD field for hours, minutes, and a single character, A or P, to indicate AM or PM. Create a variable in SRAM of this type. Write statements to initialize it to 10:45 PM.

31. Write a function that accepts a `Time` struct by reference (in r25:r25) and increments it by one minute.

32. The variable head (in SRAM) contains a pointer to the first node of a linked list. Write statements to count the number nodes in the list (use r25:r24 for the count). Each node contains a next pointer at offset 0 (low byte) and 1 (high byte).

33. If X points to a node in a linked list, write statements to insert the node pointed to by Y into the list just after node X. Each node contains a next pointer at offset 0 (low byte) and 1 (high byte).

34. If X points to a node in a linked list, write statements to remove the node immediately after that node from the list. You should assume there is such a node. Each node contains a next pointer at offset 0 (low byte) and 1 (high byte).

PROGRAMMING EXERCISES

1. Rewrite Program 12.1 to work for ASCIIZ strings.
2. Write a function to sort an array of words (signed integers) found in SRAM. It expects an array and length as arguments. Use selection, insertion, or bubble sort. Test it on several arrays defined in flash that are copied to SRAM when the program begins. You can output the arrays before and after sorting via a serial connection to a terminal program.
3. Use heap sort to sort a list of signed words found in flash. Create the heap in SRAM. Output the original list and the sorted list via a serial connection to a terminal program.
4. Write a program to accept a series of names through a serial connection with a terminal program. Place the names in an array. Sort the names and display them on the terminal. Use fixed-length strings (maximum 10 characters), padded with spaces.
5. Write a program to accept a series of names through a serial connection with a terminal program. Place the names in an array. Sort the names and display them on the terminal. Use ASCIIZ strings that are dynamically allocated. Assume all of the names are less than 20 characters in length.
6. Write a program to calculate the binomial coefficients in a table. Use a 2-dimensional array organized in row major order with nine rows. Row 0 will have one entry (1). Row k will have k + 1 entries. binom[k, 0] = binom[k, k] = 1. For all of the other entries, binom[k, j] = binom[k-1, j-1] + binom[k-1, j]. Use a function to calculate the address of any table entry (given a row and column). The largest value in the table will be binom[8,4] which is 70, so table entries can be bytes. Be sure that the unused entries in the table are zero. You can output the table to a terminal via the serial port or simply view the table in memory using the simulator.

CHAPTER 13

Real Numbers

W HEN COMPUTATIONS REQUIRE FRACTIONAL calculations, there are two common data representation options, fixed point and floating point. Fixed point calculations rely on the native integer representations and calculating units, but assume there are a fixed number of decimal places maintained during arithmetic operations. An analogy would be doing monetary calculations in pennies, rather than in dollars, with the decimal point assumed to be present. The addition and subtraction algorithms are the same for fixed point as for integers so no new hardware is needed. However, the implied decimal point creates some difficulties when multiplying or dividing, requiring additional steps to round results.

Floating point representations utilize a totally different encoding scheme, representing numbers in a manner similar to scientific notation. Floating point representations encode the sign, significand or fractional part, and the exponent as fields in a single binary code.

IEEE FLOATING POINT REPRESENTATION

One of the most popular floating point schemes is described by the IEEE 754 standard. This standard specifies both the binary encoding formats and operations that can be applied to data of this type. There are two common subdivisions, one for the 32-bit *single-precision* code, and the other for the 64-bit *double-precision* code. Java uses these representations for the primitive data types *float* and *double*. We will focus on the IEEE single-precision floating point format. Other floating point encoding methods are sometimes used; they are all similar to the format we will study in this chapter.

Range and Precision

Floating point codes are designed to represent real numbers. Because the floating point codes are fixed length, the collection of numbers that can be represented in a particular floating point format is necessarily finite. We encountered this same limitation with the integer codes, and restricted the range of representable integers based on the number of bits in the code. Each floating point code represents numbers within a specific range.

Limiting only the range of floating point numbers will not be sufficient; any nonempty interval will contain an infinite number of real values. Even if we restrict the focus to rational numbers, it will be impossible to represent every rational number within a specified range. It will be necessary therefore, to pick only a few numbers from the limited range as representable by a given floating point code. This is done by limiting the precision, or number of significant digits that are represented.

Floating point codes therefore limit both the range and the precision of numbers that may be represented. It is convenient to think of floating point numbers in scientific-like notation, that is, as a coefficient times a power of 10 ($c * 10^e$). Whereas scientific notation utilizes base 10 numerals (hence the power of 10), floating point codes are based on powers of 2. When encoding and decoding floating point codes, numbers will be expressed as a coefficient times a power of 2. The precision is determined by the number of digits (or bits) used to represent the coefficient. The range of the floating point code is primarily determined by the range of the exponent.

The available bits in a floating point code are divided into three parts. One bit represents the sign of the number; 0 means the number is positive, and 1 means the number is negative. The remaining bits are devoted to the coefficient (also called the significand or mantissa) and the exponent. This results in limited precision (the number of bits in the coefficient) and range (determined by the number of bits in the exponent). In the case of IEEE single precision (see Figure 13.1), the sign bit is in position 31 and the

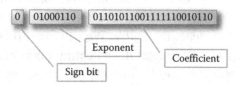

FIGURE 13.1 The sign, exponent, and coefficient fields of a single-precision IEEE floating point code.

exponent is an 8-bit biased integer code (excess-127 code) occupying bits 30 through 23. The remaining 23 bits are the fractional part of the coefficient; "1" is added to the left of these bits to complete the coefficient.

Decoding IEEE Single Precision Codes

To decode an IEEE single-precision floating point code, the 32-bit code is separated into its three parts. The least significant 23 bits are extracted and prefixed by "1" to form the significand. This represents a binary numeral m where $1 \leq m < 2$. The eight exponent bits are decoded assuming excess-127 representation. This means the bits are assumed to be a base two representation of a number from which the bias (127) is subtracted to get the exponent, e. In other words, if the exponent code represents the unsigned number k, then the actual exponent is $k-127$.

The floating point number represented by the code is then

```
n = m * 2ᵉ  or  n = -m * 2ᵉ
```

As a decoding example, consider the following single-precision code. We begin by breaking it up into three parts and establishing the meaning of each.

```
C20B999A is decoded as follows:
C20B999A = 1 10000100 00010111001100110011010
Sign bit = 1 (-)
Exponent = 0b10000100 - 127 = 132 - 127 = 5
Fraction = 1.00010111001100110011010
Number is -1.00010111001100110011010 * 2⁵
-100010.111001100110011010 = -34.90000152587890625
```

The binary number in the last step can be converted to base 10 by evaluating the equivalent polynomial. This is a sum of 24 powers of 2, some of which may be negative powers. You may prefer working with positive powers of 2. This is done by shifting the binary point to the right to get an integer. The integer can be converted and then divided by the proper power of 2 (determined by the number of bits the binary point was shifted).

```
100010.111001100110011010 (shift to the right 18 places)
   = 100010111001100110011010/2¹⁸
   = 9148826/262144
   = 34.90000152587890625
```

Encoding IEEE Single Precision Codes

Encoding is basically a reversal of the decoding process. First, the absolute value of the number is normalized. This is accomplished by dividing (or multiplying) by 2 enough times to obtain a value between 1 and 2. A number n is in *normalized form* when it is expressed as

```
n = m * 2ᵉ where 1 <= m < 2
```

The value m is converted into base two representation, then the leading "1" is stripped away and the remaining bits are used to fill in the rightmost 23 bits of the code. Trailing zeros may be added if necessary, or the value may need to be rounded. The exponent of the normalized form is converted into an 8-bit excess-127 code by adding 127 and then is converted into binary. This binary numeral fills the exponent field in the floating point code. The sign bit is set to one if the number is negative, or cleared otherwise.

Let us determine the single-precision code for 234.12. We need to normalize the number, so we repeatedly divide by 2 until we obtain a value between 1 and 2.

```
234.12 = 1.8290625 * 2⁷
```

The leading one is stripped off and the fractional part is converted into base two using repeated multiplication. As each product is found, the whole part of the product (0 or 1) is the next bit of the fractional expansion. When a 1 is obtained, it is discarded for the next multiplication. In practice, only the required number of bits is generated.

```
0.8290625 * 2 = 1.658125
0.658125 * 2 = 1.31625
0.31625 * 2 = 0.6325
0.6325 * 2 = 1.265
0.265 * 2 = 0.53
0.53 * 2 = 1.06
0.06 * 2 = 0.12
0.12 * 2 = 0.24 (this is the start of a repeating pattern)
0.24 * 2 = 0.48
0.48 * 2 = 0.96
0.96 * 2 = 1.92
0.92 * 2 = 1.84
```

```
0.84 * 2 = 1.68
0.68 * 2 = 1.36
0.36 * 2 = 0.72
0.72 * 2 = 1.44
1.44 * 2 = 0.88
0.88 * 2 = 1.76
0.76 * 2 = 1.52
0.52 * 2 = 1.04
0.04 * 2 = 0.08
0.08 * 2 = 0.16
0.16 * 2 = 0.32
0.32 * 2 = 0.64
0.64 * 2 = 1.28
0.28 * 2 = 0.56
0.56 * 2 = 1.12  (the pattern repeats after this line)
0.12 * 2 = 0.24
```

```
.8290625 = 0.1101010 00011110101110000101
           00011110101110000101...
```

We will use 23 of these bits, rounded as necessary, for the coefficient's code.

It is also possible to perform the normalization after converting the whole and fractional parts separately. The binary expansion for the whole part, 234, is determined using repeated division by 2.

```
234 = 11101010
```

The binary representation of the fractional part is determined using repeated multiplication by 2 as above.

```
0.12 * 2 = 0.24
0.24 * 2 = 0.48
0.48 * 2 = 0.96 (this is the same sequence as calculated above)
(and so on...)
```

```
0.12 = .00011110101110000101 00011110101110000101 0...
```

The bits representing the whole part are prepended to this sequence (along with a binary point) and then the binary number is normalized by shifting the binary point seven places to the left.

```
234.12 = 11101010.00011110101110000101
          00011110101110000101 0...
       = 1.110101000011110101110000101
          00011110101110000101 0... * 2⁷
```

The leading one is stripped away and 23 bits are used to encode the coefficient.

```
Code for the coefficient: 11010100001111010111000
(the next fractional bit is 0 so no rounding adjustment
is needed)
```

The exponent is encoded as excess-127

```
e = 7 + 127 = 134 = 0b10000110
```

And the code is assembled (inserting 0 as the sign bit).

```
0 10000110 11010100001111010111000 = 436A1EB8
```

Notice that the full expansion of 234.12 could not be exactly represented with 24 bits. The number represented by the resulting code is a little smaller than the actual real number we tried to encode. The correct term for this action is *discretization*, choosing the closest representable floating point number. In this case, the number actually represented is 234.1199951171875. You can check it by decoding the single-precision code we obtained in the encoding process.

Denormalized Form

The number zero requires a special case in the IEEE floating point code. It is impossible to write 0 in normalized form ($0 = m * 2^e$, $1 <= m < 2$). When the value to be normalized is smaller than 1, we repeatedly double it until a legal m is obtained. Doubling decreases the exponent. Since the smallest exponent allowed is -126 (the reason -127 is not allowed will soon be revealed), the process will eventually have to halt. In the case of zero, the best we can do in our normalization effort is the following:

```
0 = 0.0 * 2⁻¹²⁶ (m in this case is 0 but is not between 1 and 2)
```

Actually, zero is just one example of many numbers that fall into a category of floating point codes which is referred to as *denormalized*. For example, to encode the value $1.0 * 2^{-130}$, it will need to be expressed with an exponent no smaller than -126 (the lower limit for an IEEE single precision exponent).

$$1.0 * 2^{-130} = 0.0001 * 2^{-126}$$

Unfortunately, the *m* in this case is not between 1 and 2. IEEE floating point codes allow for the representation of some numbers that cannot be normalized due to being too close to zero. These values are represented in *denormalized* notation. Notice that the coefficient of denormalized values will always be zero.

Normalized floating point codes are distinguished from denormalized by the value of the exponent. When the exponent field is zero (*e* would be decoded as -127), the encoded value is in denormalized form; the bits in the coefficient field are prepended with "0" instead of "1" and the assumed exponent is -126.

Thus, an exponent code of zero represents a denormalized encoding, whereas an exponent of one or greater ($e >= -126$) represents a normalized encoding.

Consider the following very small value. The fractional part is expressed in binary.

$$0.00001000111000001000000 * 2^{-126}$$

We cannot normalize this value without decreasing the exponent below -126, the lower limit for this representation. Such numbers can still be represented in IEEE single-precision using the special *denormalized* format. For numbers smaller than $1.0 * 2^{-126}$, we express them as $m * 2^{-126}$ ($0 <= m < 1$). The "0" is stripped off the significand (m) and the remaining bits (rounded as necessary) are used in the 23 locations of the single-precision code. The exponent value of zero (00000000) is used to indicate that the floating point code is in *denormalized form*, implying the significand is to be prefaced with "0" instead of "1."

Infinity and NaN

Just as the exponent code $00 (which would represent -127) is reserved to indicate a special case, the other extreme, $FF (which would represent an exponent of +128) is also reserved to indicate another category of special cases. When the exponent code is $FF, there are two more special cases.

If the coefficient bits are all zero, then the special *infinity* values, positive or negative (determined by the sign bit), are represented. If any of the coefficient bits are nonzero, then the *NaN* or "Not a Number" value is intended.

In IEEE floating point, operations with these special values are well defined. For our purposes, it is sufficient to know that these special values exist and that they cannot be decoded using the algorithms above.

The infinity values are often the result of overflow. For example, if the value $1.0 * 2^{127}$ is doubled, the result will be too large to accurately encode in single precision format (127 is the largest exponent allowed). In this case, the result will be positive infinity and will be encoded as

```
0b01111111100000000000000000000000 or 0x7F800000
```

The NaN values are often the result of undefined or invalid mathematical operations, such as division by zero. There are two subcases of NaN, *Signaling NaN* and *Quiet NaN*, however, these concepts are beyond the scope of this discussion.

When decoding, pay careful attention to the exponent code. If it is zero, the significand is obtained by prefixing the last 23 bits with "0" and the exponent is −126. Notice that the code for zero falls into this special case. For exponent codes $01 through $FE, prefix the last 23 bits with "1" and decode the exponent as excess-127 notation. For the exponent $FF, write +Infinity, −Infinity, or NaN.

Single Precision Range and Precision

Restricting our discussion to normalized formats, the largest and smallest (positive) numbers that can be represented by IEEE single precision codes are as follows:

```
00000000100000000000000000000000
```
$$= 1.00000000000000000000000 * 2^{-126}$$
$$= (1) * 2^{-126} = 1.1754944e - 38$$

```
01111111011111111111111111111111
```
$$= 1.11111111111111111111111 * 2^{+127}$$
$$= (16777215 * 2^{-23}) * 2^{+127} = 3.4028235e + 38$$

Since the coefficient is represented as 23 bits (not including the implied leading 1), the maximum number of decimal digits of accuracy (precision) is approximately the number of digits in $2^{23} = 83,88,608$, or seven digits. Since this does not quite cover all possible seven digit numerals, we say the precision (or accuracy) of IEEE single precision values is 6–7 digits.

Since denormalized codes necessarily have leading zeros in their coefficient, they are less precise. As the values approach zero, the number of significant digits decreases.

Allowing for denormalized codes, the smallest positive value we can encode is

```
00000000000000000000000000000001
0.00000000000000000000001 * 2^-126 = 1.4012985e - 45
```

ADDITION AND SUBTRACTION OF IEEE FLOATING POINT NUMBERS

Many modern processors include floating point hardware that can perform all of the fundamental arithmetic operations on floating point data. However, if this hardware is not available, then the arithmetic operations must be accomplished through software. The AVR microcontrollers we have been studying do not include floating point hardware.

The use of sign and magnitude notation makes the addition and subtraction algorithms more complicated than the equivalent two's complement versions. When numbers of different signs are added, the magnitude of the smaller is subtracted from the magnitude of the larger and the result will have the sign of the number of greater magnitude. When the signs are the same, the magnitudes are added. The actual subtraction/addition is further complicated by the exponent. Basically, binary points must be aligned, meaning the exponents must be the same, before combining the magnitudes.

Addition

Here is a basic outline of an addition function:

```
float add (float a, float b)
if a and b are of different signs, return sub(a, -b)
isolate the sign and exponents (s, ae and be)
isolate the significands adding the leading 1's as
needed (am and bm)
```

```
while (ae < be) {ae ++; am >>= 1}
while (be < ae) {be ++; bm >>= 1}
sm = am + bm;
while (sm > 2²⁴) {sm >>= 1; ae ++}
Reassemble the sign s, sm and ae to create the result
```

Follow the steps in this example:

```
A = 0_10000111_ (1) 10100100100101110100110
B = 0_10000110_ (1) 10101100111101100000010

B is adjusted to:
B = 0_10000111_ (0) 110101100111101100000010

Add
A = 0_10000111_ (1) 10100100100101110100110
B = 0_10000111_ (0) 110101100111101100000010
- - -
S = 0_10000111_1 (0) 01111011000100100100111

Normalize
S = 0_10001000_ (1) 0011110110001001001001111  (round up)
S = 0_10001000_ (1) 00111101100010010010100
```

The actual calculations performed in this example are

```
01000011110100100100101110100110 = 420.59100341796875
01000011010101100111101100000010 = 214.48049926757812
- - -
01000100000111101100010010010100 = 635.071533203125
Actual result should be 635.07150268554687
```

The addition process required a rounding step when the final result was normalized. This is called *round-off error*. These errors are common when performing floating point computations.

Subtraction

Subtraction can be reformulated as addition

```
sub (a, b)
return add (a, -b)
```

Of course, this will create a circular definition if we use the add routine described above. Since the add routine only called subtract when the numbers had different signs (first adjusting the signs to be the same), we should deal with the subtraction of same-signed numbers directly in the subfunction. Subtraction of different signed numbers can be passed on to add after changing the sign of the second number.

```
float sub (float a, float b)
if a and b are of different signs, return add(a, -b)
isolate the sign and exponents (s, ae, and be)
isolate the significands remembering the leading 1's (am
and bm)
while (ae < be) {ae++; am >>= 1}
while (be < ae) {be++; bm >>= 1}
if (am > bm) sm = am - bm; else {sm = bm - am; s = !s;}
while (sm > 2²⁴) {sm >>= 1; ae++}
Reassemble the sign s, sm and ae to create the result
```

Comparison of Floating Point Numbers

If you list all of the nonnegative single precision IEEE codes $00000000 to $7FFFFFFF in their natural order as unsigned integers, and examine the floating point values each code represents, you will observe the following. The sequence will begin at zero, and increase gradually through the extremely small denormalized values. The values will continue to increase until the largest legal floating point number is encountered, immediately followed by the code for positive infinity. Next, many NaN codes will be seen until the code $7FFFFFFF is encountered. The next binary value is $80000000 which represents zero, in a nonstandard format (negative zero). If we continue through $FFFFFFFF, the sequence of values repeats along the negative values on the number line. The values will decrease toward negative infinity, again followed by a lot of NaN values.

00000000	0.0
00000001	1.4012985e − 45
00000002	2.8025969e − 45
. . .	. . .
007FFFFF	1.1754942e − 38
00800000	1.1754944e − 38
. . .	. . .
3F800000	1.0
3F800001	1.0000001

3F800002	1.0000002
. . .	. . .
7F7FFFFF	3.4028235e+38
7F800000	Infinity
7F800001	NaN
. . .	. . .
7FFFFFFF	NaN
80000000	-0.0
80000001	-1.4012985e-45
. . .	. . .
FF800000	-Infinity
FF800001	NaN
. . .	. . .
FFFFFFFF	NaN

This fact can be used to quickly compare floating point numbers. As long as one of the numbers is positive, a simple 32-bit signed integer (two's complement) comparison gives the correct result. Comparison of two negative values can be handled by reversing the result of the signed comparison, or by first subtracting the codes for the two negative numbers from $80,000,000. This essentially reverses the order of the codes for the negative numbers allowing for a straightforward comparison regardless of the sign of the floating point value.

MULTIPLICATION AND DIVISION OF FLOATING POINT NUMBERS

Conceptually, multiplication and division of floating point numbers follows the traditional algorithms most students learn for manipulating numbers in scientific notation. For example, $1.498 \times 10^{-3}/ - 8.760 \times 10^4$ is computed by dividing the mantissas, and subtracting the exponents, and then normalizing.

$(1.498/-8.760) \times 10^{-3-4} = -0.17100 \times 10^{-7} = -1.710 \times 10^{-8}$

When implementing the floating point arithmetic algorithm in software, all operations must be performed using integer calculations. It is not too difficult to see how this would work. Consider the following examples:

$2.75 \times 10^{12} * 6.10 \times 10^{-3} = 275 \times 10^{10} * 610 \times 10^{-5} = 167750 \times 10^5$
$\quad = 1.67750 \times 10^{10} = 1.68 \times 10^{10}$
$2.75 \times 10^{12} / 6.10 \times 10^{-3} = 275000 \times 10^7 / 610 \times 10^{-5} = 450 \times 10^2 \text{ r } 500$
$\quad = 4.51 \times 10^4$

Notice how the remainder is used for rounding of the quotient.

Of course, these examples are shown in base 10, whereas the computations performed in the floating point algorithms manipulate the mantissas and exponents in binary. Nevertheless, the basic ideas are the same.

Multiplication

Here is an example of the entire process for multiplication of two IEEE single precision floating point codes.

```
$40466666 * $40B00000  (3.1 * 5.5)
(3.1 is not stored exactly, it is approximated as 3.0999999)
Exponent: 10000000 (2¹) (128-127 = 1)
Mantissa: 1.10001100110011001100110
Exponent: 10000001 (2²) (129-127 = 2)
Mantissa: 1.01100000000000000000000
Rewrite mantissas as integers, adjusting exponents
110001100110011001100110 x 2¹⁻²³ (13002342x2⁻²²)
101100000000000000000000 x 2²⁻²³ (11534336x2⁻²¹)
Multiply
1000100001100110011001100010000000000000000000000000 x 2⁻⁴³
(149973381414912x2⁻⁴³)
Normalize and round
1.00010000110011001100110 00100000000000000000000 x 2⁴
(17.04999945) (3.1 * 5.5 = 17.05)
Hexadecimal floating point code: $41886666
```

Fast floating point arithmetic is a very complex topic. Much has been written about how to do this efficiently. The algorithms presented above are perhaps the simplest, mimicking the familiar algorithms used in the decimal system. The intent is to demonstrate the difference between integer and floating point representations and to gain an appreciation for the approximate nature and complexity of floating point arithmetic.

The AVR hardware does not support floating point representation or floating point arithmetic. Programs that are expected to run quickly need to eliminate or minimize floating point calculations. In most cases, this is a fairly straightforward process. If true floating point calculations are needed, then software must be written to accomplish them. The absence of integer division hardware in the AVR processor, and limited support for multiplication (only 8-bit multiplication is supported in hardware) further complicates the implementation of floating point routines.

It should also be noted the simplistic algorithms presented above algorithms do not treat the problems of rounding in a very careful way, and ignore the complications of denormalized formats, Infinity, and NaN. Complete implementation of floating point arithmetic must take into account a variety of special cases.

Division

A simple division example for IEEE floating point is illustrated next.

```
$40466666 / $40B00000 (3.1/5.5)
(3.1 is not stored exactly, it is approximated as 3.0999999)
Exponent: 10000000 (2¹) (128-127 = 1)
Mantissa: 1.10001100110011001100110
Exponent: 10000001 (2²) (129-127 = 2)
Mantissa: 1.01100000000000000000000
Rewrite mantissas as integers, adjusting exponents
11000110011001100110011000000000000000000000000 x 2¹⁻²³⁻²⁴
(218143100239872x2⁻⁴⁶)
1011000000000000000000000 x 2²⁻²³ (11534336x2⁻²¹)
Divide
(1001000001001010011110001 r 10100000000000000000000) x 2⁻²⁵
(18912497 r 5242880) = 18912497x2⁻²⁵ = 0.563636332750...
Normalize and round
1.001000001001010011110001 x 2⁻¹
1.00100000100101001111001 x 2⁻¹ (0.563636...)
Hexadecimal floating point code: $3F104A79
```

FIXED POINT ARITHMETIC

The absence of floating point hardware in the AVR processors makes the alternative fixed point representation for real numbers attractive. This representation uses integer representations, but assumes a decimal point (binary point) to be at a fixed location. It relies mostly on the integer operations already available with slight modifications necessary for multiplication and division.

Suppose we have an application that needs to use real numbers that are accurate to just one decimal place. Then we would need about four binary digits to the right of the binary point. This would provide accuracy to 1/16, a little better than 1/10. If we represent our numbers in 16 bits, then our range would be 0x000.0 through 0xFFF.F for unsigned data, or 0x800.0 through 0x7FF.F using a two's complement approach. Notice that this simply amounts to multiplying all of our real numbers by 16 and representing them by the nearest integer.

Encoding and Decoding Fixed Point Representations

Encoding and decoding is easily done by this approach. To encode a real number, multiply it by 16, round to the nearest integer, and then write it in binary. If signed representations are needed, and the number is negative, then apply the change sign rule after writing it in binary.

Decoding is equally simple. Apply the change sign rule if needed, then convert the value into base 10 and divide by 16.

For example, the value 10.2 would be encoded in this 4-bit fractional format as follows:

```
10.2*16 = 163.2, or 163. Converting to binary, we get
10100011. Decoding 10100011, we get 163. 163/16 = 10.1875.
```

The actual encoded value, 10.1875, is the closest representable number to 10.2 using this code. The next smaller representable value is $162/16 = 10.125$ and the next larger is $164/16 = 10.25$.

Fixed Point Addition and Subtraction

Addition and subtraction in fixed point format is accomplished by adding or subtracting the codes as if they were integer representations. For example, consider the values 10.2 and 37.9. The code for 10.2 was determined in the previous section. The code for 37.9 is determined similarly.

```
37.9*16 = 606.2 which rounds to 606
606 in binary is 1001011110
```

We can add or subtract these with no difficulty.

```
37.9 + 10.2 = 48.1
37.9 - 10.2 = 27.7
```

In code this is

```
606 + 163 = 769 (base 10 notation)
1001011110 + 10100011 = 1100000001 (unsigned base two)
769/16 = 48.0625
606-163 = 443
1001011110 - 10100011 = 110111011 (unsigned base two)
443/16 = 24.6875
```

Notice how the 0.9 + 0.2 naturally carried over into the integer part of the code. Mathematically, this simple arithmetic phenomenon is simply an illustration of the distributive law!

```
(a * 16) + (b * 16) = (a + b) * 16.
```

If signed numbers are used, two's complement notation can be employed. Consider the sum of −37.9 and 10.2 using 16-bit two's complement representation.

```
-37.9 + 10.2 = -27.7
-37.9 is encoded as 1111 1101 1010 0010
10.2 is encoded as 0000 0000 1010 0011
We add these to get 1111 1110 0100 0101 = -443
-443 / 16 = -27.6875
```

Fixed Point Multiplication and Division

Multiplication and division require a little more care. Simply multiplying the codes will result in a value 16 times too big.

```
(a * 16) * (b * 16) = (a * b) * (16 * 16)
```

It is easy to correct the result by simply dividing out the extra 16. We would of course accomplish this by shifting the result four bits to the right.

Division, (a * 16)/(b * 16) = (a/b), also creates a small problem, but shifting the dividend (numerator) left four places before dividing completely fixes the problem.

Here are two examples:

```
47.8 * 13.9 = 664.4
(765 * 222) / 16 = 169830 / 16 =
     1011111101 * 11011110 = 101001011101100110
Shift the result right 4 bits (if the last bit out is 1,
round up)
Result of multiplication is therefore 10100101110110
Converting to base 10, we get 10614, and
10614/16 = 663.375

47.8 / 13.9 = 3.4
(765 * 16) / 222 = 55 r 30
```

```
(1011111101 * 16) / 11011110
        = 10111111010000 / 11011110 = 110111 r 11110
(If the remainder is more than half the divisor, we
would round up)
Result of the division is therefore 110111
Converting to base 10, we get 55 and 55/16 = 3.4375
```

Fixed Point Notation

The AVR instruction set includes three fixed point multiply instructions that assume 1 bit for the integer part and 7 for the fractional part (called 1.7 notation). This 8-bit code can represent a limited number of real values in the range 0 up to (but not including) 2. The numbers in this range are encoded by multiplying by 128 (and rounding) to get an integer in the range 0 through 255. The implied binary point is after the leading bit.

```
0.0000000, 0.0000001, 0.0000010, . . . .1.1111111
```

The decimal equivalents are as follows:

```
0/128, 1/128, 2/128, . . ., 255/128
0, 0.00274658203125, 0.015625, . . .,1.9921875
```

Consider the value 0.35. In binary, this would be 0.01 0110 0110 0110 . . .

```
0.35 * 2 = 0.7
0.7 * 2 = 1.4
0.4 * 2 = 0.8 (pattern repeats from here)
0.8 * 2 = 1.6
0.6 * 2 = 1.2
0.2 * 2 = 0.4
```

Rounding to get eight bits, we get 0.0101101, or without the binary point, 00101101.

To decode a value represented in 1.7 format, simply convert it into an integer and divide by 2^7. The code just obtained above therefore represents the value 45/128 = 0.3515625.

Signed numbers within the interval [–1, 1) may be represented as 7.1 signed numbers using two's complement notation. The codes are the same, but are interpreted differently. For example, the code 10110010 interpreted as a signed 7.1 code represents a negative number. Applying the change sign code, we can decode it completely.

```
10110010 = a
01001110 = -a
0.1001110 is decoded as
01001110/10000000 = 78/128 = 0.609375
Thus a = -0.609375
```

Encoding a negative number, such as −0.5, requires one extra step.

0.5 in binary is 0.1000000. The 1.7 code for this value is 01000000. Applying the change sign code, we get the 1.7 signed representation for −0.5, 11000000.

AVR FMUL, FMULS, and FMULSU Instructions

The AVR microcontroller provides three instructions to support fixed point multiplication. The FMUL instruction is identical to MUL, except the result is shifted to the left by one place before storing it in R1:R0. The high byte (R1) is the result in 1.7 format; the entire 16-bit result is in 1.15 format. If the shift were not performed, the result would be 2.14 (R1 would be 2.6 format).

When using FMUL, you have to decide whether or not to ignore the extra fractional bits that are produced in R0.

The FMULS instruction is used to multiply two signed 1.7 format numbers and produce a signed 1.7 (actually 1.15) result. Note that the last bit (R0:0) will always be zero due to the way the product is computed (the left shift after the multiply).

The FMULSU instruction carries out a similar operation for a signed and unsigned operand, each in 1.7 format.

Here is an example of how −0.762 * 0.26 would be computed using the fixed point multiplication instructions. The 7.1 format value for 0.762 is $62 and applying the change sign rule yields $9E, the signed 7.1 representation. The conversion to signed 7.1 format can be performed by the assembler.

```
.equ a = int(0.26 * 128 + .5)  ;$21
.equ b = -int(0.762 * 128 + .5)  ;$9E
```

To carry out the multiplication, we need to load the operands into registers and use the FMULS or FMULSU instruction.

```
ldi r16, a
ldi r17, b
fmuls r16, r17
```

The 16-bit result will be in signed 1.15 format, in R1:R0, is \$E6BC. We discard the \$BC and get the twos'complement code \$E6 (7.1 format). As an integer, this represents −26. Dividing by 128 we get −0.203125. We can also do this in binary: 11100110, change sign to 00011010, this represents −0.0011010 or −26/128 = −0.203125.

The expected result is −0.19812. Is our value close to this? The difference is only 0.005005, which is less than 1/128, our expected precision.

SUMMARY

Using fixed point arithmetic on the AVR processor is much preferred over IEEE Floating point because of the lack of hardware support for floating point operations. A careful choice for the number of fractional bits can produce the desired precision with a minimal amount of work. Unfortunately, division still requires a rather lengthy process, but addition, subtraction, and multiplication can be implemented very efficiently.

EXERCISES

1. What are the general names for the two common representations of rational numbers.
2. What is the name of the standard used by Java to represent values of type float and double?
3. Rewrite the following decimal values in normalized form as a coefficient times a power of 2. Round the coefficient to 8 significant bits.
   (a) 10.0   (b) 0.1   (c) 19.625   (d) 0.0075
4. Write the 8-bit excess-127 code for each of the following exponents. If the exponent is out of range, say so.
   (a) −8   (b) 83   (c) −126   (d) 129   (e) −100
5. For the single precision code E57C2000, what is the sign, exponent (decoded), and base two coefficient (with leading 1)?
6. What is the base 10 equivalent of $1.0010110 * 2^{-7}$ where the coefficient is in base two?
7. Decode the following single precision codes. Give the base 10 representation of each value.
   (a) 38800000   (b) B8800000   (c) 1FA00000   (d) D0C00000
8. Encode each of the following rational numbers in single precision format. Express your answer in hexadecimal.
   (a) 32.25   (b) −0.0003   (c) 4E5   (d) $−5.9 \times 10^{-4}$

9. Consider the following 12-bit floating point format. Bit 11 is the sign encoded as usual. Bits 10 through 6 are the exponent in excess-15 format. The remaining bits represent the coefficient 0.dddddd (no leading 1). Decode the following codes (shown in hexadecimal) assuming this format.
   (a) 430   (b) 4C1   (c) C51   (d) C22

10. In question 9, what is the largest and smallest exponent? Write the code for the largest representable number in this format. What number does it represent in base 10?

11. In question 9, several codes may represent the same value. Explain how a unique representation might be enforced.

12. Decode the following IEEE single precision codes. Write them as a signed coefficient in hexadecimal times a power of 2 (if possible).
    (a) 7FD00000   (b) 80100000   (c) 0000F000   (d) FF800000

13. Add the following single precision codes. Show your work. Do not simply translate to base 10. Give your answer in the same format.
    (a) 3FE706F2 + 3FF39F50   (b) 7F024782 + 8F052312
    (c) 73860000 + 83060000   (d) 73860000 + 840C0000
    (e) 3D820000 + 2D820000   (f) 85678765 + 05678765

14. Compare the following single precision codes. Tell which is larger.
    (a) 3F24870C : 3F2087C0   (b) 3F24870C : A2093887
    (c) 800A0000 : 00090000   (d) F23C0000 : F24B0000

15. Multiply the following single precision codes. Show your work. Do not simply translate to base 10. Give your answer in the same format. After performing the multiplication, show the base 10 representation of each problem.
    (a) 3F800000 * 3F800000   (b) 3F800000 * 41800000
    (c) BFC0000 * 41600000

16. Divide the following single precision codes. Show your work. Do not simply translate to base 10. Give your answer in the same format. After performing the division, show the base 10 representation of eachproblem.
    (a) 3F800000 / 3F800000   (b) 3F800000 / BF800000
    (c) 74800000 / 7500000   (d) 75000000 / 74800000

17. If a 16-bit fixed point representation is to be used, and two decimal places of accuracy is desired, how many binary places are needed to the right of the binary point? How would you encode a number? Assuming unsigned data, what is the largest number that can be represented in this format?

18. Assuming a 12-bit fixed point representation for signed values (using two's complement), decode the following codes if the implied number of bits to the right of the binary point is 5.
    (a) 1CA   (b) F20   (c) 780   (d) 801   (e) 90C

19. Perform the following operations assuming the 12-bit representation described in question 18. Do (and show) your work in binary (or hexadecimal) without translating to base 10. When finished, show the base 10 interpretation of each problem.
    (a) 0CF + 0CF   (b) 0CF – 0CF   (c) FFF + FFF
    (d) 0CF * 040   (e) 0CF * 010   (f) 72F / F80

20. Write each decimal value in unsigned AVR 1.7 notation.
    (a) 0.75   (b) 1/3   (c) 1.46   (d) 0.001   (e) 0.05

21. Write each unsigned AVR 1.7 value as a decimal (base 10) value.
    (a) 01011101   (b) 10011101   (c) 11100000   (d) 00001111

22. Write each decimal value in signed AVR 1.7 notation.
    (a) −0.75   (b) −1   (c) 0.99   (d) −0.9

23. Write each signed AVR 1.7 value as a decimal (base 10) value.
    (a) 01011101   (b) 10011101   (c) 11100000   (d) 11111111

24. Tell the result (in R1:R0) after each instruction if R2 contains 0x7F and R3 contains 0x8C. Interpret each problem and answer in base 10 notation.
    (a) FMUL R2, R3   (b) FMULS R2, R3   (c) FMULSU R2, R3

25. Write a define byte directive to assemble the following values as unsigned AVR 1.7 format in consecutive bytes of flash: 0, 1.9, 0.85, 1.

26. Write a define byte directive to assemble the following values as signed AVR 1.7 format in consecutive bytes of flash: 0, −0.9, 0.85, −0.5.

PROGRAMMING EXERCISES

1. Write a function to add two positive numbers represented in IEEE single precision format. The 32-bit codes are stored in four consecutive bytes, beginning with the byte containing the sign. The function expects Y and Z to be pointing to the addends in SRAM, and X to be pointing to the 4 bytes where the result is to be stored. You may ignore the possibility of denormalized, infinity and NaN codes. You should use 32 bits for the coefficient when adding and then round to the required number of bits. Illustrate the correctness by simulating execution on several pairs of floating point values.

2. Write a program to find the square root of 0.5 using the method of bisection. Use unsigned AVR 1.7 notation. We know sqrt(0.5) is in the interval (0.5,1). Begin with an estimate that the answer is 0.75. Squaring the estimate gives 0.5625. (The estimate is too large, so we now know the actual square root lies in the interval (0.5, 0.75).) Bisect this interval and use the midpoint as the new estimate. Repeat the process until you get the same estimate twice. Run the program in the simulator. Compare the answer you get to the actual value.

CHAPTER 14

Programming the AVR in C

A VR STUDIO IS COMPATIBLE with a collection of C/C++ development tools that have been designed to produce machine-language programs for the AVR microcontroller. WinAVR is a suite of open source tools targeting the AVR family. It is based on the GNU GCC (GNU = GNU is Not UNIX and GCC = GNU Compiler Collection) compiler. AVR Studio will recognize the WinAVR tools once they are installed and then will allow the development of C and C++-based AVR projects. The WinAVR files are available for download at winavr.sourceforge.net.

Writing AVR programs in C allows you to focus on the algorithmic part of the solution to a problem, leaving some of the memory management and low-level details to the compiler. Statements in C programs may be translated in many ways to blocks of machine instructions. One translation is likely to be more efficient than another, in size, speed, or both. Writing in machine language can always produce the best implementation, but the process may be the least efficient (requiring more time, greater expertise, and liberal amounts of patience). You should find it very interesting to compare the program generated by a compiler to your own assembly language solution.

Documentation for the WinAVR tools is available through the AVR Studio Help menu after you begin a GCC project. You can find a variety of resources online as well. In this chapter, we will present a brief overview of writing programs in C for the AVR. Then we will explore how C and assembly language can be combined to develop applications for the

AVR platform. We will also discover the assembly language equivalents to simple C programs.

OBJECT FILES AND LINKERS

The AVR assembler takes a shortcut eliminating one of the usual steps of program translation. The skipped step is the production of intermediate files called object files that need to be linked before loading or execution. The AVR assembler assembles a single source file (perhaps after including other files via the include directive) and produces an executable file (one designed to be loaded into the program memory of an AVR microcontroller and executed).

A single source file is fine for many programming projects, but as projects grow in size and complexity, it is often desirable to compile parts of a project separately. These relatively independent parts are called compilation units. Compilers (and many assemblers) typically produce one object file for each compilation unit. These files contain detailed instructions to another program called the linker that completes the translation process. The linker's job is to take one or more object files and combine them to create an executable program.

Each object file is the result of a single compile/assemble step applied to one source document. Files included in a source file via some include mechanism are considered to be part of the single source document. If a project involves several source units, each may be compiled/assembled separately. As you are developing a project, only the source files that change need to be retranslated; the object file only changes if its associated source code changes.

Managing dependencies between source documents is a major problem in large projects. Most Integrated Development Environment (IDEs) manage dependencies through a project manager. Before the widespread use of IDEs, make files were used. A make file is a list of dependencies between program components, and actions to be taken when a change to a component is made. WinAVR uses make files to manage projects. When AVR Studio is used to invoke the WinAVR tools, dependencies are managed through the project manager. It does this by creating a make file.

Object files are not simply machine instructions and data. They are a list of linkage instructions. Object files will contain information about memory requirements for the program, including initial contents of memory. There will also be information that allows the separate object files to be connected (linked) to create a single program. Usually, the linker produces a single file that we refer to as an executable.

Standard Functions

C programmers rely heavily on the separate compilation facility of a C compiler and the associated linkage system. It is common to write a code that uses (calls) functions that are defined in a separate compilation unit. The C language includes a large number of standard functions that have already been translated to object file form. When you write programs that use these functions, the function body is located in an already compiled object file and is connected to your call by the linker. Of course, the compiler will need to have some information about the function so it can setup arguments to meet the expectations of the actual function. This information is provided in special include files called header files. To allow functions defined in one file to be used in another file, the header file is included in both. The header file defines the function's interface. That is, it tells the name of the function, its return type, and the number and types of arguments. The function body is not included in the header file.

The body of a function does not need to be known in order to translate a function call statement. Remember that calling a function requires allocating and initializing parameters. This step needs only the information in the function heading. The code following the call will handle the return value (if any). The function heading alone provides enough information to generate the machine language instructions to perform those tasks. If the location of (address of) the function body is unknown (defined in a separate compilation unit), the address portion of the actual call instruction will be filled in later by the linker.

Functions can also include statements that refer to variables defined in a different source file. The linker has the job of inserting the correct addresses in the machine instructions so the load and store instructions will function properly.

Compilers for C programs come with a large number of predefined (standard) functions. Very few C programs are written without string handling, I/O, and math related operations that rely on one or more standard functions. When you write programs using these functions, you will include the standard header file for the functions you need. The compiler will check that your function calls have the correct number and types of arguments, and that the return type matches the usage of the function.

The compile step will produce an object file containing a call to a function; the address will be missing. The linker will combine the required object files, so every function has a definition. It will also insert the addresses so everything works properly.

Executables

Compilers (and assemblers) generally produce object files. The linker is the tool that generates the executable file. In the case of an AVR program, the linker must produce a hex file containing the contents for flash. The AVR programmer will be used to load this information into flash. The microcontroller, once programmed in this way, can run the application anytime when power is applied (or the reset signal is received).

The linker combines all of the object files needed by the program. It links statements with missing addresses to the actual addresses determined when the object files are combined. The result is a single file that can be loaded into memory to allow execution.

ANATOMY OF A C PROGRAM

Each source module of a C program is written in a separate file, usually with the extension .c. For a simple console application, one of the modules must have a main function (a function named `main`). It is common for modules to require one or more include files. These are text files containing mostly declarations that are included as part of the source and compiled with the contents of your file. For AVR projects, it is customary to include the `avr/io.h` file. This is similar to the device specific include file we have used in our assembly language programs. Assuming that you specified the correct AVR device when creating the C project in AVR Studio, the `avr/io.h` file will automatically define the I/O register locations according to the specific target device so they can be accessed by name in your program. Do not forget the `avr/` in front of the include file name. This file is not a standard C include file; it is located in a subfolder (named `avr`) of the normal include file folder and is specific to the AVR devices.

Main Function

The following simple C program contains the required `main` function. In this example, `main` does nothing. Recall that the AVR programs always begin with code located in the reset interrupt. For every C program, the compiler will generate standard code for the reset interrupt. This will initialize memory, I/O devices, registers, and the stack, and then call the function called main. When main finishes its task it returns to the automatically generated reset code where an infinite loop keeps the processor busy until the microcontroller is reset.

```
#include <avr/io.h>
int main(){
...
return 0;
}
```

The main function of a C program is supposed to return an integer called the exit code to the operating system. This is why main indicates an int return type. A zero return value indicates a normal or clean exit. AVR programs are the operating system, so the return value is unimportant.

Most AVR applications are coded as an initialization section followed by an infinite loop inside main. The initialization section will include the code to initialize resources used by your program. This might include the USART, digital I/O ports, data structures, and so on. Remember that when the microcontroller is reset, the function main will be called after the basic reset tasks have been performed. A reset signal essentially restarts your program from the beginning.

```
#include <avr/io.h>
int main(){
init();
while(1){//loop forever
...
}
return 0;
}
```

Sample AVR GCC Project

The following example illustrates how to use AVR Studio to create a project in C for the AVR Microcontroller. It will simply flash the LEDs connected to port B. This assumes you are using the ATmega16A and the STK-500 development platform. The steps for the XPLAIN development kit are similar.

Begin by using the New Project Wizard in AVR Studio. Rather than selecting the AVR Assembler as the project type, select AVR GCC as

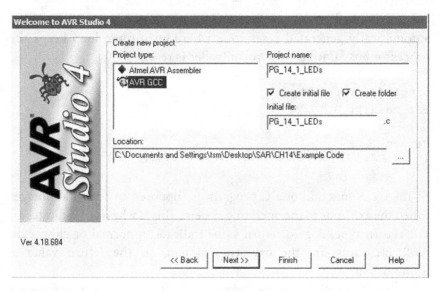

FIGURE 14.1   Starting a new C project in AVR Studio.

shown in Figure 14.1. The rest of the steps are the same as before, selecting the debug platform and the device.

The development environment will look the same as before, but you will be entering a C program rather than writing AVR Assembly language.

The beginning of the program is already shown in Figure 14.2. You can check that the compiler is correctly hooked to AVR Studio by compiling the current file. The Build menu provides the tools to compile and link programs as shown in Figure 14.3.

Remember that compiling simply produces an object file for the current source file. To compile and invoke the linker, you use the *Build* command. To ensure that all object files are up to date, the *Rebuild All*

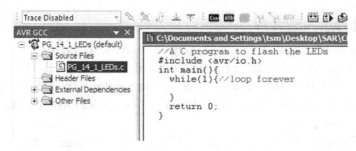

FIGURE 14.2   The beginning of a C program in the AVR Studio editor.

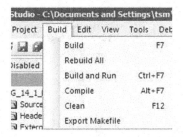

FIGURE 14.3   Compiling the project using the Build menu.

command will compile files even if they have not changed since they were last compiled. The *Clean* command will erase all of the files produced by the Build command, leaving just the source files in the project folder. Buttons for these actions are also available on the GCC Plugin toolbar above the editor area.

The compiler messages are shown in the Build window at the bottom of the screen. After compiling, the object file will be located in a subfolder of the project folder. In the current example, the object file is named default/ PG_14_1_LEDs.o. The name of the object file matches the source file name (with extension .o). Figure 14.4 shows this file (among) others in the default folder.

A make file is also created by the AVR environment. This is built by the project manager when you add files to the project. It contains the commands required to build your C project.

You should also examine the External Dependencies folder in the project window (Figure 14.5). It shows what files were included in the compile step.

The sample file we created explicitly includes only one file, avr/io.h. However, this file in turn includes other essential files. The iom16.h has definitions specific to the ATmega16A microcontroller. This file was included automatically because the ATmega16A was selected as the target device when the original project was created.

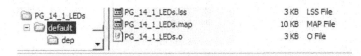

FIGURE 14.4   The files used and produced by AVR Studio when building a simple program.

FIGURE 14.5   External dependencies generated automatically by AVR Studio during the build step.

Project options (including the selection of the target device) can be modified using the Build menu and selecting Configuration Options, as shown in Figure 14.6.

In the Options dialog (Figure 14.7), you can adjust the name and location of the output folder (which defaults to *default*) and select a different target device.

It is a good idea to select the clock speed you intend to use in your application, as this allows the compiler to help with timing tasks. Note that setting the clock speed in the Project Options is declaring your intent only! You will have to select the correct clock source in the actual microcontroller when the program is downloaded.

Figure 14.7 shows a clock speed (frequency) setting of 1 MHz. In addition, the boxes at the bottom have been checked to get Map, List, and Hex files. There are additional options available by selecting one of the buttons on the left. For our purposes, we will need only the General settings.

FIGURE 14.6   Accessing the Project Configuration Options.

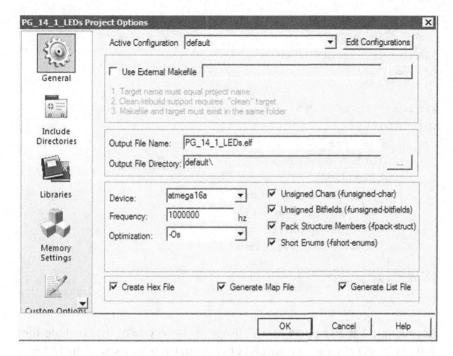

FIGURE 14.7   Specifying options in the Project Options dialog.

To complete our sample program, we need to setup port B as output, and then decide what we want to display. For this example, we will light one LED at a time, moving from LED0 to LED7 and repeating. Program 14.1 lists the entire program targeting the ATmega16A. An ATXMEGA128A version targeting the XPLAIN development kit is provided at the end of the chapter. The XMEGA version differs only in the naming and setup of the digital ports.

PROGRAM 14.1   Sequential Flashing of the LEDs

```
/*
Program 14.1
C program to flash LED's

The LED's are sequentially turned on, repeating from
LED 0.

Programmer: TM
Date: 5/2010
Platform: STK-500
```

```
Device: ATMEGA16A

Simulator execution only
*/

#include <avr/io.h>
int main() {
        DDRB = 0xFF;
        uint8_t pattern = 1;
        while (1) {
                PORTB = ~pattern;
                pattern <<= 1;
                if (pattern == 0)
                        pattern = 1;
        }
        return 0;
}
```

Accessing AVR I/O ports in a C program is very easy. The include files define the I/O registers as variables bound to the addresses of the I/O registers in the data space. When you assign a value to such a variable, it is sent to the associated I/O register. When you use one of these variables in an expression intended to be evaluated, you are reading the port value.

Here is an example of writing to DDRB (ATmega16A). The assignment statement,

```
DDRB = 0xFF;
```

is compiled to a sequence of machine-language instructions that send the byte 0xFF to I/O register DDRB. The statements actually output by the compiler depend on the optimization settings. The GCC compiler can optimize your C code to make it fast or to take up less memory. If it is not optimized, then it very conservatively translates each C statement to a standard sequence of machine-language statements. Here are two possible translations of the above assignment:

```
//Optimization option -O0 (off)
a6: e7 e3    ldi    r30, 0x37    ;55
a8: f0 e0    ldi    r31, 0x00    ;0
aa: 8f ef    ldi    r24, 0xFF    ;255
ac: 80 83    st     Z, r24
```

```
//Optimization option -Os (small)
6c: 8f ef    ldi    r24, 0xFF    ;255
6e: 87 bb    out    0x17, r24    ;23ldi r16, $FF
```

You can view the generated machine instructions (with associated assembly language interpretation) in the listing file (.lss). This file appears under Other Files in the AVR GCC window (project window) when the associated source file is compiled.

When optimization is turned off, the compiler outputs machine instructions to load the dataspace address of the I/O register (&DDRB) into Z. Indirect addressing is then used to send the specified value (which is loaded into R24 using immediate addressing) to the correct I/O register.

The optimization settings can be selected in the Project Options dialog (Figure 14.7). Selecting -O0 means no optimization. The -Os option optimizes for size, trying to use the least amount of memory possible. Options -O1 through -O3 attempt to speed up the program through various code transformations.

After changing the Optimization option, you need to recompile the project to see the changes in the listing file. The listing file produced by the compiler is a valuable tool for understanding how compilers work. In particular, you can examine how the AVR GCC compiler translates every part of your program. If there are sections that are not efficient, you may want to replace them with your own assembly language statements.

You should run this sample program in the simulator, observing the changing pattern on PORTB. To run the application on the actual microcontroller, it will be necessary to introduce a delay in the loop so the patterns do not change too quickly. There is a delay library provided with the compiler to facilitate this. You simply need to include the required header file, and then call one of the provided functions. It is also important that optimizations are turned on for the delay functions to work correctly. Additionally, the intended clock speed must be correctly configured in the Project Configuration as this is used by the compiler to calculate the correct number of clock cycles needed for specific delays.

PROGRAM 14.2 Sequential Flashing of the LEDs with Software Generated Delay

```
/*
Program 14.2
C program to flash LED's with delay loop
```

The LED's are sequentially turned on, repeating from LED 0.

Programmer: TM
Date: 5/2010
Platform: STK-500
Device: ATMEGA16A

Be sure to select the correct clock speed in the Project
Options
*/

```c
#include <avr/io.h>
#include <util/delay.h>
int main(){
        DDRB = 0xFF;
        uint8_t pattern = 1;
        while(1){
                PORTB = ~pattern;
                pattern <<= 1;
                if (pattern == 0)
                        pattern = 1;
                _delay_ms(250.0); //250 msec delay
        }
        return 0;
}
```

There are two new lines in the program. The new include file provides function headings for several functions that can be used to cause delays in a program. The function we are using accepts a single floating point argument representing the number of milliseconds it should consume. The function is called at the bottom of the display update loop, causing the delay to occur before each new value is displayed on the LEDs. In this program, the LEDs should change four times per second.

You must be careful to keep the argument to the delay function in range. In addition, the argument must be a constant (must be able to be evaluated by the compiler) and optimization must be turned on. The optimization levels are defined in the Project Configuration Options Help.

- *-O0* No optimization.

- *-O1* Optimize. Compiler performs basic optimization tasks.

- *-O2* Optimize even more for speed without sacrificing size.

- *-O3* Optimize yet more. Program size may increase.

- *-Os* Optimize for size; sacrificing speed in some cases.

Optimization should be turned off (-O0) during debugging (and delay loops like the one we just used should be commented out). If optimizations are on when debugging, some of the source lines will be skipped over when you single step through the source code. You may also see the current line marker arrow jump around in what appears to be an erratic fashion. This is due to the fact that optimization often combines several source statements to produce an efficient block of machine instructions. As a result, the current machine instruction may depend on several source statements. In such situations, there is no good way for the debugger to decide which source code line should be highlighted as the next one to be executed.

FUNDAMENTALS OF C PROGRAMMING

Many modern high-level languages are based on the syntax of C. Of course there are certain specifics that will be different. One major difference between C and Java, for example, is that C does not support object types; rather than writing methods, you write functions. The following sections summarize some important details of C programming. One thing that you will see is that programming in C requires an understanding of how data is stored and accessed. The things you have learned earlier in this book will be a valuable aid to understanding how C works. Learning about memory allocation in C will also help you understand how variables and objects are managed in other languages.

Comments

Comments in C programs are enclosed in /* and */ symbols. They may extend over multiple lines and can contain anything except a nested comment. C++ allows single line comments that start with // and extend to the end of the line. The compiler supplied with AVR Studio is both a C and C++ compiler, so either comment syntax works. Do not use a semicolon as a comment start indicator. It is the statement termination symbol in C, and will not be recognized as the start of a comment!

Include Files

There are two types of include files. Standard include files are located in a folder that is specific to the compiler installation. The compiler automatically searches preset paths for these files. Standard include files are indicated by placing the file name inside angled brackets. You may need additional include files specific to your project. These are enclosed in quotes instead of angle brackets. The compiler searches for these files in the project folder (where the other source files are located).

```
#include <avr/io.h>      //a standard AVR include file
#include "myinclude.h"   //a project specific include
                         //file
int main(){
...
return 0;
}
```

Include files generally contain one or more symbol definitions that are needed throughout a project. In large projects, include files may include other include files. As a result, it is common for a file to be included twice. Unfortunately, this can cause errors when duplicate symbol definitions are encountered. A standard design pattern is used in include files to prevent this from happening. The project include file named myinclude.h would probably contain the following statements:

```
#ifndef myinclude_h
#define myinclude_h
...
#endif
```

The #ifndef (if not defined) directive checks if the symbol after it has already been defined in the current compilation unit. If the symbol has been defined, then the compiler skips the subsequent statements up to the #endif directive (which will be at the end of the include file). If the symbol has not yet been defined, then the enclosed statements are processed. Notice that the first statement inside the #ifndef is a directive (#define) that defines the symbol myinclude_h. It is this design pattern that prevents multiple includes of this file from causing problems. The conventional symbol used to exclude multiple inclusions matches the actual file name (with periods replaced by underscores). Thus the include file myinclude.h would define the symbol myinclude_h.

Functions

C programs are basically a collection of function (and variable) definitions. The order these are listed does not make a lot of difference, however, it is required that identifiers (variables and function names) be declared before they are used. This rule allows the compiler to perform its task with a single pass through the source file. Programs normally begin with global function and variable declarations. Often these are placed in include files, so include directives are commonly found at the top of a program file. The declarations are then followed by a list of function definitions.

One of the important uses for include files is the declaration of functions. Functions in C should be declared before they are used (before a function call statement is compiled). There is a difference between a function declaration and a function definition. A function is declared by providing a prototype or heading; it is defined when its body is included. A function declaration provides essential information needed to compile function calls: the function name, return type, and number and types of parameters. The function definition provides the code for the function itself.

Here is a simple heading or prototype for a function that receives a character (byte) that is to be output on the LEDs. This prototype declares the function out2LED.

```
void out2LED(char);
```

Function definitions are made by writing a function heading (without the semicolon) and following it by a function body—a collection of statements enclosed in curly braces. If a function definition appears before a declaration is encountered, the definition also declares the function.

```
void out2LED(char c) {
    PORTB = c;
}
```

It is customary to collect all of the function headings for functions that are defined in each source file and place them in an associated header file. The source file named sample.c would have associated with it a header file named sample.h. This header file will list all of the function headings for functions defined in this file. The header file will then be included in any source file containing statements that use these functions. This ensures that all functions are declared before they are used and that the function signature matches in all files of a project.

The following example illustrates the use of a function named add that is defined in its own source file (add.c). The function heading is placed in the associated include file (add.h). This include file is included in both source files (app.c and add.c).

```
//File app.c:
#include "add.h" //declares function add
int main(){
        int x = add (2, 4); //uses function add
        return 0;
}

//File add.h:
#ifndef add_h
#define add_h
int add(int, int); //declaration of add
#endif

//File add.c:
#include "add.h" //declares function add
int add(int x, int y){ //definition of function add
        return x + y;
}
```

Variables

Variables are identifiers that represent a value stored in memory. The use of a variable name in an expression usually represents the value of the variable. Variables are usually associated with memory locations. Some variables are associated with the same memory location for the lifetime of the program. Others may be stored at different locations at different times during execution. In the C programming language, we differentiate between three main types of storage allocation: static, automatic, and dynamic.

Allocation Classes

To understand the difference between these allocation classes, you should also know that C separates memory into three major areas: data, stack, and heap. Static storage is allocated in the data segment. Variables with storage in this segment will normally be at the same address for the life of the program. The compiler basically assigns these addresses at compile time (actually, the assigned addresses are refined by the linker and loader, but this is more detail than we need to know at this time).

Automatic variables are allocated in the stack. The stack is initialized before the main program starts. In addition to being used for return addresses, interrupts, and temporary storage, the stack is also used for stack frames that will contain local storage used by a function. The compiler adds instructions to your program that take care of allocation and deallocation of automatic variables.

The last allocation class is dynamic. Dynamic variables are allocated from the area of memory called the heap. It is managed by the programmer through a collection of functions provided in a standard library. Dynamic allocation allows you the flexibility of allocating different sized containers for varying storage needs while the program is running. In C, dynamic storage is always accessed using a type of indirect addressing: pointers. Pointer variables have values that represent addresses. You cannot do much C programming without understanding pointers.

In the AVR setting, the data, stack, and heap areas are all managed in SRAM. The AVR GCC compiler comes with special library functions to allow access to program memory (flash) and EEPROM. We know it is possible in assembly language to place constants in flash that are used by our programs. The special functions provide access to such constants.

Scope

Storage classes refer to the lifetime of a variable. Scope is a related, but distinct concept. The scope of an identifier is defined as the places in a program that the identifier has meaning or can be accessed.

Variables in C programs have block (local), global (file), or program (external) scope. When variables in C are defined inside functions, they are local variables. Their scope extends from their point of declaration to the end of the block in which they are defined. A block is a set of matched curly braces. Usually local variables are defined at the beginning of a function. Parameters can also be considered to be local variables.

Local variables can be declared to be static, meaning their storage allocation occurs only once, when the program is started. If a local, static variable is initialized, it will be done so only when storage is allocated, not every time the function is activated. Static variables default to a zero initialization. Static variables, of course, retain their values between function calls. Static local variables belong to the static allocation class. Normal local variables (not static) belong to the automatic allocation class. Both have local scope.

Variables defined outside of all functions are called external variables and have program scope. This means they can be freely accessed from every function in every file of the program. Such variables, often called global variables, belong to the static allocation class. If you want a global variable to be restricted in scope to the current file, add the static attribute in front of the declaration. This gives the variable file scope.

If the keyword extern is added to the declaration of a variable, then that variable must be defined (allocated) elsewhere in the project. The extern keyword means the variable name is external, and no storage should be allocated based on its extern declaration; the variable will be bound to storage by the linker.

You may notice that no variables are assigned the dynamic storage class. This is because dynamic storage in C does not support named variables. That is, no (named) variable will belong to the dynamic allocation class. Variables in this class are sometimes called anonymous; they must be accessed through a pointer.

There are more scoping rules and allocation types in C, but those presented here are sufficient for most programming needs. Program 14.3 illustrates some of the basic scope and storage allocation concepts.

PROGRAM 14.3 Illustrate Storage Allocation Classes and Scope

```
/*Program 14.3*/
#include "ca.h"
int main(){
        extern int sum;     //declaration, but no storage
                            //allocation
        int tot = countAndAdd();   //local variable,
                                   //automatic storage
        tot = countAndAdd();
        countAndAdd();
        int x = sum; //access the external variable sum
        return 0;
}

//File ca.h
#ifndef ca_h
#define ca_h
int countAndAdd(); //declare the function
#endif

//File ca.c
#include "ca.h"
```

```
int sum = 0;  //external definition, static allocation
int countAndAdd(){ //external function definition
    static int count = 1;       //static allocation,
                                //local scope
    int tot = sum += count++; //local automatic storage
    return tot;
}
```

This program should be run in the simulator. The variable values can be watched in the watch window as each statement is executed. The watch window will display the address of each variable as well as its value.

Some things to watch for:

1. When main is about to start, the external variable sum is already allocated and initialized to 0. Storage for this variable was allocated at 0x62.

2. The local variable tot, in main, is allocated in the stack at 0x45A when function main begins executing.

3. When the function countAndAdd is entered for the first time, the static variable count is initialized. It is located at address 0x60. In addition, storage for the local variable tot is allocated at 0x452. Notice the distinct addresses for the two local variables with the same name.

4. On the second call to countAndAdd, count retains its previous value; it is not reset to 1.

5. The variables count and sum are always at the same storage locations. Since sum is global, it can be accessed by both main and countAndAdd.

6. The local variable x is located in the stack frame for main at address 0x458.

Figure 14.8 shows the memory layout for Program 14.3 when the function countAndAdd is active. The stack frame for countAndAdd is on the top of the stack; main's stack frame is immediately after. The stack frames hold automatic variables and storage for registers and the return address.

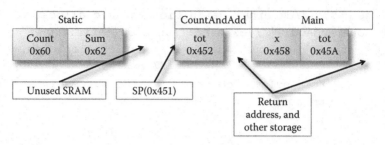

FIGURE 14.8 Memory allocation for Program 14.3.

Static storage begins at 0x60. Memory layout for every AVR Microcontroller will be similar; only the specific addresses will change.

Special Types

Named variable declarations require a type and an identifier. Standard C data types include int, unsigned long, float, char, and so on. As C does not specify exactly how many bits or bytes each of these data types require internally, special type names are used in AVR programs when it is important to have a specific number of bits. These AVR-specific types are defined when you include the standard include file, avr/io.h. The actual definitions are located in the files stdint.h and inttypes.h. Here are three examples of variable definitions using these special type names:

```
int8_t a; //signed byte
uint8_t b; // unsigned byte
int16_t c; //signed word
```

GCC Compiler and Variable Allocation

Let us look at how the compiler translates variable declarations. Begin a new project with the code from Program 14.4. You should turn off optimization when compiling this project (-O0). Be sure the listing file will be generated. Compile the program, ignoring warnings about unused variables.

PROGRAM 14.4   Illustrate Memory Allocation of Variables

```
/*
Program 14.4
C program to illustrate memory allocation
```

```
Programmer: TM
Date: 5/2010
Platform: Simulator only
Device: ATMEGA16A


*/
#include <avr/io.h>

//static (global) allocation
int8_t glob_a;
int8_t glob_b = -100;
int16_t glob_c[3] = {-1, 5, 64};


int main() {
       //static (local) allocation
       static int8_t sloc = -2;

       //automatic (stack) allocation
       int8_t loc_a = sloc;
       uint16_t loc_b;
       char loc_c[] = "4x4";
       //assignment statement
       loc_b = glob_b;
       return 0;
}
```

The global variables will be allocated from the data segment (In the ATxmega16A, this begins at address $0060.) The local variables (in main) will be allocated on the stack, but only when the function main is called. The initialization code created by the compiler will initialize the stack and then copy data (initial values for memory locations) from flash to SRAM. This will fill the memory locations allocated for the global variables with the required initial data. The listing file documents this section of the code as __do_copy_data.

```
58: cf e5    ldi    r28, 0x5F    ;95    initialize SP
5a: d4 e0    ldi    r29, 0x04    ;4
5c: de bf    out    0x3e, r29    ;62
5e: cd bf    out    0x3d, r28    ;61
```

```
00000060 <__do_copy_data>:
60: 10 e0    ldi   r17, 0x00    ;0
62: a0 e6    ldi   r26, 0x60    ;96         X = 0x0060
64: b0 e0    ldi   r27, 0x00    ;0
66: e8 ec    ldi   r30, 0xEC    ;236        Z = 0x00C8
68: f0 e0    ldi   r31, 0x00    ;0
6a: 02 c0    rjmp  .+4    ;0x70 < .do_copy_data_start>

0000006c < .do_copy_data_loop>:
6c: 05 90    lpm   r0, Z+
6e: 0d 92    st    X+, r0

00000070 < .do_copy_data_start>:
70: ac 36    cpi   r26, 0x6C    ;108
72: b1 07    cpc   r27, r17
74: d9 f7    brne  .-10   ;0x6c < .do_copy_data_loop >
```

Initialization for the copy data loop begins at address 0x0060. R17 is set to 0; it acts as the high byte for a comparison in the testing of the loop condition. The data will be copied into SRAM, starting at address 0x0060 and R27:R26 is initialized with a pointer to this address. Next, R31:R30 is initialized to point into flash at byte address 0x00EC. This is where the compiler placed the data that will be used to initialize static storage. The loop (at address 0x0070) test compares this pointer to 0x006C, the stopping address. Thus, 12 bytes (0x006C – 0x0060 = 0x000C) will be copied.

The copied bytes include 0x9C (two's complement for −100) for the glob_b, 0xFF 0xFF 0x05 0x00 0x40 0x00, for −1, 5, and 64 of the glob_c array, 0x01 for the static local sloc, and a copy of the string literal used in the function main, 0x34 0x78 0x34 0x00 ("4x4").

The initialization code then enters another loop (do_clear_bss) that initializes uninitialized global storage to zero. There is just one uninitialized global variable, glob_a, at address $006C. This is filled with a zero. C always initializes globals.

```
00000076 <__do_clear_bss > :
76: 10 e0    ldi   r17, 0x00    ;0
78: ac e6    ldi   r26, 0x6C    ;108
7a: b0 e0    ldi   r27, 0x00    ;0
7c: 01 c0    rjmp  .+2    ;0x80 < .do_clear_bss_start >

0000007e < .do_clear_bss_loop>:
7e: 1d 92    st    X+, r1
```

```
00000080 < .do_clear_bss_start>:
80: ad 36       cpi    r26, 0x6D    ;109
82: b1 07       cpc    r27, r17
84: e1 f7       brne   .-8     ;0x7e < .do_clear_bss_loop>
```

The program then calls main, and upon return, enters an infinite loop.

```
86: 0e 94 49 00     call   0x92    ;0x92 <main>
8a: 0c 94 74 00     jmp    0xe8    ;0xe8 < _exit>
```

```
        . . .
```

```
000000e8 < _exit>:
e8: f8 94     cli
```

```
000000ea <__stop_program> :
ea: ff cf     rjmp   .-2     ;0xea <__stop_program>
```

Function main follows the rules of all C functions. It begins by saving Y (R29:R28) so it can be restored before it exits. Y is used by all functions as the stack frame pointer. All local storage is accessed using indirect addressing with displacement.

```
int main(){
92: df 93  push   r29                save Y
94: cf 93  push   r28
96: cd b7  in     r28, 0x3d  ;61     Y = SP
98: de b7  in     r29, 0x3e  ;62
9a: 27 97  sbiw   r28, 0x07  ;7      allocate local storage
9c: 0f b6  in     r0, 0x3f   ;63     status register
9e: f8 94  cli
a0: de bf  out    0x3e, r29  ;62     SP = Y
a2: 0f be  out    0x3f, r0   ;63     restore status
a4: cd bf  out    0x3d, r28  ;61
```

Next it copies the SP into Y in preparation for local storage allocation. Function main requires seven bytes of storage (1 (int8_t) +2 (uint16_t) +4 (char[]), the static variable is not part of local storage). This number is subtracted from the SP address. Before storing the new SP, the SREG is copied into R0 and interrupts are disabled. This is because the storing of SP is a two-step process that must not be interrupted. The SREG is restored to restore the previous interrupt status bit (to leave interrupts enabled or disabled as before). It may look odd to restore the interrupt status before finalizing SPL (0x3D). Just remember that the next instruction will always be executed after interrupts are enabled before an interrupt can occur. The approach taken here minimizes the time interrupts may be off.

Finally, the actual body of main begins. Throughout this function, Y is used as a pointer to the stack frame. Local storage has been allocated but not yet initialized at addresses Y + 1 through Y + 7. Main begins by initializing local storage. The static local variable was already initialized in the copy_data loop. Static variables are initialized once before execution of main begins.

```
        int8_t loc_a = sloc;
a6:  80 91 67 00    lds    r24, 0x0067   r24 = sloc
aa:  8b 83 std      Y + 3, r24     ;0x03  loc_a = r24
        uint16_t loc_b;
        char loc_c[] = "4x4";
ac:  80 91 68 00    lds    r24, 0x0068   data for array
b0:  90 91 69 00    lds    r25, 0x0069
b4:  a0 91 6a 00    lds    r26, 0x006A
b8:  b0 91 6b 00    lds    r27, 0x006B
bc:  8c 83          std    Y + 4, r24     ;0x04   c[i] = data[i]
be:  9d 83          std    Y + 5, r25     ;0x05
c0:  ae 83          std    Y + 6, r26     ;0x06
c2:  bf 83          std    Y + 7, r27     ;0x07


        //assignment statement
        loc_b = glob_b;
c4:  80 91 60 00    lds  r24, 0x0060    r24 = glob_b
c8:  99 27    eor   r25, r25            (sign extended)
ca:  87 fd    sbrc  r24, 7
cc:  90 95    com   r25
ce:  9a 83    std   Y + 2, r25   ;0x02  loc_b = r25:r24
d0:  89 83    std   Y + 1, r24   ;0x01
```

From the statements in main, we can deduce that sloc is at address 0x0067, loc_a is at Y + 3, loc_c is at addresses Y + 4 through Y + 7, and the data to initialize it starts at address 0x0068. The other local variable loc_b (not initialized) is at Y + 1 and Y + 2. Note how the characters to initialize the array loc_c are copied from flash into SRAM. This is how the C compiler deals with strings. String literals are compiled into flash. The reset code (executed before main is called) copies string data to SRAM in the do_copy_data loop. In general, all data is assumed to be in SRAM during program execution. Special functions are required to access flash and EEPROM storage.

Also note the widening conversion when the assignment to loc_b (uint16_t) from glob_b (int8_t). The value at glob_b is sign extended (widened) to a word and then stored into the word reserved for loc_b. Since loc_b is unsigned, it will now represent a very large number.

The main program ends here by executing the return statement, performing the normal function exit tasks. The return value of 0 is placed in R25:R24, local storage is released, Y is restored, and the return instruction returns control to the point main was called.

```
       return 0;
d2:  80 e0   ldi    r24, 0x00    ;0  return value
d4:  90 e0   ldi    r25, 0x00    ;0

d6:  27 96   adiw   r28, 0x07    ;7  release local
d8:  0f b6   in     r0, 0x3f     ;63
da:  f8 94   cli
dc:  de bf   out    0x3e, r29    ;62
de:  0f be   out    0x3f, r0     ;63
e0:  cd bf   out    0x3d, r28    ;61
e2:  cf 91   pop    r28                 restore Y
e4:  df 91   pop    r29
e6:  08 95   ret
```

Here is the call to main and subsequent statement.

```
86:  0e 94 49 00    call   0x92    ;0x92 <main>
8a:  0c 94 74 00    jmp    0xe8    ;0xe8 <_exit>
```

The actual exit code is:

```
000000e8 <_exit>:
e8:  f8 94    cli
000000ea <__stop_program>:
ea:  ff cf    rjmp   .-2     ;0xea <__stop_program>
```

You can see that the program ends with an infinite loop.

Arrays and Pointers

Arrays can be automatic, static, or dynamic. A variable is declared to be an array by adding [] to the declaration. The size of the array is required as part of the declaration (unless it can be deduced from initialization data).

```
int16_t d[10]; //an array of 10 signed words
static uint8_t[3] e; //a static array of 3 unsigned bytes
char f[] = {'a', 'b', 'c', 0}; //Same as "abc" (see below)
```

Arrays are often managed through pointers. Pointer types are declared by adding the * character after the data type, as in sometype*. This type would be a pointer to a memory location containing a value of type sometype. Pointer variables hold addresses and point to data of a specific type (which is named in the declaration). A void* pointer is a generic pointer type; it is just an address; there is no data type information about what is stored at the address. There is no difference between a pointer to a scalar and a pointer to an array; the programmer must remember what pointers point to. Thus char* xptr; declares a variable that can point to (hold the address of) a single character or the address of an array of characters.

Addition and subtraction with pointers is possible as long as the expressions are meaningful. Adding one to a pointer calculates the address of the next data item in memory, taking into account the size of the data. Array element access can be accomplished using array subscript notation or pointer arithmetic.

```
uint16_t g[5];      //an array of unsigned words
uint16_t* h = g;    //address of an unsigned word
h += 1;             //adds 2 to address in h since
                    //uint16_t is 2 bytes
```

Notice that even though g is an array, in the assignment above, it represents the address of the first element of the array. Array names behave like a pointer value. The variable h, after the increment, will be pointing at g[1].

When using pointers, there are two operators that are very important. One is the *dereferencing* operator (*); the other is the *address of* operator (&).

If h is the pointer defined (and incremented) above, then *h is (a name for) the unsigned word g[1]. Similarly, *(h + 1), g[2], h[1], and *(g + 2) are all the same. In C, pointers and array names are virtually identical.

The *address of* operator, when applied to an expression representing a memory location, will evaluate the address of the memory location. For example, given the declarations

```
int16_t a;          //signed word
int16_t b[10];      //an array of 10 signed words
int16_t* c;         //pointer to a signed word (or array)
```

we see that &a is the address of the signed word named a. The address of b[3] would be obtained by writing &b[3]. Since c can point to a single uint16_t, or to an array of such values, all of the following assignments are legal:

```
c = $a;
c = &b[3];
c = b;
```

The operators * and & are somewhat inverses of each other; *(&a) is the same as a, and &(*c) is equal to (the value stored in) c. These operators are tricky when used with arrays and pointers; this is one place that arrays and pointers are different. An array name, or the address of an array is interpreted to be the address of the first element of the array. Thus b and &b are the same as &b[0]; all are addresses of the first array element. On the other hand, if we set c to point to the array (c = b;), then &c is the address of the pointer (address of the address of the array). We would have to write &(*c) (or simply c) to obtain the address of the first element of the array. Pointer variables live in memory, so they have addresses; array names are addresses, but they represent the address literally and (the addresses themselves) are not stored in memory.

Actually, there is a subtle difference between b and &b when b is an array. The array name, b, represents the address of the first element of the array. However, &b is the address of the entire array. Although these are the same number (same address), they have different types!

```
int b[5];
the data type of b is int * (address of an int)
the data type of *b is int
the data type of &b is int[] * (address of an array of
                                integers)
the data type of *&b is int * (address of an int)
```

When an array variable is declared, the address of the array is not placed in memory. This gets a little more complicated when arrays are declared as parameters to functions, but we will take that topic up separately. Pointer variables, on the other hand, correspond to memory locations that contain addresses. Pointers can point to data in the data segment, the stack, or the heap (or anywhere you please, even program memory).

Typedef and Struct

The `typedef` keyword is used in C to create user defined types.

```
typedef existing type specification NewTypeName;
```

Typedefs are used in AVR programs to define types such as `uint8_t` and `int16_t`. It is also used to create composite data types using structures.

The `struct`, short for structure or structured data type, allows the programmer to join several related data items together in a single block of memory. Structs use field names to refer to the components. Each field has its own type. The following `struct` and `typedef` defines a new data type called `OrderedPair` which might be used to declare variables that will represent pairs of integers.

```
typedef struct {
        int x;
        int y;
} OrderedPair;
OrderedPair aPoint;
aPoint.x = -1;
aPoint.y = 0;
```

Structures can be created without the use of `typedef`, but then you must always add the keyword `struct` in front of the structure name when declaring variables. The typedef approach simplifies use of the structure.

Structured types can sometimes act like primitives. For example, they function correctly with assignment statements (if the types are the same) and can be passed as arguments to functions.

```
OrderedPair aPoint, bPoint;
aPoint.x = -1;
```

```
aPoint.y = 0;
bPoint = aPoint;
mapit(bPoint);
```

Beware when doing assignment operations with structs or when passing structs to functions (as shown in the above example) as you are making entire copies of the contents of the struct. This is especially important when you pass a structure as an argument to a function. You will be copying the argument into a matching size storage area in the stack frame.

Structures, on the other hand, are not primitive data and cannot be compared using the usual comparison operators.

```
if (aPoint == bPoint) //illegal
```

Literals, Characters, and Strings

Literals representing strings and numbers are common elements of programs. Each language has conventions for expressing literal values in a variety of data types. Numeric literals in C programs are assumed to be in base 10, however, if a numeral begins with 0, it is octal. The 0x prefix is used for hexadecimal, and 0b for binary. Floating point literals can be expressed with a decimal point or with an exponent (as in 1e6).

Character data is always enclosed in single quotes. The backslash character is an escape code used to represent special characters such as newline ("\n") and tab ("\t"). Strings as a data type are not directly supported in C, however, a string literal such as "hello world" represents the address of an array of char(acters) that is automatically allocated and filled with the ASCII codes for the characters. A nul byte is added at the end of the array as a string terminator. String data in C is usually implemented as an array of characters with a nul byte marking the end of the string.

String Functions

C provides many standard libraries containing functions that are commonly used in programming. The string library has functions related to string processing. You can use these functions in your programs, but they must first be declared or the compiler will report them as undefined symbols. Declarations are made through an include of the string library header file.

```
#include <string.h>
```

This include file declares a variety of string related functions. The function definitions have already been compiled (from a separate source file), and only exist as part of an object file (in a folder supplied with the compiler installation). The linker will connect the calls to standard functions with the actual function addresses in these already existing object files. The function code will, of course, become part of your program and be added to the hex file that is downloaded to flash.

A few of the common string functions are illustrated in the following examples. Keep in mind that strings are actually character arrays. C does not enforce any bounds checking on arrays, so it is your responsibility to ensure that these functions access legal storage locations. Most string functions rely on strings having a nul terminating character. If you are a Java programmer, you should remember that String objects in Java are immutable. Most String methods create entirely new String objects (allocating new storage for the results). In C, strings are stored in arrays and are mutable. Many of the string functions modify the string in place. Functions that return string results will require that you provide the address of an array for the result. There is never any automatic allocation of storage for string results.

```
//a few examples    of string functions
uint16_t len = strlen(aString);
if (strcmp(s1,s2) == 0)...      //returns negative, zero,
                                  or positive
uint8_t c = aString[2];         //a string is an array!
strcpy(s1, s2);                 //s2 copied into s1
strcat(s1, s2);                 //s2 appended to end of
                                  s1 (in place)
```

As in Java, never compare strings directly. If s1 and s2 are strings (arrays of characters), then a statement such as, if (s1 == s2), will simply compare the values of these two variables, which are addresses (pointers). No comparison of the characters in the strings will occur. Use a string function to do the actual comparison.

Control Structures

C provides the common control structures found in most high-level languages. The if, if/else, while, and for statements are much like those of Java. One important variation is C's propensity to interpret any data type as a

Boolean value when necessary. This means that a loop like this is perfectly legal.

```
while(1){...}
```

Any numeric value other than zero is considered true, so this appears to represent an infinite loop. The loop body may contain a break statement that would bring about termination.

The ability to declare the loop control variable inside the for statement initialization section is not provided in C, so you must declare loop control variables outside the for loop.

Arguments and Parameters

Function calls in C always use call by value. That is, the argument is evaluated and the result is copied into the storage allocated for the parameter. C functions can never alter the actual argument. However, you are free to pass addresses of arguments; by passing an address of an argument to a function, the function can modify the original argument. Note that the actual argument is the address; the address is passed by value. This technique is sometimes called call by reference since the reference to the argument is what is actually passed.

The following function uses this call by reference technique to interchange the values of two arguments. The arguments to be changed are not passed directly (only their values would be passed and then the function could not alter their contents). Instead, the caller passes the addresses of the arguments (by value). The parameters are declared as pointers to integers.

```
void swap(int* a, int* b){
        int temp = *a;        //the *'s here dereference the
                              //addresses
        *a = *b;              //to swap the data
        *b = temp;
}
```

When you call this function, you must pass addresses of integers, not integers. Here is a sample use of the function applied to a few variables.

```
int x = 1, y = 2, z = 3;
swap(&x, &y);
swap(&y, &z);
```

It is important to understand exactly what is being passed to effect call by reference in C. It is also important to understand why the parameters are always dereferenced inside the function. There are many library functions that require the address of an argument. When calling standard functions (in the library files) you must be careful that you pass argument values or addresses as required by each function.

Passing arrays is (almost) always done by reference. That is, to pass an array, you pass its address. Consider the following program that calculates the sum of elements in an array (until a zero is encountered):

```
int sumarray(int a[]){
        int i = 0, sum = 0;
        while (a[i]){
                sum += a[i++];
        }
        return sum;
}
```

This function expects an array to be passed as an argument. A typical call might look like this.

```
int numbers[] = {1,2,3,4,0};
int sum = sumarray(numbers);
```

The argument is the array name. Remember that an array name represents the address of the array, so in fact, this will copy the address of the array only. The formal parameter is in fact a pointer variable that will receive a copy of the address. It is NOT an array! Incidentally, it is (usually) a mistake to use the address of operator when passing an array to a function.

```
int sum1 = sumarray(&numbers); //illegal - wrong type
```

The following function calls are both legal. You may need to spend a little time determining what they actually do.

```
int sum2 = sumarray(&numbers[1]);
int sum3 = sumarray(numbers + 2);
```

The function parameter can also be explicitly declared as a pointer to the array. The following function is equivalent to the first in every way:

```
int sumarray1(int* a){
        int i = 0, sum = 0;
        while (a[i]){
                sum += a[i++];
        }
        return sum;
}
```

The following function illustrates that a parameter declared as an array is actually a pointer that can be modified inside the function. In this case the pointer is used to traverse the array contents without having to compute the address of a subscripted variable.

```
int sumarray2(int a[]){
        int sum = 0;
        while (*a){
                sum += *(a++);
        }
        return sum;
}
```

When an array is "passed" to a function, the function can modify the array contents. The following function accepts the address of an array, and a size. It will store zeros into the first size elements of the array.

```
void wipe_array(int a[], int size){
        while (size > 0)
                a[--size] = 0;
}
```

AVR-Specific Syntax

When developing applications for the AVR processor in C, the ability to refer to specific hardware features, such as registers and I/O ports is essential. By including the include file, avr/io.h, the standard symbols for these resources will be appropriately defined. You use them as if they were variables. For example, the following sequence of statements sets up digital port B as output, port D as input, and then asserts a specific bit pattern on port B and reads the values on port D (ATmega16A version).

```
DDRB = 0xFF;
DDRD = 0;
```

```
PORTB = 0b01010101;
uint8_t switches = PIND;
```

The XMEGA series version would look like this:

```
/* PORTF as input, PORTE as output */
PORTCFG_MPCMASK = 0xFF;
PORTF_PIN0CTRL = 0x18;
PORTF_DIR = 0;
PORTE_DIR = 0xFF;
PORTE_OUT = 0x55;
uint8_t switches = PORTF_IN;
```

C already includes powerful bit manipulation operators. The following statements illustrate a few of the capabilities (these are ATmega16A examples):

```
GICR |= (1 << INT0); //turn on external interrupt 0
PORTB &= ~(1 << n); //clear bit n in PORTB (n is a
                      variable)
if (PIND & _BV(2)) ... //if bit 2 in PIND is set...
//_BV(2) is a macro equivalent to (1 << 2)
if (~PIND & _BV(2)) ... //if bit 2 in PIND is clear...
if (!(PIND & _BV(2))) ... //same as above
```

The last two conditions deserve some additional explanation. Consider the following two examples which focus on bit 2 of PIND:

PIND is 0b01000101; bit 2 is set.

```
~PIND & _BV(2) = 10111010 & 00000100 = 00000000 (false)
!(PIND & _BV(2)) = !(01000101 & 00000100) = !(00000100) =
false
```

PIND is 0b01000001; bit 2 is clear.

```
~PIND & _BV(2) = 10111110 & 00000100 = 00000100 (true)
!(PIND & _BV(2)) = !(01000001 & 00000100) = !(00000000) =
true
```

Be careful mixing bitwise and logical operators. The logical not (!) operator is different from the bitwise complement (~). Logical not (!) evaluates only to 0 or 1.

```
!0x01 = 0x00  (only 0 is false)
~0x01 = 0xFE  (both are true if used where a Boolean value
              is needed)
```

If interrupts are being used, it will be essential to have the capability to disable them temporarily. The include file <avr/interrupt.h> defines two functions (actually macros) that accomplish this, sei() and cli(). The following sequence disables interrupts and the restores the interrupt status (and other status flags) to its earlier state:

```
#include <avr/io.h>
#include <avr/interrupt.h>
. . .
unit8_t sreg = SREG; //read status
cli(); //disable interrupts
. . .
SREG = sreg; //restore status (including global interrupt
                                flag)
```

Function Conventions

Writing programs in C frees you to think more about the solution at a higher level. The compiler decides how to use registers and takes care of many of the details of managing memory. If you plan to mix assembly language and C, you need to be aware of how variables are stored and how the compiled code uses registers. It is especially important to understand how arguments are passed to functions and how memory is organized.

The register conventions used by the AVR-GCC compiler when translating functions are fairly simple.

- R0 is a temporary or scratch register; use it freely and never worry about preserving its contents.

- R1 is always zero. This provides a register to facilitate adding a byte to a word (e.g., when the ADC instruction needs a zero for the upper byte). If you write a function in assembly language, be sure this register is not changed or set it to zero before returning.

- R2–R17 and R28–R29 (Y) are preserved by every function. If you write a function in assembly language, you must preserve these registers. Use the stack to save and restore their contents.

- R18–R27 (which includes X) and R30–R31 (Z) may be modified freely by every function. If you call a function written in C from an assembly language function, and the contents of these registers are important, save them before the call and restore them after.

The compiler generated functions expect arguments to be placed into registers. If additional space is needed, the remaining arguments are pushed onto the stack. The arguments are assumed to be words (bytes are widened to fit). The first argument is placed in R25:R24. The next is placed in R23:R22. This continues down through R9:R8, allowing up to nine (word-sized) arguments to be passed in registers. Arguments requiring more than two bytes will utilize additional pairs.

Functions use R25:R24 for their return value. For return values requiring more than two bytes, more registers are used (up to 64-bit values in R25–R18). 8-bit data is either sign extended (signed) or zero filled (unsigned) to take up the full word.

We will need to know these conventions to write functions in assembly language that will be called from a C program, or to call C functions from an assembly language module.

Program Memory

Because the AVR Microcontroller has several memories, the C compiler recognizes some custom keywords that are used to select the memory where the variables are to reside. Normally variables will be allocated in SRAM in the data or stack segments.

The GCC compiler supports attributes of variables allowing you to specify that certain data is to be held exclusively in flash storage. Of course this will be constant data. Flash is a good place to keep string constants or tables of values that are created at compile time and never change during execution. Actually, the compiler places all of the initial values you specify for variables in flash; this data is copied into SRAM before the main function is called. The result is variables in SRAM are initialized to the values you chose every time the reset vector is executed. Special techniques are needed to instruct the compiler to keep data exclusively in flash until needed by your program.

A special include file provides access to the program memory (flash) functions and type declarations.

```
#include <avr/pgmspace.h>
```

This include file contains typedefs for flash-based data. Basically, the prefix prog_ is prepended to the existing types. Here are some examples.

```
prog_int32_t numbers[] = {298567, 2987623, -2348756,
                          9928120};
prog_char title[] = "AVR Program by Avery";
prog_uint8_t tenten = 0xAA;
```

You can declare flash-based variables only if they belong to the static allocation class. Automatic (nonstatic local variables) cannot live in flash (they live in the stack). The compiler will ignore the request to use flash-based storage with automatic variables. Instead, code will be generated to copy the initial values from flash to the stack each time such a variable is allocated.

Be careful using program memory variables in your code. You cannot use the usual assignment statements or comparison operators. Writing the comparison statement

```
if (tenten == $AA)... //tenten is a flash-based constant
```

will fail. The program will use the address of the variable tenten (which is an address in flash) as if it were an address in SRAM, comparing garbage to the literal 0xAA. To access flash data, you must use a function (actually a macro) found in the pgmspace.h header file.

```
if (pgm_read_byte(&tenten) == 0xAA)...
```

This macro expects a program memory address as an argument. Since the variable tenten is bound to a memory location in flash, the *address of* operator provides the correct argument to the macro. The resulting program uses the LPM instruction (after setting up Z to point to the byte) to retrieve the data. There are similar macros for words (pgm_read_word), and doublewords (pgm_read_dword).

To access the characters of a string in flash, you need a pointer to the string.

```
prog_char* sPtr = title;   //title is a string in flash
                     char s;
while (s = pgm_read_byte(sPtr++)){
     //do something with the character s
}
```

In this example, sPtr is an automatic variable (local) whose value represents the address of the flash data. The value represented by the variable is therefore passed to the pgm_read_byte macro. If you use the address of operator (&sPtr), you will be passing the address of the sPtr which is actually an SRAM address of a memory location somewhere in the stack. The read byte macro would not care, but you should not expect to retrieve the characters of the string!

The standard string functions (declared in string.h) only apply to strings in SRAM, but there are variants for the program memory-based strings. Two examples are strlen_P and strcpy_P. The first calculates the length of a string in flash. The latter copies a string from flash to SRAM; it requires the destination be in SRAM.

Delay Library

Writing code to introduce delays in programs is common in many AVR projects. There is a library for this purpose, util/delay.h. With this include, and a definition specifying the processor's clock speed (in Hz), you can call the following functions. The F_CPU symbol will be automatically defined for the project if you set it in the project configuration options (so it need not be specified in the code). The delay loop functions have maximum of 256 and 65,536, respectively. These are utility functions used by the other two delay functions. Be sure to respect the maximums. It is also necessary to have optimization on for these to behave properly. The argument to these functions should be a constant expression.

```
#include <util/delay.h>
#define F_CPU 1000000UL
_delay_us(100); //100 microseconds (max 768000000/F_CPU)
_delay_ms(10); //10 milliseconds (max 262140000/F_CPU)
_delay_loop_1(27); //27 * 3 clock cycles (8-bit)
_delay_loop_2(3098); //3098 * 4 clock cycles (16-bit)
```

Math Library

The C language includes a collection of math related functions such as fabs (absolute value), sqrt (square root), asin (arcsin), ceil (ceiling). The required include file is math.h. These functions require floating point formats. You can cast integer data to floating point as needed. If you use floating point data, your program will grow quite large. Remember that all floating point calculations must be simulated; there is no floating point hardware in this processor.

ASSEMBLY LANGUAGE AND C

Mixing assembly language and C can be done in two ways. The first is to embed assembly language commands directly in the C program. Called inline assembly, this is perhaps the simplest approach, but the syntax is very different from the assembly language we have already studied. Special symbols are used to allow a connection between the C-level symbols and your assembly language instructions. Since you cannot know how the compiled C program is using registers, the inline assembly language statements often allow the compiler to select a register for you. You can see that this can get quite complex.

The other way to mix C and assembly language is to place the assembly language components in a separate file (or files). The assembly language components will be functions that are designed to be called by functions written in C or assembly. They will also be able to call functions written entirely in C.

Assembly language code that is intended to be part of a C project cannot be assembled by the AVR assembler. The AVR assembler does not produce the object file needed by the linker. Instead, the GNU Assembler (GAS) must be used. AVR Studio (actually the GCC compiler) will invoke the GAS when needed in a C project. This assembler uses a slightly different syntax from the AVR assembler. The source files must use the .S (capital S) extension (instead of .asm). You will need to add such files to the project so the make utility will reflect the need to assemble and link them when the Build command is used.

In the GAS language, registers are named by number instead of by a register name (you will use 0 instead of r0). The segment directives are `.data` and `.text` (instead of `.dseg` and `.cseg`). Strings are generated using `.ascii` or `.asciiz` (the latter adds a null-terminating byte to the array of characters). The `.db` directive is replaced by `.byte` (which has an entirely different meaning in the AVR assembler).

One additional feature provided by GAS is the ability to make symbols visible to the linker. The `.global` directive is used for this purpose. Declaring a symbol global is important if it will be accessed from two different files. The linker will make the address adjustments to connect these symbols. Labels representing the entry points of functions designed to be called from outside the current assembly language file must be declared as global.

Program 14.5 illustrates a simple C and assembly language project. The C program is used to perform high-level tasks. An assembly language function is called to perform one of the subtasks. The program simply reads switches and outputs the switch number of a pressed switch on the LED display, in binary. The application turns LED6 on to indicate that a switch press is detected. When no switch or more than one switch is pressed, LED7 is illuminated instead. This is the ATmega16A version.

PROGRAM 14.5   Illustrating Mixed C and Assembly to Read Switches and Control LEDs

Main file—swread.c

```
#include <avr/io.h>
#include "switchnum.h"
int main(){
      DDRD = 0;
      DDRB = 0xFF;
      while (1){
             PORTB = ~swnum(PIND);
      }
      return 0;
}
```

Header file—switchnum.h

```
#ifndef switchnum_h
#define switchnum_h
uint8_t swnum(uint8_t);
#endif
```

Assembly file—switchnum.S

```
.global swnum

swnum:
#define swdata 24  /*raw switch data (parameter)*/
#define returnv 24 /* return value */
;These registers are scratch registers
#define temp 27    /* sliding bit to match switches */
#define data 26    /* complemented switch data */
#define count 25   /* loop counter */
```

```
        mov data, swdata
        com data      ;compare 1, 2, 4, 8, ... to this
        ldi temp, 1   ;successive compare values
        ldi returnv, (1 << 6)  ;return value has bit 6 set
        ldi count, 8 ;8 bit positions to check
lp:
        cp data, temp         ;does it match?
        breq done             ;yes!
        inc returnv           ;setup next switch number as
                              ;return value
        lsl temp              ;shift to next switch position
        dec count             ;do at most 8 times
        brne lp
        ldi returnv, 1 << 7 ;no match, return bit 7 set
done:
        ret    ;Nothing to restore, return value is already
               ;in place
```

The main program, written in C, passes raw switch data (from PIND) to the swnum function via its parameter. The return value is complemented for output on the LEDs (PORTB). The swnum function is written entirely in assembly language for GAS. The assembly module does not need to declare a function heading, but must make the name of the function a global variable. A function declaration is required by the C module to allow the call in main to be compiled, so one is provided in the usual header file.

The assembly language component is written in GAS syntax. Register names are defined in #define macros. These macros are processed by the C preprocessor before GAS is invoked. The preprocessor strips out all C comments (not assembly language comments) and processes all of the macros. GAS receives the preprocessed file, not the original source. As a result, it will be a mistake to place an assembly language comment on the same line as a #define.

```
#define swdata 24   ;raw switch data
#define data 26     ;complemented switch data
```

Doing so will cause the symbol data to include the comment. When expanded, it is (highly) probable that an assembly error will be produced. For example,

```
mov data, swdata
```

expands to

```
mov 26  ;complemented switch data, 24; raw switch data
```

which is not going to be accepted by the assembler. That explains the use of the C comment indicators, /* */ (or the single line form //comment), for comments on #define statements that appear in GAS files.

EXERCISES

1. The AVR assembler skips what usual step in the process of translating an assembly language program to executable code?
2. Explain what is the job of the linker.
3. What is a make file?
4. What is the main purpose of header files in C programs?
5. When function calls refer to functions defined in different compilation units, the address of the call instruction is determined by _____.
6. Write the include statement for a C program that will include the standard AVR I/O definitions for the targeted device. How is the actual microcontroller identified so the correct I/O definitions are used?
7. When an AVR microcontroller is configured to run a C program, from what interrupt is the function named main called?
8. The last line of the function main in a C program is usually _____.
9. When AVR Studio compiles a file named sample.c, it will produce an object file named what?
10. What command will compile and link all of the project files even if they have not been recently changed?
11. When you select the clock speed in the Project Options dialog, does the compiler generate instructions to synchronize the clock settings in the target device so the application will run at the intended speed? Explain.
12. Write a C statement to store the value 0x3F into the SREG of the CPU.
13. What is the optimization option that tells the compiler to produce the smallest program possible?
14. Write a C function call to cause a delay of approximately 1/3 s. What include statements are required for this to work?
15. What optimization level should be selected when using the integrated debugger?

16. What is the syntax for a standard C comment?
17. Write an include statement for a project-specific file named `stuff.h`.
18. Write the usual directives that prevent multiple includes for the file `stuff.h`.
19. Explain the difference between a function definition and declaration. Which is typically found in a header file?
20. What information is specified in a function declaration?
21. Write a function prototype for a function that will average three integers (each of type `int`) and return a `float`. Name the function `average`.
22. Write an include file containing the prototype specified in the previous problem. The function's definition will be placed in a file named `mathstuff.c`.
23. Name the three major storage allocation classes used in C.
24. Where is memory for automatic variables allocated from?
25. In C programs, memory in the heap is accessed through the use of special variables called what?
26. What are the three types of scope used in C programs. Explain each one.
27. In the following program segment, identify the storage class and scope of each variable.

```
int x = 0;
static float y;
int main() {
char z;
extern int w;
...}
```

28. What AVR-specific data type would be the best to hold a value in the range −4000 through +4000? 0 through 255? −100 through +100?
29. Compile the following program and use the simulator to determine the addresses of the variables x, y, and z.

```
#include <avr/io.h>
int16_t x = 0x1234;

int main() {
    static int8_t y = 0xff;
```

```
        return 0;
}
int16_t z = 0xabcd;
```

30. What addressing mode is used to access local variables?
31. Write an array declaration for the array `sizes` that will hold up to 12 signed 16-bit integers. Write a loop to initialize the array to the integer values 1 through 12.
32. Declare and initialize a pointer variable so it points to the array element `x[3]` if `x` is declared as `char x[10];`
33. Write an expression that represents the address of a variable named `size`. The address of an array of `char` named `letters`. The address of the array element, `arr[4]`.
34. If `w` is a pointer to a memory location containing an `int`, write a statement to increment the `int` value.
35. Write a type definition for a new data type named `Fract` that represents the numerator and denominator of a fraction. The numerator should be of type `int8_t` and the denominator, `uint8_t`. Declare a variable of this type and set it to the fraction −2/3.
36. The string literal "abc" represents an array of how many bytes? Explain.
37. The following function is supposed to increment its argument, but when called, the argument never changes. Rewrite the function so it works correctly. Do not change the way the function is called.

```
void increase(int x){
x++;
}


/* The function is called like this */
int a = 0;
increment(a);
/* a should be bigger now */
```

38. Write a function to find the maximum value in an array of `uint8_t` values. The function is passed the array and a `uint16_t` specifying the array size.
39. Where are arguments placed when a function is called in a C program?

40. Where is the return value for a function found if the function returns a byte value?
41. Show how to declare a string in flash memory that will represent your name as an ASCIIZ string.
42. What include statement is needed to use the AVR specific delay functions? The standard math functions?
43. It is possible to use floating point types in C programs for the AVR microcontroller. Explain why integer types are usually preferred when possible.
44. Explain what is meant by the term "inline assembly."

PROGRAMMING EXERCISES

1. Rewrite the assembly language portion of Program 14.5 in C. Test that the program works as before.
2. Write a C program to communicate serially with the PC. Use polled I/O for the USART. The AVR application should simply echo what is received on the serial line. Display a count of the number of received characters on the LEDs.
3. Write a C program that calls an assembly language function which in turn calls a function written in C. Use three program modules and appropriate header files. The main function sets up the LEDs for output and the switches for input. It passes a string (in SRAM) to the assembly language function. This function passes each character of the string to the C function which displays it on the LEDs and waits for a button to be pressed (and released). It returns a 1 if button 7 is used; it returns 0 otherwise. The assembly language function terminates immediately if button 7 was used. Otherwise, it terminates after all of the characters of the string have been displayed. This function returns a count of the number of characters that were displayed. The main function displays this number on the LEDs and then ends.
4. Write a C program to display the Fibonacci numbers on the LEDs. Pause for 3 s between values. Stop when the value would exceed 255. Use a recursive function to calculate the nth Fibonacci number. Define the function in a separate file.
5. Write a C program to display the Fibonacci numbers on the LEDs. Pause for 3 s between values. Stop when the value exceeds 255. Use an assembly language function to calculate the nth Fibonacci number iteratively. It should return a zero if the result is greater than 255. Define the assembly language function in a separate file.

6. Write a memory game that creates a random sequence of numbers in the range 0 through 7. Initially the sequence is only of length one, but after each successful turn, it is increased by another random number. On each turn, the player will attempt to repeat the sequence that is displayed on the LEDs. The program will "play" the sequence, by illuminating the corresponding LED for 1 s. When the sequence is complete, the player will press the corresponding buttons in the same order. The turn is successful if the player presses the correct buttons in the correct sequence and if the player does not take more than 3 s between button presses. When the player fails to repeat a sequence, the game ends, displaying the length of the longest sequence repeated on the LEDs. Pressing a button when the game has ended will restart the game.

Appendix A

Getting Started with the XPLAIN Evaluation Kit

THE XPLAIN EVALUATION KIT (Figure A.1) was designed by Atmel to provide a platform to evaluate the ATxmega128A1 microcontroller. The kit consists of a single circuit board hosting two AVR microcontrollers (ATxmega128A1 and AT90USB1287) in addition to a variety of I/O devices carefully chosen to demonstrate the capabilities of the Xmega processor. The kit comes with the Xmega microcontroller preprogrammed with a simple demo program. When powered up, the program flashes the eight LED's and responds to button presses by playing different sounds on a speaker.

The AT90USB1287 microcontroller serves as a proxy between the USB connector and the Xmega microcontroller. It is preloaded with software to create a bridge from the ATxmega128A1's serial communication device and the USB cable. This allows the Xmega microcontroller to send and receive data through the USB connection. At the time this text was developed, programming the ATxmega128A1 required a special programming tool and could not be accomplished via USB. However, by changing the preloaded program in the AT90USB1287, it is possible to use the USB connection for this purpose.

The developer of this replacement software is Dean Camera. The software described above is one part of a larger project managed by Dean called LUFA. LUFA stands for Lightweight USB Framework for AVRs. It is an open-source USB stack for the Atmel AT90USBxxx and ATxmegaxxUx series of microcontrollers. The project we need to use is called the XPLAIN UART-to-USB bridge/PDI Programmer and is included with the LUFA

FIGURE A.1   The Atmel XPLAIN Evaluation Kit.

package. The package is distributed in source code format, however, you need only one small file, XPLAINBridge.hex, that is obtained after building the project files. This file can be downloaded from the textbook website.

The hex file contains the machine code that will replace the program in the AT90USB1287. This program has a dual purpose. It will serve as a

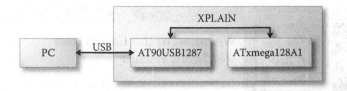

FIGURE A.2   USB connection between the PC and XPLAIN hardware.

programmer for the ATxmega128A1, and as a serial to USB bridge to allow two-way communication between a PC and an application running on the Xmega microcontroller as shown in Figure A.2.

The AT90USB1287 can be reprogrammed using the Flip Programming Utility. To reprogram the AT90USB1287, it must be placed in programming mode. This is accomplished by powering it up with a jumper across the pins labeled 1 and 2 on the J200 header. This header is also labeled JTAG USB. Pins 1 and 2 are labeled TCK and GND (Figure A.3). Some XPLAIN boards will not enter programming mode using this procedure.

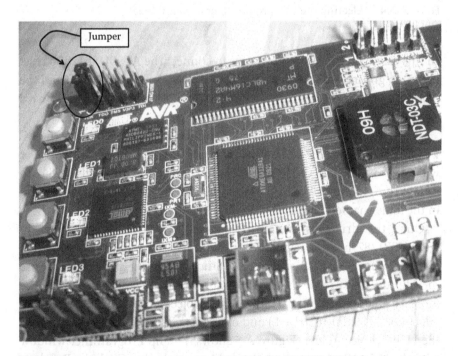

FIGURE A.3   Jumper across pins 1 and 2 of the JTAG USB (J200) header to select programming mode.

FIGURE A.4   Selecting the Flip programmer driver manually.

In this case, you can try using a wire to connect the AT90USB1287's reset pin (6) to ground (10) momentarily (with the 1–2 jumper installed and the board powered). After a reset, the AT90USB1287 on the XPLAIN board should be in bootloader mode.

The first time the XPLAIN board is connected to a USB port on the PC with the AT90USB1287 in bootloader mode, the Flip programmer driver will need to be installed. The driver should be selected manually as shown in Figure A.4. The driver information file (atmel_usb_dfu.inf) is located in the folder named USB under the Flip install directory.

Once the driver is installed, and the XPLAIN is connected in AT90USB1287 bootloader mode, the Flip Programming Utility can be started. You can start this from AVR Studio, or run it alone. We will use the Flip utility to replace the application in the AT90USB1287 with the more capable application from the LUFA project. From the Flip File menu, select Load Hex File (Ctrl + L) and open the XPLAINBridge.hex file from the LUFA project folder. Figure A.5 shows the Flip Programmer window with the LUFA Bridge HEX file loaded into the buffer. Click the Run button to accomplish the Erase, Program, and Verify cycle. This procedure

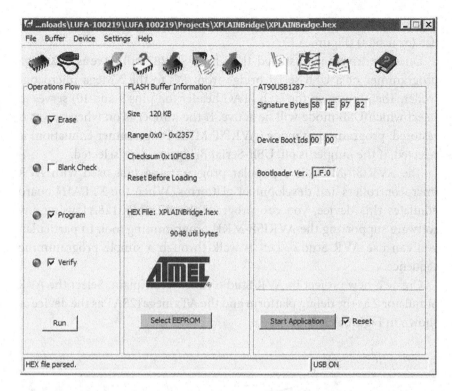

FIGURE A.5   Flip Programmer Utility ready to download the LUFA XPLAIN Bridge.hex file.

will replace the AT90USB1287's application program with the XPLAIN Bridge/PDI Programmer tool from the LUFA project. Close the Flip utility and disconnect the XPLAIN board from the USB cable.

Two new drivers need to be installed before the XPLAIN board is ready for use. Remove the jumper from the USB JTAG header and reconnect the XPLAIN to the USB port of the PC. The AT90USB1287 microcontroller should start up in LUFA Bridge mode; new hardware will be detected. The required driver is located in the LUFA project folder under the XPLAIN USB Bridge project folder. This replaces the bridge driver used by the pre-loaded software in the AT90USB1287.

Next, detach the USB cable again and place the jumper across pins 9 and 10 of the USB JTAG header (TDI and GND) as shown in Figure A.5. Note that the jumper is at the opposite end of the header. Reattach the USB cable; the AT90USB1287 should start up in AVRISP MKII Programmer emulation mode. Again, you will need to install the appropriate driver;

this time it is located in the Atmel Program Files Folder under AVR Tools/ usb (or usb64) (Figure A.6).

Once the drivers are installed, the AT90USB1287 will serve as an Xmega programmer or a USB-serial bridge from PC to the XMega microcontroller. The jumper on the USB JTAG header (on pins 9 and 10) serves to select which USB mode will be active. If the jumper is on when power is restored, programming mode (AVRISP MKII Programmer emulation) is selected; if the jumper is off, USB-Serial Bridge mode is selected.

The AVRISP-MKII is a popular programming tool used with AVR microcontrollers and development platforms. When the XPLAIN board emulates this device, you can program the ATxmega128A1 using any software supporting the AVRISP-MKII programming tool. In particular, you can use AVR Studio. Let us walk through a simple programming sequence.

Create a new project in AVR Studio called TestXplain. Select the AVR Simulator 2 as the debug platform and the ATxmega128A1 as the device as shown in Figure A.7.

FIGURE A.6 Jumper location to start the AT90USB1287 with LUFA Bridge code installed in AVRISP MKII programming mode.

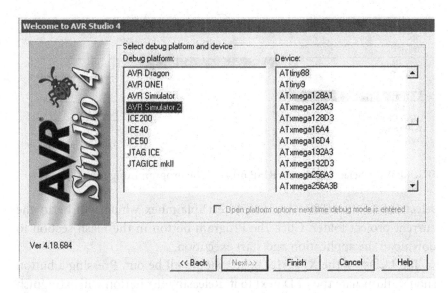

FIGURE A.7   Creating a new project for the ATxmega128A1.

Enter this program in the editor window.

```
;Simple test for programming the XPLAIN hardware
.include "ATxmega128A1def.inc"
        ldi r16, $FF
        sts PORTE_DIR, r16 ;PORTE Outputs to LED's
        sts PORTCFG_MPCMASK, r16 ;configure all 8 input
                                  ;pins
        ldi r16, 0b00011000       ;code to enable pullups
                                  ;on input pins
        sts PORTF_PIN0CTRL, r16   ;PORTF will read switches
top:
        lds r16, PORTF_IN         ;read switch state
        sts PORTE_OUT, r16        ;write switch state
        rjmp top
```

Assemble the program (correct any errors) and then choose *Program AVR/Connect* from the Tools menu (not AVR Programmer). In the dialog that opens, select the AVRISP MKII as the Programmer and USB as the Port. Be sure the XPLAIN board is connected to the PC and is in programming mode (jumper on pins 9 and 10 when powered up). The dialog should appear as shown in Figure A.8. Click Connect.

The programmer tool window should appear with title *AVRISP mkII in PDI mode with ATxmega128A1* (Figure A.9). Select the Program page and

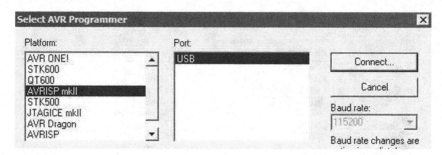

FIGURE A.8   Selecting the AVRISP mkII as the programming tool.

select the Input HEX File named TestXplain.hex which will be in the current project folder. Click the Program button in the Flash section to download the application and start execution.

The LEDs on the XPLAIN board should all be out. Pressing a button should illuminate the LED next to it. Releasing the button will extinguish the LED.

You can keep the jumper on pins 9 and 10 while testing applications that do not need to communicate with the PC while running. Some programs will need to send or receive data across the USB connection. The AT90USB1287 must be in Serial-USB Bridge mode for this communication to take place. In this case, you will need to remove the jumper after downloading your application program, then disconnect and reconnect the USB cable. This will allow serial communication to take place between the application running on the ATxmega128A1 and the PC. Remember to reconnect the jumper before downloading another application.

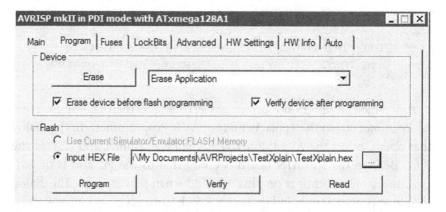

FIGURE A.9   Programming window showing a connection to the AVRISP mkII programmer.

Index

Printed in the United States
by Baker & Taylor Publisher Services

Printed in the United States
by Baker & Taylor Publisher Services